THE CONQUEST OF PERU

THE CONQUEST OF PERU

BY

WILLIAM H. PRESCOTT

Dolphin Books
Doubleday & Company, Inc.
Garden City, New York

CONTENTS

BOOK III

CONQUEST OF PERU

BOOK IV

CIVIL WARS OF THE CONQUERORS

BOOK V

SETTLEMENT OF THE COUNTRY

AUTHOR'S PREFACE

The most brilliant passages in the history of Spanish adventure in the New World are undoubtedly afforded by the conquest of Mexico and Peru,—the two states which combined with the largest extent of empire a refined social polity, and considerable progress in the arts of civilization. Indeed, so prominently do they stand out on the great canvas of history, that the name of the one, notwithstanding the contrast they exhibit in their respective institutions, most naturally suggests that of the other; and, when I sent to Spain to collect materials for an account of the Conquest of Mexico, I included in my researches those relating to the Conquest of Peru.

The larger part of the documents, in both cases, was obtained from the same great repository,—the archives of the Royal Academy of History at Madrid; a body specially intrusted with the preservation of whatever may serve to illustrate the Spanish colonial annals. The richest portion of its collection is probably that furnished by the papers of Muñoz. This eminent scholar, the historiographer of the Indies, employed nearly fifty years of his life in amassing materials for a history of Spanish discovery and conquest in America. For this, as he acted under the authority of the government, every facility was afforded him; and public offices and private depositories, in all the principal cities of the empire, both at home and throughout the wide extent of its colonial possessions, were freely opened to his inspection. The result was a magnificent collection of manuscripts, many of which he patiently transcribed with his own hand. But he did not live to reap the fruits of his persevering industry. The first volume, relative to the voyages of Columbus, was scarcely finished when he died;

and his manuscripts, at least that portion of them which have
reference to Mexico and Peru, were destined to serve the uses
of another, an inhabitant of that New World to which they
related.

Another scholar, to whose literary stores I am largely indebted, is Don Martín Fernández de Navarrete, late Director
of the Royal Academy of History. Through the greater part of
his long life he was employed in assembling original documents
to illustrate the colonial annals. Many of these have been incorporated in his great work, "Coleccion de los Viages y Des-
cubrimientos," which, although far from being completed after
the original plan of its author, is of inestimable service to the
historian. In following down the track of discovery, Navarrete
turned aside from the conquests of Mexico and Peru, to exhibit the voyages of his countrymen in the Indian seas. His
manuscripts, relating to the two former countries, he courteously allowed to be copied for me. Some of them have since
appeared in print, under the auspices of his learned coadjutors,
Salvà and Baranda, associated with him in the Academy; but
the documents placed in my hands form a most important
contribution to my materials for the present history.

The death of this illustrious man, which occurred some time
after the present work was begun, has left a void in his country
not easy to be filled; for he was zealously devoted to letters,
and few have done more to extend the knowledge of her colonial history. Far from an exclusive solicitude for his own literary projects, he was ever ready to extend his sympathy and
assistance to those of others. His reputation as a scholar was
enhanced by the higher qualities which he possessed as a man,
—by his benevolence, his simplicity of manners, and unsullied
moral worth. My own obligations to him are large; for from the
publication of my first historical work, down to the last week
of his life, I have constantly received proofs from him of his
hearty and most efficient interest in the prosecution of my historical labors; and I now the more willingly pay this well-
merited tribute to his deserts, that it must be exempt from all
suspicion of flattery.

In the list of those to whom I have been indebted for materials, I must, also, include the name of M. Ternaux-Compans,
so well known by his faithful and elegant French versions of

the Muñoz manuscripts; and that of my friend Don Pascual de Gayangos, who, under the modest dress of translation, has furnished a most acute and learned commentary on Spanish-Arabian history,—securing for himself the foremost rank in that difficult department of letters, which has been illumined by the labors of a Masdeu, a Casiri, and a Conde.

To the materials derived from these sources, I have added some manuscripts of an important character from the library of the Escurial. These, which chiefly relate to the ancient institutions of Peru, formed part of the splendid collection of Lord Kingsborough, which has unfortunately shared the lot of most literary collections, and been dispersed, since the death of its noble author. For these I am indebted to that industrious bibliographer, Mr. O. Rich, now resident in London. Lastly, I must not omit to mention my obligations, in another way, to my friend Charles Folsom, Esq., the learned librarian of the Boston Athenæum; whose minute acquaintance with the grammatical structure and the true idiom of our English tongue has enabled me to correct many inaccuracies into which I had fallen in the composition both of this and of my former works.

From these different sources I have accumulated a large amount of manuscripts, of the most various character, and from the most authentic sources; royal grants and ordinances, instructions of the Court, letters of the Emperor to the great colonial officers, municipal records, personal diaries and memoranda, and a mass of private correspondence of the principal actors in this turbulent drama. Perhaps it was the turbulent state of the country which led to a more frequent correspondence between the government at home and the colonial officers. But, whatever be the cause, the collection of manuscript materials in reference to Peru is fuller and more complete than that which relates to Mexico; so that there is scarcely a nook or corner so obscure, in the path of the adventurer, that some light has not been thrown on it by the written correspondence of the period. The historian has rather had occasion to complain of the *embarras de richesses;* for, in the multiplicity of contradictory testimony, it is not always easy to detect the truth, as the multiplicity of crosslights is apt to dazzle and bewilder the eye of the spectator.

The present History has been conducted on the same general plan with that of the Conquest of Mexico. In an Introductory Book, I have endeavored to portray the institutions of the Incas, that the reader may be acquainted with the character and condition of that extraordinary race, before he enters on the story of their subjugation. The remaining books are occupied with the narrative of the Conquest. And here, the subject, it must be allowed, notwithstanding the opportunities it presents for the display of character, strange, romantic incident, and picturesque scenery, does not afford so obvious advantages to the historian, as the Conquest of Mexico. Indeed, few subjects can present a parallel with that, for the purposes either of the historian or the poet. The natural development of the story, there, is precisely what would be prescribed by the severest rules of art. The conquest of the country is the great end always in the view of the reader. From the first landing of the Spaniards on the soil, their subsequent adventures, their battles and negotiations, their ruinous retreat, their rally and final siege all tend to this grand result, till the long series is closed by the downfall of the capital. In the march of events, all moves steadily forward to this consummation. It is a magnificent epic, in which the unity of interest is complete.

In the "Conquest of Peru," the action, so far as it is founded on the subversion of the Incas, terminates long before the close of the narrative. The remaining portion is taken up with the fierce feuds of the Conquerors, which would seem, from their very nature, to be incapable of being gathered round a central point of interest. To secure this, we must look beyond the immediate overthrow of the Indian empire. The conquest of the natives is but the first step, to be followed by the conquest of the Spaniards,—the rebel Spaniards, themselves,—till the supremacy of the Crown is permanently established over the country. It is not till this period, that the acquisition of this Transatlantic empire can be said to be completed; and, by fixing the eye on this remoter point, the successive steps of the narrative will be found leading to one great result, and that unity of interest preserved which is scarcely less essential to historic than dramatic composition. How far this has been effected, in the present work, must be left to the judgment of the reader.

No history of the conquest of Peru, founded on original documents, and aspiring to the credit of a classic composition, like the "Conquest of Mexico" by Solís, has been attempted, as far as I am aware, by the Spaniards. The English possess one of high value, from the pen of Robertson, whose masterly sketch occupies its due space in his great work on America. It has been my object to exhibit this same story, in all its romantic details; not merely to portray the characteristic features of the Conquest, but to fill up the outline with the coloring of life, so as to present a minute and faithful picture of the times. For this purpose, I have, in the composition of the work, availed myself freely of my manuscript materials, allowed the actors to speak as much as possible for themselves, and especially made frequent use of their letters; for nowhere is the heart more likely to disclose itself, than in the freedom of private correspondence.

M. Amédée Pichot, in the Preface to the French translation of the "Conquest of Mexico," infers from the plan of the composition, that I must have carefully studied the writings of his countryman, M. de Barante. The acute critic does me but justice in supposing me familiar with the principles of that writer's historical theory, so ably developed in the Preface to his "Ducs de Bourgogne." And I have had occasion to admire the skilful manner in which he illustrates this theory himself, by constructing out of the rude materials of a distant time a monument of genius that transports us at once into the midst of the Feudal Ages,—and this without the incongruity which usually attaches to a modern antique. In like manner, I have attempted to seize the characteristic expression of a distant age, and to exhibit it in the freshness of life. But in an essential particular, I have deviated from the plan of the French historian. I have suffered the scaffolding to remain after the building has been completed. In other words, I have shown to the reader the steps of the process by which I have come to my conclusions. Instead of requiring him to take my version of the story on trust, I have endeavored to give him a reason for my faith. By copious citations from the original authorities, and by such critical notices of them as would explain to him the influences to which they were subjected, I have endeavored to put him in a position for judging for himself, and thus for revising, and, if need be, reversing, the judgments of the historian. He will, at any rate, by this means, be enabled to estimate the difficulty of arriving at truth amidst the conflict of testimony; and he will learn to place little reliance on those writers who pronounce on the mysterious past with what Fontenelle calls "a frightful degree of certainty,"—a spirit the most opposite to that of the true philosophy of history.

Yet it must be admitted, that the chronicler who records the events of an earlier age has some obvious advantages in the store of manuscript materials at his command,—the statements of friends, rivals, and enemies, furnishing a wholesome counterpoise to each other; and also, in the general course of events, as they actually occurred, affording the best commentary on the true motives of the parties. The actor, engaged in the heat of the strife, finds his view bounded by the circle around him, and his vision blinded by the smoke and dust of the conflict; while the spectator, whose eye ranges over the ground from a more distant and elevated point, though the individual objects may lose somewhat of their vividness, takes in at a glance all the operations of the field. Paradoxical as it may appear, truth founded on contemporary testimony would seem, after all, as likely to be attained by the writer of a later day, as by contemporaries themselves.

Before closing these remarks, I may be permitted to add a few of a personal nature. In several foreign notices of my writings, the author has been said to be blind; and more than once I have had the credit of having lost my sight in the composition of my first history. When I have met with such erroneous accounts, I have hastened to correct them. But the present occasion affords me the best means of doing so; and I am the more desirous of this, as I fear some of my own remarks, in the Prefaces to my former histories, have led to the mistake.

While at the University, I received an injury in one of my eyes, which deprived me of the sight of it. The other, soon after, was attacked by inflammation so severely, that, for some time, I lost the sight of that also; and though it was subsequently restored, the organ was so much disordered as to remain permanently debilitated, while twice in my life, since, I have been deprived of the use of it for all purposes of reading and writing, for several years together. It was during one of these periods that I received from Madrid the materials for the "History of Ferdinand and Isabella," and in my disabled condition, with my Transatlantic treasures lying around me, I was like one pining from hunger in the midst of abundance. In this state, I resolved to make the ear, if possible, do the work of the eye. I procured the services of a secretary, who read to me the various authorities; and in time I became so far familiar with the sounds of the different foreign languages (to some of which, indeed, I had been previously accustomed by a residence abroad), that I could comprehend his reading without much difficulty. As the reader proceeded, I dictated copious notes; and, when these had swelled to a considerable amount, they were read to me repeatedly, till I had mastered their contents sufficiently for the purposes of composition. The same notes furnished an easy means of reference to sustain the text.

Still another difficulty occurred, in the mechanical labor of writing, which I found a severe trial to the eye. This was remedied by means of a writing-case, such as is used by the blind, which enabled me to commit my thoughts to paper without the aid of sight, serving me equally well in the dark as in the light. The characters thus formed made a near approach to hieroglyphics; but my secretary became expert in the art of deciphering, and a fair copy—with a liberal allowance for unavoidable blunders—was transcribed for the use of the printer. I have described the process with more minuteness, as some curiosity has been repeatedly expressed in reference to my *modus operandi* under my privations, and the knowledge of it may be of some assistance to others in similar circumstances.

Though I was encouraged by the sensible progress of my work, it was necessarily slow. But in time the tendency to inflammation diminished, and the strength of the eye was confirmed more and more. It was at length so far restored, that I could read for several hours of the day, though my labors in this way necessarily terminated with the daylight. Nor could I ever dispense with the services of a secretary, or with the writing-case; for, contrary to the usual experience, I have found writing a severer trial to the eye than reading,—a remark, however, which does not apply to the reading of manuscript; and to enable myself, therefore, to revise my composition more carefully, I caused a copy of the "History of Ferdinand and

Isabella" to be printed for my own inspection, before it was sent to the press for publication. Such as I have described was the improved state of my health during the preparation of the "Conquest of Mexico"; and, satisfied with being raised so nearly to a level with the rest of my species, I scarcely envied the superior good fortune of those who could prolong their studies into the evening, and the later hours of the night.

But a change has again taken place during the last two years. The sight of my eye has become gradually dimmed, while the sensibility of the nerve has been so far increased, that for several weeks of the last year I have not opened a volume, and through the whole time I have not had the use of it, on an average, for more than an hour a day. Nor can I cheer myself with the delusive expectation, that, impaired as the organ has become, from having been tasked, probably, beyond its strength, it can ever renew its youth, or be of much service to me hereafter in my literary researches. Whether I shall have the heart to enter, as I had proposed, on a new and more extensive field of historical labor, with these impediments, I cannot say. Perhaps long habit, and a natural desire to follow up the career which I have so long pursued, may make this, in a manner, necessary, as my past experience has already proved that it is practicable.

From this statement—too long, I fear, for his patience—the reader, who feels any curiosity about the matter, will understand the real extent of my embarrassments in my historical pursuits. That they have not been very light will be readily admitted, when it is considered that I have had but a limited use of my eye, in its best state, and that much of the time I have been debarred from the use of it altogether. Yet the difficulties I have had to contend with are very far inferior to those which fall to the lot of a blind man. I know of no historian, now alive, who can claim the glory of having overcome such obstacles, but the author of "La Conquête de l'Angleterre par les Normands"; who, to use his own touching and beautiful language, "has made himself the friend of darkness"; and who, to a profound philosophy that requires no light but that from within, unites a capacity for extensive and various research, that might well demand the severest application of the student.

The remarks into which I have been led at such length will, I trust, not be set down by the reader to an unworthy egotism, but to their true source, a desire to correct a misapprehension to which I may have unintentionally given rise myself, and which has gained me the credit with some—far from grateful to my feelings, since undeserved—of having surmounted the incalculable obstacles which lie in the path of the blind man.

WILLIAM H. PRESCOTT

BOSTON, April 2, 1847

BOOK I: INTRODUCTION

VIEW OF THE CIVILIZATION OF THE INCAS

CHAPTER I

PHYSICAL ASPECT OF THE COUNTRY—SOURCES OF
PERUVIAN CIVILIZATION—EMPIRE OF THE INCAS—
ROYAL FAMILY—NOBILITY

Of the numerous nations which occupied the great American continent at the time of its discovery by the Europeans, the two most advanced in power and refinement were undoubtedly those of Mexico and Peru. But, though resembling one another in extent of civilization, they differed widely as to the nature of it; and the philosophical student of his species may feel a natural curiosity to trace the different steps by which these two nations strove to emerge from the state of barbarism, and place themselves on a higher point in the scale of humanity.—In a former work I have endeavored to exhibit the institutions and character of the ancient Mexicans, and the story of their conquest by the Spaniards. The present will be devoted to the Peruvians; and, if their history shall be found to present less strange anomalies and striking contrasts than that of the Aztecs, it may interest us quite as much by the pleasing picture it offers of a well-regulated government and sober habits of industry under the patriarchal sway of the Incas.

The empire of Peru, at the period of the Spanish invasion, stretched along the Pacific from about the second degree north to the thirty-seventh degree of south latitude; a line, also, which describes the western boundaries of the modern republics of Ecuador, Peru, Bolivia, and Chili. Its breadth cannot so easily be determined; for, though bounded everywhere by the great ocean on the west, towards the east it spread out, in many parts, considerably beyond the mountains, to the confines of barbarous states, whose exact position is undetermined, or whose names are effaced from the map of history.

It is certain, however, that its breadth was altogether disproportioned to its length.

The topographical aspect of the country is very remarkable.
A strip of land, rarely exceeding twenty leagues in width, runs
along the coast, and is hemmed in through its whole extent by
a colossal range of mountains, which, advancing from the
Straits of Magellan, reaches its highest elevation—indeed, the
highest on the American continent—about the seventeenth degree south, and, after crossing the line, gradually subsides into
hills of inconsiderable magnitude, as it enters the Isthmus of
Panamá. This is the famous Cordillera of the Andes, or "copper mountains," as termed by the natives, though they might
with more reason have been called "mountains of gold." Arranged sometimes in a single line, though more frequently in
two or three lines running parallel or obliquely to each other,
they seem to the voyager on the ocean but one continuous
chain; while the huge volcanoes, which to the inhabitants of
the table-land look like solitary and independent masses, appear to him only like so many peaks of the same vast and
magnificent range. So immense is the scale on which Nature
works in these regions, that it is only when viewed from a
great distance, that the spectator can, in any degree, comprehend the relation of the several parts to the stupendous whole.
Few of the works of Nature, indeed, are calculated to produce
impressions of higher sublimity than the aspect of this coast,
as it is gradually unfolded to the eye of the mariner sailing on
the distant waters of the Pacific; where mountain is seen to rise
above mountain, and Chimborazo, with its glorious canopy
of snow, glittering far above the clouds, crowns the whole as
with a celestial diadem.

The face of the country would appear to be peculiarly unfavorable to the purposes both of agriculture and of internal
communication. The sandy strip along the coast, where rain
never falls, is fed only by a few scanty streams, that furnish a
remarkable contrast to the vast volumes of water which roll
down the eastern sides of the Cordilleras into the Atlantic. The
precipitous steeps of the sierra, with its splintered sides of porphyry and granite, and its higher regions wrapped in snows
that never melt under the fierce sun of the equator, unless it be
from the desolating action of its own volcanic fires, might seem

equally unpropitious to the labors of the husbandman. And all communication between the parts of the long-extended territory might be thought to be precluded by the savage character of the region, broken up by precipices, furious torrents, and impassable *quebradas,*—those hideous rents in the mountain chain, whose depths the eye of the terrified traveller, as he winds along his aërial pathway, vainly endeavors to fathom. Yet the industry, we might almost say, the genius, of the Indian was sufficient to overcome all these impediments of Nature.

By a judicious system of canals and subterraneous aqueducts, the waste places on the coast were refreshed by copious streams, that clothed them in fertility and beauty. Terraces were raised upon the steep sides of the Cordillera; and, as the different elevations had the effect of difference of latitude, they exhibited in regular gradation every variety of vegetable form, from the stimulated growth of the tropics, to the temperate products of a northern clime; while flocks of *llamas*—the Peruvian sheep—wandered with their shepherds over the broad, snow-covered wastes on the crests of the sierra, which rose beyond the limits of cultivation. An industrious population settled along the lofty regions of the plateaus, and towns and hamlets, clustering amidst orchards and widespreading gardens, seemed suspended in the air far above the ordinary elevation of the clouds. Intercourse was maintained between these numerous settlements by means of great roads which traversed the mountain passes, and opened an easy communication between the capital and the remotest extremities of the empire.

The source of this civilization is traced to the valley of Cuzco, the central region of Peru, as its name implies. The origin of the Peruvian empire, like the origin of all nations, except the very few which, like our own, have had the good fortune to date from a civilized period and people, is lost in the mists of fable, which, in fact, have settled as darkly round its history as round that of any nation, ancient or modern, in the Old World. According to the tradition most familiar to the European scholar, the time was, when the ancient races of the continent were all plunged in deplorable barbarism; when they worshipped nearly every object in nature indiscriminately; made war their pastime, and feasted on the flesh of their slaughtered captives. The Sun, the great luminary and parent of mankind, taking compassion on their degraded condition, sent two of his children, Manco Capac and Mama Oello Huaco, to gather the natives into communities, and teach them the arts of civilized life. The celestial pair, brother and sister, husband and wife, advanced along the high plains in the neighborhood of Lake Titicaca, to about the sixteenth degree south. They bore with them a golden wedge, and were directed to take up their residence on the spot where the sacred emblem should without effort sink into the ground. They proceeded accordingly but a short distance, as far as the valley of Cuzco, the spot indicated by the performance of the miracle, since there the wedge speedily sank into the earth and disappeared for ever. Here the Children of the Sun established their residence, and soon entered upon their beneficent mission among the rude inhabitants of the country; Manco Capac teaching the men the arts of agriculture, and Mama Oello initiating her own sex in the mysteries of weaving and spinning. The simple people lent a willing ear to the messengers of Heaven, and, gathering together in considerable numbers, laid the foundations of the city of Cuzco. The same wise and benevolent maxims, which regulated the conduct of the first Incas, descended to their successors, and under their mild sceptre a community gradually extended itself along the broad surface of the table-land, which asserted its superiority over the surrounding tribes. Such is the pleasing picture of the origin of the Peruvian monarchy, as portrayed by Garcilasso de la Vega, the descendant of the Incas, and through him made familiar to the European reader.

But this tradition is only one of several current among the Peruvian Indians, and probably not the one most generally received. Another legend speaks of certain white and bearded men, who, advancing from the shores of Lake Titicaca, established an ascendency over the natives, and imparted to them the blessings of civilization. It may remind us of the tradition existing among the Aztecs in respect to Quetzalcoatl, the good deity, who with a similar garb and aspect came up the great plateau from the east on a like benevolent mission to the natives. The analogy is the more remarkable, as there is no trace of any communication with, or even knowledge of, each other to be found in the two nations.

The date usually assigned for these extraordinary events was about four hundred years before the coming of the Spaniards, or early in the twelfth century. But, however pleasing to the imagination, and however popular, the legend of Manco Capac, it requires but little reflection to show its improbability, even when divested of supernatural accompaniments. On the shores of Lake Titicaca extensive ruins exist at the present day, which the Peruvians themselves acknowledge to be of older date than the pretended advent of the Incas, and to have furnished them with the models of their architecture. The date of their appearance, indeed, is manifestly irreconcilable with their subsequent history. No account assigns to the Inca dynasty more than thirteen princes before the Conquest. But this number is altogether too small to have spread over four hundred years, and would not carry back the foundations of the monarchy, on any probable computation, beyond two centuries and a half,—an antiquity not incredible in itself, and which, it may be remarked, does not precede by more than half a century the alleged foundation of the capital of Mexico. The fiction of Manco Capac and his sister-wife was devised, no doubt, at a later period, to gratify the vanity of the Peruvian monarchs, and to give additional sanction to their authority by deriving it from a celestial origin.

We may reasonably conclude that there existed in the country a race advanced in civilization before the time of the Incas; and, in conformity with nearly every tradition, we may derive this race from the neighborhood of Lake Titicaca; a conclusion strongly confirmed by the imposing architectural remains which still endure, after the lapse of so many years, on its borders. Who this race were, and whence they came, may afford a tempting theme for inquiry to the speculative antiquarian. But it is a land of darkness that lies far beyond the domain of history.

The same mists that hang round the origin of the Incas continue to settle on their subsequent annals; and, so imperfect were the records employed by the Peruvians, and so confused and contradictory their traditions, that the historian finds no firm footing on which to stand till within a century of the

Spanish conquest. At first, the progress of the Peruvians seems to have been slow, and almost imperceptible. By their wise and temperate policy, they gradually won over the neighboring tribes to their dominion, as these latter became more and more convinced of the benefits of a just and well-regulated government. As they grew stronger, they were enabled to rely more directly on force; but, still advancing under cover of the same beneficent pretexts employed by their predecessors, they proclaimed peace and civilization at the point of the sword. The rude nations of the country, without any principle of cohesion among themselves, fell one after another before the victorious arm of the Incas. Yet it was not till the middle of the fifteenth century that the famous Topa Inca Yupanqui, grandfather of the monarch who occupied the throne at the coming of the Spaniards, led his armies across the terrible desert of Atacama, and, penetrating to the southern region of Chili, fixed the permanent boundary of his dominions at the river Maule. His son, Huayna Capac, possessed of ambition and military talent fully equal to his father's, marched along the Cordillera towards the north, and, pushing his conquests across the equator, added the powerful kingdom of Quito to the empire of Peru.

The ancient city of Cuzco, meanwhile, had been gradually advancing in wealth and population, till it had become the worthy metropolis of a great and flourishing monarchy. It stood in a beautiful valley on an elevated region of the plateau, which, among the Alps, would have been buried in eternal snows, but which within the tropics enjoyed a genial and salubrious temperature. Towards the north it was defended by a lofty eminence, a spur of the great Cordillera; and the city was traversed by a river, or rather a small stream, over which bridges of timber, covered with heavy slabs of stone, furnished an easy means of communication with the opposite banks. The streets were long and narrow; the houses low, and those of the poorer sort built of clay and reeds. But Cuzco was the royal residence, and was adorned with the ample dwellings of the great nobility; and the massy fragments still incorporated in many of the modern edifices bear testimony to the size and solidity of the ancient.

The health of the city was promoted by spacious openings

and squares, in which a numerous population from the capital and the distant country assembled to celebrate the high festivals of their religion. For Cuzco was the "Holy City"; and the great Temple of the Sun, to which pilgrims resorted from the furthest borders of the empire, was the most magnificent structure in the New World, and unsurpassed, probably, in the costliness of its decorations by any building in the Old.

Towards the north, on the sierra or rugged eminence already noticed, rose a strong fortress, the remains of which at the present day, by their vast size, excite the admiration of the traveller. It was defended by a single wall of great thickness, and twelve hundred feet long on the side facing the city, where the precipitous character of the ground was of itself almost sufficient for its defence. On the other quarter, where the approaches were less difficult, it was protected by two other semicircular walls of the same length as the preceding. They were separated, a considerable distance from one another and from the fortress; and the intervening ground was raised so that the walls afforded a breastwork for the troops stationed there in times of assault. The fortress consisted of three towers, detached from one another. One was appropriated to the Inca, and was garnished with the sumptuous decorations befitting a royal residence, rather than a military post. The other two were held by the garrison, drawn from the Peruvian nobles, and commanded by an officer of the blood royal; for the position was of too great importance to be intrusted to inferior hands. The hill was excavated below the towers, and several subterraneous galleries communicated with the city and the palaces of the Inca.

The fortress, the walls, and the galleries were all built of stone, the heavy blocks of which were not laid in regular courses, but so disposed that the small ones might fill up the interstices between the great. They formed a sort of rustic work, being rough-hewn except towards the edges, which were finely wrought; and, though no cement was used, the several blocks were adjusted with so much exactness and united so closely, that it was impossible to introduce even the blade of a knife between them. Many of these stones were of vast size; some of them being full thirty-eight feet long, by eighteen broad, and six feet thick.

We are filled with astonishment, when we consider, that these enormous masses were hewn from their native bed and fashioned into shape, by a people ignorant of the use of iron; that they were brought from quarries, from four to fifteen leagues distant, without the aid of beasts of burden; were transported across rivers and ravines, raised to their elevated position on the sierra, and finally adjusted there with the nicest accuracy, without the knowledge of tools and machinery familiar to the European. Twenty thousand men are said to have been employed on this great structure, and fifty years consumed in the building. However this may be, we see in it the workings of a despotism which had the lives and fortunes of its vassals at its absolute disposal, and which, however mild in its general character, esteemed these vassals, when employed in its service, as lightly as the brute animals for which they served as a substitute.

The fortress of Cuzco was but part of a system of fortifications established throughout their dominions by the Incas. This system formed a prominent feature in their military policy; but before entering on this latter, it will be proper to give the reader some view of their civil institutions and scheme of government.

The sceptre of the Incas, if we may credit their historian, descended in unbroken succession from father to son, through their whole dynasty. Whatever we may think of this, it appears probable that the right of inheritance might be claimed by the eldest son of the *Coya*, or lawful queen, as she was styled, to distinguish her from the host of concubines who shared the affections of the sovereign. The queen was further distinguished, at least in later reigns, by the circumstance of being selected from the sisters of the Inca, an arrangement which, however revolting to the ideas of civilized nations, was recommended to the Peruvians by its securing an heir to the crown of the pure heaven-born race, uncontaminated by any mixture of earthly mould.

In his early years, the royal offspring was intrusted to the care of the *amautas*, or "wise men," as the teachers of Peruvian science were called, who instructed him in such elements of knowledge as they possessed, and especially in the cumbrous ceremonial of their religion, in which he was to take a prominent part. Great care was also bestowed on his military education, of the last importance in a state which, with its professions of peace and good-will, was ever at war for the acquisition of empire.

In this military school he was educated with such of the Inca nobles as were nearly of his own age; for the sacred name of Inca—a fruitful source of obscurity in their annals—was applied indifferently to all who descended by the male line from the founder of the monarchy. At the age of sixteen the pupils underwent a public examination, previous to their admission to what may be called the order of chivalry. This examination was conducted by some of the oldest and most illustrious Incas. The candidates were required to show their prowess in the athletic exercises of the warrior; in wrestling and boxing, in running such long courses as fully tried their agility and strength, in severe fasts of several days' duration, and in mimic combats, which, although the weapons were blunted, were always attended with wounds, and sometimes with death. During this trial, which lasted thirty days, the royal neophyte fared no better than his comrades, sleeping on the bare ground, going unshod, and wearing a mean attire,—a mode of life, it was supposed, which might tend to inspire him with more sympathy with the destitute. With all this show of impartiality, however, it will probably be doing no injustice to the judges to suppose that a politic discretion may have somewhat quickened their perceptions of the real merits of the heir-apparent.

At the end of the appointed time, the candidates selected as worthy of the honors of their barbaric chivalry were presented to the sovereign, who condescended to take a principal part in the ceremony of inauguration. He began with a brief discourse, in which, after congratulating the young aspirants on the proficiency they had shown in martial exercises, he reminded them of the responsibilities attached to their birth and station; and, addressing them affectionately as "children of the Sun," he exhorted them to imitate their great progenitor in his glorious career of beneficence to mankind. The novices then drew near, and, kneeling one by one before the Inca, he pierced their ears with a golden bodkin; and this was suffered to remain there till an opening had been made large enough

for the enormous pendants which were peculiar to their order, and which gave them, with the Spaniards, the name of
orejones. This ornament was so massy in the ears of the sovereign, that the cartilage was distended by it nearly to the
shoulder, producing what seemed a monstrous deformity in
the eyes of the Europeans, though, under the magical influence of fashion, it was regarded as a sign of beauty by the
natives.

When this operation was performed, one of the most venerable of the nobles dressed the feet of the candidates in the
sandals worn by the order, which may remind us of the ceremony of buckling on the spurs of the Christian knight. They
were then allowed to assume the girdle or sash around the
loins, corresponding with the *toga virilis* of the Romans, and
intimating that they had reached the season of manhood.
Their heads were adorned with garlands of flowers, which, by
their various colors, were emblematic of the clemency and
goodness that should grace the character of every true warrior;
and the leaves of an evergreen plant were mingled with the
flowers, to show that these virtues should endure without end.
The prince's head was further ornamented by a fillet, or tasselled fringe, of a yellow color, made of the fine threads of the
vicuña wool, which encircled the forehead as the peculiar insignia of the heir-apparent. The great body of the Inca nobility next made their appearance, and, beginning with those
nearest of kin, knelt down before the prince, and did him
homage as successor to the crown. The whole assembly then
moved to the great square of the capital, where songs, and
dances, and other public festivities closed the important ceremonial of the *huaracu*.

The reader will be less surprised by the resemblance which
this ceremonial bears to the inauguration of a Christian knight
in the feudal ages, if he reflects that a similar analogy may
be traced in the institutions of other people more or less civilized; and that it is natural that nations, occupied with the
one great business of war, should mark the period, when the
preparatory education for it was ended, by similar characteristic ceremonies.

Having thus honorably passed through his ordeal, the heir-
apparent was deemed worthy to sit in the councils of his fa-

ther, and was employed in offices of trust at home, or, more usually, sent on distant expeditions to practise in the field the lessons which he had hitherto studied only in the mimic theatre of war. His first campaigns were conducted under the renowned commanders who had grown grey in the service of his father; until, advancing in years and experience, he was placed in command himself, and, like Huayna Capac, the last and most illustrious of his line, carried the banner of the rainbow, the armorial ensign of his house, far over the borders, among the remotest tribes of the plateau.

The government of Peru was a despotism, mild in its character, but in its form a pure and unmitigated despotism. The sovereign was placed at an immeasurable distance above his subjects. Even the proudest of the Inca nobility, claiming a descent from the same divine original as himself, could not venture into the royal presence, unless barefoot, and bearing a light burden on his shoulders in token of homage. As the representative of the Sun, he stood at the head of the priesthood, and presided at the most important of the religious festivals. He raised armies, and usually commanded them in person. He imposed taxes, made laws, and provided for their execution by the appointment of judges, whom he removed at pleasure. He was the source from which every thing flowed, —all dignity, all power, all emolument. He was, in short, in the well-known phrase of the European despot, "himself the state."

The Inca asserted his claims as a superior being by assuming a pomp in his manner of living well calculated to impose on his people. His dress was of the finest wool of the vicuña, richly dyed, and ornamented with a profusion of gold and precious stones. Round his head was wreathed a turban of many-colored folds, called the *llautu;* and a tasselled fringe, like that worn by the prince, but of a scarlet color, with two feathers of a rare and curious bird, called the *coraquenque,* placed upright in it, were the distinguishing insignia of royalty. The birds from which these feathers were obtained were found in a desert country among the mountains; and it was death to destroy or to take them, as they were reserved for the exclusive purpose of supplying the royal head-gear. Every succeeding monarch was provided with a new pair of these plumes, and his credulous subjects fondly believed that only two individuals of the species had ever existed to furnish the simple ornament for the diadem of the Incas.

Although the Peruvian monarch was raised so far above the highest of his subjects, he condescended to mingle occasionally with them, and took great pains personally to inspect the condition of the humbler classes. He presided at some of the religious celebrations, and on these occasions entertained the great nobles at his table, when he complimented them, after the fashion of more civilized nations, by drinking the health of those whom he delighted to honor.

But the most effectual means taken by the Incas for communicating with their people were their progresses through the empire. These were conducted, at intervals of several years, with great state and magnificence. The sedan, or litter, in which they travelled, richly emblazoned with gold and emeralds, was guarded by a numerous escort. The men who bore it on their shoulders were provided by two cities, specially appointed for the purpose. It was a post to be coveted by no one, if, as is asserted, a fall was punished by death. They travelled with ease and expedition, halting at the *tambos*, or inns, erected by government along the route, and occasionally at the royal palaces, which in the great towns afforded ample accommodations to the whole of the monarch's retinue. The noble roads which traversed the table-land were lined with people, who swept away the stones and stubble from their surface, strewing them with sweet-scented flowers, and vying with each other in carrying forward the baggage from one village to another. The monarch halted from time to time to listen to the grievances of his subjects, or to settle some points which had been referred to his decision by the regular tribunals. As the princely train wound its way along the mountain passes, every place was thronged with spectators eager to catch a glimpse of their sovereign; and, when he raised the curtains of his litter, and showed himself to their eyes, the air was rent with acclamations as they invoked blessings on his head. Tradition long commemorated the spots at which he halted, and the simple people of the country held them in reverence as places consecrated by the presence of an Inca.

The royal palaces were on a magnificent scale, and, far from being confined to the capital or a few principal towns, were scattered over all the provinces of their vast empire. The buildings were low, but covered a wide extent of ground. Some of the apartments were spacious, but they were generally small, and had no communication with one another, except that they opened into a common square or court. The walls were made of blocks of stone of various sizes, like those described in the fortress of Cuzco, rough-hewn, but carefully wrought near the line of junction, which was scarcely visible to the eye. The roofs were of wood or rushes, which have perished under the rude touch of time, that has shown more respect for the walls of the edifices. The whole seems to have been characterized by solidity and strength, rather than by any attempt at architectural elegance.

But whatever want of elegance there may have been in the exterior of the imperial dwellings, it was amply compensated by the interior, in which all the opulence of the Peruvian princes was ostentatiously displayed. The sides of the apartments were thickly studded with gold and silver ornaments. Niches, prepared in the walls, were filled with images of animals and plants curiously wrought of the same costly materials; and even much of the domestic furniture, including the utensils devoted to the most ordinary menial services, displayed the like wanton magnificence! With these gorgeous decorations were mingled richly colored stuffs of the delicate manufacture of the Peruvian wool, which were of so beautiful a texture, that the Spanish sovereigns, with all the luxuries of Europe and Asia at their command, did not disdain to use them. The royal household consisted of a throng of menials, supplied by the neighboring towns and villages, which, as in Mexico, were bound to furnish the monarch with fuel and other necessaries for the consumption of the palace.

But the favorite residence of the Incas was at Yucay, about four leagues distant from the capital. In this delicious valley, locked up within the friendly arms of the sierra, which sheltered it from the rude breezes of the east, and refreshed by gushing fountains and streams of running water, they built the most beautiful of their palaces. Here, when wearied with the dust and toil of the city, they loved to retreat, and solace themselves with the society of their favorite concubines, wandering amidst groves and airy gardens, that shed around their soft, intoxicating odors, and lulled the senses to voluptuous repose. Here, too, they loved to indulge in the luxury of their baths, replenished by streams of crystal water which were conducted through subterraneous silver channels into basins of gold. The spacious gardens were stocked with numerous varieties of plants and flowers that grew without effort in this *temperate* region of the tropics, while parterres of a more extraordinary kind were planted by their side, glowing with the various forms of vegetable life skilfully imitated in gold and silver! Among them the Indian corn, the most beautiful of American grains, is particularly commemorated, and the curious workmanship is noticed with which the golden ear was half disclosed amidst the broad leaves of silver, and the light tassel of the same material that floated gracefully from its top.

If this dazzling picture staggers the faith of the reader, he may reflect that the Peruvian mountains teemed with gold; that the natives understood the art of working the mines, to a considerable extent; that none of the ore, as we shall see hereafter, was converted into coin, and that the whole of it passed into the hands of the sovereign for his own exclusive benefit, whether for purposes of utility or ornament. Certain it is that no fact is better attested by the Conquerors themselves, who had ample means of information, and no motive for misstatement.—The Italian poets, in their gorgeous pictures of the gardens of Alcina and Morgana, came nearer the truth than they imagined.

Our surprise, however, may reasonably be excited, when we consider that the wealth displayed by the Peruvian princes was only that which each had amassed individually for himself. He owed nothing to inheritance from his predecessors. On the decease of an Inca, his palaces were abandoned, all his treasures, except what were employed in his obsequies, his furniture and apparel, were suffered to remain as he left them, and his mansions, save one, were closed up for ever. The new sovereign was to provide himself with every thing new for his royal state. The reason of this was the popular belief, that the soul of the departed monarch would return after a time to reänimate his body on earth; and they wished that he should find again every thing to which he had been used in life.

When an Inca died, or, to use his own language, "was called home to the mansions of his father, the Sun," his obsequies were celebrated with great pomp and solemnity. The bowels were taken from the body, and deposited in the temple of Tampu, about five leagues from the capital. A quantity of his plate and jewels was buried with them, and a number of his attendants and favorite concubines, amounting sometimes, it is said, to a thousand, were immolated on his tomb. Some of them showed the natural repugnance to the sacrifice occasionally manifested by the victims of a similar superstition in India. But these were probably the menials and more humble attendants; since the women have been known, in more than one instance, to lay violent hands on themselves, when restrained from testifying their fidelity by this act of conjugal martyrdom. This melancholy ceremony was followed by a general mourning throughout the empire. At stated intervals, for a year, the people assembled to renew the expressions of their sorrow, processions were made, displaying the banner of the departed monarch; bards and minstrels were appointed to chronicle his achievements, and their songs continued to be rehearsed at high festivals in the presence of the reigning monarch,—thus stimulating the living by the glorious example of the dead.

The body of the deceased Inca was skilfully embalmed, and removed to the great Temple of the Sun at Cuzco. There the Peruvian sovereign, on entering the awful sanctuary, might behold the effigies of his royal ancestors, ranged in opposite files, —the men on the right, and their queens on the left, of the great luminary which blazed in refulgent gold on the walls of the temple. The bodies, clothed in the princely attire which they had been accustomed to wear, were placed on chairs of gold, and sat with their heads inclined downward, their hands placidly crossed over their bosoms, their countenances exhibiting their natural dusky hue,—less liable to change than the fresher coloring of a European complexion,—and their hair of raven black, or silvered over with age, according to the period at which they died! It seemed like a company of solemn worshippers fixed in devotion,—so true were the forms and lineaments to life. The Peruvians were as successful as the Egyptians in the miserable attempt to perpetuate the existence of the body beyond the limits assigned to it by nature.

They cherished a still stranger illusion in the attentions which they continued to pay to these insensible remains, as if they were instinct with life. One of the houses belonging to a deceased Inca was kept open and occupied by his guard and attendants, with all the state appropriate to royalty. On certain festivals, the revered bodies of the sovereigns were brought out with great ceremony into the public square of the capital. Invitations were sent by the captains of the guard of the respective Incas to the different nobles and officers of the court; and entertainments were provided in the names of their masters, which displayed all the profuse magnificence of their treasures,—and "such a display," says an ancient chronicler, "was there in the great square of Cuzco, on this occasion, of gold and silver plate and jewels, as no other city in the world ever witnessed." The banquet was served by the menials of the respective households, and the guests partook of the melancholy cheer in the presence of the royal phantom with the same attention to the forms of courtly etiquette as if the living monarch had presided!

The nobility of Peru consisted of two orders, the first and by far the most important of which was that of the Incas, who, boasting a common descent with their sovereign, lived, as it were, in the reflected light of his glory. As the Peruvian monarchs availed themselves of the right of polygamy to a very liberal extent, leaving behind them families of one or even two hundred children, the nobles of the blood royal, though comprehending only their descendants in the male line, came in the course of years to be very numerous. They were divided into different lineages, each of which traced its pedigree to a different member of the royal dynasty, though all terminated in the divine founder of the empire.

They were distinguished by many exclusive and very important privileges; they wore a peculiar dress; spoke a dialect, if we may believe the chronicler, peculiar to themselves; and had the choicest portion of the public domain assigned for their support. They lived, most of them, at court, near the person of the prince, sharing in his counsels, dining at his board, or supplied from his table. They alone were admissible to the great offices in the priesthood. They were invested with the command of armies, and of distant garrisons, were placed over the provinces, and, in short, filled every station of high trust and emolument. Even the laws, severe in their general tenor, seem not to have been framed with reference to them; and the people, investing the whole order with a portion of the sacred character which belonged to the sovereign, held that an Inca noble was incapable of crime.

The other order of nobility was the *Curacas*, the caciques of the conquered nations, or their descendants. They were usually continued by the government in their places, though they were required to visit the capital occasionally, and to allow their sons to be educated there as the pledges of their loyalty. It is not easy to define the nature or extent of their privileges. They were possessed of more or less power, according to the extent of their patrimony, and the number of their vassals. Their authority was usually transmitted from father to son, though sometimes the successor was chosen by the people. They did not occupy the highest posts of state, or those nearest the person of the sovereign, like the nobles of the blood. Their authority seems to have been usually local, and always in subordination to the territorial jurisdiction of the great provincial governors, who were taken from the Incas.

It was the Inca nobility, indeed, who constituted the real strength of the Peruvian monarchy. Attached to their prince by ties of consanguinity, they had common sympathies and, to a considerable extent, common interests with him. Distinguished by a peculiar dress and insignia, as well as by language and blood, from the rest of the community, they were never confounded with the other tribes and nations who were incorporated into the great Peruvian monarchy. After the lapse of centuries, they still retained their individuality as a peculiar people. They were to the conquered races of the country what the Romans were to the barbarous hordes of the Empire, or the Normans to the ancient inhabitants of the British Isles. Clustering around the throne, they formed an invincible phalanx, to shield it alike from secret conspiracy and open insurrection. Though living chiefly in the capital, they were also distributed throughout the country in all its high stations and strong military posts, thus establishing lines of communication with the court, which enabled the sovereign to act simultaneously and with effect on the most distant quarters of his empire. They possessed, moreover, an intellectual preëminence, which, no less than their station, gave them authority with the people. Indeed, it may be said to have been the principal foundation of their authority. The crania of the Inca race show a decided superiority over the other races of the land in intellectual power; and it cannot be denied that it was the fountain of the peculiar civilization and social polity, which raised the Peruvian monarchy above every other state in South America. Whence this remarkable race came, and what was its early history, are among those mysteries that meet us so frequently in the annals of the New World, and which time and the antiquary have as yet done little to explain.

CHAPTER II

ORDERS OF THE STATE—PROVISIONS FOR JUSTICE—DIVI-
SION OF LANDS—REVENUES AND REGISTERS—GREAT
ROADS AND POSTS—MILITARY TACTICS AND POLICY

If we are surprised at the peculiar and original features
of what may be called the Peruvian aristocracy, we shall be
still more so as we descend to the lower orders of the community, and see the very artificial character of their institutions,—as artificial as those of ancient Sparta, and, though in a
different way, quite as repugnant to the essential principles of
our nature. The institutions of Lycurgus, however, were designed for a petty state, while those of Peru, although originally intended for such, seemed, like the magic tent in the
Arabian tale, to have an indefinite power of expansion, and
were as well suited to the most flourishing condition of the
empire as to its infant fortunes. In this remarkable accommodation to change of circumstances we see the proofs of a contrivance that argues no slight advance in civilization.

The name of Peru was not known to the natives. It was
given by the Spaniards, and originated, it is said, in a misapprehension of the Indian name of "river." However this may
be, it is certain that the natives had no other epithet by which
to designate the large collection of tribes and nations who
were assembled under the sceptre of the Incas, than that of
Tavantinsuyu, or "four quarters of the world." This will not
surprise a citizen of the United States, who has no other name
by which to class himself among nations than what is borrowed from a quarter of the globe. The kingdom, conformably
to its name, was divided into four parts, distinguished each
by a separate title, and to each of which ran one of the four
great roads that diverged from Cuzco, the capital or *navel* of
the Peruvian monarchy. The city was in like manner divided
into four quarters; and the various races, which gathered there

from the distant parts of the empire, lived each in the quarter nearest to its respective province. They all continued to wear their peculiar national costume, so that it was easy to determine their origin; and the same order and system of arrangement prevailed in the motley population of the capital, as in the great provinces of the empire. The capital, in fact, was a miniature image of the empire.

The four great provinces were each placed under a viceroy or governor, who ruled over them with the assistance of one or more councils for the different departments. These viceroys resided, some portion of their time, at least, in the capital, where they constituted a sort of council of state to the Inca. The nation at large was distributed into decades, or small bodies of ten; and every tenth man, or head of a decade, had supervision of the rest,—being required to see that they enjoyed the rights and immunities to which they were entitled, to solicit aid in their behalf from government, when necessary, and to bring offenders to justice. To this last they were stimulated by a law that imposed on them, in case of neglect, the same penalty that would have been incurred by the guilty party. With this law hanging over his head, the magistrate of Peru, we may well believe, did not often go to sleep on his post.

The people were still further divided into bodies of fifty, one hundred, five hundred, and a thousand, each with an officer having general supervision over those beneath, and the higher ones possessing, to a certain extent, authority in matters of police. Lastly, the whole empire was distributed into sections or departments of ten thousand inhabitants, with a governor over each, from the Inca nobility, who had control over the *curacas* and other territorial officers in the district. There were, also, regular tribunals of justice, consisting of magistrates in each of the towns or small communities, with jurisdiction over petty offences, while those of a graver character were carried before superior judges, usually the governors or rulers of the districts. These judges all held their authority and received their support from the Crown, by which they were appointed and removed at pleasure. They were obliged to determine every suit in five days from the time it was brought before them; and there was no appeal from one tribunal to another. Yet there were important provisions for the security of justice. A committee of visitors patrolled the kingdom at certain times to investigate the character and conduct of the magistrates; and any neglect or violation of duty was punished in the most exemplary manner. The inferior courts were also required to make monthly returns of their proceedings to the higher ones, and these made reports in like manner to the viceroys; so that the monarch, seated in the centre of his dominions, could look abroad, as it were, to the most distant extremities, and review and rectify any abuses in the administration of the law.

The laws were few and exceedingly severe. They related almost wholly to criminal matters. Few other laws were needed by a people who had no money, little trade, and hardly any thing that could be called fixed property. The crimes of theft, adultery, and murder were all capital; though it was wisely provided that some extenuating circumstances might be allowed to mitigate the punishment. Blasphemy against the Sun, and malediction of the Inca,—offences, indeed, of the same complexion,—were also punished with death. Removing landmarks, turning the water away from a neighbor's land into one's own, burning a house, were all severely punished. To burn a bridge was death. The Inca allowed no obstacle to those facilities of communication so essential to the maintenance of public order. A rebellious city or province was laid waste, and its inhabitants exterminated. Rebellion against the "Child of the Sun" was the greatest of all crimes.

The simplicity and severity of the Peruvian code may be thought to infer a state of society but little advanced; which had few of those complex interests and relations that grow up in a civilized community, and which had not proceeded far enough in the science of legislation to economize human suffering by proportioning penalties to crimes. But the Peruvian institutions must be regarded from a different point of view from that in which we study those of other nations. The laws emanated from the sovereign, and that sovereign held a divine commission, and was possessed of a divine nature. To violate the law was not only to insult the majesty of the throne, but it was sacrilege. The slightest offence, viewed in this light, merited death; and the gravest could incur no heavier penalty. Yet, in the infliction of their punishments, they showed no

unnecessary cruelty; and the sufferings of the victim were not
prolonged by the ingenious torments so frequent among barbarous nations.

These legislative provisions may strike us as very defective,
even as compared with those of the semi-civilized races of
Anahuac, where a gradation of courts, moreover, with the
right of appeal, afforded a tolerable security for justice. But
in a country like Peru, where few but criminal causes were
known, the right of appeal was of less consequence. The law
was simple, its application easy; and, where the judge was honest, the case was as likely to be determined correctly on the
first hearing as on the second. The inspection of the board of
visitors, and the monthly returns of the tribunals, afforded no
slight guaranty for their integrity. The law which required a
decision within five days would seem little suited to the complex and embarrassing litigation of a modern tribunal. But,
in the simple questions submitted to the Peruvian judge, delay would have been useless; and the Spaniards, familiar with
the evils growing out of long-protracted suits, where the successful litigant is too often a ruined man, are loud in their
encomiums of this swift-handed and economical justice.

The fiscal regulations of the Incas, and the laws respecting
property, are the most remarkable features in the Peruvian
polity. The whole territory of the empire was divided into
three parts, one for the Sun, another for the Inca, and the
last for the people. Which of the three was the largest is
doubtful. The proportions differed materially in different
provinces. The distribution, indeed, was made on the same
general principle, as each new conquest was added to the monarchy; but the proportion varied according to the amount of
population, and the greater or less amount of land consequently required for the support of the inhabitants.

The lands assigned to the Sun furnished a revenue to support the temples, and maintain the costly ceremonial of the
Peruvian worship and the multitudinous priesthood. Those
reserved for the Inca went to support the royal state, as well
as the numerous members of his household and his kindred,
and supplied the various exigencies of government. The remainder of the lands was divided, *per capita*, in equal shares
among the people. It was provided by law, as we shall see

hereafter, that every Peruvian should marry at a certain age. When this event took place, the community or district in which he lived furnished him with a dwelling, which, as it was constructed of humble materials, was done at little cost. A lot of land was then assigned to him sufficient for his own maintenance and that of his wife. An additional portion was granted for every child, the amount allowed for a son being the double of that for a daughter. The division of the soil was renewed every year, and the possessions of the tenant were increased or diminished according to the numbers in his family. The same arrangement was observed with reference to the curacas, except only that a domain was assigned to them corresponding with the superior dignity of their stations.

A more thorough and effectual agrarian law than this cannot be imagined. In other countries where such a law has been introduced, its operation, after a time, has given way to the natural order of events, and, under the superior intelligence and thrift of some and the prodigality of others, the usual vicissitudes of fortune have been allowed to take their course, and restore things to their natural inequality. Even the iron law of Lycurgus ceased to operate after a time, and melted away before the spirit of luxury and avarice. The nearest approach to the Peruvian constitution was probably in Judea, where, on the recurrence of the great national jubilee, at the close of every half-century, estates reverted to their original proprietors. There was this important difference in Peru; that not only did the lease, if we may so call it, terminate with the year, but during that period the tenant had no power to alienate or to add to his possessions. The end of the brief term found him in precisely the same condition that he was in at the beginning. Such a state of things might be supposed to be fatal to any thing like attachment to the soil, or to that desire of improving it, which is natural to the permanent proprietor, and hardly less so to the holder of a long lease. But the practical operation of the law seems to have been otherwise; and it is probable, that, under the influence of that love of order and aversion to change which marked the Peruvian institutions, each new partition of the soil usually confirmed the occupant in his possession, and the tenant for a year was converted into a proprietor for life.

The territory was cultivated wholly by the people. The lands belonging to the Sun were first attended to. They next tilled the lands of the old, of the sick, of the widow and the orphan, and of soldiers engaged in actual service; in short, of all that part of the community who, from bodily infirmity or any other cause, were unable to attend to their own concerns. The people were then allowed to work on their own ground, each man for himself, but with the general obligation to assist his neighbor, when any circumstance—the burden of a young and numerous family, for example—might demand it. Lastly, they cultivated the lands of the Inca. This was done, with great ceremony, by the whole population in a body. At break of day, they were summoned together by proclamation from some neighboring tower or eminence, and all the inhabitants of the district, men, women, and children, appeared dressed in their gayest apparel, bedecked with their little store of finery and ornaments, as if for some great jubilee. They went through the labors of the day with the same joyous spirit, chanting their popular ballads which commemorated the heroic deeds of the Incas, regulating their movements by the measure of the chant, and all mingling in the chorus, of which the word *hailli*, or "triumph," was usually the burden. These national airs had something soft and pleasing in their character, that recommended them to the Spaniards; and many a Peruvian song was set to music by them after the Conquest, and was listened to by the unfortunate natives with melancholy satisfaction, as it called up recollections of the past, when their days glided peacefully away under the sceptre of the Incas.

A similar arrangement prevailed with respect to the different manufactures as to the agricultural products of the country. The flocks of llamas, or Peruvian sheep, were appropriated exclusively to the Sun and to the Inca. Their number was immense. They were scattered over the different provinces, chiefly in the colder regions of the country, where they were intrusted to the care of experienced shepherds, who conducted them to different pastures according to the change of season. A large number was every year sent to the capital for the consumption of the Court, and for the religious festivals and sacrifices. But these were only the males, as no female was

allowed to be killed. The regulations for the care and breeding of these flocks were prescribed with the greatest minuteness, and with a sagacity which excited the admiration of the
Spaniards, who were familiar with the management of the
great migratory flocks of merinos in their own country.

At the appointed season, they were all sheared, and the
wool was deposited in the public magazines. It was then dealt
out to each family in such quantities as sufficed for its wants,
and was consigned to the female part of the household, who
were well instructed in the business of spinning and weaving.
When this labor was accomplished, and the family was provided with a coarse but warm covering, suited to the cold
climate of the mountains,—for, in the lower country, cotton,
furnished in like manner by the Crown, took the place, to a
certain extent, of wool,—the people were required to labor for
the Inca. The quantity of the cloth needed, as well as the
peculiar kind and quality of the fabric, was first determined
at Cuzco. The work was then apportioned among the different
provinces. Officers, appointed for the purpose, superintended
the distribution of the wool, so that the manufacture of the
different articles should be intrusted to the most competent
hands. They did not leave the matter here, but entered the
dwellings, from time to time, and saw that the work was faithfully executed. This domestic inquisition was not confined to
the labors for the Inca. It included, also, those for the several
families; and care was taken that each household should employ the materials furnished for its own use in the manner
that was intended, so that no one should be unprovided with
necessary apparel. In this domestic labor all the female part
of the establishment was expected to join. Occupation was
found for all, from the child five years old to the aged matron
not too infirm to hold a distaff. No one, at least none but the
decrepit and the sick, was allowed to eat the bread of idleness
in Peru. Idleness was a crime in the eye of the law, and, as
such, severely punished; while industry was publicly commended and stimulated by rewards.

The like course was pursued with reference to the other
requisitions of the government. All the mines in the kingdom
belonged to the Inca. They were wrought exclusively for his
benefit, by persons familiar with this service, and selected

from the districts where the mines were situated. Every Peruvian of the lower class was a husbandman, and, with the exception of those already specified, was expected to provide for his own support by the cultivation of his land. A small portion of the community, however, was instructed in mechanical arts; some of them of the more elegant kind, subservient to the purposes of luxury and ornament. The demand for these was chiefly limited to the sovereign and his Court; but the labor of a larger number of hands was exacted for the execution of the great public works which covered the land. The nature and amount of the services required were all determined at Cuzco by commissioners well instructed in the resources of the country, and in the character of the inhabitants of different provinces.

This information was obtained by an admirable regulation, which has scarcely a counterpart in the annals of a semi-civilized people. A register was kept of all the births and deaths throughout the country, and exact returns of the actual population were made to government every year, by means of the *quipus*, a curious invention, which will be explained hereafter. At certain intervals, also, a general survey of the country was made, exhibiting a complete view of the character of the soil, its fertility, the nature of its products, both agricultural and mineral,—in short, of all that constituted the physical resources of the empire. Furnished with these statistical details, it was easy for the government, after determining the amount of requisitions, to distribute the work among the respective provinces best qualified to execute it. The task of apportioning the labor was assigned to the local authorities, and great care was taken that it should be done in such a manner, that, while the most competent hands were selected, it should not fall disproportionately heavy on any.

The different provinces of the country furnished persons peculiarly suited to different employments, which, as we shall see hereafter, usually descended from father to son. Thus, one district supplied those most skilled in working the mines, another the most curious workers in metals, or in wood, and so on. The artisan was provided by government with the materials; and no one was required to give more than a stipulated portion of his time to the public service. He was then succeeded by another for the like term; and it should be observed, that all who were engaged in the employment of the government—and the remark applies equally to agricultural labor—were maintained, for the time, at the public expense. By this constant rotation of labor, it was intended that no one should be overburdened, and that each man should have time to provide for the demands of his own household. It was impossible—in the judgment of a high Spanish authority—to improve on the system of distribution, so carefully was it accommodated to the condition and comfort of the artisan. The security of the working classes seems to have been ever kept in view in the regulations of the government; and these were so discreetly arranged, that the most wearing and unwholesome labors, as those of the mines, occasioned no detriment to the health of the laborer; a striking contrast to his subsequent condition under the Spanish rule.

A part of the agricultural produce and manufactures was transported to Cuzco, to minister to the immediate demands of the Inca and his Court. But far the greater part was stored in magazines scattered over the different provinces. These spacious buildings, constructed of stone, were divided between the Sun and the Inca, though the greater share seems to have been appropriated by the monarch. By a wise regulation, any deficiency in the contributions of the Inca might be supplied from the granaries of the Sun. But such a necessity could rarely have happened; and the providence of the government usually left a large surplus in the royal depositories, which was removed to a third class of magazines, whose design was to supply the people in seasons of scarcity, and, occasionally, to furnish relief to individuals, whom sickness or misfortune had reduced to poverty; thus, in a manner, justifying the assertion of a Castilian document, that a large portion of the revenues of the Inca found its way back again, through one channel or another, into the hands of the people. These magazines were found by the Spaniards, on their arrival, stored with all the various products and manufactures of the country,—with maize, *coca, quinua,* woollen and cotton stuffs of the finest quality, with vases and utensils of gold, silver, and copper, in short, with every article of luxury or use within the compass of Peruvian skill. The magazines of grain, in particular, would frequently have sufficed for the consumption of the adjoining district for several years. An inventory of the various products of the country, and the quarters whence they were obtained, was every year taken by the royal officers, and recorded by the *quipucamayus* on their registers, with surprising regularity and precision. These registers were transmitted to the capital, and submitted to the Inca, who could thus at a glance, as it were, embrace the whole results of the national industry, and see how far they corresponded with the requisitions of government.

Such are some of the most remarkable features of the Peruvian institutions relating to property, as delineated by writers who, however contradictory in the details, have a general conformity of outline. These institutions are certainly so remarkable, that it is hardly credible they should ever have been enforced throughout a great empire, and for a long period of years. Yet we have the most unequivocal testimony to the fact from the Spaniards, who landed in Peru in time to witness their operation; some of whom, men of high judicial station and character, were commissioned by the government to make investigations into the state of the country under its ancient rulers.

The impositions on the Peruvian people seem to have been sufficiently heavy. On them rested the whole burden of maintaining, not only their own order, but every other order in the state. The members of the royal house, the great nobles, even the public functionaries, and the numerous body of the priesthood, were all exempt from taxation. The whole duty of defraying the expenses of the government belonged to the people. Yet this was not materially different from the condition of things formerly existing in most parts of Europe, where the various privileged classes claimed exemption—not always with success, indeed—from bearing part of the public burdens. The great hardship in the case of the Peruvian was, that he could not better his condition. His labors were for others, rather than for himself. However industrious, he could not add a rood to his own possessions, nor advance himself one hair's breadth in the social scale. The great and universal motive to honest industry, that of bettering one's lot, was lost upon him. The great law of human progress was not for him.

As he was born, so he was to die. Even his time he could not properly call his own. Without money, with little property of any kind, he paid his taxes in labor. No wonder that the government should have dealt with sloth as a crime. It was a crime against the state, and to be wasteful of time was, in a manner, to rob the exchequer. The Peruvian, laboring all his life for others, might be compared to the convict in a tread-mill, going the same dull round of incessant toil, with the consciousness, that, however profitable the results to the state, they were nothing to him.

But this is the dark side of the picture. If no man could become rich in Peru, no man could become poor. No spendthrift could waste his substance in riotous luxury. No adventurous schemer could impoverish his family by the spirit of speculation. The law was constantly directed to enforce a steady industry and a sober management of his affairs. No mendicant was tolerated in Peru. When a man was reduced by poverty or misfortune (it could hardly be by fault), the arm of the law was stretched out to minister relief; not the stinted relief of private charity, nor that which is doled out, drop by drop, as it were, from the frozen reservoirs of "the parish," but in generous measure, bringing no humiliation to the object of it, and placing him on a level with the rest of his countrymen.

No man could be rich, no man could be poor, in Peru; but all might enjoy, and did enjoy, a competence. Ambition, avarice, the love of change, the morbid spirit of discontent, those passions which most agitate the minds of men, found no place in the bosom of the Peruvian. The very condition of his being seemed to be at war with change. He moved on in the same unbroken circle in which his fathers had moved before him, and in which his children were to follow. It was the object of the Incas to infuse into their subjects a spirit of passive obedience and tranquillity,—a perfect acquiescence in the established order of things. In this they fully succeeded. The Spanish who first visited the country are emphatic in their testimony, that no government could have been better suited to the genius of the people; and no people could have appeared more contented with their lot, or more devoted to their government.

Those who may distrust the accounts of Peruvian industry will find their doubts removed on a visit to the country. The traveller still meets, especially in the central regions of the table-land, with memorials of the past, remains of temples, palaces, fortresses, terraced mountains, great military roads, aqueducts, and other public works, which, whatever degree of science they may display in their execution, astonish him by their number, the massive character of the materials, and the grandeur of the design. Among them, perhaps the most remarkable are the great roads, the broken remains of which are still in sufficient preservation to attest their former magnificence. There were many of these roads, traversing different parts of the kingdom; but the most considerable were the two which extended from Quito to Cuzco, and, again diverging from the capital, continued in a southern direction towards Chili.

One of these roads passed over the grand plateau, and the other along the lowlands on the borders of the ocean. The former was much the more difficult achievement, from the character of the country. It was conducted over pathless sierras buried in snow; galleries were cut for leagues through the living rock; rivers were crossed by means of bridges that swung suspended in the air; precipices were scaled by stairways hewn out of the native bed; ravines of hideous depth were filled up with solid masonry; in short, all the difficulties that beset a wild and mountainous region, and which might appall the most courageous engineer of modern times, were encountered and successfully overcome. The length of the road, of which scattered fragments only remain, is variously estimated, from fifteen hundred to two thousand miles; and stone pillars, in the manner of European milestones, were erected at stated intervals of somewhat more than a league, all along the route. Its breadth scarcely exceeded twenty feet. It was built of heavy flags of freestone, and in some parts, at least, covered with a bituminous cement, which time has made harder than the stone itself. In some places, where the ravines had been filled up with masonry, the mountain torrents, wearing on it for ages, have gradually eaten a way through the base, and left the superincumbent mass—such is the cohesion of the materials—still spanning the valley like an arch!

Over some of the boldest streams it was necessary to construct suspension bridges, as they are termed, made of the tough fibres of the *maguey*, or of the osier of the country, which has an extraordinary degree of tenacity and strength. These osiers were woven into cables of the thickness of a man's body. The huge ropes, then stretched across the water, were conducted through rings or holes cut in immense buttresses of stone raised on the opposite banks of the river, and there secured to heavy pieces of timber. Several of these enormous cables, bound together, formed a bridge, which, covered with planks, well secured and defended by a railing of the same osier materials on the sides, afforded a safe passage for the traveller. The length of this aërial bridge, sometimes exceeding two hundred feet, caused it, confined, as it was, only at the extremities, to dip with an alarming inclination towards the centre, while the motion given to it by the passenger occasioned an oscillation still more frightful, as his eye wandered over the dark abyss of waters that foamed and tumbled many a fathom beneath. Yet these light and fragile fabrics were crossed without fear by the Peruvians, and are still retained by the Spaniards over those streams which, from the depth or impetuosity of the current, would seem impracticable for the usual modes of conveyance. The wider and more tranquil waters were crossed on *balsas*—a kind of raft still much used by the natives—to which sails were attached, furnishing the only instance of this higher kind of navigation among the American Indians.

The other great road of the Incas lay through the level country between the Andes and the ocean. It was constructed in a different manner, as demanded by the nature of the ground, which was for the most part low, and much of it sandy. The causeway was raised on a high embankment of earth, and defended on either side by a parapet or wall of clay; and trees and odoriferous shrubs were planted along the margin, regaling the sense of the traveller with their perfumes, and refreshing him by their shades, so grateful under the burning sky of the tropics. In the strips of sandy waste, which occasionally intervened, where the light and volatile soil was incapable of sustaining a road, huge piles, many of them to be seen at this day, were driven into the ground to indicate the route to the traveller.

All along these highways, caravansaries, or *tambos*, as they were called, were erected, at the distance of ten or twelve miles from each other, for the accommodation, more particularly, of the Inca and his suite, and those who journeyed on the public business. There were few other travellers in Peru. Some of these buildings were on an extensive scale, consisting of a fortress, barracks, and other military works, surrounded by a parapet of stone, and covering a large tract of ground. These were evidently destined for the accommodation of the imperial armies, when on their march across the country.— The care of the great roads was committed to the districts through which they passed, and a large number of hands was constantly employed under the Incas to keep them in repair. This was the more easily done in a country where the mode of travelling was altogether on foot; though the roads are said to have been so nicely constructed, that a carriage might have rolled over them as securely as on any of the great roads of Europe. Still, in a region where the elements of fire and water are both actively at work in the business of destruction, they must, without constant supervision, have gradually gone to decay. Such has been their fate under the Spanish conquerors, who took no care to enforce the admirable system for their preservation adopted by the Incas. Yet the broken portions that still survive, here and there, like the fragments of the great Roman roads scattered over Europe, bear evidence to their primitive grandeur, and have drawn forth the eulogium from so discriminating a traveller as Humboldt, usually not too profuse in his panegyric, that "the roads of the Incas were among the most useful and stupendous works ever executed by man."

The system of communication through their dominions was still further improved by the Peruvian sovereigns, by the introduction of posts, in the same manner as was done by the Aztecs. The Peruvian posts, however, established on all the great routes that conducted to the capital, were on a much more extended plan than those in Mexico. All along these routes, small buildings were erected, at the distance of less than five miles asunder, in each of which a number of runners, or *chasquis*, as they were called, were stationed to carry forward the despatches of government. These despatches were either verbal, or conveyed by means of *quipus*, and sometimes accompanied by a thread of the crimson fringe worn round the temples of the Inca, which was regarded with the same implicit deference as the signet ring of an Oriental despot.

The *chasquis* were dressed in a peculiar livery, intimating their profession. They were all trained to the employment, and selected for their speed and fidelity. As the distance each courier had to perform was small, and as he had ample time to refresh himself at the stations, they ran over the ground with great swiftness, and messages were carried through the whole extent of the long routes, at the rate of a hundred and fifty miles a day. The office of the *chasquis* was not limited to carrying despatches. They frequently brought various articles for the use of the Court; and in this way, fish from the distant ocean, fruits, game, and different commodities from the hot regions on the coast, were taken to the capital in good condition, and served fresh at the royal table. It is remarkable that this important institution should have been known to both the Mexicans and the Peruvians without any correspondence with one another; and that it should have been found among two barbarian nations of the New World, long before it was introduced among the civilized nations of Europe.

By these wise contrivances of the Incas, the most distant parts of the long-extended empire of Peru were brought into intimate relations with each other. And while the capitals of Christendom, but a few hundred miles apart, remained as far asunder as if seas had rolled between them, the great capitals Cuzco and Quito were placed by the high roads of the Incas in immediate correspondence. Intelligence from the numerous provinces was transmitted on the wings of the wind to the Peruvian metropolis, the great focus to which all the lines of communication converged. Not an insurrectionary movement could occur, not an invasion on the remotest frontier, before the tidings were conveyed to the capital, and the imperial armies were on their march across the magnificent roads of the country to suppress it. So admirable was the machinery contrived by the American despots for maintaining tranquillity throughout their dominions! It may remind us of the similar institutions of ancient Rome, when, under the Cæsars, she was mistress of half the world.

A principal design of the great roads was to serve the purposes of military communication. It formed an important item of their military policy, which is quite as well worth studying as their municipal.

Notwithstanding the pacific professions of the Incas, and the pacific tendency, indeed, of their domestic institutions, they were constantly at war. It was by war that their paltry territory had been gradually enlarged to a powerful empire. When this was achieved, the capital, safe in its central position, was no longer shaken by these military movements, and the country enjoyed, in a great degree, the blessings of tranquillity and order. But, however tranquil at heart, there is not a reign upon record in which the nation was not engaged in war against the barbarous nations on the frontier. Religion furnished a plausible pretext for incessant aggression, and disguised the lust of conquest in the Incas, probably, from their own eyes, as well as from those of their subjects. Like the followers of Mahomet, bearing the sword in one hand and the Koran in the other, the Incas of Peru offered no alternative but the worship of the Sun or war.

It is true, their fanaticism—or their policy—showed itself in a milder form than was found in the descendants of the Prophet. Like the great luminary which they adored, they operated by gentleness more potent than violence. They sought to soften the hearts of the rude tribes around them, and melt them by acts of condescension and kindness. Far from provoking hostilities, they allowed time for the salutary example of their own institutions to work its effect, trusting that their less civilized neighbors would submit to their sceptre, from a conviction of the blessings it would secure to them. When this course failed, they employed other measures, but still of a pacific character; and endeavored by negotiation, by conciliatory treatment, and by presents to the leading men, to win them over to their dominion. In short, they practised all the arts familiar to the most subtle politician of a civilized land to secure the acquisition of empire. When all these expedients failed, they prepared for war.

Their levies were drawn from all the different provinces;

though from some, where the character of the people was particularly hardy, more than from others. It seems probable that every Peruvian, who had reached a certain age, might be called to bear arms. But the rotation of military service, and the regular drills, which took place twice or thrice in a month, of the inhabitants of every village, raised the soldiers generally above the rank of a raw militia. The Peruvian army, at first inconsiderable, came, with the increase of population, in the latter days of the empire, to be very large, so that their monarchs could bring into the field, as contemporaries assure us, a force amounting to two hundred thousand men. They showed the same skill and respect for order in their military organization, as in other things. The troops were divided into bodies corresponding with our battalions and companies, led by officers, that rose, in regular gradation, from the lowest subaltern to the Inca noble, who was intrusted with the general command.

Their arms consisted of the usual weapons employed by nations, whether civilized or uncivilized, before the invention of powder,—bows and arrows, lances, darts, a short kind of sword, a battle-axe or partisan, and slings, with which they were very expert. Their spears and arrows were tipped with copper, or, more commonly, with bone, and the weapons of the Inca lords were frequently mounted with gold or silver. Their heads were protected by casques made either of wood or of the skins of wild animals, and sometimes richly decorated with metal and with precious stones, surmounted by the brilliant plumage of the tropical birds. These, of course, were the ornaments only of the higher orders. The great mass of the soldiery were dressed in the peculiar costume of their provinces, and their heads were wreathed with a sort of turban or roll of different-colored cloths, that produced a gay and animating effect. Their defensive armor consisted of a shield or buckler, and a close tunic of quilted cotton, in the same manner as with the Mexicans. Each company had its particular banner, and the imperial standard, high above all, displayed the glittering device and the rainbow,—the armorial ensign of the Incas, intimating their claims as children of the skies.

By means of the thorough system of communication established in the country, a short time sufficed to draw the levies together from the most distant quarters. The army was put under the direction of some experienced chief, of the blood royal, or, more frequently, headed by the Inca in person. The march was rapidly performed, and with little fatigue to the soldier; for, all along the great routes, quarters were provided for him, at regular distances, where he could find ample accommodations. The country is still covered with the remains of military works, constructed of porphyry or granite, which tradition assures us were designed to lodge the Inca and his army.

At regular intervals, also, magazines were established, filled with grain, weapons, and the different munitions of war, with which the army was supplied on its march. It was the especial care of the government to see that these magazines, which were furnished from the stores of the Incas, were always well filled. When the Spaniards invaded the country, they supported their own armies for a long time on the provisions found in them. The Peruvian soldier was forbidden to commit any trespass on the property of the inhabitants whose territory lay in the line of march. Any violation of this order was punished with death. The soldier was clothed and fed by the industry of the people, and the Incas rightly resolved that he should not repay this by violence. Far from being a tax on the labors of the husbandman, or even a burden on his hospitality, the imperial armies traversed the country, from one extremity to the other, with as little inconvenience to the inhabitants, as would be created by a procession of burghers, or a muster of holiday soldiers for a review.

From the moment war was proclaimed, the Peruvian monarch used all possible expedition in assembling his forces, that he might anticipate the movements of his enemies, and prevent a combination with their allies. It was, however, from the neglect of such a principle of combination, that the several nations of the country, who might have prevailed by confederated strength, fell one after another under the imperial yoke. Yet, once in the field the Inca did not usually show any disposition to push his advantages to the utmost, and urge his foe to extremity. In every stage of the war, he was open to propositions for peace; and although he sought to reduce his enemies by carrying off their harvests and distressing them by famine, he allowed his troops to commit no unnecessary outrage on person or property. "We must spare our enemies," one of the Peruvian princes is quoted as saying, "or it will be our loss, since they and all that belong to them must soon be ours." It was a wise maxim, and, like most other wise maxims, founded equally on benevolence and prudence. The Incas adopted the policy claimed for the Romans by their countryman, who tells us that they gained more by clemency to the vanquished than by their victories.

In the same considerate spirit, they were most careful to provide for the security and comfort of their own troops; and, when a war was long protracted, or the climate proved unhealthy, they took care to relieve their men by frequent reinforcements, allowing the earlier recruits to return to their homes. But while thus economical of life, both in their own followers and in the enemy, they did not shrink from sterner measures when provoked by the ferocious or obstinate character of the resistance; and the Peruvian annals contain more than one of those sanguinary pages which cannot be pondered at the present day without a shudder. It should be added that the beneficent policy, which I have been delineating as characteristic of the Incas, did not belong to all; and that there was more than one of the royal line who displayed a full measure of the bold and unscrupulous spirit of the vulgar conqueror.

The first step of the government, after the reduction of a country, was to introduce there the worship of the Sun. Temples were erected, and placed under the care of a numerous priesthood, who expounded to the conquered people the mysteries of their new faith, and dazzled them by the display of its rich and stately ceremonial. Yet the religion of the conquered was not treated with dishonor. The Sun was to be worshipped above all; but the images of their gods were removed to Cuzco and established in one of the temples, to hold their rank among the inferior deities of the Peruvian Pantheon. Here they remained as hostages for the conquered nation, which would be the less inclined to forsake its allegiance, when by doing so it must leave its own gods in the hands of its enemies.

The Incas provided for the settlement of their new conquests, by ordering a census to be taken of the population, and a careful survey to be made of the country, ascertaining its products, and the character and capacity of its soil. A division of the territory was then made on the same principle with that adopted throughout their own kingdom; and their respective portions were assigned to the Sun, the sovereign, and the people. The amount of the last was regulated by the amount of the population, but the share of each individual was uniformly the same. It may seem strange, that any people should patiently have acquiesced in an arrangement which involved such a total surrender of property. But it was a conquered nation that did so, held in awe, on the least suspicion of meditating resistance, by armed garrisons, who were established at various commanding points throughout the country. It is probable, too, that the Incas made no greater changes than was essential to the new arrangement, and that they assigned estates, as far as possible, to their former proprietors. The curacas, in particular, were confirmed in their ancient authority; or, when it was found expedient to depose the existing curaca, his rightful heir was allowed to succeed him. Every respect was shown to the ancient usages and laws of the land, as far as was compatible with the fundamental institutions of the Incas. It must also be remembered, that the conquered tribes were, many of them, too little advanced in civilization to possess that attachment to the soil which belongs to a cultivated nation. But, to whatever it be referred, it seems probable that the extraordinary institutions of the Incas were established with little opposition in the conquered territories.

Yet the Peruvian sovereigns did not trust altogether to this show of obedience in their new vassals; and, to secure it more effectually, they adopted some expedients too remarkable to be passed by in silence.—Immediately after a recent conquest, the curacas and their families were removed for a time to Cuzco. Here they learned the language of the capital, became familiar with the manners and usages of the court, as well as with the general policy of government, and experienced such marks of favor from the sovereign as would be most grateful to their feelings, and might attach them most warmly to his person. Under the influence of these sentiments, they were again sent to rule over their vassals, but still leaving their eldest sons in the capital, to remain there as a guaranty for their fidelity, as well as to grace the court of the Inca.

Another expedient was of a bolder and more original character. This was nothing less than to revolutionize the language of the country. South America, like North, was broken up into a great variety of dialects, or rather languages, having little affinity with one another. This circumstance occasioned great embarrassment to the government in the administration of the different provinces, with whose idioms they were unacquainted. It was determined, therefore, to substitute one universal language, the *Quichua*,—the language of the Court, the capital, and the surrounding country,—the richest and most comprehensive of the South American dialects. Teachers were provided in the towns and villages throughout the land, who were to give instruction to all, even the humblest classes; and it was intimated at the same time, that no one should be raised to any office of dignity or profit, who was unacquainted with this tongue. The curacas and other chiefs, who attended at the capital, became familiar with this dialect in their intercourse with the Court, and, on their return home, set the example of conversing in it among themselves. This example was imitated by their followers, and the Quichua gradually became the language of elegance and fashion, in the same manner as the Norman French was affected by all those who aspired to any consideration in England, after the Conquest. By this means, while each province retained its peculiar tongue, a beautiful medium of communication was introduced, which enabled the inhabitants of one part of the country to hold intercourse with every other, and the Inca and his deputies to communicate with all. This was the state of things on the arrival of the Spaniards. It must be admitted, that history furnishes few examples of more absolute authority than such a revolution in the language of an empire, at the bidding of a master.

Yet little less remarkable was another device of the Incas for securing the loyalty of their subjects. When any portion of the recent conquests showed a pertinacious spirit of disaffection, it was not uncommon to cause a part of the population, amounting, it might be, to ten thousand inhabitants or more, to remove to a distant quarter of the kingdom, occupied by ancient vassals of undoubted fidelity to the crown. A like number of these last was transplanted to the territory left vacant by the emigrants. By this exchange, the population was composed of two distinct races, who regarded each other with an eye of jealousy, that served as an effectual check on any mutinous proceeding. In time, the influence of the well-affected prevailed, supported, as they were, by royal authority, and by the silent working of the national institutions, to which the strange races became gradually accustomed. A spirit of loyalty sprang up by degrees in their bosoms, and, before a generation had passed away, the different tribes mingled in harmony together as members of the same community. Yet the different races continued to be distinguished by difference of dress; since, by the law of the land, every citizen was required to wear the costume of his native province. Neither could the colonist, who had been thus unceremoniously transplanted, return to his native district. For, by another law, it was forbidden to any one to change his residence without license. He was settled for life. The Peruvian government ascribed to every man his local habitation, his sphere of action, nay, the very nature and quality of that action. He ceased to be a free agent; it might be almost said, that it relieved him of personal responsibility.

In following out this singular arrangement, the Incas showed as much regard for the comfort and convenience of the colonist as was compatible with the execution of their design. They were careful that the *mitimaes*, as these emigrants were styled, should be removed to climates most congenial with their own. The inhabitants of the cold countries were not transplanted to the warm, nor the inhabitants of the warm countries to the cold. Even their habitual occupations were consulted, and the fisherman was settled in the neighborhood of the ocean, or the great lakes; while such lands were assigned to the husbandman as were best adapted to the culture with which he was most familiar. And, as migration by many, perhaps by most, would be regarded as a calamity, the government was careful to show particular marks of favor to the *mitimaes*, and, by various privileges and immunities, to ameliorate their condition, and thus to reconcile them to their lot.

The Peruvian institutions, though they may have been modified and matured under successive sovereigns, all bear the stamp of the same original,—were all cast in the same mould. The empire, strengthening and enlarging at every successive epoch of its history, was, in its latter days, but the development, on a great scale, of what it was in miniature at its commencement, as the infant germ is said to contain within itself all the ramifications of the future monarch of the forest. Each succeeding Inca seemed desirous only to tread in the path, and carry out the plans, of his predecessor. Great enterprises, commenced under one, were continued by another, and completed by a third. Thus, while all acted on a regular plan, without any of the eccentric or retrograde movements which betray the agency of different individuals, the state seemed to be under the direction of a single hand, and pursued, as if through one long reign, its great career of civilization and of conquest.

The ultimate aim of its institutions was domestic quiet. But it seemed as if this were to be obtained only by foreign war. Tranquillity in the heart of the monarchy, and war on its borders, was the condition of Peru. By this war it gave occupation to a part of its people, and, by the reduction and civilization of its barbarous neighbors, gave security to all. Every Inca sovereign, however mild and benevolent in his domestic rule, was a warrior, and led his armies in person. Each successive reign extended still wider the boundaries of the empire. Year after year saw the victorious monarch return laden with spoils, and followed by a throng of tributary chieftains to his capital. His reception there was a Roman triumph. The whole of its numerous population poured out to welcome him, dressed in the gay and picturesque costumes of the different provinces, with banners waving above their heads, and strewing branches and flowers along the path of the conqueror. The Inca, borne aloft in his golden chair on the shoulders of his nobles, moved in solemn procession, under the triumphal arches that were thrown across the way, to the great Temple of the Sun. There, without attendants,—for all but the monarch were excluded from the hallowed precincts,—the victorious prince, stripped of his royal insignia, barefooted, and with all humility, approached the awful shrine, and offered up sacrifice and thanksgiving to the glorious Deity who presided over the fortunes of the Incas. This ceremony concluded, the whole population gave itself up to festivity; music, revelry, and dancing were heard in every quarter of the capital, and illuminations and bonfires commemorated the victorious campaign of the Inca, and the accession of a new territory to his empire.

In this celebration we see much of the character of a religious festival. Indeed, the character of religion was impressed on all the Peruvian wars. The life of an Inca was one long crusade against the infidel, to spread wide the worship of the Sun, to reclaim the benighted nations from their brutish superstitions, and impart to them the blessings of a well-regulated government. This, in the favorite phrase of our day, was the "mission" of the Inca. It was also the mission of the Christian conqueror who invaded the empire of this same Indian potentate. Which of the two executed his mission most faithfully, history must decide.

Yet the Peruvian monarchs did not show a childish impatience in the acquisition of empire. They paused after a campaign, and allowed time for the settlement of one conquest before they undertook another; and, in this interval, occupied themselves with the quiet administration of their kingdom, and with the long progresses, which brought them into nearer intercourse with their people. During this interval, also, their new vassals had begun to accommodate themselves to the strange institutions of their masters. They learned to appreciate the value of a government which raised them above the physical evils of a state of barbarism, secured them protection of person, and a full participation in all the privileges enjoyed by their conquerors; and, as they became more familiar with the peculiar institutions of the country, habit, that second nature, attached them the more strongly to these institutions, from their very peculiarity. Thus, by degrees, and without violence, arose the great fabric of the Peruvian empire, composed of numerous independent and even hostile tribes, yet, under the influence of a common religion, common language, and common government, knit together as one nation, animated by a spirit of love for its institutions and devoted loyalty to its sovereign. What a contrast to the condition of the Aztec monarchy, on the neighboring continent, which, composed of the like heterogeneous materials, without any internal principle of cohesion, was only held together by the stern pressure, from without, of physical force!—Why the Peruvian monarchy should have fared no better than its rival, in its conflict with European civilization, will appear in the following pages.

CHAPTER III

PERUVIAN RELIGION—DEITIES—GORGEOUS TEMPLES—
FESTIVALS—VIRGINS OF THE SUN—MARRIAGE

It is a remarkable fact, that many, if not most, of the rude tribes inhabiting the vast American continent, however disfigured their creeds may have been in other respects by a childish superstition, had attained to the sublime conception of one Great Spirit, the Creator of the Universe, who, immaterial in his own nature, was not to be dishonored by an attempt at visible representation, and who, pervading all space, was not to be circumscribed within the walls of a temple. Yet these elevated ideas, so far beyond the ordinary range of the untutored intellect, do not seem to have led to the practical consequences that might have been expected; and few of the American nations have shown much solicitude for the maintenance of a religious worship, or found in their faith a powerful spring of action.

But, with progress in civilization, ideas more akin to those of civilized communities were gradually unfolded; a liberal provision was made, and a separate order instituted, for the services of religion, which were conducted with a minute and magnificent ceremonial, that challenged comparison, in some respects, with that of the most polished nations of Christendom. This was the case with the nations inhabiting the table-land of North America, and with the natives of Bogotá, Quito, Peru, and the other elevated regions on the great Southern continent. It was, above all, the case with the Peruvians, who claimed a divine original for the founders of their empire, whose laws all rested on a divine sanction, and whose domestic institutions and foreign wars were alike directed to preserve and propagate their faith. Religion was the basis of their polity, the very condition, as it were, of their social existence.

The government of the Incas, in its essential principles, was a theocracy.

Yet, though religion entered so largely into the fabric and conduct of the political institutions of the people, their mythology, that is, the traditionary legends by which they affected to unfold the mysteries of the universe, was exceedingly mean and puerile. Scarce one of their traditions—except the beautiful one respecting the founders of their royal dynasty—is worthy of note, or throws much light on their own antiquities, or the primitive history of man. Among the traditions of importance is one of the deluge, which they held in common with so many of the nations in all parts of the globe, and which they related with some particulars that bear resemblance to a Mexican legend.

Their ideas in respect to a future state of being deserve more attention. They admitted the existence of a soul hereafter, and connected with this a belief in the resurrection of the body. They assigned two distinct places for the residence of the good and of the wicked, the latter of which they fixed in the centre of the earth. The good they supposed were to pass a luxurious life of tranquillity and ease, which comprehended their highest notions of happiness. The wicked were to expiate their crimes by ages of wearisome labor. They associated with these ideas a belief in an evil principle or spirit, bearing the name of Cupay, whom they did not attempt to propitiate by sacrifices, and who seems to have been only a shadowy personification of sin, one that exercised little influence over their conduct.

It was this belief in the resurrection of the body, which led them to preserve the body with so much solicitude, by a simple process, however, that, unlike the elaborate embalming of the Egyptians, consisted in exposing it to the action of the cold, exceedingly dry, and highly rarefied atmosphere of the mountains. As they believed that the occupations in the future world would have great resemblance to those of the present, they buried with the deceased noble some of his apparel, his utensils, and, frequently, his treasures; and completed the gloomy ceremony by sacrificing his wives and favorite domestics, to bear him company and do him service in the happy regions beyond the clouds. Vast mounds of an irregular, or, more frequently, oblong shape, penetrated by galleries running at right angles to each other, were raised over the dead, whose dried bodies or mummies have been found in considerable numbers, sometimes erect, but more often in the sitting posture, common to the Indian tribes of both continents. Treasures of great value have also been occasionally drawn from these monumental deposits, and have stimulated speculators to repeated excavations with the hope of similar good fortune. It was a lottery like that of searching after mines, but where the chances have proved still more against the adventurers.

The Peruvians, like so many other of the Indian races, acknowledged a Supreme Being, the Creator and Ruler of the Universe, whom they adored under the different names of Pachacamac and Viracocha. No temple was raised to this invisible Being, save one only in the valley which took its name from the deity himself, not far from the Spanish city of Lima. Even this temple had existed there before the country came under the sway of the Incas, and was the great resort of Indian pilgrims from remote parts of the land; a circumstance which suggests the idea, that the worship of this Great Spirit, though countenanced, perhaps, by their accommodating policy, did not originate with the Peruvian princes.

The deity whose worship they especially inculcated, and which they never failed to establish wherever their banners were known to penetrate, was the Sun. It was he, who, in a particular manner, presided over the destinies of man; gave light and warmth to the nations, and life to the vegetable world; whom they reverenced as the father of their royal dynasty, the founder of their empire; and whose temples rose in every city and almost every village throughout the land, while his altars smoked with burnt offerings,—a form of sacrifice peculiar to the Peruvians among the semi-civilized nations of the New World.

Besides the Sun, the Incas acknowledged various objects of worship in some way or other connected with this principal deity. Such was the Moon, his sister-wife; the Stars, revered as part of her heavenly train,—though the fairest of them, Venus, known to the Peruvians by the name of Chasca, or the "youth with the long and curling locks," was adored as the page of the

Sun, whom he attends so closely in his rising and in his setting. They dedicated temples also to the Thunder and the Lightning, in whom they recognized the Sun's dread ministers, and to the Rainbow whom they worshipped as a beautiful emanation of their glorious deity.

In addition to these, the subjects of the Incas enrolled among their inferior deities many objects in nature, as the elements, the winds, the earth, the air, great mountains and rivers, which impressed them with ideas of sublimity and power, or were supposed in some way or other to exercise a mysterious influence over the destinies of man. They adopted also a notion, not unlike that professed by some of the schools of ancient philosophy, that every thing on earth had its archetype or idea, its *mother*, as they emphatically styled it, which they held sacred, as, in some sort, its spiritual essence. But their system, far from being limited even to these multiplied objects of devotion, embraced within its ample folds the numerous deities of the conquered nations, whose images were transported to the capital, where the burdensome charges of their worship were defrayed by their respective provinces. It was a rare stroke of policy in the Incas, who could thus accommodate their religion to their interests.

But the worship of the Sun constituted the peculiar care of the Incas, and was the object of their lavish expenditure. The most ancient of the many temples dedicated to this divinity was in the Island of Titicaca, whence the royal founders of the Peruvian line were said to have proceeded. From this circumstance, this sanctuary was held in peculiar veneration. Every thing which belonged to it, even the broad fields of maize, which surrounded the temple, and formed part of its domain, imbibed a portion of its sanctity. The yearly produce was distributed among the different public magazines, in small quantities to each, as something that would sanctify the remainder of the store. Happy was the man who could secure even an ear of the blessed harvest for his own granary!

But the most renowned of the Peruvian temples, the pride of the capital, and the wonder of the empire, was at Cuzco, where, under the munificence of successive sovereigns, it had become so enriched, that it received the name of *Coricancha*, or "the Place of Gold." It consisted of a principal building

and several chapels and inferior edifices, covering a large
extent of ground in the heart of the city, and completely
encompassed by a wall, which, with the edifices, was all
constructed of stone. The work was of the kind already described in the other public buildings of the country, and was
so finely executed, that a Spaniard, who saw it in its glory,
assures us, he could call to mind only two edifices in Spain,
which, for their workmanship, were at all to be compared with
it. Yet this substantial, and, in some respects, magnificent
structure, was thatched with straw!

The interior of the temple was the most worthy of admiration. It was literally a mine of gold. On the western wall was
emblazoned a representation of the deity, consisting of a human countenance, looking forth from amidst innumerable rays
of light, which emanated from it in every direction, in the
same manner as the sun is often personified with us. The
figure was engraved on a massive plate of gold of enormous
dimensions thickly powdered with emeralds and precious
stones. It was so situated in front of the great eastern portal,
that the rays of the morning sun fell directly upon it at its
rising, lighting up the whole apartment with an effulgence that
seemed more than natural, and which was reflected back from
the golden ornaments with which the walls and ceiling were
everywhere encrusted. Gold, in the figurative language of the
people was "the tears wept by the sun," and every part of the
interior of the temple glowed with burnished plates and studs
of the precious metal. The cornices, which surrounded the
walls of the sanctuary, were of the same costly material; and
a broad belt or frieze of gold, let into the stone-work, encompassed the whole exterior of the edifice.

Adjoining the principal structure were several chapels of
smaller dimensions. One of them was consecrated to the
Moon, the deity held next in reverence, as the mother of the
Incas. Her effigy was delineated in the same manner as that
of the Sun, on a vast plate that nearly covered one side of the
apartment. But this plate, as well as all the decorations of the
building, was of silver, as suited to the pale, silvery light of
the beautiful planet. There were three other chapels, one of
which was dedicated to the host of Stars, who formed the
bright court of the Sister of the Sun; another was consecrated

to his dread ministers of vengeance, the Thunder and the Lightning; and a third, to the Rainbow, whose many-colored arch spanned the walls of the edifice with hues almost as radiant as its own. There were besides several other buildings, or insulated apartments, for the accommodation of the numerous priests who officiated in the service of the temple.

All the plate, the ornaments, the utensils of every description, appropriated to the uses of religion, were of gold or silver. Twelve immense vases of the latter metal stood on the floor of the great saloon, filled with grain of the Indian corn; the censers for the perfumes, the ewers which held the water for sacrifice, the pipes which conducted it through subterraneous channels into the buildings, the reservoirs that received it, even the agricultural implements used in the gardens of the temple, were all of the same rich materials. The gardens, like those described, belonging to the royal palaces, sparkled with flowers of gold and silver, and various imitations of the vegetable kingdom. Animals, also, were to be found there,—among which the llama, with its golden fleece, was most conspicuous,—executed in the same style, and with a degree of skill, which, in this instance, probably, did not surpass the excellence of the material.

If the reader sees in this fairy picture only the romantic coloring of some fabulous *El Dorado*, he must recall what has been said before in reference to the palaces of the Incas, and consider that these "Houses of the Sun," as they were styled, were the common reservoir into which flowed all the streams of public and private benefaction throughout the empire. Some of the statements, through credulity, and others, in the desire of exciting admiration, may be greatly exaggerated; but, in the coincidence of contemporary testimony, it is not easy to determine the exact line which should mark the measure of our skepticism. Certain it is, that the glowing picture I have given is warranted by those who saw these buildings in their pride, or shortly after they had been despoiled by the cupidity of their countrymen. Many of the costly articles were buried by the natives, or thrown into the waters of the rivers and the lakes; but enough remained to attest the unprecedented opulence of these religious establishments. Such things as were in their nature portable were speedily removed, to gratify the craving of the Conquerors, who even tore away the solid cornices and frieze of gold from the great temple, filling the vacant places with the cheaper, but—since it affords no temptation to avarice—more durable, material of plaster. Yet even thus shorn of their splendor, the venerable edifices still presented an attraction to the spoiler, who found in their dilapidated walls an inexhaustible quarry for the erection of other buildings. On the very ground once crowned by the gorgeous Coricancha rose the stately church of St. Dominic, one of the most magnificent structures of the New World. Fields of maize and lucerne now bloom on the spot which glowed with the golden gardens of the temple; and the friar chants his orisons within the consecrated precincts once occupied by the Children of the Sun.

Besides the great Temple of the Sun, there was a large number of inferior temples and religious houses in the Peruvian capital and its environs, amounting, as is stated, to three or four hundred. For Cuzco was a sanctified spot, venerated not only as the abode of the Incas, but of all those deities who presided over the motley nations of the empire. It was the city beloved of the Sun; where his worship was maintained in its splendor; "where every fountain, pathway, and wall," says an ancient chronicler, "was regarded as a holy mystery." And unfortunate was the Indian noble who, at some period or other of his life, had not made his pilgrimage to the Peruvian Mecca.

Other temples and religious dwellings were scattered over the provinces; and some of them constructed on a scale of magnificence, that almost rivalled that of the metropolis. The attendants on these composed an army of themselves. The whole number of functionaries, including those of the sacerdotal order, who officiated at the Coricancha alone, was no less than four thousand.

At the head of all, both here and throughout the land, stood the great High Priest, or Villac Vmu, as he was called. He was second only to the Inca in dignity, and was usually chosen from his brothers or nearest kindred. He was appointed by the monarch, and held his office for life; and he, in turn, appointed to all the subordinate stations of his own order. This order was very numerous. Those members of it who officiated in the House of the Sun, in Cuzco, were taken exclusively from the sacred race of the Incas. The ministers in the provincial temples were drawn from the families of the curacas; but the office of high-priest in each district was reserved for one of the blood royal. It was designed by this regulation to preserve the faith in its purity, and to guard against any departure from the stately ceremonial which it punctiliously prescribed.

The sacerdotal order, though numerous, was not distinguished by any peculiar badge or costume from the rest of the nation. Neither was it the sole depository of the scanty science of the country, nor was it charged with the business of instruction, nor with those parochial duties, if they may so be called, which bring the priest in contact with the great body of the people,—as was the case in Mexico. The cause of this peculiarity may probably be traced to the existence of a superior order, like that of the Inca nobles, whose sanctity of birth so far transcended all human appointments, that they in a manner engrossed whatever there was of religious veneration in the people. They were, in fact, the holy order of the state. Doubtless, any of them might, as very many of them did, take on themselves the sacerdotal functions; and their own insignia and peculiar privileges were too well understood to require any further badge to separate them from the people.

The duties of the priest were confined to ministration in the temple. Even here his attendance was not constant, as he was relieved after a stated interval by other brethren of his order, who succeeded one another in regular rotation. His science was limited to an acquaintance with the fasts and festivals of his religion, and the appropriate ceremonies which distinguished them. This, however frivolous might be its character, was no easy acquisition; for the ritual of the Incas involved a routine of observances, as complex and elaborate as ever distinguished that of any nation, whether pagan or Christian. Each month had its appropriate festival, or rather festivals. The four principal had reference to the Sun, and commemorated the great periods of his annual progress, the solstices and equinoxes. Perhaps the most magnificent of all the national solemnities was the feast of Raymi, held at the period of the summer solstice, when the Sun, having touched the southern extremity of his course, retraced his path, as if to gladden the hearts of his chosen people by his presence. On this occasion, the Indian nobles from the different quarters of the country thronged to the capital to take part in the great religious celebration.

For three days previous, there was a general fast, and no fire was allowed to be lighted in the dwellings. When the appointed day arrived, the Inca and his court, followed by the whole population of the city, assembled at early dawn in the great square to greet the rising of the Sun. They were dressed in their gayest apparel, and the Indian lords vied with each other in the display of costly ornaments and jewels on their persons, while canopies of gaudy feather-work and richly tinted stuffs, borne by the attendants over their heads, gave to the great square, and the streets that emptied into it, the appearance of being spread over with one vast and magnificent awning. Eagerly they watched the coming of their deity, and, no sooner did his first yellow rays strike the turrets and loftiest buildings of the capital, than a shout of gratulation broke forth from the assembled multitude, accompanied by songs of triumph, and the wild melody of barbaric instruments, that swelled louder and louder as his bright orb, rising above the mountain range towards the east, shone in full splendor on his votaries. After the usual ceremonies of adoration, a libation was offered to the great deity by the Inca, from a huge golden vase, filled with the fermented liquor of maize or of maguey, which, after the monarch had tasted it himself, he dispensed among his royal kindred. These ceremonies completed, the vast assembly was arranged in order of procession, and took its way towards the Coricancha.

As they entered the street of the sacred edifice, all divested themselves of their sandals, except the Inca and his family, who did the same on passing through the portals of the temple, where none but these august personages were admitted. After a decent time spent in devotion, the sovereign, attended by his courtly train, again appeared, and preparations were made to commence the sacrifice. This, with the Peruvians, consisted of animals, grain, flowers, and sweet-scented gums; sometimes of human beings, on which occasions a child or beautiful maiden was usually selected as the victim. But such sacrifices were rare, being reserved to celebrate some great public event, as a coronation, the birth of a royal heir, or a great victory. They were never followed by those cannibal repasts familiar to the Mexicans, and to many of the fierce tribes conquered by the Incas. Indeed, the conquests of these princes might well be deemed a blessing to the Indian nations, if it were only from their suppression of cannibalism, and the diminution, under their rule, of human sacrifices.

At the feast of Raymi, the sacrifice usually offered was that of the llama; and the priest, after opening the body of his victim, sought in the appearances which it exhibited to read the lesson of the mysterious future. If the auguries were unpropitious, a second victim was slaughtered, in the hope of receiving some more comfortable assurance. The Peruvian augur might have learned a good lesson of the Roman,—to consider every omen as favorable, which served the interests of his country.

A fire was then kindled by means of a concave mirror of polished metal, which, collecting the rays of the sun into a focus upon a quantity of dried cotton, speedily set it on fire. It was the expedient used on the like occasions in ancient Rome, at least under the reign of the pious Numa. When the sky was overcast, and the face of the good deity was hidden from his worshippers, which was esteemed a bad omen, fire was obtained by means of friction. The sacred flame was intrusted to the care of the Virgins of the Sun, and if, by any neglect, it was suffered to go out in the course of the year, the event was regarded as a calamity that boded some strange disaster to the monarchy. A burnt offering of the victims was then made on the altars of the deity. This sacrifice was but the prelude to the slaughter of a great number of llamas, part of the flocks of the Sun, which furnished a banquet not only for the Inca and his Court, but for the people, who made amends at these festivals for the frugal fare to which they were usually condemned. A fine bread or cake, kneaded of maize flour by the fair hands of the Virgins of the Sun, was also placed on the royal board, where the Inca, presiding over the feast, pledged his great nobles in generous goblets of the fermented liquor of the country, and the long revelry of the day was closed at night by music and dancing. Dancing and drinking were the favorite pastimes of the Peruvians.

These amusements continued for several days, though the sacrifices terminated on the first.—Such was the great festival of Raymi; and the recurrence of this and similar festivities gave relief to the monotonous routine of toil prescribed to the lower orders of the community.

In the distribution of bread and wine at this high festival, the orthodox Spaniards, who first came into the country, saw a striking resemblance to the Christian communion; as in the practice of confession and penance, which, in a most irregular form, indeed, seems to have been used by the Peruvians, they discerned a coincidence with another of the sacraments of the Church. The good fathers were fond of tracing such coincidences, which they considered as the contrivance of Satan, who thus endeavored to delude his victims by counterfeiting the blessed rites of Christianity. Others, in a different vein, imagined that they saw in such analogies the evidence, that some of the primitive teachers of the Gospel, perhaps an apostle himself, had paid a visit to these distant regions, and scattered over them the seeds of religious truth. But it seems hardly necessary to invoke the Prince of Darkness, or the intervention of the blessed saints, to account for coincidences which have existed in countries far removed from the light of Christianity, and in ages, indeed, when its light had not yet risen on the world. It is much more reasonable to refer such casual points of resemblance to the general constitution of man, and the necessities of his moral nature.

Another singular analogy with Roman Catholic institutions is presented by the Virgins of the Sun, the "elect," as they were called, to whom I have already had occasion to refer. These were young maidens, dedicated to the service of the deity, who, at a tender age, were taken from their homes, and introduced into convents, where they were placed under the care of certain elderly matrons, *mamaconas,* who had grown grey within their walls. Under these venerable guides, the holy virgins were instructed in the nature of their religious duties. They were employed in spinning and embroidery, and, with the fine hair of the vicuña, wove the hangings for the temples, and the apparel for the Inca and his household. It was their duty, above all, to watch over the sacred fire obtained at the festival of Raymi. From the moment they entered the establishment, they were cut off from all connection with the world, even with their own family and friends. No one but the Inca, and the Coya or queen, might enter the consecrated precincts. The greatest attention was paid to their morals, and visitors were sent every year to inspect the institutions, and to report on the state of their discipline. Woe to the unhappy maiden who was detected in an intrigue! By the stern law of the Incas, she was to be buried alive, her lover was to be strangled, and the town or village to which he belonged was to be razed to the ground, and "sowed with stones," as if to efface every memorial of his existence. One is astonished to find so close a resemblance between the institutions of the American Indian, the ancient Roman, and the modern Catholic! Chastity and purity of life are virtues in woman, that would seem to be of equal estimation with the barbarian and with the civilized. —Yet the ultimate destination of the inmates of these religious houses was materially different.

The great establishment at Cuzco consisted wholly of maidens of the royal blood, who amounted, it is said, to no less than fifteen hundred. The provincial convents were supplied from the daughters of the curacas and inferior nobles, and, occasionally, where a girl was recommended by great personal attractions, from the lower classes of the people. The "Houses of the Virgins of the Sun" consisted of low ranges of stone buildings, covering a large extent of ground, surrounded by high walls, which excluded those within entirely from observation. They were provided with every accommodation for the fair inmates, and were embellished in the same sumptuous and costly manner as the palaces of the Incas, and the temples; for they received the particular care of government, as an important part of the religious establishment.

Yet the career of all the inhabitants of these cloisters was not confined within their narrow walls. Though Virgins of the Sun, they were brides of the Inca, and, at a marriageable age, the most beautiful among them were selected for the honors of his bed, and transferred to the royal seraglio. The full complement of this amounted in time not only to hundreds, but thousands, who all found accommodations in his different palaces throughout the country. When the monarch was disposed to lessen the number of his establishment, the concubine with whose society he was willing to dispense returned, not to her former monastic residence, but to her own home; where, however humble might be her original condition, she was maintained in great state, and, far from being dishonored by the situation she had filled, was held in reverence as the Inca's bride.

The great nobles of Peru were allowed, like their sovereign, a plurality of wives. The people, generally, whether by law, or by necessity stronger than law, were more happily limited to one. Marriage was conducted in a manner that gave it quite as original a character as belonged to the other institutions of the country. On an appointed day of the year, all those of marriageable age—which, having reference to their ability to take charge of a family, in the males was fixed at not less than twenty-four years, and in the women at eighteen or twenty—were called together in the great squares of their respective towns and villages, throughout the empire. The Inca presided in person over the assembly of his own kindred, and taking the hands of the different couples who were to be united, he placed them within each other, declaring the parties man and wife. The same was done by the curacas towards all persons of their own or inferior degree in their several districts. This was the simple form of marriage in Peru. No one was allowed to select a wife beyond the community to which he belonged, which generally comprehended all his own kindred; nor was any but the sovereign authorized to dispense with the law of nature—or at least, the usual law of nations—so far as to marry his own sister. No marriage was esteemed valid without the consent of the parents; and the preference of the parties, it is said, was also to be consulted; though, considering the barriers imposed by the prescribed age of the candidates, this must have been within rather narrow and whimsical limits. A dwelling was got ready for the new-married pair at the charge of the district, and the prescribed portion of land assigned for their maintenance. The law of Peru provided for the future, as well as for the present. It left nothing to chance.—The simple ceremony of marriage was followed by general festivities among the friends of the parties, which lasted several days; and as every wedding took place on the same day, and as there were few families who had not someone of their members or their kindred personally interested, there was one universal bridal jubilee throughout the empire.

The extraordinary regulations respecting marriage under the Incas are eminently characteristic of the genius of the government; which, far from limiting itself to matters of public concern, penetrated into the most private recesses of domestic life, allowing no man, however humble, to act for himself, even in those personal matters in which none but himself, or his family at most, might be supposed to be interested. No Peruvian was too low for the fostering vigilance of government. None was so high that he was not made to feel his dependence upon it in every act of his life. His very existence as an individual was absorbed in that of the community. His hopes and his fears, his joys and his sorrows, the tenderest sympathies of his nature, which would most naturally shrink from observation, were all to be regulated by law. He was not allowed even to be happy in his own way. The government of the Incas was the mildest, but the most searching of despotisms.

CHAPTER IV

EDUCATION—QUIPUS—ASTRONOMY—AGRICULTURE—
AQUEDUCTS—GUANO—IMPORTANT ESCULENTS

"Science was not intended for the people; but for those of generous blood. Persons of low degree are only puffed up by it, and rendered vain and arrogant. Neither should such meddle with the affairs of government; for this would bring high offices into disrepute, and cause detriment to the state." Such was the favorite maxim, often repeated, of Tupac Inca Yupanqui, one of the most renowned of the Peruvian sovereigns. It may seem strange that such a maxim should ever have been proclaimed in the New World, where popular institutions have been established on a more extensive scale than was ever before witnessed; where government rests wholly on the people; and education—at least, in the great northern division of the continent—is mainly directed to qualify the people for the duties of government. Yet this maxim was strictly conformable to the genius of the Peruvian monarchy, and may serve as a key to its habitual policy; since, while it watched with unwearied solicitude over its subjects, provided for their physical necessities, was mindful of their morals, and showed, throughout, the affectionate concern of a parent for his children, it yet regarded them only as children, who were never to emerge from the state of pupilage, to act or to think for themselves, but whose whole duty was comprehended in the obligation of implicit obedience.

Such was the humiliating condition of the people under the Incas, while the numerous families of the blood royal enjoyed the benefit of all the light of education, which the civilization of the country could afford; and, long after the Conquest, the spots continued to be pointed out where the seminaries had existed for their instruction. These were placed under the care of the *amautas,* or "wise men," who engrossed the scanty stock of science—if science it could be called—possessed by the Peruvians, and who were the sole teachers of youth. It was natural that the monarch should take a lively interest in the instruction of the young nobility, his own kindred. Several of the Peruvian princes are said to have built their palaces in the neighborhood of the schools, in order that they might the more easily visit them and listen to the lectures of the amautas, which they occasionally reinforced by a homily of their own. In these schools, the royal pupils were instructed in all the different kinds of knowledge in which their teachers were versed, with especial reference to the stations they were to occupy in after life. They studied the laws, and the principles of administering the government, in which many of them were to take part. They were initiated in the peculiar rites of their religion, most necessary to those who were to assume the sacerdotal functions. They learned also to emulate the achievements of their royal ancestors by listening to the chronicles compiled by the amautas. They were taught to speak their own dialect with purity and elegance; and they became acquainted with the mysterious science of the quipus, which supplied the Peruvians with the means of communicating their ideas to one another, and of transmitting them to future generations.

The quipu was a cord about two feet long, composed of different colored threads tightly twisted together, from which a quantity of smaller threads were suspended in the manner of a fringe. The threads were of different colors and were tied into knots. The word *quipu,* indeed, signifies a *knot.* The colors denoted sensible objects; as, for instance, *white* represented *silver,* and *yellow, gold.* They sometimes also stood for abstract ideas. Thus, *white* signified *peace,* and *red, war.* But the quipus were chiefly used for arithmetical purposes. The knots served instead of ciphers, and could be combined in such a manner as to represent numbers to any amount they required. By means of these they went through their calculations with great rapidity, and the Spaniards who first visited the country bear testimony to their accuracy.

Officers were established in each of the districts, who, under the title of *quipucamayus,* or "keepers of the quipus," were required to furnish the government with information on various important matters. One had charge of the revenues, reported the quantity of raw material distributed among the laborers, the quality and quantity of the fabrics made from it, and the amount of stores, of various kinds, paid into the royal magazines. Another exhibited the register of births and deaths, the marriages, the number of those qualified to bear arms, and the like details in reference to the population of the kingdom. These returns were annually forwarded to the capital, where they were submitted to the inspection of officers acquainted with the art of deciphering these mystic records. The government was thus provided with a valuable mass of statistical information, and the skeins of many-colored threads, collected and carefully preserved, constituted what might be called the national archives.

But, although the quipus sufficed for all the purposes of arithmetical computation demanded by the Peruvians, they were incompetent to represent the manifold ideas and images which are expressed by writing. Even here, however, the invention was not without its use. For, independently of the direct representation of simple objects, and even of abstract ideas, to a very limited extent, as above noticed, it afforded great help to the memory by way of association. The peculiar knot or color, in this way, suggested what it could not venture to represent; in the same manner—to borrow the homely illustration of an old writer—as the number of the Commandment calls to mind the Commandment itself. The quipus, thus used, might be regarded as the Peruvian system of mnemonics.

Annalists were appointed in each of the principal communities, whose business it was to record the most important events which occurred in them. Other functionaries of a higher character, usually the amautas, were intrusted with the history of the empire, and were selected to chronicle the great deeds of the reigning Inca, or of his ancestors. The narrative, thus concocted, could be communicated only by oral tradition; but the quipus served the chronicler to arrange the incidents with method, and to refresh his memory. The story, once treasured up in the mind, was indelibly impressed there by frequent repetition. It was repeated by the amauta to his pupils, and in this way history, conveyed partly by oral tradition, and partly by arbitrary signs, was handed down from generation to generation, with sufficient discrepancy of details, but with a general conformity of outline to the truth.

The Peruvian quipus were, doubtless, a wretched substitute for that beautiful contrivance, the alphabet, which, employing a few simple characters as the representatives of sounds, instead of ideas, is able to convey the most delicate shades of thought that ever passed through the mind of man. The Peruvian invention, indeed, was far below that of the hieroglyphics, even below the rude picture-writing of the Aztecs; for the latter art, however incompetent to convey abstract ideas, could depict sensible objects with tolerable accuracy. It is evidence of the total ignorance in which the two nations remained of each other, that the Peruvians should have borrowed nothing of the hieroglyphical system of the Mexicans, and this, notwithstanding that the existence of the maguey plant, *agave*, in South America might have furnished them with the very material used by the Aztecs for the construction of their maps.

It is impossible to contemplate without interest the struggles made by different nations, as they emerge from barbarism, to supply themselves with some visible symbols of thought,— that mysterious agency by which the mind of the individual may be put in communication with the minds of a whole community. The want of such a symbol is itself the greatest impediment to the progress of civilization. For what is it but to imprison the thought, which has the elements of immortality, within the bosom of its author, or of the small circle who come in contact with him, instead of sending it abroad to give light to thousands, and to generations yet unborn! Not only is such a symbol an essential element of civilization, but it may be assumed as the very criterion of civilization; for the intellectual advancement of a people will keep pace pretty nearly with its facilities for intellectual communication.

Yet we must be careful not to underrate the real value of the Peruvian system; nor to suppose that the quipus were as awkward an instrument, in the hand of a practised native, as they would be in ours. We know the effect of habit in all mechanical operations, and the Spaniards bear constant testimony to the adroitness and accuracy of the Peruvians in this. Their skill is not more surprising than the facility with which habit enables us to master the contents of a printed page, comprehending thousands of separate characters, by a single glance, as it were, though each character must require a distinct recognition by the eye, and that, too, without breaking the chain of thought in the reader's mind. We must not hold the invention of the quipus too lightly, when we reflect that they supplied the means of calculation demanded for the affairs of a great nation, and that, however insufficient, they afforded no little help to what aspired to the credit of literary composition.

The office of recording the national annals was not wholly confined to the amautas. It was assumed in part by the *haravecs,* or poets, who selected the most brilliant incidents for their songs or ballads, which were chanted at the royal festivals and at the table of the Inca. In this manner, a body of traditional minstrelsy grew up, like the British and Spanish ballad poetry, by means of which the name of many a rude chieftain, that might have perished for want of a chronicler, has been borne down the tide of rustic melody to later generations.

Yet history may be thought not to gain much by this alliance with poetry; for the domain of the poet extends over an ideal realm peopled with shadowy forms of fancy, that bear little resemblance to the rude realities of life. The Peruvian annals may be deemed to show somewhat of the effects of this union, since there is a tinge of the marvellous spread over them down to the very latest period, which, like a mist before the reader's eye, makes it difficult to distinguish between fact and fiction.

The poet found a convenient instrument for his purposes in the beautiful Quichua dialect. We have already seen the extraordinary measures taken by the Incas for propagating their language throughout their empire. Thus naturalized in the remotest provinces, it became enriched by a variety of exotic words and idioms, which, under the influence of the Court and of poetic culture, if I may so express myself, was gradually blended, like some finished mosaic made up of coarse and disjointed materials, into one harmonious whole. The Quichua became the most comprehensive and various, as well as the most elegant, of the South American dialects.

Besides the compositions already noticed, the Peruvians, it is said, showed some talent for theatrical exhibitions; not those barren pantomimes which, addressed simply to the eye, have formed the amusement of more than one rude nation. The Peruvian pieces aspired to the rank of dramatic compositions, sustained by character and dialogue, founded sometimes on themes of tragic interest, and at others on such as, from their light and social character, belong to comedy. Of the execution of these pieces we have now no means of judging. It was probably rude enough, as befitted an unformed people. But, whatever may have been the execution, the mere conception of such an amusement is a proof of refinement that honorably distinguishes the Peruvian from the other American races, whose pastime was war, or the ferocious sports that reflect the image of it.

The intellectual character of the Peruvians, indeed, seems to have been marked rather by a tendency to refinement than by those hardier qualities which insure success in the severer walks of science. In these they were behind several of the semi-civilized nations of the New World. They had some acquaintance with geography, so far as related to their own empire, which was indeed extensive; and they constructed maps with lines raised on them to denote the boundaries and localities, on a similar principle with those formerly used by the blind. In astronomy, they appear to have made but moderate proficiency. They divided the year into twelve lunar months, each of which, having its own name, was distinguished by its appropriate festival. They had, also, weeks; but of what length, whether of seven, nine, or ten days, is uncertain. As their lunar year would necessarily fall short of the true time, they rectified their calendar by solar observations made by means of a number of cylindrical columns raised on the high lands round Cuzco, which served them for taking azimuths; and, by measuring their shadows, they ascertained the exact times of the solstices. The period of the equinoxes they determined by the help of a solitary pillar, or gnomon, placed in the centre of a circle, which was described in the area of the great temple, and traversed by a diameter that was drawn from east to west. When the shadows were scarcely visible under the noontide rays of the sun, they said that "the god sat with all his light upon the column." Quito, which lay immediately under the equator, where the vertical rays of the sun threw no shadow at noon, was held in especial veneration as the favored abode of the great deity. The period of the equinoxes was celebrated by public rejoicings. The pillar was crowned by the golden chair of the Sun, and, both then and at the solstices, the columns were hung with garlands, and offerings of flowers and fruits were made, while high festival was kept throughout the empire. By these periods the Peruvians regulated their religious rites and ceremonial, and prescribed the nature of their agricultural labors. The year itself took its departure from the date of the winter solstice.

This meagre account embraces nearly all that has come down to us of Peruvian astronomy. It may seem strange that a nation, which had proceeded thus far in its observations, should have gone no farther; and that, notwithstanding its general advance in civilization, it should in this science have fallen so far short, not only of the Mexicans, but of the Muyscas, inhabiting the same elevated regions of the great southern plateau with themselves. These latter regulated their calendar on the same general plan of cycles and periodical series as the Aztecs, approaching yet nearer to the system pursued by the people of Asia.

It might have been expected that the Incas, the boasted Children of the Sun, would have made a particular study of the phenomena of the heavens, and have constructed a calendar on principles as scientific as that of their semi-civilized neighbors. One historian, indeed, assures us that they threw their years into cycles of ten, a hundred, and a thousand years, and that by these cycles they regulated their chronology. But this assertion—not improbable in itself—rests on a writer but little gifted with the spirit of criticism, and is counterbalanced by the silence of every higher and earlier authority, as well as by the absence of any monument, like those found among other American nations, to attest the existence of such a calendar. The inferiority of the Peruvians may be, perhaps, in part explained by the fact of their priesthood being drawn exclusively from the body of the Incas, a privileged order of nobility, who had no need, by the assumption of superior learning, to fence themselves round from the approaches of the vulgar. The little true science possessed by the Aztec priest supplied him with a key to unlock the mysteries of the heavens, and the false system of astrology which he built upon it gave him credit as a being who had something of divinity in his own nature. But the Inca noble was divine by birth. The illusory study of astrology, so captivating to the unenlightened mind, engaged no share of his attention. The only persons in Peru who claimed the power of reading the mysterious future, were the diviners, men who, combining with their pretensions some skill in the healing art, resembled the conjurors found among many of the Indian tribes. But the office was held in little repute, except among the lower classes, and was abandoned to those whose age and infirmity disqualified them for the real business of life.

The Peruvians had knowledge of one or two constellations, and watched the motions of the planet Venus, to which, as we have seen, they dedicated altars. But their ignorance of the first principles of astronomical science is shown by their ideas of eclipses, which, they supposed, denoted some great derangement of the planet; and when the moon labored under one of these mysterious infirmities, they sounded their instruments, and filled the air with shouts and lamentations, to rouse her from her lethargy. Such puerile conceits as these form a striking contrast with the real knowledge of the Mexicans, as displayed in their hieroglyphical maps, in which the true cause of this phenomenon is plainly depicted.

But, if less successful in exploring the heavens, the Incas must be admitted to have surpassed every other American race in their dominion over the earth. Husbandry was pursued by them on principles that may be truly called scientific. It was the basis of their political institutions. Having no foreign commerce, it was agriculture that furnished them with the means of their internal exchanges, their subsistence, and their revenues. We have seen their remarkable provisions for distributing the land in equal shares among the people, while they required every man, except the privileged orders, to assist in its cultivation. The Inca himself did not disdain to set the example. On one of the great annual festivals, he proceeded to the environs of Cuzco, attended by his Court, and, in the presence of all the people, turned up the earth with a golden plough,—or an instrument that served as such,—thus consecrating the occupation of the husbandman as one worthy to be followed by the Children of the Sun.

The patronage of the government did not stop with this cheap display of royal condescension, but was shown in the most efficient measures for facilitating the labors of the husbandman. Much of the country along the sea-coast suffered from want of water, as little or no rain fell there, and the few streams, in their short and hurried course from the mountains, exerted only a very limited influence on the wide extent of territory. The soil, it is true, was, for the most part, sandy and sterile; but many places were capable of being reclaimed, and, indeed, needed only to be properly irrigated to be susceptible of extraordinary production. To these spots water was conveyed by means of canals and subterraneous aqueducts, executed on a noble scale. They consisted of large slabs of freestone nicely fitted together without cement, and discharged a volume of water sufficient, by means of latent ducts or sluices, to moisten the lands in the lower level, through which they passed. Some of these aqueducts were of great length. One that traversed the district of Condesuyu measured between four and five hundred miles. They were brought from some elevated lake or natural reservoir in the heart of the mountains, and were fed at intervals by other basins which lay in their route along the slopes of the sierra. In this descent, a passage was sometimes to be opened through rocks,—and this without the aid of iron tools; impracticable mountains were to be turned; rivers and marshes to be crossed; in short, the same obstacles were to be encountered as in the construction of their mighty roads. But the Peruvians seemed to take pleasure in wrestling with the difficulties of nature. Near Caxamarca, a tunnel is still visible, which they excavated in the mountains, to give an outlet to the waters of a lake, when these rose to a height in the rainy season that threatened the country with inundation.

Most of these beneficent works of the Incas were suffered to go to decay by their Spanish conquerors. In some spots, the waters are still left to flow in their silent, subterraneous channels, whose windings and whose sources have been alike unexplored. Others, though partially dilapidated, and closed up with rubbish and the rank vegetation of the soil, still betray their course by occasional patches of fertility. Such are the remains in the valley of Nasca, a fruitful spot that lies between long tracts of desert; where the ancient water-courses of the Incas, measuring four or five feet in depth by three in width, and formed of large blocks of uncemented masonry, are conducted from an unknown distance.

The greatest care was taken that every occupant of the land through which these streams passed should enjoy the benefit of them. The quantity of water allotted to each was prescribed by law; and royal overseers superintended the distribution, and saw that it was faithfully applied to the irrigation of the ground.

The Peruvians showed a similar spirit of enterprise in their schemes for introducing cultivation into the mountainous parts of their domain. Many of the hills, though covered with a strong soil, were too precipitous to be tilled. These they cut into terraces, faced with rough stone, diminishing in regular gradation towards the summit; so that, while the lower strip, or *anden*, as it was called by the Spaniards, that belted round the base of the mountain, might comprehend hundreds of acres, the uppermost was only large enough to accommodate a few rows of Indian corn. Some of the eminences presented such a mass of solid rock, that, after being hewn into terraces, they were obliged to be covered deep with earth, before they could serve the purpose of the husbandman. With such patient toil did the Peruvians combat the formidable obstacles presented by the face of their country! Without the use of the tools or the machinery familiar to the European, each individual could have done little; but acting in large masses, and under a common direction, they were enabled by indefatigable perseverance to achieve results, to have attempted which might have filled even the European with dismay.

In the same spirit of economical husbandry which redeemed the rocky sierra from the curse of sterility, they dug below the arid soil of the valleys, and sought for a stratum where some natural moisture might be found. These excavations, called by the Spaniards *hoyas*, or "pits," were made on a great scale, comprehending frequently more than an acre, sunk to the depth of fifteen or twenty feet, and fenced round within by a wall of *adobes*, or bricks baked in the sun. The bottom of the excavation, well prepared by a rich manure of the sardines,—a small fish obtained in vast quantities along the coast, —was planted with some kind of grain or vegetable.

The Peruvian farmers were well acquainted with the different kinds of manures, and made large use of them; a circumstance rare in the rich lands of the tropics, and probably not elsewhere practised by the rude tribes of America. They made great use of *guano*, the valuable deposit of sea-fowl, that has attracted so much attention, of late, from the agriculturists both of Europe and of our own country, and the stimulating and nutritious properties of which the Indians perfectly appreciated. This was found in such immense quantities on many of the little islands along the coast, as to have the appearance of lofty hills, which, covered with a white saline incrustation, led the Conquerors to give them the name of the *sierra nevada*, or "snowy mountains."

The Incas took their usual precautions for securing the benefits of this important article to the husbandman. They assigned the small islands on the coast to the use of the respective districts which lay adjacent to them. When the island was large, it was distributed among several districts, and the boundaries for each were clearly defined. All encroachment on the rights of another was severely punished. And they secured the preservation of the fowl by penalties as stern as those by which the Norman tyrants of England protected their own game. No one was allowed to set foot on the island during the season for breeding, under pain of death; and to kill the birds at any time was punished in the like manner.

With this advancement in agricultural science, the Peruvians might be supposed to have had some knowledge of the plough, in such general use among the primitive nations of the eastern continent. But they had neither the iron ploughshare of the Old World, nor had they animals for draught, which, indeed, were nowhere found in the New. The instrument which they used was a strong, sharp-pointed stake, traversed by a horizontal piece, ten or twelve inches from the point, on which the ploughman might set his foot and force it into the ground. Six or eight strong men were attached by ropes to the stake, and dragged it forcibly along,—pulling together, and keeping time as they moved by chanting their national songs, in which they were accompanied by the women who followed in their train, to break up the sods with their rakes. The mellow soil offered slight resistance; and the laborer, by long practice, acquired a dexterity which enabled him to turn up the ground the requisite depth with astonishing facility. This substitute for the plough was but a clumsy contrivance; yet it is curious as the only specimen of the kind among the American aborigines, and was perhaps not much inferior to the wooden instrument introduced in its stead by the European conquerors.

It was frequently the policy of the Incas, after providing a deserted tract with the means for irrigation, and thus fitting it for the labors of the husbandman, to transplant there a colony of *mitimaes,* who brought it under cultivation by raising the crops best suited to the soil. While the peculiar character and capacity of the lands were thus consulted, a means of exchange of the different products was afforded to the neighboring provinces, which, from the formation of the country, varied much more than usual within the same limits. To facilitate these agricultural exchanges, fairs were instituted, which took place three times a month in some of the most populous places, where, as money was unknown, a rude kind of commerce was kept up by the barter of their respective products. These fairs afforded so many holidays for the relaxation of the industrious laborer.

Such were the expedients adopted by the Incas for the improvement of their territory; and, although imperfect, they must be allowed to show an acquaintance with the principles of agricultural science, that gives them some claim to the rank of a civilized people. Under their patient and discriminating culture, every inch of good soil was tasked to its greatest power of production; while the most unpromising spots were compelled to contribute something to the subsistence of the people. Everywhere the land teemed with evidence of agricultural wealth, from the smiling valleys along the coast to the terraced steeps of the sierra, which, rising into pyramids of verdure, glowed with all the splendors of tropical vegetation.

The formation of the country was particularly favorable, as already remarked, to an infinite variety of products, not so much from its extent as from its various elevations, which, more remarkable, even, than those in Mexico, comprehend every degree of latitude from the equator to the polar regions. Yet, though the temperature changes in this region with the degree of elevation, it remains nearly the same in the same spots throughout the year; and the inhabitant feels none of those grateful vicissitudes of season which belong to the temperate latitudes of the globe. Thus, while the summer lies in full power on the burning regions of the palm and the cocoa-tree that fringe the borders of the ocean, the broad surface of the table-land blooms with the freshness of perpetual spring, and the higher summits of the Cordilleras are white with everlasting winter.

The Peruvians turned this fixed variety of climate, if I may so say, to the best account by cultivating the productions appropriate to each; and they particularly directed their attention to those which afforded the most nutriment to man. Thus, in the lower level were to be found the cassava-tree and the banana, that bountiful plant, which seems to have relieved man from the primeval curse—if it were not rather a blessing —of toiling for his sustenance. As the banana faded from the landscape, a good substitute was found in the maize, the great agricultural staple of both the northern and southern divisions of the American continent; and which, after its exportation to the Old World, spread so rapidly there, as to suggest the idea of its being indigenous to it. The Peruvians were well acquainted with the different modes of preparing this useful vegetable, though it seems they did not use it for bread, except at festivals; and they extracted a sort of honey from the stalk, and made an intoxicating liquor from the fermented grain, to which, like the Aztecs, they were immoderately addicted.

The temperate climate of the table-land furnished them with the maguey (*agave Americana*), many of the extraordinary qualities of which they comprehended, though not its most important one of affording a material for paper. Tobacco, too, was among the products of this elevated region. Yet the Peruvians differed from every other Indian nation to whom it was known, by using it only for medicinal purposes, in the form of snuff. They may have found a substitute for its narcotic qualities in the coca (*Erythroxylum Peruvianum*), or *cuca*, as called by the natives. This is a shrub which grows to the height of a man. The leaves when gathered are dried in the sun, and, being mixed with a little lime, form a preparation for chewing, much like the betel-leaf of the East. With a small supply of this cuca in his pouch, and a handful of roasted maize, the Peruvian Indian of our time performs his wearisome journeys, day after day, without fatigue, or, at least, without complaint. Even food the most invigorating is less grateful to him than his loved narcotic. Under the Incas, it is said to have been exclusively reserved for the noble orders. If so, the people gained one luxury by the Conquest; and, after that period, it was so extensively used by them, that this article constituted a most important item of the colonial revenue of Spain. Yet, with the soothing charms of an opiate, this weed so much vaunted by the natives, when used to excess, is said to be attended with all the mischievous effects of habitual intoxication.

Higher up on the slopes of the Cordilleras, beyond the limits of the maize and of the *quinoa*,—a grain bearing some resemblance to rice, and largely cultivated by the Indians,— was to be found the potato, the introduction of which into Europe has made an era in the history of agriculture. Whether indigenous to Peru, or imported from the neighboring country of Chili, it formed the great staple of the more elevated plains, under the Incas, and its culture was continued to a height in the equatorial regions which reached many thousand feet above the limits of perpetual snow in the temperate latitudes of Europe. Wild specimens of the vegetable might be seen still higher, springing up spontaneously amidst the stunted shrubs that clothed the lofty sides of the Cordilleras, till these gradually subsided into the mosses and the short yellow grass, *pajonal*, which, like a golden carpet, was unrolled around the base of the mighty cones, that rose far into the regions of eternal silence, covered with the snows of centuries.

CHAPTER V

PERUVIAN SHEEP—GREAT HUNTS—MANUFACTURES—
MECHANICAL SKILL — ARCHITECTURE — CONCLUDING
REFLECTIONS

A nation which had made such progress in agriculture might be reasonably expected to have made, also, some proficiency in the mechanical arts,—especially when, as in the case of the Peruvians, their agricultural economy demanded in itself no inconsiderable degree of mechanical skill. Among most nations, progress in manufactures has been found to have an intimate connection with the progress of husbandry. Both arts are directed to the same great object of supplying the necessaries, the comforts, or, in a more refined condition of society, the luxuries of life; and when the one is brought to a perfection that infers a certain advance in civilization, the other must naturally find a corresponding development under the increasing demands and capacities of such a state. The subjects of the Incas, in their patient and tranquil devotion to the more humble occupations of industry which bound them to their native soil, bore greater resemblance to the Oriental nations, as the Hindoos and Chinese, than they bore to the members of the great Anglo-Saxon family, whose hardy temper has driven them to seek their fortunes on the stormy ocean, and to open a commerce with the most distant regions of the globe. The Peruvians, though lining a long extent of sea-coast, had no foreign commerce.

They had peculiar advantages for domestic manufacture in a material incomparably superior to anything possessed by the other races of the Western continent. They found a good substitute for linen in a fabric which, like the Aztecs, they knew how to weave from the tough thread of the maguey. Cotton grew luxuriantly on the low, sultry level of the coast, and furnished them with a clothing suitable to the milder latitudes of the country. But from the llama and the kindred species of Peruvian sheep they obtained a fleece adapted to the colder climate of the table-land, "more estimable," to quote a well-informed writer, Walton, "than the down of the Canadian beaver, the fleece of the *brebis des Calmoucks,* or of the Syrian goat."

Of the four varieties of the Peruvian sheep, the llama, the one most familiarly known, is the least valuable on account of its wool. It is chiefly employed as a beast of burden, for which, although it is somewhat larger than any of the other varieties, its diminutive size and strength would seem to disqualify it. It carries a load of little more than a hundred pounds, and cannot travel above three or four leagues in a day. But all this is compensated by the little care and cost required for its management and its maintenance. It picks up an easy subsistence from the moss and stunted herbage that grow scantily along the withered sides and the steeps of the Cordilleras. The structure of its stomach, like that of the camel, is such as to enable it to dispense with any supply of water for weeks, nay, months together. Its spongy hoof, armed with a claw or pointed talon to enable it to take secure hold on the ice, never requires to be shod; and the load laid upon its back rests securely in its bed of wool, without the aid of girth or saddle. The llamas move in troops of five hundred or even a thousand, and thus, though each individual carries but little, the aggregate is considerable. The whole caravan travels on at its regular pace, passing the night in the open air without suffering from the coldest temperature, and marching in perfect order, and in obedience to the voice of the driver. It is only when overloaded that the spirited little animal refuses to stir, and neither blows nor caresses can induce him to rise from the ground. He is as sturdy in asserting his rights on this occasion, as he is usually docile and unresisting.

The employment of domestic animals distinguished the Peruvians from the other races of the New World. This economy of human labor by the substitution of the brute is an important element of civilization, inferior only to what is gained by the substitution of machinery for both. Yet the ancient Peruvians seem to have made much less account of it than their Spanish conquerors, and to have valued the llama, in common with the other animals of that genus, chiefly for its fleece. Immense herds of these "large cattle," as they were called, and of the "smaller cattle," or *alpacas*, were held by the government, as already noticed, and placed under the direction of shepherds, who conducted them from one quarter of the country to another, according to the changes of the season. These migrations were regulated with all the precision with which the code of the *mesta* determined the migrations of the vast merino flocks in Spain; and the Conquerors, when they landed in Peru, were amazed at finding a race of animals so similar to their own in properties and habits, and under the control of a system of legislation which might seem to have been imported from their native land.

But the richest store of wool was obtained, not from these domesticated animals, but from the two other species, the *huanacos* and the *vicuñas*, which roamed in native freedom over the frozen ranges of the Cordilleras; where not unfrequently they might be seen scaling the snow-covered peaks which no living thing inhabits save the condor, the huge bird of the Andes, whose broad pinions bear him up in the atmosphere to the height of more than twenty thousand feet above the level of the sea. In these rugged pastures, "the flock without a fold" finds sufficient sustenance in the *ychu*, a species of grass which is found scattered all along the great ridge of the Cordilleras, from the equator to the southern limits of Patagonia. And as these limits define the territory traversed by the Peruvian sheep, which rarely, if ever, venture north of the line, it seems not improbable that this mysterious little plant is so important to their existence, that the absence of it is the principal reason why they have not penetrated to the northern latitudes of Quito and New Granada.

But, although thus roaming without a master over the boundless wastes of the Cordilleras, the Peruvian peasant was never allowed to hunt these wild animals, which were protected by laws as severe as were the sleek herds that grazed on the more cultivated slopes of the plateau. The wild game of the forest and the mountain was as much the property of the government, as if it had been inclosed within a park, or penned within a fold. It was only on stated occasions, at the great hunts, which took place once a year, under the personal superintendence of the Inca or his principal officers, that the game was allowed to be taken. These hunts were not repeated in the same quarter of the country oftener than once in four years, that time might be allowed for the waste occasioned by them to be replenished. At the appointed time, all those living in the district and its neighborhood, to the number, it might be, of fifty or sixty thousand men, were distributed round, so as to form a cordon of immense extent, that should embrace the whole country which was to be hunted over. The men were armed with long poles and spears, with which they beat up game of every description lurking in the woods, the valleys, and the mountains, killing the beasts of prey without mercy, and driving the others, consisting chiefly of the deer of the country, and the huanacos and vicuñas, towards the centre of the wide-extended circle; until, as this gradually contracted, the timid inhabitants of the forest were concentrated on some spacious plain, where the eye of the hunter might range freely over his victims, who found no place for shelter or escape.

The male deer and some of the coarser kind of the Peruvian sheep were slaughtered; their skins were reserved for the various useful manufactures to which they are ordinarily applied, and their flesh, cut into thin slices, was distributed among the people, who converted it into *charqui*, the dried meat of the country, which constituted then the sole, as it has since the principal, animal food of the lower classes of Peru.

But nearly the whole of the sheep, amounting usually to thirty or forty thousand, or even a larger number, after being carefully sheared, were suffered to escape and regain their solitary haunts among the mountains. The wool thus collected was deposited in the royal magazines, whence, in due time, it was dealt out to the people. The coarser quality was worked up into garments for their own use, and the finer for the Inca; for none but an Inca noble could wear the fine fabric of the vicuña.

The Peruvians showed great skill in the manufacture of different articles for the royal household from this delicate material, which, under the name of *vigonia* wool, is now familiar to the looms of Europe. It was wrought into shawls, robes, and other articles of dress for the monarch, and into carpets, coverlets, and hangings for the imperial palaces and the temples. The cloth was finished on both sides alike; the delicacy of the texture was such as to give it the lustre of silk; and the brilliancy of the dyes excited the admiration and the envy of the European artisan. The Peruvians produced also an article of great strength and durability by mixing the hair of animals with wool; and they were expert in the beautiful feather-work, which they held of less account than the Mexicans from the superior quality of the materials for other fabrics, which they had at their command.

The natives showed a skill in other mechanical arts similar to that displayed by their manufactures of cloth. Every man in Peru was expected to be acquainted with the various handicrafts essential to domestic comfort. No long apprenticeship was required for this, where the wants were so few as among the simple peasantry of the Incas. But, if this were all, it would imply but a very moderate advancement in the arts. There were certain individuals, however, carefully trained to those occupations which minister to the demands of the more opulent classes of society. These occupations, like every other calling and office in Peru, always descended from father to son. The division of castes, in this particular, was as precise as that which existed in Egypt or Hindostan. If this arrangement be unfavorable to originality, or to the development of the peculiar talent of the individual, it at least conduces to an easy and finished execution by familiarizing the artist with the practice of his art from childhood.

The royal magazines and the *huacas* or tombs of the Incas have been found to contain many specimens of curious and elaborate workmanship. Among these are vases of gold and silver, bracelets, collars, and other ornaments for the person; utensils of every description, some of fine clay, and many more of copper; mirrors of a hard, polished stone, or burnished silver, with a great variety of other articles made frequently on a whimsical pattern, evincing quite as much ingenuity as taste or inventive talent. The character of the Peruvian mind led to imitation, in fact, rather than invention, to delicacy and minuteness of finish, rather than to boldness or beauty of design.

That they should have accomplished these difficult works

with such tools as they possessed, is truly wonderful. It was comparatively easy to cast and even to sculpture metallic substances, both of which they did with consummate skill. But that they should have shown the like facility in cutting the hardest substances, as emeralds and other precious stones, is not so easy to explain. Emeralds they obtained in considerable quantity from the barren district of Atacames, and this inflexible material seems to have been almost as ductile in the hands of the Peruvian artist as if it had been made of clay. Yet the natives were unacquainted with the use of iron, though the soil was largely impregnated with it. The tools used were of stone, or more frequently of copper. But the material on which they relied for the execution of their most difficult tasks was formed by combining a very small portion of tin with copper. This composition gave a hardness to the metal which seems to have been little inferior to that of steel. With the aid of it, not only did the Peruvian artisan hew into shape porphyry and granite, but by his patient industry accomplished works which the European would not have ventured to undertake. Among the remains of the monuments of Cannar may be seen movable rings in the muzzles of animals, all nicely sculptured of one entire block of granite. It is worthy of remark, that the Egyptians, the Mexicans, and the Peruvians, in their progress towards civilization, should never have detected the use of iron, which lay around them in abundance; and that they should each, without any knowledge of the other, have found a substitute for it in such a curious composition of metals as gave to their tools almost the temper of steel; a secret that has been lost—or, to speak more correctly, has never been discovered—by the civilized European.

I have already spoken of the large quantity of gold and silver wrought into various articles of elegance and utility for the Incas; though the amount was inconsiderable, in comparison with what could have been afforded by the mineral riches of the land, and with what has since been obtained by the more sagacious and unscrupulous cupidity of the white man. Gold was gathered by the Incas from the deposits of the streams. They extracted the ore also in considerable quantities from the valley of Curimayo, northeast of Caxamarca, as well as from other places; and the silver mines of Porco, in particular, yielded them considerable returns. Yet they did not attempt to penetrate into the bowels of the earth by sinking a shaft, but simply excavated a cavern in the steep sides of the mountain, or, at most, opened a horizontal vein of moderate depth. They were equally deficient in the knowledge of the best means of detaching the precious metal from the dross with which it was united, and had no idea of the virtues of quicksilver,—a mineral not rare in Peru,—as an amalgam to effect this decomposition. Their method of smelting the ore was by means of furnaces built in elevated and exposed situations, where they might be fanned by the strong breezes of the mountains. The subjects of the Incas, in short, with all their patient perseverance, did little more than penetrate below the crust, the outer rind, as it were, formed over those golden caverns which lie hidden in the dark depths of the Andes. Yet what they gleaned from the surface was more than adequate for all their demands. For they were not a commercial people, and had no knowledge of money. In this they differed from the ancient Mexicans, who had an established currency of a determinate value. In one respect, however, they were superior to their American rivals, since they made use of weights to determine the quantity of their commodities, a thing wholly unknown to the Aztecs. This fact is ascertained by the discovery of silver balances, adjusted with perfect accuracy, in some of the tombs of the Incas.

But the surest test of the civilization of a people—at least, as sure as any—afforded by mechanical art is to be found in their architecture, which presents so noble a field for the display of the grand and the beautiful, and which, at the same time, is so intimately connected with the essential comforts of life. There is no object on which the resources of the wealthy are more freely lavished, or which calls out more effectually the inventive talent of the artist. The painter and the sculptor may display their individual genius in creations of surpassing excellence, but it is the great monuments of architectural taste and magnificence that are stamped in a peculiar manner by the genius of the nation. The Greek, the Egyptian, the Saracen, the Gothic,—what a key do their respective styles afford to the character and condition of the people! The monuments of China, of Hindostan, and of Central America are all indicative of an immature period, in which the imagination has not been disciplined by study, and which, therefore, in its best results, betrays only the ill-regulated aspirations after the beautiful, that belong to a semi-civilized people.

The Peruvian architecture, bearing also the general characteristics of an imperfect state of refinement, had still its peculiar character; and so uniform was that character, that the edifices throughout the country seem to have been all cast in the same mould. They were usually built of porphyry or granite; not unfrequently of brick. This, which was formed into blocks or squares of much larger dimensions than our brick, was made of a tenacious earth mixed up with reeds or tough grass, and acquired a degree of hardness with age that made it insensible alike to the storms and the more trying sun of the tropics. The walls were of great thickness, but low, seldom reaching to more than twelve or fourteen feet in height. It is rare to meet with accounts of a building that rose to a second story.

The apartments had no communication with one another, but usually opened into a court; and, as they were unprovided with windows, or apertures that served for them, the only light from without must have been admitted by the doorways. These were made with the sides approaching each other towards the top, so that the lintel was considerably narrower than the threshold, a peculiarity, also, in Egyptian architecture. The roofs have for the most part disappeared with time. Some few survive in the less ambitious edifices, of a singular bell-shape, and made of a composition of earth and pebbles. They are supposed, however, to have been generally formed of more perishable materials, of wood or straw. It is certain that some of the most considerable stone buildings were thatched with straw. Many seem to have been constructed without the aid of cement; and writers have contended that the Peruvians were unacquainted with the use of mortar, or cement of any kind. But a close, tenacious mould, mixed with lime, may be discovered filling up the interstices of the granite in some buildings; and in others, where the well-fitted blocks leave no room for this coarser material, the eye of the antiquary has detected a fine bituminous glue, as hard as the rock itself.

The greatest simplicity is observed in the construction of the buildings, which are usually free from outward ornament; though in some the huge stones are shaped into a convex form with great regularity, and adjusted with such nice precision to one another, that it would be impossible, but for the flutings, to determine the line of junction. In others, the stone is rough, as it was taken from the quarry, in the most irregular forms, with the edges nicely wrought and fitted to each other. There is no appearance of columns or of arches; though there is some contradiction as to the latter point. But it is not to be doubted, that, although they may have made some approach to this mode of construction by the greater or less inclination of the walls, the Peruvian architects were wholly unacquainted with the true principle of the circular arch reposing on its key-stone.

The architecture of the Incas is characterized, says Humboldt, "by simplicity, symmetry, and solidity." It may seem unphilosophical to condemn the peculiar fashion of a nation as indicating want of taste, because its standard of taste differs from our own. Yet there is an incongruity in the composition of the Peruvian buildings which argues a very imperfect acquaintance with the first principles of architecture. While they put together their bulky masses of porphyry and granite with the nicest art, they were incapable of mortising their timbers, and, in their ignorance of iron, knew no better way of holding the beams together than tying them with thongs of maguey. In the same incongruous spirit, the building that was thatched with straw, and unilluminated by a window, was glowing with tapestries of gold and silver! These are the inconsistencies of a rude people, among whom the arts are but partially developed. It might not be difficult to find examples of like inconsistency in the architecture and domestic arrangements of our Anglo-Saxon, and, at a still later period, of our Norman ancestors.

Yet the buildings of the Incas were accommodated to the character of the climate, and were well fitted to resist those terrible convulsions which belong to the land of volcanoes. The wisdom of their plan is attested by the number which still survive, while the more modern constructions of the Conquerors have been buried in ruins. The hand of the Conquerors, indeed, has fallen heavily on these venerable monuments, and, in their blind and superstitious search for hidden treasure, has caused infinitely more ruin than time or the earthquake. Yet enough of these monuments still remain to invite the researches of the antiquary. Those only in the most conspicuous situations have been hitherto examined. But, by the testimony of travellers, many more are to be found in the less frequented parts of the country; and we may hope they will one day call forth a kindred spirit of enterprise to that which has so successfully explored the mysterious recesses of Central America and the Yucatan Peninsula.

I cannot close this analysis of the Peruvian institutions without a few reflections on their general character and tendency, which, if they involve some repetition of previous remarks, may, I trust, be excused, from my desire to leave a correct and consistent impression on the reader. In this survey, we cannot but be struck with the total dissimilarity between these institutions and those of the Aztecs,—the other great nation who led in the march of civilization on this western continent, and whose empire in the northern portion of it was as conspicuous as that of the Incas in the south. Both nations came on the plateau, and commenced their career of conquest, at dates, it may be, not far removed from each other. And it is worthy of notice, that, in America, the elevated region along the crests of the great mountain ranges should have been the chosen seat of civilization in both hemispheres.

Very different was the policy pursued by the two races in their military career. The Aztecs, animated by the most ferocious spirit, carried on a war of extermination, signalizing their triumphs by the sacrifice of hecatombs of captives; while the Incas, although they pursued the game of conquest with equal pertinacity, preferred a milder policy, substituting negotiation and intrigue for violence, and dealt with their antagonists so that their future resources should not be crippled, and that they should come as friends, not as foes, into the bosom of the empire.

Their policy towards the conquered forms a contrast no less striking to that pursued by the Aztecs. The Mexican vassals were ground by excessive imposts and military conscriptions. No regard was had to their welfare, and the only limit to oppression was the power of endurance. They were overawed by fortresses and armed garrisons, and were made to feel every hour that they were not part and parcel of the nation, but held only in subjugation as a conquered people. The Incas, on the other hand, admitted their new subjects at once to all the rights enjoyed by the rest of the community; and, though they made them conform to the established laws and usages of the empire, they watched over their personal security and comfort with a sort of parental solicitude. The motley population, thus bound together by common interest, was animated by a common feeling of loyalty, which gave greater strength and stability to the empire, as it became more and more widely extended; while the various tribes who successively came under the Mexican sceptre, being held together only by the pressure of external force, were ready to fall asunder the moment that that force was withdrawn. The policy of the two nations displayed the principle of fear as contrasted with the principle of love.

The characteristic features of their religious systems had as little resemblance to each other. The whole Aztec pantheon partook more or less of the sanguinary spirit of the terrible war-god who presided over it, and their frivolous ceremonial almost always terminated with human sacrifice and cannibal orgies. But the rites of the Peruvians were of a more innocent cast, as they tended to a more spiritual worship. For the worship of the Creator is most nearly approached by that of the heavenly bodies, which, as they revolve in their bright orbits, seem to be the most glorious symbols of his beneficence and power.

In the minuter mechanical arts, both showed considerable skill; but in the construction of important public works, of roads, aqueducts, canals, and in agriculture in all its details, the Peruvians were much superior. Strange that they should have fallen so far below their rivals in their efforts after a higher intellectual culture, in astronomical science, more especially, and in the art of communicating thought by visible symbols. When we consider the greater refinement of the Incas, their inferiority to the Aztecs in these particulars can be explained only by the fact, that the latter in all probability were indebted for their science to the race who preceded them in the land,—that shadowy race whose origin and whose end are alike veiled from the eye of the inquirer, but who possibly may have sought a refuge from their ferocious invaders in those regions of Central America, the architectural remains of which now supply us with the most pleasing monuments of Indian civilization. It is with this more polished race, to whom the Peruvians seem to have borne some resemblance in their mental and moral organization, that they should be compared. Had the empire of the Incas been permitted to extend itself with the rapid strides with which it was advancing at the period of the Spanish conquest, the two races might have come into conflict, or, perhaps, into alliance with one another.

The Mexicans and Peruvians, so different in the character of their peculiar civilization, were, it seems probable, ignorant of each other's existence; and it may appear singular, that, during the simultaneous continuance of their empires, some of the seeds of science and of art, which pass so imperceptibly from one people to another, should not have found their way across the interval which separated the two nations. They furnish an interesting example of the opposite directions which the human mind may take in its struggle to emerge from darkness into the light of civilization.

A closer resemblance—as I have more than once taken occasion to notice—may be found between the Peruvian institutions and some of the despotic governments of Eastern Asia; those governments where despotism appears in its more mitigated form, and the whole people, under the patriarchal sway of its sovereign, seem to be gathered together like the members of one vast family. Such were the Chinese, for example, whom the Peruvians resembled in their implicit obedience to authority, their mild yet somewhat stubborn temper, their solicitude for forms, their reverence for ancient usage, their skill in the minuter manufactures, their imitative rather than inventive cast of mind, and their invincible patience, which serves instead of a more adventurous spirit for the execution of difficult undertakings.

A still closer analogy may be found with the natives of Hindostan in their division into castes, their worship of the heavenly bodies and the elements of nature, and their acquaintance with the scientific principles of husbandry. To the ancient Egyptians, also, they bore considerable resemblance in the same particulars, as well as in those ideas of a future existence which led them to attach so much importance to the permanent preservation of the body.

But we shall look in vain in the history of the East for a parallel to the absolute control exercised by the Incas over their subjects. In the East, this was founded on physical power,—on the external resources of the government. The authority of the Inca might be compared with that of the Pope in the day of his might, when Christendom trembled at the thunders of the Vatican, and the successor of St. Peter set his foot on the necks of princes. But the authority of the Pope was founded on opinion. His temporal power was nothing. The empire of the Incas rested on both. It was a theocracy more potent in its operation than that of the Jews; for, though the sanction of the law might be as great among the latter, the law was expounded by a human lawgiver, the servant and representative of Divinity. But the Inca was both the lawgiver and the law. He was not merely the representative of Divinity, or, like the Pope, its vicegerent, but he was Divinity itself. The violation of his ordinance was sacrilege. Never was there a scheme of government enforced by such terrible sanctions, or which bore so oppressively on the subjects of it. For it reached not only to the visible acts, but to the private conduct, the words, the very thoughts, of its vassals.

It added not a little to the efficacy of the government, that, below the sovereign, there was an order of hereditary nobles of the same divine original with himself, who, placed far below himself, were still immeasurably above the rest of the community, not merely by descent, but, as it would seem, by their intellectual nature. These were the exclusive depositaries of power, and, as their long hereditary training made them familiar with their vocation, and secured them implicit deference from the multitude, they became the prompt and well-practised agents for carrying out the executive measures of the administration. All that occurred throughout the wide extent of his empire—such was the perfect system of communication—passed in review, as it were, before the eyes of the monarch, and a thousand hands, armed with irresistible authority, stood ready in every quarter to do his bidding. Was it not, as we have said, the most oppressive, though the mildest, of despotisms?

It was the mildest, from the very circumstance, that the transcendent rank of the sovereign, and the humble, nay, superstitious, devotion to his will made it superfluous to assert this will by acts of violence or rigor. The great mass of the people may have appeared to his eyes as but little removed above the condition of the brute, formed to minister to his pleasures. But, from their very helplessness, he regarded them with feelings of commiseration, like those which a kind master might feel for the poor animals committed to his charge, or—to do justice to the beneficent character attributed to many of the Incas—that a parent might feel for his young and impotent offspring. The laws were carefully directed to their preservation and personal comfort. The people were not allowed to be employed on works pernicious to their health, nor to pine—a sad contrast to their subsequent destiny—under the imposition of tasks too heavy for their powers. They were never made the victims of public or private extortion; and a benevolent forecast watched carefully over their necessities, and provided for their relief in seasons of infirmity, and for their sustenance in health. The government of the Incas, however arbitrary in form, was in its spirit truly patriarchal.

Yet in this there was nothing cheering to the dignity of human nature. What the people had was conceded as a boon, not as a right. When a nation was brought under the sceptre of the Incas, it resigned every personal right, even the rights dearest to humanity. Under this extraordinary polity, a people advanced in many of the social refinements, well skilled in manufactures and agriculture, were unacquainted, as we have seen, with money. They had nothing that deserved to be called property. They could follow no craft, could engage in no labor, no amusement, but such as was specially provided by law. They could not change their residence or their dress without a license from the government. They could not even exercise the freedom which is conceded to the most abject in other countries, that of selecting their own wives. The imperative spirit of despotism would not allow them to be happy or miserable in any way but that established by law. The power of free agency—the inestimable and inborn right of every human being—was annihilated in Peru.

The astonishing mechanism of the Peruvian polity could have resulted only from the combined authority of opinion and positive power in the ruler to an extent unprecedented in the history of man. Yet that it should have so successfully gone into operation, and so long endured, in opposition to the taste, the prejudices, and the very principles of our nature, is a strong proof of a generally wise and temperate administration of the government.

The policy habitually pursued by the Incas for the *prevention* of evils that might have disturbed the order of things is well exemplified in their provisions against poverty and idleness. In these they rightly discerned the two great causes of disaffection in a populous community. The industry of the people was secured not only by their compulsory occupations at home, but by their employment on those great public works which covered every part of the country, and which still bear testimony in their decay to their primitive grandeur. Yet it may well astonish us to find, that the natural difficulty of these undertakings, sufficiently great in itself, considering the imperfection of their tools and machinery, was inconceivably enhanced by the politic contrivance of government. The royal edifices of Quito, we are assured by the Spanish conquerors, were constructed of huge masses of stone, many of which were carried all the way along the mountain roads from Cuzco, a distance of several hundred leagues. The great square of the capital was filled to a considerable depth with mould brought with incredible labor up the steep slopes of the Cordilleras from the distant shores of the Pacific Ocean. Labor was regarded not only as a means, but as an end, by the Peruvian law.

With their manifold provisions against poverty the reader has already been made acquainted. They were so perfect, that, in their wide extent of territory,—much of it smitten with the curse of barrenness,—no man, however humble, suffered from the want of food and clothing. Famine, so common a scourge in every other American nation, so common at that period in every country of civilized Europe, was an evil unknown in the dominions of the Incas.

The most enlightened of the Spaniards who first visited Peru, struck with the general appearance of plenty and prosperity, and with the astonishing order with which every thing throughout the country was regulated, are loud in their expressions of admiration. No better government, in their opinion, could have been devised for the people. Contented with their condition, and free from vice, to borrow the language of an eminent authority of that early day, the mild and docile character of the Peruvians would have well fitted them to receive the teachings of Christianity, had the love of conversion, instead of gold, animated the breasts of the Conquerors. And Carli, a philosopher of a later time, warmed by the contemplation of the picture—which his own fancy had colored—of public prosperity and private happiness under the rule of the Incas, pronounces "the *moral* man in Peru far superior to the European."

Yet such results are scarcely reconcilable with the theory of the government I have attempted to analyze. Where there is no free agency, there can be no morality. Where there is no temptation, there can be little claim to virtue. Where the routine is rigorously prescribed by law, the law, and not the man, must have the credit of the conduct. If that government is the best, which is felt the least, which encroaches on the natural liberty of the subject only so far as is essential to civil subordination, then of all governments devised by man the Peruvian has the least real claim to our admiration.

It is not easy to comprehend the genius and the full import of institutions so opposite to those of our own free republic, where every man, however humble his condition, may aspire to the highest honors of the state,—may select his own career, and carve out his fortune in his own way; where the light of knowledge, instead of being concentrated on a chosen few, is shed abroad like the light of day, and suffered to fall equally on the poor and the rich; where the collision of man with man wakens a generous emulation that calls out latent talent and tasks the energies to the utmost; where consciousness of independence gives a feeling of self-reliance unknown to the timid subjects of a despotism; where, in short, the government is made for man,—not as in Peru, where man seemed to be made only for the government. The New World is the theatre in which these two political systems, so opposite in their character, have been carried into operation. The empire of the Incas has passed away and left no trace. The other great experiment is still going on,—the experiment which is to solve the problem, so long contested in the Old World, of the capacity of man for self-government. Alas for humanity, if it should fail!

The testimony of the Spanish conquerors is not uniform in respect to the favorable influence exerted by the Peruvian institutions on the character of the people. Drinking and dancing are said to have been the pleasures to which they were immoderately addicted. Like the slaves and serfs in other lands, whose position excluded them from more serious and ennobling occupations, they found a substitute in frivolous or sensual indulgence. Lazy, luxurious, and licentious, are the epithets bestowed on them by one of those who saw them at the Conquest, but whose pen was not too friendly to the Indian. Yet the spirit of independence could hardly be strong in a people who had no interest in the soil, no personal rights to defend; and the facility with which they yielded to the Spanish invader—after every allowance for their comparative inferiority —argues a deplorable destitution of that patriotic feeling which holds life as little in comparison with freedom.

But we must not judge too hardly of the unfortunate native, because he quailed before the civilization of the European. We must not be insensible to the really great results that were achieved by the government of the Incas. We must not forget, that, under their rule, the meanest of the people enjoyed a far greater degree of personal comfort, at least, a greater exemption from physical suffering, than was possessed by similar classes in other nations on the American continent,—greater, probably, than was possessed by these classes in most of the countries of feudal Europe. Under their sceptre, the higher orders of the state had made advances in many of the arts that belong to a cultivated community. The foundations of a regular government were laid, which, in an age of rapine, secured to its subjects the inestimable blessings of tranquillity and safety. By the well-sustained policy of the Incas, the rude tribes of the forest were gradually drawn from their fast-nesses, and gathered within the folds of civilization; and of these materials was constructed a flourishing and populous empire, such as was to be found in no other quarter of the American continent. The defects of this government were those of over-refinement in legislation,—the last defects to have been looked for, certainly, in the American aborigines.

BOOK II

DISCOVERY OF PERU

CHAPTER I

ANCIENT AND MODERN SCIENCE—ART OF NAVIGATION
—MARITIME DISCOVERY—SPIRIT OF THE SPANIARDS—
POSSESSIONS IN THE NEW WORLD—RUMORS CONCERN-
ING PERU

Whatever difference of opinion may exist as to the comparative merit of the ancients and the moderns in the arts, in
poetry, eloquence, and all that depends on imagination, there
can be no doubt that in science the moderns have eminently
the advantage. It could not be otherwise. In the early ages of
the world, as in the early period of life, there was the freshness
of a morning existence, when the gloss of novelty was on every
thing that met the eye; when the senses, not blunted by familiarity, were more keenly alive to the beautiful, and the mind,
under the influence of a healthy and natural taste, was not
perverted by philosophical theory; when the simple was necessarily connected with the beautiful, and the epicurean intellect, sated by repetition, had not begun to seek for stimulants in the fantastic and capricious. The realms of fancy were
all untravelled, and its fairest flowers had not been gathered,
nor its beauties despoiled, by the rude touch of those who
affected to cultivate them. The wing of genius was not bound
to the earth by the cold and conventional rules of criticism,
but was permitted to take its flight far and wide over the
broad expanse of creation.

But with science it was otherwise. No genius could suffice
for the creation of facts,—hardly for their detection. They were
to be gathered in by painful industry; to be collected from
careful observation and experiment. Genius, indeed, might
arrange and combine these facts into new forms, and elicit
from their combinations new and important inferences; and
in this process might almost rival in originality the creations
of the poet and the artist. But if the processes of science are
necessarily slow, they are sure. There is no retrograde move-

ment in her domain. Arts may fade, the Muse become dumb, a moral lethargy may lock up the faculties of a nation, the nation itself may pass away and leave only the memory of its existence, but the stores of science it has garnered up will endure for ever. As other nations come upon the stage, and new forms of civilization arise, the monuments of art and of imagination, productions of an older time, will lie as an obstacle in the path of improvement. They cannot be built upon; they occupy the ground which the new aspirant for immortality would cover. The whole work is to be gone over again, and other forms of beauty—whether higher or lower in the scale of merit, but unlike the past—must arise to take a place by their side. But, in science, every stone that has been laid remains as the foundation for another. The coming generation takes up the work where the preceding left it. There is no retrograde movement. The individual nation may recede, but science still advances. Every step that has been gained makes the ascent easier for those who come after. Every step carries the patient inquirer after truth higher and higher towards heaven, and unfolds to him, as he rises, a wider horizon, and new and more magnificent views of the universe.

Geography partook of the embarrassments which belonged to every other department of science in the primitive ages of the world. The knowledge of the earth could come only from an extended commerce; and commerce is founded on artificial wants or an enlightened curiosity, hardly compatible with the earlier condition of society. In the infancy of nations, the different tribes, occupied with their domestic feuds, found few occasions to wander beyond the mountain chain or broad stream that formed the natural boundary of their domains. The Phœnicians, it is true, are said to have sailed beyond the Pillars of Hercules, and to have launched out on the great western ocean. But the adventures of these ancient voyagers belong to the mythic legends of antiquity, and ascend far beyond the domain of authentic record.

The Greeks, quick and adventurous, skilled in mechanical art, had many of the qualities of successful navigators, and within the limits of their little inland sea ranged fearlessly and freely. But the conquests of Alexander did more to extend the limits of geographical science, and opened an acquaintance with the remote countries of the East. Yet the march of the conqueror is slow in comparison with the movements of the unencumbered traveller. The Romans were still less enterprising than the Greeks, were less commercial in their character. The contributions to geographical knowledge grew with the slow acquisitions of empire. But their system was centralizing in its tendency; and instead of taking an outward direction and looking abroad for discovery, every part of the vast imperial domain turned towards the capital as its head and central point of attraction. The Roman conqueror pursued his path by land, not by sea. But the water is the great highway between nations, the true element for the discoverer. The Romans were not a maritime people. At the close of their empire, geographical science could hardly be said to extend farther than to an acquaintance with Europe,—and this not its more northern division,—together with a portion of Asia and Africa; while they had no other conception of a world beyond the western waters than was to be gathered from the fortunate prediction of the poet.

Then followed the Middle Ages; the dark ages, as they are called, though in their darkness were matured those seeds of knowledge, which, in fulness of time, were to spring up into new and more glorious forms of civilization. The organization of society became more favorable to geographical science. Instead of one overgrown, lethargic empire, oppressing every thing by its colossal weight, Europe was broken up into various independent communities, many of which, adopting liberal forms of government, felt all the impulses natural to freemen; and the petty republics on the Mediterranean and the Baltic sent forth their swarms of seamen in a profitable commerce, that knit together the different countries scattered along the great European waters.

But the improvements which took place in the art of navigation, the more accurate measurement of time, and, above all, the discovery of the polarity of the magnet, greatly advanced the cause of geographical knowledge. Instead of creeping timidly along the coast, or limiting his expeditions to the narrow basins of inland waters, the voyager might now spread his sails boldly on the deep, secure of a guide to direct his bark unerringly across the illimitable waste. The consciousness of this power led thought to travel in a new direction; and the mariner began to look with earnestness for another path to the Indian Spice Islands than that by which the Eastern caravans had traversed the continent of Asia. The nations on whom the spirit of enterprise, at this crisis, naturally descended, were Spain and Portugal, placed, as they were, on the outposts of the European continent, commanding the great theatre of future discovery.

Both countries felt the responsibility of their new position. The crown of Portugal was constant in its efforts, through the fifteenth century, to find a passage round the southern point of Africa into the Indian Ocean; though so timid was the navigation, that every fresh headland became a formidable barrier; and it was not till the latter part of the century that the adventurous Díaz passed quite round the Stormy Cape, as he termed it, but which John the Second, with happier augury, called the Cape of Good Hope. But, before Vasco de Gama had availed himself of this discovery to spread his sails in the Indian seas, Spain entered on her glorious career, and sent Columbus across the western waters.

The object of the great navigator was still the discovery of a route to India, but by the west instead of the east. He had no expectation of meeting with a continent in his way, and, after repeated voyages, he remained in his original error, dying, as is well known, in the conviction that it was the eastern shore of Asia which he had reached. It was the same object which directed the nautical enterprises of those who followed in the Admiral's track; and the discovery of a strait into the Indian Ocean was the burden of every order from the government, and the design of many an expedition to different points of the new continent, which seemed to stretch its leviathan length along from one pole to the other. The discovery of an Indian passage is the true key to the maritime movements of the fifteenth and the first half of the sixteenth centuries. It was the great leading idea that gave the character to the enterprise of the age.

It is not easy at this time to comprehend the impulse given to Europe by the discovery of America. It was not the gradual acquisition of some border territory, a province or a kingdom that had been gained, but a New World that was now thrown open to the Europeans. The races of animals, the mineral treasures, the vegetable forms, and the varied aspects of nature, man in the different phases of civilization, filled the mind with entirely new sets of ideas, that changed the habitual current of thought and stimulated it to indefinite conjecture. The eagerness to explore the wonderful secrets of the new hemisphere became so active, that the principal cities of Spain were, in a manner, depopulated, as emigrants thronged one after another to take their chance upon the deep. It was a world of romance that was thrown open; for, whatever might be the luck of the adventurer, his reports on his return were tinged with a coloring of romance that stimulated still higher the sensitive fancies of his countrymen, and nourished the chimerical sentiments of an age of chivalry. They listened with attentive ears to tales of Amazons which seemed to realize the classic legends of antiquity, to stories of Patagonian giants, to flaming pictures of an *El Dorado*, where the sands sparkled with gems, and golden pebbles as large as birds' eggs were dragged in nets out of the rivers.

Yet that the adventurers were no impostors, but dupes, too easy dupes of their own credulous fancies, is shown by the extravagant character of their enterprises; by expeditions in search of the magical Fountain of Health, of the golden Temple of Doboyba, of the golden sepulchres of Zenu; for gold was ever floating before their distempered vision, and the name of *Castilla del Oro*, Golden Castile, the most unhealthy and unprofitable region of the Isthmus, held out a bright promise to the unfortunate settler, who too frequently, instead of gold, found there only his grave.

In this realm of enchantment, all the accessories served to maintain the illusion. The simple natives, with their defenceless bodies and rude weapons, were no match for the European warrior armed to the teeth in mail. The odds were as great as those found in any legend of chivalry, where the lance of the good knight overturned hundreds at a touch. The perils that lay in the discoverer's path, and the sufferings he had to sustain, were scarcely inferior to those that beset the knight-errant. Hunger and thirst and fatigue, the deadly effluvia of the morass with its swarms of venomous insects, the cold of mountain snows, and the scorching sun of the tropics, these were the lot of every cavalier who came to seek his fortunes in the New World. It was the reality of romance. The life of the Spanish adventurer was one chapter more—and not the least remarkable—in the chronicles of knight-errantry.

The character of the warrior took somewhat of the exaggerated coloring shed over his exploits. Proud and vainglorious, swelled with lofty anticipations of his destiny, and an invincible confidence in his own resources, no danger could appall and no toil could tire him. The greater the danger, indeed, the higher the charm; for his soul revelled in excitement, and the enterprise without peril wanted that spur of romance which was necessary to rouse his energies into action. Yet in the motives of action meaner influences were strangely mingled with the loftier, the temporal with the spiritual. Gold was the incentive and the recompense, and in the pursuit of it his inflexible nature rarely hesitated as to the means. His courage was sullied with cruelty, the cruelty that flowed equally—strange as it may seem—from his avarice and his religion; religion as it was understood in that age,—the religion of the Crusader. It was the convenient cloak for a multitude of sins, which covered them even from himself. The Castilian, too proud for hypocrisy, committed more cruelties in the name of religion than were ever practised by the pagan idolater or the fanatical Moslem. The burning of the infidel was a sacrifice acceptable to Heaven, and the conversion of those who survived amply atoned for the foulest offences. It is a melancholy and mortifying consideration, that the most uncompromising spirit of intolerance—the spirit of the Inquisitor at home, and of the Crusader abroad—should have emanated from a religion which preached peace upon earth and good-will towards man!

What a contrast did these children of Southern Europe present to the Anglo-Saxon races who scattered themselves along the great northern division of the western hemisphere! For the principle of action with these latter was not avarice, nor the more specious pretext of proselytism; but independence—independence religious and political. To secure this, they were content to earn a bare subsistence by a life of frugality and toil. They asked nothing from the soil, but the reasonable returns of their own labor. No golden visions threw a deceitful halo around their path, and beckoned them onwards through seas of blood to the subversion of an unoffending dynasty. They were content with the slow but steady progress of their social polity. They patiently endured the privations of the wilderness, watering the tree of liberty with their tears and with the sweat of their brow, till it took deep root in the land and sent up its branches high towards the heavens; while the communities of the neighboring continent, shooting up into the sudden splendors of a tropical vegetation, exhibited, even in their prime, the sure symptoms of decay.

It would seem to have been especially ordered by Providence that the discovery of the two great divisions of the American hemisphere should fall to the two races best fitted to conquer and colonize them. Thus the northern section was consigned to the Anglo-Saxon race, whose orderly, industrious habits found an ample field for development under its colder skies and on its more rugged soil; while the southern portion, with its rich tropical products and treasures of mineral wealth, held out the most attractive bait to invite the enterprise of the Spaniard. How different might have been the result, if the bark of Columbus had taken a more northerly direction, as he at one time meditated, and landed its band of adventurers on the shores of what is now Protestant America!

Under the pressure of that spirit of nautical enterprise which filled the maritime communities of Europe in the sixteenth century, the whole extent of the mighty continent, from Labrador to Terra del Fuego, was explored in less than thirty years after its discovery; and in 1521, the Portuguese Magellan, sailing under the Spanish flag, solved the problem of the strait, and found a westerly way to the long sought Spice Islands of India,—greatly to the astonishment of the Portuguese, who, sailing from the opposite direction, there met their rivals, face to face, at the antipodes. But while the whole eastern coast of the American continent had been explored, and the central portion of it colonized,—even after the brilliant achievement of the Mexican conquest,—the veil was not yet raised that hung over the golden shores of the Pacific.

Floating rumors had reached the Spaniards, from time to time, of countries in the far west, teeming with the metal they so much coveted; but the first distinct notice of Peru was about the year 1511, when Vasco Nuñez de Balboa, the discoverer of the Southern Sea, was weighing some gold which he had collected from the natives. A young barbarian chieftain, who was present, struck the scales with his fist, and, scattering the glittering metal around the apartment, exclaimed,—"If this is what you prize so much that you are willing to leave your distant homes, and risk even life itself for it, I can tell you of a land where they eat and drink out of golden vessels, and gold is as cheap as iron is with you." It was not long after this startling intelligence that Balboa achieved the formidable adventure of scaling the mountain rampart of the Isthmus which divides the two mighty oceans from each other; when, armed with sword and buckler, he rushed into the waters of the Pacific, and cried out, in the true chivalrous vein, that "he claimed this unknown sea with all that it contained for the king of Castile, and that he would make good the claim against all, Christian or infidel, who dared to gainsay it!" All the broad continent and sunny isles washed by the waters of the Southern Ocean! Little did the bold cavalier comprehend the full import of his magnificent vaunt.

On this spot he received more explicit tidings of the Peruvian empire, heard proofs recounted of its civilization, and was shown drawings of the llama, which, to the European eye, seemed a species of the Arabian camel. But, although he steered his caravel for these golden realms, and even pushed his discoveries some twenty leagues south of the Gulf of St. Michael, the adventure was not reserved for him. The illustrious discoverer was doomed to fall a victim to that miserable jealousy with which a little spirit regards the achievements of a great one.

The Spanish colonial domain was broken up into a number of petty governments, which were dispensed sometimes to court favorites, though, as the duties of the post, at this early period, were of an arduous nature, they were more frequently reserved for men of some practical talent and enterprise. Columbus, by virtue of his original contract with the Crown, had jurisdiction over the territories discovered by himself, embracing some of the principal islands, and a few places on the continent. This jurisdiction differed from that of other functionaries, inasmuch as it was hereditary; a privilege found in the end too considerable for a subject, and commuted, therefore, for a title and a pension. These colonial governments were multiplied with the increase of empire, and by the year 1524, the period at which our narrative properly commences, were scattered over the islands, along the Isthmus of Darien, the broad tract of Terra Firma, and the recent conquests of Mexico. Some of these governments were of no great extent. Others, like that of Mexico, were of the dimensions of a kingdom; and most had an indefinite range for discovery assigned to them in their immediate neighborhood, by which each of the petty potentates might enlarge his territorial sway, and enrich his followers and himself. This politic arrangement best served the ends of the Crown, by affording a perpetual incentive to the spirit of enterprise. Thus living on their own little domains at a long distance from the mother country, these military rulers held a sort of viceregal sway, and too frequently exercised it in the most oppressive and tyrannical manner; oppressive to the native, and tyrannical towards their own followers. It was the natural consequence, when men, originally low in station, and unprepared by education for office, were suddenly called to the possession of a brief, but in its nature irresponsible, authority. It was not till after some sad experience of these results, that measures were taken to hold these petty tyrants in check by means of regular tribunals, or Royal Audiences, as they were termed, which, composed of men of character and learning, might interpose the arm of the law, or, at least, the voice of remonstrance, for the protection of both colonist and native.

Among the colonial governors, who were indebted for their situation to their rank at home, was Don Pedro Arias de Avila, or Pedrarias, as usually called. He was married to a daughter of Doña Beatriz de Bobadilla, the celebrated Marchioness of Moya, best known as the friend of Isabella the Catholic. He was a man of some military experience and considerable energy of character. But, as it proved, he was of a malignant temper; and the base qualities, which might have passed unnoticed in the obscurity of private life, were made conspicuous, and perhaps created in some measure, by sudden elevation to power; as the sunshine, which operates kindly on a generous soil, and stimulates it to production, calls forth from the unwholesome marsh only foul and pestilent vapors. This man was placed over the territory of *Castilla del Oro*, the ground selected by Nuñez de Balboa for the theatre of his discoveries. Success drew on this latter the jealousy of his superior, for it was crime enough in the eyes of Pedrarias to deserve too well. The tragical history of this cavalier belongs to a period somewhat earlier than that with which we are to be occupied. It has been traced by abler hands than mine, and, though brief, forms one of the most brilliant passages in the annals of the American conquerors.

But though Pedrarias was willing to cut short the glorious career of his rival, he was not insensible to the important consequences of his discoveries. He saw at once the unsuitableness of Darien for prosecuting expeditions on the Pacific, and, conformably to the original suggestion of Balboa, in 1519, he caused his rising capital to be transferred from the shores of the Atlantic to the ancient site of Panamá, some distance east of the present city of that name. This most unhealthy spot, the cemetery of many an unfortunate colonist, was favorably situated for the great object of maritime enterprise; and the port, from its central position, afforded the best point of departure for expeditions, whether to the north or south, along the wide range of undiscovered coast that lined the Southern Ocean. Yet in this new and more favorable position, several years were suffered to elapse before the course of discovery took the direction of Peru. This was turned exclusively towards the north, or rather west, in obedience to the orders of government, which had ever at heart the detection of a strait that, as was supposed, must intersect some part or other of the long-extended Isthmus. Armament after armament was fitted out with this chimerical object; and Pedrarias saw his domain extending every year farther and farther without deriving any considerable advantage from his acquisitions. Veragua, Costa Rica, Nicaragua, were successively occupied; and his brave cavaliers forced a way across forest and mountain and warlike tribes of savages, till, at Honduras, they came in collision with the companions of Cortés, the Conquerors of Mexico, who had descended from the great northern plateau on the regions of Central America, and thus completed the survey of this wild and mysterious land.

It was not till 1522 that a regular expedition was despatched in the direction south of Panamá, under the conduct of Pascual de Andagoya, a cavalier of much distinction in the colony. But that officer penetrated only to the Puerto de Piñas, the limit of Balboa's discoveries, when the bad state of his health compelled him to reëmbark and abandon his enterprise at its commencement.

Yet the floating rumors of the wealth and civilization of a mighty nation at the South were continually reaching the ears and kindling the dreamy imaginations of the colonists; and it may seem astonishing that an expedition in that direction should have been so long deferred. But the exact position and distance of this fairy realm were matter of conjecture. The long tract of intervening country was occupied by rude and warlike races; and the little experience which the Spanish navigators had already had of the neighboring coast and its inhabitants, and still more, the tempestuous character of the seas—for their expeditions had taken place at the most unpropitious seasons of the year—enhanced the apparent difficulties of the undertaking, and made even their stout hearts shrink from it.

Such was the state of feeling in the little community of Panamá for several years after its foundation. Meanwhile, the dazzling conquest of Mexico gave a new impulse to the ardor of discovery, and, in 1524, three men were found in the colony, in whom the spirit of adventure triumphed over every consideration of difficulty and danger that obstructed the prosecution of the enterprise. One among them was selected as fitted by his character to conduct it to a successful issue. That man was Francisco Pizarro; and as he held the same conspicuous post in the Conquest of Peru that was occupied by Cortés in that of Mexico, it will be necessary to take a brief review of his early history.

CHAPTER II

Francisco Pizarro was born at Truxillo, a city of Estremadura, in Spain. The period of his birth is uncertain; but probably it was not far from 1471. He was an illegitimate child,
and that his parents should not have taken pains to perpetuate
the date of his birth is not surprising. Few care to make a
particular record of their transgressions. His father, Gonzalo
Pizarro, was a colonel of infantry, and served with some distinction in the Italian campaigns under the Great Captain,
and afterwards in the wars of Navarre. His mother, named
Francisca Gonzalez, was a person of humble condition in the
town of Truxillo.

But little is told of Francisco's early years, and that little
not always deserving of credit. According to some, he was deserted by both his parents, and left as a foundling at the door
of one of the principal churches of the city. It is even said
that he would have perished, had he not been nursed by a
sow. This is a more discreditable fountain of supply than that
assigned to the infant Romulus. The early history of men
who have made their names famous by deeds in after-life, like
the early history of nations, affords a fruitful field for invention.

It seems certain that the young Pizarro received little care
from either of his parents, and was suffered to grow up as
nature dictated. He was neither taught to read nor write, and
his principal occupation was that of a swineherd. But this
torpid way of life did not suit the stirring spirit of Pizarro, as
he grew older, and listened to the tales, widely circulated and
so captivating to a youthful fancy, of the New World. He
shared in the popular enthusiasm, and availed himself of a

favorable moment to abandon his ignoble charge, and escape to Seville, the port where the Spanish adventurers embarked to seek their fortunes in the West. Few of them could have turned their backs on their native land with less cause for regret than Pizarro.

In what year this important change in his destiny took place we are not informed. The first we hear of him in the New World is at the island of Hispaniola, in 1510, where he took part in the expedition to Uraba in Terra Firma, under Alonzo de Ojeda, a cavalier whose character and achievements find no parallel but in the pages of Cervantes. Hernando Cortés, whose mother was a Pizarro, and related, it is said, to the father of Francis, was then in St. Domingo, and prepared to accompany Ojeda's expedition, but was prevented by a temporary lameness. Had he gone, the fall of the Aztec empire might have been postponed for some time longer, and the sceptre of Montezuma have descended in peace to his posterity. Pizarro shared in the disastrous fortunes of Ojeda's colony, and, by his discretion, obtained so far the confidence of his commander, as to be left in charge of the settlement, when the latter returned for supplies to the islands. The lieutenant continued at his perilous post for nearly two months, waiting deliberately until death should have thinned off the colony sufficiently to allow the miserable remnant to be embarked in the single small vessel that remained to it.

After this, we find him associated with Balboa, the discoverer of the Pacific, and coöperating with him in establishing the settlement at Darien. He had the glory of accompanying this gallant cavalier in his terrible march across the mountains, and of being among the first Europeans, therefore, whose eyes were greeted with the long-promised vision of the Southern Ocean.

After the untimely death of his commander, Pizarro attached himself to the fortunes of Pedrarias, and was employed by that governor in several military expeditions, which, if they afforded nothing else, gave him the requisite training for the perils and privations that lay in the path of the future Conqueror of Peru.

In 1515, he was selected, with another cavalier named Morales, to cross the Isthmus and traffic with the natives on

the shores of the Pacific. And there, while engaged in collecting his booty of gold and pearls from the neighboring islands,
as his eye ranged along the shadowy line of coast till it faded
in the distance, his imagination may have been first fired with
the idea of, one day, attempting the conquest of the mysterious regions beyond the mountains. On the removal of the seat
of government across the Isthmus to Panamá, Pizarro accompanied Pedrarias, and his name became conspicuous among
the cavaliers who extended the line of conquest to the north
over the martial tribes of Veragua. But all these expeditions,
whatever glory they may have brought him, were productive of
very little gold; and, at the age of fifty, the captain Pizarro
found himself in possession only of a tract of unhealthy land
in the neighborhood of the capital, and of such *repartimientos*
of the natives as were deemed suited to his military services.
The New World was a lottery, where the great prizes were so
few that the odds were much against the player; yet in the
game he was content to stake health, fortune, and, too often,
his fair fame.

Such was Pizarro's situation when, in 1522, Andagoya returned from his unfinished enterprise to the south of Panamá,
bringing back with him more copious accounts than any hitherto received of the opulence and grandeur of the countries
that lay beyond. It was at this time, too, that the splendid
achievements of Cortés made their impression on the public
mind, and gave a new impulse to the spirit of adventure. The
southern expeditions became a common topic of speculation
among the colonists of Panamá. But the region of gold, as it
lay behind the mighty curtain of the Cordilleras, was still
veiled in obscurity. No idea could be formed of its actual
distance; and the hardships and difficulties encountered by
the few navigators who had sailed in that direction gave a
gloomy character to the undertaking, which had hitherto de-
terred the most daring from embarking in it. There is no evidence that Pizarro showed any particular alacrity in the cause.
Nor were his own funds such as to warrant any expectation
of success without great assistance from others. He found this
in two individuals of the colony, who took too important a
part in the subsequent transactions not to be particularly
noticed.

One of them, Diego de Almagro, was a soldier of fortune, somewhat older, it seems probable, than Pizarro; though little is known of his birth, and even the place of it is disputed. It is supposed to have been the town of Almagro in New Castile, whence his own name, for want of a better source, was derived; for, like Pizarro, he was a foundling. Few particulars are known of him till the present period of our history; for he was one of those whom the working of turbulent times first throws upon the surface,—less fortunate, perhaps, than if left in their original obscurity. In his military career, Almagro had earned the reputation of a gallant soldier. He was frank and liberal in his disposition, somewhat hasty and ungovernable in his passions, but, like men of a sanguine temperament, after the first sallies had passed away, not difficult to be appeased. He had, in short, the good qualities and the defects incident to an honest nature, not improved by the discipline of early education or self-control.

The other member of the confederacy was Hernando de Luque, a Spanish ecclesiastic, who exercised the functions of vicar at Panamá, and had formerly filled the office of schoolmaster in the Cathedral of Darien. He seems to have been a man of singular prudence and knowledge of the world; and by his respectable qualities had acquired considerable influence in the little community to which he belonged, as well as the control of funds, which made his coöperation essential to the success of the present enterprise.

It was arranged among the three associates, that the two cavaliers should contribute their little stock towards defraying the expenses of the armament, but by far the greater part of the funds was to be furnished by Luque. Pizarro was to take command of the expedition, and the business of victualling and equipping the vessels was assigned to Almagro. The associates found no difficulty in obtaining the consent of the governor to their undertaking. After the return of Andagoya, he had projected another expedition, but the officer to whom it was to be intrusted died. Why he did not prosecute his original purpose, and commit the affair to an experienced captain like Pizarro, does not appear. He was probably not displeased that the burden of the enterprise should be borne by others, so long as a good share of the profit went into his own coffers. This he did not overlook in his stipulations.

Thus fortified with the funds of Luque, and the consent of the governor, Almagro was not slow to make preparations for the voyage. Two small vessels were purchased, the larger of which had been originally built by Balboa, for himself, with a view to this same expedition. Since his death, it had lain dismantled in the harbor of Panamá. It was now refitted as well as circumstances would permit, and put in order for sea, while the stores and provisions were got on board with an alacrity which did more credit, as the event proved, to Almagro's zeal than to his forecast.

There was more difficulty in obtaining the necessary complement of hands; for a general feeling of distrust had gathered round expeditions in this direction, which could not readily be overcome. But there were many idle hangers-on in the colony, who had come out to mend their fortunes, and were willing to take their chance of doing so, however desperate. From such materials as these, Almagro assembled a body of somewhat more than a hundred men; and every thing being ready, Pizarro assumed the command, and, weighing anchor, took his departure from the little port of Panamá, about the middle of November, 1524. Almagro was to follow in a second vessel of inferior size, as soon as it could be fitted out.

The time of year was the most unsuitable that could have been selected for the voyage; for it was the rainy season, when the navigation to the south, impeded by contrary winds, is made doubly dangerous by the tempests that sweep over the coast. But this was not understood by the adventurers. After touching at the Isle of Pearls, the frequent resort of navigators, at a few leagues' distance from Panamá, Pizarro held his way across the Gulf of St. Michael, and steered almost due south for the Puerto de Piñas, a headland in the province of Biruquete, which marked the limit of Andagoya's voyage. Before his departure, Pizarro had obtained all the information which he could derive from that officer in respect to the country, and the route he was to follow. But the cavalier's own experience had been too limited to enable him to be of much assistance.

Doubling the Puerto de Piñas, the little vessel entered the

river Birú, the misapplication of which name is supposed by some to have given rise to that of the empire of the Incas. After sailing up this stream for a couple of leagues, Pizarro came to anchor, and disembarking his whole force except the sailors, proceeded at the head of it to explore the country. The land spread out into a vast swamp, where the heavy rains had settled in pools of stagnant water, and the muddy soil afforded no footing to the traveller. This dismal morass was fringed with woods, through whose thick and tangled undergrowth they found it difficult to penetrate; and emerging from them, they came out on a hilly country, so rough and rocky in its character, that their feet were cut to the bone, and the weary soldier, encumbered with his heavy mail or thick-padded doublet of cotton, found it difficult to drag one foot after the other. The heat at times was oppressive; and, fainting with toil and famished for want of food, they sank down on the earth from mere exhaustion. Such was the ominous commencement of the expedition to Peru.

Pizarro, however, did not lose heart. He endeavored to revive the spirits of his men, and besought them not to be discouraged by difficulties which a brave heart would be sure to overcome, reminding them of the golden prize which awaited those who persevered. Yet it was obvious that nothing was to be gained by remaining longer in this desolate region. Returning to their vessel, therefore, it was suffered to drop down the river and proceed along its southern course on the great ocean.

After coasting a few leagues, Pizarro anchored off a place not very inviting in its appearance, where he took in a supply of wood and water. Then, stretching more towards the open sea, he held on in the same direction towards the south. But in this he was baffled by a succession of heavy tempests, accompanied with such tremendous peals of thunder and floods of rain as are found only in the terrible storms of the tropics. The sea was lashed into fury, and, swelling into mountain billows, threatened every moment to overwhelm the crazy little bark, which opened at every seam. For ten days the unfortunate voyagers were tossed about by the pitiless elements, and it was only by incessant exertions—the exertions of despair —that they preserved the ship from foundering. To add to their calamities, their provisions began to fail, and they were short of water, of which they had been furnished only with a small number of casks; for Almagro had counted on their recruiting their scanty supplies, from time to time, from the shore. Their meat was wholly consumed, and they were reduced to the wretched allowance of two ears of Indian corn a day for each man.

Thus harassed by hunger and the elements, the battered voyagers were too happy to retrace their course and regain the port where they had last taken in supplies of wood and water. Yet nothing could be more unpromising than the aspect of the country. It had the same character of low, swampy soil, that distinguished the former landing-place; while thick-matted forests, of a depth which the eye could not penetrate, stretched along the coast to an interminable length. It was in vain that the wearied Spaniards endeavored to thread the mazes of this tangled thicket, where the creepers and flowering vines, that shoot up luxuriant in a hot and humid atmosphere, had twined themselves round the huge trunks of the forest trees and made a network that could be opened only with the axe. The rain, in the meantime, rarely slackened, and the ground, strewed with leaves and saturated with moisture, seemed to slip away beneath their feet.

Nothing could be more dreary and disheartening than the aspect of these funereal forests; where the exhalations from the overcharged surface of the ground poisoned the air, and seemed to allow no life, except that, indeed, of myriads of insects, whose enamelled wings glanced to and fro, like sparks of fire, in every opening of the woods. Even the brute creation appeared instinctively to have shunned the fatal spot, and neither beast nor bird of any description was seen by the wanderers. Silence reigned unbroken in the heart of these dismal solitudes; at least, the only sounds that could be heard were the plashing of the rain-drops on the leaves, and the tread of the forlorn adventurers.

Entirely discouraged by the aspect of the country, the Spaniards began to comprehend that they had gained nothing by changing their quarters from sea to shore, and they felt the most serious apprehensions of perishing from famine in a region which afforded nothing but such unwholesome berries as they could pick up here and there in the woods. They loudly complained of their hard lot, accusing their commander as the author of all their troubles, and as deluding them with promises of a fairy-land, which seemed to recede in proportion as they advanced. It was of no use, they said, to contend against fate, and it was better to take their chance of regaining the port of Panamá in time to save their lives, than to wait where they were to die of hunger.

But Pizarro was prepared to encounter much greater evils than these, before returning to Panamá, bankrupt in credit, an object of derision as a vainglorious dreamer, who had persuaded others to embark in an adventure which he had not the courage to carry through himself. The present was his only chance. To return would be ruin. He used every argument, therefore, that mortified pride or avarice could suggest to turn his followers from their purpose; represented to them that these were the troubles that necessarily lay in the path of the discoverer; and called to mind the brilliant successes of their countrymen in other quarters, and the repeated reports, which they had themselves received, of the rich regions along the coast, of which it required only courage and constancy on their part to become the masters. Yet, as their present exigencies were pressing, he resolved to send back the vessel to the Isle of Pearls, to lay in a fresh stock of provisions for his company, which might enable them to go forward with renewed confidence. The distance was not great, and in a few days they would all be relieved from their perilous position. The officer detached on this service was named Montenegro; and taking with him nearly half the company, after receiving Pizarro's directions, he instantly weighed anchor, and steered for the Isle of Pearls.

On the departure of his vessel, the Spanish commander made an attempt to explore the country, and see if some Indian settlement might not be found, where he could procure refreshments for his followers. But his efforts were vain, and no trace was visible of a human dwelling; though, in the dense and impenetrable foliage of the equatorial regions, the distance of a few rods might suffice to screen a city from observation. The only means of nourishment left to the unfortunate adventurers were such shell-fish as they occasionally picked up on the shore, or the bitter buds of the palm-tree, and such berries and unsavory herbs as grew wild in the woods. Some of these were so poisonous, that the bodies of those who ate them swelled up and were tormented with racking pains. Others, preferring famine to this miserable diet, pined away from weakness and actually died of starvation. Yet their resolute leader strove to maintain his own cheerfulness and to keep up the drooping spirits of his men. He freely shared with them his scanty stock of provisions, was unwearied in his endeavors to procure them sustenance, tended the sick, and ordered barracks to be constructed for their accommodation, which might, at least, shelter them from the drenching storms of the season. By this ready sympathy with his followers in their sufferings, he obtained an ascendency over their rough natures, which the assertion of authority, at least in the present extremity, could never have secured to him.

Day after day, week after week, had now passed away, and no tidings were heard of the vessel that was to bring relief to the wanderers. In vain did they strain their eyes over the distant waters to catch a glimpse of their coming friends. Not a speck was to be seen in the blue distance, where the canoe of the savage dared not venture, and the sail of the white man was not yet spread. Those who had borne up bravely at first now gave way to despondency, as they felt themselves abandoned by their countrymen on this desolate shore. They pined under that sad feeling which "maketh the heart sick." More than twenty of the little band had already died, and the survivors seemed to be rapidly following.

At this crisis reports were brought to Pizarro of a light having been seen through a distant opening in the woods. He hailed the tidings with eagerness, as intimating the existence of some settlement in the neighborhood; and, putting himself at the head of a small party, went in the direction pointed out, to reconnoitre. He was not disappointed, and, after extricating himself from a dense wilderness of underbrush and foliage, he emerged into an open space, where a small Indian village was planted. The timid inhabitants, on the sudden apparition of the strangers, quitted their huts in dismay; and the famished Spaniards, rushing in, eagerly made themselves masters of their contents. These consisted of different articles of food, chiefly maize and cocoa-nuts. The supply, though small, was too seasonable not to fill them with rapture.

The astonished natives made no attempt at resistance. But, gathering more confidence as no violence was offered to their persons, they drew nearer the white men, and inquired, "Why they did not stay at home and till their own lands, instead of roaming about to rob others who had never harmed them?" Whatever may have been their opinion as to the question of right, the Spaniards, no doubt, felt then that it would have been wiser to do so. But the savages wore about their persons gold ornaments of some size, though of clumsy workmanship. This furnished the best reply to their demand. It was the golden bait which lured the Spanish adventurer to forsake his pleasant home for the trials of the wilderness. From the Indians Pizarro gathered a confirmation of the reports he had so often received of a rich country lying farther south; and at the distance of ten days' journey across the mountains they told him, there dwelt a mighty monarch whose dominions had been invaded by another still more powerful, the Child of the Sun. It may have been the invasion of Quito that was meant, by the valiant Inca Huayna Capac, which took place some years previous to Pizarro's expedition.

At length, after the expiration of more than six weeks, the Spaniards beheld with delight the return of the wandering bark that had borne away their comrades, and Montenegro sailed into port with an ample supply of provisions for his famishing countrymen. Great was his horror at the aspect presented by the latter, their wild and haggard countenances and wasted frames,—so wasted by hunger and disease, that their old companions found it difficult to recognize them. Montenegro accounted for his delay by incessant head winds and bad weather; and he himself had also a doleful tale to tell of the distress to which he and his crew had been reduced by hunger, on their passage to the Isle of Pearls. It is minute incidents like these with which we have been occupied, that enable one to comprehend the extremity of suffering to which the Spanish adventurer was subjected in the prosecution of his great work of discovery.

Revived by the substantial nourishment to which they had so long been strangers, the Spanish cavaliers, with the buoy-

ancy that belongs to men of a hazardous and roving life, forgot
their past distresses in their eagerness to prosecute their enterprise. Reëmbarking therefore on board his vessel, Pizarro bade
adieu to the scene of so much suffering, which he branded
with the appropriate name of *Puerto de la Hambre,* the Port
of Famine, and again opened his sails to a favorable breeze
that bore him onwards towards the south.

Had he struck boldly out into the deep, instead of hugging
the inhospitable shore, where he had hitherto found so little
to recompense him, he might have spared himself the repetition of wearisome and unprofitable adventures, and reached
by a shorter route the point of his destination. But the Spanish
mariner groped his way along these unknown coasts, landing
at every convenient headland, as if fearful lest some fruitful
region or precious mine might be overlooked, should a single
break occur in the line of survey. Yet it should be remembered, that, though the true point of Pizarro's destination is
obvious to us, familiar with the topography of these countries,
he was wandering in the dark, feeling his way along, inch by
inch, as it were, without chart to guide him, without knowledge of the seas or of the bearings of the coast, and even with
no better defined idea of the object at which he aimed than
that of a land teeming with gold, that lay somewhere at the
south! It was a hunt after an *El Dorado;* on information
scarcely more circumstantial or authentic than that which
furnished the basis of so many chimerical enterprises in this
land of wonders. Success only, the best argument with the
multitude, redeemed the expeditions of Pizarro from a similar
imputation of extravagance.

Holding on his southerly course under the lee of the shore,
Pizarro, after a short run, found himself abreast of an open
reach of country, or at least one less encumbered with wood,
which rose by a gradual swell, as it receded from the coast.
He landed with a small body of men, and, advancing a short
distance into the interior, fell in with an Indian hamlet. It was
abandoned by the inhabitants, who, on the approach of the
invaders, had betaken themselves to the mountains; and the
Spaniards, entering their deserted dwellings, found there a
good store of maize and other articles of food, and rude ornaments of gold of considerable value. Food was not more nec-

essary for their bodies than was the sight of gold, from time
to time, to stimulate their appetite for adventure. One spectacle, however, chilled their blood with horror. This was the
sight of human flesh, which they found roasting before the
fire, as the barbarians had left it, preparatory to their obscene
repast. The Spaniards, conceiving that they had fallen in with
a tribe of Caribs, the only race in that part of the New World
known to be cannibals, retreated precipitately to their vessel.
They were not steeled by sad familiarity with the spectacle,
like the Conquerors of Mexico.

The weather, which had been favorable, now set in tempestuous, with heavy squalls, accompanied by incessant thunder
and lightning, and the rain, as usual in these tropical tempests, descended not so much in drops as in unbroken sheets
of water. The Spaniards, however, preferred to take their
chance on the raging element rather than remain in the scene
of such brutal abominations. But the fury of the storm gradually subsided, and the little vessel held on her way along the
coast, till, coming abreast of a bold point of land named by
Pizarro Punta Quemada, he gave orders to anchor. The margin
of the shore was fringed with a deep belt of mangrove trees,
the long roots of which, interlacing one another, formed a
kind of submarine latticework that made the place difficult
of approach. Several avenues, opening through this tangled
thicket, led Pizarro to conclude that the country must be inhabited, and he disembarked, with the greater part of his
force, to explore the interior.

He had not penetrated more than a league, when he found
his conjecture verified by the sight of an Indian town of larger
size than those he had hitherto seen, occupying the brow of
an eminence, and well defended by palisades. The inhabitants, as usual, had fled; but left in their dwellings a good
supply of provisions and some gold trinkets, which the Spaniards made no difficulty of appropriating to themselves. Pizarro's flimsy bark had been strained by the heavy gales it had of
late encountered, so that it was unsafe to prosecute the voyage
further without more thorough repairs than could be given to
her on this desolate coast. He accordingly determined to send
her back with a few hands to be careened at Panamá, and
meanwhile to establish his quarters in his present position,

which was so favorable for defence. But first he despatched a small party under Montenegro to reconnoitre the country, and, if possible, to open a communication with the natives.

The latter were a warlike race. They had left their habitations in order to place their wives and children in safety. But they had kept an eye on the movements of the invaders, and, when they saw their forces divided, they resolved to fall upon each body singly before it could communicate with the other. So soon, therefore, as Montenegro had penetrated through the defiles of the lofty hills, which shoot out like spurs of the Cordilleras along this part of the coast, the Indian warriors, springing from their ambush, sent off a cloud of arrows and other missiles that darkened the air, while they made the forest ring with their shrill war-whoop. The Spaniards, astonished at the appearance of the savages, with their naked bodies gaudily painted, and brandishing their weapons as they glanced among the trees and straggling underbrush that choked up the defile, were taken by surprise and thrown for a moment into disarray. Three of their number were killed and several wounded. Yet, speedily rallying, they returned the discharge of the assailants with their crossbows,—for Pizarro's troops do not seem to have been provided with muskets on this expedition,—and then gallantly charging the enemy, sword in hand, succeeded in driving them back into the fastnesses of the mountains. But it only led them to shift their operations to another quarter, and make an assault on Pizarro before he could be relieved by his lieutenant.

Availing themselves of their superior knowledge of the passes, they reached that commander's quarters long before Montenegro, who had commenced a countermarch in the same direction. And issuing from the woods, the bold savages saluted the Spanish garrison with a tempest of darts and arrows, some of which found their way through the joints of the harness and the quilted mail of the cavaliers. But Pizarro was too well practised a soldier to be off his guard. Calling his men about him, he resolved not to abide the assault tamely in the works, but to sally out, and meet the enemy on their own ground. The barbarians, who had advanced near the defences, fell back as the Spaniards burst forth with their valiant leader at their head. But, soon returning with admirable ferocity to the charge, they singled out Pizarro, whom, by his bold bearing and air of authority, they easily recognized as the chief; and, hurling at him a storm of missiles, wounded him, in spite of his armour, in no less than seven places.

Driven back by the fury of the assault directed against his own person, the Spanish commander retreated down the slope of the hill, still defending himself as he could with sword and buckler, when his foot slipped and he fell. The enemy set up a fierce yell of triumph, and some of the boldest sprang forward to despatch him. But Pizarro was on his feet in an instant, and, striking down two of the foremost with his strong arm, held the rest at bay till his soldiers could come to the rescue. The barbarians, struck with admiration at his valor, began to falter, when Montenegro luckily coming on the ground at the moment, and falling on their rear, completed their confusion; and, abandoning the field, they made the rest of their way into the recesses of the mountains. The ground was covered with their slain; but the victory was dearly purchased by the death of two more Spaniards and a long list of wounded.

A council of war was then called. The position had lost its charm in the eyes of the Spaniards, who had met here with the first resistance they had yet experienced on their expedition. It was necessary to place the wounded in some secure spot, where their injuries could be attended to. Yet it was not safe to proceed farther, in the crippled state of their vessel. On the whole, it was decided to return and report their proceedings to the governor; and, though the magnificent hopes of the adventurers had not been realized, Pizarro trusted that enough had been done to vindicate the importance of the enterprise, and to secure the countenance of Pedrarias for the further prosecution of it.

Yet Pizarro could not make up his mind to present himself, in the present state of the undertaking, before the governor. He determined, therefore, to be set on shore with the principal part of his company at Chicamá, a place on the mainland, at a short distance west of Panamá. From this place, which he reached without any further accident, he despatched the vessel, and in it his treasurer, Nicolas de Ribera, with the gold he had collected, and with instructions to lay before the governor a full account of his discoveries, and the result of the expedition.

While these events were passing, Pizarro's associate, Almagro, had been busily employed in fitting out another vessel for the expedition at the port of Panamá. It was not till long after his friend's departure that he was prepared to follow him. With the assistance of Luque, he at length succeeded in equipping a small caravel and embarking a body of between sixty and seventy adventurers, mostly of the lowest order of the colonists. He steered in the track of his comrade, with the intention of overtaking him as soon as possible. By a signal previously concerted of notching the trees, he was able to identify the spots visited by Pizarro,—Puerto de Piñas, Puerto de la Hambre, Puerto Quemado,—touching successively at every point of the coast explored by his countrymen, though in a much shorter time. At the last-mentioned place he was received by the fierce natives with the same hostile demonstrations as Pizarro, though in the present encounter the Indians did not venture beyond their defences. But the hot blood of Almagro was so exasperated by this check, that he assaulted the place and carried it sword in hand, setting fire to the outworks and dwellings, and driving the wretched inhabitants into the forests.

His victory cost him dear. A wound from a javelin on the head caused an inflammation in one of his eyes, which, after great anguish, ended in the loss of it. Yet the intrepid adventurer did not hesitate to pursue his voyage, and, after touching at several places on the coast, some of which rewarded him with a considerable booty in gold, he reached the mouth of the *Rio de San Juan*, about the fourth degree of north latitude. He was struck with the beauty of the stream, and with the cultivation on its borders, which were sprinkled with Indian cottages showing some skill in their construction, and altogether intimating a higher civilization than any thing he had yet seen.

Still his mind was filled with anxiety for the fate of Pizarro and his followers. No trace of them had been found on the coast for a long time, and it was evident they must have foundered at sea, or made their way back to Panamá. This last he deemed most probable; as the vessel might have passed him unnoticed under the cover of the night, or of the dense fogs that sometimes hang over the coast.

Impressed with this belief, he felt no heart to continue his voyage of discovery, for which, indeed, his single bark, with its small complement of men, was altogether inadequate. He proposed, therefore, to return without delay. On his way, he touched at the Isle of Pearls, and there learned the result of his friend's expedition, and the place of his present residence. Directing his course, at once, to Chicamá, the two cavaliers soon had the satisfaction of embracing each other, and recounting their several exploits and escapes. Almagro returned even better freighted with gold than his confederate, and at every step of his progress he had collected fresh confirmation of the existence of some great and opulent empire in the South. The confidence of the two friends was much strengthened by their discoveries; and they unhesitatingly pledged themselves to one another to die rather than abandon the enterprise.

The best means of obtaining the levies requisite for so formidable an undertaking—more formidable, as it now appeared to them, than before—were made the subject of long and serious discussion. It was at length decided that Pizarro should remain in his present quarters, inconvenient and even unwholesome as they were rendered by the humidity of the climate, and the pestilent swarms of insects that filled the atmosphere. Almagro would pass over to Panamá, lay the case before the governor, and secure, if possible, his good-will towards the prosecution of the enterprise. If no obstacle were thrown in their way from this quarter, they might hope, with the assistance of Luque, to raise the necessary supplies; while the results of the recent expedition were sufficiently encouraging to draw adventurers to their standard in a community which had a craving for excitement that gave even danger a charm, and which held life cheap in comparison with gold.

THE FAMOUS CONTRACT—SECOND EXPEDITION—RUIZ
EXPLORES THE COAST—PIZARRO'S SUFFERINGS IN THE
FORESTS—ARRIVAL OF NEW RECRUITS—FRESH DISCOV-
ERIES AND DISASTERS—PIZARRO ON THE ISLE OF GALLO

On his arrival at Panamá, Almagro found that events
had taken a turn less favorable to his views than he had anticipated. Pedrarias, the governor, was preparing to lead an
expedition in person against a rebellious officer in Nicaragua;
and his temper, naturally not the most amiable, was still further soured by this defection of his lieutenant, and the necessity it imposed on him of a long and perilous march. When,
therefore, Almagro appeared before him with the request that
he might be permitted to raise further levies to prosecute his
enterprise, the governor received him with obvious dissatis-
faction, listened coldly to the narrative of his losses, turned
an incredulous ear to his magnificent promises for the future,
and bluntly demanded an account of the lives which had been
sacrificed by Pizarro's obstinacy, but which, had they been
spared, might have stood him in good stead in his present
expedition to Nicaragua. He positively declined to countenance the rash schemes of the two adventurers any longer,
and the conquest of Peru would have been crushed in the
bud, but for the efficient interposition of the remaining associate, Fernando de Luque.

This sagacious ecclesiastic had received a very different impression from Almagro's narrative, from that which had been
made on the mind of the irritable governor. The actual results of the enterprise in gold and silver, thus far, indeed, had
been small,—forming a mortifying contrast to the magnitude
of their expectations. But, in another point of view, they were
of the last importance; since the intelligence which the adventurers had gained in every successive stage of their progress
confirmed, in the strongest manner, the previous accounts, re-

ceived from Andogoya and others, of a rich Indian empire at the south, which might repay the trouble of conquering it as well as Mexico had repaid the enterprise of Cortés. Fully entering, therefore, into the feelings of his military associates, he used all his influence with the governor to incline him to a more favorable view of Almagro's petition; and no one in the little community of Panamá exercised greater influence over the councils of the executive than Father Luque, for which he was indebted no less to his discretion and acknowledged sagacity than to his professional station.

But while Pedrarias, overcome by the arguments of importunity of the churchman, yielded a reluctant assent to the application, he took care to testify his displeasure with Pizarro, on whom he particularly charged the loss of his followers, by naming Almagro as his equal in command in the proposed expedition. This mortification sunk deep into Pizarro's mind. He suspected his comrade, with what reason does not appear, of soliciting this boon from the governor. A temporary coldness arose between them, which subsided, in outward show, at least, on Pizarro's reflecting that it was better to have this authority conferred on a friend than on a stranger, perhaps an enemy. But the seeds of permanent distrust were left in his bosom, and lay waiting for the due season to ripen into a fruitful harvest of discord.

Pedrarias had been originally interested in the enterprise, at least, so far as to stipulate for a share of the gains, though he had not contributed, as it appears, a single ducat towards the expenses. He was at length, however, induced to relinquish all right to a share of the contingent profits. But, in his manner of doing so, he showed a mercenary spirit, better becoming a petty trader than a high officer of the Crown. He stipulated that the associates should secure to him the sum of one thousand *pesos de oro* in requital of his good-will, and they eagerly closed with his proposal, rather than be encumbered with his pretensions. For so paltry a consideration did he resign his portion of the rich spoil of the Incas! But the governor was not gifted with the eye of a prophet. His avarice was of that short-sighted kind which defeats itself. He had sacrificed the chivalrous Balboa just as that officer was opening to him the conquest of Peru, and he would now have quenched the spirit of enterprise, that was taking the same direction, in Pizarro and his associates.

Not long after this, in the following year, he was succeeded in his government by Don Pedro de los Rios, a cavalier of Cordova. It was the policy of the Castilian Crown to allow no one of the great colonial officers to occupy the same station so long as to render himself formidable by his authority. It had, moreover, many particular causes of disgust with Pedrarias. The functionary they sent out to succeed him was fortified with ample instructions for the good of the colony, and especially of the natives, whose religious conversion was urged as a capital object, and whose personal freedom was unequivocally asserted, as loyal vassals of the Crown. It is but justice to the Spanish government to admit that its provisions were generally guided by a humane and considerate policy, which was as regularly frustrated by the cupidity of the colonist, and the capricious cruelty of the conqueror. The few remaining years of Pedrarias were spent in petty squabbles, both of a personal and official nature; for he was still continued in office, though in one of less consideration than that which he had hitherto filled. He survived but a few years, leaving behind him a reputation not to be envied, of one who united a pusillanimous spirit with uncontrollable passions; who displayed, notwithstanding, a certain energy of character, or, to speak more correctly, an impetuosity of purpose, which might have led to good results had it taken a right direction. Unfortunately, his lack of discretion was such, that the direction he took was rarely of service to his country or to himself.

Having settled their difficulties with the governor, and obtained his sanction to their enterprise, the confederates lost no time in making the requisite preparations for it. Their first step was to execute the memorable contract which served as the basis of their future arrangements; and, as Pizarro's name appears in this, it seems probable that that chief had crossed over to Panamá so soon as the favorable disposition of Pedrarias had been secured. The instrument, after invoking in the most solemn manner the names of the Holy Trinity and Our Lady the Blessed Virgin, sets forth, that, whereas the parties have full authority to discover and subdue the countries and provinces lying south of the Gulf, belonging to the empire of Peru, and as Fernando de Luque had advanced the funds for the enterprise in bars of gold of the value of twenty thousand *pesos,* they mutually bind themselves to divide equally among them the whole of the conquered territory. This stipulation is reiterated over and over again, particularly with reference to Luque, who, it is declared, is to be entitled to one third of all lands, *repartimientos,* treasures of every kind, gold, silver, and precious stones,—to one third even of all vassals, rents, and emoluments arising from such grants as may be conferred by the Crown on either of his military associates, to be held for his own use, or for that of his heirs, assigns, or legal representative.

The two captains solemnly engage to devote themselves exclusively to the present undertaking until it is accomplished; and, in case of failure in their part of the covenant, they pledge themselves to reimburse Luque for his advances, for which all the property they possess shall be held responsible, and this declaration is to be a sufficient warrant for the execution of judgment against them, in the same manner as if it had proceeded from the decree of a court of justice.

The commanders, Pizarro and Almagro, made oath, in the name of God and the Holy Evangelists, sacredly to keep this covenant, swearing it on the missal, on which they traced with their own hands the sacred emblem of the cross. To give still greater efficacy to the compact, Father Luque administered the sacrament to the parties, dividing the consecrated wafer into three portions, of which each one of them partook; while the bystanders, says an historian, were affected to tears by this spectacle of the solemn ceremonial with which these men voluntarily devoted themselves to a sacrifice that seemed little short of insanity.

The instrument, which was dated March 10, 1526, was subscribed by Luque, and attested by three respectable citizens of Panamá, one of whom signed on behalf of Pizarro, and the other for Almagro; since neither of these parties, according to the avowal of the instrument, was able to subscribe his own name.

Such was the singular compact by which three obscure individuals coolly carved out and partitioned among themselves an empire, of whose extent, power, and resources, of whose situation, of whose existence, even, they had no sure or precise knowledge. The positive and unhesitating manner in which they speak of the grandeur of this empire, of its stores of wealth, so conformable to the event, but of which they could have really known so little, forms a striking contrast with the general skepticism and indifference manifested by nearly every other person, high and low, in the community of Panamá.

The religious tone of the instrument is not the least remarkable feature in it, especially when we contrast this with the relentless policy, pursued by the very men who were parties to it, in their conquest of the country. "In the name of the Prince of Peace," says Robertson, historian of America, "they ratified a contract of which plunder and bloodshed were the objects." The reflection seems reasonable. Yet, in criticizing what is done, as well as what is written, we must take into account the spirit of the times. The invocation of Heaven was natural, where the object of the undertaking was, in part, a religious one. Religion entered, more or less, into the theory, at least, of the Spanish conquests in the New World. That motives of a baser sort mingled largely with these higher ones, and in different proportions according to the character of the individual, no one will deny. And few are they that have proposed to themselves a long career of action without the intermixture of some vulgar personal motive,—fame, honors, or emolument. Yet that religion furnishes a key to the American crusades, however rudely they may have been conducted, is evident from the history of their origin; from the sanction openly given to them by the Head of the Church; from the throng of self-devoted missionaries, who followed in the track of the conquerors to garner up the rich harvest of souls; from the reiterated instructions of the Crown, the great object of which was the conversion of the natives; from those superstitious acts of the iron-hearted soldiery themselves, which, however they may be set down to fanaticism, were clearly too much in earnest to leave any ground for the charge of hypocrisy. It was indeed a fiery cross that was borne over the devoted land, scathing and consuming it in its terrible progress; but it was still the cross, the sign of man's salvation, the only sign by which generations and generations yet unborn were to be rescued from eternal perdition.

It is a remarkable fact, which has hitherto escaped the notice of the historian, that Luque was not the real party to this contract. He represented another, who placed in his hands the funds required for the undertaking. This appears from an instrument signed by Luque himself and certified before the same notary that prepared the original contract. The instrument declares that the sum of twenty thousand *pesos* advanced for the expedition was furnished by the Licentiate Gaspar de Espinosa, then at Panamá; that the vicar acted only as his agent and by his authority; and that, in consequence, the said Espinosa and no other was entitled to a third of all the profits and acquisitions resulting from the conquest of Peru. This instrument, attested by three persons, one of them the same who had witnessed the original contract, was dated on the 6th of August, 1531. The Licentiate Espinosa was a respectable functionary, who had filled the office of principal alcalde in Darien, and since taken a conspicuous part in the conquest and settlement of Tierra Firme. He enjoyed much consideration for his personal character and station; and it is remarkable that so little should be known of the manner in which the covenant, so solemnly made, was executed in reference to him. As in the case of Columbus, it is probable that the unexpected magnitude of the results was such as to prevent a faithful adherence to the original stipulation; and yet, from the same consideration, one can hardly doubt that the twenty thousand *pesos* of the bold speculator must have brought him a magnificent return. Nor did the worthy vicar of Panamá, as the history will show hereafter, go without his reward.

Having completed these preliminary arrangements, the three associates lost no time in making preparations for the voyage. Two vessels were purchased, larger and every way better than those employed on the former occasion. Stores were laid in, as experience dictated, on a larger scale than before, and proclamation was made of "an expedition to Peru." But the call was not readily answered by the skeptical citizens of Panamá. Of nearly two hundred men who had embarked on the former cruise, not more than three fourths now remained. This dismal mortality, and the emaciated, poverty-stricken aspect of the survivors, spoke more eloquently than the braggart promises and magnificent prospects held out by the adventurers. Still there were men in the community of such desperate circumstances, that any change seemed like a chance of bettering their condition. Most of the former company also, strange to say, felt more pleased to follow up the adventure to the end than to abandon it, as they saw the light of a better day dawning upon them. From these sources the two captains succeeded in mustering about one hundred and sixty men, making altogether a very inadequate force for the conquest of an empire. A few horses were also purchased, and a better supply of ammunition and military stores than before, though still on a very limited scale. Considering their funds, the only way of accounting for this must be by the difficulty of obtaining supplies at Panamá, which, recently founded, and on the remote coast of the Pacific, could be approached only by crossing the rugged barrier of mountains, which made the transportation of bulky articles extremely difficult. Even such scanty stock of materials as it possessed was probably laid under heavy contribution, at the present juncture, by the governor's preparations for his own expedition to the north.

Thus indifferently provided, the two captains, each in his own vessel, again took their departure from Panamá, under the direction of Bartholomew Ruiz, a sagacious and resolute pilot, well experienced in the navigation of the Southern Ocean. He was a native of Moguer, in Andalusia, that little nursery of nautical enterprise, which furnished so many seamen for the first voyages of Columbus. Without touching at the intervening points of the coast, which offered no attraction to the voyagers, they stood farther out to sea, steering direct for the Rio de San Juan, the utmost limit reached by Almagro. The season was better selected than on the former occasion, and they were borne along by favorable breezes to the place of their destination, which they reached without accident in a few days. Entering the mouth of the river, they saw the banks well lined with Indian habitations; and Pizarro, disembarking, at the head of a party of soldiers, succeeded in surprising a small village and carrying off a considerable booty of gold ornaments found in the dwellings, together with a few of the natives.

Flushed with their success, the two chiefs were confident

that the sight of the rich spoil so speedily obtained could not fail to draw adventurers to their standard in Panamá; and, as they felt more than ever the necessity of a stronger force to cope with the thickening population of the country which they were now to penetrate, it was decided that Almagro should return with the treasure and beat up for reinforcements, while the pilot Ruiz, in the other vessel, should reconnoitre the country towards the south, and obtain such information as might determine their future movements. Pizarro, with the rest of the force, would remain in the neighborhood of the river, as he was assured by the Indian prisoners, that not far in the interior was an open reach of country, where he and his men could find comfortable quarters. This arrangement was instantly put in execution. We will first accompany the intrepid pilot in his cruise towards the south.

Coasting along the great continent, with his canvas still spread to favorable winds, the first place at which Ruiz cast anchor was off the little island of Gallo, about two degrees north. The inhabitants, who were not numerous, were prepared to give him a hostile reception,—for tidings of the invaders had preceded them along the country, and even reached this insulated spot. As the object of Ruiz was to explore, not conquer, he did not care to entangle himself in hostilities with the natives; so, changing his purpose of landing, he weighed anchor, and ran down the coast as far as what is now called the Bay of St. Matthew. The country, which, as he advanced, continued to exhibit evidence of a better culture as well as of a more dense population than the parts hitherto seen, was crowded, along the shores, with spectators, who gave no signs of fear or hostility. They stood gazing on the vessel of the white men as it glided smoothly into the crystal waters of the bay, fancying it, says an old writer, some mysterious being descended from the skies.

Without staying long enough on this friendly coast to undeceive the simple people, Ruiz, standing off shore, struck out into the deep sea; but he had not sailed far in that direction, when he was surprised by the sight of a vessel, seeming in the distance like a caravel of considerable size, traversed by a large sail that carried it sluggishly over the waters. The old navigator was not a little perplexed by this phenomenon, as he was confident no European bark could have been before him in these latitudes, and no Indian nation, yet discovered, not even the civilized Mexican, was acquainted with the use of sails in navigation. As he drew near, he found it was a large vessel, or rather raft, called *balsa* by the natives, consisting of a number of huge timbers of a light, porous wood, tightly lashed together, with a frail flooring of reeds raised on them by way of deck. Two masts or sturdy poles, erected in the middle of the vessel, sustained a large square-sail of cotton, while a rude kind of rudder and a movable keel, made of plank inserted between the logs, enabled the mariner to give a direction to the floating fabric, which held on its course without the aid of oar or paddle. The simple architecture of this craft was sufficient for the purposes of the natives, and indeed has continued to answer them to the present day; for the *balsa*, surmounted by small thatched huts or cabins, still supplies the most commodious means for the transportation of passengers and luggage on the streams and along the shores of this part of the South American continent.

On coming alongside, Ruiz found several Indians, both men and women, on board, some with rich ornaments on their persons, besides several articles wrought with considerable skill in gold and silver, which they were carrying for purposes of traffic to the different places along the coast. But what most attracted his attention was the woollen cloth of which some of their dresses were made. It was of a fine texture, delicately embroidered with figures of birds and flowers, and dyed in brilliant colors. He also observed in the boat a pair of balances made to weigh the precious metals. His astonishment at these proofs of ingenuity and civilization, so much higher than any thing he had ever seen in the country, was heightened by the intelligence which he collected from some of these Indians. Two of them had come from Tumbez, a Peruvian port, some degrees to the south; and they gave him to understand, that in their neighborhood the fields were covered with large flocks of the animals from which the wool was obtained, and that gold and silver were almost as common as wood in the palaces of their monarch. The Spaniards listened greedily to reports which harmonized so well with their fond desires. Though half distrusting the exaggeration, Ruiz resolved to detain some of the Indians, including the natives of Tumbez, that they might repeat the wondrous tale to his commander, and at the same time, by learning the Castilian, might hereafter serve as interpreters with their countrymen. The rest of the party he suffered to proceed without further interruption on their voyage. Then holding on his course, the prudent pilot, without touching at any other point of the coast, advanced as far as the Punta de Pasado, about half a degree south, having the glory of being the first European who, sailing in this direction on the Pacific, had crossed the equinoctial line. This was the limit of his discoveries; on reaching which he tacked about, and standing away to the north, succeeded, after an absence of several weeks, in regaining the spot where he had left Pizarro and his comrades.

It was high time; for the spirits of that little band had been sorely tried by the perils they had encountered. On the departure of his vessels, Pizarro marched into the interior, in the hope of finding the pleasant champaign country which had been promised him by the natives. But at every step the forests seemed to grow denser and darker, and the trees towered to a height such as he had never seen, even in these fruitful regions, where Nature works on so gigantic a scale. Hill continued to rise above hill, as he advanced, rolling onward, as it were, by successive waves to join that colossal barrier of the Andes, whose frosty sides, far away above the clouds, spread out like a curtain of burnished silver, that seemed to connect the heavens with the earth.

On crossing these woody eminences, the forlorn adventurers would plunge into ravines of frightful depth, where the exhalations of a humid soil steamed up amidst the incense of sweet-scented flowers, which shone through the deep glooms in every conceivable variety of color. Birds, especially of the parrot tribe, mocked this fantastic variety of nature with tints as brilliant as those of the vegetable world. Monkeys chattered in crowds above their heads, and made grimaces like the fiendish spirits of these solitudes; while hideous reptiles, engendered in the slimy depths of the pools, gathered round the footsteps of the wanderers. Here was seen the gigantic boa, coiling his unwieldy folds about the trees, so as hardly to be distinguished from their trunks, till he was ready to dart upon his prey; and alligators lay basking on the borders of the streams, or, gliding under the waters, seized their incautious victim before he was aware of their approach. Many of the Spaniards perished miserably in this way, and others were waylaid by the natives, who kept a jealous eye on their movements, and availed themselves of every opportunity to take them at advantage. Fourteen of Pizarro's men were cut off at once in a canoe which had stranded on the bank of a stream.

Famine came in addition to other troubles, and it was with difficulty that they found the means of sustaining life on the scanty fare of the forest,—occasionally the potato, as it grew without cultivation, or the wild cocoa-nut, or, on the shore, the salt and bitter fruit of the mangrove; though the shore was less tolerable than the forest, from the swarms of mosquitos which compelled the wretched adventurers to bury their bodies up to their very faces in the sand. In this extremity of suffering, they thought only of return; and all schemes of avarice and ambition—except with Pizarro and a few dauntless spirits—were exchanged for the one craving desire to return to Panamá.

It was at this crisis that the pilot Ruiz returned with the report of his brilliant discoveries; and, not long after, Almagro sailed into port with his vessel laden with refreshments, and a considerable reinforcement of volunteers. The voyage of that commander had been prosperous. When he arrived at Panamá, he found the government in the hands of Don Pedro de los Rios; and he came to anchor in the harbor, unwilling to trust himself on shore, till he had obtained from Father Luque some account of the dispositions of the executive. These were sufficiently favorable; for the new governor had particular instructions fully to carry out the arrangements made by his predecessor with the associates. On learning Almagro's arrival, he came down to the port to welcome him, professing his willingness to afford every facility for the execution of his designs. Fortunately, just before this period, a small body of military adventurers had come to Panamá from the mother country, burning with desire to make their fortunes in the New World. They caught much more eagerly than the old and wary colonists at the golden bait held out to them; and with their addition, and that of a few supernumerary stragglers who hung about the town, Almagro found himself at the head of a reinforcement of at least eighty men, with which, having laid in a fresh supply of stores, he again set sail for the Rio de San Juan.

The arrival of the new recruits all eager to follow up the expedition, the comfortable change in their circumstances produced by an ample supply of refreshments, and the glowing pictures of the wealth that awaited them in the south, all had their effect on the dejected spirits of Pizarro's followers. Their late toils and privations were speedily forgotten, and, with the buoyant and variable feelings incident to a freebooter's life, they now called as eagerly on their commander to go forward in the voyage, as they had before called on him to abandon it. Availing themselves of the renewed spirit of enterprise, the captains embarked on board their vessels, and, under the guidance of the veteran pilot, steered in the same track he had lately pursued.

But the favorable season for a southern course, which in these latitudes lasts but a few months in the year, had been suffered to escape. The breezes blew steadily towards the north, and a strong current, not far from shore, set in the same direction. The winds frequently rose into tempests, and the unfortunate voyagers were tossed about, for many days, in the boiling surges, amidst the most awful storms of thunder and lightning, until, at length, they found a secure haven in the island of Gallo, already visited by Ruiz. As they were now too strong in numbers to apprehend an assault, the crews landed, and, experiencing no molestation from the natives, they continued on the island for a fortnight, refitting their damaged vessels, and recruiting themselves after the fatigues of the ocean. Then, resuming their voyage, the captains stood towards the south until they reached the Bay of St. Matthew. As they advanced along the coast, they were struck, as Ruiz had been before, with the evidences of a higher civilization constantly exhibited in the general aspect of the country and its inhabitants. The hand of cultivation was visible in every quarter. The natural appearance of the coast, too, had something in it more inviting; for, instead of the eternal labyrinth of mangrove trees, with their complicated roots snarled into formidable coils under the water, as if to waylay and entangle the voyager, the low margin of the sea was covered with a stately growth of ebony, and with a species of mahogany, and other hard woods that take the most brilliant and variegated polish. The sandal-wood, and many balsamic trees of unknown names, scattered their sweet odors far and wide, not in an atmosphere tainted with vegetable corruption, but on the pure breezes of the ocean, bearing health as well as fragrance on their wings. Broad patches of cultivated land intervened, disclosing hill-sides covered with the yellow maize and the potato, or check-ered, in the lower levels, with blooming plantations of cacao.

The villages became more numerous; and, as the vessels rode at anchor off the port of Tacamez, the Spaniards saw before them a town of two thousand houses or more, laid out into streets, with a numerous population clustering around it in the suburbs. The men and women displayed many ornaments of gold and precious stones about their persons, which may seem strange, considering that the Peruvian Incas claimed a mo-nopoly of jewels for themselves and the nobles on whom they condescended to bestow them. But, although the Spaniards had now reached the outer limits of the Peruvian empire, it was not Peru, but Quito, and that portion of it but recently brought under the sceptre of the Incas, where the ancient usages of the people could hardly have been effaced under the oppressive system of the American despots. The adjacent country was, moreover, particularly rich in gold, which, col-lected from the washings of the streams, still forms one of the staple products of Barbacoas. Here, too, was the fair River of Emeralds, so called from the quarries of the beautiful gem on its borders, from which the Indian monarchs enriched their treasury.

The Spaniards gazed with delight on these undeniable evi-dences of wealth, and saw in the careful cultivation of the soil a comfortable assurance that they had at length reached the land which had so long been seen in brilliant, though dis-tant, perspective before them. But here again they were doomed to be disappointed by the warlike spirit of the people, who, conscious of their own strength, showed no disposition to quail before the invaders. On the contrary, several of their canoes shot out, loaded with warriors, who, displaying a gold mask as their ensign, hovered round the vessels with looks of defiance, and, when pursued, easily took shelter under the lee of the land.

A more formidable body mustered along the shore, to the number, according to the Spanish accounts, of at least ten thousand warriors, eager, apparently, to come to close action with the invaders. Nor could Pizarro, who had landed with a party of his men in the hope of a conference with the natives, wholly prevent hostilities; and it might have gone hard with the Spaniards, hotly pressed by their resolute enemy so superior in numbers, but for a ludicrous accident reported by the historians as happening to one of the cavaliers. This was a fall from his horse, which so astonished the barbarians, who were not prepared for this division of what seemed one and the same being into two, that, filled with consternation, they fell back, and left a way open for the Christians to regain their vessels!

A council of war was now called. It was evident that the forces of the Spaniards were unequal to a contest with so numerous and well-appointed a body of natives; and, even if they should prevail here, they could have no hope of stemming the torrent which must rise against them in their progress—for the country was becoming more and more thickly settled, and towns and hamlets started into view at every new headland which they doubled. It was better, in the opinion of some,—the faint-hearted,—to abandon the enterprise at once, as beyond their strength. But Almagro took a different view of the affair. "To go home," he said, "with nothing done, would be ruin, as well as disgrace. There was scarcely one but had left creditors at Panamá, who look for payment to the fruits of this expedition. To go home now would be to deliver themselves at once into their hands. It would be to go to prison. Better to roam a freeman, though in the wilderness, than to lie bound with fetters in the dungeons of Panamá. The only course for them," he concluded, "was the one lately pursued. Pizarro might find some more commodious place where he could remain with part of the force while he himself went back for recruits to Panamá. The story they had now to tell of the riches of the land, as they had seen them with their own eyes, would put their expedition in a very different light, and could not fail to draw to their banner as many volunteers as they needed."

But this recommendation, however judicious, was not altogether to the taste of the latter commander, who did not relish the part, which constantly fell to him, of remaining behind in the swamps and forests of this wild country. "It is all very well," he said to Almagro, "for you, who pass your time pleasantly enough, careering to and fro in your vessel, or snugly sheltered in a land of plenty at Panamá; but it is quite another matter for those who stay behind to droop and die of hunger in the wilderness." To this Almagro retorted with some heat, professing his own willingness to take charge of the brave men who would remain with him, if Pizarro declined it. The controversy assuming a more angry and menacing tone, from words they would have soon come to blows, as both, laying their hands on their swords, were preparing to rush on each other, when the treasurer Ribera, aided by the pilot Ruiz, succeeded in pacifying them. It required but little effort on the part of these cooler counsellors to convince the cavaliers of the folly of a conduct which must at once terminate the expedition in a manner little creditable to its projectors. A reconciliation consequently took place, sufficient, at least in outward show, to allow the two commanders to act together in concert. Almagro's plan was then adopted; and it only remained to find out the most secure and convenient spot for Pizarro's quarters.

Several days were passed in touching at different parts of the coast, as they retraced their course; but everywhere the natives appeared to have caught the alarm, and assumed a menacing, and from their numbers a formidable, aspect. The more northerly region, with its unwholesome fens and forests, where nature wages a war even more relentless than man, was not to be thought of. In this perplexity, they decided on the little island of Gallo, as being, on the whole, from its distance from the shore, and from the scantiness of its population, the most eligible spot for them in their forlorn and destitute condition.

But no sooner was the resolution of the two captains made

known, than a feeling of discontent broke forth among their followers, especially those who were to remain with Pizarro on the island, "What!" they exclaimed, "were they to be dragged to that obscure spot to die by hunger? The whole expedition had been a cheat and a failure, from beginning to end. The golden countries, so much vaunted, had seemed to fly before them as they advanced; and the little gold they had been fortunate enough to glean had all been sent back to Panamá to entice other fools to follow their example. What had they got in return for all their sufferings? The only treasures they could boast were their bows and arrows, and they were now to be left to die on this dreary island, without so much as a rood of consecrated ground to lay their bones in!"

In this exasperated state of feeling, several of the soldiers wrote back to their friends, informing them of their deplorable condition, and complaining of the cold-blooded manner in which they were to be sacrificed to the obstinate cupidity of their leaders. But the latter were wary enough to anticipate this movement, and Almagro defeated it by seizing all the letters in the vessels, and thus cutting off at once the means of communication with their friends at home. Yet this act of unscrupulous violence, like most other similar acts, fell short of its purpose; for a soldier named Sarabia had the ingenuity to evade it by introducing a letter into a ball of cotton, which was to be taken to Panamá as a specimen of the products of the country, and presented to the governor's lady.

The letter, which was signed by several of the disaffected soldiery besides the writer, painted in gloomy colors the miseries of their condition, accused the two commanders of being the authors of this, and called on the authorities of Panamá to interfere by sending a vessel to take them from the desolate spot, while some of them might still be found surviving the horrors of their confinement. The epistle concluded with a stanza, in which the two leaders were stigmatized as partners in a slaughter-house; one being employed to drive in the cattle for the other to butcher. The verses, which had a currency in their day among the colonists to which they were certainly not entitled by their poetical merits, may be thus rendered into corresponding doggerel:

> *"Look out, Señor Governor,*
> *For the drover while he's near;*
> *Since he goes home to get the sheep*
> *For the butcher who stays here."*

CHAPTER IV [1527–1528]

Not long after Almagro's departure, Pizarro sent off the
remaining vessel, under the pretext of its being put in repair
at Panamá. It probably relieved him of a part of his followers,
whose mutinous spirit made them an obstacle rather than a
help in his forlorn condition, and with whom he was the more
willing to part because of the difficulty of finding subsistence
on the barren spot which he now occupied.

Great was the dismay occasioned by the return of Almagro
and his followers, in the little community of Panamá; for the
letter, surreptitiously conveyed in the ball of cotton, fell into
the hands for which it was intended, and the contents soon got
abroad with the usual quantity of exaggeration. The haggard
and dejected mien of the adventurers, of itself, told a tale sufficiently disheartening, and it was soon generally believed that
the few ill-fated survivors of the expedition were detained
against their will by Pizarro, to end their days with their disappointed leader on his desolate island.

Pedro de los Rios, the governor, was so much incensed at
the result of the expedition, and the waste of life it had occasioned to the colony, that he turned a deaf ear to all the
applications of Luque and Almagro for further countenance in
the affair; he derided their sanguine anticipations of the future,
and finally resolved to send an officer to the isle of Gallo, with
orders to bring back every Spaniard whom he should find still
living in that dreary abode. Two vessels were immediately despatched for the purpose, and placed under charge of a cavalier
named Tafur, a native of Cordova.

Meanwhile Pizarro and his followers were experiencing all
the miseries which might have been expected from the char-

acter of the barren spot on which they were imprisoned. They were, indeed, relieved from all apprehensions of the natives, since these had quitted the island on its occupation by the white men; but they had to endure the pains of hunger even in a greater degree than they had formerly experienced in the wild woods of the neighboring continent. Their principal food was crabs and such shell-fish as they could scantily pick up along the shores. Incessant storms of thunder and lightning, for it was the rainy season, swept over the desolate island, and drenched them with a perpetual flood. Thus, half-naked, and pining with famine, there were few in that little company who did not feel the spirit of enterprise quenched within them, or who looked for any happier termination of their difficulties than that afforded by a return to Panamá. The appearance of Tafur, therefore, with his two vessels, well stored with provisions, was greeted with all the rapture that the crew of a sinking wreck might feel on the arrival of some unexpected succour; and the only thought, after satisfying the immediate cravings of hunger, was to embark and leave the detested isle for ever.

But by the same vessel letters came to Pizarro from his two confederates, Luque and Almagro, beseeching him not to despair in his present extremity, but to hold fast to his original purpose. To return under the present circumstances would be to seal the fate of the expedition; and they solemnly engaged, if he would remain firm at his post, to furnish him in a short time with the necessary means for going forward.

A ray of hope was enough for the courageous spirit of Pizarro. It does not appear that he himself had entertained, at any time, thoughts of returning. If he had, these words of encouragement entirely banished them from his bosom, and he prepared to stand the fortune of the cast on which he had so desperately ventured. He knew, however, that solicitations or remonstrances would avail little with the companions of his enterprise; and he probably did not care to win over the more timid spirits who, by perpetually looking back, would only be a clog on his future movements. He announced his own purpose, however, in a laconic but decided manner, characteristic of a man more accustomed to act than to talk, and well calculated to make an impression on his rough followers.

Drawing his sword, he traced a line with it on the sand from east to west. Then turning towards the south, "Friends and comrades!" he said, "on that side are toil, hunger, nakedness, the drenching storm, desertion, and death; on this side, ease and pleasure. There lies Peru with its riches; here, Panamá and its poverty. Choose, each man, what best becomes a brave Castilian. For my part, I go to the south." So saying, he stepped across the line. He was followed by the brave pilot Ruiz; next by Pedro de Candia, a cavalier, born, as his name imports, in one of the isles of Greece. Eleven others successively crossed the line, thus intimating their willingness to abide the fortunes of their leader, for good or for evil. Fame, to quote the enthusiastic language of an ancient chronicler, has commemorated the names of this little band, "who thus, in the face of difficulties unexampled in history, with death rather than riches for their reward, preferred it all to abandoning their honor, and stood firm by their leader as an example of loyalty to future ages."

But the act excited no such admiration in the mind of Tafur, who looked on it as one of gross disobedience to the commands of the governor, and as little better than madness, involving the certain destruction of the parties engaged in it. He refused to give any sanction to it himself by leaving one of his vessels with the adventurers to prosecute their voyage, and it was with great difficulty that he could be persuaded even to allow them a part of the stores which he had brought for their support. This had no influence on their determination, and the little party, bidding adieu to their returning comrades, remained unshaken in their purpose of abiding the fortunes of their commander.

There is something striking to the imagination in the spectacle of these few brave spirits, thus consecrating themselves to a daring enterprise, which seemed as far above their strength as any recorded in the fabulous annals of knight-errantry. A handful of men, without food, without clothing, almost without arms, without knowledge of the land to which they were bound, without vessel to transport them, were here left on a lonely rock in the ocean with the avowed purpose of carrying on a crusade against a powerful empire, staking their lives on its success. What is there in the legends of chivalry that surpasses it? This was the crisis of Pizarro's fate. There are moments in the lives of men, which, as they are seized or neglected, decide their future destiny. Had Pizarro faltered from his strong purpose, and yielded to the occasion, now so temptingly presented, for extricating himself and his broken band from their desperate position, his name would have been buried with his fortunes, and the conquest of Peru would have been left for other and more successful adventurers. But his constancy was equal to the occasion, and his conduct here proved him competent to the perilous post he had assumed, and inspired others with a confidence in him which was surely the best assurance of success.

In the vessel that bore back Tafur and those who seceded from the expedition, the pilot Ruiz was also permitted to return, in order to coöperate with Luque and Almagro in their application for further succour.

Not long after the departure of the ships, it was decided by Pizarro to abandon his present quarters, which had little to recommend them, and which, he reflected, might now be exposed to annoyance from the original inhabitants, should they take courage and return, on learning the diminished number of the white men. The Spaniards, therefore, by his orders, constructed a rude boat or raft, on which they succeeded in transporting themselves to the little island of Gorgona, twenty-five leagues to the north of their present residence. It lay about five leagues from the continent, and was uninhabited. It had some advantages over the isle of Gallo; for it stood higher above the sea, and was partially covered with wood, which afforded shelter to a species of pheasant, and the hare or rabbit of the country, so that the Spaniards, with their cross-bows, were enabled to procure a tolerable supply of game. Cool streams that issued from the living rock furnished abundance of water, though the drenching rains that fell, without intermission, left them in no danger of perishing by thirst. From this annoyance they found protection in the rude huts which they constructed; though here, as in their former residence, they suffered from the no less intolerable annoyance of venomous insects, which multiplied and swarmed in the exhalations of the rank and stimulated soil. In this dreary abode Pizarro omitted no means by which to sustain the drooping spirits of his men. Morning prayers were duly said, and the evening hymn to the Virgin was regularly chanted; the festivals of the church were carefully commemorated, and every means taken by their commander to give a kind of religious character to his enterprise, and to inspire his rough followers with a confidence in the protection of Heaven, that might support them in their perilous circumstances.

In these uncomfortable quarters, their chief employment was to keep watch on the melancholy ocean, that they might hail the first signal of the anticipated succour. But many a tedious month passed away, and no sign of it appeared. All around was the same wide waste of waters, except to the eastward, where the frozen crest of the Andes, touched with the ardent sun of the equator, glowed like a ridge of fire along the whole extent of the great continent. Every speck in the distant horizon was carefully noticed, and the drifting timber or masses of sea-weed, heaving to and fro on the bosom of the waters, was converted by their imaginations into the promised vessel; till, sinking under successive disappointments, hope gradually gave way to doubt, and doubt settled into despair.

Meanwhile the vessel of Tafur had reached the port of Panamá. The tidings which she brought of the inflexible obstinacy of Pizarro and his followers filled the governor with indignation. He could look on it in no other light than as an act of suicide, and steadily refused to send further assistance to men who were obstinately bent on their own destruction. Yet Luque and Almagro were true to their engagements. They represented to the governor, that, if the conduct of their comrade was rash, it was at least in the service of the Crown, and in prosecuting the great work of discovery. Rios had been instructed, on his taking the government, to aid Pizarro in the enterprise; and to desert him now would be to throw away the remaining chance of success, and to incur the responsibility of his death and that of the brave men who adhered to him. These remonstrances, at length, so far operated on the mind of that functionary, that he reluctantly consented that a vessel should be sent to the island of Gorgona, but with no more hands than were necessary to work her, and with positive instructions to Pizarro to return in six months and report himself at Panamá, whatever might be the future results of his expedition.

Having thus secured the sanction of the executive, the two associates lost no time in fitting out a small vessel with stores and a supply of arms and ammunition, and despatched it to the island. The unfortunate tenants of this little wilderness, who had now occupied it for seven months, hardly dared to trust their senses when they descried the white sails of the friendly bark coming over the waters. And although, when the vessel anchored off the shore, Pizarro was disappointed to find that it brought no additional recruits for the enterprise, yet he greeted it with joy, as affording the means of solving the great problem of the existence of the rich southern empire, and of thus opening the way for its future conquest. Two of his men were so ill, that it was determined to leave them in the care of some of the friendly Indians who had continued with him through the whole of his sojourn, and to call for them on his return. Taking with him the rest of his hardy followers and the natives of Tumbez, he embarked, and, speedily weighing anchor, bade adieu to the "Hell," as it was called by the Spaniards, which had been the scene of so much suffering and such undaunted resolution.

Every heart was now elated with hope, as they found themselves once more on the waters, under the guidance of the good pilot Ruiz, who, obeying the directions of the Indians, proposed to steer for the land of Tumbez, which would bring them at once into the golden empire of the Incas,—the El Dorado, of which they had been so long in pursuit. Passing by the dreary isle of Gallo, which they had such good cause to remember, they stood farther out to sea until they made Point Tacumez, near which they had landed on their previous voyage. They did not touch at any part of the coast, but steadily held on their way, though considerably impeded by the currents, as well as by the wind, which blew with little variation from the south. Fortunately, the wind was light, and, as the weather was favorable, their voyage, though slow, was not uncomfortable. In a few days, they came in sight of Point Pasado, the limit of the pilot's former navigation; and, crossing the line, the little bark entered upon those unknown seas which had never been ploughed by European keel before. The coast, they observed, gradually declined from its former bold and rugged character, gently sloping towards the shore, and spreading out into sandy plains, relieved here and there by patches of uncommon richness and beauty; while the white cottages of the natives glistening along the margin of the sea, and the smoke that rose among the distant hills, intimated the increasing population of the country.

At length, after the lapse of twenty days from their departure from the island, the adventurous vessel rounded the point of St. Helena, and glided smoothly into the waters of the beautiful gulf of Guayaquil. The country was here studded along the shore with towns and villages, though the mighty chain of the Cordilleras, sweeping up abruptly from the coast, left but a narrow strip of emerald verdure, through which numerous rivulets, spreading fertility around them, wound their way into the sea.

The voyagers were now abreast of some of the most stupendous heights of this magnificent range; Chimborazo, with its broad round summit, towering like the dome of the Andes, and Cotopaxi, with its dazzling cone of silvery white, that knows no change except from the action of its own volcanic fires; for this mountain is the most terrible of the American volcanoes, and was in formidable activity at no great distance from the period of our narrative. Well pleased with the signs of civilization that opened on them at every league of their progress, the Spaniards, at length, came to anchor, off the island of Santa Clara, lying at the entrance of the bay of Tumbez.

The place was uninhabited, but was recognized by the Indians on board, as occasionally resorted to by the warlike people of the neighboring isle of Puná, for purpose of sacrifice and worship. The Spaniards found on the spot a few bits of gold rudely wrought into various shapes, and probably designed as offerings to the Indian deity. Their hearts were cheered, as the natives assured them they would see great abundance of the same precious metal in their own city of Tumbez.

The following morning they stood across the bay from this place. As they drew near, they beheld a town of considerable size, with many of the buildings apparently of stone and plaster, situated in the bosom of a fruitful meadow, which seemed to have been redeemed from the sterility of the surrounding country by careful and minute irrigation. When at some distance from shore, Pizarro saw standing towards him several large balsas, which were found to be filled with warriors going on an expedition against the island of Puná. Running alongside of the Indian flotilla, he invited some of the chiefs to come on board of his vessel. The Peruvians gazed with wonder on every object which met their eyes, and especially on their own countrymen, whom they had little expected to meet there. The latter informed them in what manner they had fallen into the hands of the strangers, whom they described as a wonderful race of beings, that had come thither for no harm, but solely to be made acquainted with the country and its inhabitants. This account was confirmed by the Spanish commander, who persuaded the Indians to return in their balsas and report what they had learned to their townsmen, requesting them at the same time to provide his vessel with refreshments, as it was his desire to enter into a friendly intercourse with the natives.

The people of Tumbez were gathered along the shore, and were gazing with unutterable amazement on the floating castle, which, now having dropped anchor, rode lazily at its moorings in their bay. They eagerly listened to the accounts of their countrymen, and instantly reported the affair to the *curaca* or ruler of the district, who, conceiving that the strangers must be beings of a superior order, prepared at once to comply with their request. It was not long before several balsas were seen steering for the vessel laden with bananas, plantains, yuca, Indian corn, sweet potatoes, pine-apples, cocoa-nuts, and other rich products of the bountiful vale of Tumbez. Game and fish, also, were added, with a number of llamas, of which Pizarro had seen the rude drawings belonging to Balboa, but of which till now he had met with no living specimen. He examined this curious animal, the Peruvian sheep,—or, as the Spaniards called it, the "little camel" of the Indians,—with much interest, greatly admiring the mixture of wool and hair which supplied the natives with the materials for their fabrics.

At that time there happened to be at Tumbez an Inca noble, or *orejon*—for so, as I have already noticed, men of his rank were called by the Spaniards, from the huge ornaments of gold attached to their ears. He expressed great curiosity to see the wonderful strangers, and had, accordingly, come out with the balsas for the purpose. It was easy to perceive from the superior quality of his dress, as well as from the deference paid to him by the others, that he was a person of consideration, and Pizarro received him with marked distinction. He showed him the different parts of the ship, explaining to him the uses of whatever engaged his attention, and answering his numerous queries, as well as he could, by means of the Indian interpreters. The Peruvian chief was especially desirous of knowing whence and why Pizarro and his followers had come to these shores. The Spanish captain replied, that he was the vassal of a great prince, the greatest and most powerful in the world, and that he had come to this country to assert his master's *lawful supremacy* over it. He had further come to rescue the inhabitants from the darkness of unbelief in which they were now wandering. They worshipped an evil spirit, who would sink their souls into everlasting perdition; and he would give them the knowledge of the true and only God, Jesus Christ, since to believe in him was eternal salvation.

The Indian prince listened with deep attention and apparent wonder; but answered nothing. It may be, that neither he nor his interpreters had any very distinct ideas of the doctrines thus abruptly revealed to them. It may be that he did not believe there was any other potentate on earth greater than the Inca; none, at least, who had a better right to rule over his dominions. And it is very possible he was not disposed to admit that the great luminary whom he worshipped was inferior to the God of the Spaniards. But whatever may have passed in the untutored mind of the barbarian, he did not give vent to it, but maintained a discreet silence, without any attempt to controvert or to convince his Christian antagonist.

He remained on board of the vessel till the hour of dinner, of which he partook with the Spaniards, expressing his satisfaction at the strange dishes, and especially pleased with the wine, which he pronounced far superior to the fermented liquors of his own country. On taking leave, he courteously pressed the Spaniards to visit Tumbez, and Pizarro dismissed him with the present, among other things, of an iron hatchet, which had greatly excited his admiration; for the use of iron, as we have seen, was as little known to the Peruvians as to the Mexicans.

On the day following, the Spanish captain sent one of his own men, named Alonso de Molina, on shore, accompanied by a negro who had come in the vessel from Panamá, together with a present for the curaca of some swine and poultry, neither of which were indigenous to the New World. Towards evening his emissary returned with a fresh supply of fruits and vegetables, that the friendly people sent to the vessel. Molina had a wondrous tale to tell. On landing, he was surrounded by the natives, who expressed the greatest astonishment at his dress, his fair complexion, and his long beard. The women, especially, manifested great curiosity in respect to him, and Molina seemed to be entirely won by their charms and captivating manners. He probably intimated his satisfaction by his demeanor, since they urged him to stay among them, promising in that case to provide him with a beautiful wife.

Their surprise was equally great at the complexion of his sable companion. They could not believe it was natural, and tried to rub off the imaginary dye with their hands. As the African bore all this with characteristic good-humor, displaying at the same time his rows of ivory teeth, they were prodigiously delighted. The animals were no less above their comprehension; and, when the cock crew, the simple people clapped their hands, and inquired what he was saying. Their intellects were so bewildered by sights so novel, that they seemed incapable of distinguishing between man and brute.

Molina was then escorted to the residence of the curaca, whom he found living in much state, with porters stationed at his doors, and with a quantity of gold and silver vessels, from which he was served. He was then taken to different parts of the Indian city, saw a fortress built of rough stone, and, though low, spreading over a large extent of ground. Near this was a temple; and the Spaniard's description of its decorations, blazing with gold and silver, seemed so extravagant, that Pizarro, distrusting his whole account, resolved to send a more discreet and trustworthy emissary on the following day.

The person selected was Pedro de Candia, the Greek cavalier mentioned as one of the first who intimated his intention to share the fortunes of his commander. He was sent on shore, dressed in complete mail as became a good knight, with his sword by his side, and his arquebuse on his shoulder. The Indians were even more dazzled by his appearance than by Molina's, as the sun fell brightly on his polished armour, and glanced from his military weapons. They had heard much of the formidable arquebuse from their townsmen who had come in the vessel, and they besought Candia "to let it speak to them." He accordingly set up a wooden board as a target, and, taking deliberate aim, fired off the musket. The flash of the powder and the startling report of the piece, as the board, struck by the ball, was shivered into splinters, filled the natives with dismay. Some fell on the ground, covering their faces with their hands, and others approached the cavalier with feelings of awe, which were gradually dispelled by the assurance they received from the smiling expression of his countenance.

They then showed him the same hospitable attentions which they had paid to Molina; and his description of the marvels of the place, on his return, fell nothing short of his predecessor's. The fortress, which was surrounded by a triple row of wall, was strongly garrisoned. The temple he described as literally tapestried with plates of gold and silver. Adjoining this structure was a sort of convent appropriated to the Inca's destined brides, who manifested great curiosity to see him. Whether this was gratified is not clear; but Candia described the gardens of the convent, which he entered, as glowing with imitations of fruits and vegetables all in pure gold and silver! He had seen a number of artisans at work, whose sole business seemed to be to furnish these gorgeous decorations for the religious houses.

The reports of the cavalier may have been somewhat overcolored. It was natural that men coming from the dreary wilderness, in which they had been buried the last six months, should have been vividly impressed by the tokens of civilization which met them on the Peruvian coast. But Tumbez was a favorite city of the Peruvian princes. It was the most important place on the northern borders of the empire, contiguous to the recent acquisition of Quito. The great Tupac Yupanqui had established a strong fortress there, and peopled it with a colony of *mitimaes*. The temple, and the house occupied by the Virgins of the Sun, had been erected by Huayna Capac, and were liberally endowed by that Inca, after the sumptuous fashion of the religious establishments of Peru. The town was well supplied with water by numerous aqueducts, and the fruitful valley in which it was embosomed, and the ocean which bathed its shores, supplied ample means of subsistence to a considerable population. But the cupidity of the Spaniards, after the Conquest, was not slow in despoiling the place of its glories; and the site of its proud towers and temples, in less than half a century after that fatal period, was to be traced only by the huge mass of ruins that encumbered the ground.

The Spaniards were nearly mad with joy, says an old writer, at receiving these brilliant tidings of the Peruvian city. All their fond dreams were now to be realized, and they had at length reached the realm which had so long flitted in visionary splendor before them. Pizarro expressed his gratitude to Heaven for having crowned his labors with so glorious a result; but he bitterly lamented the hard fate which, by depriving him of his followers, denied him, at such a moment, the means of availing himself of his success. Yet he had no cause for lamentation; and the devout Catholic saw in this very circumstance a providential interposition which prevented the attempt at conquest, while such attempts would have been premature. Peru was not yet torn asunder by the dissensions of rival candidates for the throne; and, united and strong under the sceptre of a warlike monarch, she might well have bid defiance to all the forces that Pizarro could muster. "It was manifestly the work of Heaven," exclaims a devout son of the Church, "that the natives of the country should have received him in so kind and loving a spirit, as best fitted to facilitate the conquest; for it was the Lord's hand which led him and his followers to this remote region for the extension of the holy faith, and for the salvation of souls."

Having now collected all the information essential to his object, Pizarro, after taking leave of the natives of Tumbez, and promising a speedy return, weighed anchor, and again turned his prow towards the south. Still keeping as near as possible to the coast, that no place of importance might escape his observation, he passed Cape Blanco, and, after sailing about a degree and a half, made the port of Payta. The inhabitants, who had notice of his approach, came out in their balsas to get sight of the wonderful strangers, bringing with them stores of fruits, fish, and vegetables, with the same hospitable spirit shown by their countrymen at Tumbez.

After staying here a short time, and interchanging presents of trifling value with the natives, Pizarro continued his cruise; and, sailing by the sandy plains of Sechura for an extent of near a hundred miles, he doubled the Punta de Aguja, and swept down the coast as it fell off towards the east, still carried forward by light and somewhat variable breezes. The weather now became unfavorable, and the voyagers encountered a succession of heavy gales, which drove them some distance out to sea, and tossed them about for many days. But they did not lose sight of the mighty ranges of the Andes, which, as they proceeded towards the south, were still seen, at nearly the same distance from the shore, rolling onwards, peak after peak, with their stupendous surges of ice, like some vast ocean, that had been suddenly arrested and frozen up in the midst of its wild and tumultuous career. With this landmark always in view, the navigator had little need of star or compass to guide his bark on her course.

As soon as the tempest had subsided, Pizarro stood in again for the continent, touching at the principal points as he coasted along. Everywhere he was received with the same spirit of generous hospitality; the natives coming out on their balsas to welcome him, laden with their little cargoes of fruits and vegetables, of all the luscious varieties that grow in the *tierra caliente*. All were eager to have a glimpse of the strangers, the "Children of the Sun," as the Spaniards began already to be called, from their fair complexions, brilliant armour, and the thunderbolts which they bore in their hands. The most favorable reports, too, had preceded them, of the urbanity and gentleness of their manners, thus unlocking the hearts of the simple natives, and disposing them to confidence and kindness. The iron-hearted soldier had not yet disclosed the darker side of his character. He was too weak to do so. The hour of conquest had not yet come.

In every place Pizarro received the same accounts of a powerful monarch who ruled over the land, and held his court on the mountain plains of the interior, where his capital was depicted as blazing with gold and silver, and displaying all the profusion of an Oriental satrap. The Spaniards, except at Tumbez, seem to have met with little of the precious metals among the natives on the coast. More than one writer asserts that they did not covet them, or, at least, by Pizarro's orders, affected not to do so. He would not have them betray their appetite for gold, and actually refused gifts when they were proffered! It is more probable that they saw little display of wealth, except in the embellishments of the temples and other sacred buildings, which they did not dare to violate. The precious metals, reserved for the uses of religion and for persons of high degree, were not likely to abound in the remote towns and hamlets on the coast.

Yet the Spaniards met with sufficient evidence of general civilization and power to convince them that there was much foundation for the reports of the natives. Repeatedly they saw structures of stone and plaster, and occasionally showing architectural skill in the execution, if not elegance of design. Wherever they cast anchor, they beheld green patches of cultivated country redeemed from the sterility of nature, and blooming with the variegated vegetation of the tropics; while a refined system of irrigation, by means of aqueducts and canals, seemed to be spread like a network over the surface of the country, making even the desert to blossom as the rose. At many places where they landed they saw the great road of the Incas which traversed the sea-coast, often, indeed, lost in the volatile sands, where no road could be maintained, but rising into a broad and substantial causeway, as it emerged on a firmer soil. Such a provision for internal communication was in itself no slight monument of power and civilization.

Still beating to the south, Pizarro passed the site of the future flourishing city of Truxillo, founded by himself some years later, and pressed on till he rode off the port of Santa. It stood on the banks of a broad and beautiful stream; but the surrounding country was so exceedingly arid that it was frequently selected as a burial-place by the Peruvians, who found the soil most favorable for the preservation of their mummies. So numerous, indeed, were the Indian *guacas*, that the place might rather be called the abode of the dead than of the living.

Having reached this point, about the ninth degree of southern latitude, Pizarro's followers besought him not to prosecute the voyage farther. Enough and more than enough had been done, they said, to prove the existence and actual position of the great Indian empire of which they had so long been in search. Yet, with their slender force, they had no power to profit by the discovery. All that remained, therefore, was to return and report the success of their enterprise to the governor at Panamá. Pizarro acquiesced in the reasonableness of this demand. He had now penetrated nine degrees farther than any former navigator in these southern seas, and, instead of the blight which, up to this hour, had seemed to hang over his fortunes, he could now return in triumph to his countrymen. Without hesitation, he prepared to retrace his course, and stood again towards the north.

On his way, he touched at several places where he had before landed. At one of these, called by the Spaniards Santa Cruz, he had been invited on shore by an Indian woman of rank, and had promised to visit her on his return. No sooner did his vessel cast anchor off the village where she lived, than she came on board, followed by a numerous train of attendants. Pizarro received her with every mark of respect, and on her departure presented her with some trinkets which had a real value in the eyes of an Indian princess. She urged the Spanish commander and his companions to return the visit, engaging to send a number of hostages on board, as security for their good treatment. Pizarro assured her that the frank confidence she had shown towards them proved that this was unnecessary. Yet, no sooner did he put off in his boat, the following day, to go on shore, than several of the principal persons in the place came alongside of the ship to be received as hostages during the absence of the Spaniards,—a singular proof of consideration for the sensitive apprehensions of her guests.

Pizarro found that preparations had been made for his reception in a style of simple hospitality that evinced some degree of taste. Arbours were formed of luxuriant and wide-spreading branches, interwoven with fragrant flowers and shrubs that diffused a delicious perfume through the air. A banquet was provided, teeming with viands prepared in the style of the Peruvian cookery, and with fruits and vegetables of tempting hue and luscious to the taste, though their names and nature were unknown to the Spaniards. After the collation was ended, the guests were entertained with music and dancing by a troop of young men and maidens simply attired, who exhibited in their favorite national amusement all the agility and grace which the supple limbs of the Peruvian Indians so well qualified them to display. Before his departure, Pizarro stated to his kind host the motives of his visit to the country, in the same manner as he had done on other occasions, and he concluded by unfurling the royal banner of Castile, which he had brought on shore, requesting her and her attendants to raise it in token of their allegiance to his sovereign. This they did with great good-humor, laughing all the while, says the chronicler, and making it clear that they had a very imperfect conception of the serious nature of the ceremony. Pizarro was contented with this outward display of loyalty, and returned to his vessel well satisfied with the entertainment he had received, and meditating, it may be, on the best mode of repaying it, hereafter, by the subjugation and conversion of the country.

The Spanish commander did not omit to touch also at Tumbez, on his homeward voyage. Here some of his followers, won by the comfortable aspect of the place and the manners of the people, intimated a wish to remain, conceiving, no doubt, that it would be better to live where they would be persons of consequence than to return to an obscure condition in the community of Panamá. One of these men was Alonso de Molina, the same who had first gone on shore at this place, and been capitivated by the charms of the Indian beauties. Pizarro complied with their wishes, thinking it would not be amiss to find, on his return, some of his own followers who would be instructed in the language and usages of the natives. He was also allowed to carry back in his vessel two or three Peruvians, for the similar purpose of instructing them in the Castilian. One of them, a youth named by the Spaniards Felipillo, plays a part of some importance in the history of subsequent events.

On leaving Tumbez, the adventurers steered directly for Panamá, touching only, on their way, at the ill-fated island of Gorgona to take on board their two companions who were left there too ill to proceed with them. One had died, and, receiving the other, Pizarro and his gallant little band continued their voyage; and, after an absence of at least eighteen months, found themselves once more safely riding at anchor in the harbor of Panamá.

The sensation caused by their arrival was great, as might have been expected. For there were few, even among the most sanguine of their friends, who did not imagine that they had long since paid for their temerity, and fallen victims to the climate or the natives, or miserably perished in a watery grave. Their joy was proportionably great, therefore, as they saw the wanderers now returned, not only in health and safety, but with certain tidings of the fair countries which had so long eluded their grasp. It was a moment of proud satisfaction to the three associates, who, in spite of obloquy, derision, and every impediment which the distrust of friends or the coldness of government could throw in their way, had persevered in their great enterprise until they had established the truth of what had been so generally denounced as a chimera. It is the misfortune of those daring spirits who conceive an idea too vast for their own generation to comprehend, or, at least, to attempt to carry out, that they pass for visionary dreamers. Such had been the fate of Luque and his associates. The existence of a rich Indian empire at the south, which, in their minds, dwelling long on the same idea and alive to all the arguments in its favor, had risen to the certainty of conviction, had been derided by the rest of their countrymen as a mere *mirage* of the fancy, which, on nearer approach, would melt into air; while the projectors, who staked their fortunes on the adventure, were denounced as madmen. But their hour of triumph, their slow and hard-earned triumph, had now arrived.

Yet the governor, Pedro de los Rios, did not seem, even at this moment, to be possessed with a conviction of the magnitude of the discovery,—or, perhaps, he was discouraged by its very magnitude. When the associates, now with more confidence, applied to him for patronage in an undertaking too vast for their individual resources, he coldly replied, "He had no desire to build up other states at the expense of his own; nor would he be led to throw away more lives than had already been sacrificed by the cheap display of gold and silver toys and a few Indian sheep!"

Sorely disheartened by this repulse from the only quarter whence effectual aid could be expected, the confederates, without funds, and with credit nearly exhausted by their past efforts, were perplexed in the extreme. Yet to stop now,—what was it but to abandon the rich mine which their own industry and perseverance had laid open, for others to work at pleasure? In this extremity the fruitful mind of Luque suggested the only expedient by which they could hope for success. This was to apply to the Crown itself. No one was so much interested in the result of the expedition. It was for the government, indeed, that discoveries were to be made, that the country was to be conquered. The government alone was competent to provide the requisite means, and was likely to take a much broader and more liberal view of the matter than a petty colonial officer.

But who was there qualified to take charge of this delicate mission? Luque was chained by his professional duties to Panamá; and his associates, unlettered soldiers, were much better fitted for the business of the camp than of the court. Almagro, blunt, though somewhat swelling and ostentatious in his address, with a diminutive stature and a countenance naturally plain, now much disfigured by the loss of an eye, was not so well qualified for the mission as his companion in arms, who, possessing a good person and altogether a commanding presence, was plausible, and, with all his defects of education, could, where deeply interested, be even eloquent in discourse. The ecclesiastic, however, suggested that the negotiation should be committed to the Licentiate Corral, a respectable functionary, then about to return on some public business to the mother country. But to this Almagro strongly objected. No one, he said, could conduct the affair so well as the party interested in it. He had a high opinion of Pizarro's prudence, his discernment of character, and his cool, deliberate policy. He knew enough of his comrade to have confidence that his presence of mind would not desert him, even in the new, and therefore embarrassing, circumstances in which he would be placed at court. No one, he said, could tell the story of their adventures with such effect, as the man who had been the chief actor in them. No one could so well paint the unparalleled sufferings and sacrifices which they had encountered; no other could tell so forcibly what had been done, what yet remained to do, and what assistance would be necessary to carry it into execution. He concluded, with characteristic frankness, by strongly urging his confederate to undertake the mission.

Pizarro felt the force of Almagro's reasoning, and, though with undisguised reluctance, acquiesced in a measure which was less to his taste than an expedition to the wilderness. But Luque came into the arrangement with more difficulty. "God grant, my children," exclaimed the ecclesiastic, "that one of you may not defraud the other of his blessing!" Pizarro engaged to consult the interests of his associates equally with his own. But Luque, it is clear, did not trust Pizarro.

There was some difficulty in raising the funds necessary for putting the envoy in condition to make a suitable appearance at court; so low had the credit of the confederates fallen, and so little confidence was yet placed in the result of their splendid discoveries. Fifteen hundred ducats were at length raised; and Pizarro, in the spring of 1528, bade adieu to Panamá, accompanied by Pedro de Candia. He took with him, also, some of the natives, as well as two or three llamas, various nice fabrics of cloth, with many ornaments and vases of gold and silver, as specimens of the civilization of the country, and vouchers for his wonderful story.

who had been the chief actor in them. No one could so well paint the unmutilated sufferings and enormities which they had endured, and other could tell so forcibly what had been done, what yet remained if the sufferers and those would be needed to carry out the design. He concluded with unwonted readiness, vehemently urging his confederate to undertake the task.

During all the time of Alminos's reasoning, and though oft indicated reluctance, he only essayed a measure which we laugh at, his state than an expedition to the wildness, knight came into the arrangement with more difficulty. "God send, my children," exclaimed the enthusiast, "that you may not attend the glory of his Majesty if I waited, replied to consult the interest of his associates equally with his own. But still more clear did this appear.

There was some difficulty in raising the funds necessary for equipping the navy in condition to make a suitable appearance. If contained how had the credit of the confederates failed, and so little confidence was yet placed in the result of their dealings and discoveries. They inquired of dross was at length raised, and, placing in the strong of steel, Pedro going to Habana accompanied by Pedro or Sandia. He took with him also some of the natives, as well as two of these human samples into tokens of faith, with their ornaments and vases of gold, and drew as spectators at the civilization of the country, and vouchers for his wonderful story.

BOOK III

CONQUEST OF PERU

CHAPTER I [1528-1531]

Pizarro and his officer, having crossed the Isthmus, embarked at Nombre de Dios for the old country, and, after a
good passage, reached Seville early in the summer of 1528.
There happened to be at that time in port a person well known
in the history of Spanish adventure as the Bachelor Enciso.
He had taken an active part in the colonization of Tierra
Firme, and had a pecuniary claim against the early colonists
of Darien, of whom Pizarro was one. Immediately on the landing of the latter, he was seized by Enciso's orders, and held
in custody for the debt. Pizarro, who had fled from his native
land as a forlorn and houseless adventurer, after an absence
of more than twenty years, passed, most of them, in unprecedented toil and suffering, now found himself on his return the
inmate of a prison. Such was the commencement of those brilliant fortunes which, as he had trusted, awaited him at home.
The circumstance excited general indignation; and no sooner
was the Court advised of his arrival in the country, and the
great purpose of his mission, than orders were sent for his
release, with permission to proceed at once on his journey.

Pizarro found the emperor at Toledo, which he was soon
to quit, in order to embark for Italy. Spain was not the favorite
residence of Charles the Fifth, in the earlier part of his reign.
He was now at that period of it when he was enjoying the full
flush of his triumphs over his gallant rival of France, whom
he had defeated and taken prisoner at the great battle of
Pavia; and the victor was at this moment preparing to pass
into Italy to receive the imperial crown from the hands of the
Roman Pontiff. Elated by his successes and his elevation to
the German throne, Charles made little account of his he-

reditary kingdom, as his ambition found so splendid a career thrown open to it on the wide field of European politics. He had hitherto received too inconsiderable returns from his transatlantic possessions to give them the attention they deserved. But, as the recent acquisition of Mexico and the brilliant anticipations in respect to the southern continent were pressed upon his notice, he felt their importance as likely to afford him the means of prosecuting his ambitious and most expensive enterprises.

Pizarro, therefore, who had now come to satisfy the royal eyes, by visible proofs, of the truth of the golden rumors which, from time to time, had reached Castile, was graciously received by the emperor. Charles examined the various objects which his officer exhibited to him with great attention. He was particularly interested by the appearance of the llama, so remarkable as the only beast of burden yet known on the new continent; and the fine fabrics of woollen cloth, which were made from its shaggy sides, gave it a much higher value, in the eyes of the sagacious monarch, than what it possessed as an animal for domestic labor. But the specimens of gold and silver manufacture, and the wonderful tale which Pizarro had to tell of the abundance of the precious metals, must have satisfied even the cravings of royal cupidity.

Pizarro, far from being embarrassed by the novelty of his situation, maintained his usual self-possession, and showed that decorum and even dignity in his address which belong to the Castilian. He spoke in a simple and respectful style, but with the earnestness and natural eloquence of one who had been an actor in the scenes he described, and who was conscious that the impression he made on his audience was to decide his future destiny. All listened with eagerness to the account of his strange adventures by sea and land, his wanderings in the forests, or in the dismal and pestilent swamps on the sea-coast, without food, almost without raiment, with feet torn and bleeding at every step, with his few companions becoming still fewer by disease and death, and yet pressing on with unconquerable spirit to extend the empire of Castile, and the name and power of her sovereign; but when he painted his lonely condition on the desolate island, abandoned by the government at home, deserted by all but a handful of devoted followers, his royal auditor, though not easily moved, was affected to tears. On his departure from Toledo, Charles commended the affairs of his vassal in the most favorable terms to the consideration of the Council of the Indies.

There was at this time another man at court, who had come there on a similar errand from the New World, but whose splendid achievements had already won for him a name that threw the rising reputation of Pizarro comparatively into the shade. This man was Hernando Cortés, the Conqueror of Mexico. He had come home to lay an empire at the feet of his sovereign, and to demand in return the redress of his wrongs, and the recompense of his great services. He was at the close of his career, as Pizarro was at the commencement of his; the conquerors of the North and of the South; the two men appointed by Providence to overturn the most potent of the Indian dynasties, and to open the golden gates by which the treasures of the New World were to pass into the coffers of Spain.

Notwithstanding the emperor's recommendation, the business of Pizarro went forward at the tardy pace with which affairs are usually conducted in the court of Castile. He found his limited means gradually sinking under the expenses incurred by his present situation, and he represented, that, unless some measures were speedily taken in reference to his suit, however favorable they might be in the end, he should be in no condition to profit by them. The queen, accordingly, who had charge of the business, on her husband's departure, expedited the affair, and on the twenty-sixth of July, 1529, she executed the memorable *Capitulation,* which defined the powers and privileges of Pizarro.

The instrument secured to that chief the right of discovery and conquest in the province of Peru, or New Castile,—as the country was then called, in the same manner as Mexico had received the name of New Spain,—for the distance of two hundred leagues south of Santiago. He was to receive the titles and rank of Governor and Captain-General of the province, together with those of Adelantado, and Alguacil Mayor, for life; and he was to have a salary of seven hundred and twenty-five thousand maravedís, with the obligation of maintaining certain officers and military retainers, corresponding with the dignity of his station. He was to have the right to erect certain fortresses, with the absolute government of them; to assign *encomiendas* of Indians, under the limitations prescribed by law; and, in fine, to exercise nearly all the prerogatives incident to the authority of a viceroy.

His associate, Almagro, was declared commander of the fortress of Tumbez, with an annual rent of three hundred thousand maravedís, and with the further rank and privileges of an hidalgo. The reverend Father Luque received the reward of his services in the Bishopric of Tumbez, and he was also declared Protector of the Indians of Peru. He was to enjoy the yearly stipend of a thousand ducats,—to be derived, like the other salaries and gratuities in this instrument, from the revenues of the conquered territory.

Nor were the subordinate actors in the expedition forgotten. Ruiz received the title of Grand Pilot of the Southern Ocean, with a liberal provision; Candia was placed at the head of the artillery; and the remaining eleven companions on the desolate island were created hidalgos and cavalleros, and raised to certain municipal dignities,—in prospect.

Several provisions of a liberal tenor were also made, to encourage emigration to the country. The new settlers were to be exempted from some of the most onerous, but customary taxes, as the *alcabala,* or to be subject to them only in a mitigated form. The tax on the precious metals drawn from mines was to be reduced, at first, to one tenth, instead of the fifth imposed on the same metals when obtained by barter or by rapine.

It was expressly enjoined on Pizarro to observe the existing regulations for the good government and protection of the natives; and he was required to carry out with him a specified number of ecclesiastics, with whom he was to take counsel in the conquest of the country, and whose efforts were to be dedicated to the service and conversion of the Indians; while lawyers and attorneys, on the other hand, whose presence was considered as boding ill to the harmony of the new settlements, were strictly prohibited from setting foot in them.

Pizarro, on his part, was bound, in six months from the date of the instrument, to raise a force, well equipped for the service, of two hundred and fifty men, of whom one hundred might be drawn from the colonies; and the government engaged to furnish some trifling assistance in the purchase of artillery and military stores. Finally, he was to be prepared, in six months after his return to Panamá, to leave that port and embark on his expedition.

Such are some of the principal provisions of this capitulation, by which the Castilian government, with the sagacious policy which it usually pursued on the like occasions, stimulated the ambitious hopes of the adventurer by high-sounding titles, and liberal promises of reward contingent on his success, but took care to stake nothing itself on the issue of the enterprise. It was careful to reap the fruits of his toil, but not to pay the cost of them.

A circumstance, that could not fail to be remarked in these provisions, was the manner in which the high and lucrative posts were accumulated on Pizarro, to the exclusion of Almagro, who, if he had not taken as conspicuous a part in personal toil and exposure, had, at least, divided with him the original burden of the enterprise, and, by his labors in another direction, had contributed quite as essentially to its success. Almagro had willingly conceded the post of honor to his confederate; but it had been stipulated, on Pizarro's departure for Spain, that, while he solicited the office of Governor and Captain-General for himself, he should secure that of Adelantado for his companion. In like manner, he had engaged to apply for the see of Tumbez for the vicar of Panamá, and the office of Alguacil Mayor for the pilot Ruiz. The bishopric took the direction that was concerted, for the soldier could scarcely claim the mitre of the prelate, but the other offices, instead of their appropriate distribution, were all concentred in himself. Yet it was in reference to his application for his friends, that Pizarro had promised on his departure to deal fairly and honorably by them all.

It is stated by the military chronicler, Pedro Pizarro, that his kinsman did, in fact, urge the suit strongly in behalf of Almagro; but that he was refused by the government, on the ground that offices of such paramount importance could not be committed to different individuals. The ill effects of such an arrangement had been long since felt in more than one of the Indian colonies, where it had led to rivalry and fatal

collision. Pizarro, therefore, finding his remonstrances unheeded, had no alternative but to combine the offices in his
own person, or to see the expedition fall to the ground. This
explanation of the affair has not received the sanction of other
contemporary historians. The apprehensions expressed by
Luque, at the time of Pizarro's assuming the mission, of some
such result as actually occurred, founded, doubtless, on a
knowledge of his associate's character, may warrant us in distrusting the alleged vindication of his conduct, and our distrust
will not be diminished by familiarity with his subsequent career. Pizarro's virtue was not of a kind to withstand temptation,—though of a much weaker sort than that now thrown in
his path.

The fortunate cavalier was also honored with the habit of
St. Jago; and he was authorized to make an important innova-
tion in his family escutcheon,—for by the father's side he might
claim his armorial bearings. The black eagle and the two pillars
emblazoned on the royal arms were incorporated with those
of the Pizarros; and an Indian city, with a vessel in the distance on the waters, and the llama of Peru, revealed the
theatre and the character of his exploits; while the legend announced, that "under the auspices of Charles, and by the industry, the genius, and the resources of Pizarro, the country
had been discovered and reduced to tranquillity,"—thus modestly intimating both the past and prospective services of the
Conqueror.

These arrangements having been thus completed to Pizarro's satisfaction, he left Toledo for Truxillo, his native
place, in Estremadura, where he thought he should be most
likely to meet with adherents for his new enterprise, and where
it doubtless gratified his vanity to display himself in the
palmy, or at least promising, state of his present circumstances.
If vanity be ever pardonable, it is certainly in a man who,
born in an obscure station in life, without family, interest, or
friends to back him, has carved out his own fortunes in the
world, and, by his own resources, triumphed over all the obstacles which nature and accident had thrown in his way. Such
was the condition of Pizarro, as he now revisited the place of
his nativity, where he had hitherto been known only as a poor
outcast, without a home to shelter, a father to own him, or a

friend to lean upon. But he now found both friends and followers, and some who were eager to claim kindred with him,
and take part in his future fortunes. Among these were four
brothers. Three of them, like himself, were illegitimate; one
of whom, named Francisco Martin de Alcántara, was related
to him by the mother's side; the other two, named Gonzalo
and Juan Pizarro, were descended from the father. "They
were all poor, and proud as they were poor," says Oviedo, who
had seen them; "and their eagerness for gain was in proportion
to their poverty."

The remaining and eldest brother, named Hernando, was a
legitimate son,—"legitimate," continues the same caustic authority, "by his pride, as well as by his birth." His features
were plain, even disagreeably so; but his figure was good. He
was large of stature, and, like his brother Francis, had on the
whole an imposing presence. In his character, he combined
some of the worst defects incident to the Castilian. He was
jealous in the extreme; impatient not merely of affront, but
of the least slight, and implacable in his resentment. He was
decisive in his measures, and unscrupulous in their execution.
No touch of pity had power to arrest his arm. His arrogance
was such, that he was constantly wounding the self-love of
those with whom he acted; thus begetting an ill-will which
unnecessarily multiplied obstacles in his path. In this he differed from his brother Francis, whose plausible manners
smoothed away difficulties, and conciliated confidence and coöperation in his enterprises. Unfortunately, the evil counsels
of Hernando exercised an influence over his brother which
more than compensated the advantages derived from his singular capacity for business.

Notwithstanding the general interest which Pizarro's adventures excited in his country, that chief did not find it easy to
comply with the provisions of the capitulation in respect to
the amount of his levies. Those who were most astonished by
his narrative were not always most inclined to take part in
his fortunes. They shrunk from the unparalleled hardships
which lay in the path of the adventurer in that direction; and
they listened with visible distrust to the gorgeous pictures of
the golden temples and gardens of Tumbez, which they looked
upon as indebted in some degree, at least, to the coloring of

his fancy, with the obvious purpose of attracting followers to his banner. It is even said that Pizarro would have found it difficult to raise the necessary funds, but for the seasonable aid of Cortés, a native of Estremadura like himself, his companion in arms in early days, and, according to report, his kinsman. No one was in a better condition to hold out a helping hand to a brother adventurer, and, probably, no one felt greater sympathy in Pizarro's fortunes, or greater confidence in his eventual success, than the man who had so lately trod the same career with renown.

The six months allowed by the capitulation had elapsed, and Pizarro had assembled somewhat less than his stipulated complement of men, with which he was preparing to embark in a little squadron of three vessels at Seville; but, before they were wholly ready, he received intelligence that the officers of the Council of the Indies proposed to inquire into the condition of the vessels, and ascertain how far the requisitions had been complied with.

Without loss of time, therefore, Pizarro, afraid, if the facts were known, that his enterprise might be nipped in the bud, slipped his cables, and crossing the bar of San Lucar, in January, 1530, stood for the isle of Gomera,—one of the Canaries, —where he ordered his brother Hernando, who had charge of the remaining vessels, to meet him.

Scarcely had he gone, before the officers arrived to institute the search. But when they objected the deficiency of men, they were easily—perhaps willingly—deceived by the pretext that the remainder had gone forward in the vessel with Pizarro. At all events, no further obstacles were thrown in Hernando's way, and he was permitted, with the rest of the squadron, to join his brother, as agreed, at Gomera.

After a prosperous voyage, the adventurers reached the northern coast of the great southern continent, and anchored off the port of Santa Marta. Here they received such discouraging reports of the countries to which they were bound, of forests teeming with insects and venomous serpents, of huge alligators that swarmed on the banks of the streams, and of hardships and perils such as their own fears had never painted, that several of Pizarro's men deserted; and their leader, thinking it no longer safe to abide in such treacherous quarters, set sail at once for Nombre de Dios.

Soon after his arrival there, he was met by his two associates, Luque and Almagro, who had crossed the mountains for the purpose of hearing from his own lips the precise import of the capitulation with the Crown. Great, as might have been expected, was Almagro's discontent at learning the result of what he regarded as the perfidious machinations of his associate. "Is it thus," he exclaimed, "that you have dealt with the friend who shared equally with you in the trials, the dangers, and the cost of the enterprise; and this, notwithstanding your solemn engagements on your departure to provide for his interests as faithfully as your own? How could you allow me to be thus dishonored in the eyes of the world by so paltry a compensation, which seems to estimate my services as nothing in comparison with your own?"

Pizarro, in reply, assured his companion that he had faithfully urged his suit, but that the government refused to confide powers which intrenched so closely on one another to different hands. He had no alternative, but to accept all himself or to decline all; and he endeavored to mitigate Almagro's displeasure by representing that the country was large enough for the ambition of both, and that the powers conferred on himself were, in fact, conferred on Almagro, since all that he had would ever be at his friend's disposal, as if it were his own. But these honeyed words did not satisfy the injured party; and the two captains soon after returned to Panamá with feelings of estrangement, if not hostility, towards one another, which did not augur well for their enterprise.

Still, Almagro was of a generous temper, and might have been appeased by the politic concessions of his rival, but for the interference of Hernando Pizarro, who, from the first hour of their meeting, showed little respect for the veteran, which, indeed, the diminutive person of the latter was not calculated to inspire, and who now regarded him as an impediment to the career of his brother.

Almagro's friends—and his frank and liberal manners had secured him many—were no less disgusted than himself with the overbearing conduct of this new ally. They loudly complained that it was quite enough to suffer from the perfidy of

Pizarro, without being exposed to the insults of his family, who had now come over with him to fatten on the spoils of conquest which belonged to their leader. The rupture soon proceeded to such a length, that Almagro avowed his intention to prosecute the expedition without further coöperation with his partner, and actually entered into negotiations for the purchase of vessels for that object. But Luque, and the Licentiate Espinosa, who had fortunately come over at that time from St. Domingo, now interposed to repair a breach which must end in the ruin of the enterprise, and the probable destruction of those most interested in its success. By their mediation, a show of reconciliation was at length effected between the parties, on Pizarro's assurance that he would relinquish the dignity of Adelantado in favor of his rival, and petition the emperor to confirm him in the possession of it;—an assurance, it may be remarked, not easy to reconcile with his former assertion in respect to the avowed policy of the Crown in bestowing this office. He was, moreover, to apply for a distinct government for his associate, so soon as he had become master of the country assigned to himself; and was to solicit no office for either of his own brothers, until Almagro had been first provided for. Lastly, the former contract in regard to the division of the spoil into three equal shares between the three original associates was confirmed in the most explicit manner. The reconciliation thus effected among the parties answered the temporary purpose of enabling them to go forward in concert in the expedition. But it was only a thin scar that had healed over the wound, which, deep and rankling within, waited only fresh cause of irritation to break out with a virulence more fatal than ever.

No time was now lost in preparing for the voyage. It found little encouragement, however, among the colonists of Panamá, who were too familiar with the sufferings on the former expeditions to care to undertake another, even with the rich bribe that was held out to allure them. A few of the old company were content to follow out the adventure to its close; and some additional stragglers were collected from the province of Nicaragua,—a shoot, it may be remarked, from the Colony of Panamá. But Pizarro made slender additions to the force brought over with him from Spain, though this body was in better condition, and, in respect to arms, ammunition, and equipment generally, was on a much better footing than his former levies. The whole number did not exceed one hundred and eighty men, with twenty-seven horses for the cavalry. He had provided himself with three vessels, two of them of a good size, to take the place of those which he had been compelled to leave on the opposite side of the Isthmus at Nombre de Dios; an armament small for the conquest of an empire, and far short of that prescribed by the capitulation with the Crown. With this the intrepid chief proposed to commence operations, trusting to his own successes, and the exertions of Almagro, who was to remain behind, for the present, to muster reinforcements.

On St. John the Evangelist's day, the banners of the company and the royal standard were consecrated in the cathedral church of Panamá; a sermon was preached before the little army by Fray Juan de Vargas, one of the Dominicans selected by the government for the Peruvian mission; and mass was performed, and the sacrament administered to every soldier previous to his engaging in the crusade against the infidel. Having thus solemnly invoked the blessing of Heaven on the enterprise, Pizarro and his followers went on board their vessels, which rode at anchor in the Bay of Panamá, and early in January, 1531, sallied forth on his third and last expedition for the conquest of Peru.

It was his intention to steer direct for Tumbez, which held out so magnificent a show of treasure on his former voyage. But head winds and currents, as usual, baffled his purpose, and after a run of thirteen days, much shorter than the period formerly required for the same distance, his little squadron came to anchor in the Bay of St. Matthew, about one degree north; and Pizarro, after consulting with his officers, resolved to disembark his forces and advance along the coast, while the vessels held their course at a convenient distance from the shore.

The march of the troops was severe and painful in the extreme; for the road was constantly intersected by streams, which, swollen by the winter rains, widened at their mouths into spacious estuaries. Pizarro, who had some previous knowledge of the country, acted as guide as well as commander of the expedition. He was ever ready to give aid where it was needed, encouraging his followers to ford or swim the torrents as they best could, and cheering the desponding by his own buoyant and courageous spirit.

At length they reached a thick-settled hamlet, or rather town, in the province of Coaque. The Spaniards rushed on the place, and the inhabitants, without offering resistance, fled in terror to the neighboring forests, leaving their effects—of much greater value than had been anticipated—in the hands of the invaders. "We fell on them, sword in hand," says one of the Conquerors, with some *naïveté;* "for, if we had advised the Indians of our approach, we should never have found there such store of gold and precious stones." The natives, however, according to another authority, stayed voluntarily; "for, as they had done no harm to the white men, they flattered themselves none would be offered to them, but that there would be only an interchange of good offices with the strangers,"—an expectation founded, it may be, on the good character which the Spaniards had established for themselves on their preceding visit, but in which the simple people now found themselves most unpleasantly deceived.

Rushing into the deserted dwellings, the invaders found there, besides stuffs of various kinds, and food most welcome in their famished condition, a large quantity of gold and silver wrought into clumsy ornaments, together with many precious stones; for this was the region of the *esmeraldas,* or emeralds, where that valuable gem was most abundant. One of these jewels that fell into the hands of Pizarro, in this neighborhood, was as large as a pigeon's egg. Unluckily, his rude followers did not know the value of their prize; and they broke many of them in pieces by pounding them with hammers. They were led to this extraordinary proceeding, it is said, by one of the Dominican missionaries, Fray Reginaldo de Pedraza, who assured them that this was the way to prove the true emerald, which could not be broken. It was observed that the good father did not subject his own jewels to this wise experiment; but, as the stones, in consequence of it, fell in value, being regarded merely as colored glass, he carried back a considerable store of them to Panamá.

The gold and silver ornaments rifled from the dwellings

were brought together and deposited in a common heap; when a fifth was deducted for the Crown, and Pizarro distributed the remainder in due proportions among the officers and privates of his company. This was the usage invariably observed on the like occasions throughout the Conquest. The invaders had embarked in a common adventure. Their interest was common, and to have allowed every one to plunder on his own account would only have led to insubordination and perpetual broils. All were required, therefore, on pain of death, to contribute whatever they obtained, whether by bargain or by rapine, to the general stock; and all were too much interested in the execution of the penalty to allow the unhappy culprit, who violated the law, any chance of escape.

Pizarro, with his usual policy, sent back to Panamá a large quantity of the gold, no less than twenty thousand *castellanos* in value, in the belief that the sight of so much treasure, thus speedily acquired, would settle the doubt of the wavering, and decide them on joining his banner. He judged right. As one of the Conquerors piously expresses it, "It pleased the Lord that we should fall in with the town of Coaque, that the riches of the land might find credit with the people, and that they should flock to it."

Pizarro, having refreshed his men, continued his march along the coast, but no longer accompanied by the vessels, which had returned for recruits to Panamá. The road, as he advanced, was checkered with strips of sandy waste, which, drifted about by the winds, blinded the soldiers, and afforded only treacherous footing for man and beast. The glare was intense; and the rays of a vertical sun beat fiercely on the iron mail and the thick quilted doublets of cotton, till the fainting troops were almost suffocated with the heat. To add to their distresses, a strange epidemic broke out in the little army. It took the form of ulcers, or rather hideous warts of great size, which covered the body, and when lanced, as was the case with some, discharged such a quantity of blood as proved fatal to the sufferer. Several died of this frightful disorder, which was so sudden in its attack, and attended with such prostration of strength, that those who lay down well at night were unable to lift their hands to their heads in the morning. The epidemic, which made its first appearance during this invasion, and which did not long survive it, spread over the country, sparing neither native nor white man. It was one of those plagues from the vial of wrath, which the destroying angel, who follows in the path of the conqueror, pours out on the devoted nations.

The Spaniards rarely experienced on their march either resistance or annoyance from the inhabitants, who, instructed by the example of Coaque, fled with their effects into the woods and neighboring mountains. No one came out to welcome the strangers and offer the rites of hospitality, as on their last visit to the land. For the white men were no longer regarded as good beings that had come from Heaven, but as ruthless destroyers, who, invulnerable to the assaults of the Indians, were borne along on the backs of fierce animals, swifter than the wind, with weapons in their hands, that scattered fire and desolation as they went. Such were the stories now circulated of the invaders, which, preceding them everywhere on their march, closed the hearts, if not the doors, of the natives against them. Exhausted by the fatigue of travel and by disease, and grievously disappointed at the poverty of the land, which now offered no compensation for their toils, the soldiers of Pizarro cursed the hour in which they had enlisted under his standard, and the men of Nicaragua, in particular, says the old chronicler, calling to mind their pleasant quarters in their luxurious land, sighed only to return to their Mahometan paradise.

At this juncture the army was gladdened by the sight of a vessel from Panamá, which brought some supplies, together with the royal treasurer, the *veedor* or inspector, the comptroller, and other high officers appointed by the Crown to attend the expedition. They had been left in Spain by Pizarro, in consequence of his abrupt departure from the country; and the Council of the Indies, on learning the circumstance, had sent instructions to Panamá to prevent the sailing of his squadron from that port. But the Spanish government, with more wisdom, countermanded the order, only requiring the functionaries to quicken their own departure, and take their place without loss of time in the expedition.

The Spaniards in their march along the coast had now advanced as far as Puerto Viejo. Here they were soon after

joined by another small reinforcement of about thirty men,
under an officer named Benalcazar, who subsequently rose to
high distinction in this service. Many of the followers of Pizarro would now have halted at this spot and established a
colony there. But that chief thought more of conquering than
of colonizing, at least for the present; and he proposed, as his
first step, to get possession of Tumbez, which he regarded as
the gate of the Peruvian empire. Continuing his march, therefore, to the shores of what is now called the Gulf of Guayaquil,
he arrived off the little island of Puná, lying at no great distance from the Bay of Tumbez. This island, he thought, would
afford him a convenient place to encamp until he was prepared
to make his descent on the Indian city.

The dispositions of the islanders seemed to favor his purpose. He had not been long in their neighborhood, before a
deputation of the natives, with their cacique at their head,
crossed over in their balsas to the mainland to welcome the
Spaniards to their residence. But the Indian interpreters of
Tumbez, who had returned with Pizarro from Spain, and continued with the camp, put their master on his guard against
the meditated treachery of the islanders, whom they accused
of designing to destroy the Spaniards by cutting the ropes that
held together the floats, and leaving those upon them to perish
in the waters. Yet the cacique, when charged by Pizarro with
this perfidious scheme, denied it with such an air of conscious
innocence, that the Spanish commander trusted himself and
his followers, without further hesitation, to his conveyance,
and was transported in safety to the shores of Puná.

Here he was received in a hospitable manner, and his troops
were provided with comfortable quarters. Well satisfied with
his present position, Pizarro resolved to occupy it until the
violence of the rainy season was passed, when the arrival of
the reinforcements he expected would put him in better condition for marching into the country of the Inca.

The island, which lies in the mouth of the river of Guayaquil, and is about eight leagues in length by four in breadth,
at the widest part, was at that time partially covered with a
noble growth of timber. But a large portion of it was subjected to cultivation, and bloomed with plantations of cacao,
of the sweet potato, and the different products of a tropical

clime, evincing agricultural knowledge as well as industry in the population. They were a warlike race; but had received from their Peruvian foes the appellation of "perfidious." It was the brand fastened by the Roman historians on their Carthaginian enemies,—with perhaps no better reason. The bold and independent islanders opposed a stubborn resistance to the arms of the Incas; and, though they had finally yielded, they had been ever since at feud, and often in deadly hostility, with their neighbors of Tumbez.

The latter no sooner heard of Pizarro's arrival on the island, than, trusting, probably, to their former friendly relations with him, they came over in some number to the Spanish quarters. The presence of their detested rivals was by no means grateful to the jealous inhabitants of Puná, and the prolonged residence of the white men on their island could not be otherwise than burdensome. In their outward demeanor they still maintained the same show of amity; but Pizarro's interpreters again put him on his guard against the proverbial perfidy of their hosts. With his suspicions thus roused, the Spanish commander was informed that a number of the chiefs had met together to deliberate on a plan of insurrection. Not caring to wait for the springing of the mine, he surrounded the place of meeting with his soldiers and made prisoners of the suspected chieftains. According to one authority, they confessed their guilt. This is by no means certain. Nor is it certain that they meditated an insurrection. Yet the fact is not improbable, in itself; though it derives little additional probability from the assertion of the hostile interpreters. It is certain, however, that Pizarro was satisfied of the existence of a conspiracy; and, without further hesitation, he abandoned his wretched prisoners, ten or twelve in number, to the tender mercies of their rivals of Tumbez, who instantly massacred them before his eyes.

Maddened by this outrage, the people of Puná sprang to arms, and threw themselves at once, with fearful yells and the wildest menaces of despair, on the Spanish camp. The odds of numbers were greatly in their favor, for they mustered several thousand warriors. But the more decisive odds of arms and discipline were on the side of their antagonists; and, as the Indians rushed forward in a confused mass to the assault, the

Castilians coolly received them on their long pikes, or swept them down by the volleys of their musketry. Their ill-protected bodies were easily cut to pieces by the sharp sword of the Spaniard; and Hernando Pizarro, putting himself at the head of the cavalry, charged boldly into the midst, and scattered them far and wide over the field, until, panic-struck by the terrible array of steel-clad horsemen, and the stunning reports and the flash of fire-arms, the fugitives sought shelter in the depths of their forests. Yet the victory was owing, in some degree, at least,—if we may credit the Conquerors,—to the interposition of Heaven; for St. Michael and his legions were seen high in the air above the combatants, contending with the arch-enemy of man, cheering on the Christians by their example!

Not more than three or four Spaniards fell in the fight; but many were wounded, and among them Hernando Pizarro, who received a severe injury in the leg from a javelin. Nor did the war end here; for the implacable islanders, taking advantage of the cover of night, or of any remissness on the part of the invaders, were ever ready to steal out of their fastnesses and spring on their enemy's camp, while, by cutting off his straggling parties, and destroying his provisions, they kept him in perpetual alarm.

In this uncomfortable situation, the Spanish commander was gladdened by the appearance of two vessels off the island. They brought a reinforcement consisting of a hundred volunteers besides horses for the cavalry. It was commanded by Hernando de Soto, a captain afterwards famous as the discoverer of the Mississippi, which still rolls its majestic current over the place of his burial,—a fitting monument for his remains, as it is of his renown.

The reinforcement was most welcome to Pizarro, who had been long discontented with his position on an island, where he found nothing to compensate the life of unintermitting hostility which he was compelled to lead. With these recruits, he felt himself in sufficient strength to cross over to the continent, and resume military operations in the proper theatre for discovery and conquest. From the Indians of Tumbez he learned that the country had been for some time distracted by a civil war between two sons of the late monarch, competitors for the throne. This intelligence he regarded as of the utmost importance, for he remembered the use which Cortés had made of similar dissensions among the tribes of Anahuac. Indeed, Pizarro seems to have had the example of his great predecessor before his eyes on more occasions than this. But he fell far short of his model; for, notwithstanding the restraint he sometimes put upon himself, his coarser nature and more ferocious temper often betrayed him into acts most repugnant to sound policy, which would never have been countenanced by the Conqueror of Mexico.

CHAPTER II

Before accompanying the march of Pizarro and his followers into the country of the Incas, it is necessary to make
the reader acquainted with the critical situation of the kingdom at that time. For the Spaniards arrived just at the consummation of an important revolution,—at a crisis most favorable to their views of conquest, and but for which, indeed,
the conquest, with such a handful of soldiers, could never have
been achieved.

In the latter part of the fifteenth century died Tupac Inca
Yupanqui, one of the most renowned of the "Children of the
Sun," who, carrying the Peruvian arms across the burning sands
of Atacama, penetrated to the remote borders of Chili, while
in the opposite direction he enlarged the limits of the empire
by the acquisition of the southern provinces of Quito. The
war in this quarter was conducted by his son Huayna Capac,
who succeeded his father on the throne, and fully equalled
him in military daring and in capacity for government.

Under this prince, the whole of the powerful state of Quito,
which rivalled that of Peru itself in wealth and refinement,
was brought under the sceptre of the Incas; whose empire received, by this conquest, the most important accession yet
made to it since the foundation of the dynasty of Manco
Capac. The remaining days of the victorious monarch were
passed in reducing the independent tribes on the remote
limits of his territory, and, still more, in cementing his conquests by the introduction of the Peruvian polity. He was
actively engaged in completing the great works of his father,
especially the highroads which led from Quito to the capital.
He perfected the establishment of posts, took great pains to

introduce the Quichua dialect throughout the empire, promoted a better system of agriculture, and, in fine, encouraged
the different branches of domestic industry and the various
enlightened plans of his predecessors for the improvement of
his people. Under his sway, the Peruvian monarchy reached
its most palmy state; and under both him and his illustrious
father it was advancing with such rapid strides in the march
of civilization as would soon have carried it to a level with
the more refined despotisms of Asia, furnishing the world, perhaps, with higher evidence of the capabilities of the American
Indian than is elsewhere to be found on the great western
continent. But other and gloomier destinies were in reserve for
the Indian races.

The first arrival of the white men on the South American
shores of the Pacific was about ten years before the death of
Huayna Capac, when Balboa crossed the Gulf of St. Michael,
and obtained the first clear report of the empire of the Incas.
Whether tidings of these adventurers reached the Indian monarch's ears is doubtful. There is no doubt, however, that he
obtained the news of the first expedition under Pizarro and
Almagro, when the latter commander penetrated as far as the
Rio de San Juan, about the fourth degree north. The accounts
which he received made a strong impression on the mind of
Huayna Capac. He discerned in the formidable prowess and
weapons of the invaders proofs of a civilization far superior to
that of his own people. He intimated his apprehension that
they would return, and that at some day, not far distant, perhaps, the throne of the Incas might be shaken by these
strangers, endowed with such incomprehensible powers. To the
vulgar eye, it was a little speck on the verge of the horizon;
but that of the sagacious monarch seemed to descry in it the
dark thunder-cloud, that was to spread till it burst in fury on
his nation!

There is some ground for believing thus much. But other
accounts, which have obtained a popular currency, not content
with this, connect the first tidings of the white men with
predictions long extant in the country, and with supernatural
appearances, which filled the hearts of the whole nation with
dismay. Comets were seem flaming athwart the heavens.
Earthquakes shook the land; the moon was girdled with rings

of fire of many colors; a thunderbolt fell on one of the royal palaces and consumed it to ashes; and an eagle, chased by several hawks, was seen, screaming in the air, to hover above the great square of Cuzco, when, pierced by the talons of his tormentors, the king of birds fell lifeless in the presence of many of the Inca nobles, who read in this an augury of their own destruction! Huayna Capac himself, calling his great officers around him, as he found he was drawing near his end, announced the subversion of his empire by the race of white and bearded strangers, as the consummation predicted by the oracles after the reign of the twelfth Inca, and he enjoined it on his vassals not to resist the decrees of Heaven, but to yield obedience to its messengers.

Such is the report of the impressions made by the appearance of the Spaniards in the country, reminding one of the similar feelings of superstitious terror occasioned by their appearance in Mexico. But the traditions of the latter land rest on much higher authority than those of the Peruvians, which, unsupported by contemporary testimony, rest almost wholly on the naked assertion of one of their own nation, who thought to find, doubtless, in the inevitable decrees of Heaven, the best apology for the supineness of his countrymen.

It is not improbable that rumors of the advent of a strange and mysterious race should have spread gradually among the Indian tribes along the great table-land of the Cordilleras, and should have shaken the hearts of the stoutest warriors with feelings of undefined dread, as of some impending calamity. In this state of mind, it was natural that physical convulsions, to which that volcanic country is peculiarly subject, should have made an unwonted impression on their minds; and that the phenomena, which might have been regarded only as extraordinary, in the usual seasons of political security, should now be interpreted by the superstitious soothsayer as the handwriting on the heavens, by which the God of the Incas proclaimed the approaching downfall of their empire.

Huayna Capac had, as usual with the Peruvian princes, a multitude of concubines, by whom he left a numerous posterity. The heir to the crown, the son of his lawful wife and sister, was named Huascar. At the period of the history at which we are now arrived, he was about thirty years of age.

Next to the heir-apparent, by another wife, a cousin of the monarch's, came Manco Capac, a young prince who will occupy an important place in our subsequent story. But the best-beloved of the Inca's children was Atahuallpa. His mother was the daughter of the last *Scyri* of Quito, who had died of grief, it was said, not long after the subversion of his kindgom by Huayna Capac. The princess was beautiful, and the Inca, whether to gratify his passion, or, as the Peruvians say, willing to make amends for the ruin of her parents, received her among his concubines. The historians of Quito assert that she was his lawful wife; but this dignity, according to the usages of the empire, was reserved for maidens of the Inca blood.

The latter years of Huayna Capac were passed in his new kingdom of Quito. Atahuallpa was accordingly brought up under his own eye, accompanied him, while in his tender years, in his campaigns, slept in the same tent with his royal father, and ate from the same plate. The vivacity of the boy, his courage and generous nature, won the affections of the old monarch to such a degree, that he resolved to depart from the established usages of the realm, and divide his empire between him and his elder brother Huascar. On his deathbed, he called the great officers of the crown around him, and declared it to be his will that the ancient kingdom of Quito should pass to Atahuallpa, who might be considered as having a natural claim on it, as the dominion of his ancestors. The rest of the empire he settled on Huascar; and he enjoined it on the two brothers to acquiesce in this arrangement, and to live in amity with each other. This was the last act of the heroic monarch; doubtless, the most impolitic of his whole life. With his dying breath he subverted the fundamental laws of the empire; and, while he recommended harmony between the successors to his authority, he left in this very division of it the seeds of inevitable discord.

His death took place, as seems probable, at the close of 1525, not quite seven years before Pizarro's arrival at Puná. The tidings of his decease spread sorrow and consternation throughout the land; for, though stern and even inexorable to the rebel and the long-resisting foe, he was a brave and magnanimous monarch, and legislated with the enlarged views of a prince who regarded every part of his dominions as equally his concern. The people of Quito, flattered by the proofs which he had given of preference for them by his permanent residence in that country, and his embellishment of their capital, manifested unfeigned sorrow at his loss; and his subjects at Cuzco, proud of the glory which his arms and his abilities had secured for his native land, held him in no less admiration; while the more thoughtful and the more timid, in both countries, looked with apprehension to the future, when the sceptre of the vast empire, instead of being swayed by an old and experienced hand, was to be consigned to rival princes, naturally jealous of one another, and, from their age, necessarily exposed to the unwholesome influence of crafty and ambitious counsellors. The people testified their regret by the unwonted honors paid to the memory of the deceased Inca. His heart was retained in Quito, and his body, embalmed after the fashion of the country, was transported to Cuzco, to take its place in the great Temple of the Sun, by the side of the remains of his royal ancestors. His obsequies were celebrated with sanguinary splendor in both the capitals of his far-extended empire; and several thousands of the imperial concubines, with numerous pages and officers of the palace, are said to have proved their sorrow, or their superstition, by offering up their own lives, that they might accompany their departed lord to the bright mansions of the Sun.

For nearly five years after the death of Huayna Capac, the royal brothers reigned, each over his allotted portion of the empire, without distrust of one another, or, at least, without collision. It seemed as if the wish of their father was to be completely realized, and that the two states were to maintain their respective integrity and independence as much as if they had never been united into one. But, with the manifold causes for jealousy and discontent, and the swarms of courtly sycophants, who would find their account in fomenting these feelings, it was easy to see that this tranquil state of things could not long endure. Nor would it have endured so long, but for the more gentle temper of Huascar, the only party who had ground for complaint. He was four to five years older than his brother, and was possessed of courage not to be doubted; but he was a prince of a generous and easy nature, and perhaps, if left to himself, might have acquiesced in an arrangement which, however unpalatable, was the will of his deified father. But Atahuallpa was of a different temper. Warlike, ambitious, and daring, he was constantly engaged in enterprises for the enlargement of his own territory, though his crafty policy was scrupulous not to aim at extending his acquisitions in the direction of his royal brother. His restless spirit, however, excited some alarm at the court of Cuzco, and Huascar, at length, sent an envoy to Atahuallpa, to remonstrate with him on his ambitious enterprises, and to require him to render him homage for his kingdom of Quito.

This is one statement. Other accounts pretend that the immediate cause of rupture was a claim instituted by Huascar for the territory of Tumebamba, held by his brother as part of his patrimonial inheritance. It matters little what was the ostensible ground of collision between persons placed by circumstances in so false a position in regard to one another, that collision must, at some time or other, inevitably occur.

The commencement, and, indeed, the whole course, of hostilities which soon broke out between the rival brothers are stated with irreconcilable, and, considering the period was so near to that of the Spanish invasion, with unaccountable discrepancy. By some it is said, that, in Atahuallpa's first encounter with the troops of Cuzco, he was defeated and made prisoner near Tumebamba, a favorite residence of his father in the ancient territory of Quito, and in the district of Cañaris. From this disaster he recovered by a fortunate escape from confinement, when, regaining his capital, he soon found himself at the head of a numerous army, led by the most able and experienced captains in the empire. The liberal manners of the young Atahuallpa had endeared him to the soldiers, with whom, as we have seen, he served more than one campaign in his father's lifetime. These troops were the flower of the great army of the Inca, and some of them had grown grey in his long military career, which had left them at the north, where they readily transferred their allegiance to the young sovereign of Quito. They were commanded by two officers of great consideration, both possessed of large experience in military affairs, and high in the confidence of the late Inca. One of them was named Quizquiz; the other, who was the maternal uncle of Atahuallpa, was called Chalicuchima.

With these practised warriors to guide him, the young monarch put himself at the head of his martial array, and directed his march towards the south. He had not advanced farther than Ambato, about sixty miles distant from his capital, when he fell in with a numerous host, which had been sent against him by his brother, under the command of a distinguished chieftain, of the Inca family. A bloody battle followed, which lasted the greater part of the day; and the theatre of combat was the skirts of the mighty Chimborazo.

The battle ended favorably for Atahuallpa, and the Peruvians were routed with great slaughter and the loss of their commander. The prince of Quito availed himself of his advantage to push forward his march until he arrived before the gates of Tumebamba, which city, as well as the whole district of Cañaris, though an ancient dependency of Quito, had sided with his rival in the contest. Entering the captive city like a conqueror, he put the inhabitants to the sword, and razed it with all its stately edifices, some of which had been reared by his own father, to the ground. He carried on the same war of extermination, as he marched through the offending district of Cañaris. In some places, it is said, the women and children came out, with green branches in their hands, in melancholy procession, to deprecate his wrath; but the vindictive conqueror, deaf to their entreaties, laid the country waste with fire and sword, sparing no man capable of bearing arms who fell into his hands.

The fate of Cañaris struck terror into the hearts of his enemies, and one place after another opened its gates to the victor, who held on his triumphant march towards the Peruvian capital. His arms experienced a temporary check before the island of Puná, whose bold warriors maintained the cause of his brother. After some days lost before this place, Atahuallpa left the contest to their old enemies, the people of Tumbez, who had early given in their adhesion to him, while he resumed his march and advanced as far as Caxamalca, about seven degrees south. Here he halted with a detachment of the army, sending forward the main body under the command of his two generals, with orders to move straight upon Cuzco. He preferred not to trust himself farther in the enemy's country, where a defeat might be fatal. By establishing his quarters at Caxamalca, he would be able to support his generals, in case of a reverse, or, at worst, to secure his retreat on Quito, until he was again in condition to renew hostilities.

The two commanders, advancing by rapid marches, at length crossed the Apurimac river, and arrived within a short distance of the Peruvian capital. Meanwhile, Huascar had not been idle. On receiving tidings of the discomfiture of his army at Ambato, he made every exertion to raise levies throughout the country. By the advice, it is said, of his priests—the most incompetent advisers in times of danger—he chose to await the approach of the enemy in his own capital; and it was not till the latter had arrived within a few leagues of Cuzco, that the Inca, taking counsel of the same ghostly monitors, sallied forth to give him battle.

The two armies met on the plains of Quipaypan, in the neighborhood of the Indian metropolis. Their numbers are stated with the usual discrepancy; but Atahuallpa's troops had considerably the advantage in discipline and experience, for many of Huascar's levies had been drawn hastily together from the surrounding country. Both fought, however, with the desperation of men who felt that every thing was at stake. It was no longer a contest for a province, but for the possession of an empire. Atahuallpa's troops, flushed with recent success, fought with the confidence of those who relied on their superior prowess; while the loyal vassals of the Inca displayed all the self-devotion of men who held their own lives cheap in the service of their master.

The fight raged with the greatest obstinacy from sunrise to sunset; and the ground was covered with heaps of the dying and the dead, whose bones lay bleaching on the battle-field long after the conquest by the Spaniards. At length, fortune declared in favor of Atahuallpa; or rather, the usual result of superior discipline and military practice followed. The ranks of the Inca were thrown into irretrievable disorder, and gave way in all directions. The conquerors followed close on the heels of the flying. Huascar himself, among the latter, endeavored to make his escape with about a thousand men who remained round his person. But the royal fugitive was discovered before he had left the field; his little party was enveloped by clouds of the enemy, and nearly every one of the devoted band perished in defence of their Inca. Huascar was made prisoner, and the victorious chiefs marched at once on his capital, which they occupied in the name of their sovereign.

These events occurred in the spring of 1532, a few months before the landing of the Spaniards. The tidings of the success of his arms and the capture of his unfortunate brother reached Atahuallpa at Caxamalca. He instantly gave orders that Huascar should be treated with the respect due to his rank, but that he should be removed to the strong fortress of Xauxa, and held there in strict confinement. His orders did not stop here, —if we are to receive the accounts of Garcilasso de la Vega, himself of the Inca race, and by his mother's side nephew of the great Huayna Capac.

According to this authority, Atahuallpa invited the Inca nobles throughout the country to assemble at Cuzco, in order to deliberate on the best means of partitioning the empire between him and his brother. When they had met in the capital, they were surrounded by the soldiery of Quito, and butchered without mercy. The motive for this perfidious act was to exterminate the whole of the royal family, who might each one of them show a better title to the crown than the illegitimate Atahuallpa. But the massacre did not end here. The illegitimate offspring, like himself, half-brothers of the monster, all, in short, who had any of the Inca blood in their veins, were involved in it; and with an appetite for carnage unparalleled in the annals of the Roman Empire or of the French Republic, Atahuallpa ordered all the females of the blood royal, his aunts, nieces, and cousins, to be put to death, and that, too, with the most refined and lingering tortures. To give greater zest to his revenge, many of the executions took place in the presence of Huascar himself, who was thus compelled to witness the butchery of his own wives and sisters, while, in the extremity of anguish, they in vain called on him to protect them!

Such is the tale told by the historian of the Incas, and received by him, as he assures us, from his mother and uncle, who, being children at the time, were so fortunate as to be among the few that escaped the massacre of their house. And such is the account repeated by many a Castilian writer since, without any symptom of distrust. But a tissue of unprovoked atrocities like these is too repugnant to the principles of human nature,—and, indeed, to common sense, to warrant our belief in them on ordinary testimony.

The annals of semi-civilized nations unhappily show that there have been instances of similar attempts to extinguish the whole of a noxious race, which had become the object of a tyrant's jealousy; though such an attempt is about as chimerical as it would be to extirpate any particular species of plant, the seeds of which had been borne on every wind over the country. But, if the attempt to exterminate the Inca race was actually made by Atahuallpa, how comes it that so many of the pure descendants of the blood royal—nearly six hundred in number—are admitted by the historian to have been in existence seventy years after the imputed massacre? Why was the massacre, instead of being limited to the legitimate members of the royal stock, who could show a better title to the crown than the usurper, extended to all, however remotely, or in whatever way, connected with the race? Why were aged women and young maidens involved in the proscription, and why were they subjected to such refined and superfluous tortures, when it is obvious that beings so impotent could have done nothing to provoke the jealousy of the tyrant? Why, when so many were sacrificed from some vague apprehension of distant danger, was his rival Huascar, together with his younger brother Manco Capac, the two men from whom the conqueror had most to fear, suffered to live? Why, in short, is the wonderful tale not recorded by others before the time of Garcilasso, and nearer by half a century to the events themselves?

That Atahuallpa may have been guilty of excesses, and abused the rights of conquest by some gratuitous acts of cruelty, may be readily believed; for no one, who calls to mind his treatment of the Cañaris,—which his own apologists do not affect to deny,—will doubt that he had a full measure of the vindictive temper which belongs to

> "Those souls of fire, and Children of the Sun,
> With whom revenge was virtue."

But there is a wide difference between this and the monstrous and most unprovoked atrocities imputed to him; implying a diabolical nature not to be admitted on the evidence of an Indian partisan, the sworn foe of his house, and repeated by Castilian chroniclers, who may naturally seek, by blazoning the enormities of Atahuallpa, to find some apology for the cruelty of their countrymen towards him.

The news of the great victory was borne on the wings of the wind to Caxamalca; and loud and long was the rejoicing, not only in the camp of Atahuallpa, but in the town and surrounding country; for all now came in, eager to offer their congratulations to the victor, and do him homage. The prince of Quito no longer hesitated to assume the scarlet *borla*, the diadem of the Incas. His triumph was complete. He had beaten his enemies on their own ground; had taken their capital; had set his foot on the neck of his rival, and won for himself the ancient sceptre of the Children of the Sun. But the hour of triumph was destined to be that of his deepest humiliation. Atahuallpa was not one of those to whom, in the language of the Grecian bard, "the Gods are willing to reveal themselves." He had not read the handwriting on the heavens. The small speck, which the clear-sighted eye of his father had discerned on the distant verge of the horizon, though little noticed by Atahuallpa, intent on the deadly strife with his brother, had now risen high towards the zenith, spreading wider and wider, till it wrapped the skies in darkness, and was ready to burst in thunders on the devoted nation.

CHAPTER III [1532]

THE SPANIARDS LAND AT TUMBEZ—PIZARRO RECON-
NOITRES THE COUNTRY—FOUNDATION OF SAN MIGUEL
—MARCH INTO THE INTERIOR—EMBASSY FROM THE
INCA—ADVENTURES ON THE MARCH—REACH THE FOOT
OF THE ANDES

We left the Spaniards at the island of Puná, preparing to
make their descent on the neighboring continent of Tumbez.
This port was but a few leagues distant, and Pizarro, with the
greater part of his followers, passed over in the ships, while
a few others were to transport the commander's baggage and
the military stores on some of the Indian balsas. One of the
latter vessels which first touched the shore was surrounded,
and three persons who were on the raft were carried off by
the natives to the adjacent woods and there massacred. The
Indians then got possession of another of the balsas, containing
Pizarro's wardrobe; but, as the men who defended it raised
loud cries for help, they reached the ears of Hernando Pizarro,
who, with a small body of horse, had effected a landing some
way farther down the shore. A broad tract of miry ground,
overflowed **at** high water, lay between him and the party thus
rudely assailed by the natives. The tide was out, and the bottom was soft and dangerous. With little regard to the danger,
however, the bold cavalier spurred his horse into the slimy
depths, and followed by his men, with the mud up to their
saddle-girths, they plunged forward until they came into the
midst of the marauders, who, terrified by the strange apparition of the horsemen, fled precipitately, without show of fight,
to the neighboring forests.

This conduct of the natives of Tumbez is not easy to be
explained; considering the friendly relations maintained with
the Spaniards on their preceding visit, and lately renewed in
the island of Puná. But Pizarro was still more astonished, on
entering their town, to find it not only deserted, but, with the
exception of a few buildings, entirely demolished. Four or five

of the most substantial private dwellings, the great temple, and the fortress—and these greatly damaged, and wholly despoiled of their interior decorations—alone survived to mark the site of the city, and attest its former splendor. The scene of desolation filled the conquerors with dismay; for even the raw recruits, who had never visited the coast before, had heard the marvellous stories of the golden treasures of Tumbez, and they had confidently looked forward to them as an easy spoil after all their fatigues. But the gold of Peru seemed only like a deceitful phantom, which, after beckoning them on through toil and danger, vanished the moment they attempted to grasp it.

Pizarro despatched a small body of troops in pursuit of the fugitives; and, after some slight skirmishing, they got possession of several of the natives, and among them, as it chanced, the curaca of the place. When brought before the Spanish commander, he exonerated himself from any share in the violence offered to the white men, saying that it was done by a lawless party of his people, without his knowledge at the time; and he expressed his willingness to deliver them up to punishment, if they could be detected. He explained the dilapidated condition of the town by the long wars carried on with the fierce tribes of Puná, who had at length succeeded in getting possession of the place, and driving the inhabitants into the neighboring woods and mountains. The Inca, to whose cause they were attached, was too much occupied with his own feuds to protect them against their enemies.

Whether Pizarro gave any credit to the cacique's exculpation of himself may be doubted. He dissembled his suspicions, however, and, as the Indian lord promised obedience in his own name, and that of his vassals, the Spanish general consented to take no further notice of the affair. He seems now to have felt for the first time, in its full force, that it was his policy to gain the good-will of the people among whom he had thrown himself in the face of such tremendous odds. It was, perhaps, the excesses of which his men had been guilty in the earlier stages of the expedition that had shaken the confidence of the people of Tumbez, and incited them to this treacherous retaliation.

Pizarro inquired of the natives who now, under promise of

impunity, came into the camp, what had become of his two
followers that remained with them in the former expedition.
The answers they gave were obscure and contradictory. Some
said, they had died of an epidemic; others, that they had perished in the war with Puná; and others intimated, that they
had lost their lives in consequence of some outrage attempted
on the Indian women. It was impossible to arrive at the truth.
The last account was not the least probable. But, whatever
the cause, there was no doubt they had both perished.

This intelligence spread an additional gloom over the
Spaniards; which was not dispelled by the flaming pictures
now given by the natives of the riches of the land, and of the
state and magnificence of the monarch in his distant capital
among the mountains. Nor did they credit the authenticity of
a scroll of paper, which Pizzaro had obtained from an Indian,
to whom it had been delivered by one of the white men left
in the country. "Know, whoever you may be," said the writing,
"that may chance to set foot in this country, that it contains
more gold and silver than there is iron in Biscay." This paper,
when shown to the soldiers, excited only their ridicule, as a
device of their captain to keep alive their chimerical hopes.

Pizarro now saw that it was not politic to protract his stay
in his present quarters, where a spirit of disaffection would
soon creep into the ranks of his followers, unless their spirits
were stimulated by novelty or a life of incessant action. Yet
he felt deeply anxious to obtain more particulars than he had
hitherto gathered of the actual condition of the Peruvian empire, of its strength and resources, of the monarch who ruled
over it, and of his present situation. He was also desirous, before taking any decisive step for penetrating the country, to
seek out some commodious place for a settlement, which
might afford him the means of a regular communication with
the colonies, and a place of strength, on which he himself
might retreat in case of disaster.

He decided, therefore, to leave part of his company at
Tumbez, including those who, from the state of their health,
were least able to take the field, and with the remainder to
make an excursion into the interior, and reconnoitre the land,
before deciding on any plan of operations. He set out early in
May, 1532; and, keeping along the more level regions himself,

sent a small detachment under the command of Hernando de Soto to explore the skirts of the vast sierra.

He maintained a rigid discipline on the march, commanding his soldiers to abstain from all acts of violence, and punishing disobedience in the most prompt and resolute manner. The natives rarely offered resistance. When they did so, they were soon reduced, and Pizarro, far from vindictive measures, was open to the first demonstrations of submission. By this lenient and liberal policy, he soon acquired a name among the inhabitants which effaced the unfavorable impressions made of him in the earlier part of the campaign. The natives, as he marched through the thick-settled hamlets which sprinkled the level region between the Cordilleras and the ocean, welcomed him with rustic hospitality, providing good quarters for his troops, and abundant supplies, which cost but little in the prolific soil of the *tierra caliente*. Everywhere Pizarro made proclamation that he came in the name of the Holy Vicar of God and of the sovereign of Spain, requiring the obedience of the inhabitants as true children of the Church, and vassals of his lord and master. And as the simple people made no opposition to a formula, of which they could not comprehend a syllable, they were admitted as good subjects of the crown of Castile, and their act of homage—or what was readily interpreted as such—was duly recorded and attested by the notary.

At the expiration of some three or four weeks spent in reconnoitring the country, Pizarro came to the conclusion that the most eligible site for his new settlement was in the rich valley of Tangarala, thirty leagues south of Tumbez, traversed by more than one stream that opens a communication with the ocean. To this spot, accordingly, he ordered the men left at Tumbez to repair at once in their vessels; and no sooner had they arrived, than busy preparations were made for building up the town in a manner suited to the wants of the colony. Timber was procured from the neighboring woods. Stones were dragged from their quarries, and edifices gradually rose, some of which made pretensions to strength, if not to elegance. Among them were a church, a magazine for public stores, a hall of justice, and a fortress. A municipal government was organized, consisting of regidores, alcaldes, and the usual civic functionaries. The adjacent territory was parcelled out among the residents, and each colonist had a certain number of the natives allotted to assist him in his labors; for, as Pizarro's secretary remarks, "it being evident that the colonists could not support themselves without the services of the Indians, the ecclesiastics and the leaders of the expedition all agreed that a *repartimiento* of the natives would serve the cause of religion, and tend greatly to their spiritual welfare, since they would thus have the opportunity of being initiated in the true faith."

Having made these arrangements with such conscientious regard to the welfare of the benighted heathen, Pizarro gave his infant city the name of San Miguel, in acknowledgment of the service rendered him by that saint in his battles with the Indians of Puná. The site originally occupied by the settlement was afterward found to be so unhealthy, that it was abandoned for another on the banks of the beautiful Piura. The town is still of some note for its manufactures, though dwindled from its ancient importance; but the name of San Miguel de Piura, which it bears, still commemorates the foundation of the first European colony in the empire of the Incas.

Before quitting the new settlement, Pizarro caused the gold and silver ornaments which he had obtained in different parts of the country to be melted down into one mass, and a fifth to be deducted for the Crown. The remainder, which belonged to the troops, he persuaded them to relinquish for the present; under the assurance of being repaid from the first spoils that fell into their hands. With these funds, and other articles collected in the course of the campaign, he sent back the vessels to Panamá. The gold was applied to paying off the ship-owners, and those who had furnished the stores for the expedition. That he should so easily have persuaded his men to resign present possession for a future contingency is proof that the spirit of enterprise was renewed in their bosoms in all its former vigor, and that they looked forward with the same buoyant confidence to the results.

In his late tour of observation, the Spanish commander had gathered much important intelligence in regard to the state of the kingdom. He had ascertained the result of the struggle between the Inca brothers, and that the victor now lay with his army encamped at the distance of only ten or twelve days' journey from San Miguel. The accounts he heard of the opulence and power of that monarch, and of his great southern capital, perfectly corresponded with the general rumors before received; and contained, therefore, something to stagger the confidence, as well as to stimulate the cupidity, of the invaders.

Pizarro would gladly have seen his little army strengthened by reinforcements, however small the amount; and on that account postponed his departure for several weeks. But no reinforcement arrived; and, as he received no further tidings from his associates, he judged that longer delay would, probably, be attended with evils greater than those to be encountered on the march; that discontents would inevitably spring up in a life of inaction, and the strength and spirits of the soldier sink under the enervating influence of a tropical climate. Yet the force at his command, amounting to less than two hundred soldiers in all, after reserving fifty for the protection of the new settlement, seemed but a small one for the conquest of an empire. He might, indeed, instead of marching against the Inca, take a southerly direction towards the rich capital of Cuzco. But this would only be to postpone the hour of reckoning. For in what quarter of the empire could he hope to set his foot, where the arm of its master would not reach him? By such a course, moreover, he would show his own distrust of himself. He would shake that opinion of his invincible prowess, which he had hitherto endeavored to impress on the natives, and which constituted a great secret of his strength; which, in short, held sterner sway over the mind than the display of numbers and mere physical force. Worse than all, such a course would impair the confidence of his troops in themselves and their reliance on himself. This would be to palsy the arm of enterprise at once. It was not to be thought of.

But while Pizarro decided to march into the interior, it is doubtful whether he had formed any more definite plan of action. We have no means of knowing his intentions, at this distance of time, otherwise than as they are shown by his actions. Unfortunately, he could not write, and he has left no record, like the inestimable Commentaries of Cortés, to enlighten us as to his motives. His secretary, and some of his companions in arms, have recited his actions in detail; but the motives which led to them they were not always so competent to disclose.

It is possible that the Spanish general, even so early as the period of his residence at San Miguel, may have meditated some daring stroke, some effective *coup-de-main*, which, like that of Cortés, when he carried off the Aztec monarch to his quarters, might strike terror into the hearts of the people, and at once decide the fortunes of the day. It is more probable, however, that he now only proposed to present himself before the Inca, as the peaceful representative of a brother monarch, and, by these friendly demonstrations, disarm any feeling of hostility, or even of suspicion. When once in communication with the Indian prince, he could regulate his future course by circumstances.

On the 24th of September, 1532, five months after landing at Tumbez, Pizarro marched out at the head of his little body of adventurers from the gates of San Miguel, having enjoined it on the colonists to treat their Indian vassals with humanity, and to conduct themselves in such a manner as would secure the good-will of the surrounding tribes. Their own existence, and with it the safety of the army and the success of the undertaking, depended on this course. In the place were to remain the royal treasurer, the *veedor*, or inspector of metals, and other officers of the crown; and the command of the garrison was intrusted to the *contador*, Antonio Navarro. Then putting himself at the head of his troops, the chief struck boldly into the heart of the country in the direction where, as he was informed, lay the camp of the Inca. It was a daring enterprise, thus to venture with a handful of followers into the heart of a powerful empire, to present himself, face to face, before the Indian monarch in his own camp, encompassed by the flower of his victorious army! Pizarro had already experienced more than once the difficulty of maintaining his ground against the rude tribes of the north, so much inferior in strength and numbers to the warlike legions of Peru. But the hazard of the game, as I have already more than once had occasion to remark, constituted its great charm with the Spaniard. The brilliant achievements of his countrymen, on the like occasions, with means so inadequate, inspired him with confidence in his own good star; and this confidence was one source of his success. Had he faltered for a moment, had he stopped to calculate chances, he must inevitably have failed; for the odds were too great to be combated by sober reason. They were only to be met triumphantly by the spirit of the knight-errant.

After crossing the smooth waters of the Piura, the little army continued to advance over a level district intersected by streams that descended from the neighboring Cordilleras. The face of the country was shagged over with forests of gigantic growth, and occasionally traversed by ridges of barren land, that seemed like shoots of the adjacent Andes, breaking up the surface of the region into little sequestered valleys of singular loveliness. The soil, though rarely watered by the rains of heaven, was naturally rich, and wherever it was refreshed with moisture, as on the margins of the streams, it was enamelled with the brightest verdure. The industry of the inhabitants, moreover, had turned these streams to the best account, and canals and aqueducts were seen crossing the low lands in all directions, and spreading over the country, like a vast network, diffusing fertility and beauty around them. The air was scented with the sweet odors of flowers, and everywhere the eye was refreshed by the sight of orchards laden with unknown fruits, and of fields waving with yellow grain and rich in luscious vegetables of every description that teem in the sunny clime of the equator. The Spaniards were among a people who had carried the refinements of husbandry to a greater extent than any yet found on the American continent; and, as they journeyed through this paradise of plenty, their condition formed a pleasing contrast to what they had before endured in the dreary wilderness of the mangroves.

Everywhere, too, they were received with confiding hospitality by the simple people; for which they were no doubt indebted, in a great measure, to their own inoffensive deportment. Every Spaniard seemed to be aware, that his only chance of success lay in conciliating the good opinion of the inhabitants, among whom he had so recklessly cast his fortunes. In most of the hamlets, and in every place of considerable size, some fortress was to be found, or royal caravansary, destined for the Inca on his progresses, the ample halls of which furnished abundant accommodations for the Spaniards;

who were thus provided with quarters along their route at the charge of the very government which they were preparing to overturn.

On the fifth day after leaving San Miguel, Pizarro halted in one of these delicious valleys, to give his troops repose, and to make a more complete inspection of them. Their number amounted in all to one hundred and seventy-seven, of which sixty-seven were cavalry. He mustered only three arquebusiers in his whole company, and a few crossbow-men, altogether not exceeding twenty. The troops were tolerably well equipped, and in good condition. But the watchful eye of their commander noticed with uneasiness, that, notwithstanding the general heartiness in the cause manifested by his followers, there were some among them whose countenances lowered with discontent, and who, although they did not give vent to it in open murmurs, were far from moving with their wonted alacrity. He was aware, that, if this spirit became contagious, it would be the ruin of the enterprise; and he thought it best to exterminate the gangrene, at once, and at whatever cost, than to wait until it had infected the whole system. He came to an extraordinary resolution.

Calling his men together, he told them that "a crisis had now arrived in their affairs, which it demanded all their courage to meet. No man should think of going forward in the expedition, who could not do so with his whole heart, or who had the least misgiving as to its success. If any repented of his share in it, it was not too late to turn back. San Miguel was but poorly garrisoned, and he should be glad to see it in greater strength. Those who chose might return to this place, and they should be entitled to the same proportion of lands and Indian vassals as the present residents. With the rest, were they few or many, who chose to take their chance with him, he should pursue the adventure to the end."

It was certainly a remarkable proposal for a commander, who was ignorant of the amount of disaffection in his ranks, and who could not safely spare a single man from his force, already far too feeble for the undertaking. Yet, by insisting on the wants of the little colony of San Miguel, he afforded a decent pretext for the secession of the malcontents, and swept away the barrier of shame which might have still held them in the camp. Notwithstanding the fair opening thus afforded, there were but few, nine in all, who availed themselves of the general's permission. Four of these belonged to the infantry, and five to the horse. The rest loudly declared their resolve to go forward with their brave leader; and, if there were some whose voices were faint amidst the general acclamation, they, at least, relinquished the right of complaining hereafter, since they had voluntarily rejected the permission to return. This stroke of policy in their sagacious captain was attended with the best effects. He had winnowed out the few grains of discontent, which, if left to themselves, might have fermented in secret till the whole mass had swelled into mutiny. Cortés had compelled his men to go forward heartily in his enterprise, by burning their vessels, and thus cutting off the only means of retreat. Pizarro, on the other hand, threw open the gates to the disaffected and facilitated their departure. Both judged right, under their peculiar circumstances, and both were perfectly successful.

Feeling himself strengthened, instead of weakened, by his loss, Pizarro now resumed his march, and, on the second day, arrived before a place called Zaran, situated in a fruitful valley among the mountains. Some of the inhabitants had been drawn off to swell the levies of Atahuallpa. The Spaniards had repeated experience on their march of the oppressive exactions of the Inca, who had almost depopulated some of the valleys to obtain reinforcements for his army. The curaca of the Indian town, where Pizarro now arrived, received him with kindness and hospitality, and the troops were quartered as usual in one of the royal *tambos* or caravansaries, which were found in all the principal places.

Yet the Spaniards saw no signs of their approach to the royal encampment, though more time had already elapsed than was originally allowed for reaching it. Shortly before entering Zaran, Pizarro had heard that a Peruvian garrison was established in a place called Caxas, lying among the hills, at no great distance from his present quarters. He immediately despatched a small party under Hernando de Soto in that direction, to reconnoitre the ground, and bring him intelligence of the actual state of things, at Zaran, where he would halt until his officer's return.

Day after day passed on, and a week had elapsed before tidings were received of his companions, and Pizarro was becoming seriously alarmed for their fate, when on the eighth morning Soto appeared, bringing with him an envoy from the Inca himself. He was a person of rank, and was attended by several followers of inferior condition. He had met the Spaniards at Caxas, and now accompanied them on their return, to deliver his sovereign's message, with a present to the Spanish commander. The present consisted of two fountains, made of stone, in the form of fortresses; some fine stuffs of woollen embroidered with gold and silver; and a quantity of goose-flesh, dried and seasoned in a peculiar manner, and much used as a perfume, in a pulverized state, by the Peruvian nobles. The Indian ambassador came charged also with his master's greeting to the strangers, whom Atahuallpa welcomed to his country, and invited to visit him in his camp among the mountains.

Pizarro well understood that the Inca's object in this diplomatic visit was less to do him courtesy, than to inform himself of the strength and condition of the invaders. But he was well pleased with the embassy, and dissembled his consciousness of its real purpose. He caused the Peruvian to be entertained in the best manner the camp could afford, and paid him the respect, says one of the Conquerors, due to the ambassador of so great a monarch. Pizarro urged him to prolong his visit for some days, which the Indian envoy declined, but made the most of his time while there, by gleaning all the information he could in respect to the uses of every strange article which he saw, as well as the object of the white men's visit to the land, and the quarter whence they came.

The Spanish captain satisfied his curiosity in all these particulars. The intercourse with the natives, it may be here remarked, was maintained by means of two of the youths who had accompanied the Conquerors on their return home from their preceding voyage. They had been taken by Pizarro to Spain, and, as much pains had been bestowed on teaching them the Castilian, they now filled the office of interpreters, and opened an easy communication with their countrymen. It was of inestimable service; and well did the Spanish commander reap the fruits of his forecast.

On the departure of the Peruvian messenger, Pizarro presented him with a cap of crimson cloth, some cheap but showy ornaments of glass, and other toys, which he had brought for the purpose from Castile. He charged the envoy to tell his master, that the Spaniards came from a powerful prince, who dwelt far beyond the waters; that they had heard much of the fame of Atahuallpa's victories, and were come to pay their respects to him, and to offer their services by aiding him with their arms against his enemies; and he might be assured, they would not halt on the road, longer than was necessary, before presenting themselves before him.

Pizarro now received from Soto a full account of his late expedition. That chief, on entering Caxas, found the inhabitants mustered in hostile array, as if to dispute his passage. But the cavalier soon convinced them of his pacific intentions, and, laying aside their menacing attitude, they received the Spaniards with the same courtesy which had been shown them in most places on their march.

Here Soto found one of the royal officers, employed in collecting the tribute for the government. From this functionary he learned that the Inca was quartered with a large army at Caxamalca, a place of considerable size on the other side of the Cordillera, where he was enjoying the luxury of the warm baths, supplied by natural springs, for which it was then famous, as it is at the present day. The cavalier gathered, also, much important information in regard to the resources and the general policy of government, the state maintained by the Inca, and the stern severity with which obedience to the law was everywhere enforced. He had some opportunity of observing this for himself, as, on entering the village, he saw several Indians hanging dead by their heels, having been executed for some violence offered to the Virgins of the Sun, of whom there was a convent in the neighborhood.

From Caxas, De Soto had passed to the adjacent town of Guancabamba, much larger, more populous, and better built than the preceding. The houses, instead of being made of clay baked in the sun, were many of them constructed of solid stone, so nicely put together, that it was impossible to detect the line of junction. A river, which passed through the town, was traversed by a bridge, and the high road of the Incas, which crossed this district, was far superior to that which the

Spaniards had seen on the seaboard. It was raised in many places, like a causeway, paved with heavy stone flags, and bordered by trees that afforded a grateful shade to the passenger, while streams of water were conducted through aqueducts along the sides to slake his thirst. At certain distances, also, they noticed small houses, which, they were told, were for the accommodation of the traveller, who might thus pass, without inconvenience, from one end of the kingdom to the other. In another quarter they beheld one of those magazines destined for the army, filled with grain, and with articles of clothing; and at the entrance of the town was a stone building, occupied by a public officer, whose business it was to collect the tolls or duties on various commodities brought into the place, or carried out of it.—These accounts of De Soto not only confirmed all that the Spaniards had heard of the Indian empire, but greatly raised their ideas of its resources and domestic policy. They might well have shaken the confidence of hearts less courageous.

Pizarro, before leaving his present quarters, despatched a messenger to San Miguel with particulars of his movements, sending, at the same time, the articles received from the Inca, as well as those obtained at different places on the route. The skill shown in the execution of some of these fabrics excited great admiration, when sent to Castile. The fine woollen cloths, especially, with their rich embroidery, were pronounced equal to silk, from which it was not easy to distinguish them. It was probably the delicate wool of the vicuña, none of which had then been seen in Europe.

Pizarro, having now acquainted himself with the most direct route to Caxamalca,—the Caxamarca of the present day,—resumed his march, taking a direction nearly south. The first place of any size at which he halted was Motupe, pleasantly situated in a fruitful valley, among hills of no great elevation, which cluster round the base of the Cordilleras. The place was deserted by its curaca, who, with three hundred of its warriors, had gone to join the standard of their Inca. Here the general, notwithstanding his avowed purpose to push forward without delay, halted four days. The tardiness of his movements can be explained only by the hope, which he may have still entertained of being joined by further reinforcements before crossing the Cordilleras. None such appeared, however; and advancing across a country in which tracts of sandy plain were occasionally relieved by a broad expanse of verdant meadow, watered by natural streams and still more abundantly by those brought through artificial channels, the troops at length arrived at the borders of a river. It was broad and deep, and the rapidity of the current opposed more than ordinary difficulty to the passage. Pizarro, apprehensive lest this might be disputed by the natives on the opposite bank, ordered his brother Hernando to cross over with a small detachment under cover of night, and secure a safe landing for the rest of the troops. At break of day Pizarro made preparations for his own passage, by hewing timber in the neighboring woods, and constructing a sort of floating bridge, on which before nightfall the whole company passed in safety, the horses swimming, being led by the bridle. It was a day of severe labor, and Pizarro took his own share in it freely, like a common soldier, having ever a word of encouragement to say to his followers.

On reaching the opposite side, they learned from their comrades that the people of the country, instead of offering resistance, had fled in dismay. One of them, having been taken and brought before Hernando Pizarro, refused to answer the questions put to him respecting the Inca and his army; till, being put to the torture, he stated that Atahuallpa was encamped, with his whole force, in three separate divisions, occupying the high grounds and plains of Caxamalca. He further stated, that the Inca was aware of the approach of the white men and of their small number, and that he was purposely decoying them into his own quarters, that he might have them more completely in his power.

This account, when reported by Hernando to his brother, caused the latter much anxiety. As the timidity of the peasantry, however, gradually wore off, some of them mingled with the troops, and among them the curaca or principal person of the village. He had himself visited the royal camp, and he informed the general that Atahuallpa lay at the strong town of Guamachucho, twenty leagues south of Caxamalca, with a large army of at least fifty thousand men.

These contradictory statements greatly perplexed the chieftain; and he proposed to one of the Indians who had borne him company during a great part of the march, to go as a spy into the Inca's quarters, and bring him intelligence of his actual position, and, as far as he could learn them, of his intentions towards the Spaniards. But the man positively declined this dangerous service, though he professed his willingness to go as an authorized messenger of the Spanish commander.

Pizarro acquiesced in this proposal, and instructed his envoy to assure the Inca that he was advancing with all convenient speed to meet him. He was to acquaint the monarch with the uniformly considerate conduct of the Spaniards towards his subjects, in their progress through the land, and to assure him that they were now coming in full confidence of finding in him the same amicable feelings towards themselves. The emissary was particularly instructed to observe if the strong passes on the road were defended, or if any preparations of a hostile character were to be discerned. This last intelligence he was to communicate to the general by means of two or three attendants, who were to accompany him on his mission.

Having taken this precaution, the wary commander again resumed his march, and at the end of three days reached the base of the mountain rampart, behind which lay the ancient town of Caxamalca. Before him rose the stupendous Andes, rock piled upon rock, their skirts below dark with evergreen forests, varied here and there by terraced patches of cultivated garden, with the peasant's cottage clinging to their shaggy sides, and their crests of snow glittering high in the heavens,— presenting altogether such a wild chaos of magnificence and beauty as no other mountain scenery in the world can show. Across this tremendous rampart, through a labyrinth of passes, easily capable of defence by a handful of men against an army, the troops were now to march. To the right ran a broad and level road, with its border of friendly shades, and wide enough for two carriages to pass abreast. It was one of the great routes leading to Cuzco, and seemed by its pleasant and easy access to invite the wayworn soldier to choose it in preference to the dangerous mountain defiles. Many were accordingly of opinion that the army should take this course, and abandon the original destination to Caxamalca. But such was not the decision of Pizarro.

The Spaniards had everywhere proclaimed their purpose, he said, to visit the Inca in his camp. This purpose had been communicated to the Inca himself. To take an opposite direction now would only be to draw on them the imputation of cowardice, and to incur Atahuallpa's contempt. No alternative remained but to march straight across the sierra to his quarters. "Let every one of you," said the bold cavalier, "take heart and go forward like a good soldier, nothing daunted by the smallness of your numbers. For in the greatest extremity God ever fights for his own; and doubt not he will humble the pride of the heathen, and bring him to the knowledge of the true faith, the great end and object of the Conquest."

Pizarro like Cortés, possessed a good share of that frank and manly eloquence which touches the heart of the soldier more than the parade of rhetoric or the finest flow of elocution. He was a soldier himself, and partook in all the feelings of the soldier, his joys, his hopes, and his disappointments. He was not raised by rank and education above sympathy with the humblest of his followers. Every chord in their bosoms vibrated with the same pulsations as his own, and the conviction of this gave him a mastery over them. "Lead on," they shouted, as he finished his brief but animating address, "lead on wherever you think best. We will follow with good-will, and you shall see that we can do our duty in the cause of God and the King!" There was no longer hesitation. All thoughts were now bent on the instant passage of the Cordilleras.

CHAPTER IV [1532]

SEVERE PASSAGE OF THE ANDES—EMBASSIES FROM
ATAHUALLPA—THE SPANIARDS REACH CAXAMALCA—
EMBASSY TO THE INCA—INTERVIEW WITH THE INCA—
DESPONDENCY OF THE SPANIARDS

That night Pizarro held a council of his principal officers,
and it was determined that he should lead the advance, consisting of forty horse and sixty foot, and reconnoitre the
ground; while the rest of the company, under his brother Hernando, should occupy their present position till they received
further orders.

At early dawn the Spanish general and his detachment were
under arms, and prepared to breast the difficulties of the sierra.
These proved even greater than had been foreseen. The path
had been conducted in the most judicious manner round the
rugged and precipitous sides of the mountains, so as best to
avoid the natural impediments presented by the ground. But
it was necessarily so steep, in many places, that the cavalry
were obliged to dismount, and, scrambling up as they could,
to lead their horses by the bridle. In many places, too, where
some huge crag or eminence overhung the road, this was
driven to the very verge of the precipice; and the traveller was
compelled to wind along the narrow ledge of rock, scarcely
wide enough for his single steed, where a misstep would pre-
cipitate him hundreds, nay, thousands, of feet into the dreadful abyss! The wild passes of the sierra, practicable for the
half-naked Indian, and even for the sure and circumspect
mule,—an animal that seems to have been created for the roads
of the Cordilleras,—were formidable to the man-at-arms encumbered with his panoply of mail. The tremendous fissures
or *quebradas*, so frightful in this mountain chain, yawned
open, as if the Andes had been split asunder by some terrible
convulsion, showing a broad expanse of the primitive rock on
their sides, partially mantled over with the spontaneous vege-

tation of ages; while their obscure depths furnished a channel for the torrents, that, rising in the heart of the sierra, worked their way gradually into light, and spread over the savannas and green valleys of the *tierra caliente* on their way to the great ocean.

Many of these passes afforded obvious points of defence; and the Spaniards, as they entered the rocky defiles, looked with apprehension lest they might rouse some foe from his ambush. This apprehension was heightened, as, at the summit of a steep and narrow gorge, in which they were engaged, they beheld a strong work, rising like a fortress, and frowning, as it were, in gloomy defiance on the invaders. As they drew near this building, which was of solid stone, commanding an angle of the road, they almost expected to see the dusky forms of the warriors rise over the battlements, and to receive their tempest of missiles on their bucklers; for it was in so strong a position, that a few resolute men might easily have held there an army at bay. But they had the satisfaction to find the place untenanted, and their spirits were greatly raised by the conviction that the Indian monarch did not intend to dispute their passage, when it would have been easy to do so with success.

Pizarro now sent orders to his brother to follow without delay; and, after refreshing his men, continued his toilsome ascent, and before nightfall reached an eminence crowned by another fortress, of even greater strength than the preceding. It was built of solid masonry, the lower part excavated from the living rock, and the whole executed with skill not inferior to that of the European architect.

Here Pizarro took up his quarters for the night. Without waiting for the arrival of the rear, on the following morning he resumed his march, leading still deeper into the intricate gorges of the sierra. The climate had gradually changed, and the men and horses, especially the latter, suffered severely from the cold, so long accustomed as they had been to the sultry climate of the tropics. The vegetation also had changed its character; and the magnificent timber which covered the lower level of the country had gradually given way to the funereal forest of pine, and, as they rose still higher, to the stunted growth of numberless Alpine plants, whose hardy natures found a congenial temperature in the icy atmosphere of the more elevated regions. These dreary solitudes seemed to be nearly abandoned by the brute creation as well as by man. The light-footed vicuña, roaming in its native state, might be sometimes seen looking down from some airy cliff, where the foot of the hunter dared not venture. But instead of the feathered tribes whose gay plumage sparkled in the deep glooms of the tropical forests, the adventurers now beheld only the great bird of the Andes, the loathsome condor, who, sailing high above the clouds, followed with doleful cries in the track of the army, as if guided by instinct in the path of blood and carnage.

At length they reached the crest of the Cordillera, where it spreads out into a bold and bleak expanse, with scarce the vestige of vegetation, except what is afforded by the *pajonal*, a dried yellow grass, which, as it is seen from below, encircling the base of the snow-covered peaks, looks, with its brilliant straw-color lighted up in the rays of an ardent sun, like a setting of gold round pinnacles of burnished silver. The land was sterile, as usual in mining districts, and they were drawing near the once famous gold quarries on the way to Caxamalca;

> "Rocks rich in gems, and mountains big with mines,
>   That on the high equator ridgy rise."

Here Pizarro halted for the coming up of the rear. The air was sharp and frosty; and the soldiers, spreading their tents, lighted fires, and, huddling round them, endeavored to find some repose after their laborious march.

They had not been long in these quarters, when a messenger arrived, one of those who had accompanied the Indian envoy sent by Pizarro to Atahuallpa. He informed the general that the road was free from enemies, and that an embassy from the Inca was on its way to the Castilian camp. Pizarro now sent back to quicken the march of the rear, as he was unwilling that the Peruvian envoy should find him with his present diminished numbers. The rest of the army were not far distant, and not long after reached the encampment.

In a short time the Indian embassy also arrived, which consisted of one of the Inca nobles and several attendants, bringing a welcome present of llamas to the Spanish commander. The Peruvian bore, also, the greetings of his master, who wished to know when the Spaniards would arrive at Caxamalca, that he might provide suitable refreshments for them. Pizarro learned that the Inca had left Guamachucho, and was now lying with a small force in the neighborhood of Caxamalca, at a place celebrated for its natural springs of warm water. The Peruvian was an intelligent person, and the Spanish commander gathered from him many particulars respecting the late contests which had distracted the empire.

As the envoy vaunted in lofty terms the military prowess and resources of his sovereign, Pizarro thought it politic to show that it had no power to overawe him. He expressed his satisfaction at the triumphs of Atahuallpa, who, he acknowledged, had raised himself high in the rank of Indian warriors. But he was as inferior, he added with more policy than politeness, to the monarch who ruled over the white men, as the petty curacas of the country were inferior to him. This was evident from the ease with which a few Spaniards had overrun this great continent, subduing one nation after another, that had offered resistance to their arms. He had been led by the fame of Atahuallpa to visit his dominions, and to offer him his services in his wars; and, if he were received by the Inca in the same friendly spirit with which he came, he was willing, for the aid he could render him, to postpone awhile his passage across the country to the opposite seas. The Indian, according to the Castilian accounts, listened with awe to this strain of glorification from the Spanish commander. Yet it is possible that the envoy was a better diplomatist than they imagined; and that he understood it was only the game of brag at which he was playing with his more civilized antagonist.

On the succeeding morning, at an early hour, the troops were again on the march, and for two days were occupied in threading the airy defiles of the Cordilleras. Soon after beginning their descent on the eastern side, another emissary arrived from the Inca, bearing a message of similar import to the preceding, and a present, in like manner, of Peruvian sheep. This was the same noble that had visited Pizarro in the valley. He now came in more state, quaffing *chicha*—the fermented juice of the maize—from golden goblets borne by his attendants, which sparkled in the eyes of the rapacious adventurers.

While he was in the camp, the Indian messenger, originally

sent by Pizarro to the Inca, returned, and no sooner did he behold the Peruvian, and the honorable reception which he met with from the Spaniards, than he was filled with wrath, which would have vented itself in personal violence, but for the interposition of the bystanders. It was hard, he said, that this Peruvian dog should be thus courteously treated, when he himself had nearly lost his life on a similar mission among his countrymen. On reaching the Inca's camp, he had been refused admission to his presence, on the ground that he was keeping a fast and could not be seen. They had paid no respect to his assertion that he came as an envoy from the white men, and would, probably, not have suffered him to escape with life, if he had not assured them that any violence offered to him would be retaliated in full measure on the persons of the Peruvian envoys, now in the Spanish quarters. There was no doubt, he continued, of the hostile intentions of Atahuallpa; for he was surrounded with a powerful army, strongly encamped about a league from Caxamalca, while that city was entirely evacuated by its inhabitants.

To all this the Inca's envoy coolly replied, that Pizarro's messenger might have reckoned on such a reception as he had found, since he seemed to have taken with him no credentials of his mission. As to the Inca's fast, that was true; and, although he would doubtless have seen the messenger, had he known there was one from the strangers, yet it was not safe to disturb him at these solemn seasons, when engaged in his religious duties. The troops by whom he was surrounded were not numerous, considering that the Inca was at that time carrying on an important war; and as to Caxamalca, it was abandoned by the inhabitants in order to make room for the white men, who were so soon to occupy it.

This explanation, however plausible, did not altogether satisfy the general; for he had too deep a conviction of the cunning of Atahuallpa, whose intentions towards the Spaniards he had long greatly distrusted. As he proposed, however, to keep on friendly relations with the monarch for the present, it was obviously not his cue to manifest suspicion. Affecting, therefore, to give full credit to the explanation of the envoy, he dismissed him with reiterated assurances of speedily presenting himself before the Inca.

The descent of the sierra, though the Andes are less precipitous on their eastern side than towards the west, was attended with difficulties almost equal to those of the upward march; and the Spaniards felt no little satisfaction, when, on the seventh day, they arrived in view of the valley of Caxamalca, which, enamelled with all the beauties of cultivation, lay unrolled like a rich and variegated carpet of verdure, in strong contrast with the dark forms of the Andes, that rose up everywhere around it. The valley is of an oval shape, extending about five leagues in length by three in breadth. It was inhabited by a population of a superior character to any which the Spaniards had met on the other side of the mountains, as was argued by the superior style of their attire, and the greater cleanliness and comfort visible both in their persons and dwellings. As far as the eye could reach, the level tract exhibited the show of a diligent and thrifty husbandry. A broad river rolled through the meadows, supplying facilities for copious irrigation by means of the usual canals and subterraneous aqueducts. The land, intersected by verdant hedge-rows, was checkered with patches of various cultivation; for the soil was rich, and the climate, if less stimulating than that of the sultry regions of the coast, was more favorable to the hardy products of the temperate latitudes. Below the adventurers, with its white houses glittering in the sun, lay the little city of Caxamalca, like a sparkling gem on the dark skirts of the sierra. At the distance of about a league farther, across the valley, might be seen columns of vapor rising up towards the heavens, indicating the place of the famous hot baths, much frequented by the Peruvian princes. And here, too, was a spectacle less grateful to the eyes of the Spaniards; for along the slope of the hills a white cloud of pavilions was seen covering the ground, as thick as snow-flakes, for the space, apparently, of several miles. "It filled us all with amazement," exclaims one of the Conquerors, "to behold the Indians occupying so proud a position! So many tents, so well appointed, as were never seen in the Indies till now! The spectacle caused something like confusion and even fear in the stoutest bosom. But it was too late to turn back, or to betray the least sign of weakness, since the natives in our own company would, in such case, have been the first to rise upon us. So, with as bold a countenance as we could, after coolly surveying the ground, we prepared for our entrance into Caxamalca."

What were the feelings of the Peruvian monarch we are not informed, when he gazed on the martial cavalcade of the Christians, as, with banners streaming, and bright panoplies glistening in the rays of the evening sun, it emerged from the dark depths of the sierra, and advanced in hostile array over the fair domain, which, to this period, had never been trodden by other foot than that of the red man. It might be, as several of the reports had stated, that the Inca had purposely decoyed the adventurers into the heart of his populous empire, that he might envelope them with his legions, and the more easily become master of their property and persons. Or was it from a natural feeling of curiosity, and relying on their professions of friendship, that he had thus allowed them, without any attempt at resistance, to come into his presence? At all events, he could hardly have felt such confidence in himself, as not to look with apprehension, mingled with awe, on the mysterious strangers, who, coming from an unknown world, and possessed of such wonderful gifts, had made their way across mountain and valley, in spite of every obstacle which man and nature had opposed to them.

Pizarro, meanwhile, forming his little corps into three divisions, now moved forward, at a more measured pace, and in order of battle, down the slopes that led towards the Indian city. As he drew near, no one came out to welcome him; and he rode through the streets without meeting with a living thing, or hearing a sound, except the echoes, sent back from the deserted dwellings, of the tramp of the soldiery.

It was a place of considerable size, containing about ten thousand inhabitants, somewhat more, probably, than the population assembled at this day within the walls of the modern city of Caxamarca. The houses, for the most part, were built of clay, hardened in the sun; the roofs thatched, or of timber. Some of the more ambitious dwellings were of hewn stone; and there was a convent in the place, occupied by the Virgins of the Sun, and a temple dedicated to the same tutelar deity, which last was hidden in the deep embowering shades of a grove on the skirts of the city. On the quarter towards

the Indian camp was a square—if square it might be called—
which was almost triangular in form, of an immense size, surrounded by low buildings. These consisted of capacious halls,
with wide doors or openings communicating with the square.
They were probably intended as a sort of barracks of the Inca's
soldiers. At the end of the *plaza,* looking towards the country,
was a fortress of stone, with a stairway leading from the city,
and a private entrance from the adjoining suburbs. There was
still another fortress on the rising ground which commanded
the town, built of hewn stone, and encompassed by three circular walls,—or rather one and the same wall, which wound
up spirally around it. It was a place of great strength, and
the workmanship showed a better knowledge of masonry, and
gave a higher impression of the architectural science of the
people, than anything the Spaniards had yet seen.

It was late in the afternoon of the fifteenth of November,
1532, when the Conquerors entered the city of Caxamalca.
The weather, which had been fair during the day, now threatened a storm, and some rain mingled with hail—for it was
unusually cold—began to fall. Pizarro, however, was so anxious
to ascertain the dispositions of the Inca, that he determined
to send an embassy, at once, to his quarters. He selected for
this, Hernando de Soto with fifteen horse, and, after his departure, conceiving that the number was too small, in case of
any unfriendly demonstrations, he ordered his brother Hernando to follow with twenty additional troopers. This captain
and one other of his party have left us an account of the
excursion.

Between the city and the imperial camp was a causeway,
built in a substantial manner across the meadow land that
intervened. Over this the cavalry galloped at a rapid pace,
and, before they had gone a league, they came in front of
the Peruvian encampment, where it spread along the gentle
slope of the mountains. The lances of the warriors were fixed
in the ground before their tents, and the Indian soldiers were
loitering without, gazing with silent astonishment at the Christian cavalcade, as with clangor of arms and shrill blast of
trumpet it swept by, like some fearful apparition, on the wings
of the wind.

The party soon came to a broad but shallow stream, which,

winding through the meadow, formed a defence for the Inca's position. Across it was a wooden bridge; but the cavaliers, distrusting its strength, preferred to dash through the waters, and without difficulty gained the opposite bank. A battalion of Indian warriors was drawn up under arms on the farther side of the bridge, but they offered no molestation to the Spaniards; and these latter had strict orders from Pizarro—scarcely necessary in their present circumstances—to treat the natives with courtesy. One of the Indians pointed out the quarter occupied by the Inca.

It was an open court-yard, with a light building or pleasure house in the centre, having galleries running around it, and opening in the rear on a garden. The walls were covered with a shining plaster, both white and colored, and in the area before the edifice was seen a spacious tank or reservoir of stone, fed by aqueducts that supplied it with both warm and cold water. A basin of hewn stone—it may be of a more recent construction—still bears, on the spot, the name of the "Inca's bath." The court was filled with Indian nobles, dressed in gayly ornamented attire, in attendance on the monarch, and with women of the royal household. Amidst this assembly it was not difficult to distinguish the person of Atahuallpa, though his dress was simpler than that of his attendants. But he wore on his head the crimson *borla* or fringe, which, surrounding the forehead, hung down as low as the eyebrow. This was the well-known badge of Peruvian sovereignty, and had been assumed by the monarch only since the defeat of his brother Huascar. He was seated on a low stool or cushion, somewhat after the Morisco or Turkish fashion, and his nobles and principal officers stood around him, with great ceremony, holding the stations suited to their rank.

The Spaniards gazed with much interest on the prince, of whose cruelty and cunning they had heard so much, and whose valor had secured to him the possession of the empire. But his countenance exhibited neither the fierce passions nor the sagacity which had been ascribed to him; and, though in his bearing he showed a gravity and a calm consciousness of authority well becoming a king, he seemed to discharge all expression from his features, and to discover only the apathy so characteristic of the American races. On the present occasion, this must have been in part, at least, assumed. For it is impossible that the Indian prince should not have contemplated with curious interest a spectacle so strange, and, in some respects, appalling, as that of these mysterious strangers, for which no previous description could have prepared him.

Hernando Pizarro and Soto, with two or three only of their followers, slowly rode up in front of the Inca; and the former, making a respectful obeisance, but without dismounting, informed Atahuallpa that he came as an ambassador from his brother, the commander of the white men, to acquaint the monarch with their arrival in his city of Caxamalca. They were the subjects of a mighty prince across the waters, and had come, he said, drawn thither by the report of his great victories, to offer their services, and to impart to him the doctrines of the true faith which they professed; and he brought an invitation from the general to Atahuallpa that the latter would be pleased to visit the Spaniards in their quarters.

To all this the Inca answered not a word; nor did he make even a sign of acknowledgment that he comprehended it; though it was translated for him by Felipillo, one of the interpreters already noticed. He remained silent, with his eyes fastened on the ground; but one of his nobles, standing by his side, answered, "It is well." This was an embarrassing situation for the Spaniards, who seemed to be as wide from ascertaining the real disposition of the Peruvian monarch towards themselves, as when the mountains were between them.

In a courteous and respectful manner, Hernando Pizarro again broke the silence by requesting the Inca to speak to them himself, and to inform them what was his pleasure. To this Atahuallpa condescended to reply, while a faint smile passed over his features,—"Tell your captain that I am keeping a fast, which will end tomorrow morning. I will then visit him, with my chieftains. In the meantime, let him occupy the public buildings on the square, and no other, till I come, when I will order what shall be done."

Soto, one of the party present at this interview, as before noticed, was the best mounted and perhaps the best rider in Pizarro's troop. Observing that Atahuallpa looked with some interest on the fiery steed that stood before him, champing the bit and pawing the ground with the natural impatience of a war-horse, the Spaniard gave him the rein, and, striking his iron heel into his side, dashed furiously over the plain; then, wheeling him round and round, displayed all the beautiful movements of his charger, and his own excellent horsemanship. Suddenly checking him in full career, he brought the animal almost on his haunches, so near the person of the Inca, that some of the foam that flecked his horse's sides was thrown on the royal garments. But Atahuallpa maintained the same marble composure as before, though several of his soldiers, whom De Soto passed in the course, were so much disconcerted by it, that they drew back in terror: an act of timidity for which they paid dearly, *if*, as the Spaniards assert, Atahuallpa caused them to be put to death that same evening for betraying such unworthy weakness to the strangers.

Refreshments were now offered by the royal attendants to the Spaniards, which they declined, being unwilling to dismount. They did not refuse, however, to quaff the sparkling chicha from golden vases of extraordinary size, presented to them by the dark-eyed beauties of the harem. Taking then a respectful leave of the Inca, the cavaliers rode back to Caxamalca, with many moody speculations on what they had seen; on the state and opulence of the Indian monarch; on the strength of his military array, their excellent appointments, and the apparent discipline in their ranks,—all arguing a much higher degree of civilization, and consequently of power, than anything they had witnessed in the lower regions of the country. As they contrasted all this with their own diminutive force, too far advanced, as they now were, for succour to reach them, they felt they had done rashly in throwing themselves into the midst of so formidable an empire, and were filled with gloomy forebodings of the result. Their comrades in the camp soon caught the infectious spirit of despondency, which was not lessened as night came on, and they beheld the watch-fires of the Peruvians lighting up the sides of the mountains, and glittering in the darkness, "as thick," says one who saw them, "as the stars of heaven."

Yet there was one bosom in that little host which was not touched with the feeling either of fear or dejection. That was Pizarro's, who secretly rejoiced that he had now brought matters to the issue for which he had so long panted. He saw the necessity of kindling a similar feeling in his followers, or all would be lost. Without unfolding his plans, he went round among his men, beseeching them not to show faint hearts at this crisis, when they stood face to face with the foe whom they had been so long seeking. "They were to rely on themselves, and on that Providence which had carried them safe through so many fearful trials. It would not now desert them, and if numbers, however great, were on the side of their enemy, it mattered little when the arm of Heaven was on theirs." The Spanish cavalier acted under the combined influence of chivalrous adventure and religious zeal. The latter was the most effective in the hour of peril; and Pizarro, who understood well the characters he had to deal with, by presenting the enterprise as a crusade, kindled the dying embers of enthusiasm in the bosoms of his followers, and restored their faltering courage.

He then summoned a council of his officers, to consider the plan of operations, or rather to propose to them the extraordinary plan on which he had himself decided. This was to lay an ambuscade for the Inca, and take him prisoner in the face of his whole army! It was a project full of peril,—bordering, as it might well seem, on desperation. But the circumstances of the Spaniards were desperate. Whichever way they turned, they were menaced by the most appalling dangers; and better was it bravely to confront the danger, than weakly to shrink from it, when there was no avenue for escape.

To fly was now too late. Whither could they fly? At the first signal of retreat, the whole army of the Inca would be upon them. Their movements would be anticipated by a foe far better acquainted with the intricacies of the sierra than themselves; the passes would be occupied, and they would be hemmed in on all sides; the mere fact of this retrograde movement would diminish the confidence and with it the effective strength of his own men, while it doubled that of his enemy.

Yet to remain long inactive in his present position seemed almost equally perilous. Even supposing that Atahuallpa should entertain friendly feelings towards the Christians, they could not confide in the continuance of such feelings. Familiarity with the white men would soon destroy the idea of anything supernatural, or even superior, in their natures. He would feel contempt for their diminutive numbers. Their horses, their arms and showy appointments, would be an attractive bait in the eye of the barbaric monarch, and when conscious that he had the power to crush their possessors, he would not be slow in finding a pretext for it. A sufficient one had already occurred in the high-handed measures of the Conquerors, on their march through his dominions.

But what reason had they to flatter themselves that the Inca cherished such a disposition towards them? He was a crafty and unscrupulous prince, and, if the accounts they had repeatedly received on their march were true, had ever regarded the coming of the Spaniards with an evil eye. It was scarcely possible he should do otherwise. His soft messages had only been intended to decoy them across the mountains, where, with the aid of his warriors, he might readily overpower them. They were entangled in the toils which the cunning monarch had spread for them.

Their only remedy, then, was to turn the Inca's arts against himself; to take him, if possible, in his own snare. There was no time to be lost; for any day might bring back the victorious legions who had recently won his battles at the south, and thus make the odds against the Spaniards far greater than now.

Yet to encounter Atahuallpa in the open field would be attended with great hazard; and even if victorious, there would be little probability that the person of the Inca, of so much importance, would fall into the hands of the victors. The invitation he had so unsuspiciously accepted to visit them in their quarters afforded the best means for securing this desirable prize. Nor was the enterprise so desperate, considering the great advantages afforded by the character and weapons of the invaders, and the unexpectedness of the assault. The mere circumstance of acting on a concerted plan would alone make a small number more than a match for a much larger one. But it was not necessary to admit the whole of the Indian force into the city before the attack; and the person of the Inca once secured, his followers, astounded by so strange an event, were they few or many, would have no heart for further resistance;—and with the Inca once in his power, Pizarro might dictate laws to the empire.

In this daring project of the Spanish chief, it was easy to

see that he had the brilliant exploit of Cortés in his mind, when he carried off the Aztec monarch in his capital. But that was not by violence,—at least not by open violence,—and it received the sanction, compulsory though it were, of the monarch himself. It was also true that the results in that case did not altogether justify a repetition of the experiment; since the people rose in a body to sacrifice both the prince and his kidnappers. Yet this was owing, in part, at least, to the indiscretion of the latter. The experiment in the outset was perfectly successful; and, could Pizarro once become master of the person of Atahuallpa, he trusted to his own discretion for the rest. It would, at least, extricate him from his present critical position, by placing in his power an inestimable guaranty for his safety; and if he could not make his own terms with the Inca at once, the arrival of reinforcements from home would, in all probability, soon enable him to do so.

Pizarro having concerted his plans for the following day, the council broke up, and the chief occupied himself with providing for the security of the camp during the night. The approaches to the town were defended; sentinels were posted at different points, especially on the summit of the fortress, where they were to observe the position of the enemy, and to report any movement that menaced the tranquillity of the night. After these precautions, the Spanish commander and his followers withdrew to their appointed quarters,—but not to sleep. At least, sleep must have come late to those who were aware of the decisive plan for the morrow; that morrow which was to be the crisis of their fate,—to crown their ambitious schemes with full success, or consign them to irretrievable ruin!

CHAPTER V [1532]

The clouds of the evening had passed away, and the sun rose bright on the following morning, the most memorable epoch in the annals of Peru. It was Saturday, the sixteenth of November, 1532. The loud cry of the trumpet called the Spaniards to arms with the first streak of dawn; and Pizarro, briefly acquainting them with the plan of the assault, made the necessary dispositions.

The *plaza*, as mentioned in the preceding chapter, was defended on its three sides by low ranges of buildings, consisting of spacious halls with wide doors or vomitories opening into the square. In these halls he stationed his cavalry in two divisions, one under his brother Hernando, the other under De Soto. The infantry he placed in another of the buildings, reserving twenty chosen men to act with himself as occasion might require. Pedro de Candia, with a few soldiers and the artillery,—comprehending under this imposing name two small pieces of ordnance, called falconets,—he established in the fortress. All received orders to wait at their posts till the arrival of the Inca. After his entrance into the great square, they were still to remain under cover, withdrawn from observation, till the signal was given by the discharge of a gun, when they were to cry their war-cries, to rush out in a body from their covert, and, putting the Peruvians to the sword, bear off the person of the Inca. The arrangement of the immense halls, opening on a level with the *plaza*, seemed to be contrived on purpose for a *coup de théâtre*. Pizarro particularly inculcated order and implicit obedience, that in the hurry of the moment there should be no confusion. Everything depended on their acting with concert, coolness, and celerity.

The chief next saw that their arms were in good order; and that the breastplates of their horses were garnished with bells, to add by their noise to the consternation of the Indians. Refreshments were, also, liberally provided, that the troops should be in condition for the conflict. These arrangements being completed, mass was performed with great solemnity by the ecclesiastics who attended the expedition; the God of battles was invoked to spread his shield over the soldiers who were fighting to extend the empire of the Cross; and all joined with enthusiasm in the chant, "*Exsurge, Domine,*" "Rise, O Lord! and judge thine own cause." One might have supposed them a company of martyrs, about to lay down their lives in defence of their faith, instead of a licentious band of adventurers, meditating one of the most atrocious acts of perfidy on the record of history! Yet, whatever were the vices of the Castilian cavalier, hypocrisy was not among the number. He felt that he was battling for the Cross, and under this conviction, exalted as it was at such a moment as this into the predominant impulse, he was blind to the baser motives which mingled with the enterprise. With feelings thus kindled to a flame of religious ardor, the soldiers of Pizarro looked forward with renovated spirits to the coming conflict; and the chieftain saw with satisfaction, that in the hour of trial his men would be true to their leader and themselves.

It was late in the day before any movement was visible in the Peruvian camp, where much preparation was making to approach the Christian quarters with due state and ceremony. A message was received from Atahuallpa, informing the Spanish commander that he should come with his warriors fully armed, in the same manner as the Spaniards had come to his quarters the night preceding. This was not an agreeable intimation to Pizarro, though he had no reason, probably, to expect the contrary. But to object might imply distrust, or, perhaps, disclose, in some measure, his own designs. He expressed his satisfaction, therefore, at the intelligence, assuring the Inca, that, come as he would, he would be received by him as a friend and brother.

It was noon before the Indian procession was on its march, when it was seen occupying the great causeway for a long extent. In front came a large body of attendants, whose office seemed to be to sweep away every particle of rubbish from the road. High above the crowd appeared the Inca, borne on the shoulders of his principal nobles, while others of the same rank marched by the sides of his litter, displaying such a dazzling show of ornaments on their persons, that, in the language of one of the Conquerors, "they blazed like the sun." But the greater part of the Inca's forces mustered along the fields that lined the road, and were spread over the broad meadows as far as the eye could reach.

When the royal procession had arrived within half a mile of the city, it came to a halt; and Pizarro saw with surprise that Atahuallpa was preparing to pitch his tents, as if to encamp there. A messenger soon after arrived, informing the Spaniards that the Inca would occupy his present station the ensuing night, and enter the city on the following morning.

This intelligence greatly disturbed Pizarro, who had shared in the general impatience of his men at the tardy movements of the Peruvians. The troops had been under arms since daylight, the cavalry mounted, and the infantry at their post, waiting in silence the coming of the Inca. A profound stillness reigned throughout the town, broken only at intervals by the cry of the sentinel from the summit of the fortress, as he proclaimed the movements of the Indian army. Nothing, Pizarro well knew, was so trying to the soldier as prolonged suspense, in a critical situation like the present; and he feared lest his ardor might evaporate, and be succeeded by that nervous feeling natural to the bravest soul at such a crisis, and which, if not fear, is near akin to it. He returned an answer, therefore, to Atahuallpa, deprecating his change of purpose; and adding that he had provided everything for his entertainment, and expected him that night to sup with him.

This message turned the Inca from his purpose; and, striking his tents again, he resumed his march, first advising the general that he should leave the greater part of his warriors behind, and enter the place with only a few of them, and without arms, as he preferred to pass the night at Caxamalca. At the same time he ordered accommodations to be provided for himself and his retinue in one of the large stone buildings, called, from a serpent sculptured on the walls, "the House of the Serpent."—No tidings could have been more grateful to the

Spaniards. It seemed as if the Indian monarch was eager to rush into the snare that had been spread for him! The fanatical cavalier could not fail to discern in it the immediate finger of Providence.

It is difficult to account for this wavering conduct of Atahuallpa, so different from the bold and decided character which history ascribes to him. There is no doubt that he made his visit to the white men in perfect good faith; though Pizarro was probably right in conjecturing that this amiable disposition stood on a very precarious footing. There is as little reason to suppose that he distrusted the sincerity of the strangers; or he would not thus unnecessarily have proposed to visit them unarmed. His original purpose of coming with all his force was doubtless to display his royal state, and perhaps, also, to show greater respect for the Spaniards; but when he consented to accept their hospitality, and pass the night in their quarters, he was willing to dispense with a great part of his armed soldiery, and visit them in a manner that implied entire confidence in their good faith. He was too absolute in his own empire easily to suspect; and he probably could not comprehend the audacity with which a few men, like those now assembled in Caxamalca, meditated an assault on a powerful monarch in the midst of his victorious army. He did not know the character of the Spaniard.

It was not long before sunset, when the van of the royal procession entered the gates of the city. First came some hundreds of the menials employed to clear the path from every obstacle, and singing songs of triumph as they came, "which, in our ears," says one of the Conquerors, "sounded like the songs of hell!" Then followed other bodies of different ranks, and dressed in different liveries. Some wore a showy stuff, checkered white and red, like the squares of a chess-board. Others were clad in pure white, bearing hammers or maces of silver or copper; and the guards, together with those in immediate attendance on the prince, were distinguished by a rich azure livery, and a profusion of gay ornaments, while the large pendants attached to the ears indicated the Peruvian noble.

Elevated high above his vassals came the Inca Atahuallpa, borne on a sedan or open litter, on which was a sort of throne made of massive gold of inestimable value. The palanquin was lined with the richly colored plumes of tropical birds, and studded with shining plates of gold and silver. The monarch's attire was much richer than on the preceding evening. Round his neck was suspended a collar of emeralds of uncommon size and brilliancy. His short hair was decorated with golden ornaments, and the imperial *borla* encircled his temples. The bearing of the Inca was sedate and dignified; and from his lofty station he looked down on the multitudes below with an air of composure, like one accustomed to command.

As the leading files of the procession entered the great square, larger, says an old chronicler, than any square in Spain, they opened to the right and left for the royal retinue to pass. Everything was conducted with admirable order. The monarch was permitted to traverse the *plaza* in silence, and not a Spaniard was to be seen. When some five or six thousand of his people had entered the place, Atahuallpa halted, and, turning round with an inquiring look, demanded, "Where are the strangers?"

At this moment Fray Vicente de Valverde, a Dominican friar, Pizarro's chaplain, and afterward Bishop of Cuzco, came forward with his breviary, or, as other accounts say, a Bible, in one hand, and a crucifix in the other, and, approaching the Inca, told him, that he came by order of his commander to expound to him the doctrines of the true faith, for which purpose the Spaniards had come from a great distance to his country. The friar then explained, as clearly as he could, the mysterious doctrine of the Trinity, and, ascending high in his account, began with the creation of man, thence passed to his fall, to his subsequent redemption by Jesus Christ, to the crucifixion, and the ascension, when the Saviour left the Apostle Peter as his Viceregent upon earth. This power had been transmitted to the successors of the Apostle, good and wise men, who, under the title of Popes, held authority over all powers and potentates on earth. One of the last of these Popes had commissioned the Spanish emperor, the most mighty monarch in the world, to conquer and convert the natives in this western hemisphere; and his general, Francisco Pizarro, had now come to execute this important mission. The friar concluded with beseeching the Peruvian monarch to receive him kindly; to abjure the errors of his own faith, and embrace that of the Christians now proffered to him, the only one by which he could hope for salvation; and, furthermore, to acknowledge himself a tributary of the Emperor Charles the Fifth, who, in that event, would aid and protect him as his loyal vassal.

Whether Atahuallpa possessed himself of every link in the curious chain of argument by which the monk connected Pizarro with St. Peter, may be doubted. It is certain, however, that he must have had very incorrect notions of the Trinity, if, as Garcilasso states, the interpreter Felipillo explained it by saying, that "the Christians believed in three Gods and one God, and that made four." But there is no doubt he perfectly comprehended that the drift of the discourse was to persuade him to resign his sceptre and acknowledge the supremacy of another.

The eyes of the Indian monarch flashed fire, and his dark brow grew darker as he replied,—"I will be no man's tributary. I am greater than any prince upon earth. Your emperor may be a great prince; I do not doubt it, when I see that he has sent his subjects so far across the waters; and I am willing to hold him as a brother. As for the Pope of whom you speak, he must be crazy to talk of giving away countries which do not belong to him. For my faith," he continued, "I will not change it. Your own God, as you say, was put to death by the very men whom he created. But mine," he concluded, pointing to his Deity,—then, alas! sinking in glory behind the mountains,—"my God still lives in the heavens, and looks down on his children."

He then demanded of Valverde by what authority he had said these things. The friar pointed to the book which he held, as his authority. Atahuallpa, taking it, turned over the pages a moment, then, as the insult he had received probably flashed across his mind, he threw it down with vehemence, and exclaimed,—"Tell your comrades that they shall give me an account of their doings in my land. I will not go from here, till they have made me full satisfaction for all the wrongs they have committed."

The friar, greatly scandalized by the indignity offered to the sacred volume, stayed only to pick it up, and, hastening to

Pizarro, informed him of what had been done, exclaiming, at the same time,—"Do you not see, that, while we stand here wasting our breath in talking with this dog, full of pride as he is, the fields are filling with Indians? Set on, at once; I absolve you." Pizarro saw that the hour had come. He waved a white scarf in the air, the appointed signal. The fatal gun was fired from the fortress. Then, springing into the square, the Spanish captain and his followers shouted the old war-cry of "St. Jago and at them." It was answered by the battle-cry of every Spaniard in the city, as, rushing from the avenues of the great halls in which they were concealed, they poured into the *plaza,* horse and foot, each in his own dark column, and threw themselves into the midst of the Indian crowd. The latter, taken by surprise, stunned by the report of artillery and muskets, the echoes of which reverberated like thunder from the surrounding buildings, and blinded by the smoke which rolled in sulphurous volumes along the square, were seized with a panic. They knew not whither to fly for refuge from the coming ruin. Nobles and commoners,—all were trampled down under the fierce charge of the cavalry, who dealt their blows, right and left, without sparing; while their swords, flashing through the thick gloom, carried dismay into the hearts of the wretched natives, who now, for the first time, saw the horse and his rider in all their terrors. They made no resistance,—as, indeed, they had no weapons with which to make it. Every avenue to escape was closed, for the entrance to the square was choked up with the dead bodies of men who had perished in vain efforts to fly; and, such was the agony of the survivors under the terrible pressure of their assailants, that a large body of Indians, by their convulsive struggles, burst through the wall of stone and dried clay which formed part of the boundary of the *plaza!* It fell, leaving an opening of more than a hundred paces, through which multitudes now found their way into the country, still hotly pursued by the cavalry, who, leaping the fallen rubbish, hung on the rear of the fugitives, striking them down in all directions.

Meanwhile the fight, or rather massacre, continued hot around the Inca, whose person was the great object of the assault. His faithful nobles, rallying about him, threw themselves in the way of the assailants, and strove, by tearing them from their saddles, or, at least, by offering their own bosoms as a mark for their vengeance, to shield their beloved master. It is said by some authorities, that they carried weapons concealed under their clothes. If so, it availed them little, as it is not pretended that they used them. But the most timid animal will defend itself when at bay. That they did not so in the present instance is proof that they had no weapons to use. Yet they still continued to force back the cavaliers, clinging to their horses with dying grasp, and, as one was cut down, another taking the place of his fallen comrade with a loyalty truly affecting.

The Indian monarch, stunned and bewildered, saw his faithful subjects falling round him without fully comprehending his situation. The litter on which he rode heaved to and fro, as the mighty press swayed backwards and forwards; and he gazed on the overwhelming ruin, like some forlorn mariner, who, tossed about in his bark by the furious elements, sees the lightning's flash and hears the thunder bursting around him with the consciousness that he can do nothing to avert his fate. At length, weary with the work of destruction, the Spaniards, as the shades of evening grew deeper, felt afraid that the royal prize might, after all, elude them; and some of the cavaliers made a desperate attempt to end the affray at once by taking Atahuallpa's life. But Pizarro, who was nearest his person, called out with stentorian voice, "Let no one, who values his life, strike at the Inca"; and, stretching out his arm to shield him, received a wound on the hand from one of his own men,—the only wound received by a Spaniard in the action.

The struggle now became fiercer than ever round the royal litter. It reeled more and more, and at length, several of the nobles who supported it having been slain, it was overturned, and the Indian prince would have come with violence to the ground, had not his fall been broken by the efforts of Pizarro and some other of the cavaliers, who caught him in their arms. The imperial *borla* was instantly snatched from his temples by a soldier named Estete, and the unhappy monarch, strongly secured, was removed to a neighboring building, where he was carefully guarded.

All attempt at resistance now ceased. The fate of the Inca

soon spread over town and country. The charm which might have held the Peruvians together was dissolved. Every man thought only of his own safety. Even the soldiery encamped on the adjacent fields took the alarm, and, learning the fatal tidings, were seen flying in every direction before their pursuers, who in the heat of triumph showed no touch of mercy. At length night, more pitiful than man, threw her friendly mantle over the fugitives, and the scattered troops of Pizarro rallied once more at the sound of the trumpet in the bloody square of Caxamalca.

The number of slain is reported, as usual, with great discrepancy. Pizarro's secretary says two thousand natives fell. A descendant of the Incas—a safer authority than Garcilasso— swells the number to ten thousand. Truth is generally found somewhere between the extremes. The slaughter was incessant, for there was nothing to check it. That there should have been no resistance will not appear strange, when we consider the fact, that the wretched victims were without arms, and that their senses must have been completely overwhelmed by the strange and appalling spectacle which burst on them so unexpectedly. "What wonder was it," said an ancient Inca to a Spaniard, who repeats it, "what wonder that our countrymen lost their wits, seeing blood run like water, and the Inca, whose person we all of us adore, seized and carried off by a handful of men?" Yet though the massacre was incessant, it was short in duration. The whole time consumed by it, the brief twilight of the tropics, did not much exceed half an hour; a short period, indeed,—yet long enough to decide the fate of Peru, and to subvert the dynasty of the Incas.

That night Pizarro kept his engagement with the Inca, since he had Atahuallpa to sup with him. The banquet was served in one of the halls facing the great square, which a few hours before had been the scene of slaughter, and the pavement of which was still encumbered with the dead bodies of the Inca's subjects. The captive monarch was placed next his conqueror. He seemed like one who did not yet fully comprehend the extent of his calamity. If he did, he showed an amazing fortitude. "It is the fortune of war," he said; and, if we may credit the Spaniards, he expressed his admiration of the adroitness with which they had contrived to entrap him in the midst of his own troops. He added, that he had been made acquainted with the progress of the white men from the hour of their landing; but that he had been led to undervalue their strength from the insignificance of their numbers. He had no doubt he should be easily able to overpower them, on their arrival at Caxamalca, by his superior strength; and, as he wished to see for himself what manner of men they were, he had suffered them to cross the mountains, meaning to select such as he chose for his own service, and, getting possession of their wonderful arms and horses, put the rest to death.

That such may have been Atahuallpa's purpose is not improbable. It explains his conduct in not occupying the mountain passes, which afforded such strong points of defence against invasion. But that a prince so astute, as by the general testimony of the Conquerors he is represented to have been, should have made so impolitic a disclosure of his hidden motives is not so probable. The intercourse with the Inca was carried on chiefly by means of the interpreter Felipillo, or *little Philip*, as he was called, from his assumed Christian name, —a malicious youth, as it appears, who bore no good-will to Atahuallpa, and whose interpretations were readily admitted by the Conquerors, eager to find some pretext for their bloody reprisals.

Atahuallpa, as elsewhere noticed, was, at this time, about thirty years of age. He was well made, and more robust than usual with his countrymen. His head was large, and his countenance might have been called handsome, but that his eyes, which were bloodshot, gave a fierce expression to his features. He was deliberate in speech, grave in manner, and towards his own people stern even to severity; though with the Spaniards he showed himself affable, sometimes even indulging in sallies of mirth.

Pizarro paid every attention to his royal captive, and endeavored to lighten, if he could not dispel, the gloom which, in spite of his assumed equanimity, hung over the monarch's brow. He besought him not to be cast down by his reverses, for his lot had only been that of every prince who had resisted the white men. They had come into the country to proclaim the gospel, the religion of Jesus Christ; and it was no wonder they had prevailed, when his shield was over them. Heaven had permitted that Atahuallpa's pride should be humbled, because of his hostile intentions towards the Spaniards, and the insults he had offered to the sacred volume. But he bade the Inca take courage and confide in him, for the Spaniards were a generous race, warring only against those who made war on them, and showing grace to all who submitted!—Atahuallpa may have thought the massacre an indifferent commentary on this vaunted lenity.

Before retiring for the night, Pizarro briefly addressed his troops on their present situation. When he had ascertained that not a man was wounded, he bade them offer up thanksgivings to Providence for so great a miracle; without its care, they could never have prevailed so easily over the host of their enemies; and he trusted their lives had been reserved for still greater things. But if they would succeed, they had much to do for themselves. They were in the heart of a powerful kingdom, encompassed by foes deeply attached to their own sovereign. They must be ever on their guard, therefore, and be prepared at any hour to be roused from their slumbers by the call of the trumpet.—Having then posted his sentinels, placed a strong guard over the apartment of Atahuallpa, and taken all the precautions of a careful commander, Pizarro withdrew to repose; and, if he could really feel, that, in the bloody scenes of the past day, he had been fighting only the good fight of the Cross, he doubtless slept sounder than on the night preceding the seizure of the Inca.

On the following morning, the first commands of the Spanish chief were to have the city cleansed of its impurities; and the prisoners, of whom there were many in the camp, were employed to remove the dead, and give them decent burial. His next care was to despatch a body of about thirty horse to the quarters lately occupied by Atahuallpa at the baths, to take possession of the spoil, and disperse the remnant of the Peruvian forces which still hung about the place.

Before noon, the party which he had detached on this service returned with a large troop of Indians, men and women, among the latter of whom were many of the wives and attendants of the Inca. The Spaniards had met with no resistance; since the Peruvian warriors, though so superior in number, excellent in appointments, and consisting mostly of able-bodied young men,—for the greater part of the veteran forces were with the Inca's generals at the south,—lost all heart from the moment of their sovereign's captivity. There was no leader to take his place; for they recognized no authority but that of the Child of the Sun, and they seemed to be held by a sort of invisible charm near the place of his confinement; while they gazed with superstitious awe on the white men, who could achieve so audacious an enterprise.

The number of Indian prisoners was so great, that some of the Conquerors were for putting them all to death, or, at least, cutting off their hands, to disable them from acts of violence, and to strike terror into their countrymen. The proposition, doubtless, came from the lowest and most ferocious of the soldiery. But that it should have been made at all shows what materials entered into the composition of Pizarro's company. The chief rejected it at once, as no less impolitic than inhuman, and dismissed the Indians to their several homes, with the assurance that none should be harmed who did not offer resistance to the white men. A sufficient number, however, were retained to wait on the Conquerors who were so well provided, in this respect, that the most common soldier was attended by a retinue of menials that would have better suited the establishment of a noble.

The Spaniards had found immense droves of llamas under the care of their shepherds in the neighborhood of the baths, destined for the consumption of the Court. Many of them were now suffered to roam abroad among their native mountains; though Pizarro caused a considerable number to be reserved for the use of the army. And this was no small quantity, if, as one of the Conquerors says, a hundred and fifty of the Peruvian sheep were frequently slaughtered in a day. Indeed, the Spaniards were so improvident in their destruction of these animals, that, in a few years, the superb flocks, nurtured with so much care by the Peruvian government, had almost disappeared from the land.

The party sent to pillage the Inca's pleasure-house brought back a rich booty in gold and silver, consisting chiefly of plate for the royal table, which greatly astonished the Spaniards by their size and weight. These, as well as some large emeralds obtained there, together with the precious spoils found on the bodies of the Indian nobles who had perished in the massacre, were placed in safe custody, to be hereafter divided. In the city of Caxamalca, the troops also found magazines stored with goods, both cotton and woollen, far superior to any they had seen, for fineness of texture, and the skill with which the various colors were blended. They were piled from the floors to the very roofs of the buildings, and in such quantity, that, after every soldier had provided himself with what he desired, it made no sensible diminution of the whole amount.

Pizarro would now gladly have directed his march on the Peruvian capital. But the distance was great, and his force was small. This must have been still further crippled by the guard required for the Inca, and the chief feared to involve himself deeper in a hostile empire so populous and powerful, with a prize so precious in his keeping. With much anxiety, therefore, he looked for reinforcements from the colonies; and he despatched a courier to San Miguel, to inform the Spaniards there of his recent successes, and to ascertain if there had been any arrival from Panamá. Meanwhile he employed his men in making Caxamalca a more suitable residence for a Christian host, by erecting a church, or, perhaps, appropriating some Indian edifice to this use, in which mass was regularly performed by the Dominican fathers, with great solemnity. The dilapidated walls of the city were also restored in a more substantial manner than before, and every vestige was soon effaced of the hurricane that had so recently swept over it.

It was not long before Atahuallpa discovered, amidst all the show of religious zeal in his Conquerors, a lurking appetite more potent in most of their bosoms than either religion or ambition. This was the love of gold. He determined to avail himself of it to procure his own freedom. The critical posture of his affairs made it important that this should not be long delayed. His brother, Huascar, ever since his defeat, had been detained as a prisoner, subject to the victor's orders. He was now at Andamarca, at no great distance from Caxamalca; and Atahuallpa feared with good reason, that, when his own imprisonment was known, Huascar would find it easy to corrupt his guards, make his escape, and put himself at the head of the contested empire, without a rival to dispute it.

In the hope, therefore, to effect his purpose by appealing

to the avarice of his keepers, he one day told Pizarro, that, if he would set him free, he would engage to cover the floor of the apartment on which they stood with gold. Those present listened with an incredulous smile; and, as the Inca received no answer, he said, with some emphasis, that "he would not merely cover the floor, but would fill the room with gold as high as he could reach"; and, standing on tiptoe, he stretched out his hand against the wall. All stared with amazement; while they regarded it as the insane boast of a man too eager to procure his liberty to weigh the meaning of his words. Yet Pizarro was sorely perplexed. As he had advanced into the country, much that he had seen, and all that he had heard, had confirmed the dazzling reports first received of the riches of Peru. Atahuallpa himself had given him the most glowing picture of the wealth of the capital, where the roofs of the temples were plated with gold, while the walls were hung with tapestry and the floors inlaid with tiles of the same precious metal. There must be some foundation for all this. At all events, it was safe to accede to the Inca's proposition; since, by so doing, he could collect, at once, all the gold at his disposal, and thus prevent its being purloined or secreted by the natives. He therefore acquiesced in Atahuallpa's offer, and, drawing a red line along the wall at the height which the Inca had indicated, he caused the terms of the proposal to be duly recorded by the notary. The apartment was about seventeen feet broad, by twenty-two feet long, and the line around the walls was nine feet from the floor. This space was to be filled with gold; but it was understood that the gold was not to be melted down into ingots, but to retain the original form of the articles into which it was manufactured, that the Inca might have the benefit of the space which they occupied. He further agreed to fill an adjoining room of smaller dimensions twice full with silver, in like manner; and he demanded two months to accomplish all this.

No sooner was this arrangement made, than the Inca despatched couriers to Cuzco and the other principal places in the kingdom, with orders that the gold ornaments and utensils should be removed from the royal palaces, and from the temples and other public buildings, and transported without loss of time to Caxamalca. Meanwhile he continued to live in the

Spanish quarters, treated with the respect due to his rank, and enjoying all the freedom that was compatible with the security of his person. Though not permitted to go abroad, his limbs were unshackled, and he had the range of his own apartments under the jealous *surveillance* of a guard, who knew too well the value of the royal captive to be remiss. He was allowed the society of his favorite wives, and Pizarro took care that his domestic privacy should not be violated. His subjects had free access to their sovereign, and every day he received visits from the Indian nobles, who came to bring presents, and offer condolence to their unfortunate master. On such occasions, the most potent of these great vassals never ventured into his presence, without first stripping off their sandals, and bearing a load on their backs in token of reverence. The Spaniards gazed with curious eyes on these acts of homage, or rather of slavish submission, on the one side, and on the air of perfect indifference with which they were received, as a matter of course, on the other; and they conceived high ideas of the character of a prince who, even in his present helpless condition, could inspire such feelings of awe in his subjects. The royal levee was so well attended, and such devotion was shown by his vassals to the captive monarch, as did not fail, in the end, to excite some feelings of distrust in his keepers.

Pizarro did not neglect the opportunity afforded him of communicating the truths of revelation to his prisoner, and both he and his chaplain, Father Valverde, labored in the same good work. Atahuallpa listened with composure and apparent attention. But nothing seemed to move him so much as the argument with which the military polemic closed his discourse,—that it could not be the true God whom Atahuallpa worshipped, since he had suffered him to fall into the hands of his enemies. The unhappy monarch assented to the force of this, acknowledging that his Deity had indeed deserted him in his utmost need.

Yet his conduct towards his brother Huascar, at this time, too clearly proves, that, whatever respect he may have shown for the teachers, the doctrines of Christianity had made little impression on his heart. No sooner had Huascar been informed of the capture of his rival, and of the large ransom he had offered for his deliverance, than, as the latter had foreseen, he made every effort to regain his liberty, and sent, or attempted to send, a message to the Spanish commander, that he would pay a much larger ransom than that promised by Atahuallpa, who, never having dwelt in Cuzco, was ignorant of the quantity of treasure there, and where it was deposited.

Intelligence of all this was secretly communicated to Atahuallpa by the persons who had his brother in charge; and his jealousy, thus roused, was further heightened by Pizarro's declaration, that he intended to have Huascar brought to Caxamalca, where he would himself examine into the controversy, and determine which of the two had best title to the sceptre of the Incas. Pizarro perceived, from the first, the advantages of a competition which would enable him, by throwing his sword into the scale he preferred, to give it a preponderance. The party who held the sceptre by his nomination would henceforth be a tool in his hands, with which to work his pleasure more effectually than he could well do in his own name. It was the game, as every reader knows, played by Edward the First in the affairs of Scotland, and by many a monarch, both before and since,—and though their examples may not have been familiar to the unlettered soldier, Pizarro was too quick in his perceptions to require, in this matter, at least, the teachings of history.

Atahuallpa was much alarmed by the Spanish commander's determination to have the suit between the rival candidates brought before him; for he feared, that, independently of the merits of the case, the decision would be likely to go in favor of Huascar, whose mild and ductile temper would make him a convenient instrument in the hands of his conquerors. Without further hesitation, he determined to remove this cause of jealousy for ever, by the death of his brother.

His orders were immediately executed, and the unhappy prince was drowned, as was commonly reported, in the river of Andamarca, declaring with his dying breath that the white men would avenge his murder, and that his rival would not long survive him.—Thus perished the unfortunate Huascar, the legitimate heir of the throne of the Incas, in the very morning of life, and the commencement of his reign; a reign, however, which had been long enough to call forth the display of many excellent and amiable qualities, though his nature was too gentle to cope with the bold and fiercer temper of his brother. Such is the portrait we have of him from the Indian and Castilian chroniclers, though the former, it should be added, were the kinsmen of Huascar, and the latter certainly bore no good-will to Atahuallpa.

That prince received the tidings of Huascar's death with every mark of surprise and indignation. He immediately sent for Pizarro, and communicated the event to him with expressions of the deepest sorrow. The Spanish commander refused, at first, to credit the unwelcome news, and bluntly told the Inca, that his brother could not be dead, and that he should be answerable for his life. To this Atahuallpa replied by renewed assurances of the fact, adding that the deed had been perpetrated, without his privity, by Huascar's keepers, fearful that he might take advantage of the troubles of the country to make his escape. Pizarro, on making further inquiries, found that the report of his death was but too true. That it should have been brought about by Atahuallpa's officers, without his express command, would only show, that, by so doing, they had probably anticipated their master's wishes. The crime, which assumes in our eyes a deeper dye from the relation of the parties, had not the same estimation among the Incas, in whose multitudinous families the bonds of brotherhood must have sat loosely,—much too loosely to restrain the arm of the despot from sweeping away any obstacle that lay in his path.

GOLD ARRIVES FOR THE RANSOM—VISIT TO PACHA-
CAMAC—DEMOLITION OF THE IDOL—THE INCA'S FAVOR-
ITE GENERAL—THE INCA'S LIFE IN CONFINEMENT—
ENVOYS' CONDUCT IN CUZCO—ARRIVAL OF ALMAGRO

Several weeks had now passed since Atahuallpa's emissaries had been despatched for the gold and silver that were
to furnish his ransom to the Spaniards. But the distances
were great, and the returns came in slowly. They consisted,
for the most part, of massive pieces of plate, some of which
weighed two or three *arrobas,*—a Spanish weight of twenty-five
pounds. On some days, articles of the value of thirty or forty
thousand *pesos de oro* were brought in, and, occasionally, of
the value of fifty or even sixty thousand *pesos*. The greedy
eyes of the Conquerors gloated on the shining heaps of treasure, which were transported on the shoulders of the Indian
porters, and, after being carefully registered, were placed in
safe deposit under a strong guard. They now began to believe
that the magnificent promises of the Inca would be fulfilled.
But, as their avarice was sharpened by the ravishing display of
wealth, such as they had hardly dared to imagine, they became
more craving and impatient. They made no allowance for the
distance and the difficulties of the way, and loudly inveighed
against the tardiness with which the royal commands were executed. They even suspected Atahuallpa of devising this
scheme only to gain a pretext for communicating with his subjects in distant places, and of proceeding as dilatorily as possible, in order to secure time for the execution of his plans.
Rumors of a rising among the Peruvians were circulated, and
the Spaniards were in apprehension of some general and sudden assault on their quarters. Their new acquisitions gave
them additional cause for solicitude; like a miser, they trembled in the midst of their treasures.

Pizarro reported to his captive the rumors that were in circulation among the soldiers, naming, as one of the places pointed out for the rendezvous of the Indians, the neighboring city of Guamachucho. Atahuallpa listened with undisguised astonishment, and indignantly repelled the charge, as false from beginning to end. "No one of my subjects," said he, "would dare to appear in arms, or to raise his finger, without my orders. You have me," he continued, "in your power. Is not my life at your disposal? And what better security can you have for my fidelity?" He then represented to the Spanish commander, that the distances of many of the places were very great; that to Cuzco, the capital, although a message might be sent by post, through a succession of couriers, in five days from Caxamalca, it would require weeks for a porter to travel over the same ground, with a heavy load on his back. "But that you may be satisfied I am proceeding in good faith," he added, "I desire you will send some of your own people to Cuzco. I will give them a safe-conduct, and, when there, they can superintend the execution of the commission, and see with their own eyes that no hostile movements are intended." It was a fair offer, and Pizarro, anxious to get more precise and authentic information of the state of the country, gladly availed himself of it.

Before the departure of these emissaries, the general had despatched his brother Hernando with about twenty horse and a small body of infantry to the neighboring town of Guama-chucho, in order to reconnoitre the country, and ascertain if there was any truth in the report of an armed force having assembled there. Hernando found every thing quiet, and met with a kind reception from the natives. But before leaving the place, he received further orders from his brother to con-tinue his march to Pachacamac, a town situated on the coast, at least a hundred leagues distant from Caxamalca. It was consecrated as the seat of the great temple of the deity of that name, whom the Peruvians worshipped as the Creator of the world. It is said that they found there altars raised to this god, on their first occupation of the country; and, such was the veneration in which he was held by the natives, that the Incas, instead of attempting to abolish his worship, deemed it more prudent to sanction it conjointly with that of their own deity, the Sun. Side by side, the two temples rose on the heights that overlooked the city of Pachacamac, and prospered in the offerings of their respective votaries. "It was a cunning arrangement," says an ancient writer, "by which the great enemy of man secured to himself a double harvest of souls."

But the temple of Pachacamac continued to maintain its ascendency; and the oracles, delivered from its dark and mysterious shrine, were held in no less repute among the natives of *Tavantinsuyu* (or "the four quarters of the world," as Peru under the Incas was called), than the oracles of Delphi obtained among the Greeks. Pilgrimages were made to the hallowed spot from the most distant regions, and the city of Pachacamac became among the Peruvians what Mecca was among the Mahometans, or Cholula with the people of Anahuac. The shrine of the deity, enriched by the tributes of the pilgrims, gradually became one of the most opulent in the land; and Atahuallpa, anxious to collect his ransom as speedily as possible, urged Pizarro to send a detachment in that direction, to secure the treasures before they could be secreted by the priests of the temple.

It was a journey of considerable difficulty. Two thirds of the route lay along the table-land of the Cordilleras, intersected occasionally by crests of the mountain range, that imposed no slight impediment to their progress. Fortunately, much of the way, they had the benefit of the great road to Cuzco, and "nothing in Christendom," exclaims Hernando Pizarro, "equals the magnificence of this road across the sierra." In some places, the rocky ridges were so precipitous, that steps were cut in them for the travellers; and though the sides were protected by heavy stone balustrades or parapets, it was with the greatest difficulty that the horses were enabled to scale them. The road was frequently crossed by streams, over which bridges of wood and sometimes of stone were thrown; though occasionally, along the declivities of the mountains, the waters swept down in such furious torrents, that the only method of passing them was by the swinging bridges of osier, of which, till now, the Spaniards had had little experience. They were secured on either bank to heavy buttresses of stone. But as they were originally designed for nothing heavier than the foot-passenger and the llama, and, as they had something exceedingly fragile in their appearance, the Spaniards hesitated to venture on them with their horses. Experience, however, soon showed they were capable of bearing a much greater weight; and though the traveller, made giddy by the vibration of the long avenue, looked with a reeling brain into the torrent that was tumbling at the depth of a hundred feet or more below him, the whole of the cavalry effected their passage without an accident. At these bridges, it may be remarked, they found persons stationed whose business it was to collect toll for the government from all travellers.

The Spaniards were amazed by the number as well as magnitude of the flocks of llamas which they saw browsing on the stunted herbage that grows in the elevated region of the Andes. Sometimes they were gathered in inclosures, but more usually were roaming at large under the conduct of their Indian shepherds; and the Conquerors now learned, for the first time, that these animals were tended with as much care, and their migrations as nicely regulated, as those of the vast flocks of merinos in their own country.

The table-land and its declivities were thickly sprinkled with hamlets and towns, some of them of considerable size; and the country in every direction bore the marks of a thrifty husbandry. Fields of Indian corn were to be seen in all its different stages, from the green and tender ear to the yellow ripeness of harvest time. As they descended into the valleys and deep ravines that divided the crests of the Cordilleras, they were surrounded by the vegetation of a warmer climate, which delighted the eye with the gay livery of a thousand bright colors, and intoxicated the senses with its perfumes. Everywhere the natural capacities of the soil were stimulated by a minute system of irrigation, which drew the fertilizing moisture from every stream and rivulet that rolled down the declivities of the Andes; while the terraced sides of the mountains were clothed with gardens and orchards that teemed with fruits of various latitudes. The Spaniards could not sufficiently admire the industry with which the natives had availed themselves of the bounty of Nature, or had supplied the deficiency where she had dealt with a more parsimonious hand.

Whether from the commands of the Inca, or from the awe which their achievements had spread throughout the land, the Conquerors were received, in every place through which they passed, with hospitable kindness. Lodgings were provided for them, with ample refreshments from the well-stored magazines, distributed at intervals along the route. In many of the towns the inhabitants came out to welcome them with singing and dancing; and, when they resumed their march, a number of able-bodied porters were furnished to carry forward their baggage.

At length, after some weeks of travel, severe even with all these appliances, Hernando Pizarro arrived before the city of Pachacamac. It was a place of considerable population, and the edifices were, many of them, substantially built. The temple of the tutelar deity consisted of a vast stone building, or rather pile of buildings, which, clustering around a conical hill, had the air of a fortress rather than a religious establishment. But, though the walls were of stone, the roof was composed of a light thatch, as usual in countries where rain seldom or never falls, and where defence, consequently, is wanted chiefly against the rays of the sun.

Presenting himself at the lower entrance of the temple, Hernando Pizarro was refused admittance by the guardians of the portal. But, exclaiming that "he had come too far to be stayed by the arm of an Indian priest," he forced his way into the passage, and, followed by his men, wound up in the gallery which led to an area on the summit of the mount, at one end of which stood a sort of chapel. This was the sanctuary of the dread deity. The door was garnished with ornaments of crystal, and with turquoises and bits of coral. Here again the Indians would have dissuaded Pizarro from violating the consecrated precincts, when, at that moment, the shock of an earthquake, that made the ancient walls tremble to their foundation, so alarmed the natives, both those of Pizarro's own company and the people of the place, that they fled in dismay, nothing doubting that their incensed deity would bury the invaders under the ruins, or consume them with his lightnings. But no such terror found its way into the breast of the Conquerors, who felt that here, at least, they were fighting the good fight of the Faith.

Tearing open the door, Pizarro and his party entered. But instead of a hall blazing, as they had fondly imagined, with gold and precious stones, offerings of the worshippers of Pachacamac, they found themselves in a small and obscure apartment, or rather den, from the floor and sides of which steamed up the most offensive odors,—like those of a slaughter-house. It was the place of sacrifice. A few pieces of gold and some emeralds were discovered on the ground, and, as their eyes became accommodated to the darkness, they discerned in the most retired corner of the room the figure of the deity. It was an uncouth monster, made of wood, with the head resembling that of a man. This was the god, through whose lips Satan had breathed forth the far-famed oracles which had deluded his Indian votaries!

Tearing the idol from its recess, the indignant Spaniards dragged it into the open air, and there broke it into a hundred fragments. The place was then purified, and a large cross, made of stone and plaster, was erected on the spot. In a few years the walls of the temple were pulled down by the Spanish settlers, who found there a convenient quarry for their own edifices. But the cross still remained spreading its broad arms over the ruins. It stood where it was planted in the very heart of the stronghold of Heathendom; and, while all was in ruins around it, it proclaimed the permanent triumphs of the Faith.

The simple natives, finding that Heaven had no bolts in store for the Conquerors, and that their god had no power to prevent the profanation of his shrine, came in gradually and tendered their homage to the strangers, whom they now regarded with feelings of superstitious awe. Pizarro profited by this temper to wean them, if possible, from their idolatry; and though no preacher himself, as he tells us, he delivered a discourse as edifying, doubtless, as could be expected from the mouth of a soldier; and, in conclusion, he taught them the sign of the cross, as an inestimable talisman to secure them against the future machinations of the Devil.

But the Spanish commander was not so absorbed in his spiritual labors as not to have an eye to those temporal concerns for which he came into this quarter. He now found, to his chagrin, that he had come somewhat too late; and that the priests of Pachacamac, being advised of his mission, had secured much the greater part of the gold, and decamped with it before his arrival. A quantity was afterwards discovered buried in the grounds adjoining. Still the amount obtained was considerable, falling little short of eighty thousand castellanos, a sum which once would have been deemed a compensation for greater fatigues than they had encountered. But the Spaniards had become familiar with gold; and their imaginations, kindled by the romantic adventures in which they had of late been engaged, indulged in visions which all the gold of Peru would scarcely have realized.

One prize, however, Hernando obtained by his expedition, which went far to console him for the loss of his treasure. While at Pachacamac, he learned that the Indian commander Challcuchima lay with a large force in the neighborhood of Xauxa, a town of some strength at a considerable distance among the mountains. This man, who was nearly related to Atahuallpa, was his most experienced general, and together with Quizquiz, now at Cuzco, had achieved those victories at the south which placed the Inca on the throne. From his birth, his talents, and his large experience, he was accounted second to no subject in the kingdom. Pizarro was aware of the importance of securing his person. Finding that the Indian noble declined to meet him on his return, he determined to march at once on Xauxa and take the chief in his own quarters. Such a scheme, considering the enormous disparity of numbers, might seem desperate even for Spaniards. But success had given them such confidence, that they hardly condescended to calculate chances.

The road across the mountains presented greater difficulties than those on the former march. To add to the troubles of the cavalry, the shoes of their horses were used up, and their hoofs suffered severely on the rough and stony ground. There was no iron at hand, nothing but gold and silver. In the present emergency they turned even these to account; and Pizarro caused the horses of the whole troop to be shod with silver. The work was done by the Indian smiths, and it answered so well, that in this precious material they found a substitute for iron during the remainder of the march.

Xauxa was a large and populous place; though we shall hardly credit the assertion of the Conquerors, that a hundred thousand persons assembled habitually in the great square of the city. The Peruvian commander was encamped, it was said, with an army of five-and-thirty thousand men at only a few miles' distance from the town. With some difficulty he was persuaded to an interview with Pizarro. The latter addressed him courteously, and urged his return with him to the Castilian quarters in Caxamalca, representing it as the command of the Inca. Ever since the capture of his master, Challcuchima had remained uncertain what course to take. The capture of the Inca in this sudden and mysterious manner by a race of beings who seemed to have dropped from the clouds, and that too in the very hour of his triumph, had entirely bewildered the Peruvian chief. He had concerted no plan for the rescue of Atahuallpa, nor, indeed, did he know whether any such movement would be acceptable to him. He now acquiesced in his commands, and was willing, at all events, to have a personal interview with his sovereign. Pizarro gained his end without being obliged to strike a single blow to effect it. The barbarian, when brought into contact with the white man, would seem to have been rebuked by his superior genius, in the same manner as the wild animal of the forest is said to quail before the steady glance of the hunter.

Challcuchima came attended by a numerous retinue. He was borne in his sedan on the shoulders of his vassals; and, as he accompanied the Spaniards on their return through the country, received everywhere from the inhabitants the homage paid only to the favorite of a monarch. Yet all this pomp vanished on his entering the presence of the Inca, whom he approached with his feet bare, while a light burden, which he had taken from one of the attendants, was laid on his back. As he drew near, the old warrior, raising his hands to heaven, exclaimed,—"Would that I had been here!—this would not then have happened"; then, kneeling down, he kissed the hands and feet of his royal master, and bathed them with his tears. Atahuallpa, on his part, betrayed not the least emotion, and showed no other sign of satisfaction at the presence of his favorite counsellor, than by simply bidding him welcome. The cold demeanor of the monarch contrasted strangely with the loyal sensibility of the subject.

The rank of the Inca placed him at an immeasurable distance above the proudest of his vassals; and the Spaniards had repeated occasion to admire the ascendency which, even in his present fallen fortunes, he maintained over his people, and the awe with which they approached him. Pedro Pizarro records an interview, at which he was present, between Atahuallpa and one of his great nobles, who had obtained leave to visit some remote part of the country on condition of returning by a certain day. He was detained somewhat beyond the appointed time, and, on entering the presence with a small propitiatory gift for his sovereign, his knees shook so violently, that it seemed, says the chronicler, as if he would have fallen to the ground. His master, however, received him kindly, and dismissed him without a word of rebuke.

Atahuallpa in his confinement continued to receive the same respectful treatment from the Spaniards as hitherto. They taught him to play with dice, and the more intricate game of chess, in which the royal captive became expert, and loved to beguile with it the tedious hours of his imprisonment. Towards his own people he maintained as far as possible his wonted state and ceremonial. He was attended by his wives and the girls of his harem, who, as was customary, waited on him at table and discharged the other menial offices about his person. A body of Indian nobles were stationed in the antechamber, but never entered the presence unbidden; and when they did enter it, they submitted to the same humiliating ceremonies imposed on the greatest of his subjects. The service of his table was gold and silver plate. His dress, which he often changed, was composed of the wool of the vicuña wrought into mantles, so fine that it had the appearance of silk. He sometimes exchanged these for a robe made of the skins of bats, as soft and sleek as velvet. Round his head he wore the *llautu,* a woollen turban or shawl of the most delicate texture, wreathed in folds of various bright colors; and he still continued to encircle his temples with the *borla,* the crimson threads of which, mingled with gold, descended so as partly to conceal his eyes. The image of royalty had charms for him, when its substance had departed. No garment or utensil that had once belonged to the Peruvian sovereign could ever be used by another. When he laid it aside, it was carefully deposited in a chest, kept for the purpose, and afterwards burned. It would have been sacrilege to apply to vulgar uses that which had been consecrated by the touch of the Inca.

Not long after the arrival of the party from Pachacamac,

in the latter part of May, the three emissaries returned from Cuzco. They had been very successful in their mission. Owing to the Inca's order, and the awe which the white men now inspired throughout the country, the Spaniards had everywhere met with a kind reception. They had been carried on the shoulders of the natives in the *hamacas*, or sedans, of the country; and, as they had travelled all the way to the capital on the great imperial road, along which relays of Indian carriers were established at stated intervals, they performed this journey of more than six hundred miles, not only without inconvenience, but with the most luxurious ease. They passed through many populous towns, and always found the simple natives disposed to venerate them as beings of a superior nature. In Cuzco they were received with public festivities, were sumptuously lodged, and had every want anticipated by the obsequious devotion of the inhabitants.

Their accounts of the capital confirmed all that Pizarro had before heard of the wealth and population of the city. Though they had remained more than a week in this place, the emissaries had not seen the whole of it. The great temple of the Sun they found literally covered with plates of gold. They had entered the interior and beheld the royal mummies, seated each in his gold-embossed chair, and in robes profusely covered with ornaments. The Spaniards had the grace to respect these, as they had been previously enjoined by the Inca; but they required that the plates which garnished the walls should be all removed. The Peruvians most reluctantly acquiesced in the commands of their sovereign to desecrate the national temple, which every inhabitant of the city regarded with peculiar pride and veneration. With less reluctance they assisted the Conquerors in stripping the ornaments from some of the other edifices, where the gold, however, being mixed with a large proportion of alloy, was of much less value.

The number of plates they tore from the Temple of the Sun was seven hundred; and though of no great thickness, probably they are compared in size to the lid of a chest, ten or twelve inches wide. A cornice of pure gold encircled the edifice, but so strongly set in the stone, that it fortunately defied the efforts of the spoilers. The Spaniards complained of the want of alacrity shown by the Indians in the work of destruction, and said that there were other parts of the city containing buildings rich in gold and silver which they had not been allowed to see. In truth, their mission, which, at best, was a most ungrateful one, had been rendered doubly annoying by the manner in which they had executed it. The emissaries were men of a very low stamp, and, puffed up by the honors conceded to them by the natives, they looked on themselves as entitled to these, and contemned the poor Indians as a race immeasurably beneath the European. They not only showed the most disgusting rapacity, but treated the highest nobles with wanton insolence. They even went so far, it is said, as to violate the privacy of the convents, and to outrage the religious sentiments of the Peruvians by their scandalous amours with the Virgins of the Sun. The people of Cuzco were so exasperated, that they would have laid violent hands on them, but for their habitual reverence for the Inca, in whose name the Spaniards had come there. As it was, the Indians collected as much gold as was necessary to satisfy their unworthy visitors, and got rid of them as speedily as possible. It was a great mistake in Pizarro to send such men. There were persons, even in his company, who, as other occasions showed, had some sense of self-respect, if not respect for the natives.

The messengers brought with them, besides silver, full two hundred *cargas* or loads of gold. This was an important accession to the contributions of Atahuallpa; and, although the treasure was still considerably below the mark prescribed, the monarch saw with satisfaction the time drawing nearer for the completion of his ransom.

Not long before this, an event had occurred which changed the condition of the Spaniards, and had an unfavorable influence on the fortunes of the Inca. This was the arrival of Almagro at Caxamalca, with a strong reinforcement. That chief had succeeded, after great efforts, in equipping three vessels, and assembling a body of one hundred and fifty men, with which he sailed from Panamá, the latter part of the preceding year. On his voyage, he was joined by a small additional force from Nicaragua, so that his whole strength amounted to one hundred and fifty foot and fifty horse, well provided with the munitions of war. His vessels were steered by the old pilot Ruiz; but after making the Bay of St. Matthew, he crept slowly along the coast, baffled as usual by winds and currents, and experiencing all the hardships incident to that protracted navigation. From some cause or other, he was not so fortunate as to obtain tidings of Pizarro; and so disheartened were his followers, most of whom were raw adventurers, that, when arrived at Puerto Viejo, they proposed to abandon the expedition, and return at once to Panamá. Fortunately, one of the little squadron which Almagro had sent forward to Tumbez brought intelligence of Pizarro and of the colony he had planted at San Miguel. Cheered by the tidings, the cavalier resumed his voyage, and succeeded, at length, towards the close of December, 1532, in bringing his whole party safe to the Spanish settlement.

He there received the account of Pizarro's march across the mountains, his seizure of the Inca, and, soon afterwards, of the enormous ransom offered for his liberation. Almagro and his companions listened with undisguised amazement to this account of his associate, and of a change in his fortunes so rapid and wonderful that it seemed little less than magic. At the same time, he received a caution from some of the colonists not to trust himself in the power of Pizarro, who was known to bear him no good-will.

Not long after Almagro's arrival at San Miguel, advices were sent of it to Caxamalca, and a private note from his secretary Perez informed Pizarro that his associate had come with no purpose of coöperating with him, but with the intention to establish an independent government. Both of the Spanish captains seem to have been surrounded by mean and turbulent spirits, who sought to embroil them with each other, trusting, doubtless, to find their own account in the rupture. However, their malicious machinations failed.

Pizarro was overjoyed at the arrival of so considerable a reinforcement, which would enable him to push his fortunes as he had desired, and go forward with the conquest of the country. He laid little stress on the secretary's communication, since, whatever might have been Almagro's original purpose, Pizarro knew that the richness of the vein he had now opened in the land would be certain to secure his coöperation in working it. He had the magnanimity, therefore,—for there is something magnanimous in being able to stifle the suggestions of a petty rivalry in obedience to sound policy,—to send at once to his ancient comrade, and invite him, with many assurances of friendship, to Caxamalca. Almagro, who was of a frank and careless nature, received the communication in the spirit in which it was made, and, after some necessary delay, directed his march into the interior. But before leaving San Miguel, having become acquainted with the treacherous conduct of his secretary, he recompensed his treason by hanging him on the spot.

Almagro reached Caxamalca about the middle of February, 1533. The soldiers of Pizarro came out to welcome their countrymen, and the two captains embraced each other with every mark of cordial satisfaction. All past differences were buried in oblivion, and they seemed only prepared to aid one another in following up the brilliant career now opened to them in the conquest of an empire.

There was one person in Caxamalca on whom this arrival of the Spaniards produced a very different impression from that made on their own countrymen. This was the Inca Atahuallpa. He saw in the new-comers only a new swarm of locusts to devour his unhappy country; and he felt, that, with his enemies thus multiplying around him, the chances were diminished of recovering his freedom, or of maintaining it, if recovered. A little circumstance, insignificant in itself, but magnified by superstition into something formidable, occurred at this time to cast an additional gloom over his situation.

A remarkable appearance, somewhat of the nature of a meteor, or it may have been a comet, was seen in the heavens by some soldiers and pointed out to Atahuallpa. He gazed on it with fixed attention for some minutes, and then exclaimed, with a dejected air, that "a similar sign had been seen in the skies a short time before the death of his father Huayna Capac." From this day a sadness seemed to take possession of him, as he looked with doubt and undefined dread to the future.—Thus it is, that, in seasons of danger, the mind, like the senses, becomes morbidly acute in its perceptions; and the least departure from the regular course of nature, that would have passed unheeded in ordinary times, to the superstitious eye seems pregnant with meaning, as in some way or other connected with the destiny of the individual.

The arrival of Almagro produced a considerable change
in Pizarro's prospects, since it enabled him to resume active
operations, and push forward his conquests in the interior. The
only obstacle in his way was the Inca's ransom, and the Spaniards had patiently waited, till the return of the emissaries from
Cuzco swelled the treasure to a large amount, though still below the stipulated limit. But now their avarice got the better
of their forbearance, and they called loudly for the immediate
division of the gold. To wait longer would only be to invite
the assault of their enemies, allured by a bait so attractive.
While the treasure remained uncounted, no man knew its
value, nor what was to be his own portion. It was better to
distribute it at once, and let every one possess and defend his
own. Several, moreover, were now disposed to return home,
and take their share of the gold with them, where they could
place it in safety. But these were few, while much the larger
part were only anxious to leave their present quarters, and
march at once to Cuzco. More gold, they thought, awaited
them in that capital, than they could get here by prolonging
their stay; while every hour was precious, to prevent the inhabitants from secreting their treasures, of which design they
had already given indication.

Pizarro was especially moved by the last consideration; and
he felt, that, without the capital, he could not hope to become
master of the empire. Without further delay, the division of
the treasure was agreed upon.

Yet, before making this, it was necessary to reduce the
whole to ingots of a uniform standard, for the spoil was composed of an infinite variety of articles, in which the gold was

of very different degrees of purity. These articles consisted of goblets, ewers, salvers, vases of every shape and size, ornaments and utensils for the temples and the royal palaces, tiles and plates for the decoration of the public edifices, curious imitations of different plants and animals. Among the plants, the most beautiful was the Indian corn, in which the golden ear was sheathed in its broad leaves of silver, from which hung a rich tassel of threads of the same precious metal. A fountain was also much admired, which sent up a sparkling jet of gold, while birds and animals of the same material played in the waters at its base. The delicacy of the workmanship of some of these, and the beauty and ingenuity of the design, attracted the admiration of better judges than the rude Conquerors of Peru.

Before breaking up these specimens of Indian art, it was determined to send a quantity, which should be deducted from the royal fifth, to the Emperor. It would serve as a sample of the ingenuity of the natives, and would show him the value of his conquests. A number of the most beautiful articles was selected, to the amount of a hundred thousand ducats, and Hernando Pizarro was appointed to be the bearer of them to Spain. He was to obtain an audience of Charles, and, at the same time that he laid the treasures before him, he was to give an account of the proceedings of the Conquerors, and to seek a further augmentation of their powers and dignities.

No man in the army was better qualified for this mission, by his address and knowledge of affairs, than Hernando Pizarro; no one would be so likely to urge his suit with effect at the haughty Castilian court. But other reasons influenced the selection of him at the present juncture.

His former jealousy of Almagro still rankled in his bosom, and he had beheld that chief's arrival at the camp with feelings of disgust, which he did not care to conceal. He looked on him as coming to share the spoils of victory, and defraud his brother of his legitimate honors. Instead of exchanging the cordial greeting proffered by Almagro at their first interview, the arrogant cavalier held back in sullen silence. His brother Francis was greatly displeased at a conduct which threatened to renew their ancient feud, and he induced Hernando to accompany him to Almagro's quarters, and make some acknowledgment for his uncourteous behavior. But, notwithstanding this show of reconciliation, the general thought the present a favorable opportunity to remove his brother from the scene of operations, where his factious spirit more than counterbalanced his eminent services.

The business of melting down the plate was intrusted to the Indian goldsmiths, who were thus required to undo the work of their own hands. They toiled day and night, but such was the quantity to be recast, that it consumed a full month. When the whole was reduced to bars of a uniform standard, they were nicely weighed, under the superintendence of the royal inspectors. The total amount of the gold was found to be one million, three hundred and twenty-six thousand, five hundred and thirty-nine *pesos de oro*, which, allowing for the greater value of money in the sixteenth century, would be equivalent, probably, at the present time, to near *three millions and a half of pounds sterling*, or somewhat less than *fifteen millions and a half of dollars*. The quantity of silver was estimated at fifty-one thousand six hundred and ten marks. History affords no parallel of such a booty—and that, too, in the most convertible form, in ready money, as it were—having fallen to the lot of a little band of military adventurers, like the Conquerors of Peru. The great object of the Spanish expeditions in the New World was gold. It is remarkable that their success should have been so complete. Had they taken the track of the English, the French, or the Dutch, on the shores of the northern continent, how different would have been the result! It is equally worthy of remark, that the wealth thus suddenly acquired, by diverting them from the slow but surer and more permanent sources of national prosperity, has in the end glided from their grasp, and left them among the poorest of the nations of Christendom.

A new difficulty now arose in respect to the division of the treasure. Almagro's followers claimed to be admitted to a share of it; which, as they equalled, and indeed, somewhat exceeded in number Pizarro's company, would reduce the gains of these last very materially. "We were not here, it is true," said Almagro's soldiers to their comrades, "at the seizure of the Inca, but we have taken our turn in mounting guard over him since his capture, have helped you to defend your treasures, and now give you the means of going forward and securing your conquests. It is a common cause," they urged, "in which all are equally embarked, and the gains should be shared equally between us."

But this way of viewing the matter was not at all palatable to Pizarro's company, who alleged that Atahuallpa's contract had been made exclusively with them; that they had seized the Inca, had secured the ransom, had incurred, in short, all the risk of the enterprise, and were not now disposed to share the fruits of it with every one who came after them.—There was much force, it could not be denied, in this reasoning, and it was finally settled between the leaders, that Almagro's followers should resign their pretensions for a stipulated sum of no great amount, and look to the career now opened to them for carving out their fortunes for themselves.

This delicate affair being thus harmoniously adjusted, Pizarro prepared, with all solemnity, for a division of the imperial spoil. The troops were called together in the great square, and the Spanish commander, "with the fear of God before his eyes," says the record, "invoked the assistance of Heaven to do the work before him conscientiously and justly." The appeal may seem somewhat out of place at the distribution of spoil so unrighteously acquired; yet, in truth, considering the magnitude of the treasure, and the power assumed by Pizarro to distribute it according to the respective deserts of the individuals, there were few acts of his life involving a heavier responsibility. On his present decision might be said to hang the future fortunes of each one of his followers,—poverty or independence during the remainder of his days.

The royal fifth was first deducted, including the remittance already sent to Spain. The share appropriated by Pizarro amounted to fifty-seven thousand two hundred and twenty-two pesos of gold, and two thousand three hundred and fifty marks of silver. He had besides this the great chair or throne of the Inca, of solid gold, and valued at twenty-five thousand *pesos de oro*. To his brother Hernando were paid thirty-one thousand and eighty pesos of gold, and two thousand three hundred and fifty marks of silver. De Soto received seventeen thousand seven hundred and forty pesos of gold, and seven hundred and twenty-four marks of silver. Most of the remaining cavalry, sixty in number, received each eight thousand eight hundred and eighty pesos of gold, and three hundred and sixty-two marks of silver, though some had more, and a few considerably less. The infantry mustered in all one hundred and five men. Almost one fifth of them were allowed, each, four thousand four hundred and forty pesos of gold, and one hundred and eighty marks of silver, half of the compensation of the troopers. The remainder received one fourth part less; though here again there were exceptions, and some were obliged to content themselves with a much smaller share of the spoil.

The new church of San Francisco, the first Christian temple in Peru, was endowed with two thousand two hundred and twenty pesos of gold. The amount assigned to Almagro's company was not excessive, if it was not more than twenty thousand pesos; and that reserved for the colonists of San Miguel, which amounted only to fifteen thousand pesos, was unaccountably small. There were among them certain soldiers, who at an early period of the expedition, as the reader may remember, abandoned the march, and returned to San Miguel. These, certainly, had little claim to be remembered in the division of booty. But the greater part of the colony consisted of invalids, men whose health had been broken by their previous hardships, but who still, with a stout and willing heart, did good service in their military post on the sea-coast. On what grounds they had forfeited their claims to a more ample remuneration, it is not easy to explain.

Nothing is said, in the partition, of Almagro himself, who, by the terms of the original contract, might claim an equal share of the spoil with his associate. As little notice is taken of Luque, the remaining partner. Luque himself, was, indeed, no longer to be benefited by worldly treasure. He had died a short time before Almagro's departure from Panamá; too soon to learn the full success of the enterprise, which, but for his exertions, must have failed; too soon to become acquainted with the achievements and the crimes of Pizarro. But the Licentiate Espinosa, whom he represented, and who, it appears, had advanced the funds for the expedition, was still living at St. Domingo, and Luque's pretensions were explicitly transferred to him. Yet it is unsafe to pronounce, at this distance of time, on the authority of mere negative testimony; and it must be admitted to form a strong presumption in favor of Pizarro's general equity in the distribution, that no complaint of it has reached us from any of the parties present, nor from contemporary chroniclers.

The division of the ransom being completed by the Spaniards, there seemed to be no further obstacle to their resuming active operations, and commencing the march to Cuzco. But what was to be done with Atahuallpa? In the determination of this question, whatever was expedient was just. To liberate him would be to set at large the very man who might prove their most dangerous enemy; one whose birth and royal station would rally round him the whole nation, place all the machinery of government at his control, and all its resources, —one, in short, whose bare word might concentrate all the energies of his people against the Spaniards, and thus delay for a long period, if not wholly defeat, the conquest of the country. Yet to hold him in captivity was attended with scarcely less difficulty; since to guard so important a prize would require such a division of their force as must greatly cripple its strength, and how could they expect, by any vigilance, to secure their prisoner against rescue in the perilous passes of the mountains?

The Inca himself now loudly demanded his freedom. The proposed amount of the ransom had, indeed, not been fully paid. It may be doubted whether it ever would have been, considering the embarrassments thrown in the way by the guardians of the temples, who seemed disposed to secrete the treasures, rather than despoil these sacred depositories to satisfy the cupidity of the strangers. It was unlucky, too, for the Indian monarch, that much of the gold, and that of the best quality, consisted of flat plates or tiles, which, however valuable, lay in a compact form that did little towards swelling the heap. But an immense amount had been already realized, and it would have been a still greater one, the Inca might allege, but for the impatience of the Spaniards. At all events, it was a magnificent ransom, such as was never paid by prince or potentate before.

These considerations Atahuallpa urged on several of the cavaliers, and especially on Hernando de Soto, who was on terms of more familiarity with him than Pizarro. De Soto reported Atahuallpa's demands to his leader; but the latter evaded a direct reply. He did not disclose the dark purposes over which his mind was brooding. Not long afterwards he caused the notary to prepare an instrument, in which he fully acquitted the Inca of further obligation in respect to the ransom. This he commanded to be publicly proclaimed in the camp, while at the same time he openly declared that the safety of the Spaniards required, that the Inca should be detained in confinement until they were strengthened by additional reinforcements.

Meanwhile the old rumors of a meditated attack by the natives began to be current among the soldiers. They were repeated from one to another, gaining something by every repetition. An immense army, it was reported, was mustering at Quito, the land of Atahuallpa's birth, and thirty thousand Caribs were on their way to support it. The Caribs were distributed by the early Spaniards rather indiscriminately over the different parts of America, being invested with peculiar horrors as a race of cannibals.

It was not easy to trace the origin of these rumors. There was in the camp a considerable number of Indians, who belonged to the party of Huascar, and who were, of course, hostile to Atahuallpa. But his worst enemy was Felipillo, the interpreter from Tumbez, already mentioned in these pages. This youth had conceived a passion, or, as some say, had been detected in an intrigue with, one of the royal concubines. The circumstance had reached the ears of Atahuallpa, who felt himself deeply outraged by it. "That such an insult should have been offered by so base a person was an indignity," he said, "more difficult to bear than his imprisonment"; and he told Pizarro, "that, by the Peruvian law, it could be expiated, not by the criminal's own death alone, but by that of his whole family and kindred." But Felipillo was too important to the Spaniards to be dealt with so summarily; nor did they probably attach such consequence to an offence which, if report be true, they had countenanced by their own example. Felipillo, however, soon learned the state of the Inca's feelings towards himself, and from that moment he regarded him with deadly hatred. Unfortunately, his malignant temper found ready means for its indulgence.

The rumors of a rising among the natives pointed to Atahuallpa as the author of it. Challcuchima was examined on the subject, but avowed his entire ignorance of any such design, which he pronounced a malicious slander. Pizarro next laid the matter before the Inca himself, repeating to him the stories in circulation, with the air of one who believed them. "What treason is this," said the general, "that you have meditated against me,—me, who have ever treated you with honor, confiding in your words, as in those of a brother?" "You jest," replied the Inca, who, perhaps, did not feel the weight of this confidence; "you are always jesting with me. How could I or my people think of conspiring against men so valiant as the Spaniards? Do not jest with me thus, I beseech you." "This," continues Pizarro's secretary, "he said in the most composed and natural manner, smiling all the while to dissemble his falsehood, so that we were all amazed to find such cunning in a barbarian."

But it was not with cunning, but with the consciousness of innocence, as the event afterwards proved, that Atahuallpa thus spoke to Pizarro. He readily discerned, however, the causes, perhaps the consequences, of the accusation. He saw a dark gulf opening beneath his feet; and he was surrounded by strangers, on none of whom he could lean for counsel or protection. The life of the captive monarch is usually short; and Atahuallpa might have learned the truth of this, when he thought of Huascar. Bitterly did he now lament the absence of Hernando Pizarro, for, strange as it may seem, the haughty spirit of this cavalier had been touched by the condition of the royal prisoner, and he had treated him with a deference which won for him the peculiar regard and confidence of the Indian. Yet the latter lost no time in endeavoring to efface the general's suspicions, and to establish his own innocence. "Am I not," said he to Pizarro, "a poor captive in your hands? How could I harbor the designs you impute to me, when I should be the first victim of the outbreak? And you little know my people, if you think that such a movement would be made without my orders; when the very birds in my dominions," said he, with somewhat of an hyperbole, "would scarcely venture to fly contrary to my will."

But these protestations of innocence had little effect on the

troops; among whom the story of a general rising of the natives continued to gain credit every hour. A large force, it was
said, was already gathered at Guamachucho, not a hundred
miles from the camp, and their assault might be hourly expected. The treasure which the Spaniards had acquired afforded a tempting prize, and their own alarm was increased
by the apprehension of losing it. The patrols were doubled.
The horses were kept saddled and bridled. The soldiers slept
on their arms; Pizarro went the rounds regularly to see that
every sentinel was on his post. The little army, in short, was
in a state of preparation for instant attack.

Men suffering from fear are not likely to be too scrupulous
as to the means of removing the cause of it. Murmurs, mingled
with gloomy menaces, were now heard against the Inca, the
author of these machinations. Many began to demand his life
as necessary to the safety of the army. Among these, the most
vehement were Almagro and his followers. They had not witnessed the seizure of Atahuallpa. They had no sympathy with
him in his fallen state. They regarded him only as an encumbrance, and their desire now was to push their fortunes in
the country, since they had got so little of the gold of Caxamalca. They were supported by Riquelme, the treasurer, and
by the rest of the royal officers. These men had been left at
San Miguel by Pizarro, who did not care to have such official
spies on his movements. But they had come to the camp with
Almagro, and they loudly demanded the Inca's death, as indispensable to the tranquillity of the country, and the interests
of the Crown.

To these dark suggestions Pizarro turned—or seemed to turn
—an unwilling ear, showing visible reluctance to proceed to
extreme measures with his prisoner. There were some few, and
among others Hernando de Soto, who supported him in these
views, and who regarded such measures as not at all justified
by the evidence of Atahuallpa's guilt. In this state of things,
the Spanish commander determined to send a small detachment to Guamachucho, to reconnoitre the country and ascertain what ground there was for the rumors of an insurrection.
De Soto was placed at the head of the expedition, which, as
the distance was not great, would occupy but a few days.

After that cavalier's departure, the agitation among the soldiers, instead of diminishing, increased to such a degree, that Pizarro, unable to resist their importunities, consented to bring Atahuallpa to trial. It was but decent, and certainly safer, to have the forms of a trial. A court was organized, over which the two captains, Pizarro and Almagro, were to preside as judges. An attorney-general was named to prosecute for the Crown, and counsel was assigned to the prisoner.

The charges preferred against the Inca, drawn up in the form of interrogatories, were twelve in number. The most important were, that he had usurped the crown and assassinated his brother Huascar; that he had squandered the public revenues since the conquest of the country by the Spaniards, and lavished them on his kindred and his minions; that he was guilty of idolatry, and of adulterous practices, indulging openly in a plurality of wives; finally, that he had attempted to excite an insurrection against the Spaniards.

These charges, most of which had reference to national usages, or to the personal relations of the Inca, over which the Spanish conquerors had clearly no jurisdiction, are so absurd, that they might well provoke a smile, did they not excite a deeper feeling. The last of the charges was the only one of moment in such a trial; and the weakness of this may be inferred from the care taken to bolster it up with the others. The mere specification of the articles must have been sufficient to show that the doom of the Inca was already sealed.

A number of Indian witnesses were examined, and their testimony, filtrated through the interpretation of Felipillo, received, it is said, when necessary, a very different coloring from that of the original. The examination was soon ended, and "a warm discussion," as we are assured by one of Pizarro's own secretaries, "took place in respect to the probable good or evil that would result from the death of Atahuallpa." It was a question of expediency. He was found guilty,—whether of all the crimes alleged we are not informed,—and he was sentenced to be burnt alive in the great square of Caxamalca. The sentence was to be carried into execution that very night. They were not even to wait for the return of De Soto, when the information he would bring would go far to establish the truth or the falsehood of the reports respecting the insurrection of the natives. It was desirable to obtain the countenance of Father Valverde to these proceedings, and a copy of the judgment was submitted to the friar for his signature, which he gave without hesitation, declaring, that, "in his opinion, the Inca, at all events, deserved death."

Yet there were some few in that martial conclave who resisted these high-handed measures. They considered them as a poor requital of all the favors bestowed on them by the Inca, who hitherto had received at their hands nothing but wrong. They objected to the evidence as wholly insufficient; and they denied the authority of such a tribunal to sit in judgment on a sovereign prince in the heart of his own dominions. If he were to be tried, he should be sent to Spain, and his cause brought before the Emperor, who alone had power to determine it.

But the great majority—and they were ten to one—overruled these objections, by declaring there was no doubt of Atahuallpa's guilt, and they were willing to assume the responsibility of his punishment. A full account of the proceedings would be sent to Castile, and the Emperor should be informed who were the loyal servants of the Crown, and who were its enemies. The dispute ran so high, that for a time it menaced an open and violent rupture; till, at length, convinced that resistance was fruitless, the weaker party, silenced, but not satisfied, contented themselves with entering a written protest against these proceedings, which would leave an indelible stain on the names of all concerned in them.

When the sentence was communicated to the Inca, he was greatly overcome by it. He had, indeed, for some time, looked to such an issue as probable, and had been heard to intimate as much to those about him. But the probability of such an event is very different from its certainty,—and that, too, so sudden and speedy. For a moment, the overwhelming conviction of it unmanned him, and he exclaimed, with tears in his eyes, —"What have I done, or my children, that I should meet such a fate? And from your hands, too," said he, addressing Pizarro; "you, who have met with friendship and kindness from my people, with whom I have shared my treasures, who have received nothing but benefits from my hands!" In the most piteous tones, he then implored that his life might be spared, promising any guaranty that might be required for the safety of every Spaniard in the army,—promising double the ransom he had already paid, if time were only given him to obtain it.

An eyewitness assures us that Pizarro was visibly affected, as he turned away from the Inca, to whose appeal he had no power to listen, in opposition to the voice of the army, and to his own sense of what was due to the security of the country. Atahuallpa, finding he had no power to turn his Conqueror from his purpose, recovered his habitual self-possession, and from that moment submitted himself to his fate with the courage of an Indian warrior.

The doom of the Inca was proclaimed by sound of trumpet in the great square of Caxamalca; and, two hours after sunset, the Spanish soldiery assembled by torch-light in the *plaza* to witness the execution of the sentence. It was on the twenty-ninth of August, 1533. Atahuallpa was led out chained hand and foot,—for he had been kept in irons ever since the great excitement had prevailed in the army respecting an assault. Father Vicente de Valverde was at his side, striving to administer consolation, and, if possible, to persuade him at this last hour to abjure his superstition and embrace the religion of his Conquerors. He was willing to save the soul of his victim from the terrible expiation in the next world, to which he had so cheerfully consigned his mortal part in this.

During Atahuallpa's confinement, the friar had repeatedly expounded to him the Christian doctrines, and the Indian monarch discovered much acuteness in apprehending the discourse of his teacher. But it had not carried conviction to his mind, and though he listened with patience, he had shown no disposition to renounce the faith of his fathers. The Dominican made a last appeal to him in this solemn hour; and, when Atahuallpa was bound to the stake, with the fagots that were to kindle his funeral pile lying around him, Valverde, holding up the cross, besought him to embrace it and be baptized, promising that, by so doing, the painful death to which he had been sentenced should be commuted for the milder form of the *garrote*,—a mode of punishment by strangulation, used for criminals in Spain.

The unhappy monarch asked if this were really so, and, on its being confirmed by Pizarro, he consented to abjure his own religion, and receive baptism. The ceremony was performed by Father Valverde, and the new convert received the name

of Juan de Atahuallpa,—the name of Juan being conferred in
honor of John the Baptist, on whose day the event took place.

Atahuallpa expressed a desire that his remains might be
transported to Quito, the place of his birth, to be preserved
with those of his maternal ancestors. Then turning to Pizarro,
as a last request, he implored him to take compassion on his
young children, and receive them under his protection. Was
there no other one in that dark company who stood grimly
around him, to whom he could look for the protection of his
offspring? Perhaps he thought there was no other so competent
to afford it, and that the wishes so solemnly expressed in that
hour might meet with respect even from his Conqueror. Then,
recovering his stoical bearing, which for a moment had been
shaken, he submitted himself calmly to his fate,—while the
Spaniards, gathering around, muttered their *credos* for the salvation of his soul! Thus by the death of a vile malefactor
perished the last of the Incas!

I have already spoken of the person and the qualities of
Atahuallpa. He had a handsome countenance, though with
an expression somewhat too fierce to be pleasing. His frame
was muscular and well-proportioned; his air commanding; and
his deportment in the Spanish quarters had a degree of refinement, the more interesting that it was touched with melancholy. He is accused of having been cruel in his wars, and
bloody in his revenge. It may be true, but the pencil of an
enemy would be likely to overcharge the shadows of the portrait. He is allowed to have been bold, high-minded, and liberal. All agree that he showed singular penetration and quick-
ness of perception. His exploits as a warrior had placed his
valor beyond dispute. The best homage to it is the reluctance
shown by the Spaniards to restore him to freedom. They
dreaded him as an enemy, and they had done him too many
wrongs to think that he could be their friend. Yet his conduct
towards them from the first had been most friendly; and they
repaid it with imprisonment, robbery, and death.

The body of the Inca remained on the place of execution
through the night. The following morning it was removed to
the church of San Francisco, where his funeral obsequies were
performed with great solemnity. Pizarro and the principal cavaliers went into mourning, and the troops listened with devout

attention to the service of the dead from the lips of Father
Valverde. The ceremony was interrupted by the sound of loud
cries and wailing, as of many voices at the doors of the church.
These were suddenly thrown open, and a number of Indian
women, the wives and sisters of the deceased, rushing up the
great aisle, surrounded the corpse. This was not the way, they
cried, to celebrate the funeral rites of an Inca; and they declared their intention to sacrifice themselves on his tomb, and
bear him company to the land of spirits. The audience, outraged by this frantic behaviour, told the intruders that Atahuallpa had died in the faith of a Christian, and that the God
of the Christians abhorred such sacrifices. They then caused
the women to be excluded from the church, and several, retiring to their own quarters, laid violent hands on themselves,
in the vain hope of accompanying their beloved lord to the
bright mansions of the Sun.

Atahuallpa's remains, notwithstanding his request, were laid
in the cemetery of San Francisco. But from thence, as is reported, after the Spaniards left Caxamalca, they were secretly
removed, and carried, as he had desired, to Quito. The colonists of a later time supposed that some treasures might have
been buried with the body. But, on excavating the ground,
neither treasure nor remains were to be discovered.

A day or two after these tragic events, Hernando de Soto
returned from his excursion. Great was his astonishment and
indignation at learning what had been done in his absence.
He sought out Pizarro at once, and found him, says the chronicler, "with a great felt hat, by way of mourning, slouched
over his eyes," and in his dress and demeanor exhibiting all
the show of sorrow. "You have acted rashly," said De Soto to
him bluntly; "Atahuallpa has been basely slandered. There
was no enemy at Guamachucho; no rising among the natives.
I have met with nothing on the road but demonstrations of
good-will, and all is quiet. If it was necessary to bring the
Inca to trial, he should have been taken to Castile and judged
by the Emperor. I would have pledged myself to see him safe
on board the vessel." Pizarro confessed that he had been pre-
cipitate, and said that he had been deceived by Riquelme,
Valverde, and the others. These charges soon reached the
ears of the treasurer and the Dominican, who, in their turn,

exculpated themselves, and upbraided Pizarro to his face, as the only one responsible for the deed. The dispute ran high; and the parties were heard by the by-standers to give one another the lie! This vulgar squabble among the leaders, so soon after the event, is the best commentary on the iniquity of their own proceedings and the innocence of the Inca.

The treatment of Atahuallpa, from first to last, forms undoubtedly one of the darkest chapters in Spanish history. There may have been massacres perpetrated on a more extended scale, and executions accompanied with a greater refinement of cruelty. But the blood-stained annals of the Conquest afford no such example of cold-hearted and systematic persecution, not of an enemy, but of one whose whole deportment had been that of a friend and a benefactor.

From the hour that Pizarro and his followers had entered within the sphere of Atahuallpa's influence, the hand of friendship had been extended to them by the natives. Their first act, on crossing the mountains, was to kidnap the monarch and massacre his people. The seizure of his person might be vindicated, by those who considered the end as justifying the means, on the ground that it was indispensable to secure the triumphs of the Cross. But no such apology can be urged for the massacre of the unarmed and helpless population,—as wanton as it was wicked.

The long confinement of the Inca had been used by the Conquerors to wring from him his treasures with the hard gripe of avarice. During the whole of this dismal period, he had conducted himself with singular generosity and good faith. He had opened a free passage to the Spaniards through every part of his empire; and had furnished every facility for the execution of their plans. When these were accomplished, and he remained an encumbrance on their hands, notwithstanding their engagement, expressed or implied, to release him,—and Pizarro, as we have seen, by a formal act, acquitted his captive of any further obligation on the score of the ransom, —he was arraigned before a mock tribunal, and, under pretences equally false and frivolous, was condemned to an excruciating death. From first to last, the policy of the Spanish conquerors towards their unhappy victim is stamped with barbarity and fraud.

It is not easy to acquit Pizarro of being in a great degree responsible for this policy. His partisans have labored to show, that it was forced on him by the necessity of the case, and that in the death of the Inca, especially, he yielded reluctantly to the importunities of others. But weak as is this apology, the historian who has the means of comparing the various testimony of the period will come to a different conclusion. To him it will appear, that Pizarro had probably long felt the removal of Atahuallpa as essential to the success of his enterprise. He foresaw the odium that would be incurred by the death of his royal captive without sufficient grounds; while he labored to establish these, he still shrunk from the responsibility of the deed, and preferred to perpetrate it in obedience to the suggestions of others, rather than his own. Like many an unprincipled politician, he wished to reap the benefit of a bad act, and let others take the blame of it.

Almagro and his followers are reported by Pizarro's secretaries to have first insisted on the Inca's death. They were loudly supported by the treasurer and the royal officers, who considered it as indispensable to the interests of the Crown; and, finally, the rumors of a conspiracy raised the same cry among the soldiers, and Pizarro, with all his tenderness for his prisoner, could not refuse to bring him to trial.—The form of a trial was necessary to give an appearance of fairness to the proceedings. That it was only form is evident from the indecent haste with which it was conducted,—the examination of evidence, the sentence, and the execution, being all on the same day. The multiplication of the charges, designed to place the guilt of the accused on the strongest ground, had, from their very number, the opposite effect, proving only the determination to convict him. If Pizarro had felt the reluctance to his conviction which he pretended, why did he send De Soto, Atahuallpa's best friend, away, when the inquiry was to be instituted? Why was the sentence so summarily executed, as not to afford opportunity, by that cavalier's return, of disproving the truth of the principal charge,—the only one, in fact, with which the Spaniards had any concern? The solemn farce of mourning and deep sorrow affected by Pizarro, who by these honors to the dead would intimate the sincere regard he had entertained for the living, was too thin a veil to impose on the most credulous.

It is not intended by these reflections to exculpate the rest of the army, and especially its officers, from their share in the infamy of the transaction. But Pizarro, as commander of the army, was mainly responsible for its measures. For he was not a man to allow his own authority to be wrested from his grasp, or to yield timidly to the impulses of others. He did not even yield to his own. His whole career shows him, whether for good or for evil, to have acted with a cool and calculating policy.

A story has been often repeated, which refers the motives of Pizarro's conduct, in some degree at least, to personal resentment. The Inca had requested one of the Spanish soldiers to write the name of God on his nail. This the monarch showed to several of his guards successively, and, as they read it, and each pronounced the same word, the sagacious mind of the barbarian was delighted with what seemed to him little short of a miracle,—to which the science of his own nation afforded no analogy. On showing the writing to Pizarro, that chief remained silent; and the Inca, finding he could not read, conceived a contempt for the commander who was even less informed than his soldiers. This he did not wholly conceal, and Pizarro, aware of the cause of it, neither forgot nor forgave it. The anecdote is reported not on the highest authority. It may be true; but it is unnecessary to look for the motives of Pizarro's conduct in personal pique, when so many proofs are to be discerned of a dark and deliberate policy.

Yet the arts of the Spanish chieftain failed to reconcile his countrymen to the atrocity of his proceedings. It is singular to observe the difference between the tone assumed by the first chroniclers of the transaction, while it was yet fresh, and that of those who wrote when the lapse of a few years had shown the tendency of public opinion. The first boldly avow the deed as demanded by expediency, if not necessity; while they deal in no measured terms of reproach with the character of their unfortunate victim. The latter, on the other hand, while they extenuate the errors of the Inca, and do justice to his good faith, are unreserved in their condemnation of the Conquerors, on whose conduct, they say, Heaven set the seal of its own reprobation, by bringing them all to an untimely and miserable end. The sentence of contemporaries has been fully ratified by that of posterity; and the persecution of Atahuallpa is regarded with justice as having left a stain, never to be effaced, on the Spanish arms in the New World.

CHAPTER VIII [1533–1534]

DISORDERS IN PERU—MARCH TO CUZCO—ENCOUNTER
WITH THE NATIVES—CHALLCUCHIMA BURNT—ARRIVAL
IN CUZCO—DESCRIPTION OF THE CITY—TREASURE
FOUND THERE

The Inca of Peru was its sovereign in a peculiar sense.
He received an obedience from his vassals more implicit than
that of any despot; for his authority reached to the most secret
conduct,—to the thoughts of the individual. He was reverenced
as more than human. He was not merely the head of the state,
but the point to which all its institutions converged, as to a
common centre,—the keystone of the political fabric, which
must fall to pieces by its own weight when that was withdrawn. So it fared on the death of Atahuallpa. His death not
only left the throne vacant, without any certain successor, but
the manner of it announced to the Peruvian people that a
hand stronger than that of their Incas had now seized the
sceptre, and that the dynasty of the Children of the Sun had
passed away for ever.

The natural consequences of such a conviction followed.
The beautiful order of the ancient institutions was broken up,
as the authority which controlled it was withdrawn. The Indians broke out into greater excesses from the uncommon restraint to which they had been before subjected. Villages were
burnt, temples and palaces were plundered, and the gold they
contained was scattered or secreted. Gold and silver acquired
an importance in the eyes of the Peruvian, when he saw the
importance attached to them by his conquerors. The precious
metals, which before served only for purposes of state or religious decoration, were now hoarded up and buried in caves
and forests. The gold and silver concealed by the natives were
affirmed greatly to exceed in quantity that which fell into the
hands of the Spaniards. The remote provinces now shook off
their allegiance to the Incas. Their great captains, at the head

of distant armies, set up for themselves. Ruminavi, a commander on the borders of Quito, sought to detach that kingdom from the Peruvian empire, and to reassert its ancient independence. The country, in short, was in that state, in which old things are passing away, and the new order of things has not yet been established. It was in a state of revolution.

The authors of the revolution, Pizarro and his followers, remained meanwhile at Caxamalca. But the first step of the Spanish commander was to name a successor to Atahuallpa. It would be easier to govern under the venerated authority to which the homage of the Indians had been so long paid; and it was not difficult to find a successor. The true heir to the crown was a second son of Huayna Capac, named Manco, a legitimate brother of the unfortunate Huascar. But Pizarro had too little knowledge of the dispositions of this prince; and he made no scruple to prefer a brother of Atahuallpa, and to present him to the Indian nobles as their future Inca. We know nothing of the character of the young Toparca, who probably resigned himself without reluctance to a destiny which, however humiliating in some points of view, was more exalted than he could have hoped to obtain in the regular course of events. The ceremonies attending a Peruvian coronation were observed, as well as time would allow; the brows of the young Inca were encircled with the imperial *borla* by the hands of his conqueror, and he received the homage of his Indian vassals. They were the less reluctant to pay it, as most of the men in the camp belonged to the faction of Quito.

All thoughts were now eagerly turned towards Cuzco, of which the most glowing accounts were circulated among the soldiers, and whose temples and royal palaces were represented as blazing with gold and silver. With imaginations thus excited, Pizarro and his entire company, amounting to almost five hundred men, of whom nearly a third, probably, were cavalry, took their departure early in September from Caxamalca,—a place ever memorable as the theatre of some of the most strange and sanguinary scenes recorded in history. All set forward in high spirits,—the soldiers of Pizarro from the expectation of doubling their present riches, and Almagro's followers from the prospect of sharing equally in the spoil with "the first conquerors." The young Inca and their old chief

Challcuchima accompanied the march in their litters, attended by a numerous retinue of vassals, and moving in as much state and ceremony as if in the possession of real power.

Their course lay along the great road of the Incas, which stretched across the elevated regions of the Cordilleras, all the way to Cuzco. It was of nearly a uniform breadth, though constructed with different degrees of care, according to the ground. Sometimes it crossed smooth and level valleys, which offered of themselves little impediment to the traveller; at other times, it followed the course of a mountain stream that wound round the base of some beetling cliff, leaving small space for the foothold; at others, again, where the sierra was so precipitous that it seemed to preclude all further progress, the road, accommodated to the natural sinuosities of the ground, wound round the heights which it would have been impossible to scale directly.

But although managed with great address, it was a formidable passage for the cavalry. The mountain was hewn into steps, but the rocky ledges cut up the hoofs of the horses; and, though the troopers dismounted and led them by the bridle, they suffered severely in their efforts to keep their footing. The road was constructed for man and the light-footed llama; and the only heavy beast of burden at all suited to it was the sagacious and sure-footed mule, with which the Spanish adventurers were not then provided. It was a singular chance that Spain was the land of the mule; and thus the country was speedily supplied with the very animal which seems to have been created for the difficult passes of the Cordilleras.

Another obstacle, often occurring, was the deep torrents that rushed down in fury from the Andes. They were traversed by the hanging bridges of osier, whose frail materials were after a time broken up by the heavy tread of the cavalry, and the holes made in them added materially to the dangers of the passage. On such occasions, the Spaniards contrived to work their way across the rivers on rafts, swimming their horses by the bridle.

All along the route, they found post-houses for the accommodation of the royal couriers, established at regular intervals; and magazines of grain and other commodities, provided in the principal towns for the Indian armies. The Spaniards profited by the prudent forecast of the Peruvian government.

Passing through several hamlets and towns of some note, the principal of which were Guamachucho and Guanuco, Pizarro, after a tedious march, came in sight of the rich valley of Xauxa. The march, though tedious, had been attended with little suffering, except in crossing the bristling crests of the Cordilleras, which occasionally obstructed their path,—a rough setting to the beautiful valleys, that lay scattered like gems along this elevated region. In the mountain passes they found some inconvenience from the cold; since, to move more quickly, they had disencumbered themselves of all superfluous baggage, and were even unprovided with tents. The bleak winds of the mountains penetrated the thick harness of the soldiers; but the poor Indians, more scantily clothed and accustomed to a tropical climate, suffered most severely. The Spaniard seemed to have a hardihood of body, as of soul, that rendered him almost indifferent to climate.

On the march they had not been molested by enemies. But more than once they had seen vestiges of them in smoking hamlets and ruined bridges. Reports, from time to time, had reached Pizarro of warriors on his track; and small bodies of Indians were occasionally seen like dusky clouds on the verge of the horizon, which vanished as the Spaniards approached. On reaching Xauxa, however, these clouds gathered into one dark mass of warriors, which formed on the opposite bank of the river that flowed through the valley.

The Spaniards advanced to the stream, which, swollen by the melting of the snows, was now of considerable width, though not deep. The bridge had been destroyed; but the Conquerors, without hesitation, dashing boldly in, advanced, swimming and wading, as they best could, to the opposite bank. The Indians, disconcerted by this decided movement, as they had relied on their watery defences, took to flight, after letting off an impotent volley of missiles. Fear gave wings to the fugitives; but the horse and his rider were swifter, and the victorious pursuers took bloody vengeance on their enemy for having dared even to meditate resistance.

Xauxa was a considerable town. It was the place already noticed as having been visited by Hernando Pizarro. It was

seated in the midst of a verdant valley, fertilized by a thousand little rills, which the thrifty Indian husbandman drew
from the parent river that rolled sluggishly through the meadows. There were several capacious buildings of rough stone in
the town, and a temple of some note in the times of the Incas.
But the strong arm of Father Valverde and his countrymen
soon tumbled the heathen deities from their pride of place,
and established, in their stead, the sacred effigies of the Virgin and Child.

Here Pizarro proposed to halt for some days, and to found a
Spanish colony. It was a favorable position, he thought, for
holding the Indian mountaineers in check, while, at the same
time, it afforded an easy communication with the sea-coast.
Meanwhile he determined to send forward De Soto, with a
detachment of sixty horse, to reconnoitre the country in
advance, and to restore the bridges where demolished by the
enemy.

That active cavalier set forward at once, but found considerable impediments to his progress. The traces of an enemy
became more frequent as he advanced. The villages were
burnt, the bridges destroyed, and heavy rocks and trees
strewed in the path to impede the march of the cavalry. As
he drew near to Bilcas, once an important place, though now
effaced from the map, he had a sharp encounter with the natives, in a mountain defile, which cost him the lives of two or
three troopers. The loss was light; but any loss was felt by the
Spaniards, so little accustomed as they had been of late, to
resistance.

Still pressing forward, the Spanish captain crossed the river
Abancay, and the broad waters of the Apurimac; and, as he
drew near the sierra of Vilcaconga, he learned that a considerable body of Indians lay in wait for him in the dangerous
passes of the mountains. The sierra was several leagues from
Cuzco; and the cavalier, desirous to reach the further side of
it before nightfall, incautiously pushed on his wearied horses.
When he was fairly entangled in its rocky defiles, a multitude
of armed warriors, springing, as it seemed, from every cavern
and thicket of the sierra, filled the air with their war-cries,
and rushed down, like one of their own mountain torrents, on
the invaders, as they were painfully toiling up the steeps.

Men and horses were overturned in the fury of the assault, and the foremost files, rolling back on those below, spread ruin and consternation in their ranks. De Soto in vain endeavored to restore order, and, if possible, to charge the assailants. The horses were blinded and maddened by the missiles, while the desperate natives, clinging to their legs, strove to prevent their ascent up the rocky pathway. De Soto saw, that, unless he gained a level ground which opened at some distance before him, all must be lost. Cheering on his men with the old battle-cry, that always went to the heart of a Spaniard, he struck his spurs deep into the sides of his wearied charger, and, gallantly supported by his troop, broke through the dark array of warriors, and, shaking them off to the right and left, at length succeeded in placing himself on the broad level.

Here both parties paused, as if by mutual consent, for a few moments. A little stream ran through the plain, at which the Spaniards watered their horses; and the animals, having recovered wind, De Soto and his men made a desperate charge on their assailants. The undaunted Indians sustained the shock with firmness; and the result of the combat was still doubtful, when the shades of evening, falling thicker around them, separated the combatants.

Both parties then withdrew from the field, taking up their respective stations within bow-shot of each other, so that the voices of the warriors on either side could be distinctly heard in the stillness of the night. But very different were the reflections of the two hosts. The Indians, exulting in their temporary triumph, looked with confidence to the morrow to complete it. The Spaniards, on the other hand, were proportionably discouraged. They were not prepared for this spirit of resistance in an enemy hitherto so tame. Several cavaliers had fallen; one of them by a blow from a Peruvian battle-axe, which clove his head to the chin, attesting the power of the weapon, and of the arm that used it. Several horses, too, had been killed; and the loss of these was almost as severely felt as that of their riders, considering the great cost and difficulty of transporting them to these distant regions. Few either of the men or horses escaped without wounds, and the Indian allies suffered still more severely.

It seemed probable, from the pertinacity and a certain order maintained in the assault, that it was directed by some leader of military experience; perhaps the Indian commander Quizquiz, who was said to be hanging round the environs of Cuzco with a considerable force.

Notwithstanding the reasonable cause of apprehension for the morrow, De Soto, like a stout-hearted cavalier, as he was, strove to keep up the spirits of his followers. If they had beaten off the enemy when their horses were jaded, and their own strength nearly exhausted, how much easier it would be to come off victorious when both were restored by a night's rest; and he told them to "trust in the Almighty, who would never desert his faithful followers in their extremity." The event justified De Soto's confidence in this seasonable succour.

From time to time, on his march, he had sent advices to Pizarro of the menacing state of the country, till his commander, becoming seriously alarmed, was apprehensive that the cavalier might be overpowered by the superior numbers of the enemy. He accordingly detached Almagro with nearly all the remaining horse, to his support,—unencumbered by infantry, that he might move the lighter. That efficient leader advanced by forced marches, stimulated by the tidings which met him on the road; and was so fortunate as to reach the foot of the sierra of Vilcaconga the very night of the engagement.

There hearing of the encounter, he pushed forward without halting, though his horses were spent with travel. The night was exceedingly dark, and Almagro, afraid of stumbling on the enemy's bivouac, and desirous to give De Soto information of his approach, commanded his trumpets to sound, till the notes, winding through the defiles of the mountains, broke the slumbers of his countrymen, sounding like blithest music in their ears. They quickly replied with their own bugles, and soon had the satisfaction to embrace their deliverers.

Great was the dismay of the Peruvian host, when the morning light discovered the fresh reinforcement of the ranks of the Spaniards. There was no use in contending with an enemy who gathered strength from the conflict, and who seemed to multiply his numbers at will. Without further attempt to renew the fight, they availed themselves of a thick fog, which hung over the lower slopes of the hills, to effect their retreat, and left the passes open to the invaders. The two cavaliers then continued their march until they extricated their forces from the sierra, when, taking up a secure position, they proposed to await there the arrival of Pizarro.

The commander-in-chief, meanwhile, lay at Xauxa, where he was greatly disturbed by the rumors which reached him of the state of the country. His enterprise, thus far, had gone forward so smoothly, that he was no better prepared than his lieutenant to meet with resistance from the natives. He did not seem to comprehend that the mildest nature might at last be roused by oppression; and that the massacre of their Inca, whom they regarded with such awful veneration, would be likely, if any thing could do it, to wake them from their apathy.

The tidings which he now received of the retreat of the Peruvians were most welcome; and he caused mass to be said, and thanksgivings to be offered up to Heaven, "which had shown itself thus favorable to the Christians throughout this mighty enterprise." The Spaniard was ever a Crusader. He was, in the sixteenth century, what *Cœur de Lion* and his brave knights were in the twelfth, with this difference: the cavalier of that day fought for the Cross and for glory, while gold and the Cross were the watchwords of the Spaniard. The spirit of chivalry had waned somewhat before the spirit of trade; but the fire of religious enthusiasm still burned as bright under the quilted mail of the American Conqueror, as it did of yore under the iron panoply of the soldier of Palestine.

It seemed probable that some man of authority had organized, or at least countenanced, this resistance of the natives, and suspicion fell on the captive chief Challcuchima, who was accused of maintaining a secret correspondence with his confederate, Quizquiz. Pizarro waited on the Indian noble, and, charging him with the conspiracy, reproached him, as he had formerly done his royal master, with ingratitude towards the Spaniards, who had dealt with him so liberally. He concluded by the assurance, that, if he did not cause the Peruvians to lay down their arms, and tender their submission at once, he should be burnt alive, so soon as they reached Almagro's quarters.

The Indian chief listened to the terrible menace with the utmost composure. He denied having had any communication with his countrymen, and said, that, in his present state of confinement, at least, he could have no power to bring them to submission. He then remained doggedly silent, and Pizarro did not press the matter further. But he placed a strong guard over his prisoner, and caused him to be put in irons. It was an ominous proceeding, and had been the precursor of the death of Atahuallpa.

Before quitting Xauxa, a misfortune befell the Spaniards in the death of their creature, the young Inca Toparca. Suspicion, of course, fell on Challcuchima, now selected as the scape-goat for all the offences of his nation. It was a disappointment to Pizarro, who hoped to find a convenient shelter for his future proceedings under this shadow of royalty.

The general considered it most prudent not to hazard the loss of his treasures by taking them on the march, and he accordingly left them at Xauxa, under a guard of forty soldiers, who remained there in garrison. No event of importance occurred on the road, and Pizarro, having effected a junction with Almagro, their united forces soon entered the vale of Xaquixaguana, about five leagues from Cuzco. This was one of those bright spots, so often found embosomed amidst the Andes, the more beautiful from contrast with the savage character of the scenery around it. A river flowed through the valley, affording the means of irrigating the soil, and clothing it in perpetual verdure; and the rich and flowering vegetation spread out like a cultivated garden. The beauty of the place and its delicious coolness commended it as a residence for the Peruvian nobles, and the sides of the hills were dotted with their villas, which afforded them a grateful retreat in the heats of summer. Yet the centre of the valley was disfigured by a quagmire of some extent, occasioned by the frequent overflowing of the waters; but the industry of the Indian architects had constructed a solid causeway, faced with heavy stone, and connected with the great road, which traversed the whole breadth of the morass.

In this valley Pizarro halted for several days, while he refreshed his troops from the well-stored magazines of the Incas. His first act was to bring Challcuchima to trial; if trial that could be called, where sentence may be said to have gone hand in hand with accusation. We are not informed of the nature of the evidence. It was sufficient to satisfy the Spanish captains of the chieftain's guilt. Nor is it at all incredible that Challcuchima should have secretly encouraged a movement among the people, designed to secure his country's freedom and his own. He was condemned to be burnt alive on the spot. "Some thought it a hard measure," says Herrera; "but those who are governed by reasons of state policy are apt to shut their eyes against every thing else." Why this cruel mode of execution was so often adopted by the Spanish Conquerors is not obvious; unless it was that the Indian was an infidel, and fire seems to have been considered the fitting doom of the infidel, as the type of that inextinguishable flame which awaited him in the regions of the damned.

Father Valverde accompanied the Peruvian chieftain to the stake. He seems always to have been present at this dreary moment, anxious to profit by it, if possible, to work the conversion of the victim. He painted in gloomy colors the dreadful doom of the unbeliever, to whom the waters of baptism could alone secure the ineffable glories of paradise. It does not appear that he promised any commutation of punishment in this world. But his arguments fell on a stony heart, and the chief coldly replied, he "did not understand the religion of the white men." He might be pardoned for not comprehending the beauty of a faith which, as it would seem, had borne so bitter fruits to him. In the midst of his tortures, he showed the characteristic courage of the American Indian, whose power of endurance triumphs over the power of persecution in his enemies, and he died with his last breath invoking the name of Pachacamac. His own followers brought the fagots to feed the flames that consumed him.

Soon after this tragic event, Pizarro was surprised by a visit from a Peruvian noble, who came in great state, attended by a numerous and showy retinue. It was the young prince Manco, brother of the unfortunate Huascar, and the rightful successor to the crown. Being brought before the Spanish commander, he announced his pretensions to the throne, and claimed the protection of the strangers. It is said he had meditated resisting them by arms, and had encouraged the assaults made on them on their march; but, finding resistance ineffectual, he had taken this politic course, greatly to the displeasure of his more resolute nobles. However this may be, Pizarro listened to his application with singular contentment, for he saw in this new scion of the true royal stock, a more effectual instrument for his purposes than he could have found in the family of Quito, with whom the Peruvians had but little sympathy. He received the young man, therefore, with great cordiality, and did not hesitate to assure him that he had been sent into the country by his master, the Castilian sovereign, in order to vindicate the claims of Huascar to the crown, and to punish the usurpation of his rival.

Taking with him the Indian prince, Pizarro now resumed his march. It was interrupted for a few hours by a party of the natives, who lay in wait for him in the neighboring sierra. A sharp skirmish ensued, in which the Indians behaved with great spirit, and inflicted some little injury on the Spaniards; but the latter, at length, shaking them off, made good their passage through the defile, and the enemy did not care to follow them into the open country.

It was late in the afternoon when the Conquerors came in sight of Cuzco. The descending sun was streaming his broad rays full on the imperial city, where many an altar was dedicated to his worship. The low ranges of buildings, showing in his beams like so many lines of silvery light, filled up the bosom of the valley and the lower slopes of the mountains, whose shadowy forms hung darkly over the fair city, as if to shield it from the menaced profanation. It was so late, that Pizarro resolved to defer his entrance till the following morning.

That night vigilant guard was kept in the camp, and the soldiers slept on their arms. But it passed away without annoyance from the enemy, and early on the following day, November 15, 1533, Pizarro prepared for his entrance into the Peruvian capital.

The little army was formed into three divisions, of which the centre, or "battle," as it was called, was led by the general. The suburbs were thronged with a countless multitude of the natives, who had flocked from the city and the surrounding country to witness the showy, and, to them, startling pageant. All looked with eager curiosity on the strangers, the fame of whose terrible exploits had spread to the remotest parts of the empire. They gazed with astonishment on their dazzling arms and fair complexions, which seemed to proclaim them the true Children of the Sun; and they listened with feelings of mysterious dread, as the trumpet sent forth its prolonged notes through the streets of the capital, and the solid ground shook under the heavy tramp of the cavalry.

The Spanish commander rode directly up the great square. It was surrounded by low piles of buildings, among which were several palaces of the Incas. One of these, erected by Huayna Capac, was surmounted by a tower, while the ground-floor was occupied by one or more immense halls, like those described in Caxamalca, where the Peruvian nobles held their *fêtes* in stormy weather. These buildings afforded convenient barracks for the troops, though, during the first few weeks, they remained under their tents in the open *plaza*, with their horses picketed by their side, ready to repulse any insurrection of the inhabitants.

The capital of the Incas, though falling short of the *El Dorado* which had engaged their credulous fancies, astonished the Spaniards by the beauty of its edifices, the length and regularity of its streets, and the good order and appearance of comfort, even luxury, visible in its numerous population. It far surpassed all they had yet seen in the New World. The population of the city is computed by one of the Conquerors at two hundred thousand inhabitants, and that of the suburbs at as many more. This account is not confirmed, as far as I have seen, by any other writer. But however it may be exaggerated, it is certain that Cuzco was the metropolis of a great empire, the residence of the Court and the chief nobility; frequented by the most skilful mechanics and artisans of every description, who found a demand for their ingenuity in the royal precincts; while the place was garrisoned by a numerous soldiery, and was the resort, finally, of emigrants from the most distant provinces. The quarters whence this motley population came were indicated by their peculiar dress, and especially their head-gear, so rarely found at all on the American Indian, which, with its variegated colors, gave a picturesque effect to the groups and masses in the streets. The habitual order and decorum maintained in this multifarious assembly showed the excellent police of the capital, where

the only sounds that disturbed the repose of the Spaniards
were the noises of feasting and dancing, which the natives,
with happy insensibility, constantly prolonged to a late hour
of the night.

The edifices of the better sort—and they were very numerous—were of stone, or faced with stone. Among the principal
were the royal residences; as each sovereign built a new palace
for himself, covering, though low, a large extent of ground.
The walls were sometimes stained or painted with gaudy tints,
and the gates, we are assured, were sometimes of colored
marble. "In the delicacy of the stone-work," says another of
the Conquerors, "the natives far excelled the Spaniards,
though the roofs of their dwellings, instead of tiles, were only
of thatch, but put together with the nicest art." The sunny
climate of Cuzco did not require a very substantial material
for defence against the weather.

The most important building was the fortress, planted on
a solid rock, that rose boldly above the city. It was built of
hewn stone, so finely wrought that it was impossible to detect
the line of junction between the blocks; and the approaches
to it were defended by three semicircular parapets, composed
of such heavy masses of rock, that it bore resemblance to the
kind of work known to architects as the Cyclopean. The fortress was raised to a height rare in Peruvian architecture; and
from the summit of the tower the eye of the spectator ranged
over a magnificent prospect, in which the wild features of the
mountain scenery, rocks, woods, and waterfalls, were mingled
with the rich verdure of the valley, and the shining city filling
up the foreground,—all blended in sweet harmony under the
deep azure of a tropical sky.

The streets were long and narrow. They were arranged with
perfect regularity, crossing one another at right angles; and
from the great square diverged four principal streets connect-
ing with the high roads of the empire. The square itself, and
many parts of the city, were paved with a fine pebble. Through
the heart of the capital ran a river of pure water, if it might
not be rather termed a canal, the banks or sides of which, for
the distance of twenty leagues, were faced with stone. Across
this stream, bridges, constructed of similar broad flags, were

thrown, at intervals, so as to afford an easy communication between the different quarters of the capital.

The most sumptuous edifice in Cuzco, in the times of the Incas, was undoubtedly the great temple dedicated to the Sun, which, studded with gold plates, as already noticed, was surrounded by convents and dormitories for the priests, with their gardens and broad parterres sparkling with gold. The exterior ornaments had been already removed by the Conquerors,—all but the frieze of gold, which, embedded in the stones, still encircled the principal building. It is probable that the tales of wealth, so greedily circulated among the Spaniards, greatly exceeded the truth. If they did not, the natives must have been very successful in concealing their treasures from the invaders. Yet much still remained, not only in the great House of the Sun, but in the inferior temples which swarmed in the capital.

Pizarro, on entering Cuzco, had issued an order forbidding any soldier to offer violence to the dwellings of the inhabitants. But the palaces were numerous, and the troops lost no time in plundering them of their contents, as well as in despoiling the religious edifices. The interior decorations supplied them with considerable booty. They stripped off the jewels and rich ornaments that garnished the royal mummies in the temple of Coricancha. Indignant at the concealment of their treasures, they put the inhabitants, in some instances, to the torture, and endeavored to extort from them a confession of their hiding-places. They invaded the repose of the sepulchres, in which the Peruvians often deposited their valuable effects, and compelled the grave to give up its dead. No place was left unexplored by the rapacious Conquerors, and they occasionally stumbled on a mine of wealth that rewarded their labors.

In a cavern near the city they found a number of vases of pure gold, richly embossed with the figures of serpents, locusts, and other animals. Among the spoil were four golden llamas and ten or twelve statues of women, some of gold, others of silver, "which merely to see," says one of the Conquerors, with some naïveté, "was truly a great satisfaction." The gold was probably thin, for the figures were all as large as life; and several of them, being reserved for the royal fifth, were not recast, but sent in their original form to Spain. The magazines were stored with curious commodities; richly tinted robes of cotton and feather-work, gold sandals, and slippers of the same material, for the women, and dresses composed entirely of beads of gold. The grain and other articles of food, with which the magazines were filled, were held in contempt by the Conquerors, intent only on gratifying their lust for gold. The time came when the grain would have been of far more value.

Yet the amount of treasure in the capital did not equal the sanguine expectations that had been formed by the Spaniards. But the deficiency was supplied by the plunder which they had collected at various places on their march. In one place, for example, they met with ten planks or bars of solid silver, each piece being twenty feet in length, one foot in breadth, and two or three inches thick. They were intended to decorate the dwelling of an Inca noble.

The whole mass of treasure was brought into a common heap, as in Caxamalca; and after some of the finer specimens had been deducted for the Crown, the remainder was delivered to the Indian goldsmiths to be melted down into ingots of a uniform standard. The division of the spoil was made on the same principle as before. There were four hundred and eighty soldiers, including the garrison of Xauxa, who were each to receive a share, that of the cavalry being double that of the infantry. The amount of booty is stated variously by those present at the division of it. According to some it considerably exceeded the ransom of Atahuallpa. Others state it as less. Pedro Pizarro says that each horseman got six thousand *pesos de oro*, and each one of the infantry half that sum; though the same discrimination was made by Pizarro as before, in respect to the rank of the parties, and their relative services. But Sancho, the royal notary, and secretary of the commander, estimates the whole amount as far less,—not exceeding five hundred and eighty thousand and two hundred *pesos de oro*, and two hundred and fifteen thousand marks of silver. In the absence of the official returns, it is impossible to determine which is correct. But Sancho's narrative is countersigned, it may be remembered, by Pizarro and the royal treasurer Riquelme, and doubtless, therefore, shows the actual amount for which the Conquerors accounted to the Crown.

Whichever statement we receive, the sum, combined with that obtained at Caxamalca, might well have satisfied the cravings of the most avaricious. The sudden influx of so much wealth, and that, too, in so transferable a form, among a party of reckless adventurers little accustomed to the possession of money, had its natural effect. It supplied them with the means of gaming, so strong and common a passion with the Spaniards, that it may be considered a national vice. Fortunes were lost and won in a single day, sufficient to render the proprietors independent for life; and many a desperate gamester, by an unlucky throw of the dice or turn of the cards, saw himself stripped in a few hours of the fruits of years of toil, and obliged to begin over again the business of rapine. Among these, one in the cavalry service is mentioned, named Leguizano, who had received as his share of the booty the image of the Sun, which, raised on a plate of burnished gold, spread over the walls in a recess of the great temple, and which, for some reason or other,—perhaps because of its superior fineness,—was not recast like the other ornaments. This rich prize the spendthrift lost in a single night; whence it came to be a proverb in Spain, *Juega el Sol antes que amanezca*, "Play away the Sun before sunrise."

The effect of such a surfeit of the precious metals was instantly felt on prices. The most ordinary articles were only to be had for exorbitant sums. A quire of paper sold for ten *pesos de oro;* a bottle of wine, for sixty; a sword, for forty or fifty; a cloak, for a hundred,—sometimes more; a pair of shoes cost thirty or forty *pesos de oro*, and a good horse could not be had for less than twenty-five hundred. Some brought a still higher price. Every article rose in value, as gold and silver, the representatives of all, declined. Gold and silver, in short, seemed to be the only things in Cuzco that were not wealth. Yet there were some few wise enough to return contented with their present gains to their native country. Here their riches brought them consideration and competence, and, while they excited the envy of their countrymen, stimulated them to seek their own fortunes in the like path of adventure.

NEW INCA CROWNED—MUNICIPAL REGULATIONS—TER-
RIBLE MARCH OF ALVARADO—INTERVIEW WITH PI-
ZARRO—FOUNDATION OF LIMA—HERNANDO PIZARRO
REACHES SPAIN—SENSATION AT COURT—FEUDS OF AL-
MAGRO AND THE PIZARROS

The first care of the Spanish general, after the division
of the booty, was to place Manco on the throne, and to obtain
for him the recognition of his countrymen. He, accordingly,
presented the young prince to them as their future sovereign,
the legitimate son of Huayna Capac, and the true heir of the
Peruvian sceptre. The annunciation was received with enthusiasm by the people, attached to the memory of his illustrious
father, and pleased that they were still to have a monarch rule
over them of the ancient line of Cuzco.

Everything was done to maintain the illusion with the Indian population. The ceremonies of a coronation were studi-
ously observed. The young prince kept the prescribed fasts
and vigils; and on the appointed day, the nobles and the people, with the whole Spanish soldiery, assembled in the great
square of Cuzco to witness the concluding ceremony. Mass
was publicly performed by Father Valverde, and the Inca
Manco received the fringed diadem of Peru, not from the hand
of the high-priest of his nation, but from his conqueror, Pizarro. The Indian lords then tendered their obeisance in the
customary form; after which the royal notary read aloud the
instrument asserting the supremacy of the Castilian Crown,
and requiring the homage of all present to its authority. This
address was explained by an interpreter, and the ceremony
of homage was performed by each one of the parties waving
the royal banner of Castile twice or thrice with his hands.
Manco then pledged the Spanish commander in a golden
goblet of the sparkling *chicha;* and, the latter having cordially
embraced the new monarch, the trumpets announced the conclusion of the ceremony. But it was not the note of triumph,

but of humiliation; for it proclaimed that the armed foot of the stranger was in the halls of the Peruvian Incas; that the ceremony of coronation was a miserable pageant; that their prince himself was but a puppet in the hands of his conquerors; and that the glory of the Children of the Sun had departed for ever!

Yet the people readily gave in to the illusion, and seemed willing to accept this image of their ancient independence. The accession of the young monarch was greeted by all the usual *fêtes* and rejoicings. The mummies of his royal ancestors, with such ornaments as were still left to them, were paraded in the great square. They were attended each by his own numerous retinue, who performed all the menial offices, as if the object of them were alive and could feel their import. Each ghostly form took its seat at the banquet-table— now, alas! stripped of the magnificent service with which it was wont to blaze at these high festivals—and the guests drank deep to the illustrious dead. Dancing succeeded the carousal, and the festivities, prolonged to a late hour, were continued night after night by the giddy population, as if their conquerors had not been intrenched in the capital!—What a contrast to the Aztecs in the conquest of Mexico!

Pizarro's next concern was to organize a municipal government for Cuzco, like those in the cities of the parent country. Two *alcaldes* were appointed, and eight *regidores,* among which last functionaries were his brothers Gonzalo and Juan. The oaths of office were administered with great solemnity, on the twenty-fourth of March, 1534, in the presence both of Spaniards and Peruvians, in the public square; as if the general were willing by this ceremony to intimate to the latter, that, while they retained the semblance of their ancient institutions, the real power was henceforth vested in their conquerors. He invited Spaniards to settle in the place by liberal grants of land and houses, for which means were afforded by the numerous palaces and public buildings of the Incas; and many a cavalier, who had been too poor in his own country to find a place to rest in, now saw himself the proprietor of a spacious mansion that might have entertained the retinue of a prince. From this time, says an old chronicler, Pizarro, who had hitherto been distinguished by his military title of "Captain-General," was addressed by that of "Governor." Both had been bestowed on him by the royal grant.

Nor did the chief neglect the interests of religion. Father Valverde, whose nomination as Bishop of Cuzco not long afterwards received the Papal sanction, prepared to enter on the duties of his office. A place was selected for the cathedral of his diocese, facing the *plaza*. A spacious monastery subsequently rose on the ruins of the gorgeous House of the Sun; its walls were constructed of the ancient stones; the altar was raised on the spot where shone the bright image of the Peruvian deity, and the cloisters of the Indian temple were trodden by the friars of St. Dominic. To make the metamorphosis more complete, the House of the Virgins of the Sun was replaced by a Roman Catholic nunnery. Christian churches and monasteries gradually supplanted the ancient edifices, and such of the latter as were suffered to remain, despoiled of their heathen insignia, were placed under the protection of the Cross.

The Fathers of St. Dominic, the Brethren of the Order of Mercy, and other missionaries, now busied themselves in the good work of conversion. We have seen that Pizarro was required by the Crown to bring out a certain number of these holy men in his own vessels; and every succeeding vessel brought an additional reinforcement of ecclesiastics. They were not all like the Bishop of Cuzco, with hearts so seared by fanaticism as to be closed against sympathy with the unfortunate natives. They were, many of them, men of singular humility, who followed in the track of the conqueror to scatter the seeds of spiritual truth, and, with disinterested zeal, devoted themselves to the propagation of the Gospel. Thus did their pious labors prove them the true soldiers of the Cross, and showed that the object so ostentatiously avowed of carrying its banner among the heathen nations was not an empty vaunt.

The effort to Christianize the heathen is an honorable characteristic of the Spanish conquests. The Puritan, with equal religious zeal, did comparatively little for the conversion of the Indian, content, as it would seem, with having secured to himself the inestimable privilege of worshipping God in his own way. Other adventurers who have occupied the New World have often had too little regard for religion themselves, to be very solicitous about spreading it among the savages. But the Spanish missionary, from first to last, has shown a keen interest in the spiritual welfare of the natives. Under his auspices, churches on a magnificent scale have been erected, schools for elementary instruction founded, and every rational means taken to spread the knowledge of religious truth, while he has carried his solitary mission into remote and almost inaccessible regions, or gathered his Indian disciples into communities, like the good Las Casas in Cumaná, or the Jesuits in California and Paraguay. At all times, the courageous ecclesiastic has been ready to lift his voice against the cruelty of the conqueror, and the no less wasting cupidity of the colonist; and when his remonstrances, as was too often the case, have proved unavailing, he has still followed to bind up the broken-hearted, to teach the poor Indian resignation under his lot, and light up his dark intellect with the revelation of a holier and happier existence.—In reviewing the blood-stained records of Spanish colonial history, it is but fair, and at the same time cheering, to reflect, that the same nation which sent forth the hard-hearted conqueror from its bosom sent forth the missionary to do the work of beneficence, and spread the light of Christian civilization over the farthest regions of the New World.

While the governor, as we are henceforth to style him, lay at Cuzco, he received repeated accounts of a considerable force in the neighborhood, under the command of Atahuallpa's officer, Quizquiz. He accordingly detached Almagro, with a small body of horse and a large Indian force under the Inca Manco, to disperse the enemy, and, if possible, to capture their leader. Manco was the more ready to take part in the expedition, as the enemy were soldiers of Quito, who, with their commander, bore no good-will to himself.

Almagro, moving with his characteristic rapidity, was not long in coming up with the Indian chieftain. Several sharp encounters followed, as the army of Quito fell back on Xauxa, near which a general engagement decided the fate of the war by the total discomfiture of the natives. Quizquiz fled to the elevated plains of Quito, where he still held out with undaunted spirit against a Spanish force in that quarter, till at

length his own soldiers, wearied by these long and ineffectual
hostilities, massacred their commander in cold blood. Thus
fell the last of the two great officers of Atahuallpa, who, if
their nation had been animated by a spirit equal to their own,
might long have successfully maintained their soil against the
invader.

Some time before this occurrence, the Spanish governor,
while in Cuzco, received tidings of an event much more alarming to him than any Indian hostilities. This was the arrival
on the coast of a strong Spanish force, under command of Don
Pedro de Alvarado, the gallant officer who had served under
Cortés with such renown in the war of Mexico. That cavalier,
after forming a brilliant alliance in Spain, to which he was
entitled by his birth and military rank, had returned to his
government of Guatemala, where his avarice had been roused
by the magnificent reports he daily received of Pizarro's conquests. These conquests, he learned, had been confined to
Peru; while the northern kingdom of Quito, the ancient residence of Atahuallpa, and, no doubt, the principal depository
of his treasures, yet remained untouched. Affecting to consider this country as falling without the governor's jurisdiction,
he immediately turned a large fleet, which he had intended
for the Spice Islands, in the direction of South America; and
in March, 1534, he landed in the Bay of Caraques, with five
hundred followers, of whom half were mounted, and all ad-
mirably provided with arms and ammunition. It was the best
equipped and the most formidable array that had yet appeared
in the southern seas.

Although manifestly an invasion of the territory conceded
to Pizarro by the Crown, the reckless cavalier determined to
march at once on Quito. With the assistance of an Indian
guide, he proposed to take the direct route across the mountains, a passage of exceeding difficulty, even at the most favorable season.

After crossing the Rio Dable, Alvarado's guide deserted
him, so that he was soon entangled in the intricate mazes of
the sierra; and, as he rose higher and higher into the regions
of winter, he became surrounded with ice and snow, for which
his men, taken from the warm countries of Guatemala, were
but ill prepared. As the cold grew more intense, many of them

were so benumbed, that it was with difficulty they could proceed. The infantry, compelled to make exertions, fared best. Many of the troopers were frozen stiff in their saddles. The Indians, still more sensible to the cold, perished by hundreds. As the Spaniards huddled round their wretched bivouacs, with such scanty fuel as they could glean, and almost without food, they waited in gloomy silence the approach of morning. Yet the morning light, which gleamed coldly on the cheerless waste, brought no joy to them. It only revealed more clearly the extent of their wretchedness. Still struggling on through the winding Puertos Nevados, or Snowy Passes, their track was dismally marked by fragments of dress, broken harness, golden ornaments, and other valuables plundered on their march,— by the dead bodies of men, or by those less fortunate, who were left to die alone in the wilderness. As for the horses, their carcasses were not suffered long to cumber the ground, as they were quickly seized and devoured half raw by the starving soldiers, who, like the famished condors, now hovering in troops above their heads, greedily banqueted on the most offensive offal to satisfy the gnawings of hunger.

Alvarado, anxious to secure the booty which had fallen into his hands at an earlier part of his march, encouraged every man to take what gold he wanted from the common heap, reserving only the royal fifth. But they only answered, with a ghastly smile of derision, "that food was the only gold for them." Yet in this extremity, which might seem to have dissolved the very ties of nature, there are some affecting instances recorded of self-devotion; of comrades who lost their lives in assisting others, and of parents and husbands (for some of the cavaliers were accompanied by their wives) who, instead of seeking their own safety, chose to remain and perish in the snows with the objects of their love.

To add to their distress, the air was filled for several days with thick clouds of earthy particles and cinders, which blinded the men, and made respiration exceedingly difficult. This phenomenon, it seems probable, was caused by an eruption of the distant Cotopaxi, which, about twelve leagues southeast of Quito, rears up its colossal, and perfectly symmetrical cone far above the limits of eternal snow,—the most beautiful and the most terrible of the American volcanoes.

At the time of Alvarado's expedition, it was in a state of eruption, the earliest instance of the kind on record, though doubtless not the earliest. Since that period, it has been in frequent commotion, sending up its sheets of flame to the height of half a mile, spouting forth cataracts of lava that have overwhelmed towns and villages in their career, and shaking the earth with subterraneous thunders, that, at the distance of more than a hundred leagues, sounded like the reports of artillery! Alvarado's followers, unacquainted with the cause of the phenomenon, as they wandered over tracts buried in snow, —the sight of which was strange to them,—in an atmosphere laden with ashes, became bewildered by this confusion of the elements, which Nature seemed to have contrived purposely for their destruction. Some of these men were the soldiers of Cortés, steeled by many a painful march, and many a sharp encounter with the Aztecs. But this war of the elements, they now confessed, was mightier than all.

At length, Alvarado, after sufferings which even the most hardy, probably, could have endured but a few days longer, emerged from the Snowy Pass, and came on the elevated table-land, which spreads out, at the height of more than nine thousand feet above the ocean, in the neighborhood of Riobamba. But one fourth of his gallant army had been left to feed the condor in the wilderness, besides the greater part, at least two thousand, of his Indian auxiliaries. A great number of his horses, too, had perished; and the men and horses that escaped were all of them more or less injured by the cold and the extremity of suffering.—Such was the terrible passage of the Puertos Nevados, which I have only briefly noticed as an episode to the Peruvian conquest, but the account of which, in all its details, though it occupied but a few weeks in duration, would give one a better idea of the difficulties encountered by the Spanish cavaliers, than volumes of ordinary narrative.

As Alvarado, after halting some time to restore his exhausted troops, began his march across the broad plateau, he was astonished by seeing the prints of horses' hoofs on the soil. Spaniards, then, had been there before him, and, after all his toil and suffering, others had forestalled him in the enterprise against Quito! It is necessary to say a few words in explanation of this.

When Pizarro quitted Caxamalca, being sensible of the growing importance of San Miguel, the only port of entry then in the country, he despatched a person in whom he had great confidence to take charge of it. This person was Sebastian Benalcazar, a cavalier who afterwards placed his name in the first rank of the South American conquerors, for courage, capacity,—and cruelty. But this cavalier had hardly reached his government, when, like Alvarado, he received such accounts of the riches of Quito, that he determined, with the force at his command, though without orders, to undertake its reduction.

At the head of about a hundred and forty soldiers, horse and foot, and a stout body of Indian auxiliaries, he marched up the broad range of the Andes, to where it spreads out into the table-land of Quito, by a road safer and more expeditious than that taken by Alvarado. On the plains of Riobamba, he encountered the Indian general Ruminavi. Several engagements followed, with doubtful success, when, in the end, science prevailed where courage was well matched, and the victorious Benalcazar planted the standard of Castile on the ancient towers of Atahuallpa. The city, in honor of his general, Francisco Pizarro, he named San Francisco del Quito. But great was his mortification on finding that either the stories of its riches had been fabricated, or that these riches were secreted by the natives. The city was all that he gained by his victories,—the shell without the pearl of price which gave it its value. While devouring his chagrin, as he best could, the Spanish captain received tidings of the approach of his superior, Almagro.

No sooner had the news of Alvarado's expedition reached Cuzco, than Almagro left the place with a small force for San Miguel, proposing to strengthen himself by a reinforcement from that quarter, and to march at once against the invaders. Greatly was he astonished, on his arrival in that city, to learn the departure of its commander. Doubting the loyalty of his motives, Almagro, with the buoyancy of spirit which belongs to youth, though in truth somewhat enfeebled by the infirmi-

ties of age, did not hesitate to follow Benalcazar at once across
the mountains.

With his wonted energy, the intrepid veteran, overcoming
all the difficulties of his march, in a few weeks placed himself
and his little company on the lofty plains which spread around
the Indian city of Riobamba; though in his progress he had
more than one hot encounter with the natives, whose courage
and perseverance formed a contrast sufficiently striking to the
apathy of the Peruvians. But the fire only slumbered in the
bosom of the Peruvian. His hour had not yet come.

At Riobamba, Almagro was soon joined by the commander
of San Miguel, who disclaimed, perhaps sincerely, any disloyal
intent in his unauthorized expedition. Thus reinforced, the
Spanish captain coolly awaited the coming of Alvarado. The
forces of the latter, though in a less serviceable condition,
were much superior in number and appointments to those of
his rival. As they confronted each other on the broad plains
of Riobamba, it seemed probable that a fierce struggle must
immediately follow, and the natives of the country have the
satisfaction to see their wrongs avenged by the very hands that
inflicted them. But it was Almagro's policy to avoid such an
issue.

Negotiations were set on foot, in which each party stated
his claims to the country. Meanwhile Alvarado's men mingled
freely with their countrymen in the opposite army, and heard
there such magnificent reports of the wealth and wonders of
Cuzco, that many of them were inclined to change their present service for that of Pizarro. Their own leader, too, satisfied
that Quito held out no recompense worth the sacrifices he had
made, and was like to make, by insisting on his claim, became
now more sensible of the rashness of a course which must
doubtless incur the censure of his sovereign. In this temper,
it was not difficult for them to effect an adjustment of difficulties; and it was agreed, as the basis of it, that the governor
should pay one hundred thousand *pesos de oro* to Alvarado,
in consideration of which the latter was to resign to him his
fleet, his forces, and all his stores and munitions. His vessels,
great and small, amounted to twelve in number, and the sum
he received, though large, did not cover his expenses. This

treaty being settled, Alvarado proposed, before leaving the country, to have an interview with Pizarro.

The governor, meanwhile, had quitted the Peruvian capital for the sea-coast, from his desire to repel any invasion that might be attempted in that direction by Alvarado, with whose real movements he was still unacquainted. He left Cuzco in charge of his brother Juan, a cavalier whose manners were such as, he thought, would be likely to gain the good-will of the native population. Pizarro also left ninety of his troops, as the garrison of the capital, and the nucleus of his future colony. Then, taking the Inca Manco with him, he proceeded as far as Xauxa. At this place he was entertained by the Indian prince with the exhibition of a great national hunt,—such as has been already described in these pages,—in which immense numbers of wild animals were slaughtered, and the vicuñas, and other races of Peruvian sheep, which roam over the mountains, driven into inclosures and relieved of their delicate fleeces.

The Spanish governor then proceeded to Pachacamac, where he received the grateful intelligence of the accommodation with Alvarado; and not long afterwards he was visited by that cavalier himself, previously to his embarkation.

The meeting was conducted with courtesy and a show, at least, of good-will, on both sides, as there was no longer real cause for jealousy between the parties; and each, as may be imagined, looked on the other with no little interest, as having achieved such distinction in the bold path of adventure. In the comparison, Alvarado had somewhat the advantage; for Pizarro, though of commanding presence, had not the brilliant exterior, the free and joyous manner, which, no less than his fresh complexion and sunny locks, had won for the conqueror of Guatemala, in his campaigns against the Aztecs, the *sobriquet* of *Tonatiuh*, or "Child of the Sun."

Blithe were the revels that now rang through the ancient city of Pachacamac; where, instead of songs, and of the sacrifices so often seen there in honor of the Indian deity, the walls echoed to the noise of tourneys and Moorish tilts of reeds, with which the martial adventurers loved to recall the sports of their native land. When these were concluded, Alvarado reëmbarked for his government of Guatemala, where his restless spirit soon involved him in other enterprises that cut short his adventurous career. His expedition to Peru was eminently characteristic of the man. It was founded in injustice, conducted with rashness, and ended in disaster.

The reduction of Peru might now be considered as, in a manner, accomplished. Some barbarous tribes in the interior, it is true, still held out, and Alonso de Alvarado, a prudent and able officer, was employed to bring them into subjection. Benalcazar was still at Quito, of which he was subsequently appointed governor by the Crown. There he was laying deeper the foundation of the Spanish power, while he advanced the line of conquest still higher towards the north. But Cuzco, the ancient capital of the Indian monarchy, had submitted. The armies of Atahuallpa had been beaten and scattered. The empire of the Incas was dissolved; and the prince who now wore the Peruvian diadem was but the shadow of a king, who held his commission from his conqueror.

The first act of the governor was to determine on the site of the future capital of this vast colonial empire. Cuzco, withdrawn among the mountains, was altogether too far removed from the sea-coast for a commercial people. The little settlement of San Miguel lay too far to the north. It was desirable to select some more central position, which could be easily found in one of the fruitful valleys that bordered the Pacific. Such was that of Pachacamac, which Pizarro now occupied. But, on further examination, he preferred the neighboring valley of Rimac, which lay to the north, and which took its name, signifying in the Quichua tongue "one who speaks," from a celebrated idol, whose shrine was much frequented by the Indians for the oracles it delivered. Through the valley flowed a broad stream, which, like a great artery, was made, as usual by the natives, to supply a thousand finer veins that meandered through the beautiful meadows.

On this river Pizarro fixed the site of his new capital, at somewhat less than two leagues' distance from its mouth, which expanded into a commodious haven for the commerce that the prophetic eye of the founder saw would one day— and no very distant one—float on its waters. The central situation of the spot recommended it as a suitable residence for the Peruvian viceroy, whence he might hold easy communication with the different parts of the country, and keep vigilant watch over his Indian vassals. The climate was delightful, and, though only twelve degrees south of the line, was so far tempered by the cool breezes that generally blow from the Pacific, or from the opposite quarter down the frozen sides of the Cordilleras, that the heat was less than in corresponding latitudes on the continent. It never rained on the coast; but this dryness was corrected by a vaporous cloud, which, through the summer months, hung like a curtain over the valley, sheltering it from the rays of a tropical sun, and imperceptibly distilling a refreshing moisture, that clothed the fields in the brightest verdure.

The name bestowed on the infant capital was *Ciudad de los Reyes,* or City of the Kings, in honor of the day, being the sixth of January, 1535,—the festival of Epiphany,—when it was said to have been founded, or more probably when its site was determined, as its actual foundation seems to have been twelve days later. But the Castilian name ceased to be used even within the first generation, and was supplanted by that of Lima, into which the original Indian name of Rimac was corrupted by the Spaniards.

The city was laid out on a very regular plan. The streets were to be much wider than usual in Spanish towns, and perfectly straight, crossing one another at right angles, and so far asunder as to afford ample space for gardens to the dwellings, and for public squares. It was arranged in a triangular form, having the river for its base, the waters of which were to be carried, by means of stone conduits, through all the principal streets, affording facilities for irrigating the grounds around the houses.

No sooner had the governor decided on the site and on the plan of the city, than he commenced operations with his characteristic energy. The Indians were collected from the distance of more than a hundred miles to aid in the work. The Spaniards applied themselves with vigor to the task, under the eye of their chief. The sword was exchanged for the tool of the artisan. The camp was converted into a hive of diligent laborers; and the sounds of war were succeeded by the peaceful hum of a busy population. The *plaza*, which was extensive, was to be surrounded by the cathedral, the palace of the viceroy, that of the municipality, and other public buildings; and their foundations were laid on a scale, and with a solidity, which defied the assaults of time, and, in some instances, even the more formidable shock of earthquakes, that, at different periods, have laid portions of the fair capital in ruins.

While these events were going on, Almagro, the Marshal, as he is usually termed by chroniclers of the time, had gone to Cuzco, whither he was sent by Pizarro to take command of that capital. He received also instructions to undertake, either by himself or by his captains, the conquest of the countries towards the south, forming part of Chili. Almagro, since his arrival at Caxamalca, had seemed willing to smother his ancient feelings of resentment towards his associate, or, at least, to conceal the expression of them, and had consented to take command under him in obedience to the royal mandate. He had even, in his despatches, the magnanimity to make honorable mention of Pizarro, as one anxious to promote the interests of government. Yet he did not so far trust his companion, as to neglect the precaution of sending a confidential agent to represent his own services, when Hernando Pizarro undertook his mission to the mother-country.

That cavalier, after touching at St. Domingo, had arrived without accident at Seville, in January, 1534. Besides the royal fifth, he took with him gold, to the value of half a million of *pesos*, together with a large quantity of silver, the property of private adventurers, some of whom, satisfied with their gains, had returned to Spain in the same vessel with himself. The custom-house was filled with solid ingots, and with vases of different forms, imitations of animals, flowers, fountains, and other objects, executed with more or less skill, and all of pure gold, to the astonishment of the spectators, who flocked from the neighboring country to gaze on these marvellous productions of Indian art. Most of the manufactured articles were the property of the Crown; and Hernando Pizarro, after a short stay at Seville, selected some of the most gorgeous specimens, and crossed the country to Calatayud, where the emperor was holding the cortes of Aragon.

Hernando was instantly admitted to the royal presence, and obtained a gracious audience. He was more conversant with courts than either of his brothers, and his manners, when in situations that imposed a restraint on the natural arrogance of his temper, were graceful and even attractive. In a respectful tone, he now recited the stirring adventures of his brother and his little troop of followers, the fatigues they had endured, the difficulties they had overcome, their capture of the Peruvian Inca, and his magnificent ransom. He had not to tell of the massacre of the unfortunate prince, for that tragic event, which had occurred since his departure from the country, was still unknown to him. The cavalier expatiated on the productiveness of the soil, and on the civilization of the people, evinced by their proficiency in various mechanic arts; in proof of which he displayed the manufactures of wool and cotton, and the rich ornaments of gold and silver. The monarch's eyes sparkled with delight as he gazed on these last. He was too sagacious not to appreciate the advantages of a conquest which secured to him a country so rich in agricultural resources. But the returns from these must necessarily be gradual and long deferred; and he may be excused for listening with still greater satisfaction to Pizarro's tales of its mineral stores; for his ambitious projects had drained the imperial treasury, and he saw in the golden tide thus unexpectedly poured in upon him the immediate means of replenishing it.

Charles made no difficulty, therefore, in granting the petitions of the fortunate adventurer. All the previous grants of Francis Pizarro and his associates were confirmed in the fullest manner; and the boundaries of the governor's jurisdiction were extended seventy leagues further towards the south. Nor did Almagro's services, this time, go unrequited. He was empowered to discover and occupy the country for the distance of two hundred leagues, beginning at the southern limit of Pizarro's territory. Charles, in proof, still further, of his satisfaction, was graciously pleased to address a letter to the two commanders, in which he complimented them on their prowess, and thanked them for their services. This act of justice to Almagro would have been highly honorable to Hernando Pizarro, considering the unfriendly relations in which they stood to each other, had it not been made necessary by the presence of the marshal's own agents at court, who, as already noticed, stood ready to supply any deficiency in the statements of the emissary.

In this display of the royal bounty, the envoy, as will readily be believed, did not go without his reward. He was lodged as an attendant of the Court; was made a knight of Santiago, the most prized of the chivalric orders in Spain; was empowered to equip an armament, and to take command of it; and the royal officers at Seville were required to aid him in his views and facilitate his embarkation for the Indies.

The arrival of Hernando Pizarro in the country, and the reports spread by him and his followers, created a sensation among the Spaniards such as had not been felt since the first voyage of Columbus. The discovery of the New World had filled the minds of men with indefinite expectations of wealth, of which almost every succeeding expedition had proved the fallacy. The conquest of Mexico, though calling forth general admiration as a brilliant and wonderful exploit, had as yet failed to produce those golden results which had been so fondly anticipated. The splendid promises held out by Francis Pizarro on his recent visit to the country had not revived the confidence of his countrymen, made incredulous by repeated disappointment. All that they were assured of was the difficulties of the enterprise; and their distrust of its results was sufficiently shown by the small number of followers, and those only of the most desperate stamp, who were willing to take their chance in the adventure.

But now these promises were realized. It was no longer the golden reports that they were to trust; but the gold itself, which was displayed in such profusion before them. All eyes were now turned towards the West. The broken spendthrift saw in it the quarter where he was to repair his fortunes as speedily as he had ruined them. The merchant, instead of seeking the precious commodities of the East, looked in the opposite direction, and counted on far higher gains, where the most common articles of life commanded so exorbitant prices. The cavalier, eager to win both gold and glory at the point of his lance, thought to find a fair field for his prowess on the mountain plains of the Andes. Hernando Pizarro found that his brother had judged rightly in allowing as many of his company as chose to return home, confident that the display of their wealth would draw ten to his banner for every one that quitted it.

In a short time that cavalier saw himself at the head of one of the most numerous and well-appointed armaments, probably, that had left the shores of Spain since the great fleet of Ovando, in the time of Ferdinand and Isabella. It was scarcely more fortunate than this. Hardly had Hernando put to sea, when a violent tempest fell on the squadron, and compelled him to return to port and refit. At length he crossed the ocean, and reached the little harbor of Nombre de Dios in safety. But no preparations had been made for his coming, and, as he was detained here some time before he could pass the mountains, his company suffered greatly from scarcity of food. In their extremity, the most unwholesome articles were greedily devoured, and many a cavalier spent his little savings to procure himself a miserable subsistence. Disease, as usual, trod closely in the track of famine, and numbers of the unfortunate adventurers, sinking under the unaccustomed heats of the climate, perished on the very threshold of discovery.

It was the tale often repeated in the history of Spanish enterprise. A few, more lucky than the rest, stumble on some unexpected prize, and hundreds, attracted by their success, press forward in the same path. But the rich spoil which lay on the surface has been already swept away by the first comers, and those who follow are to win treasure by long-protracted and painful exertion.—Broken in spirit and in fortune, many returned in disgust to their native shores, while others remained where they were, to die in despair. They thought to dig for gold; but they dug only their graves.

Yet it fared not thus with all Pizarro's company. Many of them, crossing the Isthmus with him to Panamá, came in time to Peru, where, in the desperate chances of its revolutionary struggles, some few arrived at posts of profit and distinction. Among those who first reached the Peruvian shore was an emissary sent by Almagro's agents to inform him of the important grant made to him by the Crown. The tidings reached him just as he was making his entry into Cuzco, where he was received with all respect by Juan and Gonzalo Pizarro, who, in obedience to their brother's commands, instantly resigned the government of the capital into the marshal's hands. But Almagro was greatly elated on finding himself now placed by his sovereign in a command that made him independent of the man who had so deeply wronged him; and he intimated that in the exercise of his present authority he acknowledged no superior. In this lordly humor he was confirmed by several of his followers, who insisted that Cuzco fell to the south of the territory ceded to Pizarro, and consequently came within that now granted to the marshal. Among these followers were several of Alvarado's men, who, though of better condition than the soldiers of Pizarro, were under much worse discipline, and had acquired, indeed, a spirit of unbridled license under that unscrupulous chief. They now evinced little concern for the native population of Cuzco; and, not content with the public edifices, seized on the dwellings of individuals, where it suited their conveniences, appropriating their contents without ceremony,—showing as little respect, in short, for person or property, as if the place had been taken by storm.

While these events were passing in the ancient Peruvian capital, the governor was still at Lima, where he was greatly disturbed by the accounts he received of the new honors conferred on his associate. He did not know that his own jurisdiction had been extended seventy leagues further to the south, and he entertained the same suspicion with Almagro, that the capital of the Incas did not rightly come within his present limits. He saw all the mischief likely to result from this opulent city falling into the hands of his rival, who would thus have an almost indefinite means of gratifying his own cupidity, and that of his followers. He felt, that, under the present circumstances, it was not safe to allow Almagro to anticipate the possession of power, to which, as yet, he had no legitimate right; for the despatches containing the warrant for it still remained with Hernando Pizarro, at Panamá, and all that had reached Peru was a copy of a garbled extract.

Without loss of time, therefore, he sent instructions to Cuzco for his brothers to resume the government, while he defended the measure to Almagro on the ground, that, when he should hereafter receive his credentials, it would be unbecoming to be found already in possession of the post. He concluded by urging him to go forward without delay in his expedition to the south.

But neither the marshal nor his friends were pleased with the idea of so soon relinquishing the authority which they now considered as his right. The Pizarros, on the other hand, were pertinacious in reclaiming it. The dispute grew warmer and warmer. Each party had its supporters; the city was split into factions; and the municipality, the soldiers, and even the Indian population, took sides in the struggle for power. Matters were proceeding to extremity, menacing the capital with violence and bloodshed, when Pizarro himself appeared among them.

On receiving tidings of the fatal consequences of his mandates, he had posted in all haste to Cuzco, where he was greeted with undisguised joy by the natives, as well as by the more temperate Spaniards, anxious to avert the impending storm. The governor's first interview was with Almagro, whom he embraced with a seeming cordiality in his manner; and, without any show of resentment, inquired into the cause of the present disturbances. To this the marshal replied, by throwing the blame on Pizarro's brothers; but, although the governor reprimanded them with some asperity for their violence, it was soon evident that his sympathies were on their side, and the dangers of a feud between the two associates seemed greater than ever. Happily, it was postponed by the intervention of some common friends, who showed more discretion than their leaders. With their aid a reconciliation was at length effected, on the grounds substantially of their ancient compact.

It was agreed that their friendship should be maintained inviolate; and, by a stipulation that reflects no great credit on the parties, it was provided that neither should malign nor disparage the other, especially in their despatches to the emperor; and that neither should hold communication with the government without the knowledge of his confederate; lastly, that both the expenditures and the profits of future discovery should be shared equally by the associates. The wrath of Heaven was invoked by the most solemn imprecations on the head of whichever should violate this compact, and the Almighty was implored to visit the offender with loss of property and of life in this world, and with eternal perdition in that to come! The parties further bound themselves to the observance of this contract by a solemn oath taken on the sacrament, as it was held in the hands of Father Bartolomé de Segovia, who concluded the ceremony by performing mass. The whole proceeding, and the articles of agreement, were carefully recorded by the notary, in an instrument bearing date June 12, 1535, and attested by a long list of witnesses.

Thus did these two ancient comrades, after trampling on the ties of friendship and honor, hope to knit themselves to each other by the holy bands of religion. That it should have been necessary to resort to so extraordinary a measure might have furnished them with the best proof of its inefficacy.

Not long after this accommodation of their differences, the marshal raised his standard for Chili; and numbers, won by his popular manners, and by his liberal largesses,—liberal to prodigality,—eagerly joined in the enterprise, which they fondly trusted would lead even to greater riches than they had found in Peru. Two Indians, Paullo Topa, a brother of the Inca Manco, and Villac Umu, the high-priest of the nation, were sent in advance, with three Spaniards, to prepare the way for the little army. A detachment of a hundred and fifty men, under an officer named Saavedra, next followed. Almagro remained behind to collect further recruits; but before his levies were completed, he began his march, feeling himself insecure, with his diminished strength, in the neighborhood of Pizarro! The remainder of his forces, when mustered, were to follow him.

Thus relieved of the presence of his rival, the governor returned without further delay to the coast, to resume his labors in the settlement of the country. Besides the principal city of "The Kings," he established others along the Pacific, destined to become hereafter the flourishing marts of commerce. The most important of these, in honor of his birthplace, he named Truxillo, planting it on a site already indicated by Almagro. He made also numerous *repartimientos* both of lands and Indians among his followers, in the usual manner of the Spanish Conquerors;—though here the ignorance of the real resources of the country led to very different results from what he had intended, as the territory smallest in extent, not unfrequently, from the hidden treasures in its bosom, turned out greatest in value.

But nothing claimed so much of Pizarro's care as the rising metropolis of Lima; and, so eagerly did he press forward the

work, and so well was he seconded by the multitude of laborers at his command, that he had the satisfaction to see his
young capital, with its stately edifices and its pomp of gardens,
rapidly advancing towards completion. It is pleasing to contemplate the softer features in the character of the rude soldier,
as he was thus occupied with healing up the ravages of war,
and laying the broad foundations of an empire more civilized
than that which he had overthrown. This peaceful occupation
formed a contrast to the life of incessant turmoil in which he
had been hitherto engaged. It seemed, too, better suited to his
own advancing age, which naturally invited to repose. And,
if we may trust his chroniclers, there was no part of his career
in which he took greater satisfaction. It is certain there is no
part which has been viewed with greater satisfaction by posterity; and, amidst the woe and desolation which Pizarro and
his followers brought on the devoted land of the Incas, Lima,
the beautiful City of the Kings, still survives as the most glorious work of his creation, the fairest gem on the shores of the
Pacific.

CHAPTER X [1535-1536]

While the absence of his rival Almagro relieved Pizarro
from all disquietude from that quarter, his authority was menaced in another, where he had least expected it. This was from
the native population of the country. Hitherto the Peruvians
had shown only a tame and submissive temper, that inspired
their conquerors with too much contempt to leave room for
apprehension. They had passively acquiesced in the usurpation of the invaders; had seen one monarch butchered, another
placed on the vacant throne, their temples despoiled of their
treasures, their capital and country appropriated and parcelled
out among the Spaniards; but, with the exception of an occasional skirmish in the mountain passes, not a blow had been
struck in defence of their rights. Yet this was the warlike nation which had spread its conquests over so large a part of
the continent!

In his career, Pizarro, though he scrupled at nothing to effect
his object, had not usually countenanced such superfluous acts
of cruelty as had too often stained the arms of his countrymen
in other parts of the continent, and which, in the course of a
few years, had exterminated nearly a whole population in
Hispaniola. He had struck one astounding blow, by the seizure
of Atahuallpa; and he seemed willing to rely on this to strike
terror into the natives. He even affected some respect for the
institutions of the country, and had replaced the monarch he
had murdered by another of the legitimate line. Yet this was
but a pretext. The kingdom had experienced a revolution of
the most decisive kind. Its ancient institutions were subverted.
Its heaven-descended aristocracy was levelled almost to the
condition of the peasant. The people became the serfs of the
Conquerors. Their dwellings in the capital—at least, after the

arrival of Alvarado's officers—were seized and appropriated. The temples were turned into stables; the royal residences into barracks for the troops. The sanctity of the religious houses was violated. Thousands of matrons and maidens, who, however erroneous their faith, lived in chaste seclusion in the conventual establishments, were now turned abroad, and became the prey of a licentious soldiery. A favorite wife of the young Inca was debauched by the Castilian officers. The Inca, himself treated with contemptuous indifference, found that he was a poor dependant, if not a tool, in the hands of his conquerors.

Yet the Inca Manco was a man of a lofty spirit and a courageous heart; such a one as might have challenged comparison with the bravest of his ancestors in the prouder days of the empire. Stung to the quick by the humiliations to which he was exposed, he repeatedly urged Pizarro to restore him to the real exercise of power, as well as to the show of it. But Pizarro evaded a request so incompatible with his own ambitious schemes, or, indeed, with the policy of Spain, and the young Inca and his nobles were left to brood over their injuries in secret, and await patiently the hour of vengeance.

The dissensions among the Spaniards themselves seemed to afford a favorable opportunity for this. The Peruvian chiefs held many conferences together on the subject, and the high-priest Villac Umu urged the necessity of a rising so soon as Almagro had withdrawn his forces from the city. It would then be comparatively easy, by assaulting the invaders on their several posts, scattered as they were over the country, to overpower them by superior numbers, and shake off their detested yoke before the arrival of fresh reinforcements should rivet it for ever on the necks of his countrymen. A plan for a general rising was formed, and it was in conformity to it that the priest was selected by the Inca to bear Almagro company on the march, that he might secure the coöperation of the natives in the country, and then secretly return—as in fact he did—to take a part in the insurrection.

To carry their plans into effect, it became necessary that the Inca Manco should leave the city and present himself among his people. He found no difficulty in withdrawing from Cuzco, where his presence was scarcely heeded by the Spaniards, as his nominal power was held in little deference by the haughty and confident Conquerors. But in the capital there was a body of Indian allies more jealous of his movements. These were from the tribe of the Cañares, a warlike race of the north, too recently reduced by the Incas to have much sympathy with them or their institutions. There were about a thousand of this people in the place, and as they had conceived some suspicion of the Inca's purposes, they kept an eye on his movements, and speedily reported his absence to Juan Pizarro.

That cavalier, at the head of a small body of horse, instantly marched in pursuit of the fugitive, whom he was so fortunate as to discover in a thicket of reeds, in which he sought to conceal himself, at no great distance from the city. Manco was arrested, brought back a prisoner to Cuzco, and placed under a strong guard in the fortress. The conspiracy seemed now at an end; and nothing was left to the unfortunate Peruvians but to bewail their ruined hopes, and to give utterance to their disappointment in doleful ballads, which rehearsed the captivity of their Inca, and the downfall of his royal house.

While these things were in progress, Hernando Pizarro returned to Ciudad de los Reyes, bearing with him the royal commission for the extension of his brother's powers, as well as of those conceded to Almagro. The envoy also brought the royal patent conferring on Francisco Pizarro the title of *Marques de los Atavillos,*—a province in Peru. Thus was the fortunate adventurer placed in the ranks of the proud aristocracy of Castile, few of whose members could boast—if they had the courage to boast—their elevation from so humble an origin, as still fewer could justify it by a show of greater services to the Crown.

The new marquess resolved not to forward the commission, at present, to the marshal, whom he designed to engage still deeper in the conquest of Chili, that his attention might be diverted from Cuzco, which, however, his brother assured him, now fell, without doubt, within the newly extended limits of his own territory. To make more sure of this important prize, he despatched Hernando to take the government of the capital into his own hands, as the one of his brothers on whose talents and practical experience he placed greatest reliance.

Hernando, notwithstanding his arrogant bearing towards his

countrymen, had ever manifested a more than ordinary sympathy with the Indians. He had been the friend of Atahuallpa; to such a degree, indeed, that it was said, if he had been in the camp at the time, the fate of that unhappy monarch would probably have been averted. He now showed a similar friendly disposition towards his successor, Manco. He caused the Peruvian prince to be liberated from confinement, and gradually admitted him into some intimacy with himself. The crafty Indian availed himself of his freedom to mature his plans for the rising, but with so much caution, that no suspicion of them crossed the mind of Hernando. Secrecy and silence are characteristic of the American, almost as invariably as the peculiar color of his skin. Manco disclosed to his conqueror the existence of several heaps of treasure, and the places where they had been secreted; and, when he had thus won his confidence, he stimulated his cupidity still further by an account of a statue of pure gold of his father Huayna Capac, which the wily Peruvian requested leave to bring from a secret cave in which it was deposited, among the neighboring Andes. Hernando, blinded by his avarice, consented to the Inca's departure.

He sent with him two Spanish soldiers, less as a guard than to aid him in the object of his expedition. A week elapsed, and yet he did not return, nor were there any tidings to be gathered of him. Hernando now saw his error, especially as his own suspicions were confirmed by the unfavorable reports of his Indian allies. Without further delay, he despatched his brother Juan, at the head of sixty horse, in quest of the Peruvian prince, with orders to bring him back once more a prisoner to his capital.

That cavalier, with his well-armed troops, soon traversed the environs of Cuzco without discovering any vestige of the fugitive. The country was remarkably silent and deserted, until, as he approached the mountain range that hems in the valley of Yucay, about six leagues from the city, he was met by the two Spaniards who had accompanied Manco. They informed Pizarro that it was only at the point of the sword he could recover the Inca, for the country was all in arms, and the Peruvian chief at its head was preparing to march on the capital. Yet he had offered no violence to their persons, but had allowed them to return in safety.

The Spanish captain found this story fully confirmed when he arrived at the river Yucay, on the opposite bank of which were drawn up the Indian battalions to the number of many thousand men, who, with their young monarch at their head, prepared to dispute his passage. It seemed that they could not feel their position sufficiently strong, without placing a river, as usual, between them and their enemy. The Spaniards were not checked by this obstacle. The stream, though deep, was narrow; and plunging in, they swam their horses boldly across, amidst a tempest of stones and arrows that rattled thick as hail on their harness, finding occasionally some crevice or vulnerable point,—although the wounds thus received only goaded them to more desperate efforts. The barbarians fell back as the cavaliers made good their landing; but, without allowing the latter time to form, they returned with a spirit which they had hitherto seldom displayed, and enveloped them on all sides with their greatly superior numbers. The fight now raged fiercely. Many of the Indians were armed with lances headed with copper tempered almost to the hardness of steel, and with huge maces and battle-axes of the same metal. Their defensive armour, also, was in many respects excellent, consisting of stout doublets of quilted cotton, shields covered with skins, and casques richly ornamented with gold and jewels, or sometimes made like those of the Mexicans, in the fantastic shape of the heads of wild animals, garnished with rows of teeth that grinned horribly above the visage of the warrior. The whole army wore an aspect of martial ferocity, under the control of much higher military discipline than the Spaniards had before seen in the country.

The little band of cavaliers, shaken by the fury of the Indian assault, were thrown at first into some disorder, but at length, cheering on one another with the old war-cry of "St. Jago," they formed in solid column, and charged boldly into the thick of the enemy. The latter, incapable of withstanding the shock, gave way, or were trampled down under the feet of the horses, or pierced by the lances of the riders. Yet their flight was conducted with some order; and they turned at intervals, to let off a volley of arrows, or to deal furious blows with their pole-axes and war-clubs. They fought as if conscious that they were under the eye of their Inca.

It was evening before they had entirely quitted the level ground, and withdrawn into the fastnesses of the lofty range of hills which belt round the beautiful valley of Yucay. Juan Pizarro and his little troop encamped on the level at the base of the mountains. He had gained a victory, as usual, over immense odds; but he had never seen a field so well disputed, and his victory had cost him the lives of several men and horses, while many more had been wounded, and were nearly disabled by the fatigues of the day. But he trusted the severe lesson he had inflicted on the enemy, whose slaughter was great, would crush the spirit of resistance. He was deceived.

The following morning, great was his dismay to see the passes of the mountains filled up with dark lines of warriors, stretching as far as the eye could penetrate into the depths of the sierra, while dense masses of the enemy were gathered like thunder-clouds along the slopes and summits, as if ready to pour down in fury on the assailants. The ground, altogether unfavorable to the manœuvres of cavalry, gave every advantage to the Peruvians, who rolled down huge rocks from their elevated position, and sent off incessant showers of missiles on the heads of the Spaniards. Juan Pizarro did not care to entangle himself further in the perilous defile; and, though he repeatedly charged the enemy, and drove them back with considerable loss, the second night found him with men and horses wearied and wounded, and as little advanced in the object of his expedition as on the preceding evening. From this embarrassing position, after a day or two more spent in unprofitable hostilities, he was surprised by a summons from his brother to return with all expedition to Cuzco, which was now besieged by the enemy!

Without delay, he began his retreat, recrossed the valley, the recent scene of slaughter, swam the river Yucay, and, by a rapid countermarch, closely followed by the victorious enemy, who celebrated their success with songs or rather yells of triumph, he arrived before nightfall in sight of the capital.

But very different was the sight which there met his eye from what he had beheld on leaving it a few days before. The extensive environs, as far as the eye could reach, were occupied by a mighty host, which an indefinite computation swelled to the number of two hundred thousand warriors. The dusky lines of the Indian battalions stretched out to the very verge of the mountains; while, all around, the eye saw only the crests and waving banners of chieftains, mingled with rich panoplies of feather-work, which reminded some few who had served under Cortés of the military costume of the Aztecs. Above all rose a forest of long lances and battle-axes edged with copper, which, tossed to and fro in wild confusion, glittered in the rays of the setting sun, like light playing on the surface of a dark and troubled ocean. It was the first time that the Spaniards had beheld an Indian army in all its terrors; such an army as the Incas led when the banner of the Sun was borne triumphant over the land.

Yet the bold hearts of the cavaliers, if for a moment dismayed by the sight, soon gathered courage as they closed up their files, and prepared to open a way for themselves through the beleaguering host. But the enemy seemed to shun the encounter; and, falling back at their approach, left a free entrance into the capital. The Peruvians were, probably, not unwilling to draw as many victims as they could into the toils, conscious that, the greater the number, the sooner they would become sensible to the approaches of famine.

Hernando Pizarro greeted his brother with no little satisfaction; for he brought an important addition to his force, which now, when all were united, did not exceed two hundred, horse and foot, besides a thousand Indian auxiliaries; an insignificant number, in comparison with the countless multitudes that were swarming at the gates. That night was passed by the Spaniards with feelings of the deepest anxiety, as they looked forward with natural apprehension to the morrow. It was early in February, 1536, when the siege of Cuzco commenced; a siege memorable as calling out the most heroic displays of Indian and European valor, and bringing the two races in deadlier conflict with each other than had yet occurred in the conquest of Peru.

The numbers of the enemy seemed no less formidable during the night than by the light of day; far and wide their watch-fires were to be seen gleaming over valley and hill-top, as thickly scattered, says an eyewitness, as "the stars of heaven in a cloudless summer night." Before these fires had become pale in the light of the morning, the Spaniards were roused by the hideous clamor of conch, trumpet, and atabal, mingled with the fierce war-cries of the barbarians, as they let off volleys of missiles of every description, most of which fell harmless within the city. But others did more serious execution. These were burning arrows, and red-hot stones wrapped in cotton that had been steeped in some bituminous substance, which scattered long trains of light through the air, fell on the roofs of the buildings, and speedily set them on fire. These roofs, even of the better sort of edifices, were uniformly of thatch, and were ignited as easily as tinder. In a moment the flames burst forth from the most opposite quarters of the city. They quickly communicated to the wood-work in the interior of the buildings, and broad sheets of flames mingled with smoke rose up towards the heavens, throwing a fearful glare over every object. The rarefied atmosphere heightened the previous impetuosity of the wind, which, fanning the rising flames, they rapidly spread from dwelling to dwelling, till the whole fiery mass, swayed to and fro by the tempest, surged and roared with the fury of a volcano. The heat became intense, and clouds of smoke, gathering like a dark pall over the city, produced a sense of suffocation and almost blindness in those quarters where it was driven by the winds.

The Spaniards were encamped in the great square, partly under awnings, and partly in the hall of the Inca Viracocha, on the ground since covered by the cathedral. Three times in the course of that dreadful day, the roof of the building was on fire; but, although no efforts were made to extinguish it, the flames went out without doing much injury. This miracle was ascribed to the Blessed Virgin, who was distinctly seen by several of the Christian combatants, hovering over the spot on which was to be raised the temple dedicated to her.

Fortunately, the open space around Hernando's little company separated them from the immediate scene of conflagration. It afforded a means of preservation similar to that employed by the American hunter, who endeavors to surround himself with a belt of wasted land, when overtaken by a conflagration in the prairies. All day the fire continued to rage, and at night the effect was even more appalling; for by the lurid flames the unfortunate Spaniards could read the consternation depicted in each other's ghastly countenances, while in the suburbs, along the slopes of the surrounding hills, might be seen the throng of besiegers, gazing with fiendish exultation on the work of destruction. High above the town to the north, rose the grey fortress, which now showed ruddy in the glare, looking grimly down on the ruins of the fair city which it was no longer able to protect; and in the distance were to be discerned the shadowy forms of the Andes, soaring up in solitary grandeur into the regions of eternal silence, far beyond the wild tumult that raged so fearfully at their base.

Such was the extent of the city, that it was several days before the fury of the fire was spent. Tower and temple, hut, palace, and hall, went down before it. Fortunately, among the buildings that escaped were the magnificent House of the Sun and the neighboring Convent of the Virgins. Their insulated position afforded the means, of which the Indians from motives of piety were willing to avail themselves, for their preservation. Full one half of the capital, so long the chosen seat of Western civilization, the pride of the Incas, and the bright abode of their tutelar deity, was laid in ashes by the hands of his own children. It was some consolation for them to reflect, that it burned over the heads of its conquerors,—their trophy and their tomb!

During the long period of the conflagration, the Spaniards made no attempt to extinguish the flames. Such an attempt would have availed nothing. Yet they did not tamely submit to the assaults of the enemy, and they sallied forth from time to time to repel them. But the fallen timbers and scattered rubbish of the houses presented serious impediments to the movements of horse; and, when these were partially cleared away by the efforts of the infantry and the Indian allies, the Peruvians planted stakes and threw barricades across the path, which proved equally embarrassing. To remove them was a work of time and no little danger, as the pioneers were exposed to the whole brunt of the enemy's archery, and the aim of the Peruvian was sure. When at length the obstacles were cleared away, and a free course was opened to the cavalry, they rushed with irresistible impetuosity on their foes, who, falling back in confusion, were cut to pieces by the riders, or pierced through with their lances. The slaughter on these occasions was great; but the Indians, nothing disheartened, usually returned with renewed courage to the attack, and, while fresh reinforcements met the Spaniards in front, others, lying in ambush among the ruins, threw the troops into disorder by assailing them on the flanks. The Peruvians were expert both with bow and sling; and these encounters, notwithstanding the superiority of their arms, cost the Spaniards more lives than in their crippled condition they could afford to spare,—a loss poorly compensated by that of tenfold the number of the enemy. One weapon, peculiar to South American warfare, was used with some effect by the Peruvians. This was the *lasso*, a long rope with a noose at the end, which they adroitly threw over the rider, or entangled with it the legs of his horse, so as to bring them both to the ground. More than one Spaniard fell into the hands of the enemy by this expedient.

Thus harassed, sleeping on their arms, with their horses picketed by their side, ready for action at any and every hour, the Spaniards had no rest by night or by day. To add to their troubles, the fortress which overlooked the city, and completely commanded the great square in which they were quartered, had been so feebly garrisoned in their false sense of security, that, on the approach of the Peruvians, it had been abandoned without a blow in its defence. It was now occupied by a strong body of the enemy, who, from his elevated position, sent down showers of missiles, from time to time, which added greatly to the annoyance of the besieged. Bitterly did their captain now repent the improvident security which had led him to neglect a post so important.

Their distresses were still further aggravated by the rumors, which continually reached their ears, of the state of the country. The rising, it was said, was general throughout the land; the Spaniards living on their insulated plantations had all been massacred; Lima and Truxillo and the principal cities were besieged, and must soon fall into the enemy's hands; the Peruvians were in possession of the passes, and all communications were cut off, so that no relief was to be expected from their countrymen on the coast. Such were the dismal stories (which, however exaggerated, had too much foundation in fact), that now found their way into the city from the camp of the besiegers. And to give greater credit to the rumors, eight or ten human heads were rolled into the *plaza*, in whose bloodstained visages the Spaniards recognized with horror the lineaments of their companions, who they knew had been dwelling in solitude on their estates!

Overcome by these horrors, many were for abandoning the place at once, as no longer tenable, and for opening a passage for themselves to the coast with their own good swords. There was a daring in the enterprise which had a charm for the adventurous spirit of the Castilian. Better, they said, to perish in a manly struggle for life, than to die thus ignominiously, pent up like foxes in their holes, to be suffocated by the hunter!

But the Pizarros, De Rojas, and some other of the principal cavaliers, refused to acquiesce in a measure which, they said, must cover them with dishonor. Cuzco had been the great prize for which they had contended; it was the ancient seat of empire, and, though now in ashes, would again rise from its ruins as glorious as before. All eyes would be turned on them, as its defenders, and their failure, by giving confidence to the enemy, might decide the fate of their countrymen throughout the land. They were placed in that post as the post of honor, and better would it be to die there than to desert it.

There seemed, indeed, no alternative; for every avenue to escape was cut off by an enemy who had perfect knowledge of the country, and possession of all its passes. But this state of things could not last long. The Indian could not, in the long run, contend with the white man. The spirit of insurrection would die out of itself. Their great army would melt away, unaccustomed as the natives were to the privations incident to a protracted campaign. Reinforcements would be daily coming in from the colonies; and, if the Castilians would be but true to themselves for a season, they would be relieved by their own countrymen, who would never suffer them to die like outcasts among the mountains.

The cheering words and courageous bearing of the cavaliers went to the hearts of their followers; for the soul of the Spaniard readily responded to the call of honor, if not of humanity. All now agreed to stand by their leader to the last. But, if they would remain longer in their present position, it was absolutely necessary to dislodge the enemy from the fortress; and, before venturing on this dangerous service, Pizarro resolved to strike such a blow as should intimidate the besiegers from further attempt to molest his present quarters.

He communicated his plan of attack to his officers; and, forming his little troop into three divisions, he placed them under command of his brother Gonzalo, of Gabriel de Rojas, an officer in whom he reposed great confidence, and Hernan Ponce de Leon. The Indian pioneers were sent forward to clear away the rubbish, and the several divisions moved simultaneously up the principal avenues towards the camp of the besiegers. Such stragglers as they met in their way were easily cut to pieces, and the three bodies, bursting impetuously on the disordered lines of the Peruvians, took them completely by surprise. For some moments there was little resistance, and the slaughter was terrible. But the Indians gradually rallied, and, coming into something like order, returned to the fight with the courage of men who had long been familiar with danger. They fought hand to hand with their copper-headed war-clubs and pole-axes, while a storm of darts, stones, and arrows rained on the well-defended bodies of the Christians.

The barbarians showed more discipline than was to have been expected; for which, it is said, they were indebted to some Spanish prisoners, from several of whom, the Inca, having generously spared their lives, took occasional lessons in the art of war. The Peruvians had, also, learned to manage with some degree of skill the weapons of their conquerors; and they were seen armed with bucklers, helmets, and swords of European workmanship, and even, in a few instances, mounted on the horses which they had taken from the white men. The young Inca, in particular, accoutred in the European fashion, rode a war-horse which he managed with considerable address, and, with a long lance in his hand, led on his followers to the attack.—This readiness to adopt the superior arms and tactics of the Conquerors intimates a higher civilization than that which belonged to the Aztec, who, in his long collision with the Spaniards, was never so far divested of his terrors for the horse as to venture to mount him.

But a few days or weeks of training were not enough to give familiarity with weapons, still less with tactics, so unlike those to which the Peruvians had been hitherto accustomed. The fight, on the present occasion, though hotly contested, was not of long duration. After a gallant struggle, in which the natives threw themselves fearlessly on the horsemen, endeavoring to tear them from their saddles, they were obliged to give way before the repeated shock of their chargers. Many were trampled under foot, others cut down by the Spanish broadswords, while the arquebusiers, supporting the cavalry, kept up a running fire that did terrible execution on the flanks and rear of the fugitives. At length, sated with slaughter, and trusting that the chastisement he had inflicted on the enemy would secure him from further annoyance for the present, the Castilian general drew back his forces to their quarters in the capital.

His next step was the recovery of the citadel. It was an enterprise of danger. The fortress, which overlooked the northern section of the city, stood high on a rocky eminence, so steep as to be inaccessible on this quarter, where it was defended only by a single wall. Towards the open country, it was more easy of approach; but there it was protected by two semicircular walls, each about twelve hundred feet in length, and of great thickness. They were built of massive stones, or rather rocks, put together without cement, so as to form a kind of rustic-work. The level of the ground between these lines of defence was raised up so as to enable the garrison to discharge its arrows at the assailants, while their own persons were protected by the parapet. Within the interior wall was the fortress, consisting of three strong towers, one of great height, which, with a smaller one, was now held by the enemy, under the command of an Inca noble, a warrior of well-tried valor, prepared to defend it to the last extremity.

The perilous enterprise was intrusted by Hernando Pizarro to his brother Juan, a cavalier in whose bosom burned the adventurous spirit of a knight-errant of romance. As the fortress was to be approached through the mountain passes, it became necessary to divert the enemy's attention to another quarter. A little while before sunset Juan Pizarro left the city with a picked corps of horsemen, and took a direction opposite to that of the fortress, that the besieging army might suppose the object was a foraging expedition. But secretly countermarching in the night, he fortunately found the passes un-protected, and arrived before the outer wall of the fortress, without giving the alarm to the garrison.

The entrance was through a narrow opening in the centre of the rampart; but this was now closed up with heavy stones, that seemed to form one solid work with the rest of the ma-sonry. It was an affair of time to dislodge these huge masses, in such a manner as not to rouse the garrison. The Indian nations, who rarely attacked in the night, were not sufficiently acquainted with the art of war even to provide against surprise by posting sentinels. When the task was accomplished, Juan Pizarro and his gallant troop rode through the gateway, and advanced towards the second parapet.

But their movements had not been conducted so secretly as to escape notice, and they now found the interior court swarming with warriors, who, as the Spaniards drew near, let off clouds of missiles that compelled them to come to a halt. Juan Pizarro, aware that no time was to be lost, ordered one half of his corps to dismount, and, putting himself at their head, prepared to make a breach as before in the fortifications. He had been wounded some days previously in the jaw, so that, finding his helmet caused him pain, he rashly dispensed with it, and trusted for protection to his buckler. Leading on his men, he encouraged them in the work of demolition, in the face of such a storm of stones, javelins, and arrows, as might have made the stoutest heart shrink from encountering it. The good mail of the Spaniards did not always protect them; but others took the place of such as fell, until a breach was made, and the cavalry, pouring in, rode down all who opposed them.

The parapet was now abandoned, and the enemy, hurrying with disorderly flight across the inclosure, took refuge on a kind of platform or terrace, commanded by the principal tower. Here rallying, they shot off fresh volleys of missiles against the Spaniards, while the garrison in the fortress hurled down fragments of rock and timber on their heads. Juan Pizarro, still among the foremost, sprang forward on the terrace, cheering on his men by his voice and example; but at this moment he was struck by a large stone on the head, not then protected by his buckler, and was stretched on the ground. The dauntless chief still continued to animate his followers by his voice, till the terrace was carried, and its miserable defenders were put to the sword. His sufferings were then too much for him, and he was removed to the town below, where, notwithstanding every exertion to save him, he survived the injury but a fortnight, and died in great agony. —To say that he was a Pizarro is enough to attest his claim to valor. But it is his praise, that his valor was tempered by courtesy. His own nature appeared mild by contrast with the haughty temper of his brothers, and his manners made him a favorite of the army. He had served in the conquest of Peru from the first, and no name on the roll of its conquerors is less tarnished by the reproach of cruelty, or stands higher in all the attributes of a true and valiant knight.

Though deeply sensible to his brother's disaster, Hernando Pizarro saw that no time was to be lost in profiting by the advantages already gained. Committing the charge of the town to Gonzalo, he put himself at the head of the assailants, and laid vigorous siege to the fortresses. One surrendered after a short resistance. The other and more formidable of the two still held out under the brave Inca noble who commanded it. He was a man of an athletic frame, and might be seen striding along the battlements, armed with a Spanish buckler and cuirass, and in his hand wielding a formidable mace, garnished with points or knobs of copper. With this terrible weapon he struck down all who attempted to force a passage into the fortress. Some of his own followers who proposed a surrender he is said to have slain with his own hand. Hernando prepared to carry the place by escalade. Ladders were planted against the walls, but no sooner did a Spaniard gain the topmost round, than he was hurled to the ground by the strong arm of the Indian warrior. His activity was equal to his strength; and he seemed to be at every point the moment that his presence was needed.

The Spanish commander was filled with admiration at this display of valor; for he could admire valor even in an enemy. He gave orders that the chief should not be injured, but be taken alive, if possible. This was not easy. At length, numerous ladders having been planted against the tower, the Spaniards scaled it on several quarters at the same time, and, leaping into the place, overpowered the few combatants who still made a show of resistance. But the Inca chieftain was not to be taken; and, finding further resistance ineffectual, he sprang to the edge of the battlements, and, casting away his war-club, wrapped his mantle around him and threw himself headlong from the summit. He died like an ancient Roman. He had struck his last stroke for the freedom of his country, and he scorned to survive her dishonor.—The Castilian commander left a small force to secure his conquest, and returned in triumph to his quarters.

Week after week rolled away, and no relief came to the beleaguered Spaniards. They had long since begun to feel the approaches of famine. Fortunately, they were provided with water from the streams which flowed through the city. But, though they had well husbanded their resources, their provisions were exhausted, and they had for some time depended on such scanty supplies of grain as they could gather from the ruined magazines and dwellings, mostly consumed by the fire, or from the produce of some successful foray. This latter resource was attended with no little difficulty; for every expedition led to a fierce encounter with the enemy, which usually cost the lives of several Spaniards, and inflicted a much heavier injury on the Indian allies. Yet it was at least one good result of such loss, that it left fewer to provide for. But the whole number of the besieged was so small, that any loss greatly increased the difficulties of defence by the remainder.

As months passed away without bringing any tidings of their countrymen, their minds were haunted with still gloomier apprehensions as to their fate. They well knew that the governor would make every effort to rescue them from their desperate condition. That he had not succeeded in this made it probable, that his own situation was no better than theirs, or, perhaps, he and his followers had already fallen victims to the fury of the insurgents. It was a dismal thought, that they alone were left in the land, far from all human succour, to perish miserably by the hands of the barbarians among the mountains.

Yet the actual state of things, though gloomy in the extreme, was not quite so desperate as their imaginations had painted it. The insurrection, it is true, had been general throughout the country, at least that portion of it occupied by the Spaniards. It had been so well concerted, that it broke out almost simultaneously, and the Conquerors, who were living in careless security on their estates, had been massacred to the number of several hundreds. An Indian force had sat down before Xauxa, and a considerable army had occupied the valley of Rimac and laid siege to Lima. But the country around that capital was of an open, level character, very favorable to the action of cavalry. Pizarro no sooner saw himself menaced by the hostile array, than he sent such a force against the Peruvians as speedily put them to flight; and, following up his advantage, he inflicted on them such a severe chastisement, that, although they still continued to hover in the distance and cut off his communications with the interior, they did not care to trust themselves on the other side of the Rimac.

The accounts that the Spanish commander now received of the state of the country filled him with the most serious alarm. He was particularly solicitous for the fate of the garrison at Cuzco, and he made repeated efforts to relieve that capital. Four several detachments, amounting to more than four hundred men in all, half of them cavalry, were sent by him at different times, under some of his bravest officers. But none of them reached their place of destination. The wily natives permitted them to march into the interior of the country, until they were fairly entangled in the passes of the Cordilleras. They then enveloped them with greatly superior numbers, and, occupying the heights, showered down their fatal missiles on the heads of the Spaniards, or crushed them under the weight of fragments of rock which they rolled on them from the mountains. In some instances, the whole detachment was cut off to a man. In others, a few stragglers only survived to return and tell the bloody tale to their countrymen at Lima.

Pizarro was now filled with consternation. He had the most dismal forebodings of the fate of the Spaniards dispersed throughout the country, and even doubted the possibility of maintaining his own foothold in it without assistance from abroad. He despatched a vessel to the neighboring colony at Truxillo, urging them to abandon the place, with all their effects, and to repair to him at Lima. The measure was, fortunately, not adopted. Many of his men were for availing themselves of the vessels which rode at anchor in the port to make their escape from the country at once, and take refuge in Panamá. Pizarro would not hearken to so dastardly a counsel, which involved the desertion of the brave men in the interior who still looked to him for protection. He cut off the hopes of these timid spirits by despatching all the vessels then in port on a very different mission. He sent letters by them to the governors of Panamá, Nicaragua, Guatemala, and Mexico, representing the gloomy state of his affairs, and invoking their aid. His epistle to Alvarado, then established at Guatemala, is preserved. He conjures him by every sentiment of honor and patriotism to come to his assistance, and this before it was too late. Without assistance, the Spaniards could no longer maintain their footing in Peru, and that great empire would be lost to the Castilian Crown. He finally engages to share with him such conquests as they may make with their united arms.—Such concessions, to the very man whose absence from the country, but a few months before, Pizarro would have been willing to secure at almost any price, are sufficient evidence of the extremity of his distress. The succours thus earnestly solicited arrived in time, not to quell the Indian insurrection, but to aid him in a struggle quite as formidable with his own countrymen.

It was now August. More than five months had elapsed since the commencement of the siege of Cuzco, yet the Peruvian legions still lay encamped around the city. The siege had been protracted much beyond what was usual in Indian warfare, and showed the resolution of the natives to exterminate the white men. But the Peruvians themselves had for some time been straitened by the want of provisions. It was no easy matter to feed so numerous a host; and the obvious resource of the magazines of grain, so providently prepared by the Incas, did them but little service, since their contents had been most prodigally used, and even dissipated, by the Spaniards, on their first occupation of the country. The season for planting had now arrived, and the Inca well knew, that, if his followers were to neglect it, they would be visited by a scourge even more formidable than their invaders. Disbanding the greater part of his forces, therefore, he ordered them to withdraw to their homes, and, after the labors of the field were over, to return and resume the blockade of the capital. The

Inca reserved a considerable force to attend on his own person, with which he retired to Tambo, a strongly fortified place south of the valley of Yucay, the favorite residence of his ancestors. He also posted a large body as a corps of observation in the environs of Cuzco, to watch the movements of the enemy, and to intercept supplies.

The Spaniards beheld with joy the mighty host, which had so long encompassed the city, now melting away. They were not slow in profiting by the circumstance, and Hernando Pizarro took advantage of the temporary absence to send out foraging parties to scour the country, and bring back supplies to his famishing soldiers. In this he was so successful that on one occasion no less than two thousand head of cattle—the Peruvian sheep—were swept away from the Indian plantations and brought safely to Cuzco. This placed the army above all apprehensions on the score of want for the present.

Yet these forays were made at the point of the lance, and many a desperate contest ensued, in which the best blood of the Spanish chivalry was shed. The contests, indeed, were not confined to large bodies of troops, but skirmishes took place between smaller parties, which sometimes took the form of personal combats. Nor were the parties so unequally matched as might have been supposed in these single rencontres; and the Peruvian warrior, with his sling, his bow, and his *lasso,* proved no contemptible antagonist for the mailed horseman, whom he sometimes even ventured to encounter, hand to hand, with his formidable battle-axe. The ground around Cuzco became a battle-field, like the *vega* of Granada, in which Christian and Pagan displayed the characteristics of their peculiar warfare; and many a deed of heroism was performed, which wanted only the song of the minstrel to shed around it a glory like that which rested on the last days of the Moslem of Spain.

But Hernando Pizarro was not content to act wholly on the defensive; and he meditated a bold stroke, by which at once to put an end to the war. This was the capture of the Inca Manco, whom he hoped to surprise in his quarters at Tambo.

For this service he selected about eighty of his best-mounted cavalry, with a small body of foot; and, making a large détour through the less frequented mountain defiles, he arrived before Tambo without alarm to the enemy. He found the place more strongly fortified than he had imagined. The palace, or rather fortress, of the Incas stood on a lofty eminence, the steep sides of which, on the quarter where the Spaniards approached, were cut into terraces, defended by strong walls of stone and sunburnt brick. The place was impregnable on this side. On the opposite, it looked towards the Yucay, and the ground descended by a gradual declivity towards the plain through which rolled its deep but narrow current. This was the quarter on which to make the assault.

Crossing the stream without much difficulty, the Spanish commander advanced up the smooth *glacis* with as little noise as possible. The morning light had hardly broken on the mountains; and Pizarro, as he drew near the outer defences, which, as in the fortress of Cuzco, consisted of a stone parapet of great strength drawn round the inclosure, moved quickly forward, confident that the garrison were still buried in sleep. But thousands of eyes were upon him; and as the Spaniards came within bowshot, a multitude of dark forms suddenly rose above the rampart, while the Inca, with his lance in hand, was seen on horseback in the inclosure, directing the operations of his troops. At the same moment the air was darkened with innumerable missiles, stones, javelins, and arrows, which fell like a hurricane on the troops, and the mountains rang to the wild war-whoop of the enemy. The Spaniards, taken by surprise, and many of them sorely wounded, were staggered; and, though they quickly rallied, and made two attempts to renew the assault, they were at length obliged to fall back, unable to endure the violence of the storm. To add to their confusion, the lower level in their rear was flooded by the waters, which the natives, by opening the sluices, had diverted from the bed of the river, so that their position was no longer tenable. A council of war was then held, and it was decided to abandon the attack as desperate, and to retreat in as good order as possible.

The day had been consumed in these ineffectual operations; and Hernando, under cover of the friendly darkness, sent forward his infantry and baggage, taking command of the centre himself, and trusting the rear to his brother Gonzalo. The river was happily recrossed without accident, although the

enemy, now confident in their strength, rushed out of their
defences, and followed up the retreating Spaniards, whom
they annoyed with repeated discharges of arrows. More than
once they pressed so closely on the fugitives, that Gonzalo
and his chivalry were compelled to turn and make one of those
desperate charges that effectually punished their audacity, and
stayed the tide of pursuit. Yet the victorious foe still hung on
the rear of the discomfited cavaliers, till they had emerged
from the mountain passes, and come within sight of the blackened walls of the capital. It was the last triumph of the Inca.

BOOK IV

CIVIL WARS OF THE CONQUERORS

CHAPTER I [1535–1537]

ALMAGRO'S MARCH TO CHILI—SUFFERING OF THE
TROOPS—HE RETURNS AND SEIZES CUZCO—ACTION OF
ABANCAY—GASPAR DE ESPINOSA—ALMAGRO LEAVES
CUZCO—NEGOTIATIONS WITH PIZARRO

While the events recorded in the preceding chapter were
passing, the Marshal Almagro was engaged in his memorable
expedition to Chili. He had set out, as we have seen, with
only part of his forces, leaving his lieutenant to follow him
with the remainder. During the first part of the way, he profited by the great military road of the Incas, which stretched
across the table-land far towards the south. But as he drew
near to Chili, the Spanish commander became entangled in
the defiles of the mountains, where no vestige of a road was
to be discerned. Here his progress was impeded by all the obstacles which belong to the wild scenery of the Cordilleras;
deep and ragged ravines, round whose sides a slender sheep-
path wound up to a dizzy height over the precipices below;
rivers rushing in fury down the slopes of the mountains, and
throwing themselves in stupendous cataracts into the yawn-
ing abyss; dark forests of pine that seemed to have no end,
and then again long reaches of desolate table-land, without so
much as a bush or shrub to shelter the shivering traveller from
the blast that swept down from the frozen summits of the
sierra.

The cold was so intense, that many lost the nails of their
fingers, their fingers themselves, and sometimes their limbs.
Others were blinded by the dazzling waste of snow, reflecting
the rays of a sun made intolerably brilliant in the thin atmosphere of these elevated regions. Hunger came, as usual, in
the train of woes; for in these dismal solitudes no vegetation
that would suffice for the food of man was visible, and no living thing, except only the great bird of the Andes, hovering
over their heads in expectation of his banquet. This was too

frequently afforded by the number of wretched Indians, who, unable, from the scantiness of their clothing, to encounter the severity of the climate, perished by the way. Such was the pressure of hunger, that the miserable survivors fed on the dead bodies of their countrymen, and the Spaniards forced a similar sustenance from the carcasses of their horses, literally frozen to death in the mountain passes.—Such were the terrible penalties which Nature imposed on those who rashly intruded on these her solitary and most savage haunts.

Yet their own sufferings do not seem to have touched the hearts of the Spaniards with any feeling of compassion for the weaker natives. Their path was everywhere marked by burnt and desolated hamlets, the inhabitants of which were compelled to do them service as beasts of burden. They were chained together in gangs of ten or twelve, and no infirmity or feebleness of body excused the unfortunate captive from his full share of the common toil, till he sometimes dropped dead, in his very chains, from mere exhaustion! Alvarado's company are accused of having been more cruel than Pizarro's; and many of Almagro's men, it may be remembered, were recruited from that source. The commander looked with displeasure, it is said, on these enormities, and did what he could to repress them. Yet he did not set a good example in his own conduct, if it be true that he caused no less than thirty Indian chiefs to be burnt alive, for the massacre of three of his followers! The heart sickens at the recital of such atrocities perpetrated on an unoffending people, or, at least, guilty of no other crime than that of defending their own soil too well.

There is something in the possession of superior strength most dangerous, in a moral view, to its possessor. Brought in contact with semi-civilized man, the European, with his endowments and effective force so immeasurably superior, holds him as little higher than the brute, and as born equally for his service. He feels that he has a natural right, as it were, to his obedience, and that this obedience is to be measured, not by the powers of the barbarian, but by the will of his conqueror. Resistance becomes a crime to be washed out only in the blood of the victim. The tale of such atrocities is not confined to the Spaniard. Wherever the civilized man and the savage have come in contact, in the East or in the West, the story has been too often written in blood.

From the wild chaos of mountain scenery the Spaniards emerged on the green vale of Coquimbo, about the thirtieth degree of south latitude. Here they halted to refresh themselves in its abundant plains, after their unexampled sufferings and fatigues. Meanwhile Almagro despatched an officer with a strong party in advance, to ascertain the character of the country towards the south. Not long after, he was cheered by the arrival of the remainder of his forces under his lieutenant Rodrigo de Orgoñez. This was a remarkable person, and intimately connected with the subsequent fortunes of Almagro.

He was a native of Oropesa, had been trained in the Italian wars, and held the rank of ensign in the army of the Constable of Bourbon at the famous sack of Rome. It was a good school in which to learn his iron trade, and to steel the heart against any too ready sensibility to human suffering. Orgoñez was an excellent soldier; true to his commander, prompt, fearless, and unflinching in the execution of his orders. His services attracted the notice of the Crown, and, shortly after this period, he was raised to the rank of Marshal of New Toledo. Yet it may be doubted whether his character did not qualify him for an executive and subordinate station rather than for one of higher responsibility.

Almagro received also the royal warrant, conferring on him his new powers and territorial jurisdiction. The instrument had been detained by the Pizarros to the very last moment. His troops, long since disgusted with their toilsome and unprofitable march, were now clamorous to return. Cuzco, they said, undoubtedly fell within the limits of his government, and it was better to take possession of its comfortable quarters than to wander like outcasts in this dreary wilderness. They reminded their commander that thus only could he provide for the interests of his son Diego. This was an illegitimate son of Almagro, on whom his father doted with extravagant fondness, justified more than usual by his promising character.

After an absence of about two months, the officer sent on the exploring expedition returned, bringing unpromising accounts of the southern regions of Chili. The only land of promise for the Castilian was one that teemed with gold. He had penetrated to the distance of a hundred leagues, to the limits, probably, of the conquests of the Incas on the river Maule. The Spaniards had fortunately stopped short of the land of Arauco, where the blood of their countrymen was soon after to be poured out like water, and which still maintains a proud independence amidst the general humiliation of the Indian races around it.

Almagro now yielded, with little reluctance, to the renewed importunities of the soldiers, and turned his face towards the North. It is unnecessary to follow his march in detail. Disheartened by the difficulty of the mountain passage, he took the road along the coast, which led him across the great desert of Atacama. In crossing this dreary waste, which stretches for nearly a hundred leagues to the northern borders of Chili, with hardly a green spot in its expanse to relieve the fainting traveller, Almagro and his men experienced as great sufferings, though not of the same kind, as those which they had encountered in the passes of the Cordilleras. Indeed, the captain would not easily be found at this day, who would venture to lead his army across this dreary region. But the Spaniard of the sixteenth century had a strength of limb and a buoyancy of spirit which raised him to a contempt of obstacles, almost justifying the boast of the historian, that "he contended indifferently, at the same time, with man, with the elements, and with famine!"

After traversing the terrible desert, Almagro reached the ancient town of Arequipa, about sixty leagues from Cuzco. Here he learned with astonishment the insurrection of the Peruvians, and further, that the young Inca Manco still lay with a formidable force at no great distance from the capital. He had once been on friendly terms with the Peruvian prince, and he now resolved, before proceeding farther, to send an embassy to his camp, and arrange an interview with him in the neighborhood of Cuzco.

Almagro's emissaries were well received by the Inca, who alleged his grounds of complaint against the Pizarros, and named the vale of Yucay as the place where he would confer with the marshal. The Spanish commander accordingly resumed his march, and, taking one half of his force, whose whole number fell somewhat short of five hundred men, he repaired in person to the place of rendezvous; while the remainder of his army established their quarters at Urcos, about six leagues from the capital.

The Spaniards in Cuzco, startled by the appearance of this fresh body of troops in their neighborhood, doubted, when they learned the quarter whence they came, whether it betided them good or evil. Hernando Pizarro marched out of the city with a small force, and, drawing near to Urcos, heard with no little uneasiness of Almagro's purpose to insist on his pretensions to Cuzco. Though much inferior in strength to his rival, he determined to resist him.

Meanwhile, the Peruvians, who had witnessed the conference between the soldiers of the opposite camps, suspected some secret understanding between the parties, which would compromise the safety of the Inca. They communicated their distrust to Manco, and the latter, adopting the same sentiments, or perhaps, from the first, meditating a surprise of the Spaniards, suddenly fell upon the latter in the valley of Yucay with a body of fifteen thousand men. But the veterans of Chili were too familiar with Indian tactics to be taken by surprise. And though a sharp engagement ensued, which lasted more than an hour, in which Orgoñez had a horse killed under him, the natives were finally driven back with great slaughter, and the Inca was so far crippled by the blow, that he was not likely for the present to give further molestation.

Almagro, now joining the division left at Urcos, saw no further impediment to his operations on Cuzco. He sent, at once, an embassy to the municipality of the place, requiring the recognition of him as its lawful governor, and presenting at the same time a copy of his credentials from the Crown. But the question of jurisdiction was not one easy to be settled, depending, as it did, on a knowledge of the true parallels of latitude, not very likely to be possessed by the rude followers of Pizarro. The royal grant had placed under his jurisdiction all the country extending two hundred and seventy leagues south of the river at Santiago, situated one degree and twenty minutes north of the equator. Two hundred and seventy leagues on the meridian, by our measurement, would fall more than a degree short of Cuzco, and, indeed, would barely include the city of Lima itself. But the Spanish leagues, of only seventeen and a half to a degree, would remove the southern boundary to nearly half a degree beyond the capital of the Incas, which would thus fall within the jurisdiction of Pizarro. Yet the division-line ran so close to the disputed ground, that the true result might reasonably be doubted, where no careful scientific observations had been made to obtain it; and each party was prompt to assert, as they always are in such cases, that its own claim was clear and unquestionable.

Thus summoned by Almagro, the authorities of Cuzco, unwilling to give umbrage to either of the contending chiefs, decided that they must wait until they could take counsel—which they promised to do at once—with certain pilots better instructed than themselves in the position of the Santiago. Meanwhile, a truce was arranged between the parties, each solemnly engaging to abstain from hostile measures, and to remain quiet in their present quarters.

The weather now set in cold and rainy. Almagro's soldiers, greatly discontented with their position, flooded as it was by the waters, were quick to discover that Hernando Pizarro was busily employed in strengthening himself in the city, contrary to agreement. They also learned with dismay, that a large body of men, sent by the governor from Lima, under command of Alonso de Alvarado, was on the march to relieve Cuzco. They exclaimed that they were betrayed, and that the truce had been only an artifice to secure their inactivity until the arrival of the expected succours. In this state of excitement, it was not very difficult to persuade their commander—too ready to surrender his own judgment to the rash advisers around him—to violate the treaty, and take possession of the capital.

Under cover of a dark and stormy night (April 8th, 1537), he entered the place without opposition, made himself master of the principal church, established strong parties of cavalry at the head of the great avenues to prevent surprise, and detached Orgoñez with a body of infantry to force the dwelling of Hernando Pizarro. That captain was lodged with his brother Gonzalo in one of the large halls built by the Incas for public diversions, with immense doors of entrance that opened on the *plaza*. It was garrisoned by about twenty soldiers, who, as the gates were burst open, stood stoutly to the defence of their leader. A smart struggle ensued, in which some lives were lost, till at length Orgoñez, provoked by the obstinate resistance, set fire to the combustible roof of the building. It was speedily in flames, and the burning rafters falling on the heads of the inmates, they forced their reluctant leader to an unconditional surrender. Scarcely had the Spaniards left the building, when the whole roof fell in with a tremendous crash.

Almagro was now master of Cuzco. He ordered the Pizarros, with fifteen or twenty of the principal cavaliers, to be secured and placed in confinement. Except so far as required for securing his authority, he does not seem to have been guilty of acts of violence to the inhabitants, and he installed one of Pizarro's most able officers, Gabriel de Rojas, in the government of the city. The municipality, whose eyes were now open to the validity of Almagro's pretensions, made no further scruple to recognize his title to Cuzco.

The marshal's first step was to send a message to Alonso de Alvarado's camp, advising that officer of his occupation of the city, and requiring his obedience to him as its legitimate master. Alvarado was lying, with a body of five hundred men, horse and foot, at Xauxa, about thirteen leagues from the capital. He had been detached several months previously for the relief of Cuzco; but had, most unaccountably, and, as it proved, most unfortunately for the Peruvian capital, remained at Xauxa with the alleged motive of protecting that settlement and the surrounding country against the insurgents. He now showed himself loyal to his commander; and, when Almagro's ambassadors reached his camp, he put them in irons, and sent advice of what had been done to the governor at Lima.

Almagro, offended by the detention of his emissaries, prepared at once to march against Alonso de Alvarado, and take more effectual means to bring him to submission. His lieutenant, Orgoñez, strongly urged him before his departure to strike off the heads of the Pizarros, alleging, "that, while they lived, his commander's life would never be safe"; and concluding with the Spanish proverb, "Dead men never bite." But the marshal, though he detested Hernando in his heart, shrunk from so violent a measure; and, independently of other considerations, he had still an attachment for his old associate, Francis Pizarro, and was unwilling to sever the ties between them for ever. Contenting himself, therefore, with placing his prisoners under strong guard in one of the stone buildings belonging to the House of the Sun, he put himself at the head of his forces, and left the capital in quest of Alvarado.

That officer had now taken up a position on the farther side of the *Rio de Abancay*, where he lay, with the strength of his little army, in front of a bridge, by which its rapid waters are traversed, while a strong detachment occupied a spot commanding a ford lower down the river. But in this detachment was a cavalier of much consideration in the army, Pedro de Lerma, who, from some pique against his commander, had entered into treasonable correspondence with the opposite party. By his advice, Almagro, on reaching the border of the river, established himself against the bridge in face of Alvarado, as if prepared to force a passage, thus concentrating his adversary's attention on that point. But, when darkness had set in, he detached a large body under Orgoñez to pass the ford, and operate in concert with Lerma. Orgoñez executed this commission with his usual promptness. The ford was crossed, though the current ran so swiftly, that several of his men were swept away by it, and perished in the waters. Their leader received a severe wound himself in the mouth, as he was gaining the opposite bank, but, nothing daunted, he cheered on his men, and fell with fury on the enemy. He was speedily joined by Lerma, and such of the soldiers as he had gained over, and, unable to distinguish friend from foe, the enemy's confusion was complete.

Meanwhile, Alvarado, roused by the noise of the attack on this quarter, hastened to the support of his officer, when Almagro, seizing the occasion, pushed across the bridge, dispersed the small body left to defend it, and, falling on Alvarado's rear, that general saw himself hemmed in on all sides. The struggle did not last long; and the unfortunate chief, uncertain on whom he could rely, surrendered with all his force,—those only excepted who had already deserted to the enemy. Such was the battle of Abancay, as it was called, from the river on whose banks it was fought, on the twelfth of July, 1537. Never was a victory more complete, or achieved with less cost of life; and Almagro marched back, with an array of prisoners scarcely inferior to his own army in number, in triumph to Cuzco.

While the events related in the preceding pages were passing, Francisco Pizarro had remained at Lima, anxiously awaiting the arrival of the reinforcements which he had requested to enable him to march to the relief of the beleaguered capital of the Incas. His appeal had not been unanswered. Among the rest was a corps of two hundred and fifty men, led by the Licentiate Gaspar de Espinosa, one of the three original associates, it may be remembered, who engaged in the conquest of Peru. He had now left his own residence at Panamá, and came in person, for the first time, it would seem, to revive the drooping fortunes of his confederates. Pizarro received also a vessel laden with provisions, military stores, and other necessary supplies, besides a rich wardrobe for himself, from Cortés, the Conqueror of Mexico, who generously stretched forth his hand to aid his kinsman in the hour of need.

With a force amounting to four hundred and fifty men, half of them cavalry, the governor quitted Lima, and began his march on the Inca capital. He had not advanced far, when he received tidings of the return of Almagro, the seizure of Cuzco, and the imprisonment of his brothers; and, before he had time to recover from this astounding intelligence, he learned the total defeat and capture of Alvarado. Filled with consternation at these rapid successes of his rival, he now returned in all haste to Lima, which he put in the best posture of defence, to secure it against the hostile movements, not unlikely, as he thought, to be directed against that capital itself. Meanwhile, far from indulging in impotent sallies of resentment, or in complaints of his ancient comrade, he only lamented that Almagro should have resorted to these violent measures for the settlement of their dispute, and this less—if we may take his word for it—from personal considerations than from the prejudice it might do to the interests of the Crown.

But, while busily occupied with warlike preparations, he did not omit to try the effect of negotiation. He sent an embassy to Cuzco, consisting of several persons in whose discretion he placed the greatest confidence, with Espinosa at their head, as the party most interested in an amicable arrangement.

The licentiate, on his arrival, did not find Almagro in as favorable a mood for an accommodation as he could have wished. Elated by his recent successes, he now aspired not only to the possession of Cuzco, but of Lima itself, as falling within the limits of his jurisdiction. It was in vain that Espinosa urged the propriety, by every argument which prudence could suggest, of moderating his demands. His claims upon Cuzco, at least, were not to be shaken, and he declared himself ready to peril his life in maintaining them. The licentiate coolly replied by quoting the pithy Castilian proverb, *El vencido vencido, y el vencidor perdido;* "The vanquished vanquished, and the victor undone."

What influence the temperate arguments of the licentiate might eventually have had on the heated imagination of the soldier is doubtful; but unfortunately for the negotiation, it was abruptly terminated by the death of Espinosa himself, which took place most unexpectedly, though, strange to say, in those times, without the imputation of poison. He was a great loss to the parties in the existing fermentation of their minds; for he had the weight of character which belongs to wise and moderate counsels, and a deeper interest than any other man in recommending them.

The name of Espinosa is memorable in history from his early connection with the expedition to Peru, which, but for the seasonable, though secret, application of his funds, could not then have been compassed. He had long been a resident in the Spanish colonies of Tierra Firme and Panamá, where he had served in various capacities, sometimes as a legal functionary presiding in the courts of justice, and not unfrequently as an efficient leader in the early expeditions of conquest and discovery. In these manifold vocations he acquired high reputation for probity, intelligence, and courage, and his death at the present crisis was undoubtedly the most unfortunate event that could befall the country.

All attempt at negotiation was now abandoned; and Almagro announced his purpose to descend to the sea-coast, where he could plant a colony and establish a port for himself. This would secure him the means, so essential, of communication with the mother-country, and here he would resume negotiations for the settlement of his dispute with Pizarro. Before quitting Cuzco, he sent Orgoñez with a strong force against the Inca, not caring to leave the capital exposed in his absence to further annoyance from that quarter.

But the Inca, discouraged by his late discomfiture, and unable, perhaps, to rally in sufficient strength for resistance, abandoned his stronghold at Tambo, and retreated across the mountains. He was hotly pursued by Orgoñez over hill and valley, till, deserted by his followers, and with only one of his wives to bear him company, the royal fugitive took shelter in the remote fastnesses of the Andes.

Before leaving the capital, Orgoñez again urged his commander to strike off the heads of the Pizarros, and then march at once upon Lima. By this decisive step he would bring the war to an issue, and for ever secure himself from the insidious machinations of his enemies. But, in the mean time, a new friend had risen up to the captive brothers. This was Diego de Alvarado, brother of that Pedro, who, as mentioned in a preceding chapter, had conducted the unfortunate expedition to Quito. After his brother's departure, Diego had attached himself to the fortunes of Almagro, had accompanied him to Chili, and, as he was a cavalier of birth, and possessed of some truly noble qualities, he had gained deserved ascendency over his commander. Alvarado had frequently visited Hernando Pizarro in his confinement, where, to beguile the tediousness of captivity, he amused himself with gaming,—the passion of the Spaniard. They played deep, and Alvarado lost the enormous sum of eighty thousand gold castellanos. He was prompt in paying the debt, but Hernando Pizarro peremptorily declined to receive the money. By this politic generosity, he secured an important advocate in the council of Almagro. It stood him now in good stead. Alvarado represented to the marshal, that such a measure as that urged by Orgoñez would not only outrage the feelings of his followers, but would ruin his fortunes by the indignation it must excite at court. When Almagro acquiesced in these views, as in truth most grateful to his own nature, Orgoñez, chagrined at his determination, declared that the day would come when he would repent this mistaken lenity. "A Pizarro," he said, "was never known to forget an injury; and that which they had already received from Almagro was too deep for them to forgive." Prophetic words!

On leaving Cuzco, the marshal gave orders that Gonzalo

Pizarro and the other prisoners should be detained in strict custody. Hernando he took with him, closely guarded, on his march. Descending rapidly towards the coast, he reached the pleasant vale of Chincha in the latter part of August. Here he occupied himself with laying the foundations of a town bearing his own name, which might serve as a counterpart to the City of the Kings,—thus bidding defiance, as it were, to his rival on his own borders. While occupied in this manner, he received the unwelcome tidings, that Gonzalo Pizarro, Alonso de Alvarado, and the other prisoners, having tampered with their guards, had effected their escape from Cuzco, and he soon after heard of their safe arrival in the camp of Pizarro.

Chafed by this intelligence, the marshal was not soothed by the insinuations of Orgoñez, that it was owing to his ill-advised lenity; that it might have gone hard with Hernando, but that Almagro's attention was diverted by the negotiation which Francisco Pizarro now proposed to resume.

After some correspondence between the parties, it was agreed to submit the arbitration of the dispute to a single individual, Fray Francisco de Bovadilla, a Brother of the Order of Mercy. Though living in Lima, and, as might be supposed, under the influence of Pizarro, he had a reputation for integrity that disposed Almagro to confide the settlement of the question exclusively to him. In this implicit confidence in the friar's impartiality, Orgoñez, of a less sanguine temper than his chief, did not participate.

An interview was arranged between the rival chiefs. It took place at Mala, November 13th, 1537; but very different was the deportment of the two commanders towards each other from that which they had exhibited at their former meetings. Almagro, indeed, doffing his bonnet, advanced in his usual open manner to salute his ancient comrade; but Pizarro, hardly condescending to return the salute, haughtily demanded why the marshal had seized upon his city of Cuzco, and imprisoned his brothers. This led to a recrimination on the part of his associate. The discussion assumed the tone of an angry altercation, till Almagro, taking a hint—or what he conceived to be such—from an attendant, that some treachery was intended, abruptly quitted the apartment, mounted his horse, and galloped back to his quarters at Chincha. The conference closed, as might have been anticipated from the heated temper of their minds when they began it, by widening the breach it was intended to heal. The friar, now left wholly to himself, after some deliberation, gave his award. He decided that a vessel, with a skilful pilot on board, should be sent to determine the exact latitude of the river of Santiago, the northern boundary of Pizarro's territory, by which all the measurements were to be regulated. In the mean time, Cuzco was to be delivered up by Almagro, and Hernando Pizarro to be set at liberty, on condition of his leaving the country in six weeks for Spain. Both parties were to retire within their undisputed territories, and to abandon all further hostilities.

This award, as may be supposed, highly satisfactory to Pizarro, was received by Almagro's men with indignation and scorn. They had been sold, they cried, by their general, broken, as he was, by age and infirmities. Their enemies were to occupy Cuzco and its pleasant places, while they were to be turned over to the barren wilderness of Charcas. Little did they dream that under this poor exterior were hidden the rich treasures of Potosí. They denounced the umpire as a hireling of the governor, and murmurs were heard among the troops, stimulated by Orgoñez, demanding the head of Hernando. Never was that cavalier in greater danger. But his good genius in the form of Alvarado again interposed to protect him. His life in captivity was a succession of reprieves.

Yet his brother, the governor, was not disposed to abandon him to his fate. On the contrary, he was now prepared to make every concession to secure his freedom. Concessions, that politic chief well knew, cost little to those who are not concerned to abide by them. After some preliminary negotiation, another award, more equitable, or, at all events, more to the satisfaction of the discontented party, was given. The principal articles of it were, that, until the arrival of some definitive instructions on the point from Castile, the city of Cuzco, with its territory, should remain in the hands of Almagro; and that Hernando Pizarro should be set at liberty, on the condition, above stipulated, of leaving the country in six weeks.—When the terms of this agreement were communicated to Orgoñez, that officer intimated his opinion of them, by passing his finger across his throat, and exclaiming, "What has my fidelity to my commander cost me!"

Almagro, in order to do greater honor to his prisoner, visited him in person, and announced to him that he was from that moment free. He expressed a hope, at the same time, that "all past differences would be buried in oblivion, and that henceforth they should live only in the recollection of their ancient friendship." Hernando replied, with apparent cordiality, that "he desired nothing better for himself." He then swore in the most solemn manner, and pledged his knightly honor,—the latter, perhaps, a pledge of quite as much weight in his own mind as the former,—that he would faithfully comply with the terms stipulated in the treaty. He was next conducted by the marshal to his quarters, where he partook of a collation in company with the principal officers; several of whom, together with Diego Almagro, the general's son, afterwards escorted the cavalier to his brother's camp, which had been transferred to the neighboring town of Mala. Here the party received a most cordial greeting from the governor, who entertained them with a courtly hospitality, and lavished many attentions, in particular, on the son of his ancient associate. In short, such, on their return, was the account of their reception, that it left no doubt in the mind of Almagro that all was at length amicably settled.—He did not know Pizarro.

CHAPTER II [1537–1538]

Scarcely had Almagro's officers left the governor's quarters, when the latter, calling his little army together, briefly
recapitulated the many wrongs which had been done him by
his rival, the seizure of his capital, the imprisonment of his
brothers, the assault and defeat of his troops; and he concluded
with the declaration,—heartily echoed back by his military
audience,—that the time had now come for revenge. All the
while that the negotiations were pending, Pizarro had been
busily occupied with military preparations. He had mustered
a force considerably larger than that of his rival, drawn from
various quarters, but most of them familiar with service. He
now declared, that, as he was too old to take charge of the
campaign himself, he should devolve that duty on his brothers;
and he released Hernando from all his engagements to Almagro, as a measure justified by necessity. That cavalier, with
graceful pertinacity, intimated his design to abide by the
pledges he had given, but, at length, yielded a reluctant assent
to the commands of his brother, as to a measure imperatively
demanded by his duty to the Crown.

The governor's next step was to advise Almagro that the
treaty was at an end. At the same time, he warned him to
relinquish his pretensions to Cuzco, and withdraw into his own
territory, or the responsibility of the consequences would lie on
his own head.

Reposing in his false security, Almagro was now fully awakened to the consciousness of the error he had committed; and
the warning voice of his lieutenant may have risen to his recollection. The first part of the prediction was fulfilled. And what
should prevent the latter from being so? To add to his distress,

he was laboring at this time under a grievous malady, the result of early excesses, which shattered his constitution, and made him incapable alike of mental and bodily exertion.

In this forlorn condition, he confided the management of his affairs to Orgoñez, on whose loyalty and courage he knew he might implicitly rely. The first step was to secure the passes of the Guaitara, a chain of hills that hemmed in the valley of Zangalla, where Almagro was at present established. But, by some miscalculation, the passes were not secured in season; and the active enemy, threading the dangerous defiles, effected a passage across the sierra, where a much inferior force to his own might have taken him at advantage. The fortunes of Almagro were on the wane.

His thoughts were now turned towards Cuzco, and he was anxious to get possession of this capital before the arrival of the enemy. Too feeble to sit on horseback, he was obliged to be carried in a litter; and, when he reached the ancient town of Bilcas, not far from Guamanga, his indisposition was so severe that he was compelled to halt and remain there three weeks before resuming his march.

The governor and his brothers, in the mean time, after traversing the pass of Guaitara, descended into the valley of Ica, where Pizarro remained a considerable while, to get his troops into order and complete his preparations for the campaign. Then, taking leave of the army, he returned to Lima, committing the prosecution of the war, as he had before announced, to his younger and more active brothers. Hernando, soon after quitting Ica, kept along the coast as far as Nasca, proposing to penetrate the country by a circuitous route in order to elude the enemy, who might have greatly embarrassed him in some of the passes of the Cordilleras. But unhappily for him, this plan of operations, which would have given him such manifest advantage, was not adopted by Almagro; and his adversary, without any other impediment than that arising from the natural difficulties of the march, arrived, in the latter part of April, 1538, in the neighborhood of Cuzco.

But Almagro was already in possession of that capital, which he had reached ten days before. A council of war was held by him respecting the course to be pursued. Some were for making good the defence of the city. Almagro would have tried what could be done by negotiation. But Orgoñez bluntly replied,—"It is too late; you have liberated Hernando Pizarro, and nothing remains but to fight him." The opinion of Orgoñez finally prevailed, to march out and give the enemy battle on the plains. The marshal, still disabled by illness from taking the command, devolved it on his trusty lieutenant, who, mustering his forces, left the city, and took up a position at Las Salinas, less than a league distant from Cuzco. The place received its name from certain pits or vats in the ground, used for the preparation of salt, that was obtained from a natural spring in the neighborhood. It was an injudicious choice of ground, since its broken character was most unfavorable to the free action of cavalry, in which the strength of Almagro's force consisted. But, although repeatedly urged by the officers to advance into the open country, Orgoñez persisted in his position, as the most favorable for defence, since the front was protected by a marsh, and by a little stream that flowed over the plain. His forces amounted in all to about five hundred, more than half of them horse. His infantry was deficient in fire-arms, the place of which was supplied by the long pike. He had also six small cannon, or falconets, as they were called, which, with his cavalry, formed into two equal divisions, he disposed on the flanks of his infantry. Thus prepared, he calmly awaited the approach of the enemy.

It was not long before the bright arms and banners of the Spaniards under Hernando Pizarro were seen emerging from the mountain passes. The troops came forward in good order, and like men whose steady step showed that they had been spared in the march, and were now fresh for action. They advanced slowly across the plain, and halted on the opposite border of the little stream which covered the front of Orgoñez. Here Hernando, as the sun had set, took up his quarters for the night, proposing to defer the engagement till daylight.

The rumors of the approaching battle had spread far and wide over the country; and the mountains and rocky heights around were thronged with multitudes of natives, eager to feast their eyes on a spectacle, where, whichever side were victorious, the defeat would fall on their enemies. The Castilian women and children, too, with still deeper anxiety, had thronged out from Cuzco to witness the deadly strife in which brethren and kindred were to contend for mastery. The whole number of the combatants was insignificant; though not as compared with those usually engaged in these American wars. It is not, however, the number of the players, but the magnitude of the stake, that gives importance and interest to the game; and in this bloody game, they were to play for the possession of an empire.

The night passed away in silence, unbroken by the vast assembly which covered the surrounding hill-tops. Nor did the soldiers of the hostile camps, although keeping watch within hearing of one another, and with the same blood flowing in their veins, attempt any communication. So deadly was the hate in their bosoms!

The sun rose bright, as usual in this beautiful climate, on Saturday, the twenty-sixth day of April, 1538. But long before his beams were on the plain, the trumpet of Hernando Pizarro had called his men to arms. His forces amounted in all to about seven hundred. They were drawn from various quarters, the veterans of Pizarro, the followers of Alonso de Alvarado,—many of whom, since their defeat, had found their way back to Lima,—and the late reinforcement from the isles, most of them seasoned by many a toilsome march in the Indian campaigns, and many a hard-fought field. His mounted troops were inferior to those of Almagro; but this was more than compensated by the strength of his infantry, comprehending a well-trained corps of arquebusiers, sent from St. Domingo, whose weapons were of the improved construction recently introduced from Flanders. They were of a large calibre, and threw double-headed shot, consisting of bullets linked together by an iron chain. It was doubtless a clumsy weapon compared with modern fire-arms, but, in hands accustomed to wield it, proved a destructive instrument.

Hernando Pizarro drew up his men in the same order of battle as that presented by the enemy,—throwing his infantry into the centre, and disposing his horse on the flanks; one corps of which he placed under command of Alonso de Alvarado, and took charge of the other himself. The infantry was headed by his brother Gonzalo, supported by Pedro de Valdivia, the future hero of Arauco, whose disastrous story forms the burden of romance as well as of chronicle.

Mass was said, as if the Spaniards were about to fight what they deemed the good fight of the faith, instead of imbruing their hands in the blood of their countrymen. Hernando Pizarro then made a brief address to his soldiers. He touched on the personal injuries he and his family had received from Almagro; reminded his brother's veterans that Cuzco had been wrested from their possession; called up the glow of shame on the brows of Alvarado's men as he talked of the rout of Abancay, and, pointing out the Inca metropolis that sparkled in the morning sunshine, he told them that there was the prize of the victor. They answered his appeal with acclamations; and the signal being given, Gonzalo Pizarro, heading his battalion of infantry, led it straight across the river. The water was neither broad nor deep, and the soldiers found no difficulty in gaining a landing, as the enemy's horse was prevented by the marshy ground from approaching the borders. But, as they worked their way across the morass, the heavy guns of Orgoñez played with effect on the leading files, and threw them into disorder. Gonzalo and Valdivia threw themselves into the midst of their followers, menacing some, encouraging others, and at length led them gallantly forward to the firm ground. Here the arquebusiers, detaching themselves from the rest of the infantry, gained a small eminence, whence, in their turn, they opened a galling fire on Orgoñez, scattering his array of spearmen, and sorely annoying the cavalry on the flanks.

Meanwhile, Hernando, forming his two squadrons of horse into one column, crossed under cover of this well-sustained fire, and, reaching the firm ground, rode at once against the enemy. Orgoñez, whose infantry was already much crippled, advancing his horse, formed the two squadrons into one body, like his antagonist, and spurred at full gallop against the assailants. The shock was terrible; and it was hailed by the swarms of Indian spectators on the surrounding heights with a fiendish yell of triumph, that rose far above the din of battle, till it was lost in echoes among the mountains.

The struggle was desperate. For it was not that of the white men against the defenceless Indian, but of Spaniard against Spaniard; both parties cheering on their comrades with their battle-cries of *"El Rey y Almagro,"* or *"El Rey y Pizarro,"*

—while they fought with a hate, to which national antipathy was as nothing; a hate strong in proportion to the strength of the ties that had been rent asunder.

In this bloody field well did Orgoñez do his duty, fighting like one to whom battle was the natural element. Singling out a cavalier, whom from the color of the sobre-vest on his armour, he erroneously supposed to be Hernando Pizarro, he charged him in full career, and overthrew him with his lance. Another he ran through in like manner, and a third he struck down with his sword, as he was prematurely shouting "Victory!" But while thus doing the deeds of a paladin of romance, he was hit by a chain-shot from an arquebuse, which, penetrating the bars of his visor, grazed his forehead, and deprived him for a moment of reason. Before he had fully recovered, his horse was killed under him, and though the fallen cavalier succeeded in extricating himself from the stirrups, he was surrounded, and soon overpowered by numbers. Still refusing to deliver up his sword, he asked "if there was no knight to whom he could surrender." One Fuentes, a menial of Pizarro, presenting himself as such, Orgoñez gave his sword into his hands,—and the dastard, drawing his dagger, stabbed his defenceless prisoner to the heart! His head, then struck off, was stuck on a pike, and displayed, a bloody trophy, in the great square of Cuzco, as the head of a traitor. Thus perished as loyal a cavalier, as decided in council, and as bold in action, as ever crossed to the shores of America.

The fight had now lasted more than an hour, and the fortune of the day was turning against the followers of Almagro. Orgoñez being down, their confusion increased. The infantry, unable to endure the fire of the arquebusiers, scattered and took refuge behind the stone-walls, that here and there straggled across the country. Pedro de Lerma, vainly striving to rally the cavalry, spurred his horse against Hernando Pizarro, with whom he had a personal feud. Pizarro did not shrink from the encounter. The lances of both the knights took effect. That of Hernando penetrated the thigh of his opponent, while Lerma's weapon, glancing by his adversary's saddlebow, struck him with such force above the groin, that it pierced the joints of his mail, slightly wounding the cavalier, and forcing his horse back on his haunches. But the press of the fight soon

parted the combatants, and, in the turmoil that ensued, Lerma
was unhorsed, and left on the field covered with wounds.

There was no longer order, and scarcely resistance, among
the followers of Almagro. They fled, making the best of their
way to Cuzco, and happy was the man who obtained quarter
when he asked it. Almagro himself, too feeble to sit so long on
his horse, reclined on a litter, and from a neighboring eminence surveyed the battle, watching its fluctuations with all
the interest of one who felt that honor, fortune, life itself, hung
on the issue. With agony not to be described, he had seen his
faithful followers, after their hard struggle, borne down by
their opponents, till, convinced that all was lost, he succeeded
in mounting a mule, and rode off for a temporary refuge to
the fortress of Cuzco. Thither he was speedily followed, taken,
and brought in triumph to the capital, where, ill as he was, he
was thrown into irons, and confined in the same apartment of
the stone building in which he had imprisoned the Pizarros.

The action lasted not quite two hours. The number of
killed, variously stated, was probably not less than a hundred
and fifty,—one of the combatants calls it two hundred,—a great
number, considering the shortness of the time, and the small
amount of forces engaged. No account is given of the wounded.
Wounds were the portion of the cavalier. Pedro de Lerma is
said to have received seventeen, and yet was taken alive from
the field! The loss fell chiefly on the followers of Almagro. But
the slaughter was not confined to the heat of the action. Such
was the deadly animosity of the parties, that several were murdered in cold blood, like Orgoñez, after they had surrendered.
Pedro de Lerma himself, while lying on his sick couch in the
quarters of a friend in Cuzco, was visited by a soldier, named
Samaniego, whom he had once struck for an act of disobedience. This person entered the solitary chamber of the wounded
man, took his place by his bed-side, and then, upbraiding him
for the insult, told him that he had come to wash it away in
his blood! Lerma in vain assured him, that, when restored to
health, he would give him the satisfaction he desired. The mis-
creant, exclaiming "Now is the hour!", plunged his sword into
his bosom. He lived several years to vaunt this atrocious exploit, which he proclaimed as a reparation to his honor. It is
some satisfaction to know that the insolence of this vaunt cost

him his life.—Such anecdotes, revolting as they are, illustrate not merely the spirit of the times, but that peculiarly ferocious spirit which is engendered by civil wars,—the most unforgiving in their character of any, but wars of religion.

In the hurry of the flight of one party, and the pursuit by the other, all pouring towards Cuzco, the field of battle had been deserted. But it soon swarmed with plunderers, as the Indians, descending like vultures from the mountains, took possession of the bloody ground, and, despoiling the dead, even to the minutest article of dress, left their corpses naked on the plain. It has been thought strange that the natives should not have availed themselves of their superior numbers to fall on the victors after they had been exhausted by the battle. But the scattered bodies of the Peruvians were without a leader; they were broken in spirit, moreover, by recent reverses, and the Castilians, although weakened for the moment by the struggle, were in far greater strength in Cuzco than they had ever been before.

Indeed, the number of troops now assembled within its walls, amounting to full thirteen hundred, composed, as they were, of the most discordant materials, gave great uneasiness to Hernando Pizarro. For there were enemies glaring on each other and on him with deadly though smothered rancor, and friends, if not so dangerous, not the less troublesome from their craving and unreasonable demands. He had given the capital up to pillage, and his followers found good booty in the quarters of Almagro's officers. But this did not suffice the more ambitious cavaliers; and they clamorously urged their services, and demanded to be placed in charge of some expedition, nothing doubting that it must prove a golden one. All were in quest of an *El Dorado.* Hernando Pizarro acquiesced as far as possible in these desires, most willing to relieve himself of such importunate creditors. The expeditions, it is true, usually ended in disaster; but the country was explored by them. It was the lottery of adventure; the prizes were few, but they were splendid; and in the excitement of the game, few Spaniards paused to calculate the chances of success.

Among those who left the capital was Diego, the son of Almagro. Hernando was mindful to send him, with a careful escort, to his brother the governor, desirous to remove him at this crisis from the neighborhood of his father. Meanwhile the marshal himself was pining away in prison under the combined influence of bodily illness and distress of mind. Before the battle of Salinas, it had been told to Hernando Pizarro that Almagro was like to die. "Heaven forbid," he exclaimed, "that this should come to pass before he falls into my hands!" Yet the gods seemed now disposed to grant but half of this pious prayer, since his captive seemed about to escape him just as he had come into his power. To console the unfortunate chief, Hernando paid him a visit in his prison, and cheered him with the assurance that he only waited for the governor's arrival to set him at liberty; adding, "that, if Pizarro did not come soon to the capital, he himself would assume the responsibility of releasing him, and would furnish him with a conveyance to his brother's quarters." At the same time, with considerate attention to his comfort, he inquired of the marshal "what mode of conveyance would be best suited to his state of health." After this he continued to send him delicacies from his own table to revive his faded appetite. Almagro, cheered by these kind attentions, and by the speedy prospect of freedom, gradually mended in health and spirits.

He little dreamed that all this while a process was industriously preparing against him. It had been instituted immediately on his capture, and every one, however humble, who had any cause of complaint against the unfortunate prisoner, was invited to present it. The summons was readily answered; and many an enemy now appeared in the hour of his fallen fortunes, like the base reptiles crawling into light amidst the ruins of some noble edifice; and more than one, who had received benefits from his hands, were willing to court the favor of his enemy by turning on their benefactor. From these loathsome sources a mass of accusations was collected which spread over two thousand folio pages! Yet Almagro was the idol of his soldiers!

Having completed the process (July 8th, 1538), it was not difficult to obtain a verdict against the prisoner. The principal charges on which he was pronounced guilty were those of levying war against the Crown, and thereby occasioning the death of many of his Majesty's subjects; of entering into conspiracy with the Inca; and finally, of dispossessing the royal governor of the city of Cuzco. On these charges he was condemned to suffer death as a traitor, by being publicly beheaded in the great square of the city. Who were the judges, or what was the tribunal that condemned him, we are not informed. Indeed, the whole trial was a mockery; if that can be called a trial, where the accused himself is not even aware of the accusation.

The sentence was communicated by a friar deputed for the purpose to Almagro. The unhappy man, who all the while had been unconsciously slumbering on the brink of a precipice, could not at first comprehend the nature of his situation. Recovering from the first shock, "It was impossible," he said, "that such wrong could be done him,—he would not believe it." He then besought Hernando Pizarro to grant him an interview. That cavalier, not unwilling, it would seem, to witness the agony of his captive, consented; and Almagro was so humbled by his misfortunes, that he condescended to beg for his life with the most piteous supplications. He reminded Hernando of his ancient relations with his brother, and the good offices he had rendered him and his family in the earlier part of their career. He touched on his acknowledged services to his country, and besought his enemy "to spare his grey hairs, and not to deprive him of the short remnant of an existence from which he had now nothing more to fear."—To this the other coldly replied, that "he was surprised to see Almagro demean himself in a manner so unbecoming a brave cavalier; that his fate was no worse than had befallen many a soldier before him; and that, since God had given him the grace to be a Christian, he should employ his remaining moments in making up his account with Heaven!"

But Almagro was not to be silenced. He urged the service he had rendered Hernando himself. "This was a hard requital," he said, "for having spared his life so recently under similar circumstances, and that, too, when he had been urged again and again by those around him to take it away." And he concluded by menacing his enemy with the vengeance of the emperor, who would never suffer this outrage on one who had rendered such signal services to the Crown to go unrequited. It was all in vain; and Hernando abruptly closed the conference by repeating, that "his doom was inevitable, and he must prepare to meet it."

Almagro, finding that no impression was to be made on his iron-hearted conqueror, now seriously addressed himself to the settlement of his affairs. By the terms of the royal grant he was empowered to name his successor. He accordingly devolved his office on his son, appointing Diego de Alvarado, on whose integrity he had great reliance, administrator of the province during his minority. All his property and possessions in Peru, of whatever kind, he devised to his master the emperor, assuring him that a large balance was still due to him in his unsettled accounts with Pizarro. By this politic bequest, he hoped to secure the monarch's protection for his son, as well as a strict scrutiny into the affairs of his enemy.

The knowledge of Almagro's sentence produced a deep sensation in the community of Cuzco. All were amazed at the presumption with which one, armed with a little brief authority, ventured to sit in judgment on a person of Almagro's station. There were few who did not call to mind some generous or good-natured act of the unfortunate veteran. Even those who had furnished materials for the accusation, now startled by the tragic result to which it was to lead, were heard to denounce Hernando's conduct as that of a tyrant. Some of the principal cavaliers, and among them Diego de Alvarado, to whose intercession, as we have seen, Hernando Pizarro, when a captive, had owed his own life, waited on that commander, and endeavored to dissuade him from so high-handed and atrocious a proceeding. It was in vain. But it had the effect of changing the mode of execution, which, instead of the public square, was now to take place in prison.

On the day appointed, a strong corps of arquebusiers was drawn up in the *plaza*. The guards were doubled over the houses where dwelt the principal partisans of Almagro. The executioner, attended by a priest, stealthily entered his prison; and the unhappy man, after confessing and receiving the sacrament, submitted without resistance to the *garrote*. Thus obscurely, in the gloomy silence of a dungeon, perished the hero of a hundred battles! His corpse was removed to the great square of the city, where, in obedience to the sentence, the head was severed from the body. A herald proclaimed aloud the nature of the crimes for which he had suffered; and his remains, rolled in their bloody shroud, were borne to the house of his friend Hernan Ponce de Leon, and the next day laid with all due solemnity in the church of Our Lady of Mercy. The Pizarros appeared among the principal mourners. It was remarked, that their brother had paid similar honors to the memory of Atahuallpa.

Almagro, at the time of his death, was probably not far from seventy years of age. But this is somewhat uncertain; for Almagro was a foundling, and his early history is lost in obscurity. He had many excellent qualities by nature; and his defects, which were not few, may reasonably be palliated by the circumstances of his situation. For what extenuation is not authorized by the position of a *foundling,*—without parents, or early friends, or teacher to direct him,—his little bark set adrift on the ocean of life, to take its chance among the rude billows and breakers, without one friendly hand stretched forth to steer or to save it! The name of "foundling" comprehends an apology for much, very much, that is wrong in after life.

He was a man of strong passions, and not too well used to control them. But he was neither vindictive nor habitually cruel. I have mentioned one atrocious outrage which he committed on the natives. But insensibility to the rights of the Indians he shared with many a better-instructed Spaniard. Yet the Indians, after his conviction, bore testimony to his general humanity, by declaring that they had no such friend among the white men. Indeed, far from being vindictive, he was placable and easily yielded to others. The facility with which he yielded, the result of good-natured credulity, made him too often the dupe of the crafty; and it showed, certainly, a want of that self-reliance which belongs to great strength of character. Yet his facility of temper, and the generosity of his nature, made him popular with his followers. No commander was ever more beloved by his soldiers. His generosity was often carried to prodigality. When he entered on the campaign of Chili, he lent a hundred thousand gold ducats to the poorer cavaliers to equip themselves and afterwards gave them up the debt. He was profuse to ostentation. But his extravagance did him no harm among the roving spirits of the camp, with whom prodigality is apt to gain more favor than a strict and well-regulated economy.

He was a good soldier, careful and judicious in his plans,

patient and intrepid in their execution. His body was covered with the scars of his battles, till the natural plainness of his person was converted almost into deformity. He must not be judged by his closing campaign, when, depressed by disease, he yielded to the superior genius of his rival; but by his numerous expeditions by land and by water for the conquest of Peru and the remote Chili. Yet it may be doubted whether he possessed those uncommon qualities, either as a warrior or as a man, that, in ordinary circumstances, would have raised him to distinction. He was one of the three, or, to speak more strictly, of the two associates, who had the good fortune and the glory to make one of the most splendid discoveries in the Western World. He shares largely in the credit of this with Pizarro; for, when he did not accompany that leader in his perilous expeditions, he contributed no less to their success by his exertions in the colonies.

Yet his connection with that chief can hardly be considered a fortunate circumstance in his career. A partnership between individuals for discovery and conquest is not likely to be very scrupulously observed, especially by men more accustomed to govern others than to govern themselves. If causes for discord do not arise before, they will be sure to spring up on division of the spoil. But this association was particularly ill-assorted. For the free, sanguine, and confiding temper of Almagro was no match for the cool and crafty policy of Pizarro; and he was invariably circumvented by his companion, whenever their respective interests came in collision.

Still the final ruin of Almagro may be fairly imputed to himself. He made two capital blunders. The first was his appeal to arms by the seizure of Cuzco. The determination of a boundary-line was not to be settled by arms. It was a subject for arbitration; and, if arbitrators could not be trusted, it should have been referred to the decision of the Crown. But, having once appealed to arms, he should not then have resorted to negotiation,—above all, to negotiation with Pizarro. This was his second and greatest error. He had seen enough of Pizarro to know that he was not to be trusted. Almagro did trust him, and he paid for it with his life.

CHAPTER III [1539–1540]

PIZARRO REVISITS CUZCO—HERNANDO RETURNS TO CAS-
TILE—HIS LONG IMPRISONMENT—COMMISSIONER SENT
TO PERU—HOSTILITIES WITH THE INCA—PIZARRO'S AC-
TIVE ADMINISTRATION—GONZALO PIZARRO

On the departure of his brother in pursuit of Almagro, the
Marquess Francisco Pizarro, as we have seen, returned to
Lima. There he anxiously awaited the result of the campaign;
and on receiving the welcome tidings of the victory of Las
Salinas, he instantly made preparations for his march to Cuzco.
At Xauxa, however, he was long detained by the distracted
state of the country, and still longer, as it would seem, by a
reluctance to enter the Peruvian capital while the trial of Almagro was pending.

He was met at Xauxa by the marshal's son Diego, who had
been sent to the coast by Hernando Pizarro. The young man
was filled with the most gloomy apprehensions respecting his
father's fate, and he besought the governor not to allow his
brother to do him any violence. Pizarro, who received Diego
with much apparent kindness, bade him take heart, as no
harm should come to his father; adding, that he trusted their
ancient friendship would soon be renewed. The youth, com-
forted by these assurances, took his way to Lima, where, by
Pizarro's orders, he was received into his house, and treated
as a son.

The same assurances respecting the marshal's safety were
given by the governor to Bishop Valverde, and some of the
principal cavaliers who interested themselves in behalf of the
prisoner. Still Pizarro delayed his march to the capital; and
when he resumed it, he had advanced no farther than the *Rio
de Abancay* when he received tidings of the death of his rival.
He appeared greatly shocked by the intelligence, his whole
frame was agitated, and he remained for some time with his
eyes bent on the ground showing signs of strong emotion.

Such is the account given by his friends. A more probable version of the matter represents him to have been perfectly aware of the state of things at Cuzco. When the trial was concluded, it is said he received a message from Hernando, inquiring what was to be done with the prisoner. He answered in a few words:—"Deal with him so that he shall give us no more trouble." It is also stated that Hernando, afterwards, when laboring under the obloquy caused by Almagro's death, shielded himself under instructions affirmed to have been received from the governor. It is quite certain, that, during his long residence at Xauxa, the latter was in constant communication with Cuzco; and that had he, as Valverde repeatedly urged him, quickened his march to that capital, he might easily have prevented the consummation of the tragedy. As commander-in-chief, Almagro's fate was in his hands; and, whatever his own partisans may affirm of his innocence, the impartial judgment of history must hold him equally accountable with Hernando for the death of his associate.

Neither did his subsequent conduct show any remorse for these proceedings. He entered Cuzco, says one who was present there to witness it, amidst the flourish of clarions and trumpets, at the head of his martial cavalcade, and dressed in the rich suit presented him by Cortés, with the proud bearing and joyous mien of a conqueror. When Diego de Alvarado applied to him for the government of the southern provinces, in the name of the young Almagro, whom his father, as we have seen, had consigned to his protection, Pizarro answered, that "the marshal, by his rebellion, had forfeited all claims to the government." And, when he was still further urged by the cavalier, he bluntly broke off the conversation by declaring that "his own territory covered all on this side of Flanders"! —intimating, no doubt, by this magnificent vaunt, that he would endure no rival on this side of the water.

In the same spirit, he had recently sent to supersede Benalcazar, the conqueror of Quito, who, he was informed, aspired to an independent government. Pizarro's emissary had orders to send the offending captain to Lima; but Benalcazar, after pushing his victorious career far into the north, had returned to Castile to solicit his guerdon from the emperor.

To the complaints of the injured natives, who invoked his

protection, he showed himself strangely insensible, while the followers of Almagro he treated with undisguised contempt. The estates of all the leaders were confiscated, and transferred without ceremony to his own partisans. Hernando had made attempts to conciliate some of the opposite faction by acts of liberality, but they had refused to accept any thing from the man whose hands were stained with the blood of their commander. The governor held to them no such encouragement; and many were reduced to such abject poverty, that, too proud to expose their wretchedness to the eyes of their conquerors, they withdrew from the city, and sought a retreat among the neighboring mountains.

For his own brothers he provided by such ample *repartimientos,* as excited the murmurs of his adherents. He appointed Gonzalo to the command of a strong force destined to act against the natives of Charcas, a hardy people occupying the territory assigned by the Crown to Almagro. Gonzalo met with a sturdy resistance, but, after some severe fighting, succeeded in reducing the province to obedience. He was recompensed, together with Hernando, who aided him in the conquest by a large grant in the neighborhood of Porco, the productive mines of which had been partially wrought under the Incas. The territory, thus situated, embraced part of those silver hills of Potosí which have since supplied Europe with such stores of the precious metals. Hernando comprehended the capabilities of the ground, and he began working the mines on a more extensive scale than that hitherto adopted, though it does not appear that any attempt was then made to penetrate the rich crust of Potosí. A few years more were to elapse before the Spaniards were to bring to light the silver quarries that lay hidden in the bosom of its mountains.

It was now the great business of Hernando to collect a sufficient quantity of treasure to take with him to Castile. Nearly a year had elapsed since Almagro's death; and it was full time that he should return and present himself at court, where Diego de Alvarado and other friends of the marshal, who had long since left Peru, were industriously maintaining the claims of the younger Almagro, as well as demanding redress for the wrongs done to his father. But Hernando looked confidently to his gold to dispel the accusations against him.

Before his departure, he counselled his brother to beware of the "men of Chili," as Almagro's followers were called; desperate men, who would stick at nothing, he said, for revenge. He besought the governor not to allow them to consort together in any number within fifty miles of his person; if he did, it would be fatal to him. And he concluded by recommending a strong body-guard; "for I," he added, "shall not be here to watch over you." But the governor laughed at the idle fears, as he termed them, of his brother, bidding the latter take no thought of him, "as every hair in the heads of Almagro's followers was a guaranty for his safety." He did not know the character of his enemies so well as Hernando.

The latter soon after embarked at Lima in the summer of 1539. He did not take the route of Panamá, for he had heard that it was the intention of the authorities there to detain him. He made a circuitous passage, therefore, by way of Mexico, landed in the Bay of Tecoantepec, and was making his way across the narrow strip that divides the great oceans, when he was arrested and taken to the capital. But the Viceroy Mendoza did not consider that he had a right to detain him, and he was suffered to embark at Vera Cruz, and to proceed on his voyage. Still he did not deem it safe to trust himself in Spain without further advices. He accordingly put in at one of the Azores, where he remained until he could communicate with home. He had some powerful friends at court, and by them he was encouraged to present himself before the emperor. He took their advice, and shortly after, reached the Spanish coast in safety.

The Court was at Valladolid; but Hernando, who made his entrance into that city, with great pomp and a display of his Indian riches, met with a reception colder than he had anticipated. For this he was mainly indebted to Diego de Alvarado, who was then residing there, and who, as a cavalier of honorable standing, and of high connections, had considerable influence. He had formerly, as we have seen, by his timely interposition, more than once saved the life of Hernando; and he had consented to receive a pecuniary obligation from him to a large amount. But all were now forgotten in the recollection of the wrong done to his commander; and, true to the trust reposed in him by that chief in his dying hour, he had come to Spain to vindicate the claims of the young Almagro.

But although coldly received at first, Hernando's presence, and his own version of the dispute with Almagro, aided by the golden arguments which he dealt with no stinted hand, checked the current indignation, and the opinion of his judges seemed for a time suspended. Alvarado, a cavalier more accustomed to the prompt and decisive action of a camp than to the tortuous intrigues of a court, chafed at the delay, and challenged Hernando to settle their quarrel by single combat. But his prudent adversary had no desire to leave the issue to such an ordeal; and the affair was speedily terminated by the death of Alvarado himself, which happened five days after the challenge. An event so opportune naturally suggested the suspicion of poison.

But his accusations had not wholly fallen to the ground; and Hernando Pizarro had carried measures with too high a hand, and too grossly outraged public sentiment, to be permitted to escape. He received no formal sentence, but he was imprisoned in the strong fortress of Medina del Campo, where he was allowed to remain for twenty years, when in 1560, after a generation had nearly passed away, and time had, in some measure, thrown its softening veil over the past, he was suffered to regain his liberty. But he came forth an aged man, bent down with infirmities and broken in spirit,—an object of pity, rather than indignation. Rarely has retributive justice been meted out in fuller measure to offenders so high in authority,—most rarely in Castile.

Yet Hernando bore this long imprisonment with an equanimity which, had it been founded on principle, might command our respect. He saw brothers and kindred, all on whom he leaned for support, cut off one after another; his fortune, in part, confiscated, while he was involved in expensive litigation for the remainder; his fame blighted, his career closed in an untimely hour, himself an exile in the heart of his own country;—yet he bore it all with the constancy of a courageous spirit. Though very old when released, he still survived several years, and continued to the extraordinary age of a hundred. He lived long enough to see friends, rivals, and foes all called away to their account before him.

Hernando Pizarro was in many respects a remarkable character. He was the eldest of the brothers, to whom he was related only by the father's side, for he was born in wedlock of honorable parentage on both sides of his house. In his early years, he received a good education,—good for the time. He was taken by his father, while quite young, to Italy, and there learned the art of war under the Great Captain. Little is known of his history after his return to Spain; but, when his brother had struck out for himself his brilliant career of discovery in Peru, Hernando consented to take part in his adventures.

He was much deferred to by Francisco, not only as his elder brother, but from his superior education and his knowledge of affairs. He was ready in his perceptions, fruitful in resources, and possessed of great vigor in action. Though courageous, he was cautious; and his counsels, when not warped by passion, were wise and wary. But he had other qualities, which more than counterbalanced the good resulting from excellent parts and attainments. His ambition and avarice were insatiable. He was supercilious even to his equals; and he had a vindictive temper, which nothing could appease. Thus, instead of aiding his brother in the Conquest, he was the evil genius that blighted his path. He conceived from the first an unwarrantable contempt for Almagro, whom he regarded as his brother's rival, instead of what he then was, the faithful partner of his fortunes. He treated him with personal indignity, and, by his intrigues at court, had the means of doing him sensible injury. He fell into Almagro's hands, and had nearly paid for these wrongs with his life. This was not to be forgiven by Hernando, and he coolly waited for the hour of revenge. Yet the execution of Almagro was a most impolitic act; for an evil passion can rarely be gratified with impunity. Hernando thought to buy off justice with the gold of Peru. He had studied human nature on its weak and wicked side, and he expected to profit from it. Fortunately, he was deceived. He had, indeed, his revenge; but the hour of his revenge was that of his ruin.

The disorderly state of Peru was such as to demand the immediate interposition of government. In the general license that prevailed there, the rights of the Indian and of the Spaniard were equally trampled under foot. Yet the subject was one of

great difficulty; for Pizarro's authority was now firmly established over the country, which itself was too remote from Castile to be readily controlled at home. Pizarro, moreover, was
a man not easy to be approached, confident in his own
strength, jealous of interference, and possessed of a fiery temper, which would kindle into a flame at the least distrust of
the government. It would not answer to send out a commission to suspend him from the exercise of his authority until
his conduct could be investigated, as was done with Cortés,
and other great colonial officers, on whose rooted loyalty the
Crown could confidently rely. Pizarro's loyalty sat, it was
feared, too lightly on him to be a powerful restraint on his
movements; and there were not wanting those among his reckless followers, who, in case of extremity, would be prompt to
urge him to throw off his allegiance altogether, and set up an
independent government for himself.

Some one was to be sent out, therefore, who should possess,
in some sort, a controlling, or, at least, concurrent power with
the dangerous chief, while ostensibly he should act only in
subordination to him. The person selected for this delicate mission, was the Licentiate Vaca de Castro, a member of the Royal
Audience of Valladolid. He was a learned judge, a man of
integrity and wisdom, and, though not bred to arms, had so
much address, and such knowledge of character, as would enable him readily to turn the resources of others to his own
account.

His commission was guarded in a way which showed the
embarrassment of the government. He was to appear before
Pizarro in the capacity of a royal judge; to consult with him
on the redress of grievances, especially with reference to the
unfortunate natives; to concert measures for the prevention of
future evils; and above all, to possess himself faithfully of the
condition of the country in all its details, and to transmit intelligence of it to the Court of Castile. But, in case of Pizarro's
death, he was to produce his warrant as royal governor, and
as such to claim the obedience of the authorities throughout
the land.—Events showed the wisdom of providing for this latter contingency.

The licentiate, thus commissioned, quitted his quiet residence at Valladolid, embarked at Seville, in the autumn of

1540, and, after a tedious voyage across the Atlantic, he traversed the Isthmus, and, encountering a succession of tempests on the Pacific, that had nearly sent his frail bark to the bottom, put in with her, a mere wreck, at the northerly port of Buenaventura. The affairs of the country were in a state to require his presence.

The civil war which had lately distracted the land had left it in so unsettled a state, that the agitation continued long after the immediate cause had ceased. This was especially the case among the natives. In the violent transfer of *repartimientos,* the poor Indian hardly knew to whom he was to look as his master. The fierce struggles between the rival chieftains left him equally in doubt whom he was to regard as the rulers of the land. As to the authority of a common sovereign, across the waters, paramount over all, he held that in still greater distrust; for what was the authority which could not command the obedience even of its own vassals? The Inca Manco was not slow in taking advantage of this state of feeling. He left his obscure fastnesses in the depths of the Andes, and established himself with a strong body of followers in the mountain country lying between Cuzco and the coast. From this retreat, he made descents on the neighboring plantations, destroying the houses, sweeping off the cattle, and massacring the people. He fell on travellers, as they were journeying singly or in caravans from the coast, and put them to death—it is told by his enemies—with cruel tortures. Single detachments were sent against him, from time to time, but without effect. Some he eluded, others he defeated; and, on one occasion, cut off a party of thirty troopers, to a man.

At length, Pizarro found it necessary to send a considerable force under his brother Gonzalo against the Inca. The hardy Indian encountered his enemy several times in the rough passes of the Cordilleras. He was usually beaten, and sometimes with heavy loss, which he repaired with astonishing facility, for he always contrived to make his escape, and so true were his followers, that, in defiance of pursuit and ambuscade, he found a safe shelter in the secret haunts of the sierra.

Thus baffled, Pizarro determined to try the effect of pacific overtures. He sent to the Inca, both in his own name, and in that of the Bishop of Cuzco, whom the Peruvian prince held in reverence, to invite him to enter into negotiation. Manco acquiesced, and indicated, as he had formerly done with Almagro, the valley of Yucay, as the scene of it. The governor repaired thither, at the appointed time, well guarded, and, to propitiate the barbarian monarch, sent him a rich present by the hands of an African slave. The slave was met on the route by a party of the Inca's men, who, whether with or without their master's orders, cruelly murdered him, and bore off the spoil to their quarters. Pizarro resented this outrage by another yet more atrocious.

Among the Indian prisoners was one of the Inca's wives, a young and beautiful woman, to whom he was said to be fondly attached. The governor ordered her to be stripped naked, bound to a tree, and, in presence of the camp, to be scourged with rods, and then shot to death with arrows. The wretched victim bore the execution of the sentence with surprising fortitude. She did not beg for mercy, where none was to be found. Not a complaint, scarcely a groan, escaped her under the infliction of these terrible torments. The iron Conquerors were amazed at this power of endurance in a delicate woman, and they expressed their admiration, while they condemned the cruelty of their commander,—in their hearts. Yet constancy under the most excruciating tortures that human cruelty can inflict is almost the universal characteristic of the American Indian.

Pizarro now prepared, as the most effectual means of checking these disorders among the natives, to establish settlements in the heart of the disaffected country. These settlements, which received the dignified name of cities, might be regarded in the light of military colonies. The houses were usually built of stone, to which were added the various public offices, and sometimes a fortress. A municipal corporation was organized. Settlers were invited by the distribution of large tracts of land in the neighborhood, with a stipulated number of Indian vassals to each. The soldiers then gathered there, sometimes accompanied by their wives and families; for the women of Castile seem to have disdained the impediments of sex, in the ardor of conjugal attachment, or, it may be, of romantic adventure. A populous settlement rapidly grew up in the wilderness, affording protection to the surrounding territory, and furnishing a commercial *dépôt* for the country, and an armed force ready at all times to maintain public order.

Such a settlement was that now made at Guamanga, midway between Cuzco and Lima, which effectually answered its purpose by guarding the communications with the coast. Another town was founded in the mining district of Charcas, under the appropriate name of the Villa de la Plata, the "City of Silver." And Pizarro, as he journeyed by a circuitous route along the shores of the southern sea towards Lima, planted there the city of Arequipa, since arisen to such commercial celebrity.

Once more in his favorite capital of Lima, the governor found abundant occupation in attending to its municipal concerns, and in providing for the expansive growth of its population. Nor was he unmindful of the other rising settlements on the Pacific. He encouraged commerce with the remoter colonies north of Peru, and took measures for facilitating internal intercourse. He stimulated industry in all its branches, paying great attention to husbandry, and importing seeds of the different European grains, which he had the satisfaction, in a short time, to see thriving luxuriantly in a country where the variety of soil and climate afforded a home for almost every product. Above all, he promoted the working of the mines, which already began to make such returns, that the most common articles of life rose to exorbitant prices, while the precious metals themselves seemed the only things of little value. But they soon changed hands, and found their way to the mother-country, where they rose to their true level as they mingled with the general currency of Europe. The Spaniards found that they had at length reached the land of which they had been so long in search,—the land of gold and silver. Emigrants came in greater numbers to the country, and, spreading over its surface, formed in the increasing population the most effectual barrier against the rightful owners of the soil.

Pizarro, strengthened by the arrival of fresh adventurers, now turned his attention to the remoter quarters of the country. Pedro de Valdivia was sent on his memorable expedition to Chili; and to his own brother Gonzalo the governor assigned the territory of Quito, with instructions to explore the unknown country towards the east, where, as report said, grew the cinnamon. As this chief, who had hitherto acted but a subordinate part in the Conquest, is henceforth to take the most conspicuous, it may be well to give some account of him.

Little is known of his early life, for he sprang from the same obscure origin with Francisco, and seems to have been as little indebted as his elder brother to the fostering care of his parents. He entered early on the career of a soldier; a career to which every man in that iron age, whether cavalier or vagabond, seems, if left to himself, to have most readily inclined. Here he soon distinguished himself by his skill in martial exercises, was an excellent horseman, and, when he came to the New World, was esteemed the best lance in Peru.

In talent and in expansion of views, he was inferior to his brothers. Neither did he discover the same cool and crafty policy; but he was equally courageous, and in the execution of his measures quite as unscrupulous. He had a handsome person, with open, engaging features, a free, soldier-like address, and a confiding temper, which endeared him to his followers. His spirit was high and adventurous, and, what was equally important, he could inspire others with the same spirit, and thus do much to insure the success of his enterprises. He was an excellent captain in *guerilla* warfare, an admirable leader in doubtful and difficult expeditions; but he had not the enlarged capacity for a great military chief, still less for a civil ruler. It was his misfortune to be called to fill both situations.

CHAPTER IV [1540-1542]

GONZALO PIZARRO'S EXPEDITION—PASSAGE ACROSS THE
MOUNTAINS—DISCOVERS THE NAPO—INCREDIBLE SUF-
FERINGS—ORELLANA SAILS DOWN THE AMAZON—DE-
SPAIR OF THE SPANIARDS—THE SURVIVORS RETURN TO
QUITO

Gonzalo Pizarro received the news of his appointment to
the government of Quito with undisguised pleasure; not so
much for the possession that it gave him of this ancient Indian
province, as for the field that it opened for discovery towards
the east,—the fabled land of Oriental spices, which had long
captivated the imagination of the Conquerors. He repaired to
his government without delay, and found no difficulty in awak-
ening a kindred enthusiasm to his own in the bosoms of his
followers. In a short time, he mustered three hundred and
fifty Spaniards, and four thousand Indians. One hundred and
fifty of his company were mounted, and all were equipped in
the most thorough manner for the undertaking. He provided,
moreover, against famine by a large stock of provisions, and
an immense drove of swine which followed in the rear.

It was the beginning of 1540, when he set out on this celebrated expedition. The first part of the journey was attended
with comparatively little difficulty, while the Spaniards were
yet in the land of the Incas; for the distractions of Peru had
not been felt in this distant province, where the simple people
still lived as under the primitive sway of the Children of the
Sun. But the scene changed as they entered the territory of
Quixos, where the character of the inhabitants, as well as of
the climate, seemed to be of another description. The country
was traversed by lofty ranges of the Andes, and the adventurers were soon entangled in their deep and intricate passes.
As they rose into the more elevated regions, the icy winds
that swept down the sides of the Cordilleras benumbed their
limbs, and many of the natives found a wintry grave in the
wilderness. While crossing this formidable barrier, they experi-

enced one of those tremendous earthquakes which, in these volcanic regions, so often shake the mountains to their base. In one place, the earth was rent asunder by the terrible throes of Nature, while streams of sulphurous vapor issued from the cavity, and a village with some hundreds of houses was precipitated into the frightful abyss!

On descending the eastern slopes, the climate changed; and, as they came on the lower level, the fierce cold was succeeded by a suffocating heat, while tempests of thunder and lightning, rushing from out of the gorges of the sierra, poured on their heads with scarcely any intermission day or night, as if the offended deities of the place were willing to take vengeance on the invaders of their mountain solitudes. For more than six weeks the deluge continued unabated, and the forlorn wanderers, wet, and weary with incessant toil, were scarcely able to drag their limbs along the soil broken up and saturated with the moisture. After some months of toilsome travel, in which they had to cross many a morass and mountain stream, they at length reached *Canelas,* the Land of Cinnamon. They saw the trees bearing the precious bark, spreading out into broad forests; yet, however valuable an article for commerce it might have proved in accessible situations, in these remote regions it was of little worth to them. But, from the wandering tribes of savages whom they occasionally met in their path, they learned that at ten days' distance was a rich and fruitful land abounding with gold, and inhabited by populous nations. Gonzalo Pizarro had already reached the limits originally proposed for the expedition. But this intelligence renewed his hopes, and he resolved to push the adventure farther. It would have been well for him and his followers, had they been content to return on their footsteps.

Continuing their march, the country now spread out into broad savannas terminated by forests, which, as they drew near, seemed to stretch on every side to the very verge of the horizon. Here they beheld trees of that stupendous growth seen only in the equinoctial regions. Some were so large, that sixteen men could hardly encompass them with extended arms! The wood was thickly matted with creepers and parasitical vines, which hung in gaudy-colored festoons from tree to tree, clothing them in a drapery beautiful to the eye, but forming an impenetrable network. At every step of their way, they were obliged to hew open a passage with their axes, while their garments, rotting from the effects of the drenching rains to which they had been exposed, caught in every bush and bramble, and hung about them in shreds. Their provisions, spoiled by the weather, had long since failed, and the live stock which they had taken with them had either been consumed or made their escape in the woods and mountain passes. They had set out with nearly a thousand dogs, many of them of the ferocious breed used in hunting down the unfortunate natives. These they now gladly killed, but their miserable carcasses furnished a lean banquet for the famishing travellers; and, when these were gone, they had only such herbs and dangerous roots as they could gather in the forest.

At length the way-worn company came on a broad expanse of water formed by the Napo, one of the great tributaries of the Amazon, and which, though only a third or fourth rate river in America, would pass for one of the first magnitude in the Old World. The sight gladdened their hearts, as, by winding along its banks, they hoped to find a safer and more practicable route. After traversing its borders for a considerable distance, closely beset with thickets which it taxed their strength to the utmost to overcome, Gonzalo and his party came within hearing of a rushing noise that sounded like subterranean thunder. The river, lashed into fury, tumbled along over rapids with frightful velocity, and conducted them to the brink of a magnificent cataract, which, to their wondering fancies, rushed down in one vast volume of foam to the depth of twelve hundred feet! The appalling sounds which they had heard for the distance of six leagues were rendered yet more oppressive to the spirits by the gloomy stillness of the surrounding forests. The rude warriors were filled with sentiments of awe. Not a bark dimpled the waters. No living thing was to be seen but the wild tenants of the wilderness, the unwieldy boa, and the loathsome alligator basking on the borders of the stream. The trees towering in wide-spread magnificence towards the heavens, the river rolling on in its rocky bed as it had rolled for ages, the solitude and silence of the scene, broken only by the hoarse fall of waters, or the faint rustling of the woods,—all seemed to spread out around them in the same wild and primitive state as when they came from the hands of the Creator.

For some distance above and below the falls, the bed of the river contracted so that its width did not exceed twenty feet. Sorely pressed by hunger, the adventurers determined, at all hazards, to cross to the opposite side, in hopes of finding a country that might afford them sustenance. A frail bridge was constructed by throwing the huge trunks of trees across the chasm, where the cliffs, as if split asunder by some convulsion of nature, descended sheer down a perpendicular depth of several hundred feet. Over this airy causeway the men and horses succeeded in effecting their passage with the loss of a single Spaniard, who, made giddy by heedlessly looking down, lost his footing and fell into the boiling surges below.

Yet they gained little by the exchange. The country wore the same unpromising aspect, and the river-banks were studded with gigantic trees, or fringed with impenetrable thickets. The tribes of Indians, whom they occasionally met in the pathless wilderness, were fierce and unfriendly, and they were engaged in perpetual skirmishes with them. From these they learned that a fruitful country was to be found down the river at the distance of only a few days' journey, and the Spaniards held on their weary way, still hoping and still deceived, as the promised land flitted before them, like the rainbow, receding as they advanced.

At length, spent with toil and suffering, Gonzalo resolved to construct a bark large enough to transport the weaker part of his company and his baggage. The forest furnished him with timber; the shoes of the horses which had died on the road or been slaughtered for food, were converted into nails; gum distilled from the trees took the place of pitch; and the tattered garments of the soldiers supplied a substitute for oakum. It was a work of difficulty; but Gonzalo cheered his men in the task, and set an example by taking part in their labors. At the end of two months a brigantine was completed, rudely put together, but strong and of sufficient burden to carry half the company,—the first European vessel to float on these inland waters.

Gonzalo gave the command to Francisco de Orellana, a cavalier from Truxillo, on whose courage and devotion to himself he thought he could rely. The troops now moved forward, still following the descending course of the river, while the brigantine kept alongside; and when a bold promontory or more impracticable country intervened, it furnished timely aid by the transportation of the feebler soldiers. In this way they journeyed, for many a wearisome week, through the dreary wilderness on the borders of the Napo. Every scrap of provisions had been long since consumed. The last of their horses had been devoured. To appease the gnawings of hunger, they were fain to eat the leather of their saddles and belts. The woods supplied them with scanty sustenance, and they greedily fed upon toads, serpents, and such other reptiles as they occasionally found.

They were now told of a rich district, inhabited by a populous nation, where the Napo emptied into a still greater river that flowed towards the east. It was, as usual, at the distance of several days' journey; and Gonzalo Pizarro resolved to halt where he was and send Orellana down in his brigantine to the confluence of the waters to procure a stock of provisions, with which he might return and put them in condition to resume their march. That cavalier, accordingly, taking with him fifty of the adventurers, pushed off into the middle of the river, where the stream ran swiftly, and his bark, taken by the current, shot forward with the speed of an arrow, and was soon out of sight.

Days and weeks passed away, yet the vessel did not return; and no speck was to be seen on the waters, as the Spaniards strained their eyes to the farthest point, where the line of light faded away in the dark shadows of the foliage on the borders. Detachments were sent out, and, though absent several days, came back without intelligence of their comrades. Unable longer to endure this suspense, or, indeed, to maintain themselves in their present quarters, Gonzalo and his famishing followers now determined to proceed towards the junction of the rivers. Two months elapsed before they accomplished this terrible journey,—those of them who did not perish on the way,—although the distance probably did not exceed two hundred leagues; and they at length reached the spot so long desired, where the Napo pours its tide into the Amazon, that mighty stream, which, fed by its thousand tributaries, rolls on towards the ocean, for many hundred miles, through the heart of the great continent,—the most majestic of American rivers.

But the Spaniards gathered no tidings of Orellana, while the country, though more populous than the region they had left, was as little inviting in its aspect, and was tenanted by a race yet more ferocious. They now abandoned the hope of recovering their comrades, who they supposed must have miserably perished by famine or by the hands of the natives. But their doubts were at length dispelled by the appearance of a white man wandering half-naked in the woods, in whose famine-stricken countenance they recognized the features of one of their countrymen. It was Sanchez de Vargas, a cavalier of good descent, and much esteemed in the army. He had a dismal tale to tell.

Orellana, borne swiftly down the current of the Napo, had reached the point of its confluence with the Amazon in less than three days; accomplishing in this brief space of time what had cost Pizarro and his company two months. He had found the country altogether different from what had been represented, and, so far from supplies for his countrymen, he could barely obtain sustenance for himself. Nor was it possible for him to return as he had come, and make head against the current of the river; while the attempt to journey by land was an alternative scarcely less formidable. In this dilemma, an idea flashed across his mind. It was to launch his bark at once on the bosom of the Amazon, and descend its waters to its mouth. He would then visit the rich and populous nations that, as report said, lined its borders, sail out on the great ocean, cross to the neighboring isles, and return to Spain to claim the glory and the guerdon of discovery. The suggestion was eagerly taken up by his reckless companions, welcoming any course that would rescue them from the wretchedness of their present existence, and fired with the prospect of new and stirring adventure,—for the love of adventure was the last feeling to become extinct in the bosom of the Castilian cavalier. They heeded little their unfortunate comrades, whom they were to abandon in the wilderness!

This is not the place to record the circumstances of Orellana's extraordinary expedition. He succeeded in his enterprise. But it is marvellous that he should have escaped shipwreck in the perilous and unknown navigation of that river. Many times his vessel was nearly dashed to pieces on its rocks and in its furious rapids; and he was in still greater peril from the warlike tribes on its borders, who fell on his little troop whenever he attempted to land, and followed in his wake for miles in their canoes. He at length emerged from the great river; and, once upon the sea, Orellana made for the isle of Cubagua; thence passing over to Spain, he repaired to court, and told the circumstances of his voyage,—of the nations of Amazons whom he had found on the banks of the river, the El Dorado which report assured him existed in the neighborhood, and other marvels,—the exaggeration rather than the coinage of a credulous fancy. His audience listened with willing ears to the tales of the traveller; and in an age of wonders, when the mysteries of the East and West were hourly coming to light, they might be excused for not discerning the true line between romance and reality.

He found no difficulty in obtaining a commission to conquer and colonize the realms he had discovered. He soon saw himself at the head of five hundred followers, prepared to share the perils and the profits of his expedition. But neither he, nor his country, was destined to realize these profits. He died on his outward passage, and the lands washed by the Amazon fell within the territories of Portugal. The unfortunate navigator did not even enjoy the undivided honor of giving his name to the waters he had discovered. He enjoyed only the barren glory of the discovery, surely not balanced by the iniquitous circumstances which attended it.

One of Orellana's party maintained a stout opposition to his proceedings, as repugnant both to humanity and honor. This was Sanchez de Vargas; and the cruel commander was revenged on him by abandoning him to his fate in the desolate region where he was now found by his countrymen.

The Spaniards listened with horror to the recital of Vargas, and their blood almost froze in their veins as they saw themselves thus deserted in the heart of this remote wilderness, and deprived of their only means of escape from it. They made an effort to prosecute their journey along the banks, but, after some toilsome days, strength and spirits failed, and they gave up in despair!

Then it was that the qualities of Gonzalo Pizarro, as a fit leader in the hour of despondency and danger, shone out conspicuous. To advance farther was hopeless. To stay where they were, without food or raiment, without defence from the fierce animals of the forest and the fiercer natives, was impossible. One only course remained; it was to return to Quito. But this brought with it the recollection of the past, of sufferings which they could too well estimate,—hardly to be endured even in imagination. They were now at least four hundred leagues from Quito, and more than a year had elapsed since they had set out on their painful pilgrimage. How could they encounter these perils again!

Yet there was no alternative. Gonzalo endeavored to reassure his followers by dwelling on the invincible constancy they had hitherto displayed; adjuring them to show themselves still worthy of the name of Castilians. He reminded them of the glory they would for ever acquire by their heroic achievement, when they should reach their own country. He would lead them back, he said, by another route, and it could not be but that they should meet somewhere with those abundant regions of which they had so often heard. It was something, at least, that every step would take them nearer home; and as, at all events, it was clearly the only course now left, they should prepare to meet it like men. The spirit would sustain the body; and difficulties encountered in the right spirit were half vanquished already!

The soldiers listened eagerly to his words of promise and encouragement. The confidence of their leader gave life to the desponding. They felt the force of his reasoning, and, as they lent a willing ear to his assurances, the pride of the old Castilian honor revived in their bosoms, and every one caught somewhat of the generous enthusiasm of their commander. He was, in truth, entitled to their devotion. From the first hour of the expedition, he had freely borne his part in its privations. Far from claiming the advantage of his position, he had taken his lot with the poorest soldiers; ministering to the wants of the sick, cheering up the spirits of the desponding, sharing his stinted allowance with his famished followers, bearing his full part in the toil and burden of the march, ever showing himself their faithful comrade, no less than their captain. He found the benefit of this conduct in a trying hour like the present.

I will spare the reader the recapitulation of the sufferings endured by the Spaniards on their retrograde march to Quito. They took a more northerly route than that by which they had approached the Amazon; and, if it was attended with fewer difficulties, they experienced yet greater distresses from their greater inability to overcome them. Their only nourishment was such scanty fare as they could pick up in the forest, or happily meet with in some forsaken Indian settlement, or wring by violence from the natives. Some sickened and sank down by the way, for there was none to help them. Intense misery had made them selfish; and many a poor wretch was abandoned to his fate, to die alone in the wilderness, or, more probably, to be devoured, while living, by the wild animals which roamed over it.

At length, in June, 1542, after somewhat more than a year consumed in their homeward march, the way-worn company came on the elevated plains in the neighborhood of Quito. But how different their aspect from that which they had exhibited on issuing from the gates of the same capital, two years and a half before, with high romantic hope and in all the pride of military array! Their horses gone, their arms broken and rusted, the skins of wild animals instead of clothes hanging loosely about their limbs, their long and matted locks streaming wildly down their shoulders, their faces burned and blackened by the tropical sun, their bodies wasted by famine and sorely disfigured by scars,—it seemed as if the charnel-house had given up its dead, as, with uncertain step, they glided slowly onwards like a troop of dismal spectres! More than half of the four thousand Indians who had accompanied the expedition had perished, and of the Spaniards only eighty, and many of these irretrievably broken in constitution, returned to Quito.

The few Christian inhabitants of the place, with their wives and children, came out to welcome their countrymen. They ministered to them all the relief and refreshment in their power; and, as they listened to the sad recital of their sufferings, they mingled their tears with those of the wanderers. The whole company then entered the capital, where their first act —to their credit be it mentioned—was to go in a body to the church, and offer up thanksgiving to the Almighty for their miraculous preservation through their long and perilous pilgrimage. Such was the end of the expedition to the Amazon; an expedition which, for its dangers and hardships, the length of their duration, and the constancy with which they were endured, stands, perhaps, unmatched in the annals of American discovery.

CHAPTER V [1541]

THE ALMAGRO FACTION—THEIR DESPERATE CONDITION
—CONSPIRACY AGAINST FRANCISCO PIZARRO—ASSAS-
SINATION OF PIZARRO—ACTS OF THE CONSPIRATORS—
PIZARRO'S CHARACTER

When Gonzalo Pizarro reached Quito, he received tidings
of an event which showed that his expedition to the Amazon
had been even more fatal to his interests than he had imagined.
A revolution had taken place during his absence, which had
changed the whole condition of things in Peru.

In a preceding chapter we have seen, that, when Hernando
Pizarro returned to Spain, his brother the marquess repaired
to Lima, where he continued to occupy himself with building
up his infant capital, and watching over the general interests
of the country. While thus employed, he gave little heed to a
danger that hourly beset his path, and this, too, in despite of
repeated warnings from more circumspect friends.

After the execution of Almagro, his followers, to the number
of several hundred, remained scattered through the country;
but, however scattered, still united by a common sentiment
of indignation against the Pizarros, the murderers, as they regarded them, of their leader. The governor was less the object
of these feelings than his brother Hernando, as having been
less instrumental in the perpetration of the deed. Under these
circumstances, it was clearly Pizarro's policy to do one of two
things; to treat the opposite faction either as friends, or as open
enemies. He might conciliate the most factious by acts of kindness, efface the remembrance of past injury, if he could, by
present benefits; in short, prove to them that his quarrel had
been with their leader, not with themselves, and that it was
plainly for their interest to come again under his banner. This
would have been the most politic, as well as the most magnanimous course; and, by augmenting the number of his adherents, would have greatly strengthened his power in the

land. But, unhappily, he had not the magnanimity to pursue it. It was not in the nature of a Pizarro to forgive an injury, or the man whom he had injured. As he would not, therefore, try to conciliate Almagro's adherents, it was clearly the governor's policy to regard them as enemies,—not the less so for being in disguise,—and to take such measures as should disqualify them for doing mischief. He should have followed the counsel of his more prudent brother Hernando, and distributed them in different quarters, taking care that no great number should assemble at any one point, or, above all, in the neighborhood of his own residence.

But the governor despised the broken followers of Almagro too heartily to stoop to precautionary measures. He suffered the son of his rival to remain in Lima, where his quarters soon became the resort of the disaffected cavaliers. The young man was well known to most of Almagro's soldiers, having been trained along with them in the camp under his father's eye, and, now that his parent was removed, they naturally transferred their allegiance to the son who survived him.

That the young Almagro, however, might be less able to maintain this retinue of unprofitable followers, he was deprived by Pizarro of a great part of his Indians and lands, while he was excluded from the government of New Toledo, which had been settled on him by his father's testament. Stripped of all means of support, without office or employment of any kind, the men of Chili, for so Almagro's adherents continued to be called, were reduced to the utmost distress. So poor were they, as is the story of the time, that twelve cavaliers, who lodged in the same house, could muster only one cloak among them all; and, with the usual feeling of pride that belongs to the poor *hidalgo*, unwilling to expose their poverty, they wore this cloak by turns, those who had no right to it remaining at home. Whether true or not, the anecdote well illustrates the extremity to which Almagro's faction was reduced. And this distress was rendered yet more galling by the effrontery of their enemies, who, enriched by their forfeitures, displayed before their eyes all the insolent bravery of equipage and apparel that could annoy their feelings.

Men thus goaded by insult and injury were too dangerous to be lightly regarded. But, although Pizarro received various intimations intended to put him on his guard, he gave no heed to them. "Poor devils!" he would exclaim, speaking with contemptuous pity of the men of Chili; "they have had bad luck enough. We will not trouble them further." And so little did he consider them, that he went freely about, as usual, riding without attendants to all parts of the town and to its immediate environs.

News now reached the colony of the appointment of a judge by the Crown to take cognizance of the affairs of Peru. Pizarro, although alarmed by the intelligence, sent orders to have him well entertained on his landing, and suitable accommodations prepared for him on the route. The spirits of Almagro's followers were greatly raised by the tidings. They confidently looked to this high functionary for the redress of their wrongs; and two of their body, clad in suits of mourning, were chosen to go to the north, where the judge was expected to land, and to lay their grievances before him.

But months elapsed, and no tidings came of his arrival, till, at length, a vessel, coming into port, announced that most of the squadron had foundered in the heavy storms on the coast, and that the commissioner had probably perished with them. This was disheartening intelligence to the men of Chili, whose "miseries," to use the words of their young leader, "had become too grievous to be borne." Symptoms of disaffection had already begun openly to manifest themselves. The haughty cavaliers did not always doff their bonnets, on meeting the governor in the street; and on one occasion, three ropes were found suspended from the public gallows, with labels attached to them, bearing the names of Pizarro, Velasquez the judge, and Picado the governor's secretary. This last functionary was peculiarly odious to Almagro and his followers. As his master knew neither how to read nor write, all his communications passed through Picado's hands; and, as the latter was of a hard and arrogant nature, greatly elated by the consequence which his position gave him, he exercised a mischievous influence on the governor's measures. Almagro's poverty-stricken followers were the objects of his open ridicule, and he revenged the insult now offered him by riding before their young leader's residence, displaying a tawdry magnificence in his dress, sparkling with gold and silver, and with the inscription, "For the

Men of Chili," set in his bonnet. It was a foolish taunt; but the
poor cavaliers who were the object of it, made morbidly sensitive by their sufferings, had not the philosophy to despise it.

At length, disheartened by the long protracted coming of
Vaca de Castro, and still more by the recent reports of his
loss, Almagro's faction, despairing of redress from a legitimate
authority, determined to take it into their own hands. They
came to the desperate resolution of assassinating Pizarro. The
day named for this was Sunday, the twenty-sixth of June,
1541. The conspirators, eighteen or twenty in number, were
to assemble in Almagro's house, which stood in the great
square next to the cathedral, and, when the governor was returning from mass, they were to issue forth and fall on him in
the street. A white flag, unfurled at the same time from an
upper window in the house, was to be the signal for the rest
of their comrades to move to the support of those immediately
engaged in the execution of the deed.

These arrangements could hardly have been concealed from
Almagro, since his own quarters were to be the place of rendezvous. Yet there is no good evidence of his having taken part
in the conspiracy. He was, indeed, too young to make it probable that he took a leading part in it. He is represented by
contemporary writers to have given promise of many good
qualities, though, unhappily, he was not placed in a situation
favorable for their development. He was the son of an Indian
woman of Panamá; but from early years had followed the
troubled fortunes of his father, to whom he bore much resemblance in his free and generous nature, as well as in the violence of his passions. His youth and inexperience disqualified
him from taking the lead in the perplexing circumstances in
which he was placed, and made him little more than a puppet
in the hands of others.

The most conspicuous of his advisers was Juan de Herrada,
or Rada, as his name is more usually spelt,—a cavalier of respectable family, but who, having early enlisted as a common
soldier, had gradually risen to the highest posts in the army by
his military talents. At this time he was well advanced in years;
but the fires of youth were not quenched in his bosom, and
he burned with desire to avenge the wrongs done to his ancient
commander. The attachment which he had ever felt for the

elder Almagro he seems to have transferred in full measure to his son; and it was apparently with reference to him, even more than to himself, that he devised this audacious plot, and prepared to take the lead in the execution of it.

There was one, however, in the band of conspirators who felt some compunctions of conscience at the part he was acting, and who relieved his bosom by revealing the whole plot to his confessor. The latter lost no time in reporting it to Picado, by whom in turn it was communicated to Pizarro. But, strange to say, it made little more impression on the governor's mind than the vague warnings he had so frequently received. "It is a device of the priest," said he; "he wants a mitre." Yet, he repeated the story to the judge Velasquez, who, instead of ordering the conspirators to be seized, and the proper steps taken for learning the truth of the accusation, seemed to be possessed with the same infatuation as Pizarro; and he bade the governor be under no apprehension, "for no harm should come to him, while the rod of justice," not a metaphorical badge of authority in Castile, "was in his hands." Still, to obviate every possibility of danger, it was deemed prudent for Pizarro to abstain from going to mass on Sunday, and to remain at home on pretence of illness.

On the day appointed, Rada and his companions met in Almagro's house, and waited with anxiety for the hour when the governor should issue from the church. But great was their consternation, when they learned that he was not there, but was detained at home, as currently reported, by illness. Little doubting that their design was discovered, they felt their own ruin to be the inevitable consequence, and that, too, without enjoying the melancholy consolation of having struck the blow for which they had incurred it. Greatly perplexed, some were for disbanding, in the hope that Pizarro might, after all, be ignorant of their designs. But most were for carrying it into execution at once, by assaulting him in his own house. The question was summarily decided by one of the party, who felt that in this latter course lay their only chance of safety. Throwing open the doors, he rushed out, calling on his comrades "to follow him, or he would proclaim the purpose for which they had met." There was no longer hesitation, and the cavaliers issued forth, with Rada at their head, shouting, "Long live the king! Death to the tyrant!"

It was the hour of dinner, which, in this primitive age of the Spanish colonies, was at noon. Yet numbers, roused by the cries of the assailants, came out into the square to inquire the cause. "They are going to kill the marquess," some said very coolly; others replied, "It is Picado." No one stirred in their defence. The power of Pizarro was not seated in the hearts of his people.

As the conspirators traversed the *plaza*, one of the party made a circuit to avoid a little pool of water that lay in their path. "What!" exclaimed Rada, "afraid of wetting your feet, when you are to wade up to your knees in blood!" And he ordered the man to give up the enterprise and go home to his quarters. The anecdote is characteristic.

The governor's palace stood on the opposite side of the square. It was approached by two courtyards. The entrance to the outer one was protected by a massive gate, capable of being made good against a hundred men or more. But it was left open, and the assailants, hurrying through to the inner court, still shouting their fearful battle-cry, were met by two domestics loitering in the yard. One of these they struck down. The other, flying in all haste towards the house, called out, "Help, help! the men of Chili are all coming to murder the marquess!"

Pizarro at this time was at dinner, or, more probably, had just dined. He was surrounded by a party of friends, who had dropped in, it seems, after mass, to inquire after the state of his health, some of whom had remained to partake of his repast. Among these was Don Martinez de Alcantara, Pizarro's half-brother by the mother's side, the judge Velasquez, the bishop elect of Quito, and several of the principal cavaliers in the place, to the number of fifteen or twenty. Some of them, alarmed by the uproar in the courtyard, left the saloon, and, running down to the first landing on the stairway, inquired into the cause of the disturbance. No sooner were they informed of it by the cries of the servant, than they retreated with precipitation into the house; and, as they had no mind to abide the storm unarmed, or at best imperfectly armed, as most of them were, they made their way to a corridor that overlooked the gardens, into which they easily let themselves down without injury. Velasquez, the judge, the better to have the use of his hands in the descent, held his rod of office in his mouth, thus taking care, says a caustic old chronicler, not to falsify his assurance, that "no harm should come to Pizarro while the rod of justice was in his hands"!

Meanwhile, the marquess, learning the nature of the tumult, called out to Francisco de Chaves, an officer high in his confidence, and who was in the outer apartment opening on the staircase, to secure the door, while he and his brother Alcantara buckled on their armour. Had this order, coolly given, been as coolly obeyed, it would have saved them all, since the entrance could easily have been maintained against a much larger force, till the report of the cavaliers who had fled had brought support to Pizarro. But unfortunately, Chaves, disobeying his commander, half opened the door, and attempted to enter into a parley with the conspirators. The latter had now reached the head of the stairs, and cut short the debate by running Chaves through the body, and tumbling his corpse down into the area below. For a moment they were kept at bay by the attendants of the slaughtered cavalier, but these, too, were quickly despatched; and Rada and his companions, entering the apartment, hurried across it, shouting out, "Where is the marquess? Death to the tyrant!"

Martinez de Alcantara, who in the adjoining room was assisting his brother to buckle on his mail, no sooner saw that the entrance to the antechamber had been gained, than he sprang to the doorway of the apartment, and, assisted by two young men, pages of Pizarro, and by one or two cavaliers in attendance, endeavored to resist the approach of the assailants. A desperate struggle now ensued. Blows were given on both sides, some of which proved fatal, and two of the conspirators were slain, while Alcantara and his brave companions were repeatedly wounded.

At length, Pizarro, unable, in the hurry of the moment, to adjust the fastenings of his cuirass, threw it away, and, enveloping one arm in his cloak, with the other seized his sword, and sprang to his brother's assistance. It was too late; for Alcantara was already staggering under the loss of blood, and soon fell to the ground. Pizarro threw himself on his invaders, like a lion roused in his lair, and dealt his blows with as much rapidity and force, as if age had no power to stiffen his limbs. "What ho!" he cried, "traitors! have you come to kill me in my own house?" The conspirators drew back for a moment, as two of their body fell under Pizarro's sword; but they quickly rallied, and, from their superior numbers, fought at great advantage by relieving one another in the assault. Still the passage was narrow, and the struggle lasted for some minutes, till both of Pizarro's pages were stretched by his side, when Rada, impatient of the delay, called out, "Why are we so long about it? Down with the tyrant!" and taking one of his companions, Narvaez, in his arms, he thrust him against the marquess. Pizarro, instantly grappling with his opponent, ran him through with his sword. But at that moment he received a wound in the throat, and reeling, he sank on the floor, while the swords of Rada and several of the conspirators were plunged into his body. "Jesu!" exclaimed the dying man, and, tracing a cross with his finger on the bloody floor, he bent down his head to kiss it, when a stroke, more friendly than the rest, put an end to his existence.

The conspirators, having accomplished their bloody deed, rushed into the street, and, brandishing their dripping weapons, shouted out, "The tyrant is dead! The laws are restored! Long live our master the emperor, and his governor, Almagro!" The men of Chili, roused by the cheering cry, now flocked in from every side to join the banner of Rada, who soon found himself at the head of nearly three hundred followers, all armed and prepared to support his authority. A guard was placed over the houses of the principal partisans of the late governor, and their persons were taken into custody. Pizarro's house, and that of his secretary Picado, were delivered up to pillage, and a large booty in gold and silver was found in the former. Picado himself took refuge in the dwelling of Riquelme, the treasurer; but his hiding-place was detected,—betrayed, according to some accounts, by the looks, though not the words, of the treasurer himself,—and he was dragged forth and committed to a secure prison. The whole city was thrown into consternation, as armed bodies hurried to and fro on their several errands, and all who were not in the faction of Almagro trembled lest they should be involved in the proscription of their enemies. So great was the disorder, that the Brothers of Mercy, turning out in a body, paraded the streets in solemn procession, with the host elevated in the air, in hopes by the presence of the sacred symbol to calm the passions of the multitude.

But no other violence was offered by Rada and his followers than to apprehend a few suspected persons, and to seize upon horses and arms wherever they were to be found. The municipality was then summoned to recognize the authority of Almagro; the refractory were ejected without ceremony from their offices, and others of the Chili faction were substituted. The claims of the new aspirant were fully recognized; and young Almagro, parading the streets on horseback, and escorted by a well-armed body of cavaliers, was proclaimed by sound of trumpet governor and captain-general of Peru.

Meanwhile, the mangled bodies of Pizarro and his faithful adherents were left weltering in their blood. Some were for dragging forth the governor's corpse to the market-place, and fixing his head upon a gibbet. But Almagro was secretly prevailed on to grant the entreaties of Pizarro's friends, and allow his interment. This was stealthily and hastily performed, in the fear of momentary interruption. A faithful attendant and his wife, with a few black domestics, wrapped the body in a cotton cloth and removed it to the cathedral. A grave was hastily dug in an obscure corner, the services were hurried through, and, in secrecy, and in darkness dispelled only by the feeble glimmering of a few tapers furnished by these humble menials, the remains of Pizarro, rolled in their bloody shroud, were consigned to their kindred dust. Such was the miserable end of the Conqueror of Peru,—of the man who but a few hours before had lorded it over the land with as absolute a sway as was possessed by its hereditary Incas. Cut off in the broad light of day, in the heart of his own capital, in the very midst of those who had been his companions in arms and shared with him his triumphs and his spoils, he perished like a wretched outcast. "There was none, even," in the expressive language of the chronicler, "to say, God forgive him!"

A few years later, when tranquillity was restored to the country, Pizarro's remains were placed in a sumptuous coffin and deposited under a monument in a conspicuous part of the cathedral. And in 1607, when time had thrown its friendly mantle over the past, and the memory of his errors and his crimes was merged in the consideration of the great services he had rendered to the Crown by the extension of her colonial empire, his bones were removed to the new cathedral, and allowed to repose side by side with those of Mendoza, the wise and good viceroy of Peru.

Pizarro was, probably, not far from sixty-five years of age at the time of his death; though this, it must be added, is but loose conjecture, since there exists no authentic record of the date of his birth. He was never married; but by an Indian princess of the Inca blood, daughter of Atahuallpa and grand-daughter of the great Huayna Capac, he had two children, a son and a daughter. Both survived him; but the son did not live to manhood. Their mother, after Pizarro's death, wedded a Spanish cavalier, named Ampuero, and removed with him to Spain. Her daughter Francisca accompanied her, and was there subsequently married to her uncle Hernando Pizarro, then a prisoner in the Mota del Medina. Neither the title nor estates of the Marquess Francisco descended to his illegiti-mate offspring. But in the third generation, in the reign of Philip the Fourth, the title was revived in favor of Don Juan Hernando Pizarro, who, out of gratitude for the services of his ancestor, was created Marquess of the Conquest, *Marques de la Conquista*, with a liberal pension from government. His de-scendants, bearing the same title of nobility, are still to be found, it is said, at Truxillo, in the ancient province of Estremadura, the original birthplace of the Pizarros.

Pizarro's person has been already described. He was tall in stature, well-proportioned, and with a countenance not un-pleasing. Bred in camps, with nothing of the polish of a court, he had a soldier-like bearing, and the air of one accustomed to command. But though not polished, there was no embar-rassment or rusticity in his address, which, where it served his purpose, could be plausible and even insinuating. The proof of it is the favorable impression made by him, on presenting himself, after his second expedition—stranger as he was to all its forms and usages—at the punctilious court of Castile.

Unlike many of his countrymen, he had no passion for os-tentatious dress, which he regarded as an encumbrance. The costume which he most affected on public occasions was a black cloak, with a white hat, and shoes of the same color; the last, it is said, being in imitation of the Great Captain, whose character he had early learned to admire in Italy, but to which his own, certainly, bore very faint resemblance.

He was temperate in eating, drank sparingly, and usually rose an hour before dawn. He was punctual in attendance to business, and shrunk from no toil. He had, indeed, great powers of patient endurance. Like most of his nation, he was fond of play, and cared little for the quality of those with whom he played; though, when his antagonist could not afford to lose, he would allow himself, it is said, to be the loser; a mode of conferring an obligation much commended by a Castilian writer, for its delicacy.

Though avaricious, it was in order to spend and not to hoard. His ample treasures, more ample than those, probably, that ever before fell to the lot of an adventurer, were mostly dissipated in his enterprises, his architectural works, and schemes of public improvement, which, in a country where gold and silver might be said to have lost their value from their abundance, absorbed an incredible amount of money. While he regarded the whole country, in a manner, as his own, and distributed it freely among his captains, it is certain that the princely grant of a territory with twenty thousand vassals, made to him by the Crown, was never carried into effect; nor did his heirs ever reap the benefit of it.

To a man possessed of the active energies of Pizarro, sloth was the greatest evil. The excitement of play was in a manner necessary to a spirit accustomed to the habitual stimulants of war and adventure. His uneducated mind had no relish for more refined, intellectual recreation. The deserted foundling had neither been taught to read nor write. This has been disputed by some, but it is attested by unexceptionable authorities. Montesinos says, indeed, that Pizarro, on his first voyage, tried to learn to read; but the impatience of his temper prevented it, and he contented himself with learning to sign his name. But Montesinos was not a contemporary historian. Pedro Pizarro, his companion in arms, expressly tells us he could neither read nor write; and Zarate, another contemporary, well acquainted with the Conquerors, confirms this statement, and adds, that Pizarro could not so much as sign his name. This was done by his secretary—Picado, in his latter years—while the governor merely made the customary *rúbrica* or flourish at the sides of his name. This is the case with the instruments I have examined, in which his signature, written probably by his secretary, or his title of *Marques*, in later life substituted for his name, is garnished with a flourish at the ends, executed in as bungling a manner as if done by the hand of a ploughman. Yet we must not estimate this deficiency as we should in this period of general illumination,—general, at least, in our own fortunate country. Reading and writing, so universal now, in the beginning of the sixteenth century might be regarded in the light of accomplishments; and all who have occasion to consult the autograph memorials of that time will find the execution of them, even by persons of the highest rank, too often such as would do little credit to a schoolboy of the present day.

Though bold in action and not easily turned from his purpose, Pizarro was slow in arriving at a decision. This gave him an appearance of irresolution foreign to his character. Perhaps the consciousness of this led him to adopt the custom of saying "No," at first, to applicants for favor; and afterwards, at leisure, to revise his judgment, and grant what seemed to him expedient. He took the opposite course from his comrade Almagro, who, it was observed, generally said "Yes," but too often failed to keep his promise. This was characteristic of the careless and easy nature of the latter, governed by impulse rather than principle.

It is hardly necessary to speak of the courage of a man pledged to such a career as that of Pizarro. Courage, indeed, was a cheap quality among the Spanish adventurers, for danger was their element. But he possessed something higher than mere animal courage, in that constancy of purpose which was rooted too deeply in his nature to be shaken by the wildest storms of fortune. It was this inflexible constancy which formed the key to his character, and constituted the secret of his success. A remarkable evidence of it was given in his first expedition, among the mangroves and dreary marshes of Choco. He saw his followers pining around him under the blighting malaria, wasting before an invisible enemy, and unable to strike a stroke in their own defence. Yet his spirit did not yield, nor did he falter in his enterprise.

There is something oppressive to the imagination in this war against nature. In the struggle of man against man, the spirits are raised by a contest conducted on equal terms; but in a war with the elements, we feel, that, however bravely we may contend, we can have no power to control. Nor are we cheered on by the prospect of glory in such a contest; for, in the capricious estimate of human glory, the silent endurance of privations, however painful, is little, in comparison with the ostentatious trophies of victory. The laurel of the hero grows best on the battle-field.

This inflexible spirit of Pizarro was shown still more strongly, when, in the little island of Gallo, he drew the line on the sand, which was to separate him and his handful of followers from their country and from civilized man. He trusted that his own constancy would give strength to the feeble, and rally brave hearts around him for the prosecution of his enterprise. He looked with confidence to the future, and he did not miscalculate. This was heroic, and wanted only a nobler motive for its object to constitute the true moral sublime.

Yet the same feature in his character was displayed in a manner scarcely less remarkable, when, landing on the coast, and ascertaining the real strength and civilization of the Incas, he persisted in marching into the interior at the head of a force of less than two hundred men. In this he undoubtedly proposed to himself the example of Cortés, so contagious to the adventurous spirits of that day, and especially to Pizarro, engaged, as he was, in a similar enterprise. Yet the hazard assumed by Pizarro was far greater than that of the Conqueror of Mexico, whose force was nearly three times as large, while the terrors of the Inca name—however justified by the result —were as widely spread as those of the Aztecs.

It was doubtless in imitation of the same captivating model, that Pizarro planned the seizure of Atahuallpa. But the situations of the two Spanish captains were as dissimilar as the manner in which their acts of violence were conducted. The wanton massacre of the Peruvians resembled that perpetrated by Alvarado in Mexico, and might have been attended with consequences as disastrous, if the Peruvian character had been as fierce as that of the Aztecs. But the blow which roused the latter to madness broke the tamer spirits of the Peruvians. It was a bold stroke, which left so much to chance, that it scarcely merits the name of policy.

When Pizarro landed in the country, he found it distracted by a contest for the crown. It would seem to have been for his interest to play off one party against the other, throwing his own weight into the scale that suited him. Instead of this, he resorted to an act of audacious violence which crushed them both at a blow. His subsequent career afforded no scope for the profound policy displayed by Cortés, when he gathered conflicting nations under his banner, and directed them against a common foe. Still less did he have the opportunity of displaying the tactics and admirable strategy of his rival. Cortés conducted his military operations on the scientific principles of a great captain at the head of a powerful host. Pizarro appears only as an adventurer, a fortunate knight-errant. By one bold stroke, he broke the spell which had so long held the land under the dominion of the Incas. The spell was broken, and the airy fabric of their empire, built on the superstition of ages, vanished. This was good fortune, rather than the result of policy.

Pizarro was eminently perfidious. Yet nothing is more opposed to sound policy. One act of perfidy fully established becomes the ruin of its author. The man who relinquishes confidence in his good faith gives up the best basis for future operations. Who will knowingly build on a quicksand? By his perfidious treatment of Almagro, Pizarro alienated the minds of the Spaniards. By his perfidious treatment of Atahuallpa, and subsequently of the Inca Manco, he disgusted the Peruvians. The name of Pizarro became a by-word for perfidy. Almagro took his revenge in a civil war; Manco in an insurrection which nearly cost Pizarro his dominion. The civil war terminated in a conspiracy which cost him his life. Such were the fruits of his policy. Pizarro may be regarded as a cunning man; but not, as he has been often eulogized by his countrymen, as a politic one.

When Pizarro obtained possession of Cuzco, he found a country well advanced in the arts of civilization; institutions under which the people lived in tranquillity and personal safety; the mountains and the uplands whitened with flocks; the valleys teeming with the fruits of a scientific husbandry; the granaries and warehouses filled to overflowing; the whole land rejoicing in its abundance; and the character of the nation, softened under the influence of the mildest and most innocent form of superstition, well prepared for the reception of a higher and a Christian civilization. But, far from introducing this, Pizarro delivered up the conquered races to his brutal soldiery; the sacred cloisters were abandoned to their lust; the towns and villages were given up to pillage; the wretched natives were parcelled out like slaves, to toil for their conquerors in the mines; the flocks were scattered, and wantonly destroyed; the granaries were dissipated; the beautiful contrivances for the more perfect culture of the soil were suffered to fall into decay; the paradise was converted into a desert. Instead of profiting by the ancient forms of civilization, Pizarro preferred to efface every vestige of them from the land, and on their ruin to erect the institutions of his own country. Yet these institutions did little for the poor Indian, held in iron bondage. It was little to him that the shores of the Pacific were studded with rising communities and cities, the marts of a flourishing commerce. He had no share in the goodly heritage. He was an alien in the land of his fathers.

The religion of the Peruvian, which directed him to the worship of that glorious luminary which is the best representative of the might and beneficence of the Creator, is perhaps the purest form of superstition that has existed among men. Yet it was much, that, under the new order of things, and through the benevolent zeal of the missionaries, some glimmerings of a nobler faith were permitted to dawn on his darkened soul. Pizarro, himself, cannot be charged with manifesting any overweening solicitude for the propagation of the Faith. He was no bigot, like Cortés. Bigotry is the perversion of the religious principle; but the principle itself was wanting in Pizarro. The conversion of the heathen was a predominant motive with Cortés in his expedition. It was not a vain boast. He would have sacrificed his life for it at any time; and more than once, by his indiscreet zeal, he actually did place his life and the success of his enterprise in jeopardy. It was his great purpose to purify the land from the brutish abominations of the Aztecs, by substituting the religion of Jesus. This gave to his expedition the character of a crusade. It furnished the best apology for the Conquest, and does more towards enlisting our sympathies on the side of the Conquerors.

But Pizarro's ruling motives, so far as they can be scanned by human judgment, were avarice and ambition. The good missionaries, indeed, followed in his train to scatter the seeds of spiritual truth, and the Spanish government, as usual, directed its beneficent legislation to the conversion of the natives. But the moving power with Pizarro and his followers was the lust of gold. This was the real stimulus to their toil, the price of perfidy, the true guerdon of their victories. This gave a base and mercenary character to their enterprise; and when we contrast the ferocious cupidity of the conquerors with the mild and inoffensive manners of the conquered, our sympathies, the sympathies even of the Spaniard, are necessarily thrown into the scale of the Indian.

But as no picture is without its lights, we must not, in justice to Pizarro, dwell exclusively on the darker features of his portrait. There was no one of her sons to whom Spain was under larger obligations for extent of empire; for his hand won for her the richest of the Indian jewels that once sparkled in her imperial diadem. When we contemplate the perils he braved, the sufferings he patiently endured, the incredible obstacles he overcame, the magnificent results he effected with his single arm, as it were, unaided by the government,—though neither a good, nor a great man in the highest sense of that term, it is impossible not to regard him as a very extraordinary one.

Nor can we fairly omit to notice, in extenuation of his errors, the circumstances of his early life; for, like Almagro, he was the son of sin and sorrow, early cast upon the world to seek his fortunes as he might. In his young and tender age he was to take the impression of those into whose society he was thrown. And when was it the lot of the needy outcast to fall into that of the wise and the virtuous? His lot was cast among the licentious inmates of a camp, the school of rapine, whose only law was the sword, and who looked on the wretched Indian as their rightful spoil.

Who does not shudder at the thought of what his own fate might have been, trained in such a school? The amount of crime does not necessarily show the criminality of the agent. History, indeed, is concerned with the former, that it may be recorded as a warning to mankind; but it is He alone who knoweth the heart, the strength of the temptation, and the means of resisting it, that can determine the measure of the guilt.

CHAPTER VI [1541–1543]

MOVEMENTS OF THE CONSPIRATORS—ADVANCE OF VACA
DE CASTRO—PROCEEDINGS OF ALMAGRO—PROGRESS OF
THE GOVERNOR—THE FORCES APPROACH EACH OTHER—
BLOODY PLAINS OF CHUPAS—CONDUCT OF VACA DE
CASTRO

The first step of the conspirators, after securing possession
of the capital, was to send to the different cities, proclaiming
the revolution which had taken place, and demanding the
recognition of the young Almagro as governor of Peru. Where
the summons was accompanied by a military force, as at
Truxillo and Arequipa, it was obeyed without much cavil. But
in other cities a colder assent was given, and in some the
requisition was treated with contempt. In Cuzco, the place of
most importance next to Lima, a considerable number of the
Almagro faction secured the ascendency of their party; and
such of the magistracy as resisted were ejected from their
offices to make room for others of a more accommodating
temper. But the loyal inhabitants of the city, dissatisfied with
this proceeding, privately sent to one of Pizarro's captains,
named Alvarez de Holguin, who lay with a considerable force
in the neighborhood; and that officer, entering the place, soon
dispossessed the new dignitaries of their honors, and restored
the ancient capital to its allegiance.

The conspirators experienced a still more determined opposition from Alonso de Alvarado, one of the principal captains of Pizarro,—defeated, as the reader will remember, by
the elder Almagro at the bridge of Abancay,—and now lying
in the north with a corps of about two hundred men, as good
troops as any in the land. That officer, on receiving tidings of
his general's assassination, instantly wrote to the Licentiate
Vaca de Castro, advising him of the state of affairs in Peru,
and urging him to quicken his march towards the south.

This functionary had been sent out by the Spanish Crown,
as noticed in a preceding chapter, to coöperate with Pizarro

in restoring tranquillity to the country, with authority to assume the government himself, in case of that commander's death. After a long and tempestuous voyage, he had landed, in the spring of 1541, at the port of Buenaventura, and, disgusted with the dangers of the sea, preferred to continue his wearisome journey by land. But so enfeebled was he by the hardships he had undergone, that it was full three months before he reached Popayan, where he received the astounding tidings of the death of Pizarro. This was the contingency which had been provided for, with such judicious forecast, in his instructions. Yet he was sorely perplexed by the difficulties of his situation. He was a stranger in the land, with a very imperfect knowledge of the country, without an armed force to support him, without even the military science which might be supposed necessary to avail himself of it. He knew nothing of the degree of Almagro's influence, or of the extent to which the insurrection had spread,—nothing, in short, of the dispositions of the people among whom he was cast.

In such an emergency, a feebler spirit might have listened to the counsels of those who advised to return to Panamá, and stay there until he had mustered a sufficient force to enable him to take the field against the insurgents with advantage. But the courageous heart of Vaca de Castro shrunk from a step which would proclaim his incompetency to the task assigned him. He had confidence in his own resources, and in the virtue of the commission under which he acted. He relied, too, on the habitual loyalty of the Spaniards; and, after mature deliberation, he determined to go forward, and trust to events for accomplishing the objects of his mission.

He was confirmed in this purpose by the advices he now received from Alvarado; and without longer delay, he continued his march towards Quito. Here he was well received by Gonzalo Pizarro's lieutenant, who had charge of the place during his commander's absence on his expedition to the Amazon. The licentiate was also joined by Benalcazar, the Conqueror of Quito, who brought a small reinforcement, and offered personally to assist him in the prosecution of his enterprise. He now displayed the royal commission, empowering him, on Pizarro's death, to assume the government. That contingency had arrived, and Vaca de Castro declared his purpose to ex-

ercise the authority conferred on him. At the same time, he
sent emissaries to the principal cities, requiring their obedience to him as the lawful representative of the Crown,—taking
care to employ discreet persons on the mission, whose character would have weight with the citizens. He then continued
his march slowly towards the south.

He was willing by his deliberate movements to give time
for his summons to take effect, and for the fermentation
caused by the late extraordinary events to subside. He reckoned confidently on the loyalty which made the Spaniard unwilling, unless in cases of the last extremity, to come into collision with the royal authority; and, however much this
popular sentiment might be disturbed by temporary gusts of
passion, he trusted to the habitual current of their feelings for
giving the people a right direction. In this he did not miscalculate; for so deep-rooted was the principle of loyalty in
the ancient Spaniard, that ages of oppression and misrule
could alone have induced him to shake off his allegiance. Sad
it is, but not strange, that the length of time passed under a
bad government has not qualified him for devising a good one.

While these events were passing in the north, Almagro's
faction at Lima was daily receiving new accessions of strength.
For, in addition to those who, from the first, had been avow-
edly of his father's party, there were many others who, from
some cause or other, had conceived a disgust for Pizarro, and
who now willingly enlisted under the banner of the chief that
had overthrown him.

The first step of the young general, or rather of Rada, who
directed his movements, was to secure the necessary supplies
for the troops, most of whom, having long been in indigent
circumstances, were wholly unprepared for service. Funds to a
considerable amount were raised, by seizing on the moneys of
the Crown in the hands of the treasurer. Pizarro's secretary,
Picado, was also drawn from his prison, and interrogated as
to the place where his master's treasures were deposited. But,
although put to the torture, he would not—or, as is probable,
could not—give information on the subject; and the conspirators, who had a long arrear of injuries to settle with him, closed
their proceedings by publicly beheading him in the great
square of Lima.

Valverde, Bishop of Cuzco, as he himself assures us, vainly interposed in his behalf. It is singular, that, the last time this fanatical prelate appears on the stage, it should be in the benevolent character of a supplicant for mercy. Soon afterwards, he was permitted, with the judge, Velasquez, and some other adherents of Pizarro, to embark from the port of Lima. We have a letter from him, dated at Tumbez, in November, 1541; almost immediately after which he fell into the hands of the Indians, and with his companions was massacred at Puná. A violent death not unfrequently closed the stormy career of the American adventurer. Valverde was a Dominican friar, and, like Father Olmedo in the suite of Cortés, had been by his commander's side throughout the whole of his expedition. But he did not always, like the good Olmedo, use his influence to stay the uplifted hand of the warrior. At least, this was not the mild aspect in which he presented himself at the terrible massacre of Caxamalca. Yet some contemporary accounts represent him, after he had been installed in his episcopal office, as unwearied in his labors to convert the natives, and to ameliorate their condition; and his own correspondence with the government, after that period, shows great solicitude for these praiseworthy objects. Trained in the severest school of monastic discipline, which too often closes the heart against the common charities of life, he could not, like the benevolent Las Casas, rise so far above its fanatical tenets as to regard the heathen as his brother, while in the state of infidelity; and, in the true spirit of that school, he doubtless conceived that the sanctity of the end justified the means, however revolting in themselves. Yet the same man, who thus freely shed the blood of the poor native to secure the triumph of his faith, would doubtless have as freely poured out his own in its defence. The character was no uncommon one in the sixteenth century.

Almagro's followers, having supplied themselves with funds, made as little scruple to appropriate to their own use such horses and arms, of every description, as they could find in the city. And this they did with the less reluctance, as the inhabitants for the most part testified no good-will to their cause. While thus employed, Almagro received intelligence that Holguin had left Cuzco with a force of near three hundred men, with which he was preparing to effect a junction with Alvarado in the north. It was important to Almagro's success that he should defeat this junction. If to procrastinate was the policy of Vaca de Castro, it was clearly that of Almagro to quicken operations, and to bring matters to as speedy an issue as possible; to march at once against Holguin, whom he might expect easily to overcome with his superior numbers; then to follow up the stroke by the still easier defeat of Alvarado, when the new governor would be, in a manner, at his mercy. It would be easy to beat these several bodies in detail, which, once united, would present formidable odds. Almagro and his party had already arrayed themselves against the government by a proceeding too atrocious, and which struck too directly at the royal authority, for its perpetrators to flatter themselves with the hopes of pardon. Their only chance was boldly to follow up the blow, and, by success, to place themselves in so formidable an attitude as to excite the apprehensions of government. The dread of its too potent vassal might extort terms that would never be conceded to his prayers.

But Almagro and his followers shrunk from this open collision with the Crown. They had taken up rebellion because it lay in their path, not because they had wished it. They had meant only to avenge their personal wrongs on Pizarro, and not to defy the royal authority. When, therefore, some of the more resolute, who followed things fearlessly to their consequences, proposed to march at once against Vaca de Castro, and, by striking at the head, settle the contest by a blow, it was almost universally rejected; and it was not till after long debate that it was finally determined to move against Holguin, and cut off his communication with Alonso de Alvarado.

Scarcely had Almagro commenced his march on Xauxa, where he proposed to give battle to his enemy, than he met with a severe misfortune in the death of Juan de Rada. He was a man somewhat advanced in years; and the late exciting scenes, in which he had taken the principal part, had been too much for a frame greatly shattered by a life of extraordinary hardship. He was thrown into a fever, of which he soon after died. By his death, Almagro sustained an inestimable loss; for, besides his devoted attachment to his young leader, he was, by his large experience, and his cautious though courageous character, better qualified than any other cavalier in the army to conduct him safely through the stormy sea on which he had led him to embark.

Among the cavaliers of highest consideration after Rada's death, the two most aspiring were Christoval de Sotelo, and Garcia de Alvarado; both possessed of considerable military talent, but the latter marked by a bold, presumptuous manner, which might remind one of his illustrious namesake, who achieved much higher renown under the banner of Cortés. Unhappily, a jealousy grew up between these two officers; that jealousy, so common among the Spaniards, that it may seem a national characteristic; an impatience of equality, founded on a false principle of honor, which has ever been the fruitful source of faction among them, whether under a monarchy or a republic.

This was peculiarly unfortunate for Almagro, whose inexperience led him to lean for support on others, and who, in the present distracted state of his council, knew scarcely where to turn for it. In the delay occasioned by these dissensions, his little army did not reach the valley of Xauxa till after the enemy had passed it. Almagro followed close, leaving behind his baggage and artillery that he might move the lighter. But the golden opportunity was lost. The rivers, swollen by autumnal rains, impeded his pursuit; and, though his light troops came up with a few stragglers of the rear-guard, Holguin succeeded in conducting his forces through the dangerous passes of the mountains, and in effecting a junction with Alonso de Alvarado, near the northern seaport of Huaura.

Disappointed in his object, Almagro prepared to march on Cuzco,—the capital, as he regarded it, of his own jurisdiction,—to get possession of that city, and there make preparations to meet his adversary in the field. Sotelo was sent forward with a small corps in advance. He experienced no opposition from the now defenceless citizens; the government of the place was again restored to the hands of the men of Chili, and their young leader soon appeared at the head of his battalions, and established his winter-quarters in the Inca capital.

Here, the jealousy of the rival captains broke out into an open feud. It was ended by the death of Sotelo, treacherously assassinated in his own apartment by Garcia de Alvarado. Almagro, greatly outraged by this atrocity, was the more indignant, as he felt himself too weak to punish the offender. He smothered his resentment for the present, affecting to treat the dangerous officer with more distinguished favor. But Alvarado was not the dupe of this specious behaviour. He felt that he had forfeited the confidence of his commander. In revenge, he laid a plot to betray him; and Almagro, driven to the necessity of self-defence, imitated the example of his officer, by entering his house with a party of armed men, who, laying violent hands on the insurgent, slew him on the spot.

This irregular proceeding was followed by the best consequences. The seditious schemes of Alvarado perished with him. The seeds of insubordination were eradicated, and from that moment Almagro experienced only implicit obedience and the most loyal support from his followers. From that hour, too, his own character seemed to be changed; he relied far less on others than on himself, and developed resources not to have been anticipated in one of his years; for he had hardly reached the age of twenty-two. From this time he displayed an energy and forecast, which proved him, in despite of his youth, not unequal to the trying emergencies of the situation in which it was his unhappy lot to be placed.

He instantly set about providing for the wants of his men, and strained every nerve to get them in good fighting order for the approaching campaign. He replenished his treasury with a large amount of silver which he drew from the mines of La Plata. Saltpetre, obtained in abundance in the neighborhood of Cuzco, furnished the material for gunpowder. He caused cannon, some of large dimensions, to be cast under the superintendence of Pedro de Candia, the Greek, who, it may be remembered, had first come into the country with Pizarro, and who with a number of his countrymen,—Levantines, as they were called,—was well acquainted with this manufacture. Under their care, fire-arms were made, together with cuirasses and helmets, in which silver was mingled with copper, and of so excellent a quality, that they might vie, says an old soldier of the time, with those from the workshops of Milan. Almagro received a seasonable supply, moreover, from a source scarcely to have been expected. This was from Manco, the wandering

Inca, who, detesting the memory of Pizarro, transferred to the young Almagro the same friendly feelings which he had formerly borne to his father; heightened, it may be, by the consideration that Indian blood flowed in the veins of the young commander. From this quarter Almagro obtained a liberal supply of swords, spears, shields, and arms and armour of every description, chiefly taken by the Inca at the memorable siege of Cuzco. He also received the gratifying assurance, that the latter would support him with a detachment of native troops when he opened the campaign.

Before making a final appeal to arms, however, Almagro resolved to try the effect of negotiation with the new governor. In the spring, or early in the summer, of 1542, he sent an embassy to the latter, then at Lima, in which he deprecated the necessity of taking arms against an officer of the Crown. His only desire, he said, was to vindicate his own rights; to secure the possession of New Toledo, the province bequeathed to him by his father, and from which he had been most unjustly excluded by Pizarro. He did not dispute the governor's authority over New Castile, as the country was designated which had been assigned to the marquess; and he concluded by proposing that each party should remain within his respective territory until the determination of the Court of Castile could be made known to them. To this application, couched in respectful terms, Almagro received no answer.

Frustrated in his hopes of a peaceful accommodation, the young captain now saw that nothing was left but the arbitrament of arms. Assembling his troops, preparatory to his departure from the capital, he made them a brief address. He protested that the step which he and his brave companions were about to take was not an act of rebellion against the Crown. It was forced on them by the conduct of the governor himself. The commission of that officer gave him no authority over the territory of New Toledo, settled on Almagro's father, and by his father bequeathed to him. If Vaca de Castro, by exceeding the limits of his authority, drove him to hostilities, the blood spilt in the quarrel would lie on the head of that commander, not on his. "In the assassination of Pizarro," he continued, "we took that justice into our own hands which elsewhere was denied us. It is the same now, in our contest

with the royal governor. We are as true-hearted and loyal subjects of the Crown as he is." And he concluded by invoking
his soldiers to stand by him heart and hand in the approaching
contest, in which they were all equally interested with himself.

The appeal was not made to an insensible audience. There
were few among them who did not feel that their fortunes
were indissolubly connected with those of their commander;
and while they had little to expect from the austere character
of the governor, they were warmly attached to the person of
their young chief, who, with all the popular qualities of his
father, excited additional sympathy from the circumstances of
his age and his forlorn condition. Laying their hands on the
cross, placed on an altar raised for the purpose, the officers and
soldiers severally swore to brave every peril with Almagro, and
remain true to him to the last.

In point of numbers, his forces had not greatly strengthened
since his departure from Lima. He mustered but little more
than five hundred in all; but among them were his father's
veterans, well seasoned by many an Indian campaign. He had
about two hundred horse, many of them clad in complete
mail, a circumstance not too common in these wars, where a
stuffed doublet of cotton was often the only panoply of the
warrior. His infantry, formed of pikemen and arquebusiers,
was excellently armed. But his strength lay in his heavy ordnance, consisting of sixteen pieces, eight large and eight
smaller guns, or falconets, as they were called, forming, says
one who saw it, a beautiful park of artillery, that would have
made a brave show on the citadel of Burgos. The little army,
in short, though not imposing from its numbers, was under as
good discipline, and as well appointed, as any that ever fought
on the fields of Peru; much better than any which Almagro's
own father or Pizarro ever led into the field and won their
conquests with. Putting himself at the head of his gallant
company, the chieftain sallied forth from the walls of Cuzco
about midsummer, in 1542, and directed his march towards
the coast in expectation of meeting the enemy.

While the events detailed in the preceding pages were passing, Vaca de Castro, whom we left at Quito in the preceding
year, was advancing slowly towards the south. His first act,
after leaving that city, showed his resolution to enter into no

compromise with the assassins of Pizarro. Benalcazar, the distinguished officer whom I have mentioned as having early given in his adherence to him, had protected one of the principal conspirators, his personal friend, who had come into his power, and had facilitated his escape. The governor, indignant at the proceeding, would listen to no explanation, but ordered the offending officer to return to his own district of Popayan. It was a bold step, in the precarious state of his own fortunes.

As the governor pursued his march, he was well received by the people on the way; and when he entered the cities of San Miguel and of Truxillo, he was welcomed with loyal enthusiasm by the inhabitants, who readily acknowledged his authority, though they showed little alacrity to take their chance with him in the coming struggle.

After lingering a long time in each of these places, he resumed his march and reached the camp of Alonso de Alvarado at Huaura, early in 1542. Holguin had established his quarters at some little distance from his rival; for a jealousy had sprung up, as usual, between these two captains, who both aspired to the supreme command of Captain-General of the army. The office of governor, conferred on Vaca de Castro, might seem to include that of commander-in-chief of the forces. But De Castro was a scholar, bred to the law; and, whatever authority he might arrogate to himself in civil matters, the two captains imagined that the military department he would resign into the hands of others. They little knew the character of the man.

Though possessed of no more military science than belonged to every cavalier in that martial age, the governor knew that to avow his ignorance, and to resign the management of affairs into the hands of others, would greatly impair his authority, if not bring him into contempt with the turbulent spirits among whom he was now thrown. He had both sagacity and spirit, and trusted to be able to supply his own deficiencies by the experience of others. His position placed the services of the ablest men in the country at his disposal, and with the aid of their counsels he felt quite competent to decide on his plan of operations, and to enforce the execution of it. He knew, moreover, that the only way to allay the jealousy of the two parties in the present crisis was to assume himself the office which was the cause of their dissension.

Still he approached his ambitious officers with great caution; and the representations, which he made through some judicious persons who had the most intimate access to them, were so successful, that both were in a short time prevailed on to relinquish their pretensions in his favor. Holguin, the more unreasonable of the two, then waited on him in his rival's quarters, where the governor had the further satisfaction to reconcile him to Alonso de Alvarado. It required some address, as their jealousy of each other had proceeded to such lengths that a challenge had passed between them.

Harmony being thus restored, the licentiate passed over to Holguin's camp, where he was greeted with salvoes of artillery, and loud acclamations of "Viva el Rey" from the loyal soldiery. Ascending the platform covered with velvet, he made an animated harangue to the troops; his commission was read aloud by the secretary; and the little army tendered their obedience to him as the representative of the Crown.

Vaca de Castro's next step was to send off the greater part of his force, in the direction of Xauxa, while, at the head of a small corps, he directed his march towards Lima. Here he was received with lively demonstrations of joy by the citizens, who were generally attached to the cause of Pizarro, the founder and constant patron of their capital. Indeed, the citizens had lost no time after Almagro's departure in expelling his creatures from the municipality, and reasserting their allegiances. With these favorable dispositions towards himself, the governor found no difficulty in obtaining a considerable loan of money from the wealthier inhabitants. But he was less successful, at first, in his application for horses and arms, since the harvest had been too faithfully gleaned, already, by the men of Chili. As, however, he prolonged his stay some time in the capital, he obtained important supplies, before he left it, both of arms and ammunition, while he added to his force by a considerable body of recruits.

As he was thus employed, he received tidings that the enemy had left Cuzco, and was on his march towards the coast. Quitting Los Reyes, therefore, with his trusty followers, Vaca de Castro marched at once to Xauxa, the appointed place of rendezvous. Here he mustered his forces, and found that they amounted to about seven hundred men. The cavalry, in which lay his strength, was superior in numbers to that of his antagonist, but neither so well mounted or armed. It included many cavaliers of birth, and well-tried soldiers, besides a number who, having great interests at stake, as possessed of large estates in the country, had left them at the call of government, to enlist under its banners. His infantry, besides pikes, was indifferently well supplied with fire-arms; but he had nothing to show in the way of artillery except three or four ill-mounted falconets. Yet, notwithstanding these deficiencies, the royal army, if so insignificant a force can deserve that name, was so far superior in numbers to that of his rival, that the one might be thought, on the whole, to be no unequal match for the other.

The reader, familiar with the large masses employed in European warfare, may smile at the paltry forces of the Spaniards. But in the New World, where a countless host of natives went for little, five hundred well-trained Europeans were regarded as a formidable body. No army, up to the period before us, had ever risen to a thousand. Yet it is not numbers, as I have already been led to remark, that give importance to a conflict; but the consequences that depend on it,—the magnitude of the stake, and the skill and courage of the players. The more limited the means, even, the greater may be the science shown in the use of them; until, forgetting the poverty of the materials, we fix our attention on the conduct of the actors, and the greatness of the results.

While at Xauxa, Vaca de Castro received an embassy from Gonzalo Pizarro, returned from his expedition from the "Land of Cinnamon," in which that chief made an offer of his services in the approaching contest. The governor's answer showed that he was not wholly averse to an accommodation with Almagro, provided it could be effected without compromising the royal authority. He was willing, perhaps, to avoid the final trial by battle, when he considered, that, from the equality of the contending forces, the issue must be extremely doubtful. He knew that the presence of Pizarro in the camp, the detested enemy of the Almagrians, would excite distrust in their bosoms that would probably baffle every effort at accommodation. Nor is it likely that the governor cared to have so restless a spirit introduced into his own councils. He accordingly sent to Gonzalo, thanking him for the promptness of his support, but courteously declined it, while he advised him to remain in his province, and repose after the fatigues of his wearisome expedition. At the same time, he assured him that he would not fail to call for his services when occasion required it.—The haughty cavalier was greatly disgusted by the repulse.

The governor now received such an account of Almagro's movements as led him to suppose that he was preparing to occupy Guamanga, a fortified place of considerable strength, about thirty leagues from Xauxa. Anxious to secure this post, he broke up his encampment, and by forced marches, conducted in so irregular a manner as must have placed him in great danger if his enemy had been near to profit by it, he succeeded in anticipating Almagro, and threw himself into the place while his antagonist was at Bilcas, some ten leagues distant.

At Guamanga, Vaca de Castro received another embassy from Almagro, of similar import with the former. The young chief again deprecated the existence of hostilities between brethren of the same family, and proposed an accommodation of the quarrel on the same basis as before. To these proposals the governor now condescended to reply. It might be thought, from his answer, that he felt some compassion for the youth and inexperience of Almagro, and that he was willing to distinguish between him and the principal conspirators, provided he could detach him from their interests. But it is more probable that he intended only to amuse his enemy by a show of negotiation, while he gained time for tampering with the fidelity of his troops.

He insisted that Almagro should deliver up to him all those immediately implicated in the death of Pizarro, and should then disband his forces. On these conditions the government would pass over his treasonable practices, and he should be reinstated in the royal favor. Together with this mission, Vaca de Castro, it is reported, sent a Spaniard, disguised as an Indian, who was instructed to communicate with certain officers in Almagro's camp, and prevail on them, if possible, to abandon his cause and return to their allegiance. Unfortunately, the disguise of the emissary was detected. He was seized, put to the torture, and, having confessed the whole of the transaction, was hanged as a spy.

Almagro laid the proceeding before his captains. The terms proffered by the governor were such as no man with a particle of honor in his nature could entertain for a moment; and Almagro's indignation, as well as that of his companions, was heightened by the duplicity of their enemy, who could practise such insidious arts, while ostensibly engaged in a fair and open negotiation. Fearful, perhaps, lest the tempting offers of their antagonist might yet prevail over the constancy of some of the weaker spirits among them, they demanded that all negotiation should be broken off, and that they should be led at once against the enemy.

The governor, meanwhile, finding the broken country around Guamanga unfavorable for his cavalry, on which he mainly relied, drew off his forces to the neighboring lowlands, known as the Plains of Chupas. It was the tempestuous season of the year, and for several days the storm raged wildly among the hills, and, sweeping along their sides into the valley, poured down rain, sleet, and snow on the miserable bivouacs of the soldiers, till they were drenched to the skin and nearly stiffened by the cold. At length, on the sixteenth of September, 1542, the scouts brought in tidings that Almagro's troops were advancing, with the intention, apparently, of occupying the highlands around Chupas. The war of the elements had at last subsided, and was succeeded by one of those brilliant days which are found only in the tropics. The royal camp was early in motion, as Vaca de Castro, desirous to secure the heights that commanded the valley, detached a body of arquebusiers on that service, supported by a corps of cavalry, which he soon followed with the rest of the forces. On reaching the eminence, news was brought that the enemy had come to a halt, and established himself in a strong position at less than a league's distance.

It was now late in the afternoon, and the sun was not more than two hours above the horizon. The governor hesitated to begin the action when they must so soon be overtaken by night. But Alonso de Alvarado assured him that "now was the time; for the spirits of his men were hot for fight, and it was better to take the benefit of it than to damp their ardor by delay." The governor acquiesced, exclaiming at the same time,—"O for the might of Joshua, to stay the sun in his course!" He then drew up his army in order of battle, and made dispositions for the attack.

In the centre he placed his infantry, consisting of arquebusiers and pikemen, constituting the *battle*, as it was called. On the flanks, he established his cavalry, placing the right wing, together with the royal standard, under charge of Alonso de Alvarado, and the left under Holguin, supported by a gallant body of cavaliers. His artillery, too insignificant to be of much account, was also in the centre. He proposed himself to lead the van, and to break the first lance with the enemy; but from this chivalrous display he was dissuaded by his officers, who reminded him that too much depended on his life to have it thus wantonly exposed. The governor contented himself, therefore, with heading a body of reserve, consisting of forty horse, to act on any quarter as occasion might require. This corps, comprising the flower of his chivalry, was chiefly drawn from Alvarado's troop, greatly to the discontent of that captain. The governor himself rode a coal-black charger, and wore a rich surcoat of brocade over his mail, through which the habit and emblems of the knightly order of St. James, conferred on him just before his departure from Castile, were conspicuous. It was a point of honor with the chivalry of the period to court danger by displaying their rank in the splendor of their military attire and the caparisons of their horses.

Before commencing the assault, Vaca de Castro addressed a few remarks to his soldiers, in order to remove any hesitation that some might yet feel, who recollected the displeasure shown by the emperor to the victors as well as the vanquished after the battle of Salinas. He told them that their enemies were rebels. They were in arms against him, the representative of the Crown, and it was his duty to quell this rebellion and punish the authors of it. He then caused the law to be read aloud, proclaiming the doom of traitors. By this law, Almagro and his followers had forfeited their lives and property, and the governor promised to distribute the latter among such of his men as showed the best claim to it by their conduct in the battle. This last politic promise vanquished the scruples of the most fastidious; and, having completed his dispositions in the most judicious and soldier-like manner, Vaca de Castro gave the order to advance.

As the forces turned a spur of the hills, which had hitherto screened them from their enemies, they came in sight of the latter, formed along the crest of a gentle eminence, with their snow-white banners, the distinguishing color of the Almagrians, floating above their heads, and their bright arms flinging back the broad rays of the evening sun. Almagro's disposition of his troops was not unlike that of his adversary. In the centre was his excellent artillery, covered by his arquebusiers and spearmen; while his cavalry rode on the flanks. The troops on the left he proposed to lead in person. He had chosen his position with judgment, as the character of the ground gave full play to his guns, which opened an effective fire on the assailants as they drew near. Shaken by the storm of shot, Vaca de Castro saw the difficulty of advancing in open view of the hostile battery. He took the counsel, therefore, of Francisco de Carbajal, who undertook to lead the forces by a circuitous, but safer, route. This is the first occasion on which the name of this veteran appears in these American wars, where it was afterwards to acquire a melancholy notoriety. He had come to the country after the campaigns of forty years in Europe, where he had studied the art of war under the Great Captain, Gonsalvo de Cordova. Though now far advanced in age, he possessed all the courage and indomitable energy of youth, and well exemplified the lessons he had studied under his great commander.

Taking advantage of a winding route that sloped around the declivity of the hills, he conducted the troops in such a manner, that, until they approached quite near the enemy, they were protected by the intervening ground. While thus advancing, they were assailed on the left flank by the Indian battalions under Paullo, the Inca Manco's brother; but a corps of musketeers, directing a scattering fire among them, soon rid the Spaniards of this annoyance. When, at length, the royal troops, rising above the hill, again came into view of Almagro's lines, the artillery opened on them with fatal effect. It was but for a moment, however, as, from some unaccountable cause, the guns were pointed at such an angle, that, although presenting an obvious mark, by far the greater part of the shot passed over their heads. Whether this was the result of treachery, or merely of awkwardness, is uncertain. The artillery was under charge of the engineer, Pedro de Candia. This man, who, it may be remembered, was one of the thirteen that so gallantly stood by Pizarro in the island of Gallo, had fought side by side with his leader through the whole of the Conquest. He had lately, however, conceived some disgust with him, and had taken part with the faction of Almagro. The death of his old commander, he may perhaps have thought, had settled all their differences, and he was now willing to return to his former allegiance. At least, it is said, that, at this very time, he was in correspondence with Vaca de Castro. Almagro himself seems to have had no doubt of his treachery. For, after remonstrating in vain with him on his present conduct, he ran him through the body, and the unfortunate cavalier fell lifeless on the field. Then, throwing himself on one of the guns, Almagro gave it a new direction, and that so successfully, that, when it was discharged, it struck down several of the cavalry.

The firing now took better effect, and by one volley a whole file of the royal infantry was swept off, and though others quickly stepped in to fill up the ranks, the men, impatient of their sufferings, loudly called on the troopers, who had halted for a moment, to quicken their advance. This delay had been caused by Carbajal's desire to bring his own guns to bear on the opposite columns. But the design was quickly abandoned; the clumsy ordnance was left on the field, and orders were given to the cavalry to charge; the trumpets sounded, and, crying their war-cries, the bold cavaliers struck their spurs into their steeds, and rode at full speed against the enemy.

Well had it been for Almagro, if he had remained firm on the post which gave him such advantage. But from a false point of honor, he thought it derogatory to a brave knight passively to await the assault, and, ordering his own men to charge, the hostile squadrons, rapidly advancing against each other, met midway on the plain. The shock was terrible. Horse and rider reeled under the force of it. The spears flew into shivers; and the cavaliers, drawing their swords, or wielding their maces and battle-axes,—though some of the royal troopers were armed only with a common axe,—dealt their blows with all the fury of civil hate. It was a fearful struggle, not merely of man against man, but, to use the words of an eyewitness, of brother against brother, and friend against friend. No quarter was asked; for the wrench that had been strong enough to tear asunder the dearest ties of kindred left no hold for humanity. The excellent arms of the Almagrians counterbalanced the odds of numbers; but the royal partisans gained some advantage by striking at the horses instead of the mailed bodies of their antagonists.

The infantry, meanwhile, on both sides, kept up a sharp cross-fire from their arquebuses, which did execution on the ranks of the cavaliers, as well as on one another. But Almagro's battery of heavy guns, now well directed, mowed down the advancing columns of foot. The latter, staggering, began to fall back from the terrible fire, when Francisco de Carbajal, throwing himself before them, cried out, "Shame on you, my men! Do you give way now? I am twice as good a mark for the enemy as any of you!" He was a very large man; and, throwing off his steel helmet and cuirass, that he might have no advantage over his followers, he remained lightly attired in his cotton doublet, when, swinging his partisan over his head, he sprang boldly forward through blinding volumes of smoke and a tempest of musket-balls, and, supported by the bravest of his troops, overpowered the gunners, and made himself master of their pieces.

The shades of night had now, for some time been coming thicker and thicker over the field. But still the deadly struggle went on in the darkness, as the red and white badges intimated the respective parties, and their war-cries rose above the din, —"Vaca de Castro y el Rey,"—"Almagro y el Rey,"—while both invoked the aid of their military apostle St. James. Holguin, who commanded the royalists on the left, pierced through by two musket-balls, had been slain early in the action. He had made himself conspicuous by a rich sobre-vest of white velvet over his armour. Still a gallant band of cavaliers maintained the fight so valiantly on that quarter, that the Almagrians found it difficult to keep their ground.

It fared differently on the right, where Alonso de Alvarado commanded. He was there encountered by Almagro in person, who fought worthy of his name. By repeated charges on his opponent, he endeavored to bear down his squadrons, so much worse mounted and worse armed than his own. Alvarado resisted with undiminished courage; but his numbers had been thinned, as we have seen, before the battle, to supply the governor's reserve, and, fairly overpowered by the superior strength of his adversary, who had already won two of the royal banners, he was slowly giving ground. "Take, but kill not!" shouted the young chief, who felt himself sure of victory.

But at this crisis, Vaca de Castro, who, with his reserve, had occupied a rising ground that commanded the field of action, was fully aware that the time had now come for him to take part in the struggle. He had long strained his eyes through the gloom to watch the movements of the combatants, and received constant tidings how the fight was going. He no longer hesitated, but, calling on his men to follow, led off boldly into the thickest of the *mêlée* to the support of his stout-hearted officer. The arrival of a new corps on the field, all fresh for action, gave another turn to the tide. Alvarado's men took heart and rallied. Almagro's, though driven back by the fury of the assault, quickly returned against their assailants. Thirteen of Vaca de Castro's cavaliers fell dead from their saddles. But it was the last effort of the Almagrians. Their strength, though not their spirit, failed them. They gave way in all directions, and, mingling together in the darkness, horse, foot, and artillery, they trampled one another down, as they made the best of their way from the press of their pursuers. Almagro used every effort to stay them. He performed miracles of valor, says one who witnessed them; but he was borne along by the tide, and, though he seemed to court death, by the freedom with which he exposed his person to danger, yet he escaped without a wound.

Others there were of his company, and among them a young cavalier named Gerónimo de Alvarado, who obstinately refused to quit the field; and shouting out,—"We slew Pizarro! we killed the tyrant!" they threw themselves on the lances of their conquerors, preferring death on the battle-field to the ignominious doom of the gibbet.

It was nine o'clock when the battle ceased, though the firing was heard at intervals over the field at a much later hour, as some straggling party of fugitives were overtaken by their pursuers. Yet many succeeded in escaping in the obscurity of night, while some, it is said, contrived to elude pursuit in a more singular way; tearing off the badges from the corpses of their enemies, they assumed them for themselves, and, mingling in the ranks as followers of Vaca de Castro, joined in the pursuit.

That commander, at length, fearing some untoward accident, and that the fugitives, should they rally again under cover of the darkness, might inflict some loss on their pursuers, caused his trumpets to sound, and recalled his scattered forces under their banners. All night they remained under arms on the field, which, so lately the scene of noisy strife, was now hushed in silence, broken only by the groans of the wounded and the dying. The natives, who had hung, during the fight, like a dark cloud, round the skirts of the mountains, contemplating with gloomy satisfaction the destruction of their enemies, now availed themselves of the obscurity to descend, like a pack of famished wolves, upon the plains, where they stripped the bodies of the slain, and even of the living, but disabled wretches, who had in vain dragged themselves into the bushes for concealment. The following morning, Vaca de Castro gave orders that the wounded—those who had not perished in the cold damps of the night—should be committed to the care of the surgeons, while the priests were occupied with administering confession and absolution to the dying. Four large graves or pits were dug, in which the bodies of the slain —the conquerors and the conquered—were heaped indiscriminately together. But the remains of Alvarez de Holguin and several other cavaliers of distinction were transported to Guamanga, where they were buried with the solemnities suited to their rank; and the tattered banners won from their vanquished countrymen waved over their monuments, the trophies of their victory.

The number of killed is variously reported,—from three hundred to five hundred on both sides. The mortality was greatest among the Conquerors, who suffered more from the cannon of the enemy before the action, than the latter suffered in the rout that followed it. The number of wounded was still greater; and full half of the survivors of Almagro's party were made prisoners. Many, indeed, escaped from the field to the neighboring town of Guamanga, where they took refuge in the churches and monasteries. But their asylum was not respected, and they were dragged forth and thrown into prison. Their brave young commander fled with a few followers only to Cuzco, where he was instantly arrested by the magistrates whom he had himself placed over the city.

At Guamanga, Vaca de Castro appointed a commission, with the Licentiate de la Gama at its head, for the trial of the prisoners; and *justice* was not satisfied, till forty had been condemned to death, and thirty others—some of them with the loss of one or more of their members—sent into banishment. Such severe reprisals have been too common with the Spaniards in their civil feuds. Strange that they should so blindly plunge into these, with this dreadful doom for the vanquished!

From the scene of this bloody tragedy, the governor proceeded to Cuzco, which he entered at the head of his victorious battalions, with all the pomp and military display of a conqueror. He maintained a corresponding state in his way of living, at the expense of a sneer from some, who sarcastically contrasted this ostentatious profusion with the economical reforms he subsequently introduced into the finances. But Vaca de Castro was sensible of the effect of this outward show on the people generally, and disdained no means of giving authority to his office. His first act was to determine the fate of his prisoner, Almagro. A council of war was held. Some were for sparing the unfortunate chief, in consideration of his youth, and the strong cause of provocation he had received. But the majority were of opinion that such mercy could not be extended to the leader of the rebels, and that his death was indispensable to the permanent tranquillity of the country.

When led to execution in the great square of Cuzco,—the same spot where his father had suffered but a few years before,—Almagro exhibited the most perfect composure, though, as the herald proclaimed aloud the doom of the traitor, he indignantly denied that he was one. He made no appeal for mercy to his judges, but simply requested that his bones might be laid by the side of his father's. He objected to having his eyes bandaged, as was customary on such occasions, and, after confession, he devoutly embraced the cross, and submitted his neck to the stroke of the executioner. His remains, agreeably to his request, were transported to the monastery of La

Merced, where they were deposited side by side with those of his unfortunate parent.

There have been few names, indeed, in the page of history, more unfortunate than that of Almagro. Yet the fate of the son excites a deeper sympathy than that of the father; and this, not merely on account of his youth, and the peculiar circumstances of his situation. He possessed many of the good qualities of the elder Almagro, with a frank and manly nature, in which the bearing of the soldier was somewhat softened by the refinement of a better education than is to be found in the license of a camp. His career, though short, gave promise of considerable talent, which required only a fair field for its development. But he was the child of misfortune, and his morning of life was overcast by clouds and tempests. If his character, naturally benignant, sometimes showed the fiery sparkles of the vindictive Indian temper, some apology may be found, not merely in his blood, but in the circumstances of his situation. He was more sinned against than sinning; and, if conspiracy could ever find a justification, it must be in a case like his, where, borne down by injuries heaped on his parent and himself, he could obtain no redress from the only quarter whence he had a right to look for it. With him, the name of Almagro became extinct and the faction of Chili, so long the terror of the land, passed away for ever.

While these events were occurring in Cuzco, the governor learned that Gonzalo Pizarro had arrived at Lima, where he showed himself greatly discontented with the state of things in Peru. He loudly complained that the government of the country, after his brother's death, had not been placed in his hands; and, as reported by some, he was now meditating schemes for getting possession of it. Vaca de Castro well knew that there would be no lack of evil counsellors to urge Gonzalo to this desperate step; and, anxious to extinguish the spark of insurrection before it had been fanned by these turbulent spirits into a flame, he detached a strong body to Lima to secure that capital. At the same time he commanded the presence of Gonzalo Pizarro in Cuzco.

That chief did not think it prudent to disregard the summons; and shortly after entered the Inca capital, at the head of a well-armed body of cavaliers. He was at once admitted into the governor's presence, when the latter dismissed his guard, remarking that he had nothing to fear from a brave and loyal knight like Pizarro. He then questioned him as to his late adventures in Canelas, and showed great sympathy for his extraordinary sufferings. He took care not to alarm his jealousy by any allusion to his ambitious schemes, and concluded by recommending him, now that the tranquillity of the country was re-established, to retire and seek the repose he so much needed, on his valuable estates at Charcas. Gonzalo Pizarro, finding no ground opened for a quarrel with the cool and politic governor, and probably feeling that he was, at least not now, in sufficient strength to warrant it, thought it prudent to take the advice, and withdrew to La Plata, where he busied himself in working those rich mines of silver that soon put him in condition for more momentous enterprise than any he had yet attempted.

Thus rid of his formidable competitor, Vaca de Castro occupied himself with measures for the settlement of the country. He began with his army, a part of which he had disbanded. But many cavaliers still remained, pressing their demands for a suitable recompense for their services. These they were not disposed to undervalue, and the governor was happy to rid himself of their importunities by employing them on distant expeditions, among which was the exploration of the country watered by the great Río de la Plata. The boiling spirits of the high-mettled cavaliers, without some such vent, would soon have thrown the whole country again into a state of fermentation.

His next concern was to provide laws for the better government of the colony. He gave especial care to the state of the Indian population; and established schools for teaching them Christianity. By various provisions, he endeavored to secure them from the exactions of their conquerors, and he encouraged the poor natives to transfer their own residence to the communities of the white men. He commanded the caciques to provide supplies for the *tambos*, or houses for the accommodation of travellers, which lay in their neighborhood, by which regulation he took away from the Spaniards a plausible apology for rapine, and greatly promoted facility of intercourse. He was watchful over the finances, much dilapidated in the late troubles, and in several instances retrenched what he deemed excessive *repartimientos* among the Conquerors. This last act exposed him to much odium from the objects of it. But his measures were so just and impartial, that he was supported by public opinion.

Indeed, Vaca de Castro's conduct, from the hour of his arrival in the country, had been such as to command respect, and prove him competent to the difficult post for which he had been selected. Without funds, without troops, he had found the country, on his landing, in a state of anarchy; yet, by courage and address, he had gradually acquired sufficient strength to quell the insurrection. Though no soldier, he had shown undaunted spirit and presence of mind in the hour of action, and made his military preparations with a forecast and discretion that excited the admiration of the most experienced veteran.

If he may be thought to have abused the advantages of victory by cruelty towards the conquered, it must be allowed that he was not influenced by any motives of a personal nature. He was a lawyer, bred in high notions of royal prerogative. Rebellion he looked upon as an unpardonable crime; and, if his austere nature was unrelenting in the exaction of justice, he lived in an iron age, when justice was rarely tempered by mercy.

In his subsequent regulations for the settlement of the country, he showed equal impartiality and wisdom. The colonists were deeply sensible of the benefits of his administration, and afforded the best commentary on his services by petitioning the Court of Castile to continue him in the government of Peru. Unfortunately, such was not the policy of the Crown.

CHAPTER VII [1543–1544]

ABUSES BY THE CONQUERORS—CODE FOR THE COLONIES
—GREAT EXCITEMENT IN PERU—BLASCO NUÑEZ THE
VICEROY—HIS SEVERE POLICY—OPPOSED BY GONZALO
PIZARRO

Before continuing the narrative of events in Peru, we must turn to the mother-country, where important changes were in progress in respect to the administration of the colonies.

Since his accession to the Crown, Charles the Fifth had been chiefly engrossed by the politics of Europe, where a theatre was opened more stimulating to his ambition than could be found in a struggle with the barbarian princes of the New World. In this quarter, therefore, an empire almost unheeded, as it were, had been suffered to grow up, until it had expanded into dimensions greater than those of his European dominions and destined soon to become far more opulent. A scheme of government had, it is true, been devised, and laws enacted from time to time for the regulation of the colonies. But these laws were often accommodated less to the interests of the colonies themselves, than to those of the parent country; and, when contrived in a better spirit, they were but imperfectly executed; for the voice of authority, however loudly proclaimed at home, too often died away in feeble echoes before it had crossed the waters.

This state of things, and, indeed, the manner in which the Spanish territories in the New World had been originally acquired, were most unfortunate both for the conquered races and their masters. Had the provinces gained by the Spaniards been the fruit of peaceful acquisition,—of barter and negotiation,—or had their conquest been achieved under the immediate direction of government, the interests of the natives would have been more carefully protected. From the superior civilization of the Indians in the Spanish American colonies, they still continued after the Conquest to remain on the ground, and to mingle in the same communities, with the white men; in this forming an obvious contrast to the condition of our own aborigines, who, shrinking from the contact of civilization, have withdrawn, as the latter has advanced, deeper and deeper into the heart of the wilderness. But the South American Indian was qualified by his previous institutions for a more refined legislation than could be adapted to the wild hunters of the forest; and, had the sovereign been there in person to superintend his conquests, he could never have suffered so large a portion of his vassals to be wantonly sacrificed to the cupidity and cruelty of the handful of adventurers who subdued them.

But, as it was, the affair of reducing the country was committed to the hands of irresponsible individuals, soldiers of fortune, desperate adventurers, who entered on conquest as a game, which they were to play in the most unscrupulous manner, with little care but to win it. Receiving small encouragement from the government, they were indebted to their own valor for success; and the right of conquest, they conceived, extinguished every existing right in the unfortunate natives. The lands, the persons, of the conquered races were parcelled out and appropriated by the victors as the legitimate spoils of victory; and outrages were perpetrated every day, at the contemplation of which humanity shudders.

These outrages, though nowhere perpetrated on so terrific a scale as in the islands, where, in a few years, they had nearly annihilated the native population, were yet of sufficient magnitude in Peru to call down the vengeance of Heaven on the heads of their authors; and the Indian might feel that this vengeance was not long delayed, when he beheld his oppressors, wrangling over their miserable spoil, and turning their swords against each other. Peru, as already mentioned, was subdued by adventurers, for the most part, of a lower and more ferocious stamp than those who followed the banner of Cortés. The character of the followers partook, in some measure, of that of the leaders in their respective enterprises. It was a sad fatality for the Incas; for the reckless soldiers of Pizarro were better suited to contend with the fierce Aztec than with the more refined and effeminate Peruvian. Intoxicated by the unaccustomed possession of power, and without the least notion of the responsibilities which attached to their situation as masters of the land, they too often abandoned themselves to the indulgence of every whim which cruelty or caprice could dictate. "Not unfrequently," says an unsuspicious witness, "I have seen the Spaniards, long after the Conquest, amuse themselves by hunting down the natives with bloodhounds for mere sport, or in order to train their dogs to the game!" The most unbounded scope was given to licentiousness. The young maiden was torn without remorse from the arms of her family to gratify the passion of her brutal conqueror. The sacred houses of the Virgins of the Sun were broken open and violated, and the cavalier swelled his harem with a troop of Indian girls, making it seem that the Crescent would have been a much more fitting symbol for his banner than the immaculate Cross.

But the dominant passion of the Spaniard was the lust of gold. For this he shrunk from no toil himself, and was merciless in his exactions of labor from his Indian slave. Unfortunately, Peru abounded in mines which too well repaid this labor; and human life was the item of least account in the estimate of the Conquerors. Under his Incas, the Peruvian was never suffered to be idle; but the task imposed on him was always proportioned to his strength. He had his seasons of rest and refreshment, and was well protected against the inclemency of the weather. Every care was shown for his personal safety. But the Spaniards, while they taxed the strength of the native to the utmost, deprived him of the means of repairing it, when exhausted. They suffered the provident arrangements of the Incas to fall into decay. The granaries were emptied; the flocks were wasted in riotous living. They were slaughtered to gratify a mere epicurean whim, and many a llama was destroyed solely for the sake of the brains,—a dainty morsel, much coveted by the Spaniards. So reckless was the spirit of destruction after the Conquest, says Ondegardo, the wise governor of Cuzco, that in four years more of these animals perished than in four hundred, in the times of the Incas. The flocks, once so numerous over the broad table-lands, were now thinned to a scanty number, that sought shelter in the fastnesses of the Andes. The poor Indian, without food, without the warm fleece which furnished him a defence against the cold, now wandered half-starved and naked over the plateau. Even those who had aided the Spaniards in the Conquest fared no better; and many an Inca noble roamed a mendicant over the lands where he once held rule, and if driven, perchance, by his necessities, to purloin something from the superfluity of his conquerors, he expiated it by a miserable death.

It is true, there were good men, missionaries, faithful to their calling, who wrought hard in the spiritual conversion of the native, and who, touched by his misfortunes, would gladly have interposed their arm to shield him from his oppressors. But too often the ecclesiastic became infected by the general spirit of licentiousness; and the religious fraternities, who led a life of easy indulgence on the lands cultivated by their Indian slaves, were apt to think less of the salvation of their souls than of profiting by the labor of their bodies.

Yet still there were not wanting good and wise men in the colonies, who, from time to time, raised the voice of remonstrance against these abuses, and who carried their complaints to the foot of the throne. To the credit of the government, it must also be confessed, that it was solicitous to obtain such information as it could, both from its own officers, and from commissioners deputed especially for the purpose, whose voluminous communications throw a flood of light on the internal condition of the country, and furnish the best materials for the historian. But it was found much easier to get this information than to profit by it.

In 1541, Charles the Fifth, who had been much occupied by the affairs of Germany, revisited his ancestral dominions, where his attention was imperatively called to the state of the colonies. Several memorials in relation to it were laid before him; but no one pressed the matter so strongly on the royal conscience as Las Casas, afterwards Bishop of Chiapa. This good ecclesiastic, whose long life had been devoted to those benevolent labors which gained him the honorable title of Protector of the Indians, had just completed his celebrated treatise on the Destruction of the Indies, the most remarkable record, probably, to be found, of human wickedness, but which, unfortunately, loses much of its effect from the credulity of the writer, and his obvious tendency to exaggerate.

In 1542, Las Casas placed his manuscript in the hands of his royal master. That same year, a council was called at

Valladolid, composed chiefly of jurists and theologians, to devise a system of laws for the regulation of the American
colonies.

Las Casas appeared before this body, and made an elaborate argument, of which a part only has been given to the public. He there assumes, as a fundamental proposition, that the
Indians were by the law of nature free; that, as vassals of the
Crown, they had a right to its protection, and should be declared free from that time, without exception and for ever. He
sustains this proposition by a great variety of arguments, comprehending the substance of most that has been since urged
in the same cause by the friends of humanity. He touches on
the ground of expediency, showing, that, without the interference of government, the Indian race must be gradually exterminated by the systematic oppression of the Spaniards. In
conclusion, he maintains, that, if the Indians, as it was pretended, would not labor unless compelled, the white man
would still find it for his interest to cultivate the soil; and that
if he should not be able to do so, that circumstance would
give him no right over the Indian, since *God does not allow
evil that good may come of it*.—This lofty morality, it will be
remembered, was from the lips of a Dominican, in the sixteenth century, one of the order that founded the Inquisition,
and in the very country where the fiery tribunal was then in
most active operation.

The arguments of Las Casas encountered all the opposition
naturally to be expected from indifference, selfishness, and
bigotry. They were also resisted by some persons of just and
benevolent views in his audience, who, while they admitted
the general correctness of his reasoning, and felt deep sympathy for the wrongs of the natives, yet doubted whether his
scheme of reform was not fraught with greater evils than those
it was intended to correct. For Las Casas was the uncompromising friend of freedom. He intrenched himself strongly on
the ground of natural right; and, like some of the reformers
of our own day, disdained to calculate the consequences of
carrying out the principle to its full and unqualified extent.
His earnest eloquence, instinct with the generous love of humanity, and fortified by a host of facts, which it was not easy
to assail, prevailed over his auditors. The result of their de-

liberations was a code of ordinances, which, however, far from being limited to the wants of the natives, had particular reference to the European population, and the distractions of the country. It was of general application to all the American colonies. It will be necessary here only to point out some of the provisions having immediate reference to Peru.

The Indians were declared true and loyal vassals of the Crown, and their freedom as such was fully recognized. Yet, to maintain inviolate the guaranty of the government to the Conquerors, it was decided, that those lawfully possessed of slaves might still retain them; but, at the death of the present proprietors, they were to revert to the Crown.

It was provided, however, that slaves, in any event, should be forfeited by all those who had shown themselves unworthy to hold them by neglect or ill-usage; by all public functionaries, or such as had held offices under the government; by ecclesiastics and religious corporations; and lastly,—a sweeping clause, —by all who had taken a criminal part in the feuds of Almagro and Pizarro.

It was further ordered, that the Indians should be moderately taxed; that they should not be compelled to labor where they did not choose, and that where, from particular circumstances, this was made necessary, they should receive a fair compensation. It was also decreed, that, as the *repartimientos* of land were often excessive, they should in such cases be reduced; and that, where proprietors had been guilty of a notorious abuse of their slaves, their estates should be forfeited altogether.

As Peru had always shown a spirit of insubordination, which required a more vigorous interposition of authority than was necessary in the other colonies, it was resolved to send a viceroy to that country, who should display a state, and be armed with powers, that might make him a more fitting representative of the sovereign. He was to be accompanied by a Royal Audience, consisting of four judges, with extensive powers of jurisdiction, both criminal and civil, who, besides a court of justice, should constitute a sort of council to advise with and aid the viceroy. The Audience of Panamá was to be dissolved, and the new tribunal, with the vice-king's court, was to be established at Los Reyes, or Lima, as it now began to be called,

—henceforth the metropolis of the Spanish empire on the Pacific.

Such were some of the principal features of this remarkable code, which, touching on the most delicate relations of society, broke up the very foundations of property, and, by a stroke of the pen, as it were, converted a nation of slaves into freemen. It would have required, we may suppose, but little forecast to divine, that in the remote regions of America, and especially in Peru, where the colonists had been hitherto accustomed to unbounded license, a reform, so salutary in essential points, could be enforced thus summarily only at the price of a revolution.—Yet the ordinances received the sanction of the emperor that same year, and in November, 1543, were published at Madrid.

No sooner was their import known than it was conveyed by numerous letters to the colonists, from their friends in Spain. The tidings flew like wildfire over the land, from Mexico to Chili. Men were astounded at the prospect of the ruin that awaited them. In Peru, particularly, there was scarcely one that could hope to escape the operation of the law. Few there were who had not taken part, at some time or other, in the civil feuds of Almagro and Pizarro; and still fewer of those that remained that would not be entangled in some one or other of the insidious clauses that seemed spread out, like a web, to ensnare them.

The whole country was thrown into commotion. Men assembled tumultuously in the squares and public places, and, as the regulations were made known they were received with universal groans and hisses. "Is this the fruit," they cried, "of all our toil? Is it for this that we have poured out our blood like water? Now that we are broken down by hardships and sufferings, to be left at the end of our campaigns as poor as at the beginning! Is this the way government rewards our services in winning for it an empire? The government has done little to aid us in making the conquest, and for what we have we may thank our own good swords; and with these same swords," they continued, warming into menace, "we know how to defend it." Then, stripping up his sleeve, the war-worn veteran bared his arm, or, exposing his naked bosom, pointed to his scars, as the best title to his estates.

The governor, Vaca de Castro, watched the storm thus gathering from all quarters, with the deepest concern. He was himself in the very heart of disaffection; for Cuzco, tenanted by a mixed and lawless population, was so far removed into the depths of the mountains, that it had much less intercourse with the parent country, and was consequently much less under her influence, than the great towns on the coast. The people now invoked the governor to protect them against the tyranny of the Court; but he endeavored to calm the agitation by representing, that by these violent measures they would only defeat their own object. He counselled them to name deputies to lay their petition before the Crown, stating the impracticability of the present scheme of reform, and praying for the repeal of it; and he conjured them to wait patiently for the arrival of the viceroy, who might be prevailed on to suspend the ordinances till further advices could be received from Castile.

But it was not easy to still the tempest; and the people now eagerly looked for some one whose interests and sympathies might lie with theirs, and whose position in the community might afford them protection. The person to whom they naturally turned in this crisis was Gonzalo Pizarro, the last in the land of that family who had led the armies of the Conquest, —a cavalier whose gallantry and popular manners had made him always a favorite with the people. He was beset with applications to interpose in their behalf with the government, and shield them from the oppressive ordinances.

But Gonzalo Pizarro was at Charcas, busily occupied in exploring the rich veins of Potosí, whose silver fountains, just brought into light, were soon to pour such streams of wealth over Europe. Though gratified with this appeal to his protection, the cautious cavalier was more intent on providing for the means of enterprise than on plunging prematurely into it; and, while he secretly encouraged the malcontents, he did not commit himself by taking part in any revolutionary movement. At the same period, he received letters from Vaca de Castro,—whose vigilant eye watched all the aspects of the time, —cautioning Gonzalo and his friends not to be seduced, by any wild schemes of reform, from their allegiance. And, to check still further these disorderly movements, he ordered his alcaldes to arrest every man guilty of seditious language, and bring him at once to punishment. By this firm yet temperate conduct the minds of the populace were overawed, and there was a temporary lull in the troubled waters, while all looked anxiously for the coming of the viceroy.

The person selected for this critical post was a knight of Avila, named Blasco Nuñez Vela. He was a cavalier of ancient family, handsome in person, though now somewhat advanced in years, and reputed brave and devout. He had filled some offices of responsibility to the satisfaction of Charles the Fifth, by whom he was now appointed to this post in Peru. The selection did no credit to the monarch's discernment.

It may seem strange that this important place should not have been bestowed on Vaca de Castro, already on the spot, and who had shown himself so well qualified to fill it. But ever since that officer's mission to Peru, there had been a series of assassinations, insurrections, and civil wars, that menaced the wretched colony with ruin; and, though his wise administration had now brought things into order, the communication with the Indies was so tardy, that the results of his policy were not yet fully disclosed. As it was designed, moreover, to make important innovations in the government, it was thought better to send some one who would have no personal prejudices to encounter, from the part he had already taken, and who, coming directly from the Court, and clothed with extraordinary powers, might present himself with greater authority than could one who had become familiar to the people in an inferior capacity. The monarch, however, wrote a letter with his own hand to Vaca de Castro, in which he thanked that officer for his past services, and directed him, after aiding the new viceroy with the fruits of his large experience, to return to Castile, and take his seat in the Royal Council. Letters of a similar complimentary kind were sent to the loyal colonists who had stood by the governor in the late troubles of the country. Freighted with these testimonials, and with the ill-starred ordinances, Blasco Nuñez embarked at San Lucar, on the 3rd of November, 1543. He was attended by the four judges of the Audience, and by a numerous retinue, that he might appear in the state befitting his distinguished rank.

About the middle of the following January, 1544, the viceroy, after a favorable passage, landed at Nombre de Dios. He found there a vessel laden with silver from the Peruvian mines, ready to sail for Spain. His first act was to lay an embargo on it for the government, as containing the proceeds of slave labor. After this extraordinary measure, taken in opposition to the advice of the Audience, he crossed the Isthmus to Panamá. Here he gave sure token of his future policy, by causing more than three hundred Indians, who had been brought by their owners from Peru, to be liberated and sent back to their own country. This high-handed measure created the greatest sensation in the city, and was strongly resisted by the judges of the Audience. They besought him not to begin thus precipitately to execute his commission, but to wait till his arrival in the colony, when he should have taken time to acquaint himself somewhat with the country, and with the temper of the people. But Blasco Nuñez coldly replied, that "he had come, not to tamper with the laws, nor to discuss their merits, but to execute them,—and execute them he would, to the letter, whatever might be the consequence." This answer, and the peremptory tone in which it was delivered, promptly adjourned the debate; for the judges saw that debate was useless with one who seemed to consider all remonstrance as an attempt to turn him from his duty, and whose ideas of duty precluded all discretionary exercise of authority, even where the public good demanded it.

Leaving the Audience, as one of its body was ill, at Panamá, the viceroy proceeded on his way, and, coasting down the shores of the Pacific, on the fourth of March he disembarked at Tumbez. He was well received by the loyal inhabitants; his authority was publicly proclaimed, and the people were overawed by the display of a magnificence and state such as had not till then been seen in Peru. He took an early occasion to intimate his future line of policy by liberating a number of Indian slaves on the application of their caciques. He then proceeded by land towards the south, and showed his determination to conform in his own person to the strict letter of the ordinances, by causing his baggage to be carried by mules, where it was practicable; and where absolutely necessary to make use of Indians, he paid them fairly for their services.

The whole country was thrown into consternation by reports of the proceedings of the viceroy, and of his conversations, most unguarded, which were eagerly circulated, and, no doubt, often exaggerated. Meetings were again called in the cities. Discussions were held on the expediency of resisting his further progress, and a deputation of citizens from Cuzco, who were then in Lima, strongly urged the people to close the gates of that capital against him. But Vaca de Castro had also left Cuzco for the latter city, on the earliest intimation of the viceroy's approach, and, with some difficulty, he prevailed on the inhabitants not to swerve from their loyalty, but to receive their new ruler with suitable honors, and trust to his calmer judgment for postponing the execution of the law till the case could be laid before the throne.

But the great body of the Spaniards, after what they had heard, had slender confidence in the relief to be obtained from this quarter. They now turned with more eagerness than ever towards Gonzalo Pizarro; and letters and addresses poured in upon him from all parts of the country, inviting him to take on himself the office of their protector. These applications found a more favorable response than on the former occasion.

There were, indeed, many motives at work to call Gonzalo into action. It was to his family, mainly, that Spain was indebted for this extension of her colonial empire; and he had felt deeply aggrieved that the government of the colony should be trusted to other hands than his. He had felt this on the arrival of Vaca de Castro, and much more so when the appointment of a viceroy proved it to be the settled policy of the Crown to exclude his family from the management of affairs. His brother Hernando still languished in prison, and he himself was now to be sacrificed as the principal victim of the fatal ordinances. For who had taken so prominent a part in the civil war with the elder Almagro? And the viceroy was currently reported—it may have been scandal—to have intimated that Pizarro would be dealt with accordingly. Yet there was no one in the country who had so great a stake, who had so much to lose by the revolution. Abandoned thus by the government, he conceived that it was now time to take care of himself.

Assembling together some eighteen or twenty cavaliers in

whom he most trusted, and taking a large amount of silver, drawn from the mines, he accepted the invitation to repair to Cuzco. As he approached this capital, he was met by a numerous body of the citizens, who came out to welcome him, making the air ring with their shouts, as they saluted him with the title of Procurator-General of Peru. The title was speedily confirmed by the municipality of the city, who invited him to head a deputation to Lima, in order to state their grievances to the viceroy, and solicit the present suspension of the ordinances.

But the spark of ambition was kindled in the bosom of Pizarro. He felt strong in the affections of the people; and, from the more elevated position in which he now stood, his desires took a loftier and more unbounded range. Yet, if he harbored a criminal ambition in his breast, he skilfully veiled it from others—perhaps from himself. The only object he professed to have in view was the good of the people; a suspicious phrase, usually meaning the good of the individual. He now demanded permission to raise and organize an armed force, with the further title of Captain-General. His views were entirely pacific; but it was not safe, unless strongly protected, to urge them on a person of the viceroy's impatient and arbitrary temper. It was further contended by Pizarro's friends, that such a force was demanded, to rid the country of their old enemy, the Inca Manco, who hovered in the neighboring mountains with a body of warriors, ready, at the first opportunity, to descend on the Spaniards. The municipality of Cuzco hesitated, as well it might, to confer powers so far beyond its legitimate authority. But Pizarro avowed his purpose, in case of refusal, to decline the office of Procurator; and the efforts of his partisans, backed by those of the people, at length silenced the scruples of the magistrates, who bestowed on the ambitious chief the military command to which he aspired. Pizarro accepted it with the modest assurance, that he did so "purely from regard to the interests of the king, of the Indies, and, above all, of Peru!"

THE VICEROY ARRIVES AT LIMA—GONZALO PIZARRO
MARCHES FROM CUZCO—DEATH OF THE INCA MANCO—
RASH CONDUCT OF THE VICEROY—SEIZED AND DEPOSED
BY THE AUDIENCE—GONZALO PROCLAIMED GOVERNOR
OF PERU

While the events recorded in the preceding pages were
in progress, Blasco Nuñez had been journeying towards Lima.
But the alienation which his conduct had already caused in
the minds of the colonists was shown in the cold reception
which he occasionally experienced on the route, and in the
scanty accommodations provided for him and his retinue. In
one place where he took up his quarters, he found an ominous
inscription over the door:—"He that takes my property must
expect to pay for it with his life." Neither daunted, nor diverted from his purpose, the inflexible viceroy held on his way
towards the capital, where the inhabitants, preceded by Vaca
de Castro and the municipal authorities, came out to receive
him. He entered in great state, under a canopy of crimson
cloth, embroidered with the arms of Spain, and supported by
stout poles or staves of solid silver, which were borne by the
members of the municipality. A cavalier, holding a mace, the
emblem of authority, rode before him; and after the oaths of
office were administered in the council-chamber, the procession moved towards the cathedral, where *Te Deum* was sung,
and Blasco Nuñez was installed in his new dignity of viceroy
of Peru.

His first act was to proclaim his determination in respect
to the ordinances. He had no warrant to suspend their execution. He should fulfil his commission; but he offered to join
the colonists in a memorial to the emperor, soliciting the repeal of a code which he now believed would be for the interests neither of the country nor of the Crown. With this
avowed view of the subject, it may seem strange that Blasco
Nuñez should not have taken the responsibility of suspending

the law until his sovereign could be assured of the inevitable consequences of enforcing it. The pacha of a Turkish despot, who had allowed himself this latitude for the interests of his master, might, indeed, have reckoned on the bowstring. But the example of Mendoza, the prudent viceroy of Mexico, who adopted this course in a similar crisis, and precisely at the same period, showed its propriety under existing circumstances. The ordinances were suspended by him till the Crown could be warned of the consequences of enforcing them,—and Mexico was saved from revolution. But Blasco Nuñez had not the wisdom of Mendoza.

The public apprehension was now far from being allayed. Secret cabals were formed in Lima, and communications held with the different towns. No distrust, however, was raised in the breast of the viceroy, and, when informed of the preparations of Gonzalo Pizarro, he took no other step than to send a message to his camp, announcing the extraordinary powers with which he was himself invested, and requiring that chief to disband his forces. He seemed to think that a mere word from him would be sufficient to dissipate rebellion. But it required more than a breath to scatter the iron soldiery of Peru.

Gonzalo Pizarro, meanwhile, was busily occupied in mustering his army. His first step was to order from Guamanga sixteen pieces of artillery, sent there by Vaca de Castro, who, in the present state of excitement, was unwilling to trust the volatile people of Cuzco with these implements of destruction. Gonzalo, who had no scruples as to Indian labor, appropriated six thousand of the natives to the service of transporting this train of ordnance across the mountains.

By his exertions and those of his friends, the active chief soon mustered a force of nearly four hundred men, which, if not very imposing in the outset, he conceived would be swelled, in his descent to the coast, by tributary levies from the towns and villages on the way. All his own funds were expended in equipping his men and providing for the march; and, to supply deficiencies, he made no scruple—since, to use his words, it was for the public interest—to appropriate the moneys in the royal treasury. With this seasonable aid, his troops, well mounted and thoroughly equipped, were put in excellent fighting order; and, after making them a brief harangue, in which he was careful to insist on the pacific character of his enterprise, somewhat at variance with its military preparations, Gonzalo Pizarro sallied forth from the gates of the capital.

Before leaving it, he received an important accession of strength in the person of Francisco de Carbajal, the veteran who performed so conspicuous a part in the battle of Chupas. He was at Charcas when the news of the ordinances reached Peru; and he instantly resolved to quit the country and return to Spain, convinced that the New World would be no longer the land for him,—no longer the golden Indies. Turning his effects into money, he prepared to embark them on board the first ship that offered. But no opportunity occurred, and he could have little expectation now of escaping the vigilant eye of the viceroy. Yet, though solicited by Pizarro to take command under him in the present expedition, the veteran declined, saying, he was eighty years old, and had no wish but to return home, and spend his few remaining days in quiet. Well had it been for him, had he persisted in his refusal. But he yielded to the importunities of his friend; and the short space that yet remained to him of life proved long enough to brand his memory with perpetual infamy.

Soon after quitting Cuzco, Pizarro learned the death of the Inca Manco. He was massacred by a party of Spaniards, of the faction of Almagro, who, on the defeat of their young leader, had taken refuge in the Indian camp. They, in turn, were all slain by the Peruvians. It is impossible to determine on whom the blame of the quarrel should rest, since no one present at the time has recorded it.

The death of Manco Inca, as he was commonly called, is an event not to be silently passed over in Peruvian history; for he was the last of his race that may be said to have been animated by the heroic spirit of the ancient Incas. Though placed on the throne by Pizarro, far from remaining a mere puppet in his hands, Manco soon showed that his lot was not to be cast with that of his conquerors. With the ancient institutions of his country lying a wreck around him, he yet struggled bravely, like Guatemozin, the last of the Aztecs, to uphold her tottering fortunes, or to bury his oppressors under her ruins. By the assault on his own capital of Cuzco, in which so large a portion of it was demolished, he gave a check to the arms of Pizarro, and, for a season, the fate of the Conquerors trembled in the balance. Though foiled, in the end, by the superior science of his adversary, the young barbarian still showed the same unconquerable spirit as before. He withdrew into the fastnesses of his native mountains, whence sallying forth as occasion offered, he fell on the caravan of the traveller, or on some scattered party of the military; and, in the event of a civil war, was sure to throw his own weight into the weaker scale, thus prolonging the contest of his enemies, and feeding his revenge by the sight of their calamities. Moving lightly from spot to spot, he eluded pursuit amidst the wilds of the Cordilleras; and, hovering in the neighborhood of the towns, or lying in ambush on the great thoroughfares of the country, the Inca Manco made his name a terror to the Spaniards. Often did they hold out to him terms of accommodation; and every succeeding ruler, down to Blasco Nuñez, bore instructions from the Crown to employ every art to conciliate the formidable warrior. But Manco did not trust the promises of the white man; and he chose rather to maintain his savage independence in the mountains, with the few brave spirits around him, than to live a slave in the land which had once owned the sway of his ancestors.

The death of the Inca removed one of the great pretexts for Gonzalo Pizarro's military preparations; but it had little influence on him, as may be readily imagined. He was much more sensible to the desertion of some of his followers, which took place early on the march. Several of the cavaliers of Cuzco, startled by his unceremonious appropriation of the public moneys, and by the belligerent aspect of affairs, now for the first time seemed to realize that they were in the path of rebellion. A number of these, including some principal men of the city, secretly withdrew from the army, and, hastening to Lima, offered their services to the viceroy. The troops were disheartened by this desertion, and even Pizarro for a moment faltered in his purpose, and thought of retiring with some fifty followers to Charcas, and there making his composition with government. But a little reflection, aided by the remonstrances of the courageous Carbajal, who never turned his back on an enterprise which he had once assumed, convinced him that he had gone too far to recede,—that his only safety was to advance.

He was reassured by more decided manifestations, which he soon after received, of the public opinion. An officer named Puelles, who commanded at Guanuco, joined him, with a body of horse with which he had been intrusted by the viceroy. This defection was followed by that of others, and Gonzalo, as he descended the sides of the table-land, found his numbers gradually swelled to nearly double the amount with which he had left the Indian capital.

As he traversed with a freer step the bloody field of Chupas, Carbajal pointed out the various localities of the battle-ground, and Pizarro might have found food for anxious reflection, as he meditated on the fortunes of a rebel. At Guamanga he was received with open arms by the inhabitants, many of whom eagerly enlisted under his banner; for they trembled for their property, as they heard from all quarters of the inflexible temper of the viceroy.

That functionary began now to be convinced that he was in a critical position. Before Puelles's treachery, above noticed, had been consummated, the viceroy had received some vague intimation of his purpose. Though scarcely crediting it, he detached one of his company, named Diaz, with a force to intercept him. But, although that cavalier undertook the mission with alacrity, he was soon after prevailed on to follow the example of his comrade, and, with the greater part of the men under his command, went over to the enemy. In the civil feuds of this unhappy land, parties changed sides so lightly, that treachery to a commander had almost ceased to be a stain on the honor of a cavalier. Yet all, on whichever side they cast their fortunes, loudly proclaimed their loyalty to the Crown.

Thus betrayed by his own men, by those apparently most devoted to his service, Blasco Nuñez became suspicious of every one around him. Unfortunately, his suspicions fell on some who were most deserving of his confidence. Among these was his predecessor, Vaca de Castro. That officer had conducted himself, in the delicate situation in which he had been placed, with his usual discretion, and with perfect integrity and honor. He had frankly communicated with the viceroy, and well had it been for Blasco Nuñez, if he had known how to profit by it. But he was too much puffed up by the arrogance of office, and by the conceit of his own superior wisdom, to defer much to the counsels of his experienced predecessor. The latter was now suspected by the viceroy of maintaining a secret correspondence with his enemies at Cuzco,—a suspicion which seems to have had no better foundation than the personal friendship which Vaca de Castro was known to entertain for these individuals. But, with Blasco Nuñez, to suspect was to be convinced; and he ordered De Castro to be placed under arrest, and confined on board of a vessel lying in the harbor. This high-handed measure was followed by the arrest and imprisonment of several other cavaliers, probably on grounds equally frivolous.

He now turned his attention towards the enemy. Notwithstanding his former failure, he still did not altogether despair of effecting something by negotiation, and he sent another embassy, having the bishop of Lima at its head, to Gonzalo Pizarro's camp, with promises of a general amnesty, and some proposals of a more tempting character to the commander. But this step, while it proclaimed his own weakness, had no better success than the preceding.

The viceroy now vigorously prepared for war. His first care was to put the capital in a posture of defence, by strengthening its fortifications, and throwing barricades across the streets. He ordered a general enrolment of the citizens, and called in levies from the neighboring towns,—a call not very promptly answered. A squadron of eight or ten vessels was got ready in the port to act in concert with the land forces. The bells were taken from the churches, and used in the manufacture of muskets; and funds were procured from the fifths which had accumulated in the royal treasury. The most extravagant bounty was offered to the soldiers, and prices were paid for mules and horses, which showed that gold, or rather silver, was the commodity of least value in Peru. By these efforts, the active commander soon assembled a force considerably larger than that of his adversary. But how could he confide in it?

While these preparations were going forward, the judges of the Audience arrived at Lima. They had shown, throughout their progress, no great respect either for the ordinances, or the will of the viceroy; for they had taxed the poor natives as freely and unscrupulously as any of the Conquerors. We have

seen the entire want of cordiality subsisting between them and
their principal in Panamá. It became more apparent, on their
landing at Lima. They disapproved of his proceedings in every
particular; of his refusal to suspend the ordinances,—although,
in fact, he had found no opportunity, of late, to enforce them;
of his preparations for defence, declaring that he ought rather
trust to the effect of negotiation; and, finally, of his imprisonment of so many loyal cavaliers, which they pronounced an
arbitrary act, altogether beyond the bounds of his authority;
and they did not scruple to visit the prison in person, and discharge the captives from their confinement.

This bold proceeding, while it conciliated the good-will of
the people, severed, at once, all relations with the viceroy.
There was in the Audience a lawyer, named Cepeda, a cunning, ambitious man, with considerable knowledge in the way
of his profession, and with still greater talent for intrigue. He
did not disdain the low arts of a demagogue to gain the favor
of the populace, and trusted to find his own account in fomenting a misunderstanding with Blasco Nuñez. The latter,
it must be confessed, did all in his power to aid his counsellor
in this laudable design.

A certain cavalier in the place, named Suarez de Carbajal,
who had long held an office under the government, fell under
the viceroy's displeasure, on suspicion of conniving at the secession of some of his kinsmen, who had lately taken part with
the malcontents. The viceroy summoned Carbajal to attend
him at his palace, late at night; and when conducted to his
presence, he bluntly charged him with treason. The latter
stoutly denied the accusation, in tones as haughty as those of
his accuser. The altercation grew warm, until, in the heat of
passion, Blasco Nuñez struck him with his poniard. In an instant, the attendants, taking this as a signal, plunged their
swords into the body of the unfortunate man, who fell lifeless on the floor.

Greatly alarmed for the consequences of his rash act,—for
Carbajal was much beloved in Lima,—Blasco Nuñez ordered
the corpse of the murdered man to be removed by a private
stairway from the house, and carried to the cathedral, where,
rolled in his bloody cloak, it was laid in a grave hastily dug to
receive it. So tragic a proceeding, known to so many witnesses,

could not long be kept secret. Vague rumors of the fact explained the mysterious disappearance of Carbajal. The grave was opened, and the mangled remains of the slaughtered cavalier established the guilt of the viceroy.

From this hour Blasco Nuñez was held in universal abhorrence; and his crime, in this instance, assumed the deeper dye of ingratitude, since the deceased was known to have had the greatest influence in reconciling the citizens early to his government. No one knew where the blow would fall next, or how soon he might himself become the victim of the ungovernable passions of the viceroy. In this state of things, some looked to the Audience, and yet more to Gonzalo Pizarro, to protect them.

That chief was slowly advancing towards Lima, from which, indeed, he was removed but a few days' march. Greatly perplexed, Blasco Nuñez now felt the loneliness of his condition. Standing aloof, as it were, from his own followers, thwarted by the Audience, betrayed by his soldiers, he might well feel the consequences of his misconduct. Yet there seemed no other course for him, but either to march out and meet the enemy, or to remain in Lima and defend it. He had placed the town in a posture of defence, which argued this last to have been his original purpose. But he felt he could no longer rely on his troops, and he decided on a third course, most unexpected.

This was to abandon the capital, and withdraw to Truxillo, about eighty leagues distant. The women would embark on board the squadron, and with the effects of the citizens, be transported by water. The troops, with the rest of the inhabitants, would march by land, laying waste the country as they proceeded. Gonzalo Pizarro, when he arrived at Lima, would find it without supplies for his army, and, thus straitened he would not care to take a long march across a desert in search of his enemy.

What the viceroy proposed to effect by this movement is not clear, unless it were to gain time; and yet the more time he had gained, thus far, the worse it had proved for him. But he was destined to encounter a decided opposition from the judges. They contended that he had no warrant for such an act, and that the Audience could not lawfully hold its sessions out of the capital. Blasco Nuñez persisted in his determination, menacing that body with force, if necessary. The judges appealed to the citizens to support them in resisting such an arbitrary measure. They mustered a force for their own protection, and that same day passed a decree that the viceroy should be arrested.

Late at night, Blasco Nuñez was informed of the hostile preparations of the judges. He instantly summoned his followers, to the number of more than two hundred, put on his armour, and prepared to march out at the head of his troops against the Audience. This was the true course; for in a crisis like that in which he was placed, requiring promptness and decision, the presence of the leader is essential to insure success. But, unluckily, he yielded to the remonstrances of his brother and other friends, who dissuaded him from rashly exposing his life in such a venture.

What Blasco Nuñez neglected to do was done by the judges. They sallied forth at the head of their followers, whose number, though small at first, they felt confident would be swelled by volunteers as they advanced. Rushing forward, they cried out,—"Liberty! Liberty! Long live the king and the Audience!" It was early dawn, and the inhabitants, startled from their slumbers, ran to the windows and balconies, and, learning the object of the movement, some snatched up their arms and joined in it, while the women, waving their scarfs and kerchiefs, cheered on the assault.

When the mob arrived before the viceroy's palace, they halted for a moment, uncertain what to do. Orders were given to fire on them from the windows, and a volley passed over their heads. No one was injured; and the greater part of the viceroy's men, with most of the officers,—including some of those who had been so anxious for his personal safety,—now openly joined the populace. The palace was then entered, and abandoned to pillage. Blasco Nuñez, deserted by all but a few faithful adherents, made no resistance. He surrendered to the assailants, was led before the judges, and by them was placed in strict confinement. The citizens, delighted with the result, provided a collation for the soldiers; and the affair ended without the loss of a single life. Never was there so bloodless a revolution.

The first business of the judges was to dispose of the prisoner. He was sent, under a strong guard, to a neighboring island, till some measures could be taken respecting him. He was declared to be deposed from his office; a provisional government was established, consisting of their own body, with Cepeda at its head, as president; and its first act was to pronounce the detested ordinances suspended, till instructions could be received from Court. It was also decided to send Blasco Nuñez back to Spain with one of their own body, who should explain to the emperor the nature of the late disturbances, and vindicate the measures of the Audience. This was soon put in execution. The Licentiate Alvarez was the person selected to bear the viceroy company; and the unfortunate commander, after passing several days on the desolate island, with scarcely any food, and exposed to all the inclemencies of the weather, took his departure for Panamá.

A more formidable adversary yet remained in Gonzalo Pizarro, who had now advanced to Xauxa, about ninety miles from Lima. Here he halted, while numbers of the citizens prepared to join his banner, choosing rather to take service under him than to remain under the self-constituted authority of the Audience. The judges, meanwhile, who had tasted the sweets of office too short a time to be content to resign them, after considerable delay, sent an embassy to the Procurator. They announced to him the revolution that had taken place, and the suspension of the ordinances. The great object of his mission had been thus accomplished; and, as a new government was now organized, they called on him to show his obedience to it, by disbanding his forces, and withdrawing to the unmolested enjoyment of his estates. It was a bold demand,—though couched in the most courteous and complimentary phrase,—to make of one in Pizarro's position. It was attempting to scare away the eagle just ready to swoop on his prey. If the chief had faltered, however, he would have been reassured by his lion-hearted lieutenant. "Never show faint heart," exclaimed the latter, "when you are so near the goal. Success has followed every step of your path. You have now only to stretch forth your hand, and seize the government. Every thing else will follow."—The envoy who brought the message from the judges was sent back with the answer, that "the people had called Gonzalo Pizarro to the government of the country, and, if the Audience did not at once invest him with it, the city should be delivered up to pillage."

The bewildered magistrates were thrown into dismay by this decisive answer. Yet loth to resign, they took counsel in their perplexity of Vaca de Castro, still detained on board of one of the vessels. But that commander had received too little favor at the hands of his successors to think it necessary to peril his life on their account by thwarting the plans of Pizarro. He maintained a discreet silence, therefore, and left the matter to the wisdom of the Audience.

Meanwhile, Carbajal was sent into the city to quicken their deliberations. He came at night, attended only by a small party of soldiers, intimating his contempt of the power of the judges. His first act was to seize a number of cavaliers, whom he dragged from their beds, and placed under arrest. They were men of Cuzco, the same already noticed as having left Pizarro's ranks soon after his departure from that capital. While the Audience still hesitated as to the course they should pursue, Carbajal caused three of his prisoners, persons of consideration and property, to be placed on the backs of mules, and escorted out of town to the suburbs, where, with brief space allowed for confession, he hung them all on the branches of a tree. He superintended the execution himself, and tauntingly complimented one of his victims, by telling him, that, "in consideration of his higher rank, he should have the privilege of selecting the bough on which to be hanged!" The ferocious officer would have proceeded still further in his executions, it is said, had it not been for orders received from his leader. But enough was done to quicken the perceptions of the Audience as to their course, for they felt their own lives suspended by a thread in such unscrupulous hands. Without further delay, therefore, they sent to invite Gonzalo Pizarro to enter the city, declaring that the security of the country and the general good required the government to be placed in his hands.

That chief had now advanced within half a league of the capital, which soon after, on the twenty-eighth of October, 1544, he entered in battle-array. His whole force was little short of twelve hundred Spaniards, besides several thousand Indians, who dragged his heavy guns in the advance. Then came the files of spearmen and arquebusiers, making a formidable corps of infantry for a colonial army; and lastly, the cavalry, at the head of which rode Pizarro himself, on a powerful charger, gaily caparisoned. The rider was in complete mail, over which floated a richly embroidered surcoat, and his head was protected by a crimson cap, highly ornamented,—his showy livery setting off his handsome, soldier-like person to advantage. Before him was borne the royal standard of Castile; for every one, royalist or rebel, was careful to fight under that sign. This emblem of loyalty was supported on the right by a banner, emblazoned with the arms of Cuzco, and by another on the left, displaying the armorial bearings granted by the Crown to the Pizarros. As the martial pageant swept through the streets of Lima, the air was rent with acclamations from the populace, and from the spectators in the balconies. The cannon sounded at intervals, and the bells of the city—those that the viceroy had spared—rang out a joyous peal, as if in honor of a victory!

The oaths of office were duly administered by the judges of the Royal Audience, and Gonzalo Pizarro was proclaimed Governor and Captain-General of Peru, till his Majesty's pleasure could be known in respect to the government. The new ruler then took up his quarters in the palace of his brother,—where the stains of that brother's blood were not yet effaced. *Fêtes*, bull-fights, and tournaments graced the ceremony of inauguration, and were prolonged for several days, while the giddy populace of the capital abandoned themselves to jubilee, as if a new and more auspicious order of things had commenced for Peru!

CHAPTER IX [1544-1546]

The first act of Gonzalo Pizarro was to cause those persons to be apprehended who had taken the most active part against him in the late troubles. Several he condemned to death; but afterwards commuted the sentence, and contented himself with driving them into banishment and confiscating their estates. His next concern was to establish his authority on a firm basis. He filled the municipal government of Lima with his own partisans. He sent his lieutenants to take charge of the principal cities. He caused galleys to be built at Arequipa to secure the command of the seas; and brought his forces into the best possible condition, to prepare for future emergencies.

The Royal Audience existed only in name; for its powers were speedily absorbed by the new ruler, who desired to place the government on the same footing as under the marquess, his brother. Indeed, the Audience necessarily fell to pieces, from the position of its several members. Alvarez had been sent with the viceroy to Castile. Cepeda, the most aspiring of the court, now that he had failed in his own schemes of ambition, was content to become a tool in the hands of the military chief who had displaced him. Zarate, a third judge, who had, from the first, protested against the violent measures of his colleagues, was confined to his house by a mortal illness; and Tepeda, the remaining magistrate, Gonzalo now proposed to send back to Castile with such an account of the late transactions as should vindicate his own conduct in the eyes of the emperor. This step was opposed by Carbajal, who bluntly told his commander that "he had gone too far to expect favor from the Crown; and that he had better rely for his vindication on his pikes and muskets!"

But the ship which was to transport Tepeda was found to have suddenly disappeared from the port. It was the same in which Vaca de Castro was confined; and that officer, not caring to trust to the forbearance of one whose advances, on a former occasion, he had so unceremoniously repulsed, and convinced, moreover, that his own presence could profit nothing in a land where he held no legitimate authority, had prevailed on the captain to sail with him to Panamá. He then crossed the Isthmus, and embarked for Spain. The rumors of his coming had already preceded him, and charges were not wanting against him from some of those whom he had offended by his administration. He was accused of having carried measures with a high hand, regardless of the rights, both of the colonist and of the native; and, above all, of having embezzled the public moneys, and of returning with his coffers richly freighted to Castile. This last was an unpardonable crime.

No sooner had the governor set foot in his own country than he was arrested, and hurried to the fortress of Arevalo; and, though he was afterwards removed to better quarters, where he was treated with the indulgence due to his rank, he was still kept a prisoner of state for twelve years, when the tardy tribunals of Castile pronounced a judgment in his favor. He was acquitted of every charge that had been brought against him, and, so far from peculation, was proved to have returned home no richer than he went. He was released from confinement, reinstated in his honors and dignities, took his seat anew in the royal council, and Vaca de Castro enjoyed, during the remainder of his days, the consideration to which he was entitled by his deserts. The best eulogium on the wisdom of his administration was afforded by the troubles brought on the colonies by that of his successor.

The nation became gradually sensible of the value of his services; though the manner in which they were requited by the government must be allowed to form a cold commentary on the gratitude of princes.

Gonzalo Pizarro was doomed to experience a still greater disappointment than that caused by the escape of Vaca de Castro, in the return of Blasco Nuñez. The vessel which bore him from the country had hardly left the shore, when Alvarez, the judge, whether from remorse at the part which he had taken, or apprehensive of the consequences of carrying back the viceroy to Spain, presented himself before that dignitary, and announced that he was no longer a prisoner. At the same time he excused himself for the part he had taken, by his desire to save the life of Blasco Nuñez, and extricate him from his perilous situation. He now placed the vessel at his disposal, and assured him it should take him wherever he chose.

The viceroy, whatever faith he may have placed in the judge's explanation, eagerly availed himself of his offer. His proud spirit revolted at the idea of returning home in disgrace, foiled, as he had been, in every object of his mission. He determined to try his fortune again in the land, and his only doubt was, on what point to attempt to rally his partisans around him. At Panamá he might remain in safety, while he invoked assistance from Nicaragua, and other colonies at the north. But this would be to abandon his government at once; and such a confession of weakness would have a bad effect on his followers in Peru. He determined, therefore, to direct his steps towards Quito, which, while it was within his jurisdiction, was still removed far enough from the theatre of the late troubles to give him time to rally, and make head against his enemies.

In pursuance of this purpose, the viceroy and his suite disembarked at Tumbez, about the middle of October, 1544. On landing, he issued a manifesto setting forth the violent proceedings of Gonzalo Pizarro and his followers, whom he denounced as traitors to their prince, and he called on all true subjects in the colony to support him in maintaining the royal authority. The call was not unheeded; and volunteers came in, though tardily, from San Miguel, Puerto Viejo, and other places on the coast, cheering the heart of the viceroy with the conviction that the sentiment of loyalty was not yet extinct in the bosoms of the Spaniards.

But, while thus occupied, he received tidings of the arrival of one of Pizarro's captains on the coast, with a force superior to his own. Their number was exaggerated; but Blasco Nuñez, without waiting to ascertain the truth, abandoned his position at Tumbez, and, with as much expedition as he could make across a wild and mountainous country half-buried in snow, he marched to Quito. But this capital, situated at the northern extremity of his province, was not a favorable point for the rendezvous of his followers; and, after prolonging his stay till he had received assurance from Benalcazar, the loyal commander at Popayan, that he would support him with all his strength in the coming conflict, he made a rapid counter-march to the coast, and took up his position at the town of San Miguel. This was a spot well suited to his purposes, as lying on the great high road along the shores of the Pacific, besides being the chief mart for commercial intercourse with Panamá and the north.

Here the viceroy erected his standard, and in a few weeks found himself at the head of a force amounting to nearly five hundred in all, horse and foot, ill provided with arms and ammunition, but apparently zealous in the cause. Finding himself in sufficient strength to commence active operations, he now sallied forth against several of Pizarro's captains in the neighborhood, over whom he obtained some decided advantages, which renewed his confidence, and flattered him with the hopes of reëstablishing his ascendency in the country.

During this time, Gonzalo Pizarro was not idle. He had watched with anxiety the viceroy's movements; and was now convinced that it was time to act, and that, if he would not be unseated himself, he must dislodge his formidable rival. He accordingly placed a strong garrison under a faithful officer in Lima, and, after sending forward a force of some six hundred men by land to Truxillo, he embarked for the same port himself, on the 4th of March, 1545, the very day on which the viceroy had marched from Quito.

At Truxillo, Pizarro put himself at the head of his little army, and moved without loss of time against San Miguel. His rival, eager to bring their quarrel to an issue, would fain have marched out to give him battle; but his soldiers, mostly young and inexperienced levies, hastily brought together, were intimidated by the name of Pizarro. They loudly insisted on being led into upper country, where they would be reinforced by Benalcazar; and their unfortunate commander, like the rider of some unmanageable steed, to whose humors he is obliged to submit, was hurried away in a direction contrary to his wishes. It was the fate of Blasco Nuñez to have his purposes baffled alike by his friends and his enemies.

On arriving before San Miguel, Gonzalo Pizarro found, to his great mortification, that his antagonist had left it. Without entering the town, he quickened his pace, and, after traversing a valley of some extent, reached the skirts of a mountain chain, into which Blasco Nuñez had entered but a few hours before. It was late in the evening; but Pizarro, knowing the importance of despatch, sent forward Carbajal with a party of light troops to overtake the fugitives. That captain succeeded in coming up with their lonely bivouac among the mountains at midnight, when the weary troops were buried in slumber. Startled from their repose by the blast of the trumpet, which, strange to say, their enemy had incautiously sounded, the viceroy and his men sprang to their feet, mounted their horses, grasped their arquebuses, and poured such a volley into the ranks of their assailants, that Carbajal, disconcerted by his reception, found it prudent, with his inferior force, to retreat. The viceroy followed, till, fearing an ambuscade in the darkness of the night, he withdrew, and allowed his adversary to rejoin the main body of the army under Pizarro.

This conduct of Carbajal, by which he allowed the game to slip through his hands, from mere carelessness, is inexplicable. It forms a singular exception to the habitual caution and vigilance displayed in his military career. Had it been the act of any other captain, it would have cost him his head. But Pizarro, although greatly incensed, set too high a value on the services and well-tried attachment of his lieutenant, to quarrel with him. Still it was considered of the last importance to overtake the enemy, before he had advanced much farther to the north, where the difficulties of the ground would greatly embarrass the pursuit. Carbajal, anxious to retrieve his error, was accordingly again placed at the head of a corps of light troops, with instructions to harass the enemy's march, cut off his stores, and keep him in check, if possible, till the arrival of Pizarro.

But the viceroy had profited by the recent delay to gain considerably on his pursuers. His road led across the valley of Caxas, a broad, uncultivated district, affording little sustenance for man or beast. Day after day, his troops held on their march through this dreary region, intersected with *barrancas* and rocky ravines that added incredibly to their toil. Their principal food was the parched corn, which usually formed the nourishment of the travelling Indians, though held of much less account by the Spaniards; and this meagre fare was reinforced by such herbs as they found on the way-side, which, for want of better utensils, the soldiers were fain to boil in their helmets. Carbajal, meanwhile, pressed on them so close, that their baggage, ammunition, and sometimes their mules, fell into his hands. The indefatigable warrior was always on their track, by day and by night, allowing them scarcely any repose. They spread no tent, and lay down in their arms, with their steeds standing saddled beside them; and hardly had the weary soldier closed his eyes, when he was startled by the cry that the enemy was upon him.

At length, the harassed followers of Blasco Nuñez reached the *depoblado*, or desert of Paltos, which stretches towards the north for many a dreary league. The ground, intersected by numerous streams, has the character of a great quagmire, and men and horses floundered about in the stagnant waters, or with difficulty worked their way over the marsh, or opened a passage through the tangled underwood that shot up in rank luxuriance from the surface. The way-worn horses, without food, except such as they could pick up in the wilderness, were often spent with travel, and, becoming unserviceable, were left to die on the road, with their hamstrings cut, that they might be of no use to the enemy; though more frequently they were despatched to afford a miserable banquet to their masters. Many of the men now fainted by the way from mere exhaustion, or loitered in the woods, unable to keep up with the march. And woe to the straggler who fell into the hands of Carbajal, at least if he had once belonged to the party of Pizarro. The mere suspicion of treason sealed his doom with the unrelenting soldier.

The sufferings of Pizarro and his troop were scarcely less than those of the viceroy; though they were somewhat mitigated by the natives of the country, who, with ready instinct, discerned which party was the strongest, and, of course, the most to be feared. But, with every alleviation, the chieftain's sufferings were terrible. It was repeating the dismal scenes of the expedition to the Amazon. The soldiers of the Conquest must be admitted to have purchased their triumphs dearly.

Yet the viceroy had one source of disquietude, greater, perhaps, than any arising from physical suffering. This was the distrust of his own followers. There were several of the principal cavaliers in his suite whom he suspected of being in correspondence with the enemy, and even of designing to betray him into their hands. He was so well convinced of this, that he caused two of these officers to be put to death on the march; and their dead bodies, as they lay by the roadside, meeting the eye of the soldier, told him that there were others to be feared in these frightful solitudes besides the enemy in his rear.

Another cavalier, who held the chief command under the viceroy, was executed, after a more formal investigation of his case, at the first place where the army halted. At this distance of time, it is impossible to determine how far the suspicions of Blasco Nuñez were founded on truth. The judgments of contemporaries are at variance. In times of political ferment, the opinion of the writer is generally determined by the complexion of his party. To judge from the character of Blasco Nuñez, jealous and irritable, we might suppose him to have acted without sufficient cause. But this consideration is counterbalanced by that of the facility with which his followers swerved from their allegiance to their commander, who seems to have had so light a hold on their affections, that they were shaken off by the least reverse of fortune. Whether his suspicions were well or ill founded, the effect was the same on the mind of the viceroy. With an enemy in his rear whom he dared not fight, and followers whom he dared not trust, the cup of his calamities was nearly full.

At length, he issued forth on firm ground, and, passing through Tomebamba, Blasco Nuñez reëntered his northern capital of Quito. But his reception was not so cordial as that which he had before experienced. He now came as a fugitive, with a formidable enemy in pursuit; and he was soon made to feel that the surest way to receive support is not to need it.

Shaking from his feet the dust of the disloyal city, whose superstitious people were alive to many an omen that boded his approaching ruin, the unfortunate commander held on his way towards Pastos, in the jurisdiction of Benalcazar. Pizarro and his forces entered Quito not long after, disappointed, that, with all his diligence, the enemy still eluded his pursuit. He halted only to breathe his men, and, declaring that "he would follow up the viceroy to the North Sea but he would overtake him," he resumed his march. At Pastos, he nearly accomplished his object. His advance-guard came up with Blasco Nuñez as the latter was halting on the opposite bank of a rivulet. Pizarro's men, fainting from toil and heat, staggered feebly to the water-side, to slake their burning thirst, and it would have been easy for the viceroy's troops, refreshed by repose, and superior in number to their foes, to have routed them. But Blasco Nuñez could not bring his soldiers to the charge. They had fled so long before their enemy, that the mere sight of him filled their hearts with panic, and they would have no more thought of turning against him than the hare would turn against the hound that pursues her. Their safety, they felt, was to fly, not to fight, and they profited by the exhaustion of their pursuers only to quicken their retreat.

Gonzalo Pizarro continued the chase some leagues beyond Pastos; when, finding himself carried farther than he desired into the territories of Benalcazar, and not caring to encounter this formidable captain at disadvantage, he came to a halt, and, notwithstanding his magnificent vaunt about the North Sea, ordered a retreat, and made a rapid countermarch on Quito. Here he found occupation in repairing the wasted spirits of his troops, and in strengthening himself with fresh rein-forcements, which much increased his numbers; though these were again diminished by a body that he detached under Carbajal to suppress an insurrection, which he now learned had broken out in the south. It was headed by Diego Centeno, one of his own officers, whom he had established in La Plata, the inhabitants of which place had joined in the revolt and raised the standard for the Crown. With the rest of his forces, Pizarro resolved to remain at Quito, waiting the hour when the viceroy would reënter his dominions; as the tiger crouches by some spring in the wilderness, patiently waiting the return of his victims.

Meanwhile Blasco Nuñez had pushed forward his retreat to Popayan, the capital of Benalcazar's province. Here he was kindly received by the people; and his soldiers, reduced by desertion and disease to one fifth of their original number, rested from the unparalleled fatigues of a march which had continued for more than two hundred leagues. It was not long before he was joined by Cabrera, Benalcazar's lieutenant, with a stout reinforcement, and, soon after, by that chieftain himself. His whole force now amounted to near four hundred men, most of them in good condition, and well trained in the school of American warfare. His own men were sorely deficient both in arms and ammunition; and he set about repairing the want by building furnaces for manufacturing arquebuses and pikes.—One familiar with the history of these times is surprised to see the readiness with which the Spanish adventurers turned their hands to various trades and handicrafts usually requiring a long apprenticeship. They displayed the dexterity so necessary to settlers in a new country, where every man must become in some degree his own artisan. But this state of things, however favorable to the ingenuity of the artist, is not very propitious to the advancement of the art; and there can be little doubt that the weapons thus made by the soldiers of Blasco Nuñez were of the most rude and imperfect construction.

As week after week rolled away, Gonzalo Pizarro, though fortified with the patience of a Spanish soldier, felt uneasy at the protracted stay of Blasco Nuñez in the north, and he resorted to stratagem to decoy him from his retreat. He marched out of Quito with the greater part of his forces, pretending that he was going to support his lieutenants in the south, while he left a garrison in the city under the command of Puelles, the same officer who had formerly deserted from the viceroy. These tidings he took care should be conveyed to the enemy's camp. The artifice succeeded as he wished. Blasco Nuñez and his followers, confident in their superiority over Puelles, did not hesitate for a moment to profit by the supposed absence of Pizarro. Abandoning Popayan, the viceroy, early in January, 1546, moved by rapid marches towards the south. But before he reached the place of his destination, he became apprised of the snare into which he had been drawn. He communicated the fact to his officers; but he had already suffered so much from suspense, that his only desire now was, to bring his quarrel with Pizarro to the final arbitrament of arms.

That chief, meanwhile, had been well informed, through his spies, of the viceroy's movements. On learning the departure of the latter from Popayan, he had reëntered Quito, joined his forces with those of Puelles, and, issuing from the capital, had taken up a strong position about three leagues to the north, on a high ground that commanded a stream, across which the enemy must pass. It was not long before the latter came in sight, and Blasco Nuñez, as night beagn to fall, established himself on the opposite bank of the rivulet. It was so near to the enemy's quarters, that the voices of the sentinels could be distinctly heard in the opposite camps, and they did not fail to salute one another with the epithet of "traitors." In these civil wars, as we have seen, each party claimed for itself the exclusive merit of loyalty.

But Benalcazar soon saw that Pizarro's position was too strong to be assailed with any chance of success. He proposed, therefore, to the viceroy, to draw off his forces secretly in the night; and, making a détour round the hills, to fall on the enemy's rear, where he would be least prepared to receive them. The counsel was approved; and, no sooner were the two hosts shrouded from each other's eyes by the darkness, than, leaving his camp-fires burning to deceive the enemy, Blasco Nuñez broke up his quarters, and began his circuitous march in the direction of Quito. But either he had been misinformed, or his guides misled him; for the roads proved so impracticable, that he was compelled to make a circuit of such extent, that dawn broke before he drew near the point of attack. Finding that he must now abandon the advantage of a surprise, he pressed forward to Quito, where he arrived with men and horses sorely fatigued by a night-march of eight leagues, from a point which, by the direct route, would not have exceeded three. It was a fatal error on the eve of an engagement.

He found the capital nearly deserted by the men. They had all joined the standard of Pizarro; for they had now caught the general spirit of disaffection, and looked upon that chief as their protector from the oppressive ordinances. Pizarro was the representative of the people. Greatly moved at this desertion, the unhappy viceroy, lifting his hands to heaven, exclaimed,— "Is it thus, Lord, that thou abandonest thy servants?" The women and children came out, and in vain offered him food, of which he stood obviously in need, asking him, at the same time, "Why he had come there to die?" His followers, with more indifference than their commander, entered the houses of the inhabitants, and unceremoniously appropriated whatever they could find to appease the cravings of appetite.

Benalcazar, who saw the temerity of giving battle, in their present condition, recommended the viceroy to try the effect of negotiation, and offered himself to go to the enemy's camp, and arrange, if possible, terms of accommodation with Pizarro. But Blasco Nuñez, if he had desponded for a moment, had now recovered his wonted constancy, and he proudly replied,— "There is no faith to be kept with traitors. We have come to fight, not to parley; and we must do our duty like good and loyal cavaliers. I will do mine," he continued, "and be assured I will be the first man to break a lance with the enemy."

He then called his troops together, and addressed to them a few words preparatory to marching. "You are all brave men," he said, "and loyal to your sovereign. For my own part, I hold life as little in comparison with my duty to my prince. Yet let us not distrust our success; the Spaniard, in a good cause, has often overcome greater odds than these. And we are fighting for the right; it is the cause of God,—the cause of God," he concluded, and the soldiers, kindled by his generous ardor, answered him with huzzas that went to the head of the unfortunate commander, little accustomed of late to this display of enthusiasm.

It was the eighteenth of January, 1546, when Blasco Nuñez marched out at the head of his array, from the ancient city of Quito. He had proceeded but a mile, when he came in view of the enemy, formed along the crest of some high lands, which, by a gentle swell, rose gradually from the plains of Añaquito. Gonzalo Pizarro, greatly chagrined on ascertaining the departure of the viceroy, early in the morning, had broken up his camp, and directed his march on the capital, fully resolved that his enemy should not escape him.

The viceroy's troops, now coming to a halt, were formed in order of battle. A small body of arquebusiers was stationed in the advance to begin the fight. The remainder of that corps was distributed among the spearmen, who occupied the centre, protected on the flanks by the horse drawn up in two nearly equal squadrons. The cavalry amounted to about one hundred and forty, being little inferior to that on the other side, though the whole number of the viceroy's forces, being less than four hundred, did not much exceed the half of his rival's. On the right, and in front of the royal banner, Blasco Nuñez, supported by thirteen chosen cavaliers, took his station, prepared to head the attack.

Pizarro had formed his troops in a corresponding manner with that of his adversary. They mustered about seven hundred in all, well appointed, in good condition, and officered by the best knights in Peru. As, notwithstanding his superiority of numbers, Pizarro did not seem inclined to abandon his advantageous position, Blasco Nuñez gave orders to advance. The action commenced with the arquebusiers, and in a few moments the dense clouds of smoke, rolling over the field, obscured every object; for it was late in the day when the action began, and the light was rapidly fading.

The infantry, now levelling their pikes, advanced under cover of the smoke, and were soon hotly engaged with the opposite files of spearmen. Then came the charge of the cavalry, which—notwithstanding they were thrown into some disorder by the fire of Pizarro's arquebusiers, far superior in number to their own—was conducted with such spirit that the enemy's horse were compelled to reel and fall back before it. But it was only to recoil with greater violence, as, like an overwhelming wave, Pizarro's troopers rushed on their foes, driving them along the slope, and bearing down man and horse in indiscriminate ruin. Yet these, in turn, at length rallied, cheered on by the cries and desperate efforts of their officers. The lances were shivered, and they fought hand to hand with swords and battle-axes mingled together in wild confusion. But the struggle was of no long duration; for, though the numbers were nearly equal, the viceroy's cavalry, jaded by the severe march of the previous night, were no match for their antagonists. The ground was strewn with the wreck of their bodies; and horses and riders, the dead and the dying, lay heaped on one another. Cabrera, the brave lieutenant of Benalcazar, was slain, and that commander was thrown under his horse's feet, covered with wounds, and left for dead on the field. Alvarez, the judge, was mortally wounded. Both he and his colleague Cepeda were in the action, though ranged on opposite sides, fighting as if they had been bred to arms, not to the profession of the law.

Yet Blasco Nuñez and his companions maintained a brave struggle on the right of the field. The viceroy had kept his word by being the first to break his lance against the enemy, and by a well-directed blow had borne a cavalier, named Alonso de Montalvo, clean out of his saddle. But he was at length overwhelmed by numbers, and, as his companions, one after another, fell by his side, he was left nearly unprotected. He was already wounded, when a blow on the head from the battle-axe of a soldier struck him from his horse, and he fell stunned on the ground. Had his person been known, he might have been taken alive, but he wore a sobre-vest of Indian cotton over his armour, which concealed the military order of St. James, and the other badges of his rank.

His person, however, was soon recognized by one of Pizarro's followers, who, not improbably, had once followed the viceroy's banner. The soldier immediately pointed him out to the Licentiate Carbajal. This person was the brother of the cavalier whom, as the reader may remember, Blasco Nuñez had so rashly put to death in his palace at Lima. The licentiate had afterwards taken service under Pizarro, and, with several of his kindred, was pledged to take vengeance on the viceroy. Instantly riding up, he taunted the fallen commander with the murder of his brother, and was in the act of dismounting to despatch him with his own hand, when Puelles remonstrating on this, as an act of degradation, commanded one of his attendants, a black slave, to cut off the viceroy's head. This the fellow executed with a single stroke of his sabre, while the wretched man, perhaps then dying of his wounds, uttered no word, but with eyes imploringly turned up towards heaven, received the fatal blow. The head was then borne aloft on a pike, and some were brutal enough to pluck out the grey hairs from the beard and set them in their caps, as grisly trophies of their victory. The fate of the day was now decided. Yet still the infantry made a brave stand, keeping Pizarro's horse at bay with their bristling array of pikes. But their numbers were thinned by the arquebusiers; and, thrown into disorder, they could no longer resist the onset of the horse, who broke into their column, and soon scattered and drove them off the ground. The pursuit was neither long nor bloody; for darkness came on, and Pizarro bade his trumpets sound, to call his men together under their banners.

Though the action lasted but a short time, nearly one third of the viceroy's troops had perished. The loss of their opponents was inconsiderable. Several of the vanquished cavaliers took refuge in the churches of Quito. But they were dragged from the sanctuary, and some—probably those who had once espoused the cause of Pizarro—were led to execution, and others banished to Chili. The greater part were pardoned by the Conqueror. Benalcazar, who recovered from his wounds, was permitted to return to his government, on condition of no more bearing arms against Pizarro. His troops were invited to take service under the banner of the victor, who, however, never treated them with the confidence shown to his ancient partisans. He was greatly displeased at the indignities offered to the viceroy; whose mangled remains he caused to be buried with the honors due to his rank in the cathedral of Quito. Gonzalo Pizarro, attired in black, walked as chief mourner in the procession.—It was usual with Pizarros, as we have seen, to pay these obituary honors to their victims.

Such was the sad end of Blasco Nuñez Vela, first viceroy of Peru. It was less than two years since he had set foot in the country, a period of unmitigated disaster and disgrace. His misfortunes may be imputed partly to circumstances, and partly to his own character. The minister of an odious and oppressive law, he was intrusted with no discretionary power in the execution of it. Yet every man may, to a certain extent, claim the right to such a power; since, to execute a commission, which circumstances show must certainly defeat the object for which it was designed, would be absurd. But it requires sagacity to determine the existence of such a contingency, and moral courage to assume the responsibility of acting on it. Such a crisis is the severest test of character. To dare to disobey from a paramount sense of duty is a paradox that a little soul can hardly comprehend. Unfortunately, Blasco Nuñez was a pedantic martinet, a man of narrow views, who could not feel himself authorized under any circumstances to swerve from the letter of the law. Puffed up by his brief authority

moreover, he considered opposition to the ordinances as treason to himself; and thus, identifying himself with his commission, he was prompted by personal feelings, quite as much as
by those of a public and patriotic nature.

Neither was the viceroy's character of a kind that tended to
mitigate the odium of his measures, and reconcile the people
to their execution. It afforded a strong contrast to that of his
rival, Pizarro, whose frank, chivalrous bearing, and generous
confidence in his followers, made him universally popular,
blinding their judgments, and giving to the worse the semblance of the better cause. Blasco Nuñez, on the contrary, irritable and suspicious, placed himself in a false position with all
whom he approached; for a suspicious temper creates an
atmosphere of distrust around it that kills every kindly affec-
tion. His first step was to alienate the members of the Audience who were sent to act in concert with him. But this was
their fault as well as his, since they were as much too lax, as
he was too severe, in the interpretation of the law. He next
alienated and outraged the people whom he was appointed to
govern. And, lastly, he disgusted his own friends, and too often
turned them into enemies; so that, in his final struggle for
power and for existence, he was obliged to rely on the arm of
the stranger. Yet in the catalogue of his qualities we must not
pass in silence over his virtues. There are two to the credit of
which he is undeniably entitled,—a loyalty, which shone the
brighter amidst the general defection around him, and a
constancy under misfortune, which might challenge the respect even of his enemies. But with the most liberal allowance
for his merits, it can scarcely be doubted that a person more
incompetent to the task assigned him could not have been
found in Castile.

The victory of Añaquito was received with general joy in
the neighboring capital; all the cities of Peru looked on it as
sealing the downfall of the detested ordinances, and the name
of Gonzalo Pizarro was sounded from one end of the country
to the other as that of its deliverer. That chief continued to
prolong his stay in Quito during the wet season, dividing his
time between the licentious pleasures of the reckless adventurer and the cares of business that now pressed on him as

ruler of the state. His administration was stained with fewer acts of violence than might have been expected from the circumstances of his situation. So long as Carbajal, the counsellor in whom he unfortunately placed greatest reliance, was absent, Gonzalo sanctioned no execution, it was observed, but according to the forms of law. He rewarded his followers by new grants of land, and detached several on expeditions, to no greater distance, however, than would leave it in his power readily to recall them. He made various provisions for the welfare of the natives, and some, in particular, for instructing them in the Christian faith. He paid attention to the faithful collection of the royal dues, urging on the colonists that they should deport themselves so as to conciliate the good-will of the Crown, and induce a revocation of the ordinances. His administration, in short, was so conducted, that even the austere Gasca, his successor, allowed "it was a good government,—for a tyrant."

At length, in July, 1546, the new governor bade adieu to Quito, and, leaving there a sufficient garrison under his officer Puelles, began his journey to the south. It was a triumphal progress, and everywhere he was received on the road with enthusiasm by the people. At Truxillo, the citizens came out in a body to welcome him, and the clergy chanted anthems in his honor, extolling him as the "victorious prince," and imploring the Almighty "to lengthen his days, and give him honor." At Lima, it was proposed to clear away some of the buildings, and open a new street for his entrance, which might ever after bear the name of the victor. But the politic chieftain declined this flattering tribute, and modestly preferred to enter the city by the usual way. A procession was formed of the citizens, the soldiers, and the clergy, and Pizarro made his entry into the capital with two of his principal captains on foot, holding the reins of his charger, while the archbishop of Lima, and the bishops of Cuzco, Quito, and Bogotá, the last of whom had lately come to the city to be consecrated, rode by his side. The streets were strewn with boughs, the walls of the houses hung with showy tapestries, and triumphal arches were thrown over the way in honor of the victor. Every balcony, veranda, and house-top was crowded with spectators, who sent up huzzas, loud and long, saluting the victorious soldier with the titles of "Liberator, and Protector of the People." The bells rang out their joyous peal, as on his former entrance into the capital; and amidst strains of enlivening music, and the blithe sounds of jubilee, Gonzalo held on his way to the palace of his brother. Peru was once more placed under the dynasty of the Pizarros.

Deputies came from different parts of the country, tending the congratulations of their respective cities; and every one eagerly urged his own claims to consideration for the services he had rendered in the revolution. Pizarro, at the same time, received the welcome intelligence of the success of his arms in the south. Diego Centeno, as before stated, had there raised the standard of rebellion, or rather, of loyalty to his sovereign. He had made himself master of La Plata, and the spirit of insurrection had spread over the broad province of Charcas. Carbajal, who had been sent against him from Quito, after repairing to Lima, had passed at once to Cuzco, and there, strengthening his forces, had descended by rapid marches on the refractory district. Centeno did not trust himself in the field against this formidable champion. He retreated with his troops into the fastnesses of the sierra. Carbajal pursued, following on his track with the pertinacity of a bloodhound; over mountain and moor, through forests and dangerous ravines, allowing him no respite, by day or by night. Eating, drinking, sleeping in his saddle, the veteran, eighty years of age, saw his own followers tire one after another, while he urged on the chase, like the wild huntsman of Bürger, as if endowed with an unearthly frame, incapable of fatigue! During this terrible pursuit, which continued for more than two hundred leagues over a savage country, Centeno found himself abandoned by most of his followers. Such of them as fell into Carbajal's hands were sent to speedy execution, for that inexorable chief had no mercy on those who had been false to their party. At length, Centeno, with a handful of men, arrived on the borders of the Pacific, and there, separating from one another, they provided, each in the best way he could, for their own safety. Their leader found an asylum in a cave in the mountains, where he was secretly fed by an Indian curaca, till the time again came for him to unfurl the standard of revolt.

Carbajal, after some further decisive movements, which fully established the ascendency of Pizarro over the south, returned in triumph to La Plata. There he occupied himself with working the silver mines of Potosí, in which a vein, recently opened, promised to make richer returns than any yet discovered in Mexico or Peru; and he was soon enabled to send large remittances to Lima, deducting no stinted commission for himself,—for the cupidity of the lieutenant was equal to his cruelty.

Gonzalo Pizarro was now undisputed master of Peru. From Quito to the northern confines of Chili, the whole country acknowledged his authority. His fleet rode triumphant on the Pacific, and gave him the command of every city and hamlet on its borders. His admiral, Hinojosa, a discreet and gallant officer, had secured him Panamá, and, marching across the Isthmus, had since obtained for him the possession of Nombre de Dios,—the principal key of communication with Europe. His forces were on an excellent footing, including the flower of the warriors who had fought under his brother, and who now eagerly rallied under the name of Pizarro; while the tide of wealth that flowed in from the mines of Potosí supplied him with the resources of an European monarch.

The new governor now began to assume a state correspondent with his full-blown fortunes. He was attended by a bodyguard of eighty soldiers. He dined always in public, and usually with not less than a hundred guests at table. He even affected, it was said, the most decided etiquette of royalty, giving his hand to be kissed, and allowing no one, of whatever rank, to be seated in his presence. But this is denied by others. It would not be strange that a vain man like Pizarro, with a superficial, undisciplined mind, when he saw himself thus raised from an humble condition to the highest post in the land, should be somewhat intoxicated by the possession of power, and treat with superciliousness those whom he had once approached with deference. But one who had often seen him in his prosperity assures us, that it was not so, and that the governor continued to show the same frank and soldier-like bearing as before his elevation, mingling on familiar terms with his comrades, and displaying the same qualities which had hitherto endeared him to the people.

However this may be, it is certain there were not wanting those who urged him to throw off his allegiance to the Crown, and set up an independent government for himself. Among these was his lieutenant, Carbajal, whose daring spirit never shrunk from following things to their consequences. He plainly counselled Pizarro to renounce his allegiance at once. "In fact, you have already done so," he said. "You have been in arms against a viceroy, have driven him from the country, beaten and slain him in battle. What favor, or even mercy, can you expect from the Crown? You have gone too far either to halt, or to recede. You must go boldly on, proclaim yourself king; the troops, the people, will support you." And he concluded, it is said, by advising him to marry the Coya, the female representative of the Incas, that the two races might henceforth repose in quiet under a common sceptre!

The advice of the bold counsellor was, perhaps, the most politic that could have been given to Pizarro under existing circumstances. For he was like one who had heedlessly climbed far up a dizzy precipice,—too far to descend safely, while he had no sure hold where he was. His only chance was to climb still higher, till he had gained the summit. But Gonzalo Pizarro shrunk from the attitude, in which this placed him, of avowed rebellion. Notwithstanding the criminal course into which he had been, of late, seduced, the sentiment of loyalty was too deeply implanted in his bosom to be wholly eradicated. Though in arms against the measures and ministers of his sovereign, he was not prepared to raise the sword against that sovereign himself. He, doubtless, had conflicting emotions in his bosom; like Macbeth, and many a less noble nature,

> "Would not play false,
> And yet would wrongly win."

And however grateful to his vanity might be the picture of the air-drawn sceptre thus painted to his imagination, he had not the audacity—we may, perhaps, say, the criminal ambition —to attempt to grasp it.

Even at this very moment, when urged to this desperate extremity, he was preparing a mission to Spain, in order to vindicate the course he had taken, and to solicit an amnesty for the past, with a full confirmation of his authority, as successor to his brother in the government of Peru.—Pizarro did not read the future with the calm, prophetic eye of Carbajal.

BOOK V

SETTLEMENT OF THE COUNTRY

CHAPTER I [1545–1547]

GREAT SENSATION IN SPAIN—PEDRO DE LA GASCA—HIS
EARLY LIFE—HIS MISSION TO PERU—HIS POLITIC CON-
DUCT—HIS OFFERS TO PIZARRO—GAINS THE FLEET

While the important revolution detailed in the preceding
pages was going forward in Peru, rumors of it, from time to
time, found their way to the mother-country; but the distance
was so great, and opportunities for communication so rare, that
the tidings were usually very long behind the occurrence of the
events to which they related. The government heard with dismay of the troubles caused by the ordinances and the intem-
perate conduct of the viceroy; and it was not long before it
learned that this functionary was deposed and driven from his
capital, while the whole country, under Gonzalo Pizarro, was
arrayed in arms against him. All classes were filled with consternation at this alarming intelligence; and many that had before approved the ordinances now loudly condemned the
ministers, who, without considering the inflammable temper
of the people, had thus rashly fired a train which menaced a
general explosion throughout the colonies. No such rebellion,
within the memory of man, had occurred in the Spanish empire. It was compared with the famous war of the *comunidades*, in the beginning of Charles the Fifth's reign. But the
Peruvian insurrection seemed the more formidable of the two.
The troubles of Castile, being under the eye of the Court,
might be the more easily managed; while it was difficult to
make the same power felt on the remote shores of the Indies.
Lying along the distant Pacific, the principle of attraction
which held Peru to the parent country was so feeble, that this
colony might, at any time, with a less impulse than that now
given to it, fly from its political orbit. It seemed as if the fairest
of its jewels was about to fall from the imperial diadem!
Such was the state of things in the summer of 1545, when

Charles the Fifth was absent in Germany, occupied with the religious troubles of the empire. The government was in the hands of his son, who, under the name of Philip the Second, was soon to sway the sceptre over the largest portion of his father's dominions, and who was then holding his court at Valladolid. He called together a council of prelates, jurists, and military men of greatest experience, to deliberate on the measures to be pursued for restoring order in the colonies. All agreed in regarding Pizarro's movement in the light of an audacious rebellion; and there were few, at first, who were not willing to employ the whole strength of government to vindicate the honor of the Crown,—to quell the insurrection, and bring the authors of it to punishment.

But, however desirable this might appear, a very little reflection showed that it was not easy to be done, if, indeed, it were practicable. The great distance of Peru required troops to be transported not merely across the ocean, but over the broad extent of the great continent. And how was this to be effected, when the principal ports, the keys of communication with the country, were in the hands of the rebels, while their fleet rode in the Pacific, the mistress of its waters, cutting off all approach to the coast? Even if a Spanish force could be landed in Peru, what chance would it have, unaccustomed, as it would be, to the country and the climate, of coping with the veterans of Pizarro, trained to war in the Indies and warmly attached to the person of their commander? The new levies thus sent out might become themselves infected with the spirit of insurrection, and cast off their own allegiance.

Nothing remained, therefore, but to try conciliatory measures. The government, however mortifying to its pride, must retrace its steps. A free grace must be extended to those who submitted, and such persuasive arguments should be used, and such politic concessions made, as would convince the refractory colonists that it was their interest, as well as their duty, to return to their allegiance.

But to approach the people in their present state of excitement, and to make those concessions without too far compromising the dignity and permanent authority of the Crown, was a delicate matter, for the success of which they must rely wholly on the character of the agent. After much deliberation, a competent person, as it was thought, was found in an ecclesiastic, by the name of Pedro de la Gasca,—a name which, brighter by contrast with the gloomy times in which it first appeared, still shines with undiminished splendor after the lapse of ages.

Pedro de la Gasca was born, probably, towards the close of the fifteenth century, in a small village in Castile, named Barco de Avila. He came, both by father's and mother's side, from an ancient and noble lineage; ancient indeed, if, as his biographers contend, he derived his descent from Gasca, one of the conspirators against Julius Cæsar! Having the misfortune to lose his father early in life, he was placed by his uncle in the famous seminary of Alcalá de Henares, founded by the great Ximénes. Here he made rapid proficiency in liberal studies, especially in those connected with his profession, and at length received the degree of Master of Theology.

The young man, however, discovered other talents than those demanded by his sacred calling. The war of the *comunidades* was then raging in the country; and the authorities of his college showed a disposition to take the popular side. But Gasca, putting himself at the head of an armed force, seized one of the gates of the city, and, with assistance from the royal troops, secured the place to the interests of the Crown. This early display of loyalty was probably not lost on his vigilant sovereign.

From Alcalá, Gasca was afterwards removed to Salamanca; where he distinguished himself by his skill in scholastic disputation, and obtained the highest academic honors in that ancient university, the fruitful nursery of scholarship and genius. He was subsequently intrusted with the management of some important affairs of an ecclesiastical nature, and made a member of the Council of the Inquisition.

In this latter capacity he was sent to Valencia, about 1540, to examine into certain alleged cases of heresy in that quarter of the country. These were involved in great obscurity, and, although Gasca had the assistance of several eminent jurists in the investigation, it occupied him nearly two years. In the conduct of this difficult matter, he showed so much penetration, and such perfect impartiality, that he was appointed by the Cortes of Valencia to the office of *visitador* of that kingdom;

a highly responsible post, requiring great discretion in the person who filled it, since it was his province to inspect the condition of the courts of justice and of finance, throughout the land, with authority to reform abuses. It was proof of extraordinary consideration, that it should have been bestowed on Gasca; since it was a departure from the established usage—and that in a nation most wedded to usage—to confer the office on any but a subject of the Aragonese crown.

Gasca executed the task assigned to him with independence and ability. While he was thus occupied, the people of Valencia were thrown into consternation by a meditated invasion of the French and the Turks, who, under the redoubtable Barbarossa, menaced the coast and the neighboring Balearic isles. Fears were generally entertained of a rising of the Morisco population; and the Spanish officers who had command in that quarter, being left without the protection of a navy, despaired of making head against the enemy. In this season of general panic, Gasca alone appeared calm and self-possessed. He remonstrated with the Spanish commanders on their unsoldier-like despondency; encouraged them to confide in the loyalty of the Moriscos; and advised the immediate erection of fortifications along the shores for their protection. He was, in consequence, named one of a commission to superintend these works, and to raise levies for defending the sea-coast; and so faithfully was the task performed, that Barbarossa, after some ineffectual attempts to make good his landing, was baffled at all points, and compelled to abandon the enterprise as hopeless. The chief credit of this resistance must be assigned to Gasca, who superintended the construction of the defences, and who was enabled to contribute a large part of the requisite funds by the economical reforms he had introduced into the administration of Valencia.

It was at this time, the latter part of the year 1545, that the council of Philip selected Gasca as the person most competent to undertake the perilous mission to Peru. His character, indeed, seemed especially suited to it. His loyalty had been shown through his whole life. With great suavity of manners he combined the most intrepid resolution. Though his demeanor was humble, as beseemed his calling, it was far from abject; for he was sustained by a conscious rectitude of pur-

pose, that impressed respect on all with whom he had intercourse. He was acute in his perceptions, had a shrewd knowledge of character, and, though bred to the cloister, possessed
an acquaintance with affairs, and even with military science,
such as was to have been expected only from one reared in
courts and camps.

Without hesitation, therefore, the council unanimously recommended him to the emperor, and requested his approbation
of their proceedings. Charles had not been an inattentive ob-
server of Gasca's course. His attention had been particularly
called to the able manner in which he had conducted the judicial process against the heretics of Valencia. The monarch saw,
at once, that he was the man for the present emergency; and
he immediately wrote to him, with his own hand, expressing
his entire satisfaction at the appointment, and intimating his
purpose to testify his sense of his worth by preferring him to
one of the principal sees then vacant.

Gasca accepted the important mission now tendered to him
without hesitation; and, repairing to Madrid, received the instructions of the government as to the course to be pursued.
They were expressed in the most benign and conciliatory tone,
perfectly in accordance with the suggestions of his own benevolent temper. But, while he commended the tone of the instructions, he considered the powers with which he was to be
intrusted as wholly incompetent to their object. They were conceived in the jealous spirit with which the Spanish government
usually limited the authority of its great colonial officers, whose
distance from home gave peculiar cause for distrust. On every
strange and unexpected emergency, Gasca saw that he should
be obliged to send back for instructions. This must cause delay,
where promptitude was essential to success. The Court, moreover, as he represented to the council, was, from its remote-
ness from the scene of action, utterly incompetent to pronounce as to the expediency of the measures to be pursued.
Some one should be sent out in whom the king could implicitly
confide, and who should be invested with powers competent
to every emergency; powers not merely to decide on what was
best, but to carry that decision into execution; and he boldly
demanded that he should go not only as the representative of
the sovereign, but clothed with all the authority of the sover-

eign himself. Less than this would defeat the very object for which he was to be sent. "For myself," he concluded, "I ask neither salary nor compensation of any kind. I covet no display of state or military array. With my stole and breviary I trust to do the work that is committed to me. Infirm as I am in body, the repose of my own home would have been more grateful to me than this dangerous mission; but I will not shrink from it at the bidding of my sovereign, and if, as is very probable, I may not be permitted again to see my native land, I shall, at least, be cheered by the consciousness of having done my best to serve its interests."

The members of the council, while they listened with admiration to the disinterested avowal of Gasca, were astounded by the boldness of his demands. Not that they distrusted the purity of his motives, for these were above suspicion. But the powers for which he stipulated were so far beyond those hitherto delegated to a colonial viceroy, that they felt they had no warrant to grant them. They even shrank from soliciting them from the emperor, and required that Gasca himself should address the monarch, and state precisely the grounds on which demands so extraordinary were founded.

Gasca readily adopted the suggestion, and wrote in the most full and explicit manner to his sovereign, who had then transferred his residence to Flanders. But Charles was not so tenacious, or, at least, so jealous, of authority, as his ministers. He had been too long in possession of it to feel that jealousy; and, indeed, many years were not to elapse, before, oppressed by its weight, he was to resign it altogether into the hands of his son. His sagacious mind, moreover, readily comprehended the difficulties of Gasca's position. He felt that the present extraordinary crisis was to be met only by extraordinary measures. He assented to the force of his vassal's arguments, and, on the sixteenth of February, 1546, wrote him another letter expressive of his approbation, and intimated his willingness to grant him powers as absolute as those he had requested.

Gasca was to be styled President of the Royal Audience. But, under this simple title, he was placed at the head of every department in the colony, civil, military, and judicial. He was empowered to make new *repartimientos*, and to confirm those already made. He might declare war, levy troops, appoint to all offices, or remove from them, at pleasure. He might exercise the royal prerogative of pardoning offences, and was especially authorized to grant an amnesty to all, without exception, implicated in the present rebellion. He was, moreover, to proclaim at once the revocation of the odious ordinances. These two last provisions might be said to form the basis of all his operations.

Since ecclesiastics were not to be reached by the secular arm, and yet were often found fomenting troubles in the colonies, Gasca was permitted to banish from Peru such as he thought fit. He might even send home the viceroy, if the good of the country required it. Agreeably to his own suggestion, he was to receive no specified stipend; but he had unlimited orders on the treasuries both of Panamá and Peru. He was furnished with letters from the emperor to the principal authorities, not only in Peru, but in Mexico and the neighboring colonies, requiring their countenance and support; and, lastly, blank letters, bearing the royal signature, were delivered to him, which he was to fill up at his pleasure.

While the grant of such unbounded powers excited the warmest sentiments of gratitude in Gasca towards the sovereign who could repose in him so much confidence, it seems—which is more extraordinary—not to have raised corresponding feelings of envy in the courtiers. They knew well that it was not for himself that the good ecclesiastic had solicited them. On the contrary, some of the council were desirous that he should be preferred to the bishopric, as already promised him, before his departure; conceiving that he would thus go with greater authority than as an humble ecclesiastic, and fearing, moreover, that Gasca himself, were it omitted, might feel some natural disappointment. But the president hastened to remove these impressions. "The honor would avail me little," he said, "where I am going; and it would be manifestly wrong to appoint me to an office in the Church, while I remain at such a distance that I cannot discharge the duties of it. The consciousness of my insufficiency," he continued, "should I never return, would lie heavy on my soul in my last moments." The politic reluctance to accept the mitre has passed into a proverb. But there was no affectation here; and Gasca's friends, yielding to his arguments, forbore to urge the matter further.

The new president now went forward with his preparation. They were few and simple; for he was to be accompanied by a slender train of followers, among whom the most conspicuous was Alonso de Alvarado, the gallant officer who, as the reader may remember, long commanded under Francisco Pizarro. He had resided of late years at court; and now at Gasca's request accompanied him to Peru, where his presence might facilitate negotiations with the insurgents, while his military experience would prove no less valuable in case of an appeal to arms. Some delay necessarily occurred in getting ready his little squadron, and it was not till the 26th of May, 1546, that the president embarked at San Lucar for the New World.

After a prosperous voyage, and not a long one for that day, he landed, about the middle of July, at the port of Santa Martha. Here he received the astounding intelligence of the battle of Añaquito, of the defeat and death of the viceroy, and of the manner in which Gonzalo Pizarro had since established his absolute rule over the land. Although these events had occurred several months before Gasca's departure from Spain, yet, so imperfect was the intercourse, no tidings of them had then reached that country.

They now filled the president with great anxiety; as he reflected that the insurgents, after so atrocious an act as the slaughter of the viceroy, might well despair of grace, and become reckless of consequences. He was careful, therefore, to have it understood, that the date of his commission was subsequent to that of the fatal battle, and that it authorized an entire amnesty of all offences hitherto committed against the government.

Yet, in some points of view, the death of Blasco Nuñez might be regarded as an auspicious circumstance for the settlement of the country. Had he lived till Gasca's arrival, the latter would have been greatly embarrassed by the necessity of acting in concert with a person so generally detested in the colony, or by the unwelcome alternative of sending him back to Castile. The insurgents, moreover, would, in all probability, be now more amenable to reason, since all personal animosity might naturally be buried in the grave of their enemy.

The president was much embarrassed by deciding in what quarter he should attempt to enter Peru. Every port was in the hands of Pizarro, and was placed under the care of his officers, with strict charge to intercept any communications from Spain, and to detain such persons as bore a commission from that country until his pleasure could be known respecting them. Gasca, at length, decided on crossing over to Nombre de Dios, then held with a strong force by Hernan Mexia, an officer to whose charge Gonzalo had committed this strong gate to his dominions, as to a person on whose attachment to his cause he could confidently rely.

Had Gasca appeared off this place in a menacing attitude, with a military array, or, indeed, with any display of official pomp that might have awakened distrust in the commander, he would doubtless have found it no easy matter to effect a landing. But Mexia saw nothing to apprehend in the approach of a poor ecclesiastic, without an armed force, with hardly even a retinue to support him, coming solely, as it seemed, on an errand of mercy. No sooner, therefore, was he acquainted with the character of the envoy, and his mission, than he prepared to receive him with the honors due to his rank, and marched out at the head of his soldiers, together with a considerable body of ecclesiastics resident in the place. There was nothing in the person of Gasca, still less in his humble clerical attire and modest retinue, to impress the vulgar spectator with feelings of awe or reverence. Indeed, the poverty-stricken aspect, as it seemed, of himself and his followers, so different from the usual state affected by the Indian viceroys, excited some merriment among the rude soldiery, who did not scruple to break their coarse jests on his appearance, in hearing of the president himself. "If this is the sort of governor his Majesty sends over to us," they exclaimed, "Pizarro need not trouble his head much about it."

Yet the president, far from being ruffled by this ribaldry, or from showing resentment to its authors, submitted to it with the utmost humility, and only seemed the more grateful to his own brethren, who, by their respectful demeanor, appeared anxious to do him honor.

But, however plain and unpretending the manners of Gasca, Mexia, on his first interview with him soon discovered that he had no common man to deal with. The president, after briefly explaining the nature of his commission, told him that he had come as a messenger of peace; and that it was on peaceful measures he relied for his success. He then stated the general scope of his commission, his authority to grant a free pardon to all, without exception, who at once submitted to government, and, finally, his purpose to proclaim the revocation of the ordinances. The objects of the revolution were thus attained. To contend longer would be manifest rebellion, and that without a motive; and he urged the commander by every principle of loyalty and patriotism to support him in settling the distractions of the country, and bringing it back to its allegiance.

The candid and conciliatory language of the president, so different from the arrogance of Blasco Nuñez, and the austere demeanor of Vaca de Castro, made a sensible impression on Mexia. He admitted the force of Gasca's reasoning, and flattered himself that Gonzalo Pizarro would not be insensible to it. Though attached to the fortunes of that leader, he was loyal in heart, and, like most of the party, had been led by accident, rather than by design, into rebellion; and now that so good an opportunity occurred to do it with safety, he was not unwilling to retrace his steps, and secure the royal favor by thus early returning to his allegiance. This he signified to the president, assuring him of his hearty coöperation in the good work of reform.

This was an important step for Gasca. It was yet more important for him to secure the obedience of Hinojosa, the governor of Panamá, in the harbor of which city lay Pizarro's navy, consisting of two-and-twenty vessels. But it was not easy to approach this officer. He was a person of much higher character than was usually found among the reckless adventurers in the New World. He was attached to the interests of Pizarro, and the latter had requited him by placing him in command of his armada and of Panamá, the key to his territories on the Pacific.

The president first sent Mexia and Alonso de Alvarado to prepare the way for his own coming, by advising Hinojosa of the purport of his mission. He soon after followed, and was received by that commander with every show of outward respect. But while the latter listened with deference to the representations of Gasca, they failed to work the change in him

which they had wrought in Mexia; and he concluded by asking the president to show him his powers, and by inquiring
whether they gave him authority to confirm Pizarro in his
present post, to which he was entitled no less by his own services than by the general voice of the people.

This was an embarrassing question. Such a concession would
have been altogether too humiliating to the Crown; but to
have openly avowed this at the present juncture to so stanch
an adherent of Pizarro might have precluded all further negotiation. The president evaded the question, therefore, by simply stating, that the time had not yet come for him to produce
his powers, but that Hinojosa might be assured they were such
as to secure an ample recompense to every loyal servant of
his country.

Hinojosa was not satisfied; and he immediately wrote to Pizarro, acquainting him with Gasca's arrival and with the object of his mission, at the same time plainly intimating his
own conviction that the president had no authority to confirm
him in the government. But before the departure of the ship,
Gasca secured the services of a Dominican friar, who had
taken his passage on board for one of the towns on the coast.
This man he intrusted with manifestos, setting forth the purport of his visit, and proclaiming the abolition of the ordinances, with a free pardon to all who returned to their obedience. He wrote, also, to the prelates and to the corporations of
the different cities. The former he requested to coöperate with
him in introducing a spirit of loyalty and subordination among
the people, while he intimated to the towns his purpose to
confer with them hereafter, in order to devise some effectual
measures for the welfare of the country. These papers the
Dominican engaged to distribute, himself, among the principal cities of the colony; and he faithfully kept his word,
though, as it proved, at no little hazard of his life. The seeds
thus scattered might many of them fall on barren ground. But
the greater part, the president trusted, would take root in the
hearts of the people; and he patiently waited for the harvest.

Meanwhile, though he failed to remove the scruples of
Hinojosa, the courteous manners of Gasca, and his mild, persuasive discourse, had a visible effect on other individuals with
whom he had daily intercourse. Several of these, and among

them some of the principal cavaliers in Panamá, as well as in the squadron, expressed their willingness to join the royal cause, and aid the president in maintaining it. Gasca profited by their assistance to open a communication with the authorities of Guatemala and Mexico, whom he advised of his mission, while he admonished them to allow no intercourse to be carried on with the insurgents on the coast of Peru. He, at length, also prevailed on the governor of Panamá to furnish him with the means of entering into communication with Gonzalo Pizarro himself; and a ship was despatched to Lima, bearing a letter from Charles the Fifth, addressed to that chief, with an epistle also from Gasca.

The emperor's communication was couched in the most condescending and even conciliatory terms. Far from taxing Gonzalo with rebellion, his royal master affected to regard his conduct as in a manner imposed on him by circumstances, especially by the obduracy of the viceroy Nuñez in denying the colonists the inalienable right of petition. He gave no intimation of an intent to confirm Pizarro in the government, or, indeed, to remove him from it; but simply referred him to Gasca as one who would acquaint him with the royal pleasure, and with whom he was to coöperate in restoring tranquillity to the country.

Gasca's own letter was pitched on the same politic key. He remarked, however, that the exigencies which had hitherto determined Gonzalo's line of conduct existed no longer. All that had been asked was conceded. There was nothing now to contend for; and it only remained for Pizarro and his followers to show their loyalty and the sincerity of their principles by obedience to the Crown. Hitherto, the president said, Pizarro had been in arms against the viceroy; and the people had supported him as against a common enemy. If he prolonged the contest, that enemy must be his sovereign. In such a struggle, the people would be sure to desert him; and Gasca conjured him, by his honor as a cavalier, and his duty as a loyal vassal, to respect the royal authority, and not rashly provoke a contest which must prove to the world that his conduct hitherto had been dictated less by patriotic motives than by selfish ambition.

This letter, which was conveyed in language the most courteous and complimentary to the subject of it, was of great length. It was accompanied by another much more concise, to Cepeda, the intriguing lawyer, who, as Gasca knew, had the greatest influence over Pizarro, in the absence of Carbajal, then employed in reaping the silver harvest from the newly discovered mines of Potosí. In this epistle, Gasca affected to defer to the cunning politician as a member of the Royal Audience, and he conferred with him on the best manner of supplying a vacancy in that body. These several despatches were committed to a cavalier, named Paniagua, a faithful adherent of the president, and one of those who had accompanied him from Castile. To this same emissary he also gave manifestos and letters, like those intrusted to the Dominican, with orders to distribute them in Lima, before he quitted that capital.

Weeks and months rolled away, while the president still remained at Panamá, where, indeed, as his communications were jealously cut off with Peru, he might be said to be detained as a sort of prisoner of state. Meanwhile, both he and Hinojosa were looking with anxiety for the arrival of some messenger from Pizarro, who should indicate the manner in which the president's mission was to be received by that chief. The governor of Panamá was not blind to the perilous position in which he was himself placed, nor to the madness of provoking a contest with the Court of Castile. But he had a reluctance—not too often shared by the cavaliers of Peru—to abandon the fortunes of the commander who had reposed in him so great confidence. Yet he trusted that this commander would embrace the opportunity now offered, of placing himself and the country in a state of permanent security.

Several of the cavaliers who had given in their adhesion to Gasca, displeased by this obstinacy, as they termed it, of Hinojosa, proposed to seize his person and then get possession of the armada. But the president at once rejected this offer. His mission, he said, was one of peace, and he would not stain it at the outset by an act of violence. He even respected the scruples of Hinojosa; and a cavalier of so honorable a nature, he conceived, if once he could be gained by fair means, would be much more likely to be true to his interests, than if overcome either by force or fraud. Gasca thought he might safely abide his time. There was policy, as well as honesty, in this; indeed, they always go together.

Meantime, persons were occasionally arriving from Lima and the neighboring places, who gave accounts of Pizarro, varying according to the character and situation of the parties. Some represented him as winning all hearts by his open temper and the politic profusion with which, though covetous of wealth, he distributed *repartimientos* and favors among his followers. Others spoke of him as carrying matters with a high hand, while the greatest timidity and distrust prevailed among the citizens of Lima. All agreed that his power rested on too secure a basis to be shaken; and that, if the president should go to Lima, he must either consent to become Pizarro's instrument and confirm him in the government, or forfeit his own life.

It was undoubtedly true, that Gonzalo, while he gave attention, as his friends say, to the public business, found time for free indulgence in those pleasures which wait on the soldier of fortune in his hour of triumph. He was the object of flattery and homage; courted even by those who hated him. For such as did not love the successful chieftain had good cause to fear him; and his exploits were commemorated in *romances* or ballads, as rivalling—it was not far from truth—those of the most doughty paladins of chivalry.

Amidst this burst of adulation, the cup of joy commended to Pizarro's lips had one drop of bitterness in it that gave its flavor to all the rest; for, notwithstanding his show of confidence, he looked with unceasing anxiety to the arrival of tidings that might assure him in what light his conduct was regarded by the government at home. This was proved by his jealous precautions to guard the approaches to the coast, and to detain the persons of the royal emissaries. He learned, therefore, with no little uneasiness, from Hinojosa, the landing of President Gasca, and the purport of his mission. But his discontent was mitigated, when he understood that the new envoy had come without military array, without any of the ostentatious trappings of office to impose on the minds of the vulgar, but alone, as it were, in the plain garb of an humble missionary. Pizarro could not discern, that under this modest exterior lay a moral power, stronger than his own steel-clad battalions, which, operating silently on public opinion, —the more sure that it was silent,—was even now undermining his strength, like a subterraneous channel eating away the foundations of some stately edifice, that stands secure in its pride of place!

But, although Gonzalo Pizarro could not foresee this result, he saw enough to satisfy him that it would be safest to exclude the president from Peru. The tidings of his arrival, moreover, quickened his former purpose of sending an embassy to Spain to vindicate his late proceedings, and request the royal confirmation of his authority. The person placed at the head of this mission was Lorenzo de Aldana, a cavalier of discretion as well as courage, and high in the confidence of Pizarro, as one of his most devoted partisans. He had occupied some important posts under that chief, one secret of whose successes was the sagacity he showed in the selection of his agents.

Besides Aldana and one or two cavaliers, the bishop of Lima was joined in the commission, as likely, from his position, to have a favorable influence on Gonzalo's fortunes at court. Together with the despatches for the government, the envoys were intrusted with a letter to Gasca from the inhabitants of Lima; in which, after civilly congratulating the president on his arrival, they announced their regret that he had come too late. The troubles of the country were now settled by the overthrow of the viceroy, and the nation was reposing in quiet under the rule of Pizarro. An embassy, they stated, was on its way to Castile, *not to solicit pardon*, for they had committed no crime, but to petition the emperor to confirm their leader in the government, as the man in Peru best entitled to it by his virtues. They expressed the conviction that Gasca's presence would only serve to renew the distractions of the country, and they darkly intimated that his attempt to land would probably cost him his life.—The language of this singular document was more respectful than might be inferred from its import. It was dated the 14th of October, 1546, and was subscribed by seventy of the principal cavaliers in the city. It was not improbably dictated by Cepeda, whose hand is visible in most of the intrigues of Pizarro's little court. It is also said,—the authority is somewhat questionable,—that Aldana received instructions from Gonzalo secretly to offer a bribe of fifty thousand *pesos de oro* to the president, to prevail on him to return to Castile; and in case of his refusal, some darker and more effectual way was to be devised to rid the country of his presence.

Aldana, fortified with his despatches, sped swiftly on his voyage to Panamá. Through him the governor learned the actual state of feeling in the councils of Pizarro; and he listened with regret to the envoy's conviction, that no terms would be admitted by that chief or his companions, that did not confirm him in the possession of Peru.

Aldana was soon admitted to an audience by the president. It was attended with very different results from what had followed from the conferences with Hinojosa; for Pizarro's envoy was not armed by nature with that stubborn panoply which had hitherto made the other proof against all argument. He now learned with surprise the nature of Gasca's powers, and the extent of the royal concessions to the insurgents. He had embarked with Gonzalo Pizarro on a desperate venture, and he found that it had proved successful. The colony had nothing more, in reason, to demand; and, though devoted in heart to his leader, he did not feel bound by any principle of honor to take part with him, solely to gratify his ambition, in a wild contest with the Crown that must end in inevitable ruin. He consequently abandoned his mission to Castile, probably never very palatable to him, and announced his purpose to accept the pardon proffered by government, and support the president in settling the affairs of Peru. He subsequently wrote, it should be added, to his former commander in Lima, stating the course he had taken, and earnestly recommending the latter to follow his example.

The influence of this precedent in so important a person as Aldana, aided, doubtless, by the conviction that no change was now to be expected in Pizarro, while delay would be fatal to himself, at length prevailed over Hinojosa's scruples, and he intimated to Gasca his willingness to place the fleet under his command. The act was performed with great pomp and ceremony. Some of Pizarro's stanchest partisans were previously removed from the vessels; and on the nineteenth of November, 1546, Hinojosa and his captains resigned their commissions into the hands of the president. They next took the oaths of allegiance to Castile; a free pardon for all past offences was proclaimed by the herald from a scaffold erected in the great square of the city; and the president, greeting them as true and loyal vassals of the Crown, restored their several commissions to the cavaliers. The royal standard of Spain was then unfurled on board the squadron, and proclaimed that this stronghold of Pizarro's power had passed away from him for ever.

The return of their commissions to the insurgent captains was a politic act in Gasca. It secured the services of the ablest officers in the country, and turned against Pizarro the very arm on which he had most leaned for support. Thus was this great step achieved, without force or fraud, by Gasca's patience and judicious forecast. He was content to bide his time; and he now might rely with well-grounded confidence on the ultimate success of his mission.

CHAPTER II [1547]

GASCA ASSEMBLES HIS FORCES—DEFECTION OF PIZAR-
RO'S FOLLOWERS—HE MUSTERS HIS LEVIES—AGITATION
IN LIMA—HE ABANDONS THE CITY—GASCA SAILS FROM
PANAMÁ—BLOODY BATTLE OF HUARINA

No sooner was Gasca placed in possession of Panamá and
the fleet, than he entered on a more decisive course of policy
than he had been hitherto allowed to pursue. He raised levies
of men, and drew together supplies from all quarters. He took
care to discharge the arrears already due to the soldiers, and
promised liberal pay for the future; for, though mindful that
his personal charges should cost little to the Crown, he did
not stint his expenditure when the public good required it.
As the funds in the treasury were exhausted, he obtained loans
on the credit of the government from the wealthy citizens of
Panamá, who, relying on his good faith, readily made the necessary advances. He next sent letters to the authorities of
Guatemala and Mexico, requiring their assistance in carrying
on hostilities, if necessary, against the insurgent; and he despatched a summons, in like manner, to Benalcazar, in the
provinces north of Peru, to meet him, on his landing in that
country, with his whole available force.

The greatest enthusiasm was shown by the people of Panamá in getting the little navy in order for his intended voyage;
and prelates and commanders did not disdain to prove their
loyalty by taking part in the good work, along with the soldiers
and sailors. Before his own departure, however, Gasca proposed to send a small squadron of four ships under Aldana,
to cruise off the port of Lima, with instructions to give protection to those well affected to the royal cause, and receive
them, if need be, on board his vessels. He was also intrusted
with authenticated copies of the president's commission, to be
delivered to Gonzalo, that the chief might feel, there was yet
time to return before the gates of mercy were closed against
him.

While these events were going on, Gasca's proclamations and letters were doing their work in Peru. It required but little sagacity to perceive that the nation at large, secured in the protection of person and property, had nothing to gain by revolution. Interest and duty, fortunately, now lay on the same side; and the ancient sentiment of loyalty, smothered for a time, but not extinguished, revived in the breasts of the people. Still this was not manifested, at once, by any overt act; for, under a strong military rule, men dared hardly think for themselves, much less communicate their thoughts to one another. But changes of public opinion, like changes in the atmosphere that come on slowly and imperceptibly, make themselves more and more widely felt, till, by a sort of silent sympathy, they spread to the remotest corners of the land. Some intimations of such a change of sentiment at length found their way to Lima, although all accounts of the president's mission had been jealously excluded from that capital. Gonzalo Pizarro himself became sensible of these symptoms of disaffection, though almost too faint and feeble, as yet, for the most experienced eye to descry in them the coming tempest.

Several of the president's proclamations had been forwarded to Gonzalo by his faithful partisans; and Carbajal, who had been summoned from Potosí, declared they were "more to be dreaded than the lances of Castile." Yet Pizarro did not, for a moment, lose his confidence in his own strength; and with a navy like that now in Panamá at his command, he felt he might bid defiance to any enemy on his coasts. He had implicit confidence in the fidelity of Hinojosa.

It was at this period that Paniagua arrived off the port with Gasca's despatches to Pizarro, consisting of the emperor's letter and his own. They were instantly submitted by that chieftain to his trusty counsellors, Carbajal and Cepeda, and their opinions asked as to the course to be pursued. It was the crisis of Pizarro's fate.

Carbajal, whose sagacious eye fully comprehended the position in which they stood, was in favor of accepting the royal grace on the terms proposed; and he intimated his sense of their importance by declaring, that "he would pave the way for the bearer of them into the capital with ingots of gold and silver." Cepeda was of a different way of thinking. He was a judge of the Royal Audience; and had been sent to Peru as the immediate counsellor of Blasco Nuñez. But he had turned against the viceroy, had encountered him in battle, and his garments might be said to be yet wet with his blood! What grace was there, then, for him? Whatever respect might be shown to the letter of the royal provisions, in point of fact, he must ever live under the Castilian rule a ruined man. He accordingly, strongly urged the rejection of Gasca's offers. "They will cost you your government," he said to Pizarro; "the smooth-tongued priest is not so simple a person as you take him to be. He is deep and politic. He knows well what promises to make; and, once master of the country, he will know, too, how to keep them."

Carbajal was not shaken by the arguments or the sneers of his companions; and as the discussion waxed warm, Cepeda taxed his opponent with giving counsel suggested by fears for his own safety,—a foolish taunt, sufficiently disproved by the whole life of the doughty old warrior. Carbajal did not insist further on his own views, however, as he found them unwelcome to Pizarro, and contented himself with coolly remarking, that "he had, indeed, no relish for rebellion; but he had as long a neck for a halter, he believed, as any of his companions; and as he could hardly expect to live much longer, at any rate, it was, after all, of little moment to him."

Pizarro, spurred on by a fiery ambition that overleaped every obstacle, did not condescend to count the desperate chances of a contest with the Crown. He threw his own weight into the scale with Cepeda. The offer of grace was rejected; and he thus cast away the last tie which held him to his country, and, by the act, proclaimed himself a rebel.

It was not long after the departure of Paniagua, that Pizarro received tidings of the defection of Aldana and Hinojosa, and of the surrender of the fleet, on which he had expended an immense sum, as the chief bulwark of his power. This unwelcome intelligence was followed by accounts of the further defection of some of the principal towns in the north, and of the assassination of Puelles, the faithful lieutenant to whom he had confided the government of Quito. It was not very long, also, before he found his authority assailed in the opposite quarter at Cuzco; for Centeno, the loyal chieftain who, as the reader may remember, had been driven by Carbajal to take refuge in a cave near Arequipa, had issued from his concealment after remaining there a year, and, on learning the arrival of Gasca, had again raised the royal standard. Then collecting a small body of followers, and falling on Cuzco by night, he made himself master of that capital, defeated the garrison who held it, and secured it for the Crown. Marching soon after into the province of Charcas, the bold chief allied himself with the officer who commanded for Pizarro in La Plata; and their combined forces, to the number of a thousand, took up a position on the borders of Lake Titicaca, where the two cavaliers coolly waited an opportunity to take the field against their ancient commander.

Gonzalo Pizarro, touched to the heart by the desertion of those in whom he most confided, was stunned by the dismal tidings of his losses coming so thick upon him. Yet he did not waste his time in idle crimination or complaint; but immediately set about making preparations to meet the storm with all his characteristic energy. He wrote, at once, to such of his captains as he believed still faithful, commanding them to be ready with their troops to march to his assistance at the shortest notice. He reminded them of their obligations to him, and that their interests were identical with his own. The president's commission, he added, had been made out before the news had reached Spain of the battle of Añaquito, and could never cover a pardon to those concerned in the death of the viceroy.

Pizarro was equally active in enforcing his levies in the capital, and in putting them in the best fighting order. He soon saw himself at the head of a thousand men, beautifully equipped, and complete in all their appointments; "as gallant an array," says an old writer, "though so small in number, as ever trod the plains of Italy,"—displaying in the excellence of their arms, their gorgeous uniforms, and the caparisons of their horses, a magnificence that could be furnished only by the silver of Peru. Each company was provided with a new stand of colors, emblazoned with its peculiar device. Some bore the initials and arms of Pizarro, and one or two of these were audaciously surmounted by a crown, as if to intimate the rank to which their commander might aspire.

Among the leaders most conspicuous on this occasion was Cepeda, "who," in the words of a writer of his time, "had exchanged the robe of the licentiate for the plumed casque and mailed harness of the warrior." But the cavalier to whom Pizarro confided the chief care of organizing his battalions was the veteran Carbajal, who had studied the art of war under the best captains of Europe, and whose life of adventure had been a practical commentary on their early lessons. It was on his arm that Gonzalo most leaned in the hour of danger; and well had it been for him, if he had profited by his counsels at an earlier period.

It gives one some idea of the luxurious accommodations of Pizarro's forces, that he endeavored to provide each of his musketeers with a horse. The expenses incurred by him were enormous. The immediate cost of his preparations, we are told, was not less than half a million of *pesos de oro;* and his pay to the cavaliers, and, indeed, to the common soldiers, in his little army, was on an extravagant scale, nowhere to be met with but on the silver soil of Peru.

When his own funds were exhausted, he supplied the deficiency by fines imposed on the rich citizens of Lima as the price of exemption from service, by forced loans, and various other schemes of military exaction. From this time, it is said, the chieftain's temper underwent a visible change. He became more violent in his passions, more impatient of control, and indulged more freely in acts of cruelty and license. The desperate cause in which he was involved made him reckless of consequences. Though naturally frank and confiding, the frequent defection of his followers filled him with suspicion. He knew not in whom to confide. Every one who showed himself indifferent to his cause, or was suspected of being so, was dealt with as an open enemy. The greatest distrust prevailed in Lima. No man dared confide in his neighbor. Some concealed their effects; others contrived to elude the vigilance of the sentinels, and hid themselves in the neighboring woods and mountains. No one was allowed to enter or leave the city without a license. All commerce, all intercourse, with other places was cut off. It was long since the fifths belonging to the Crown had been remitted to Castile; as Pizarro had appropriated them for his own use. He now took possession of the mints, broke up the royal stamps, and issued a debased coin, emblazoned with his own cipher. It was the most decisive act of sovereignty.

At this gloomy period, the lawyer Cepeda contrived a solemn farce, the intent of which was to give a sort of legal sanction to the rebel cause in the eyes of the populace. He caused a process to be prepared against Gasca, Hinojosa, and Aldana, in which they were accused of treason against the existing government of Peru, were convicted, and condemned to death. This instrument he submitted to a number of jurists in the capital, requiring their signatures. But they had no mind thus inevitably to implicate themselves, by affixing their names to such a paper; and they evaded it by representing, that it would only serve to cut off all chance, should any of the accused be so disposed, of their again embracing the cause they had deserted. Cepeda was the only man who signed the document. Carbajal treated the whole thing with ridicule. "What is the object of your process?" said he to Cepeda. "Its object," replied the latter, "is to prevent delay, that, if taken at any time, the guilty party may be at once led to execution." "I cry you mercy," retorted Carbajal; "I thought there must be some virtue in the instrument, that would have killed them outright. Let but one of these same traitors fall into my hands, and I will march him off to execution, without waiting for the sentence of a court, I promise you!"

While this paper war was going on, news was brought that Aldana's squadron was off the port of Callao. That commander had sailed from Panamá, the middle of February, 1547. On his passage down the coast he had landed at Truxillo, where the citizens welcomed him with enthusiasm, and eagerly proclaimed their submission to the royal authority. He received, at the same time, messages from several of Pizarro's officers in the interior, intimating their return to their duty, and their readiness to support the president. Aldana named Caxamalca as a place of rendezvous, where they should concentrate their forces, and wait the landing of Gasca. He then continued his voyage towards Lima.

No sooner was Pizarro informed of his approach, than, fear-

ful lest it might have a disastrous effect in seducing his followers from their fidelity, he marched them about a league out
of the city, and there encamped. He was two leagues from the
coast, and he posted a guard on the shore to intercept all
communication with the vessels. Before leaving the capital,
Cepeda resorted to an expedient for securing the inhabitants
more firmly, as he conceived, in Pizarro's interests. He caused
the citizens to be assembled, and made them a studied harangue, in which he expatiated on the services of their governor, and the security which the country had enjoyed under
his rule. He then told them that every man was at liberty to
choose for himself; to remain under the protection of their
present ruler, or, if they preferred, to transfer their allegiance
to his enemy. He invited them to speak their minds, but required every one who would still continue under Pizarro to
take an oath of fidelity to his cause, with the assurance, that, if
any should be so false hereafter as to violate this pledge, he
should pay for it with his life. There was no one found bold
enough—with his head thus in the lion's mouth—to swerve
from his obedience to Pizarro; and every man took the oath
prescribed, which was administered in the most solemn and
imposing form by the licentiate. Carbajal, as usual, made a
jest of the whole proceeding. "How long," he asked his companion, "do you think these same oaths will stand? The first
wind that blows off the coast after we are gone will scatter
them in air!" His prediction was soon verified.

Meantime, Aldana anchored off the port, where there was
no vessel of the insurgents to molest him. By Cepeda's advice,
some four or five had been burnt a short time before, during
the absence of Carbajal, in order to cut off all means by which
the inhabitants could leave the place. This was deeply de-
plored by the veteran soldier on his return. "It was destroying," he said, "the guardian angels of Lima." And certainly,
under such a commander, they might now have stood Pizarro
in good stead; but his star was on the wane.

The first act of Aldana was to cause the copy of Gasca's
powers, with which he had been intrusted, to be conveyed to
his ancient commander, by whom it was indignantly torn in
pieces. Aldana next contrived, by means of his agents, to cir-
culate among the citizens, and even the soldiers of the camp,

the president's manifestos. They were not long in producing their effect. Few had been at all aware of the real purport of Gasca's mission, of the extent of his powers, or of the generous terms offered by government. They shrunk from the desperate course into which they had been thus unwarily seduced, and they sought only in what way they could, with least danger, extricate themselves from their present position, and return to their allegiance. Some escaped by night from the camp, eluded the vigilance of the sentinels, and effected their retreat on board the vessels. Some were taken, and found no quarter at the hands of Carbajal and his merciless ministers. But, where the spirit of disaffection was abroad, means of escape were not wanting.

As the fugitives were cut off from Lima and the neighboring coast, they secreted themselves in the forests and mountains, and watched their opportunity for making their way to Truxillo and other ports at a distance; and so contagious was the example, that it not unfrequently happened that the very soldiers sent in pursuit of the deserters joined with them. Among those that fled was the Licentiate Carbajal, who must not be confounded with his military namesake. He was the same cavalier whose brother had been put to death in Lima by Blasco Nuñez, and who revenged himself, as we have seen, by imbruing his own hands in the blood of the viceroy. That a person thus implicated should trust to the royal pardon showed that no one need despair of it; and the example proved most disastrous to Pizarro.

Carbajal, who made a jest of every thing, even of the misfortunes which pinched him the sharpest, when told of the desertion of his comrades, amused himself by humming the words of a popular ditty:

"The wind blows the hairs off my head, mother;
Two at a time, it blows them away!"

But the defection of his followers made a deeper impression on Pizarro, and he was sorely distressed as he beheld the gallant array, to which he had so confidently looked for gaining his battles, thus melting away like a morning mist. Bewildered by the treachery of those in whom he had most trusted, he knew not where to turn, nor what course to take. It was evident that he must leave his present dangerous quarters without loss of time. But whither should he direct his steps? In the north, the great towns had abandoned his cause, and the president was already marching against him; while Centeno held the passes of the south, with a force double his own. In this emergency, he at length resolved to occupy Arequipa, a seaport still true to him, where he might remain till he had decided on some future course of operations.

After a painful but rapid march, Gonzalo arrived at this place, where he was speedily joined by a reinforcement that he had detached for the recovery of Cuzco. But so frequent had been the desertions from both companies,—though in Pizarro's corps these had greatly lessened since the departure from the neighborhood of Lima,—that his whole number did not exceed five hundred men, less than half of the force which he had so recently mustered in the capital. To such humble circumstances was the man now reduced, who had so lately lorded it over the land with unlimited sway! Still the chief did not despond. He had gathered new spirit from the excitement of his march and his distance from Lima; and he seemed to recover his former confidence, as he exclaimed,—"It is misfortune that teaches us who are our friends. If but ten only remain true to me, fear not but I will again be master of Peru!"

No sooner had the rebel forces withdrawn from the neighborhood of Lima, than the inhabitants of that city, little troubled, as Carbajal had predicted, by their compulsory oaths of allegiance to Pizarro, threw open their gates to Aldana, who took possession of this important place in the name of the president. That commander, meanwhile, had sailed with his whole fleet from Panamá, on the tenth of April, 1547. The first part of his voyage was prosperous; but he was soon perplexed by contrary currents, and the weather became rough and tempestuous. The violence of the storm continuing day after day, the sea was lashed into fury, and the fleet was tossed about on the billows, which ran mountain high, as if emulating the wild character of the region they bounded. The rain descended in torrents, and the lightning was so incessant, that the vessels, to quote the lively language of the chronicler, "seemed to be driving through seas of flame!" The hearts of the stoutest mariners were filled with dismay. They considered it hopeless to struggle against the elements, and they loudly demanded to return to the continent, and postpone the voyage till a more favorable season of the year.

But the president saw in this the ruin of his cause, as well as of the loyal vassals who had engaged, on his landing, to support it. "I am willing to die," he said, "but not to return"; and, regardless of the remonstrances of his more timid followers, he insisted on carrying as much sail as the ships could possibly bear, at every interval of the storm. Meanwhile, to divert the minds of the seamen from their present danger, Gasca amused them by explaining some of the strange phenomena exhibited by the ocean in the tempest, which had filled their superstitious minds with mysterious dread.

Signals had been given for the ships to make the best of their way, each for itself, to the island of Gorgona. Here they arrived, one after another, with but a single exception, though all more or less shattered by the weather. The president waited only for the fury of the elements to spend itself, when he again embarked, and, on smoother waters, crossed over to Manta. From this place he soon after continued his voyage to Tumbez, and landed at that port on the thirteenth of June. He was everywhere received with enthusiasm, and all seemed anxious to efface the remembrance of the past by professions of future fidelity to the Crown. Gasca received, also, numerous letters of congratulation from cavaliers in the interior, most of whom had formerly taken service under Pizarro. He made courteous acknowledgments for their offers of assistance, and commanded them to repair to Caxamalca, the general place of rendezvous.

To this same spot he sent Hinojosa, so soon as that officer had disembarked with the land forces from the fleet, ordering him to take command of the levies assembled there, and then join him at Xauxa. Here he determined to establish his headquarters. It lay in a rich and abundant territory, and by its central position afforded a point for acting with greatest advantage against the enemy.

He then moved forward, at the head of a small detachment of cavalry, along the level road on the coast towards Truxillo. After halting for a short time in that loyal city, he traversed the mountain range on the southeast, and soon entered the fruitful valley of Xauxa. There he was presently joined by reinforcements from the north, as well as from the principal places on the coast; and, not long after his arrival, received a message from Centeno, informing him that he held the passes by which Gonzalo Pizarro was preparing to make his escape from the country, and that the insurgent chief must soon fall into his hands.

The royal camp was greatly elated by these tidings. The war, then, was at length terminated, and that without the president having been called upon so much as to lift his sword against a Spaniard. Several of his counsellors now advised him to disband the greater part of his forces, as burdensome and no longer necessary. But the president was too wise to weaken his strength before he had secured the victory. He consented, however, to countermand the requisition for levies from Mexico and the adjoining colonies, as now feeling sufficiently strong in the general loyalty of the country. But, concentrating his forces at Xauxa, he established his quarters in that town, as he had first intended, resolved to await there tidings of the operations in the south. The result was different from what he had expected.

Pizarro, meanwhile, whom we left at Arequipa, had decided, after much deliberation, to evacuate Peru, and pass into Chili. In this territory, beyond the president's jurisdiction, he might find a safe retreat. The fickle people, he thought, would soon weary of their new ruler; and he would then rally in sufficient strength to resume active operations for the recovery of his domain. Such were the calculations of the rebel chieftain. But how was he to effect his object, while the passes among the mountains, where his route lay, were held by Centeno with a force more than double his own? He resolved to try negotiation; for that captain had once served under him, and had, indeed, been most active in persuading Pizarro to take on himself the office of procurator. Advancing, accordingly, in the direction of Lake Titicaca, in the neighborhood of which Centeno had pitched his camp, Gonzalo despatched an emissary to his quarters to open a negotiation. He called to his adversary's recollection the friendly relations that had once subsisted between them; and reminded him of one occasion in particular, in which he had spared his life, when convicted of a conspiracy against himself. He harbored no sentiments of unkindness, he said, for Centeno's recent conduct, and had not now come to seek a quarrel with him. His purpose was to abandon Peru; and the only favor he had to request of his former associate was to leave him a free passage across the mountains.

To this communication Centeno made answer in terms as courtly as those of Pizarro himself, that he was not unmindful of their ancient friendship. He was now ready to serve his former commander in any way not inconsistent with honor, or obedience to his sovereign. But he was there in arms for the royal cause, and he could not swerve from his duty. If Pizarro would but rely on his faith and surrender himself up, he pledged his knightly word to use all his interest with the government, to secure as favorable terms for him and his followers as had been granted to the rest of their countrymen.—Gonzalo listened to the smooth promises of his ancient comrade with bitter scorn depicted in his countenance, and, snatching the letter from his secretary, cast it away from him with indignation. There was nothing left but an appeal to arms.

He at once broke up his encampment, and directed his march on the borders of Lake Titicaca, near which lay his rival. He resorted, however, to stratagem, that he might still, if possible, avoid an encounter. He sent forward his scouts in a different direction from that which he intended to take, and then quickened his march on Huarina. This was a small town situated on the southeastern extremity of Lake Titicaca, the shores of which, the seat of the primitive civilization of the Incas, were soon to resound with the murderous strife of their more civilized conquerors!

But Pizarro's movements had been secretly communicated to Centeno, and that commander, accordingly, changing his ground, took up a position not far from Huarina, on the same day on which Gonzalo reached this place. The videttes of the two camps came in sight of each other that evening, and the rival forces, lying on their arms, prepared for action on the following morning.

It was the twenty-sixth of October, 1547, when the two commanders, having formed their troops in order of battle, advanced to the encounter on the plains of Huarina. The ground, defended on one side by a bold spur of the Andes, and not far removed on the other from the waters of Titicaca, was an open and level plain, well suited to military manœuvres. It seemed as if prepared by Nature as the lists for an encounter.

Centeno's army amounted to about a thousand men. His cavalry consisted of near two hundred and fifty, well equipped and mounted. Among them were several gentlemen of family, some of whom had once followed the banners of Pizarro; the whole forming an efficient corps, in which rode some of the best lances of Peru. His arquebusiers were less numerous, not exceeding a hundred and fifty, indifferently provided with ammunition. The remainder, and much the larger part of Centeno's army, consisted of spearmen, irregular levies hastily drawn together, and possessed of little discipline.

This corps of infantry formed the centre of his line, flanked by the arquebusiers in two nearly equal divisions, while his cavalry were also disposed in two bodies on the right and left wings. Unfortunately, Centeno had been for the past week ill of pleurisy,—so ill, indeed, that on the preceding day he had been bled several times. He was now too feeble to keep his saddle, but was carried in a litter, and when he had seen his men formed in order, he withdrew to a distance from the field, unable to take part in the action. But Solano, the militant bishop of Cuzco, who, with several of his followers, took part in the engagement,—a circumstance, indeed, of no strange occurrence,—rode along the ranks with the crucifix in his hand, bestowing his benediction on the soldiers, and exhorting each man to do his duty.

Pizarro's forces were less than half of his rival's, not amounting to more than four hundred and eighty men. The horse did not muster above eighty-five in all, and he posted them in a single body on the right of his battalion. The strength of his army lay in his arquebusiers, about three hundred and fifty in number. It was an admirable corps, commanded by Carbajal, by whom it had been carefully drilled. Considering the excellence of its arms, and its thorough discipline, this little body of infantry might be considered as the flower of the Peruvian soldiery, and on it Pizarro mainly relied for the success of the day. The remainder of his force, consisting of pikemen, not formidable for their numbers, though, like the rest of the infantry, under excellent discipline, he distributed on the left of his musketeers, so as to repel the enemy's horse.

Pizarro himself had charge of the cavalry, taking his place, as usual, in the foremost rank. He was superbly accoutred. Over his shining mail he wore a sobre-vest of slashed velvet of a rich crimson color; and he rode a high-mettled charger, whose gaudy caparisons, with the showy livery of his rider, made the fearless commander the most conspicuous object in the field.

His lieutenant, Carbajal, was equipped in a very different style. He wore armour of proof of the most homely appearance, but strong and serviceable; and his steel bonnet, with its closely barred visor of the same material, protected his head from more than one desperate blow on that day. Over his arms he wore a surcoat of a greenish color, and he rode an active, strong-boned jennet, which, though capable of enduring fatigue, possessed neither grace nor beauty. It would not have been easy to distinguish the veteran from the most ordinary cavalier.

The two hosts arrived within six hundred paces of each other, when they both halted. Carbajal preferred to receive the attack of the enemy, rather than advance further; for the ground he now occupied afforded a free range for his musketry, unobstructed by the trees or bushes that were sprinkled over some other parts of the field. There was a singular motive, in addition, for retaining his present position. The soldiers were encumbered, some with two, some with three, arquebuses each, being the arms left by those who, from time to time, had deserted the camp. This uncommon supply of muskets, however serious an impediment on a march, might afford great advantage to troops waiting an assault; since, from the imperfect knowledge as well as construction of fire-arms at that day, much time was wasted in loading them.

Preferring, therefore, that the enemy should begin the attack, Carbajal came to a halt, while the opposite squadron, after a short respite, continued their advance a hundred paces farther. Seeing that they then remained immovable, Carbajal detached a small party of skirmishers to the front, in order to provoke them; but it was soon encountered by a similar party of the enemy, and some shots were exchanged, though with little damage to either side. Finding this manœuvre fail, the veteran ordered his men to advance a few paces, still hoping to provoke his antagonist to the charge. This succeeded. "We lose honor," exclaimed Centeno's soldiers; who, with a bastard sort of chivalry, belonging to undisciplined troops, felt it a disgrace to await an assault. In vain their officers called out to them to remain at their post. Their commander was absent, and they were urged on by the cries of a frantic friar, named Domingo Ruiz, who, believing the Philistines were delivered into their hands, called out,—"Now is the time! Onward, onward, fall on the enemy!" They needed nothing further, and the men rushed forward in tumultuous haste, the pikemen carrying their levelled weapons so heedlessly as to interfere with one another, and in some instances to wound their comrades. The musketeers, at the same time, kept up a disorderly fire as they advanced, which, from their rapid motion and the distance, did no execution.

Carbajal was well pleased to see his enemies thus wasting their ammunition. Though he allowed a few muskets to be discharged, in order to stimulate his opponents the more, he commanded the great body of his infantry to reserve their fire till every shot could take effect. As he knew the tendency of marksmen to shoot above the mark, he directed his men to aim at the girdle, or even a little below it; adding, that a shot that fell short might still do damage, while one that passed a hair's breadth above the head was wasted.

The veteran's company stood calm and unmoved, as Centeno's rapidly advanced; but when the latter had arrived within a hundred paces of their antagonists, Carbajal gave the word to fire. An instantaneous volley ran along the line, and a tempest of balls was poured into the ranks of the assailants, with such unerring aim, that more than a hundred fell dead on the field, while a still greater number were wounded. Before they could recover from their disorder, Carbajal's men, snatching up their remaining pieces, discharged them with the like dreadful effect into the thick of the enemy. The confusion of the latter was now complete. Unable to sustain the incessant shower of balls which fell on them from the scattering fire kept up by the arquebusiers, they were seized with a panic, and fled, scarcely making a show of further fight, from the field.

But very different was the fortune of the day in the cavalry combat. Gonzalo Pizarro had drawn up his troop somewhat in the rear of Carbajal's right, in order to give the latter a freer range for the play of his musketry. When the enemy's horse on the left galloped briskly against him, Pizarro, still favoring Carbajal,—whose fire, moreover, inflicted some loss on the assailants,—advanced but a few rods to receive the charge. Centeno's squadron, accordingly, came thundering on in full career, and, notwithstanding the mischief sustained from their enemy's musketry, fell with such fury on their adversaries as to overturn them, man and horse, in the dust; "riding over their prostrate bodies," says the historian, "as if they had been a flock of sheep!" The latter, with great difficulty recovering from the first shock, attempted to rally and sustain the fight on more equal terms.

Yet the chief could not regain the ground he had lost. His men were driven back at all points. Many were slain, many more wounded, on both sides, and the ground was covered with the dead bodies of men and horses. But the loss fell much the most heavily on Pizarro's troop; and the greater part of those who escaped with life were obliged to surrender as prisoners. Cepeda, who fought with the fury of despair, received a severe cut from a sabre across the face, which disabled him and forced him to yield. Pizarro, after seeing his best and bravest fall around him, was set upon by three or four cavaliers at once. Disentangling himself from the *mêlée*, he put spurs to his horse, and the noble animal, bleeding from a severe wound across the back, outstripped all his pursuers except one, who stayed him by seizing the bridle. It would have gone hard with Gonzalo, but, grasping a light battle-axe, which hung by his side, he dealt such a blow on the head of his enemy's horse that he plunged violently, and compelled his rider to release his hold. A number of arquebusiers, in the mean time, seeing Pizarro's distress, sprang forward to his rescue, slew two of his assailants who had now come up with him, and forced the others to fly in their turn.

The rout of the cavalry was complete; and Pizarro considered the day as lost, as he heard the enemy's trumpet sending forth the note of victory. But the sounds had scarcely died away, when they were taken up by the opposite side. Centeno's infantry had been discomfited, as we have seen, and driven off the ground. But his cavalry on the right had charged Carbajal's left, consisting of spearmen mingled with arquebusiers. The horse rode straight against this formidable phalanx. But they were unable to break through the dense array of pikes, held by the steady hands of troops who stood firm and fearless on their post; while, at the same time, the assailants were greatly annoyed by the galling fire of the arquebusiers in the rear of the spearmen. Finding it impracticable to make a breach, the horsemen rode round the flanks in much disorder, and finally joined themselves with the victorious squadron of Centeno's cavalry in the rear. Both parties now attempted another charge on Carbajal's battalion. But his men facing about with the promptness and discipline of well-trained soldiers, the rear was converted into the front. The same forest of spears was presented to the attack; while an incessant discharge of balls punished the audacity of the cavaliers, who, broken and completely dispirited by their ineffectual attempt, at length imitated the example of the panic-struck foot, and abandoned the field.

Pizarro and a few of his comrades still fit for action followed up the pursuit for a short distance only, as, indeed, they were in no condition themselves, nor sufficiently strong in numbers, long to continue it. The victory was complete, and the insurgent chief took possession of the deserted tents of the enemy, where an immense booty was obtained in silver; and where he also found the tables spread for the refreshment of Centeno's soldiers after their return from the field. So confident were they of success! The repast now served the necessities of their conquerors. Such is the fortune of war! It was, indeed, a most decisive action; and Gonzalo Pizarro, as he rode over the field strewed with the corpses of his enemies, was observed several times to cross himself and exclaim,—"Jesu! what a victory!"

No less than three hundred and fifty of Centeno's followers were killed, and the number of wounded was even greater. More than a hundred of these are computed to have perished from exposure during the following night; for, although the climate in this elevated region is temperate, yet the night winds blowing over the mountains are sharp and piercing, and many a wounded wretch, who might have been restored by careful treatment, was chilled by the damps, and found a stiffened corpse at sunrise. The victory was not purchased without a heavy loss on the part of the Conquerors, a hundred or more of whom were left on the field. Their bodies lay thick on that part of the ground occupied by Pizarro's cavalry, where the fight raged hottest. In this narrow space were found, also the bodies of more than a hundred horses, the greater part of which, as well as those of their riders, usually slain with them, belonged to the victorious army. It was the most fatal battle that had yet been fought on the blood-stained soil of Peru.

The glory of the day—the melancholy glory—must be referred almost wholly to Carbajal and his valiant squadron. The judicious arrangements of the old warrior, with the thorough discipline and unflinching courage of his followers, retrieved the fortunes of the fight, when it was nearly lost by the cavalry, and secured the victory.

Carbajal, proof against all fatigue, followed up the pursuit with those of his men that were in condition to join him. Such of the unhappy fugitives as fell into his hands—most of whom had been traitors to the cause of Pizarro—were sent to instant execution. The laurels he had won in the field against brave men in arms, like himself, were tarnished by cruelty towards his defenceless captives. Their commander, Centeno, more fortunate, made his escape. Finding the battle lost, he quitted his litter, threw himself upon his horse, and, notwithstanding his illness, urged on by the dreadful doom that awaited him, if taken, he succeeded in making his way into the neighboring sierra. Here he vanished from his pursuers, and, like a wounded stag, with the chase close upon his track, he still contrived to elude it, by plunging into the depths of the forests, till, by a circuitous route, he miraculously succeeded in effecting his escape to Lima. The bishop of Cuzco, who went off in a different direction, was no less fortunate. Happy for him that he did not fall into the hands of the ruthless Carbajal, who, as the bishop had once been a partisan of Pizarro, would, to judge from the little respect he usually showed those of his cloth, have felt as little compunction in sentencing him to the gibbet as if he had been the meanest of the common file.

On the day following the action, Gonzalo Pizarro caused the bodies of the soldiers, still lying side by side on the field where they had been so lately engaged together in mortal strife, to be deposited in a common sepulchre. Those of higher rank—for distinctions of rank were not to be forgotten in the grave—were removed to the church of the village of Huarina, which gave its name to the battle. There they were interred with all fitting solemnity. But in later times they were transported to the cathedral church of La Paz, "The City of Peace," and laid under a mausoleum erected by general subscription in that quarter. For few there were who had not to mourn the loss of some friend or relative on that fatal day.

The victor now profited by his success to send detachments to Arequipa, La Plata, and other cities in that part of the country, to raise funds and reinforcements for the war. His own losses were more than compensated by the number of the vanquished party who were content to take service under his banner. Mustering his forces, he directed his march to Cuzco, which capital, though occasionally seduced into a display of loyalty to the Crown, had early manifested an attachment to his cause.

Here the inhabitants were prepared to receive him in triumph, under arches thrown across the streets, with bands of music, and minstrelsy commemorating his successes. But Pizarro, with more discretion, declined the honors of an ovation while the country remained in the hands of his enemies. Sending forward the main body of his troops, he followed on foot, attended by a slender retinue of friends and citizens, and proceeded at once to the cathedral, where thanksgivings were offered up, and *Te Deum* was chanted in honor of his victory. He then withdrew to his residence, announcing his purpose to establish his quarters, for the present, in the venerable capital of the Incas.

All thoughts of a retreat into Chili were abandoned; for his recent success had kindled new hopes in his bosom, and revived his ancient confidence. He trusted that it would have a similar effect on the vacillating temper of those whose fidelity had been shaken by fears for their own safety, and their distrust of his ability to cope with the president. They would now see that his star was still in the ascendant. Without further apprehensions for the event, he resolved to remain in Cuzco, and there quietly await the hour when a last appeal to arms should decide which of the two was to remain master of Peru.

CHAPTER III [1547-1548]

While the events recorded in the preceding chapter were passing, President Gasca had remained at Xauxa, awaiting further tidings from Centeno, little doubting that they would inform him of the total discomfiture of the rebels. Great was his dismay, therefore, on learning the issue of the fatal conflict at Huarina,—that the royalists had been scattered far and wide before the sword of Pizarro, while their commander had vanished like an apparition, leaving the greatest uncertainty as to his fate.

The intelligence spread general consternation among the soldiers, proportioned to their former confidence; and they felt it was almost hopeless to contend with a man who seemed protected by a charm that made him invincible against the greatest odds. The president, however sore his disappointment, was careful to conceal it, while he endeavored to restore the spirits of his followers. "They had been too sanguine," he said, "and it was in this way that Heaven rebuked their presumption. Yet it was but in the usual course of events, that Providence, when it designed to humble the guilty, should allow him to reach as high an elevation as possible, that his fall might be the greater!"

But while Gasca thus strove to reassure the superstitious and the timid, he bent his mind, with his usual energy, to repair the injury which the cause had sustained by the defeat at Huarina. He sent a detachment under Alvarado to Lima, to collect such of the royalists as had fled thither from the field of battle, and to dismantle the ships of their cannon, and bring them to the camp. Another body was sent to Guamanga, about sixty leagues from Cuzco, for the similar purpose of protecting the fugitives, and also of preventing the Indian caciques from forwarding supplies to the insurgent army in Cuzco. As his own forces now amounted to considerably more than any his opponent could bring against him, Gasca determined to break up his camp without further delay, and march on the Inca capital.

Quitting Xauxa, December 29, 1547, he passed through Guamanga, and after a severe march, rendered particularly fatiguing by the inclement state of the weather and the badness of the roads, he entered the province of Andaguaylas. It was a fair and fruitful country, and since the road beyond would take him into the depths of a gloomy sierra, scarcely passable in the winter snows, Gasca resolved to remain in his present quarters until the severity of the season was mitigated. As many of the troops had already contracted diseases from exposure to the incessant rains, he established a camp hospital; and the good president personally visited the quarters of the sick, ministering to their wants, and winning their hearts by his sympathy.

Meanwhile, the royal camp was strengthened by the continual arrival of reinforcements; for notwithstanding the shock that was caused throughout the country by the first tidings of Pizarro's victory, a little reflection convinced the people that the right was the strongest, and must eventually prevail. There came, also, with these levies, several of the most distinguished captains in the country. Centeno, burning to retrieve his late disgrace, after recovering from his illness, joined the camp with his followers from Lima. Benalcazar, the conqueror of Quito, who, as the reader will remember, had shared in the defeat of Blasco Nuñez in the north, came with another detachment; and was soon after followed by Valdivia, the famous conqueror of Chili, who, having returned to Peru to gather recruits for his expedition, had learned the state of the country, and had thrown himself, without hesitation, into the same scale with the president, though it brought him into collison with his old friend and comrade, Gonzalo Pizarro. The arrival of this last ally was greeted with general rejoicing by the camp; for Valdivia, schooled in the Italian wars, was esteemed the most accomplished soldier in Peru; and Gasca complimented him by declaring "he would rather see him than a reinforcement of eight hundred men!"

Besides these warlike auxiliaries, the president was attended by a train of ecclesiastics and civilians, such as was rarely found in the martial fields of Peru. Among them were the bishops of Quito, Cuzco, and Lima, the four judges of the new Audience, and a considerable number of churchmen and monkish missionaries. However little they might serve to strengthen his arm in battle, their presence gave authority and something of a sacred character to the cause, which had their effect on the minds of the soldiers.

The wintry season now began to give way before the mild influence of spring, which makes itself early felt in these tropical, but from their elevation temperate, regions; and Gasca, after nearly three months' detention in Andaguaylas, mustered his levies for the final march upon Cuzco. Their whole number fell little short of two thousand,—the largest European force yet assembled in Peru. Nearly half were provided with firearms; and infantry were more available than horse in the mountain countries which they were to traverse. But his cavalry was also numerous, and he carried with him a train of eleven heavy guns. The equipment and discipline of the troops were good; they were well provided with ammunition and military stores; and were led by officers whose names were associated with the most memorable achievements in the New World. All who had any real interest in the weal of the country were to be found, in short, under the president's banner, making a striking contrast to the wild and reckless adventurers who now swelled the ranks of Pizarro.

Gasca, who did not affect a greater knowledge of military affairs than he really possessed, had given the charge of his forces to Hinojosa, naming the Marshal Alvarado as second in command. Valdivia, who came after these dispositions had been made, accepted a colonel's commission, with the understanding that he was to be consulted and employed in all matters of moment.—Having completed his arrangements, the president broke up his camp in March, 1548, and moved upon Cuzco.

The first obstacle of his progress was the river Abancay, the bridge over which had been broken down by the enemy. But as there was no force to annoy them on the opposite bank, the army was not long in preparing a new bridge, and throwing it across the stream, which in this place had nothing formidable in its character. The road now struck into the heart of a mountain region, where woods, precipices, and ravines were mingled together in a sort of chaotic confusion, with here and there a green and sheltered valley, glittering like an island of verdure amidst the wild breakers of a troubled ocean! The bold peaks of the Andes, rising far above the clouds, were enveloped in snow, which, descending far down their sides, gave a piercing coldness to the winds that swept over their surface, until men and horses were benumbed and stiffened under their influence. The roads, in these regions, were in some places so narrow and broken, as to be nearly impracticable for cavalry. The cavaliers were compelled to dismount; and the president, with the rest, performed the journey on foot, so hazardous, that, even, in later times, it has been no uncommon thing for the sure-footed mule to be precipitated, with its cargo of silver, thousands of feet down the sheer sides of a precipice.

By these impediments of the ground, the march was so retarded, that the troops seldom accomplished more than two leagues a day. Fortunately, the distance was not great; and the president looked with more apprehension to the passage of the Apurimac, which he was now approaching. This river, one of the most formidable tributaries of the Amazon, rolls its broad waters through the gorges of the Cordilleras, that rise up like an immense rampart of rock on either side, presenting a natural barrier which it would be easy for an enemy to make good against a force much superior to his own. The bridges over this river, as Gasca learned before his departure from Andaguaylas, had been all destroyed by Pizarro. The president, accordingly, had sent to explore the banks of the stream, and determine the most eligible spot for reëstablishing communications with the opposite side.

The place selected was near the Indian village of Cotapampa, about nine leagues from Cuzco; for the river, though rapid and turbulent from being compressed within more narrow limits, was here less than two hundred paces in width; a distance, however, not inconsiderable. Directions had been given to collect materials in large quantities in the neighborhood of this spot as soon as possible; and at the same time, in order to perplex the enemy and compel him to divide his forces, should he be disposed to resist, materials in smaller quantities were assembled on three other points of the river. The officer stationed in the neighborhood of Cotapampa was instructed not to begin to lay the bridge, till the arrival of a sufficient force should accelerate the work, and insure its success.

The structure in question, it should be remembered, was one of those suspension bridges formerly employed by the Incas, and still used in crossing the deep and turbulent rivers of South America. They are made of osier withes, twisted into enormous cables, which, when stretched across the water, are attached to heavy blocks of masonry, or, where it will serve, to the natural rock. Planks are laid transversely across these cables, and a passage is thus secured, which, notwithstanding the light and fragile appearance of the bridge, as it swings at an elevation sometimes of several hundred feet above the abyss, affords a tolerably safe means of conveyance for men, and even for such heavy burdens as artillery.

Notwithstanding the peremptory commands of Gasca, the officer intrusted with collecting the materials for the bridge was so anxious to have the honor of completing the work himself, that he commenced it at once. The president, greatly displeased at learning this, quickened his march, in order to cover the work with his whole force. But, while toiling through the mountain labyrinth, tidings were brought him that a party of the enemy had demolished the small portion of the bridge already made, by cutting the cables on the opposite bank. Valdivia, accordingly, hastened forward at the head of two hundred arquebusiers, while the main body of the army followed with as much speed as practicable.

That officer, on reaching the spot, found that the interruption had been caused by a small party of Pizarro's followers, not exceeding twenty in number, assisted by a stronger body of Indians. He at once caused *balsas*, broad and clumsy barks, or rather, rafts of the country, to be provided, and by this means passed his men over, without opposition, to the other side of the river. The enemy, disconcerted by the arrival of such a force, retreated and made the best of their way to report the affair to their commander at Cuzco. Meanwhile, Valdivia, who saw the importance of every moment in the present crisis, pushed forward the work with the greatest vigor. Through all that night his weary troops continued the labor, which was already well advanced, when the president and his battalions, emerging from the passes of the Cordilleras, presented themselves at sunrise on the opposite bank.

Little time was given for repose, as all felt assured that the success of their enterprise hung on the short respite now given them by the improvident enemy. The president, with his principal officers, took part in the labor with the common soldiers; and before ten o'clock in the evening, Gasca had the satisfaction to see the bridge so well secured, that the leading files of the army, unencumbered by their baggage, might venture to cross it. A short time sufficed to place several hundred men on the other bank. But here a new difficulty, not less formidable than that of the river, presented itself to the troops. The ground rose up with an abrupt, almost precipitous, swell from the river-side, till, in the highest peaks, it reached an elevation of several thousand feet. This steep ascent, though not to its full height, indeed, was now to be surmounted. The difficulties of the ground, broken up into fearful chasms and watercourses, and tangled with thickets, were greatly increased by the darkness of the night; and the soldiers, as they toiled slowly upward, were filled with apprehension, akin to fear, from the uncertainty whether each successive step might not bring them into an ambuscade, for which the ground was so favorable. More than once, the Spaniards were thrown into a panic by false reports that the enemy were upon them. But Hinojosa and Valdivia were at hand to rally their men, and cheer them on, until, at length, before dawn broke, the bold cavaliers and their followers placed themselves on the highest point traversed by the road, where they waited the arrival of the president. This was not long delayed; and in the course of the following morning, the royalists were already in sufficient strength to bid defiance to their enemy.

The passage of the river had been effected with less loss than might have been expected, considering the darkness of the night, and the numbers that crowded over the aërial causeway. Some few, indeed, fell into the water, and were drowned;

and more than sixty horses, in the attempt to swim them across the river, were hurried down the current, and dashed against the rocks below. It still required time to bring up the heavy train of ordnance and the military wagons; and the president encamped on the strong ground which he now occupied, to await their arrival, and to breathe his troops after their extraordinary efforts. In these quarters we must leave him, to acquaint the reader with the state of things in the insurgent army, and with the cause of its strange remissness in guarding the passes of the Apurimac.

From the time of Pizarro's occupation of Cuzco, he had lived in careless luxury in the midst of his followers, like a soldier of fortune in the hour of prosperity; enjoying the present, with as little concern for the future as if the crown of Peru were already fixed irrevocably upon his head. It was otherwise with Carbajal. He looked on the victory at Huarina as the commencement, not the close, of the struggle for empire; and he was indefatigable in placing his troops in the best condition for maintaining their present advantage. At the first streak of dawn, the veteran might be seen mounted on his mule, with the garb and air of a common soldier, riding about in the different quarters of the capital, sometimes superintending the manufacture of arms, or providing military stores, and sometimes drilling his men, for he was most careful always to maintain the strictest discipline. His restless spirit seemed to find no pleasure but in incessant action; living, as he had always done, in the turmoil of military adventure, he had no relish for any thing unconnected with war, and in the city saw only the materials for a well-organized camp.

With these feelings, he was much dissatisfied at the course taken by his younger leader, who now professed his intention to abide where he was, and, when the enemy advanced, to give him battle. Carbajal advised a very different policy. He had not that full confidence, it would seem, in the loyalty of Pizarro's partisans, at least, not of those who had once followed the banner of Centeno. These men, some three hundred in number, had been in a manner compelled to take service under Pizarro. They showed no heartiness in the cause, and the veteran strongly urged his commander to disband them at once; since it was far better to go to battle with a few faithful followers than with a host of the false and faint-hearted.

But Carbajal thought, also, that his leader was not sufficiently strong in numbers to encounter his opponent, supported as he was by the best captains of Peru. He advised, accordingly, that he should abandon Cuzco, carrying off all the treasure, provisions, and stores of every kind from the city, which might, in any way, serve the necessities of the royalists. The latter, on their arrival, disappointed by the poverty of a place where they had expected to find so much booty, would become disgusted with the service. Pizarro, meanwhile, might take refuge with his men in the neighboring fastnesses, where, familiar with the ground, it would be easy to elude the enemy; and if the latter persevered in the pursuit, with numbers diminished by desertion, it would not be difficult in the mountain passes to find an opportunity for assailing him at advantage.— Such was the wary counsel of the old warrior. But it was not to the taste of his fiery commander, who preferred to risk the chances of a battle, rather than turn his back on a foe.

Neither did Pizarro show more favor to a proposition, said to have been made by the Licentiate Cepeda,—that he should avail himself of his late success to enter into negotiations with Gasca. Such advice, from the man who had so recently resisted all overtures of the president, could only have proceeded from a conviction, that the late victory placed Pizarro on a vantage-ground for demanding terms far better than would have been before conceded to him. It may be that subsequent experience had also led him to distrust the fidelity of Gonzalo's followers, or, possibly, the capacity of their chief to conduct them through the present crisis. Whatever may have been the motives of the slippery counsellor, Pizarro gave little heed to the suggestion, and even showed some resentment, as the matter was pressed on him. In every contest, with Indian or European, whatever had been the odds, he had come off victorious. He was not now for the first time to despond; and he resolved to remain in Cuzco, and hazard all on the chances of a battle. There was something in the hazard itself captivating to his bold and chivalrous temper. In this, too, he was confirmed by some of the cavaliers who had followed him through all his fortunes; reckless young adventurers, who, like himself, would

rather risk all on a single throw of the dice, than adopt the
cautious, and, as it seemed to them, timid, policy of graver
counsellors. It was by such advisers, then, that Pizarro's future
course was to be shaped.

Such was the state of affairs in Cuzco, when Pizarro's soldiers returned with the tidings, that a detachment of the
enemy had crossed the Apurimac, and were busy in reëstablishing the bridge. Carbajal saw at once the absolute necessity
of maintaining this pass. "It is my affair," he said; "I claim to
be employed on this service. Give me but a hundred picked
men, and I will engage to defend the pass against an army,
and bring back the *chaplain*"—the name by which the president was known in the rebel camp—"a prisoner to Cuzco." "I
cannot spare you, father," said Gonzalo, addressing him by
this affectionate epithet, which he usually applied to his aged
follower, "I cannot spare you so far from my own person"; and
he gave the commission to Juan de Acosta, a young cavalier
warmly attached to his commander, and who had given undoubted evidence of his valor on more than one occasion, but
who, as the event proved, was signally deficient in the qualities
demanded for so critical an undertaking as the present. Acosta,
accordingly, was placed at the head of two hundred mounted
musketeers, and, after much wholesome counsel from Carbajal,
set out on his expedition.

But he soon forgot the veteran's advice, and moved at so
dull a pace over the difficult roads, that, although the distance
was not more than nine leagues, he found, on his arrival, the
bridge completed, and so large a body of the enemy already
crossed, that he was in no strength to attack them. Acosta did,
indeed, meditate an ambuscade by night; but the design was
betrayed by a deserter, and he contented himself with retreating to a safe distance, and sending for a further reinforcement
from Cuzco. Three hundred men were promptly detached to
his support; but when they arrived, the enemy was already
planted in full force on the crest of the eminence. The golden
opportunity was irrecoverably lost; and the disconsolate cavalier rode back in all haste to report the failure of his enterprise
to his commander in Cuzco.

The only question now to be decided was as to the spot
where Gonzalo Pizarro should give battle to his enemies. He

determined at once to abandon the capital, and wait for his opponents in the neighboring valley of Xaquixaguana. It was about five leagues distant, and the reader may remember it as the place where Francis Pizarro burned the Peruvian general Challcuchima, on his first occupation of Cuzco. The valley, fenced round by the lofty rampart of the Andes, was, for the most part, green and luxuriant, affording many picturesque points of view; and, from the genial temperature of the climate, had been a favorite summer residence of the Indian nobles, many of whose pleasure-houses still dotted the sides of the mountains. A river, or rather stream, of no great volume, flowed through one end of this inclosure, and the neighboring soil was so wet and miry as to have the character of a morass.

Here the rebel commander arrived, after a tedious march over roads not easily traversed by his train of heavy wagons and artillery. His forces amounted in all to about nine hundred men, with some half-dozen pieces of ordnance. It was a well-appointed body, and under excellent discipline, for it had been schooled by the strictest martinet in the Peruvian service. But it was the misfortune of Pizarro that his army was composed, in part, at least, of men on whose attachment to his cause he could not confidently rely. This was a deficiency which no courage nor skill in the leader could supply.

On entering the valley, Pizarro selected the eastern quarter of it, towards Cuzco, as the most favorable spot for his encampment. It was crossed by the stream above mentioned, and he stationed his army in such a manner, that, while one extremity of the camp rested on a natural barrier formed by the mountain cliffs that here rose up almost perpendicularly, the other was protected by the river. While it was scarcely possible, therefore, to assail his flanks, the approaches in front were so extremely narrowed by these obstacles, that it would not be easy to overpower him by numbers in that direction. In the rear, his communications remained open with Cuzco, furnishing a ready means for obtaining supplies. Having secured this strong position, he resolved patiently to wait the assault of the enemy.

Meanwhile, the royal army had been toiling up the steep sides of the Cordilleras, until, at the close of the third day, the president had the satisfaction to find himself surrounded by his whole force, with their guns and military stores. Having now sufficiently refreshed his men, he resumed his march, and all went forward with the buoyant confidence of bringing their quarrel with the *tyrant*, as Pizarro was called, to a speedy issue.

Their advance was slow, as in the previous part of the march, for the ground was equally embarrassing. It was not long, however, before the president learned that his antagonist had pitched his camp in the neighboring valley of Xaquixaguana. Soon afterward, two friars, sent by Gonzalo himself, appeared in the army, for the ostensible purpose of demanding a sight of the powers with which Gasca was intrusted. But as their conduct gave reason to suspect they were spies, the president caused the holy men to be seized, and refused to allow them to return to Pizarro. By an emissary of his own, whom he despatched to the rebel chief, he renewed the assurance of pardon already given him, in case he would lay down his arms and submit. Such an act of generosity, at this late hour, must be allowed to be highly creditable to Gasca, believing, as he probably did, that the game was in his own hands.—It is a pity that the anecdote does not rest on the best authority.

After a march of a couple of days, the advanced guard of the royalists came suddenly on the outposts of the insurgents, from whom they had been concealed by a thick mist, and a slight skirmish took place between them. At length, on the morning of the eighth of April, the royal army, turning the crest of the lofty range that belts around the lovely valley of Xaquixaguana, beheld far below on the opposite side the glittering lines of the enemy, with their white pavilions, looking like clusters of wild fowl nestling among the cliffs of the mountains. And still further off might be descried a host of Indian warriors, showing gaudily in their variegated costumes; for the natives, in this part of the country, with little perception of their true interests, manifested great zeal in the cause of Pizarro.

Quickening their step, the royal army now hastily descended the steep sides of the sierra; and notwithstanding every effort of their officers, they moved in so little order, each man picking his way as he could, that the straggling column presented many a vulnerable point to the enemy; and the descent would not have been accomplished without considerable loss, had Pizarro's cannon been planted on any of the favorable positions which the ground afforded. But that commander, far from attempting to check the president's approach, remained doggedly in the strong position he had occupied, with the full confidence that his adversaries would not hesitate to assail it, strong as it was, in the same manner as they had done at Huarina.

Yet he did not omit to detach a corps of arquebusiers to secure a neighboring eminence or spur of the Cordilleras, which in the hands of the enemy might cause some annoyance to his own camp, while it commanded still more effectually the ground soon to be occupied by the assailants. But his manœuvre was noticed by Hinojosa; and he defeated it by sending a stronger detachment of the royal musketeers, who repulsed the rebels, and, after a short skirmish, got possession of the heights. Gasca's general profited by this success to plant a small battery of cannon on the eminence, from which, although the distance was too great for him to do much execution, he threw some shot into the hostile camp. One ball, indeed, struck down two men, one of them Pizarro's page, killing a horse, at the same time, which he held by the bridle; and the chief instantly ordered the tents to be struck, considering that they afforded too obvious a mark for the artillery.

Meanwhile, the president's forces had descended into the valley, and as they came on the plain were formed into line by their officers. The ground occupied by the army was somewhat lower than that of their enemy, whose shot, as discharged, from time to time, from his batteries, passed over their heads. Information was now brought by a deserter, one of Centeno's old followers, that Pizarro was getting ready for a night attack. The president, in consequence, commanded his whole force to be drawn up in battle array, prepared, at any instant, to repulse the assault. But if such were meditated by the insurgent chief, he abandoned it,—and, as it is said, from a distrust of the fidelity of some of the troops, who, under cover of the darkness, he feared, would go over to the opposite side. If this be true, he must have felt the full force of Carbajal's admonition, when too late to profit by it. The unfortunate commander was in the situation of some bold, high-mettled cavalier, rushing to battle on a war-horse whose tottering joints threaten to give way under him at every step, and leave his rider to the mercy of his enemies!

The president's troops stood to their arms the greater part of the night, although the air from the mountains was so keen, that it was with difficulty they could hold their lances in their hands. But before the rising sun had kindled into a glow the highest peaks of the sierra, both camps were in motion, and busily engaged in preparations for the combat. The royal army was formed into two battalions of infantry, one to attack the enemy in front, and the other, if possible, to operate on his flank. These battalions were protected by squadrons of horse on the wings and in the rear, while reserves both of horse and arquebusiers were stationed to act as occasion might require. The dispositions were made in so masterly a manner, as to draw forth a hearty eulogium from old Carbajal, who exclaimed, "Surely the Devil or Valdivia must be among them!" —an undeniable compliment to the latter, since the speaker was ignorant of that commander's presence in the camp.

Gasca, leaving the conduct of the battle to his officers, withdrew to the rear with his train of clergy and licentiates, the last of whom did not share in the ambition of their rebel brother, Cepeda, to break a lance in the field.

Gonzalo Pizarro formed his squadron in the same manner as he had done on the plains of Huarina; except that the increased number of his horse now enabled him to cover both flanks of his infantry. It was still on his fire-arms, however, that he chiefly relied. As the ranks were formed, he rode among them, encouraging his men to do their duty like brave cavaliers, and true soldiers of the Conquest. Pizarro was superbly armed, as usual, and wore a complete suit of mail, of the finest manufacture, which, as well as his helmet, was richly inlaid with gold. He rode a chestnut horse of great strength and spirit, and as he galloped along the line, brandishing his lance, and displaying his easy horsemanship, he might be thought to form no bad personification of the Genius of Chivalry. To complete his dispositions, he ordered Cepeda to lead up the infantry; for the licentiate seems to have had a larger share in the conduct of his affairs of late, or at least in the present military arrangements, than Carbajal. The latter, indeed, whether from disgust at the course taken by his leader, or from a distrust, which, it is said, he did not affect to conceal, of the success of the present operations, disclaimed all responsibility for them, and chose to serve rather as a private cavalier than as a commander. Yet Cepeda, as the event showed, was no less shrewd in detecting the coming ruin.

When he had received his orders from Pizarro, he rode forward as if to select the ground for his troops to occupy; and in doing so disappeared for a few moments behind a projecting cliff. He soon reappeared, however, and was seen galloping at full speed across the plain. His men looked with astonishment, yet not distrusting his motives, till, as he continued his course direct towards the enemy's lines, his treachery became apparent. Several pushed forward to overtake him, and among them a cavalier, better mounted than Cepeda. The latter rode a horse of no great strength or speed, quite unfit for this critical manœuvre of his master. The animal, was, moreover, encumbered by the weight of the caparisons with which his ambitious rider had loaded him, so that, on reaching a piece of miry ground that lay between the armies, his pace was greatly retarded. Cepeda's pursuers rapidly gained on him, and the cavalier above noticed came, at length, so near as to throw a lance at the fugitive, which, wounding him in the thigh, pierced his horse's flank, and they both came headlong to the ground. It would have fared ill with the licentiate, in this emergency, but fortunately a small party of troopers on the other side, who had watched the chase, now galloped briskly forward to the rescue, and, beating off his pursuers, they recovered Cepeda from the mire, and bore him to the president's quarters.

He was received by Gasca with the greatest satisfaction,—so great, that, according to one chronicler, he did not disdain to show it by saluting the licentiate on the cheek. The anecdote is scarcely reconcilable with the characters and relations of the parties, or with the president's subsequent conduct. Gasca, however, recognized the full value of his prize, and the effect which his desertion at such a time must have on the spirits of the rebels. Cepeda's movement, so unexpected by his own party, was the result of previous deliberation, as he had secretly given assurance, it is said, to the prior of

Arequipa, then in the royal camp, that, if Gonzalo Pizarro could not be induced to accept the pardon offered him, he would renounce his cause. The time selected by the crafty counsellor for doing so was that most fatal to the interests of his commander.

The example of Cepeda was contagious. Garcilasso de la Vega, father of the historian, a cavalier of old family, and probably of higher consideration than any other in Pizarro's party, put spurs to his horse, at the same time with the licentiate, and rode over to the enemy. Ten or a dozen of the arquebusiers followed in the same direction, and succeeded in placing themselves under the protection of the advanced guard of the royalists.

Pizarro stood aghast at this desertion, in so critical a juncture, of those in whom he had most trusted. He was, for a moment, bewildered. The very ground on which he stood seemed to be crumbling beneath him. With this state of feeling among his soldiers, he saw that every minute of delay was fatal. He dared not wait for the assault, as he had intended, in his strong position, but instantly gave the word to advance. Gasca's general, Hinojosa, seeing the enemy in motion, gave similar orders to his own troops. Instantly the skirmishers and arquebusiers on the flanks moved rapidly forward, the artillery prepared to open their fire, and "the whole army," says the president in his own account of the affair, "advanced with steady step and perfect determination."

But before a shot was fired, a column of arquebusiers, composed chiefly of Centeno's followers, abandoned their post, and marched directly over to the enemy. A squadron of horse, sent in pursuit of them, followed their example. The president instantly commanded his men to halt, unwilling to spill blood unnecessarily, as the rebel host was like to fall to pieces of itself.

Pizarro's faithful adherents were seized with a panic, as they saw themselves and their leader thus betrayed into the enemy's hands. Further resistance was useless. Some threw down their arms, and fled in the direction of Cuzco. Others sought to escape to the mountains; and some crossed to the opposite side, and surrendered themselves prisoners, hoping it was not too late to profit by the promises of grace. The Indian allies, on seeing the Spaniards falter, had been the first to go off the ground.

Pizarro, amidst the general wreck, found himself left with only a few cavaliers who disdained to fly. Stunned by the unexpected reverse of fortune, the unhappy chief could hardly comprehend his situation. "What remains for us?" said he to Acosta, one of those who still adhered to him. "Fall on the enemy, since nothing else is left," answered the lion-hearted soldier, "and die like Romans!" "Better to die like Christians," replied his commander; and, slowly turning his horse, he rode off in the direction of the royal army.

He had not proceeded far, when he was met by an officer, to whom, after ascertaining his name and rank, Pizarro delivered up his sword, and yielded himself prisoner. The officer, overjoyed at his prize, conducted him, at once, to the president's quarters. Gasca was on horseback, surrounded by his captains, some of whom, when they recognized the person of the captive, had the grace to withdraw, that they might not witness his humiliation. Even the best of them, with a sense of right on their side, may have felt some touch of compunction at the thought that their desertion had brought their benefactor to this condition.

Pizarro kept his seat in his saddle, but, as he approached, made a respectful obeisance to the president, which the latter acknowledged by a cold salute. Then, addressing his prisoner in a tone of severity, Gasca abruptly inquired,—"Why he had thrown the country into such confusion;—raising the banner of revolt; killing the viceroy; usurping the government; and obstinately refusing the offers of grace that had been repeatedly made him?"

Gonzalo attempted to justify himself by referring the fate of the viceroy to his misconduct, and his own usurpation, as it was styled, to the free election of the people, as well as that of the Royal Audience. "It was my family," he said, "who conquered the country; and, as their representative here, I felt I had a right to the government." To this Gasca replied, in a still severer tone, "Your brother did, indeed, conquer the land; and for this the emperor was pleased to raise both him and you from the dust. He lived and died a true and loyal subject; and it only makes your ingratitude to your sovereign

the more heinous." Then, seeing his prisoner about to reply,
the president cut short the conference, ordering him into close
confinement. He was committed to the charge of Centeno,
who had sought the office, not from any unworthy desire to
gratify his revenge,—for he seems to have had a generous nature,—but for the honorable purpose of ministering to the
comfort of the captive. Though held in strict custody by this
officer, therefore, Pizarro was treated with the deference due
to his rank, and allowed every indulgence by his keeper, except
his freedom.

In this general wreck of their fortunes, Francisco de Carbajal fared no better than his chief. As he saw the soldiers
deserting their posts and going over to the enemy, one after
another, he coolly hummed the words of his favorite old
ballad:

"The wind blows the hairs off my head, mother!"

But when he found the field nearly empty, and his stout-
hearted followers vanished like a wreath of smoke, he felt it
was time to provide for his own safety. He knew there could
be no favor for him; and, putting spurs to his horse, he be-
took himself to flight with all the speed he could make. He
crossed the stream that flowed, as already mentioned, by the
camp, but, in scaling the opposite bank, which was steep and
stony, his horse, somewhat old, and oppressed by the weight
of his rider, who was large and corpulent, lost his footing and
fell with him into the water. Before he could extricate himself, Carbajal was seized by some of his own followers, who
hoped, by such a prize, to make their peace with the victor,
and hurried off towards the president's quarters.

The convoy was soon swelled by a number of the common
file from the royal army, some of whom had long arrears to
settle with the prisoner; and, not content with heaping reproaches and imprecations on his head, they now threatened
to proceed to acts of personal violence, which Carbajal, far
from deprecating, seemed rather to court, as the speediest way
of ridding himself of life. When he approached the president's
quarters, Centeno, who was near, rebuked the disorderly rab-
ble, and compelled them to give way. Carbajal, on seeing this,
with a respectful air demanded to whom he was indebted for

this courteous protection. To which his ancient comrade replied, "Do you not know me?—Diego Centeno!" "I crave your pardon," said the veteran, sarcastically alluding to his long flight in the Charcas, and his recent defeat at Huarina; "it is so long since I have seen any thing but your back, that I had forgotten your face!"

Among the president's suite was the martial bishop of Cuzco, who, it will be remembered had shared with Centeno in the disgrace of his defeat. His brother had been taken by Carbajal, in his flight from the field, and instantly hung up by that fierce chief, who, as we have had more than one occasion to see, was no respecter of persons. The bishop now reproached him with his brother's murder, and, incensed by his cool replies, was ungenerous enough to strike the prisoner on the face. Carbajal made no attempt at resistance. Nor would he return a word to the queries put to him by Gasca; but, looking haughtily round on the circle, maintained a contemptuous silence. The president, seeing that nothing further was to be gained from his captive, ordered him, together with Acosta, and the other cavaliers who had surrendered, into strict custody, until their fate should be decided.

Gasca's next concern was to send an officer to Cuzco, to restrain his partisans from committing excesses in consequence of the late victory,—if victory that could be called, where not a blow had been struck. Every thing belonging to the vanquished, their tents, arms, ammunition, and military stores, became the property of the victors. Their camp was well victualled, furnishing a seasonable supply to the royalists, who had nearly expended their own stock of provisions. There was, moreover, considerable booty in the way of plate and money; for Pizarro's men, as was not uncommon in those turbulent times, went, many of them, to the war with the whole of their worldly wealth, not knowing of any safe place in which to bestow it. An anecdote is told of one of Gasca's soldiers, who, seeing a mule running over the field, with a large pack on his back, seized the animal, and mounted him, having first thrown away the burden, supposing it to contain armour, or something of little worth. Another soldier, more shrewd, picked up the parcel, as his share of the spoil, and found it contained several thousand gold ducats! It was the fortune of war.

Thus terminated the battle, or rather rout, of Xaquixaguana. The number of killed and wounded—for some few perished in the pursuit—was not great; according to most accounts, not exceeding fifteen killed on the rebel side, and one only on that of the royalists! and that one, by the carelessness of a comrade. Never was there a cheaper victory; so bloodless a termination of a fierce and bloody rebellion! It was gained not so much by the strength of the victors as by the weakness of the vanquished. They fell to pieces of their own accord, because they had no sure ground to stand on. The arm, not nerved by the sense of right, became powerless in the hour of battle. It was better that they should thus be overcome by moral force than by a brutal appeal to arms. Such a victory was more in harmony with the beneficent character of the conqueror and of his cause. It was the triumph of order; the best homage to law and justice.

CHAPTER IV [1548–1550]

EXECUTION OF CARBAJAL—GONZALO PIZARRO BE-
HEADED—SPOILS OF VICTORY—WISE REFORMS BY
GASCA—HE RETURNS TO SPAIN—HIS DEATH AND CHAR-
ACTER

It was now necessary to decide on the fate of the prisoners; and Alonso de Alvarado, with the Licentiate Cianca,
one of the new Royal Audience, was instructed to prepare
the process. It did not require a long time. The guilt of the
prisoners was too manifest, taken, as they had been, with arms
in their hands. They were all sentenced to be executed, and
their estates were confiscated to the use of the Crown. Gonzalo
Pizarro was to be beheaded, and Carbajal to be drawn and
quartered. No mercy was shown to him who had shown none
to others. There was some talk of deferring the execution till
the arrival of the troops in Cuzco; but the fear of disturbances
from those friendly to Pizarro determined the president to
carry the sentence into effect the following day, on the field
of battle.

When his doom was communicated to Carbajal, he heard it
with his usual indifference. "They can but kill me," he said,
as if he had already settled the matter in his own mind. During the day, many came to see him in his confinement; some
to upbraid him with his cruelties; but most, from curiosity to
see the fierce warrior who had made his name so terrible
through the land. He showed no unwillingness to talk with
them, though it was in those sallies of caustic humor in which
he usually indulged at the expense of his hearer. Among these
visitors was a cavalier of no note, whose life, it appears, Carbajal had formerly spared, when in his power. This person expressed to the prisoner his strong desire to serve him; and as
he reiterated his professions, Carbajal cut them short by exclaiming,—"And what service can you do me? Can you set me
free? If you cannot do that, you can do nothing. If I spared

your life, as you say, it was probably because I did not think it worth while to take it."

Some piously disposed persons urged him to see a priest, if it were only to unburden his conscience before leaving the world. "But of what use would that be?" asked Carbajal. "I have nothing that lies heavy on my conscience, unless it be, indeed, the debt of half a real to a shopkeeper in Seville, which I forgot to pay before leaving the country!"

He was carried to execution on a hurdle, or rather in a basket, drawn by two mules. His arms were pinioned, and, as they forced his bulky body into this miserable conveyance, he exclaimed,—"Cradles for infants, and a cradle for the old man too, it seems!" Notwithstanding the disinclination he had manifested to a confessor, he was attended by several ecclesiastics on his way to the gallows; and one of them repeatedly urged him to give some token of penitence at this solemn hour, if it were only by repeating the *Pater Noster* and *Ave Maria*. Carbajal, to rid himself of the ghostly father's importunity, replied by coolly repeating the words, *"Pater Noster,"* *"Ave Maria"*! He then remained obstinately silent. He died, as he had lived, with a jest, or rather a scoff, upon his lips.

Francisco de Carbajal was one of the most extraordinary characters of these dark and turbulent times; the more extraordinary from his great age; for, at the period of his death, he was in his eighty-fourth year;—an age when the bodily powers, and, fortunately, the passions, are usually blunted; when, in the witty words of the French moralist, "We flatter ourselves we are leaving our vices, whereas it is our vices that are leaving us." But the fires of youth glowed fierce and unquenchable in the bosom of Carbajal.

The date of his birth carries us back towards the middle of the fifteenth century, before the times of Ferdinand and Isabella. He was of obscure parentage, and born, as it is said, at Arevalo. For forty years he served in the Italian wars, under the most illustrious captains of the day, Gonsalvo de Cordova, Navarro, and the Colonnas. He was an ensign at the battle of Ravenna; witnessed the capture of Francis the First at Pavia; and followed the banner of the ill-starred Bourbon at the sack of Rome. He got no gold for his share of the booty, on this occasion, but simply the papers of a notary's office, which,

Carbajal shrewdly thought, would be worth gold to him. And so it proved; for the notary was fain to redeem them at a price which enabled the adventurer to cross the seas to Mexico, and seek his fortune in the New World. On the insurrection of the Peruvians, he was sent to the support of Francis Pizarro, and was rewarded by that chief with a grant of land in Cuzco. Here he remained for several years, busily employed in increasing his substance; for the love of lucre was a ruling passion in his bosom. On the arrival of Vaca de Castro, we find him doing good service under the royal banner; and at the breaking out of the great rebellion under Gonzalo Pizarro, he converted his property into gold, and prepared to return to Castile. He seemed to have a presentiment that to remain where he was would be fatal. But, although he made every effort to leave Peru, he was unsuccessful, for the viceroy had laid an embargo on the shipping. He remained in the country, therefore, and took service, as we have seen, though reluctantly, under Pizarro. It was his destiny.

The tumultuous life on which he now entered roused all the slumbering passions of his soul, which lay there, perhaps unconsciously to himself; cruelty, avarice, revenge. He found ample exercise for them in the war with his countrymen; for civil war is proverbially the most sanguinary and ferocious of all. The atrocities recorded of Carbajal, in his new career, and the number of his victims, are scarcely credible. For the honor of humanity, we may trust the accounts are greatly exaggerated; but that he should have given rise to them at all is sufficient to consign his name to infamy.

He even took a diabolical pleasure, it is said, in amusing himself with the sufferings of his victims, and in the hour of execution would give utterance to frightful jests, that made them taste more keenly the bitterness of death! He had a sportive vein, if such it could be called, which he freely indulged on every occasion. Many of his sallies were preserved by the soldiery; but they are, for the most part, of a coarse, repulsive character, flowing from a mind familiar with the weak and wicked side of humanity, and distrusting every other. He had his jest for every thing,—for the misfortunes of others, and for his own. He looked on life as a farce,—though he too often made it a tragedy.

Carbajal must be allowed one virtue; that of fidelity to his party. This made him less tolerant to perfidy in others. He was never known to show mercy to a renegade. This undeviating fidelity, though to a bad cause, may challenge something like a feeling of respect, where fidelity was so rare.

As a military man, Carbajal takes a high rank among the soldiers of the New World. He was strict, even severe, in enforcing discipline, so that he was little loved by his followers. Whether he had the genius for military combinations requisite for conducting war on an extended scale may be doubted; but in the shifts and turns of guerilla warfare he was unrivalled. Prompt, active, and persevering, he was insensible to danger or fatigue, and, after days spent in the saddle, seemed to attach little value to the luxury of a bed.

He knew familiarly every mountain pass, and, such were the sagacity and the resources displayed in his roving expeditions, that he was vulgarly believed to be attended by a *familiar*. With a character so extraordinary, with powers prolonged so far beyond the usual term of humanity, and passions so fierce in one tottering on the verge of the grave, it was not surprising that many fabulous stories should be eagerly circulated respecting him, and that Carbajal should be clothed with mysterious terrors as a sort of supernatural being,—the demon of the Andes!

Very different were the circumstances attending the closing scene of Gonzalo Pizarro. At his request, no one had been allowed to visit him in his confinement. He was heard pacing his tent during the greater part of the day, and when night came, having ascertained from Centeno that his execution was to take place on the following noon, he laid himself down to rest. He did not sleep long, however, but soon rose, and continued to traverse his apartment, as if buried in meditation, till dawn. He then sent for a confessor, and remained with him till after the hour of noon, taking little or no refreshment. The officers of justice became impatient; but their eagerness was sternly rebuked by the soldiery, many of whom, having served under Gonzalo's banner, were touched with pity for his misfortunes.

When the chieftain came forth to execution, he showed in his dress the same love of magnificence and display as in happier days. Over his doublet he wore a superb cloak of yellow velvet, stiff with gold embroidery, while his head was protected by a cap of the same materials, richly decorated, in like manner, with ornaments of gold. In this gaudy attire he mounted his mule, and the sentence was so far relaxed that his arms were suffered to remain unshackled. He was escorted by a goodly number of priests and friars, who held up the crucifix before his eyes, while he carried in his own hand an image of the Virgin. She had ever been the peculiar object of Pizarro's devotion; so much so, that those who knew him best in the hour of his prosperity were careful, when they had a petition, to prefer it in the name of the blessed Mary.

Pizarro's lips were frequently pressed to the emblem of his divinity, while his eyes were bent on the crucifix in apparent devotion, heedless of the objects around him. On reaching the scaffold, he ascended it with a firm step, and asked leave to address a few words to the soldiery gathered round it. "There are many among you," said he, "who have grown rich on my brother's bounty, and my own. Yet, of all my riches, nothing remains to me but the garments I have on; and even these are not mine, but the property of the executioner. I am without means, therefore, to purchase a mass for the welfare of my soul; and I implore you, by the remembrance of past benefits, to extend this charity to me when I am gone, that it may be well with you in the hour of death." A profound silence reigned throughout the martial multitude, broken only by sighs and groans, as they listened to Pizarro's request; and it was faithfully responded to, since, after his death, masses were said in many of the towns for the welfare of the departed chieftain.

Then, kneeling down before a crucifix placed on a table, Pizarro remained for some minutes absorbed in prayer; after which, addressing the soldier who was to act as the minister of justice, he calmly bade him "do his duty with a steady hand." He refused to have his eyes bandaged, and, bending forward his neck, submitted it to the sword of the executioner, who struck off the head with a single blow, so true that the body remained for some moments in the same erect posture as in life. The head was taken to Lima, where it was set in a cage or frame, and then fixed on a gibbet by the side of Carbajal's. On it was placed a label, bearing,—"This is the head of the traitor Gonzalo Pizarro, who rebelled in Peru against his sovereign, and battled in the cause of tyranny and treason against the royal standard in the valley of Xaquixaguana." His large estates, including the rich mines in Potosí, were confiscated; his mansion in Lima was razed to the ground, the place strewed with salt, and a stone pillar set up, with an inscription interdicting any one from building on a spot which had been profaned by the residence of a traitor.

Gonzalo's remains were not exposed to the indignities inflicted on Carbajal's, whose quarters were hung in chains on the four great roads leading to Cuzco. Centeno saved Pizarro's body from being stripped, by redeeming his costly raiment from the executioner, and in this sumptuous shroud it was laid in the chapel of the convent of Our Lady of Mercy in Cuzco. It was the same spot where, side by side, lay the bloody remains of the Almagros, father and son, who in like manner had perished by the hand of justice, and were indebted to private charity for their burial. All these were now consigned "to the same grave," says the historian, with some bitterness, "as if Peru could not afford land enough for a burial-place to its conquerors."

Gonzalo Pizarro had reached only his forty-second year at the time of his death,—being just half the space allotted to his follower Carbajal. He was the youngest of the remarkable family to whom Spain was indebted for the acquisition of Peru. He came over to the country with his brother Francisco, on the return of the latter from his visit to Castile. Gonzalo was present in all the remarkable passages of the Conquest. He witnessed the seizure of Atahuallpa, took an active part in suppressing the insurrection of the Incas, and especially in the reduction of Charcas. He afterwards led the disastrous expedition to the Amazon; and, finally, headed the memorable rebellion which ended so fatally to himself. There are but few men whose lives abound in such wild and romantic adventure, and, for the most part, crowned with success. The space which he occupies in the page of history is altogether disproportioned to his talents. It may be in some measure ascribed to fortune, but still more to those showy qualities which form a sort of substitute for mental talent, and which secured his popularity with the vulgar.

He had a brilliant exterior; excelled in all martial exercises; rode well, fenced well, managed his lance to perfection, was a first-rate marksman with the arquebuse, and added the accomplishment of being an excellent draughtsman. He was bold and chivalrous, even to temerity; courted adventure, and was always in the front of danger. He was a knight-errant, in short, in the most extravagant sense of the term, and, "mounted on his favorite charger," says one who had often seen him, "made no more account of a squadron of Indians than of a swarm of flies."

While thus, by his brilliant exploits and showy manners, he captivated the imaginations of his countrymen, he won their hearts no less by his soldier-like frankness, his trust in their fidelity,—too often abused,—and his liberal largesses; for Pizarro, though avaricious of the property of others, was, like the Roman conspirator, prodigal of his own. This was his portrait in happier days, when his heart had not been corrupted by success; for that some change was wrought on him by his prosperity is well attested. His head was made giddy by his elevation; and it is proof of a want of talent equal to his success, that he knew not how to profit by it. Obeying the dictates of his own rash judgment, he rejected the warnings of his wisest counsellors, and relied with blind confidence on his destiny. Garcilasso imputes this to the malignant influence of the stars. But the superstitious chronicler might have better explained it by a common principle of human nature; by the presumption nourished by success; the insanity, as the Roman, or rather Grecian, proverb calls it, with which the gods afflict men when they design to ruin them.

Gonzalo was without education, except such as he had picked up in the rough school of war. He had little even of that wisdom which springs from natural shrewdness and insight into character. In all this he was inferior to his elder brothers, although he fully equalled them in ambition. Had he possessed a tithe of their sagacity, he would not have madly persisted in rebellion, after the coming of the president. Before this period, he represented the people. Their interests and his were united. He had their support, for he was contending for the redress of their wrongs. When these were redressed by the government, there was nothing to contend for. From that time, he was battling only for himself. The people had no part nor interest in the contest. Without a common sympathy to bind them together, was it strange that they should fall off from him, like leaves in winter, and leave him exposed, a bare and sapless trunk, to the fury of the tempest?

Cepeda, more criminal than Pizarro, since he had both superior education and intelligence, which he employed only to mislead his commander, did not long survive him. He had come to the country in an office of high responsibility. His first step was to betray the viceroy whom he was sent to support; his next was to betray the Audience with whom he should have acted; and lastly, he betrayed the leader whom he most affected to serve. His whole career was treachery to his own government. His life was one long perfidy.

After his surrender, several of the cavaliers, disgusted at his cold-blooded apostasy, would have persuaded Gasca to send him to execution along with his commander; but the president refused, in consideration of the signal service he had rendered the Crown by his defection. He was put under arrest, however, and sent to Castile. There he was arraigned for high treason. He made a plausible defence, and as he had friends at court, it is not improbable he would have been acquitted; but, before the trial was terminated, he died in prison. It was the retributive justice not always to be found in the affairs of this world.

Indeed, it so happened, that several of those who had been most forward to abandon the cause of Pizarro survived their commander but a short time. The gallant Centeno, and the Licentiate Carbajal, who deserted him near Lima, and bore the royal standard on the field of Xaquixaguana, both died within a year after Pizarro. Hinojosa was assassinated but two years later in La Plata; and his old comrade Valdivia, after a series of brilliant exploits in Chili, which furnished her most glorious theme to the epic Muse of Castile, was cut off by the invincible warriors of Arauco. The Manes of Pizarro were amply avenged.

Acosta, and three or four other cavaliers who surrendered with Gonzalo, were sent to execution on the same day with their chief; and Gasca, on the morning following the dismal tragedy, broke up his quarters and marched with his whole army to Cuzco, where he was received by the politic people with the same enthusiasm which they had so recently shown to his rival. He found there a number of the rebel army who had taken refuge in the city after their late defeat, where they were immediately placed under arrest. Proceedings, by Gasca's command, were instituted against them. The principal cavaliers, to the number of ten or twelve, were executed; others were banished or sent to the galleys; and the estates of all were confiscated. The estates of the rebels supplied a fund for the recompense of the loyal. The execution of justice may seem to have been severe; but Gasca was willing that the rod should fall heavily on those who had so often rejected his proffers of grace. Lenity was wasted on a rude, licentious soldiery, who hardly recognized the existence of government, unless they felt its rigor.

A new duty now devolved on the president,—that of rewarding his faithful followers,—not less difficult, as it proved, than that of punishing the guilty. The applicants were numerous; since every one who had raised a finger in behalf of the government claimed his reward. They urged their demands with a clamorous importunity which perplexed the good president, and consumed every moment of his time.

Disgusted with this unprofitable state of things, Gasca resolved to rid himself of the annoyance at once, by retiring to the valley of Guaynarima, about twelve leagues distant from the city, and there digesting, in quiet, a scheme of compensation, adjusted to the merits of the parties. He was accompanied only by his secretary, and by Loaysa, now archbishop of Lima, a man of sense, and well acquainted with the affairs of the country. In this seclusion the president remained three months, making a careful examination into the conflicting claims, and apportioning the forfeitures among the parties according to their respective services. The *repartimientos*, it should be remarked, were usually granted only for life, and, on the death of the incumbent, reverted to the Crown, to be reassigned or retained at its pleasure.

When his arduous task was completed, Gasca determined to withdraw to Lima, leaving the instrument of partition with the archbishop, to be communicated to the army. Notwithstanding all the care that had been taken for an equitable adjustment, Gasca was aware that it was impossible to satisfy the demands of a jealous and irritable soldiery, where each man would be likely to exaggerate his own deserts, while he underrated those of his comrades; and he did not care to expose himself to importunities and complaints that could serve no other purpose than to annoy him.

On his departure, the troops were called together by the archbishop in the cathedral, to learn the contents of the schedule intrusted to him. A discourse was first preached by a worthy Dominican, the prior of Arequipa, in which the reverend father expatiated on the virtue of contentment, the duty of obedience, and the folly, as well as wickedness, of an attempt to resist the constituted authorities,—topics, in short, which he conceived might best conciliate the good-will and conformity of his audience.

A letter from the president was then read from the pulpit. It was addressed to the officers and soldiers of the army. The writer began with briefly exposing the difficulties of his task, owing to the limited amount of the gratuities, and the great number and services of the claimants. He had given the matter the most careful consideration, he said, and endeavored to assign to each his share, according to his deserts, without prejudice or partiality. He had, no doubt, fallen into errors, but he trusted his followers would excuse them, when they reflected that he had done according to the best of his poor abilities; and all, he believed, would do him the justice to acknowledge he had not been influenced by motives of personal interest. He bore emphatic testimony to the services they had rendered to the good cause, and concluded with the most affectionate wishes for their future prosperity and happiness. The letter was dated at Guaynarima, August 17, 1548, and bore the simple signature of the Licentiate Gasca.

The archbishop next read the paper containing the president's award. The annual rent of the estates to be distributed amounted to a hundred and thirty thousand *pesos ensayados;* a large amount, considering the worth of money in that day,— in any other country than Peru, where money was a drug.

The *repartimientos* thus distributed varied in value from one hundred to thirty-five hundred *pesos* of yearly rent; all, apparently, graduated with the nicest precision to the merits of the parties. The number of pensioners was about two hundred and fifty; for the fund would not have sufficed for general distribution, nor were the services of the greater part deemed worthy of such a mark of consideration.

The effect produced by the document, on men whose minds were filled with the most indefinite expectations, was just such as had been anticipated by the president. It was received with a general murmur of disapprobation. Even those who had got more than they expected were discontented, on comparing their condition with that of their comrades, whom they thought still better remunerated in proportion to their deserts. They especially inveighed against the preference shown to the old partisans of Gonzalo Pizarro—as Hinojosa, Centeno, and Aldana—over those who had always remained loyal to the Crown. There was some ground for such a preference; for none had rendered so essential services in crushing the rebellion; and it was these services that Gasca proposed to recompense. To reward every man who had proved himself loyal, simply for his loyalty, would have frittered away the donative into fractions that would be of little value to any.

It was in vain, however, that the archbishop, seconded by some of the principal cavaliers, endeavored to infuse a more contented spirit into the multitude. They insisted that the award should be rescinded, and a new one made on more equitable principles; threatening, moreover, that, if this were not done by the president, they would take the redress of the matter into their own hands. Their discontent, fomented by some mischievous persons who thought to find their account in it, at length proceeded so far as to menace a mutiny; and it was not suppressed till the commander of Cuzco sentenced one of the ringleaders to death, and several others to banishment. The iron soldiery of the Conquest required an iron hand to rule them.

Meanwhile, the president had continued his journey towards Lima; and on the way was everywhere received by the people with an enthusiasm, the more grateful to his heart that he felt he had deserved it. As he drew near the capital, the loyal inhabitants prepared to give him a magnificent reception. The whole population came forth from the gates, led by the au-

thorities of the city, with Aldana as corregidor at their head.
Gasca rode on a mule, dressed in his ecclesiastical robes. On
his right, borne on a horse richly caparisoned, was the royal
seal, in a box curiously chased and ornamented. A gorgeous
canopy of brocade was supported above his head by the officers of the municipality, who, in their robes of crimson velvet,
walked bareheaded by his side. Gay troops of dancers, clothed
in fantastic dresses of gaudy-colored silk, followed the procession, strewing flowers and chanting verses as they went, in
honor of the president. They were designed as emblematical
of the different cities of the colony; and they bore legends or
mottoes in rhyme on their caps, intimating their loyal devotion
to the Crown, and evincing much more loyalty in their composition, it may be added, than poetical merit. In this way, without beat of drum, or noise of artillery, or any of the rude accompaniments of war, the good president made his peaceful
entry into the City of the Kings, while the air was rent with
the acclamations of the people, who hailed him as their "Father and Deliverer, the Savior of their country!"

But, however grateful was this homage to Gasca's heart, he
was not a man to waste his time in idle vanities. He now
thought only by what means he could eradicate the seeds of
disorder which shot up so readily in this fruitful soil, and how
he could place the authority of the government on a permanent basis. By virtue of his office, he presided over the Royal
Audience, the great judicial, and, indeed, executive tribunal
of the colony; and he gave great despatch to the business,
which had much accumulated during the late disturbances.
In the unsettled state of property, there was abundant subject
for litigation; but, fortunately, the new Audience was composed of able, upright judges, who labored diligently with
their chief to correct the mischief caused by the misrule of
their predecessors.

Neither was Gasca unmindful of the unfortunate natives;
and he occupied himself earnestly with that difficult problem,
—the best means practicable of ameliorating their condition.
He sent a number of commissioners, as visitors, into different
parts of the country, whose business it was to inspect the *encomiendas*, and ascertain the manner in which the Indians
were treated, by conversing not only with the proprietors, but

with the natives themselves. They were also to learn the nature and extent of the tributes paid in former times by the vassals of the Incas.

In this way, a large amount of valuable information was obtained, which enabled Gasca, with the aid of a council of ecclesiastics and jurists, to digest a uniform system of taxation for the natives, lighter even than that imposed on them by the Peruvian princes. The president would gladly have relieved the conquered races from the obligations of personal service; but, on mature consideration, this was judged impracticable in the present state of the country, since the colonists, more especially in the tropical regions, looked to the natives for the performance of labor, and the latter, it was found from experience, would not work at all, unless compelled to do so. The president, however, limited the amount of service to be exacted with great precision, so that it was in the nature of a moderate personal tax. No Peruvian was to be required to change his place of residence, from the climate to which he had been accustomed, to another; a fruitful source of discomfort, as well as of disease, in past times. By these various regulations, the condition of the natives, though not such as had been contemplated by the sanguine philanthropy of Las Casas, was improved far more than was compatible with the craving demands of the colonists; and all the firmness of the Audience was required to enforce provisions so unpalatable to the latter. Still they were enforced. Slavery, in its most odious sense, was no longer tolerated in Peru. The term "slave" was not recognized as having relation to her institutions; and the historian of the Indies makes the proud boast,—it should have been qualified by the limitations I have noticed,—that every Indian vassal might aspire to the rank of a freeman.

Besides these reforms, Gasca introduced several in the municipal government of the cities, and others yet more important in the management of the finances, and in the mode of keeping the accounts. By these and other changes in the internal economy of the colony, he placed the administration on a new basis, and greatly facilitated the way for a more sure and orderly government by his successors. As a final step, to secure the repose of the country after he was gone, he detached some of the more aspiring cavaliers on distant expeditions, trusting that they would draw off the light and restless spirits, who might otherwise gather together and disturb the public tranquillity; as we sometimes see the mists which have been scattered by the genial influence of the sun become condensed, and settle into a storm, on his departure.

Gasca had been now more than fifteen months in Lima, and nearly three years had elapsed since his first entrance into Peru. In that time, he had accomplished the great objects of his mission. When he landed, he found the colony in a state of anarchy, or rather organized rebellion under a powerful and popular chief. He came without funds or forces to support him. The former he procured through the credit which he established in his good faith; the latter he won over by argument and persuasion from the very persons to whom they had been confided by his rival. Thus he turned the arms of that rival against himself. By a calm appeal to reason he wrought a change in the hearts of the people; and, without costing a drop of blood to a single loyal subject, he suppressed a rebellion which had menaced Spain with the loss of the wealthiest of her provinces. He had punished the guilty, and in their spoils found the means to recompense the faithful. He had, moreover, so well husbanded the resources of the country, that he was enabled to pay off the large loan he had negotiated with the merchants of the colony, for the expenses of the war, exceeding nine hundred thousand *pesos de oro*. Nay, more, by his economy he had saved a million and a half of ducats for the government, which for some years had received nothing from Peru; and he now proposed to carry back this acceptable treasure to swell the royal coffers. All this had been accomplished without the cost of outfit or salary, or any charge to the Crown except that of his own frugal expenditure. The country was now in a state of tranquillity. Gasca felt that his work was done; and that he was free to gratify his natural longing to return to his native land.

Before his departure, he arranged a distribution of those *repartimientos* which had lapsed to the Crown during the past year by the death of the incumbents. Life was short in Peru; since those who lived by the sword, if they did not die by the sword, too often fell early victims to the hardships incident to their adventurous career. Many were the applicants for the new bounty of government; and, as among them were some of those who had been discontented with the former partition, Gasca was assailed by remonstrances, and sometimes by reproaches couched in no very decorous or respectful language. But they had no power to disturb his equanimity; he patiently listened, and replied to all in the mild tone of expostulation best calculated to turn away wrath; "by this victory over himself," says an old writer, "acquiring more real glory, than by all his victories over his enemies."

An incident occurred on the eve of his departure, touching in itself, and honorable to the parties concerned. The Indian caciques of the neighboring country, mindful of the great benefits he had rendered their people, presented him with a considerable quantity of plate in token of their gratitude. But Gasca refused to receive it, though in doing so he gave much concern to the Peruvians, who feared they had unwittingly fallen under his displeasure.

Many of the principal colonists, also, from the same wish to show their sense of his important services, sent to him, after he had embarked, a magnificent donative of fifty thousand gold *castellanos*. "As he had taken leave of Peru," they said, "there could be no longer any ground for declining it." But Gasca was as decided in his rejection of this present, as he had been of the other. "He had come to the country," he remarked, "to serve the king, and to secure the blessings of peace to the inhabitants; and now that, by the favor of Heaven, he had been permitted to accomplish this, he would not dishonor the cause by any act that might throw suspicion on the purity of his motives." Notwithstanding his refusal, the colonists contrived to secrete the sum of twenty thousand *castellanos* on board his vessel, with the idea, that, once in his own country, with his mission concluded, the president's scruples would be removed. Gasca did, indeed, accept the donative; for he felt that it would be ungracious to send it back; but it was only till he could ascertain the relatives of the donors, when he distributed it among the most needy.

Having now settled all his affairs, the president committed the government, until the arrival of a viceroy, to his faithful partners of the Royal Audience; and in January, 1550, he embarked with the royal treasure on board of a squadron for

Panamá. He was accompanied to the shore by a numerous crowd of the inhabitants, cavaliers and common people, persons of all ages and conditions, who followed to take their last look of their benefactor, and watch with straining eyes the vessel that bore him away from their land.

His voyage was prosperous, and early in March the president reached his destined port. He stayed there only till he could muster horses and mules sufficient to carry the treasure across the mountains; for he knew that this part of the country abounded in wild, predatory spirits, who would be sorely tempted to some act of violence by a knowledge of the wealth which he had with him. Pushing forward, therefore, he crossed the rugged Isthmus, and, after a painful march, arrived in safety at Nombre de Dios.

The event justified his apprehensions. He had been gone but three days, when a ruffian horde, after murdering the bishop of Guatemala, broke into Panamá with the design of inflicting the same fate on the president, and of seizing the booty. No sooner were the tidings communicated to Gasca, than, with his usual energy, he levied a force and prepared to march to the relief of the invaded capital. But Fortune—or, to speak more correctly, Providence—favored him here, as usual; and, on the eve of his departure, he learned that the marauders had been met by the citizens, and discomfited with great slaughter. Disbanding his forces, therefore, he equipped a fleet of nineteen vessels to transport himself and the royal treasure to Spain, where he arrived in safety, entering the harbor of Seville after a little more than four years from the period when he had sailed from the same port.

Great was the sensation throughout the country caused by his arrival. Men could hardly believe that results so momentous had been accomplished in so short a time by a single individual,—a poor ecclesiastic, who, unaided by government, had, by his own strength, as it were, put down a rebellion which had so long set the arms of Spain at defiance!

The emperor was absent in Flanders. He was overjoyed on learning the complete success of Gasca's mission; and not less satisfied with the tidings of the treasure he had brought with him; for the exchequer, rarely filled to overflowing, had been exhausted by the recent troubles in Germany. Charles instantly wrote to the president, requiring his presence at court, that he might learn from his own lips the particulars of his expedition. Gasca, accordingly, attended by a numerous retinue of nobles and cavaliers,—for who does not pay homage to him whom the king delighteth to honor?—embarked at Barcelona, and, after a favorable voyage, joined the Court in Flanders.

He was received by his royal master, who fully appreciated his services, in a manner most grateful to his feelings; and not long afterward he was raised to the bishopric of Palencia,—a mode of acknowledgment best suited to his character and deserts. Here he remained till 1561, when he was promoted to the vacant see of Siguenza. The rest of his days he passed peacefully in the discharge of his episcopal functions; honored by his sovereign, and enjoying the admiration and respect of his countrymen.

In his retirement, he was still consulted by the government in matters of importance relating to the Indies. The disturbances of that unhappy land were renewed, though on a much smaller scale than before, soon after the president's departure. They were chiefly caused by discontent with the *repartimientos*, and with the constancy of the Audience in enforcing the benevolent restrictions as to the personal services of the natives. But these troubles subsided, after a very few years, under the wise rule of the Mendozas,—two successive viceroys of that illustrious house which has given so many of its sons to the service of Spain. Under their rule, the mild yet determined policy was pursued, of which Gasca had set the example. The ancient distractions of the country were permanently healed. With peace, prosperity returned within the borders of Peru; and the consciousness of the beneficent results of his labors may have shed a ray of satisfaction, as it did of glory, over the evening of the president's life.

That life was brought to a close in November, 1567, at an age, probably, not far from the one fixed by the sacred writer as the term of human existence. He died at Valladolid, and was buried in the church of Santa Maria Magdalena, in that city, which he had built and liberally endowed. His monument, surmounted by the sculptured effigy of a priest in his sacerdotal robes, is still to be seen there, attracting the admiration of the traveller by the beauty of its execution. The banners taken from Gonzalo Pizarro on the field of Xaquixaguana were suspended over his tomb, as the trophies of his memorable mission to Peru. The banners have long since mouldered into dust, with the remains of him who slept beneath them; but the memory of his good deeds will endure for ever.

Gasca was plain in person, and his countenance was far from comely. He was awkward and ill-proportioned; for his limbs were too long for his body,—so that when he rode, he appeared to be much shorter than he really was. His dress was humble, his manners simple, and there was nothing imposing in his presence. But, on a nearer intercourse, there was a charm in his discourse that effaced every unfavorable impression produced by his exterior, and won the hearts of his hearers.

The president's character may be thought to have been sufficiently portrayed in the history already given of his life. It presented a combination of qualities which generally serve to neutralize each other, but which were mixed in such proportions in him as to give it additional strength. He was gentle, yet resolute; by nature intrepid, yet preferring to rely on the softer arts of policy. He was frugal in his personal expenditure, and economical in the public; yet caring nothing for riches on his own account, and never stinting his bounty when the public good required it. He was benevolent and placable, yet could deal sternly with the impenitent offender; lowly in his deportment, yet with a full measure of that self-respect which springs from conscious rectitude of purpose; modest and unpretending, yet not shrinking from the most difficult enterprises; deferring greatly to others, yet, in the last resort, relying mainly on himself; moving with deliberation,—patiently waiting his time; but, when that came, bold, prompt, and decisive.

Gasca was not a man of genius, in the vulgar sense of that term. At least, no one of his intellectual powers seems to have received an extraordinary development, beyond what is found in others. He was not a great writer, nor a great orator, nor a great general. He did not affect to be either. He committed the care of his military matters to military men; of ecclesiastical to the clergy; and his civil and judicial concerns he reposed on the members of the Audience. He was not one of those little great men who aspire to do every thing themselves, under the conviction that nothing can be done so well by others. But the president was a keen judge of character. Whatever might be the office, he selected the best man for it. He did more. He assured himself of the fidelity of his agents, presided at their deliberations; dictated a general line of policy, and thus infused a spirit of unity into their plans, which made all move in concert to the accomplishment of one grand result.

A distinguishing feature of his mind was his common sense, —the best substitute for genius in a ruler who has the destinies of his fellowmen at his disposal, and more indispensable than genius itself. In Gasca, the different qualities were blended in such harmony, that there was no room for excess. They seemed to regulate each other. While his sympathy with mankind taught him the nature of their wants, his reason suggested to what extent these were capable of relief, as well as the best mode of effecting it. He did not waste his strength on illusory schemes of benevolence, like Las Casas, on the one hand; nor did he countenance the selfish policy of the colonists, on the other. He aimed at the practicable,—the greatest good practicable.

In accomplishing his objects, he disclaimed force equally with fraud. He trusted for success to his power over the convictions of his hearers; and the source of this power was the confidence he inspired in his own integrity. Amidst all the calumnies of faction, no imputation was ever cast on the integrity of Gasca. No wonder that a virtue so rare should be of high price in Peru.

There are some men whose characters have been so wonderfully adapted to the peculiar crisis in which they appeared, that they seem to have been specially designed for it by Providence. Such was Washington, in our own country, and Gasca, in Peru. We can conceive of individuals with higher qualities, at least with higher intellectual qualities, than belonged to either of these great men. But it was the wonderful conformity of their characters to the exigencies of their situation, the perfect adaptation of the means to the end, that constituted the secret of their success; that enabled Gasca so gloriously to crush revolution, and Washington still more gloriously to achieve it.

Gasca's conduct on his first coming to the colonies affords the best illustration of his character. Had he come backed by a military array, or even clothed in the paraphernalia of authority, every heart and hand would have been closed against him. But the humble ecclesiastic excited no apprehension; and his enemies were already disarmed, before he had begun his approaches. Had Gasca, impatient of Hinojosa's tardiness, listened to the suggestions of those who advised his seizure, he would have brought his cause into jeopardy by this early display of violence. But he wisely chose to win over his enemy by operating on his conviction.

In like manner, he waited his time for making his entry into Peru. He suffered his communications to do their work in the minds of the people, and was careful not to thrust in the sickle before the harvest was ripe. In this way, wherever he went, every thing was prepared for his coming; and when he set foot in Peru, the country was already his own.

After the dark and turbulent spirits with which we have been hitherto occupied, it is refreshing to dwell on a character like that of Gasca. In the long procession which has passed in review before us, we have seen only the mail-clad cavalier, brandishing his bloody lance, and mounted on his war-horse, riding over the helpless natives, or battling with his own friends and brothers; fierce, arrogant, and cruel, urged on by the lust of gold, or the scarce more honorable love of a bastard glory. Mingled with these qualities, indeed, we have seen sparkles of the chivalrous and romantic temper which belongs to the heroic age of Spain. But, with some honorable exceptions, it was the scum of her chivalry that resorted to Peru, and took service under the banner of the Pizarros. At the close of this long array of iron warriors, we behold the poor and humble missionary coming into the land on an errand of mercy, and everywhere proclaiming the glad tidings of peace. No warlike trumpet heralds his approach, nor is his course to be tracked by the groans of the wounded and the dying. The means he employs are in perfect harmony with his end. His weapons are argument and mild persuasion. It is the reason he would conquer, not the body. He wins his way by conviction, not by violence. It is a moral victory to which he aspires, more potent, and happily more permanent, than that of the blood-stained conqueror. As he thus calmly, and imperceptibly, as it were, comes to his great results, he may remind us of the